Director 8.5 Studio

Andrew Allenson
Joel Baumann
Sham Bhangal
Thomas Blaha
Andrew Cameron
Justin Clayden
Rob Dillon
Brian Douglas
Tota Hasegawa
Kenneth Orr
Darrel Plant
Alan Queen
Christopher Robbins
José Rodriguez
Tomas Roope
Karsten Schmidt
Kevin Sutherland
Don Synstelien
Leif Wells

friendsof

DESIGNER TO DESIGNER™

Director 8.5 Studio

© 2001 friends of ED

First printed in August 2001

Trademark Acknowledgments

friends of ED has endeavored to provide trademark information about all the companies and products mentioned in this book by the appropriate use of capitals. However, friends of ED cannot guarantee the accuracy of this information.

Published by friends of ED
30 Lincoln Road, Olton, Birmingham. B27 6PA. UK.

Printed in USA

ISBN: 1-903450-69-1

Director 8.5 Studio

Credits

Authors Andrew Allenson, Joel Baumann, Sham Bhangal, Thomas Blaha, Andrew Cameron, Justin Clayden, Rob Dillon, Brian Douglas, Tota Hasegawa, Kenneth Orr, Darrel Plant, Alan Queen, Christopher Robbins, José Rodriguez, Tomas Roope, Karsten Schmidt, Kevin Sutherland, Don Synstelien, Leif Wells

Content Architect Eleanor Baylis

Editors Eleanor Baylis, Jon Bounds, Dan Britton, Lumbotharan Thevathasan

Technical Reviewers Simone Baboni, Manno Bult, Todd Darling, Neal (Iggy) Davis, Corné van Dooren, Simon Edwards, Brian K James, Daniel Kent, Jeroen Meeuwissen, James Penberthy, Vibha Roy, Todd Simon, Gabrielle Smith, Jon Steer, Peter Walker

Graphic Editors William Fallon, Katy Freer, Deb Murray

Author Agent Jeremy Booker

Project Administator Fionnuala Meacher

Index Andrew Criddle, Simon Collins

Cover Design Katy Freer

Proof Readers Jeremy Booker, David Chambers, Faye Claridge, Joanna Farmer, Shabnam Hussain, Mel Jehs, Laurent Lafon, Fionnuala Meacher, Deborah Murray, Mel Orgee, Paul Thewlis, Robert Tidy

CD Kristian Besley

Team Leader Mel Orgee

Director 8.5 Studio

Andrew Allenson   www.pickledonion.com
Andrew Allenson was born in Bedfordshire and studied at Goldsmiths' College in London. He divides his time between teaching, consultancy and developing personal projects. Andrew helped start ANTIROM and then ROM+SON studios, and teaches at the Royal College of Art. His is currently working on pickledonion.com, a collection of simple toys that explore complexity, emergence and group behaviour using sound and light.

Joel Baumann   www.tomato.co.uk
When I left my farm in Arizona in 1983 I would have never thought that I'd be working on computers one day. Now after 3 years of evening classes in computer related design at the Mississippi University of particle physics and educational technology, I have finally achieved the level of skill needed to be a true professional in this industry. Most of my work relates in some way to animal behavioural patterns, because I have been observing cattle throughout my youth. Herding and non-hierarchical herd systems are interesting and I use them as the basis for all my designs.

Sham Bhangal
Sham Bhangal originally started out as an engineer, specializing in industrial computer based display and control systems. His spare time was partly taken up by freelance web design, something that slowly took up more and more of his time until the engineering had to go. He is now also writing for friends of ED, something that is taking more and more time away from web design...funny how life repeats itself! Sham lives in Manchester, England, with his partner Karen.

Thomas Blaha   www.ncimedia.com
I have been involved in computers and media since the early 1980's and began working with Director as a hobby while attending graduate school in 1993. In the fall of 1994, it became a fulltime career when I started North Coast Interactive, Inc., a development company focusing on the Business to Business communication needs of the Industrial marketplace. Since its inception, I have been involved in the development of many leading edge projects from interactive CD-ROMs to e-Commerce websites for companies large and small.

Andrew Cameron   www.romandson.com
Andy Cameron is a founder member of the antirom collective. He founded the Hypermedia Research Centre at the University of Westminster in 1996 and started Romandson Ltd in 1999. He has been active in commercial and experimental interactive media design since the early 1990s, as well as writing extensively on the aesthetics and political economy of interactive media. Andy currently divides his time between the Romandson studio in London and the Benetton Fabrica studio in North Italy where he is Creative Director of New Media.

About the Authors

Justin Clayden   www.coolfusion.com.au

Justin was born in December of 1970, and is thus a likely candidate for the inheritance of Jimi Hendrix's soul, if not guitar playing ability. He started programming at the age of 11, despite those around him telling him he was "past it". He's been writing games since 1983, on a number of platforms that include the Vic-20, Commodore 64, Apple II, Amigas, Macs, PCs, etc. These days he writes games mostly for online use. When he can bear to pull himself away from games, he enjoys surfing, writing and recording music. He holds a Bachelor of Informatics from Griffith University, and just completed a Masters of Philosophy at the University of Sydney, where he also lectures in 3d Modelling and Photorealism.

Rob Dillon   www.r-effects.com

Rob Dillon has been a media developer for more than 20 years, founding the Digital Design Group in 1993, which has produced CD and web based digital media for businesses. Rob has written two "Survival Guides" for Apple Computer's Multimedia Program, and contributed to the CD based product, "Lingo TimeSavers", a tool for Director users. Rob is the Pittsburgh area user group representative for the Macromedia User Groups, has a BA in Mass Communication, and teaches Interactive Media Authoring at the Art Institute of Pittsburgh. He will begin teaching an Interactive Media survey course at Carnegie Mellon University this Fall.

Brian Douglas   www.imaginarystudio.com

I am the head programmer for Imaginary Studio (http://www.imaginarystudio.com) in New York City. I prefer the outdoors to my computer. If you really want to learn programming, go look at nature and how it organizes itself. My thanks to Chris Robbins for getting me involved in this book, and my wife, Margi, for being patient while I spent days off working on this.

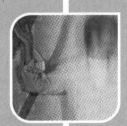

Tota Hasegawa   www.tota.ne.jp/www.tomato.co.uk

Born in 1972. Gained a BA Hon's in Contemporary Media Practice from Harrow University of Westminster, London. Attended the Royal College of Art to do an MA in Computer Related Design. From 1997 - 99 worked as an Interaction Designer at the Sony Creative Center Human Interface Group, Tokyo. From 1999 – 01 based at the Sony Computer Science Lab. Ltd/Interaction Lab, Tokyo working as a Research Designer. Currently with Tomato Interactive, London.

Kenneth Orr   www.kenorr.co.uk

Born and currently living in The West of Scotland, Ken is a Systems Designer working full-time at a local wholesale company. His duties included Technical Illustration, Instruction Manuals, component design (SolidWorks and AutoCAD) in addition to Multimedia assignments. During the mid 90s, Ken completed a BSc in Computer Aided Engineering and a PgD in Maintenance Systems Engineering and Management. Ken enjoys participating in on-line communities particularly were-here.com helping other developers through his role as Moderator. Ken hopes to continually increase his Multimedia skills while improving his knowledge of new technologies.

Director 8.5 Studio

Darrel Plant   www.moshplant.com

Darrel Plant is Publisher at Moshofsky/Plant Creative Services in Portland, Oregon, and the Technical Editor of the Director Online User Group (www.director-online.com) where he oversees the production of three to five articles a week on Director and Flash. He's the author/co-author of four books on multimedia and a contributor to two others (including this one); written numerous articles for magazines including WIRED; published a short-lived book review magazine; worked as a radio DJ playing alternative music back when it was still known as 'college rock'; and once offered himself up to the voters as a candidate for the Oregon State Legislature.

Alan Queen   www.alanqueen.com

Alan started life as a starving musician, and recording engineer. He got into computer programming by making Enhanced CD's for an Atlanta based record company. He eventually cut his hair, and "injected the blue dye" at IBM, where he made CD roms, kiosks, and games. After 5 years at IBM he packed his bags and headed for the front lines of the dot-com wars in San Francisco. There he made multiplayer games for Shockwave.com. He's now back in Atlanta, (having barely escaped the explosion of the dot bomb), making games, playing games, and trying to find more time for music.

Christopher Robbins   www.webactivism.org

When he returned to the U.S. after several years in West Africa as a Peace Corps Volunteer, his choice was simple: work with farmers in Cambodia or stay in New York and "do" art. Several years later, he is kind of doing both, but really doing neither. He'd like to thank Shelly for putting up with his countless hours in front of that screen and for pretending to care what sprites are, and the web industry for forcing him to see more sunrises than he ever thought possible. He is currently speaking about himself in the third person..

José Rodriguez   www.JRVisuals.com

Born in Puerto Rico, Jose is the founder of JRVisuals (www.JRVisuals.com) which he runs from his apartment in the Bronx, New York where he lives with his wife Jennifer and son Julian. Jose is also developing a Collective of Media Developers under the name Media-OP (www.Media-OP.com) and currently runs the New York Metro Macromedia User Group (www.NYMMUG.org). His work combines programming, audio, and art into a seamless blend that has gained notoriety in the field for nearly a decade.

Tomas Roope   www.tomato.co.uk

After studying a degree in Film, Video and Photography in 1991 and several freelance roles including technical and creative director, he started working at Tomato, heading up their first CD-ROM project. At the same time he was involved with the arts collective Antirom that published a CD-ROM in 1995, this developed into a commercial venture and continued till spring 1999 when Tomas and two of his colleagues began Tomato Interactive. He's won several design awards including three D&AD silvers and has given several talks around the world. As well as his commercial undertakings, he is currently teaching on product design at the Royal College of Art as well as producing installations for several international exhibitions.

About the Authors

Karsten Schmidt   www.toxi.co.uk

Taught myself Assembler on Atari 800XL, got involved in the European Demo scene and wrote a commercial game. All this daylight robbery made me more interested in both design and music, so I set up my own home studio and begun organising and playing live PAs on raves in '95. The same year I also started a college course of Computer Science of Media and worked as freelance web designer. Left Germany and have been living and working in London for the last 3 years. My colour synthesis project SpectraCol.com was Macromedia Site of Day. Currently helping to set up a Director section on Ultrashock.com.

Kevin Sutherland   www.professional-i.com

A Senior Associate at London & New York based Company-i, specialising in Internet development and technology. The boom of the "Corporate Portal" is keeping him busy at present with no end of client challenges to resolve.

"The simple approach is always the best way to go, the art is in finding a simple approach to a complex challenge, break them down into their smallest components and even the greatest of challenges can be resolved"

Don Synstelien   www.synstelien.com

Don Synstelien has been an Interactive Creative Director, Design Director and a Freelance Interactive Developer since 1992. In addition, he served some time doing print design before computers became popular and teaching teachers how to best use digital media in their classrooms when computers were first introduced into the classroom. He has produced work for companies such as 3M, Trilogy, IBM, Lucent, AT&T, Pillsbury, Motorola and many others and currently works and resides in Atlanta Georgia where he is busy helping to create dot-com failures and is seriously considering buying a boat and becoming a pirate for a living.

Leif Wells   www.leifcom.com

After spending a year stealing computer time from a local university, Leif E. Wells earned his first interactive gig with IBM Eduquest assisting in the creation of "A Book of Shadowboxes", a children's storybook. From there he went on to become the lead developer of the award winning "The 1994 IBM Interactive Annual Report" – a project that nearly killed him. After a brief stay in the Betty Ford Clinic for Interactive Developers, Leif went on to freelance for the next several years creating interesting work for IBM, The Coca-Cola Company, and Red Sky Interactive.

Palette
and
Table of
Contents

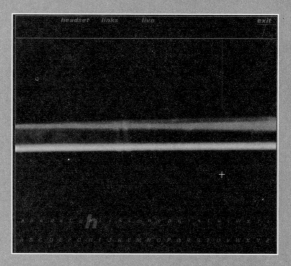

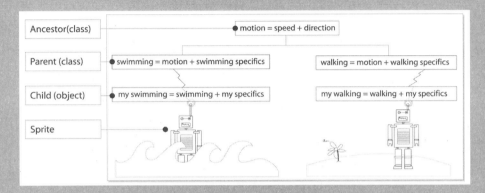

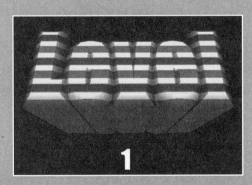

3D IN DIRECTOR 8.5

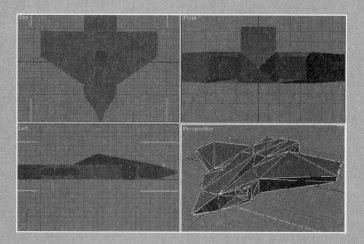

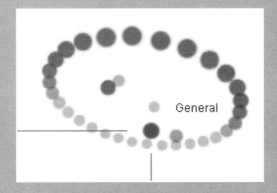

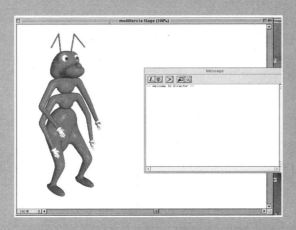

INTEGRATING WITH DIRECTOR

Learn how to really work with sound in Director, all the way
from import to full throttle 3D, interactive sound applications.

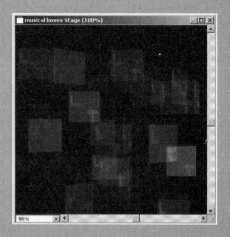

Incorporating, and manipulating Video effects in Director.

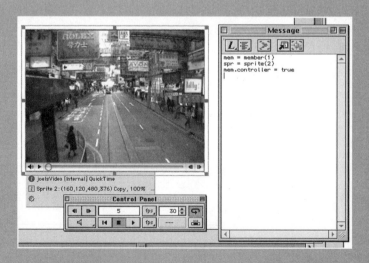

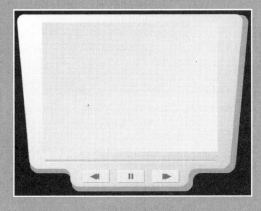

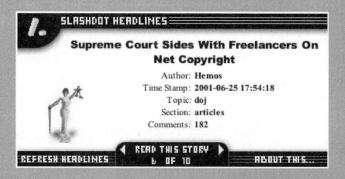

DIRECTOR IN THE REAL WORLD

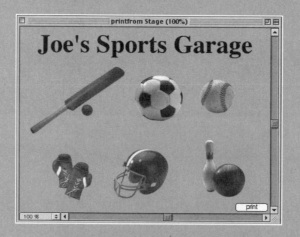

Director 8.5 Studio

Table of Contents

4   Gaming with OOP

5   Imaging Lingo

Director 8.5 Studio

Table of Contents

Director 8.5 Studio

Table of Contents

12 Flash

13 The Multiuser Server

Table of Contents

15 Plan and Process

16 Publishing Shockwave

Table of Contents

17 Projectors and Printing

18 Designing for Interaction

Director 8.5 Studio

A Director for Flash Users

Index

Table of Contents

Chapter 1
Introduction

Why a book about Director?

I've been told that a watched pot will never boil, and it seems to me that the same thing must be true for software. The mountain of attention that has been paid to Flash managed to distract the industry, albeit temporarily, from a pot that is just beginning to boil over with renewed possibility: Director. All of a sudden, a program that appeared to be on its last legs only a year ago is awash with recharged interest.

Director has long been regarded as the industry's powerhouse for multimedia creation. It has been used to create thousands of interactive titles. Director has long been capable of using externally programmed resources to interact with everything from Quicktime video to external DVD (video) players in custom created hardware kiosks. In short, it's capable of minor miracles.

So with all that functionality, what could possibly have been added to shake the design world up with such renewed vigor? The answer is simple: 3D, a multiuser environment, and the Flash Asset Xtra.

We wrote this book because we are, every single author, dedicated to Director, and we love to design and program with it. We all understand the magic that is possible when you're using Director, and we have first–hand experience of the excitement and the frustration that comes with each version release. We've written this book in anticipation of the applications that you will create once you've worked with it; knowing that we have contributed in some small way to helping you build them was the inspiration that we needed to get started. We all hope that the book we have compiled here is inspiring and instructive enough to enable you to create some truly amazing work, and that you'll share it with us when you've finished.

Our primary goal with Director Studio is to highlight the features that have been added to Director, while covering the fundamentals that will help you get the best out of these new features. Whenever possible, we have been extensive with our code samples and techniques, so you should be able to implement immediately any project that may have prompted you to buy this book.

As you work through, try to pay close attention to the techniques that the authors use to solve the problems they are presented with in the chapter. You will notice that some of the authors work in what might at first appear to be unusual, if not downright strange, ways to accomplish their goals. They aren't crazy, they're just thinking outside the box. It's precisely because Director is so extensible that you'll often find yourself thinking outside the box to solve a simple problem. I can't recall how many different ways to play video I have seen incorporated into projects over the years, but none of the ways that *really* work are as simple as the documentation would have you believe. It's not so unusual to find yourself at that point in development where the rules don't appear to apply.

So, we'll begin this introduction to Director 8.5 with a little history.

A brief history of Director

In the beginning there was Hypercard, Apple Computer's simple multimedia layout and control environment, and Storyboard LIVE! from IBM. Then came Macromind Video Works, which soon became Director. Although it was a Macintosh only application, the corporate environment quickly began to see that dynamic presentations created using Director really did deliver their messages effectively.

I began using Director 3 in 1992. Compared to the program we're used to nowadays, version 3 was very primitive. It was also Macintosh only, so Macromind introduced the Director Player for Windows. Although this move complicated the development process it did open up the playback of presentations and games to thousand of computers. Remember, these were the days of double density floppy disks – the process for development was to create on Macintosh, test on Macintosh, transfer to the PC, test on the PC, then bug fix on the Macintosh. Ouch!

Director's theatre metaphor was popular even back then. The score, the stage, the cast members taking their instructions from (text files called) scripts, and performing on the stage – from the very beginning, the work environment has been easy to understand and well received. And even in the days of version 3, Lingo was a popular and powerful scripting language.

By the time the cross–platform Director 4 was introduced, several award winning multimedia commercial titles had been created. Multimedia had hit the mainstream, and Director users could now develop on the Windows 3.1 platform, which made the software more acceptable in the corporate environment. Other tools had been developed as well, like Icon Author, Kalida ScriptX, Toolbox and many more, but Director had already been embraced as the industry standard.

With Director 4, Lingo became a more mature language. The introduction of the `on mouseDown`, and `on enterFrame` events prompted script wrapping. In earlier versions, you simply put a script into a frame for it to be called, but with the more formal `on enterFrame` call you could instruct Director to interpret your scripts as you wanted them interpreted.

Good though Director 4 was, there was still plenty of room for advancement in Director 5. Anti-alias typefaces were incorporated, along with leading, kerning and other areas of typeface control. This helped lower file size by allowing developers to use system fonts instead of graphics (which couldn't be edited) for every piece of text. This was a real timesaver when it came to textual changes.

The technical improvements were even more extensive: many new additions to Lingo, (like the keyword `member`), multiple casts, and Xtras. Like XCMDs on the Macintosh platform, these pieces of code added things like new transitions, and additional cast types. Almost instantaneously third party Xtras for Director began to appear.

The release of Director 5 also brought with it Shockwave. Although Shockwave is a simple enough idea: a reduced size Director file transported across the Internet and played by a browser plug-in, at the time it was revolutionary. The 28.8 modem had yet to become the industry standard, so files had to be worked and reworked to get them small enough to be useful. But the work was worth it; suddenly the Internet was a multimedia vehicle, alive with motion graphics, audio, and games.

> *I'm skipping version 6 and going straight to 6.5. I would tell you why, but I still have a headache from the time I spent working in 6...*

Lingo is great if you're happy programming, or work exclusively with programmers, but most of us work with at least one designer who could crash a computer with a `go to the frame` script. That's where Director 6.5's behaviors come in. By simply giving a sprite a behavior the designer could animate a graphic, change the tab order of an input text, or select a button action. A behavior is, in essence, a sprite script that makes the sprite an **object**. If you attach a button behavior to a graphic on the stage, you might be presented with a dialog box asking you to select a graphic to display when the cursor rolls over the button. Or you can select a sound for mouse clicks and a frame to go to after the click.

In addition to the new Lingo that made behaviors possible, Director 6.5 brought with it the 120 channel score. Before you had to make do with the 48, which brought about some very interesting workarounds, like using Lingo to swap cast members. This was the release that also gave us on-screen animation path editing, where the path of a sprite was represented with blue squares for every frame, and a line connected each square. This visual editing method was a real boon for the animation impaired.

Big changes were also made to Shockwave as it matured as a delivery platform. Better streaming was developed, and with it came some powerful new Network Lingo commands and keywords.

Flash, a new vector–based Web animation product purchased by Macromedia in 1997, was added to the list of importable file formats. This made Flash animation files built for use on the Web re–useable in Director CD–ROM projects and presentations.

By the time version 7 of Director was due to come out, the old code from previous versions was piling up and Lingo was badly in need of retuning and updating. The new engine that debuted in Director 7 added remarkable speed improvements. Alpha channels were introduced, and with them the functionality that had previously only been available in Xtras became a standard feature. If you imported a 24–bit graphic with an alpha channel into Director 7, the only thing you would see once that graphic was on screen was the area left uncovered by the alpha channel. This made it easier to handle transparent areas around graphics. Instead of having to edit 8–bit graphics, or put several versions of the same graphic in the cast, you just placed an alpha channel around it, (and enhanced compression enabled you to bring the larger image size down.)

Another new feature with Director 7 was the ability to embed fonts into the cast. Although version 5 had made it possible to anti–alias text in Director, a lot of designers and developers felt that choosing between system fonts and requiring the delivery system to install the desired font didn't make this capability terribly functional. Director 7 allowed you to import the font and be assured that it would look great on any system, Macintosh or PC. Also placed into semi–retirement were quick draw shapes. These were replaced by vector shapes, which behaved like Adobe Illustrator or Macromedia Freehand shapes.

Director 7 integrated more of the development process within the authoring environment. Instead of saving a file and opening up Afterburner to convert and compress your files to the

Shockwave format, all you needed to do was **save it as a Shockwave movie**. This release also featured the Multiuser Server (MUS).

By the time it hit version 8, Director had become a mature, well-rounded interactive media tool – a tool without competition. Up until this point, one of the few things you *couldn't* do with Director was create images. You could move images, shrink them, overlap them, and replace them, but you couldn't create them. Enter Imaging Lingo.

Take a look at the First Annual Director Demo Competition at Charles Foreman's SetPixel Web site www.setpixel.com/content/democomp/. The contest illustrates what Director programmers can do with Imaging Lingo.

Director 8 also came with new debugging functions for the director.ini and shockwave.ini files that work with Director and Shockwave. Using those files properly helps developers clear bugs from their code more efficiently. The zoomable stage came along too, with more sprite channels, and some much needed audio features. I believe that sound is often the most neglected area of multimedia. No one spends enough time or money on music or sound, absence of audio, or worse, poor audio, can really undo a piece of interactive media.

Director Today

Director has taken quite a leap in imaging power. Version 8 gave us much more control over 2D graphics, and now we have 3D graphic image rendering and manipulation. Macromedia and Intel collaborated to put 3D into Director, allowing us to use the tools that we already know, like 3D Studio MAX, and use them in combination with Flash, Quicktime, Real Media, and Imaging Lingo to create a whole new experience. Now, with Director 8.5, developers can create games that in previous years could only be accomplished by teams of programmers on gaming consoles. We've also been given a huge amount of 3D Lingo. Take a look at some of the great games developed to showcase the power of Shockwave 3D at the Macromedia site.

Since this book is essentially about Director 8.5, I'll let the other developers tell you how powerful this tool has become. What they have to tell you could change the way you see interactive media and the Web.

OK, Director isn't dead, but it lost the war to Flash, right?

Didn't Flash take over the Internet? And don't most designers today have enough basic knowledge of Flash to produce *most* of what we were creating in Director a couple years ago? Is there really room for Director anymore?

Well, let's look at that. First, Flash is a great tool, but it hardly took over the Internet, at least, it didn't take over from Director, because Director never really 'owned' the Internet. Oh sure, it made a good play for it when Shockwave first came out. The promise was that it would give new life to the web. The truth was that the files that it produced were a little too big for the modems at the time, which were generally limited to a widely available 14.4 and a slightly less available 28.8. The bandwidth available back then just could not handle the files that fledgling Internet designers were producing – or the plug-in for that matter. Flash was perfectly timed: modems may have been slow, but Flash files were small. Little wonder, then, that Flash became the dominant Internet delivery platform for multimedia.

Keep in mind that the Internet isn't everything. Flash cannot (and will not) replace Director. It doesn't have the robust features that developers expect from a tool that they use and trust everyday. Just recently I was talking to a Flash developer friend of mine who spent the day working on a project in Flash only to realize that the Flash player was incapable of the functionality essential to the project.

The problem with Flash, from this perspective, is that it is designed for web delivery. That is where its strengths are, and that is where it should be used. Once you start using Flash for desktop delivery, even though it *can* be used that way, you start to run into areas that are better suited to Director. The biggest problem that we Director users have today is that so many clients, having heard so much about Flash on the web, superimpose the word 'Interactive' with 'Flash'.

Currently Director has some really great features that are still beyond Flash's capabilities, despite some rather inventive workarounds by some very creative individuals and companies. These areas are pretty important to desktop multimedia; areas like Video. Flash does not currently possess the ability to playback video unless you do some really ugly or nonsensical things to make it play – open it in a browser window, or trace each frame and make the movie into a gigantic frame-by-frame vector file. While these approaches will *play* the video, many companies have become accustomed to seamless integration of video into their presentations, and won't accept this kind of delivery in a professional environment.

Another area is extensibility. If you stay with either program for long enough you'll get to a point where you need more than it can give you. I've been there many times. The principle difference between Flash and Director, though, is that you can draw from a deep library of third party Xtra programs that take Director's capabilities into almost every area. There are so many Xtras that you can find books entirely devoted to Xtras and what they do.

So, now we've established that there probably is a place for both Director and Flash, let's take a look at where Director really excels.

Where should I use Director?

Director is a very versatile product. I've seen it used for any number of applications – from presentations to promotions, hugely successful commercial CD–ROM games to computer–based education, productivity applications to collaboration applications, product demonstrations to music videos.

CD-ROM Projects: If I had a nickel for every CD–ROM based project I've ever been a part of, why, I'd have a couple of bucks. Let's face it – Director sings when it comes to CD–ROM work. It is as if Director was created to do just that. Well, kids, that's because it *was*!

With Director and a CD–ROM there isn't much you cannot do. Usually, CD–ROMs are used to distribute content created in Director when there is too much content to reliably distribute any other way. Six hundred and some odd megabytes of space, a huge install base (do you know anyone who can't use a CD?), and cross–platform delivery, all in a small coaster sized disc of pure digital joy. Try getting that kind of bandwidth through a modem!

The reason that Director is so powerful on a CD–ROM is the projector, the runtime distribution application. Projectors have none of the limitations that exist with Shockwave: you can read and write files on the hard drive, show various kinds of video and audio, open other applications, and even install applications. In other words, a projector is just like any other application you run on your computer.

The earliest interactive project I remember being delivered on CD-ROM was VERBUM magazine's Verbum Interactive 1.0 in 1991. This was in the days of 16-color presentations delivered on diskette. The folks at Verbum magazine were on a mission to create the world's first integrated multimedia magazine. It featured articles that the user could read onscreen, a tutorial, demonstrations of products, and a video roundtable discussion of the state of the infant multimedia market. Incredible! Imagine what they might have done if they'd had Director 8.5 back in 1991.

Today, Director can deliver almost anything: annual reports, electronic marketing brochures, games, and training. All you have to do is make sure your project fits into 640 Megabytes of space.

Updateable CD/Internet hybrids: Now, just because you have decided to distribute your content on a CD–ROM, that doesn't mean the content has to be static. Director's inbuilt connectivity functions make it possible for you to reach out to the Internet to extend and update your content. You can open a browser to view your Web site or send e–mail – but really that's child's play. You can navigate somewhere online seamlessly, by issuing a simple network Lingo command. Your web server and your CD-ROM can be made to work as one.

Shockwave content: Well, as much as I know and love CD–ROM content delivery, it does have its drawbacks. The costs of replication and distribution can be a problem. The advantage that Shockwave has over CD–ROM is that there are no replication costs. Period. And the distribution scheme is simple – you just tell everyone to come and get it. And, of course, millions of users have the Shockwave plug–in on their computer.

Games: The obvious place to look for Shockwave entertainment is Shockwave.com. Check some of them out, and have a think about how you might go about coding them. Many of them are modern day replicas of the arcade games of my youth. Director games are wonderful things – I'm sure you don't need me to tell you that!

Kiosks: Kiosks are a great way to provide information. They're used in malls, hotels, business lobbies, and museums. Director is a great tool if it's a kiosk you need to create. After all, a kiosk is really just a CD–ROM project running on a fast hard drive with a touch screen monitor attached. Just imagine what you could do if you added a modem to the mix. Can you say "e-commerce"? I knew you could!

Demos: Don't be confused by the word 'demo'. I don't actually mean something that demonstrates a piece of software. A good demo, Imaging Lingo skills and a lot of creativity can get a developer a great deal of respect in the community. Not to mention catching the eye of potential employers.

Demonstrations: Now we are talking about software demonstrations. If you have some decent screenshots and a good script, you can give a potential customer an excellent idea of how a piece of software works. I've created demonstrations for both electronic banking software and Web publishing software, because clients have wanted to give their customers a guided tour of the software without actually having to install it, or create a mini version.

Prototyping: Creating a game or an application in a programming language like C++ can be a quite a struggle if you're starting from scratch. One of the hardest parts is creating a user interface that is friendly and efficient. Director comes to the rescue here, too. With Director, developers can create and test a user interface without getting in the way of the programmers.

Presentations: While most people use a product like Microsoft PowerPoint to create and show presentations, Director can really supercharge a presentation.

Kobe Steel had a problem. A Japanese company had a multi-billion dollar product that was difficult to sell. Every developing country needed it, and it was remarkably good value. The problem was that Kobe Steel needed to let the government agents with buying power know about it, and he had a langue barrier problem. Enter Bill Whitley and the Whitley Group with an award-winning solution: a multimedia presentation.

Using English as the common language, the presentation was narrated from a script that had been painstakingly created to remove any potential cultural misunderstandings. The engineer who gave the presentation would participate, playing go-between with the audience and presentation segments, answering questions and giving additional details. This made the presentation more like interactive theater. The presentation also included a graphical predictor, showing the returns on investments according to suggestions from the audience.

The presentation began getting rave reviews – so much so that representatives from countries who had not seen the presentation began contacting Kobe Steel. As a result the decision makers for these countries attended the presentation, and the sales cycle was reduced from eighteen months down to six months. And all this by creating a dynamic presentation using Director.

Well, a little idealized maybe, but you get the point.

Animations: Now, I'm no scientist. I find simple engineering feats like can openers ingenious. But some of the folks in this sort of field have something in common with me, and that's Director. They use Director to present complex animations that prove their theories and showing how their product will look once it's manufactured.

Educational products: Director shines in computer-based training. You may have heard, it said that people remember 10% of what they hear, 30% of what they see, and 90% of what they hear, see, and do. Well, *good* computer-based training uses the eyes, ears and minds of students. As you know, presenting the content is one of things that Director does very well. You can also create tests of all kinds; multiple choice, and matching tests are fairly simple to create with Director, and with a little more work, you can create visual puzzles that help people learn to solve complex problems.

Screensavers: There's something of a wave of screen savers being created with Director. Trivia games, animated characters, clocks, corporate branding – a screen saver can be anything.

Of course this isn't a comprehensive list – there are plenty of other applications you can create using Director – but I hope it gives you a good idea of the scope of the possibilities Director lays at your fingertips.

Knowing when to use Director

So as you can see, Director is a powerful and versatile tool. It's important, though, to know when you *shouldn't* turn to Director.

As a developer, I strongly believe that you should always use the right tool for a job. No one wants to fix a television with a can opener (well, nobody but MacGuyver, but he is a fictitious character *on* television). And, although Director is my all time favorite tool, and I've used it to support myself over the past few years, there are times when even I wouldn't use it. Let's take a look at a few examples.

Some Web based animations and Interfaces: yes, you can create some fabulous animations and wonderful interfaces using Director, but there will be times when Flash is a better solution. Make sure you're using the right tool.

Hardcore 3D Games: some games are harder to create than others. Thinking about creating the next Doom or Unreal Tournament? You may be able to use Director to prototype the interface, or even a mockup to show potential investors, but the performance required by some games is currently unattainable with the Director engine, and it can be too much for the most modern of machines. Know what you're aiming for and whether it's possible before you begin.

High–resolution imagery: If you're planning to create the next 'A Bug's Life' or some high–resolution imagery, then don't start with Director. High–resolution imagery should be left to the 3D Studio MAXs and Mayas of the world. Shockwave 3D was created with a lower (but not the lowest) common denominator in mind. The engineers at Macromedia and Intel wanted to bring you 3D, so they did. But currently, video or still images are the best format for high–resolution imagery.

And on the next slide we have: As you know, Director can supercharge a presentation. But if you are giving a presentation to five people at your office about how the new parking permits work, use a presentation product like Microsoft PowerPoint. Using Director for a small job is something akin to using a high–rise crane to prize a rock out of your shoe.

Creating Professional Graphics: Director has powerful imaging capabilities, (which you'll be working with in the book) and a paint window. That doesn't mean that you should use Director to create logos, buttons or other graphics. Macromedia Fireworks or Adobe Photoshop have always done these things better than Director does. Remember: Director is a great tool for assembling all kinds of media into an interactive product. Keep your focus, people!

Who uses Director?

An awful lot of people. In the world of multimedia creation, Director is pretty long in the tooth. While most of the tools around today have histories ranging from a few weeks to a few short years, Director's history stretches back to the origins of the multimedia revolution. Indeed, there are people who have already retired from careers that were largely based on the work that they did in Director.

With all that time in the field, Director users have had a lot of time to perfect their art. That saying about no man being an island rings very true when you're working with Director. The skills required to produce a fully featured project these days have increased exponentially. There are very few people who have all the required abilities that it takes to produce a finished CD–ROM or kiosk today.

Back when I started using Director I used to pride myself on being able to design, program and troubleshoot most of the work that I did. As time went on the features list grew and the manuals thickened, and I soon found that I had to start specializing if I was to keep up.

That kind of specialization happened all over the industry and ended up creating jobs that have become pretty standard as time has gone on. While the veracity of this list will vary from company to company (not to mention being totally irrelevant at companies where they have new age Internet titles like 'Agent of Change' or 'Master of Art Stuff'), you should recognize many of the titles and functions.

Project Managers and Interactive Producers: Guides a project from inception to completion by tracking workflow and allocating resources where needed. In some companies this person is the project owner, and responsible for its profitability and success.

One would think that a project manager would have little use for Director, and indeed, most of the time this person is working in programs like Visio and Microsoft Word, locked into debates about funding with management, or ordering pizza for the programming team. But it's not so unusual for the project manger to suddenly find herself thoroughly engaged during the debugging or proofing stage, making minor changes to text, or uncovering those ever present bugs that plague a project near the end of its life. That's when knowing Director comes in handy.

Interactive Creative Director: commands a small army of Interactive Designers and controls the creative vision for the project. Usually responsible for writing the creative brief, or creating the initial designs. In some companies, this person is the owner of a project and its ultimate quality and success.

It's vital that someone in this position has a realistic understanding of the capabilities of Director and Lingo, because they are the ones most likely to invent something that will confound and infuriate the Lingo Programmer when the project actually has to be built. As a result, many Interactive Creative Directors have a good working knowledge of Director. While it's rare to find one that knows how to program, you can count on a good Interactive Creative Director to know what Director is capable of, and many have done at least a little work inside the score and typed up at least a few lines of Lingo during their careers.

Interactive Designer: Hours and hours of Photoshop work and Flash production, designing everything from intros to dialog boxes. The Interactive Designer is responsible for carrying out the vision set forth by the Interactive Creative Director.

With all the work that is required of an Interactive Designer, many often do at least a little work inside Director at some point of a project. In fact, since Director was born from an animation program, it's common sense that many designers use the program for both that and related tasks.

Lingo Programmer: A good Lingo Programmer is like a subject in a sleep deprivation experiment – projects seem to rely on their ability to be able to make up the time overused elsewhere in the project. The Lingo programmer is responsible for producing the mechanics of any working interactive project, and is frequently called upon to work miracles and do the impossible after someone else has promised it.

The workhorse of any project, the programmer is the member of the team who gets to hold a sign saying *the buck stops here!* Which is just as well, really, as they will be the ones putting in late nights at the final stages of any project.

The Shockwave Developer: The Shockwave programmer is someone who works in Director to create online or Internet enabled projects. They dedicate their lives to making Director files more compressed, stream across the Internet better, load faster and perform to perfection in any browser. Director by its nature is not adept at generating small files like those created by Flash, so the Shockwave developer is going to spend a lot of their time thinking about how they can make things smaller and their animations programmatic.

There is a payoff for all this hard work: it seems that Shockwave, while not necessarily brilliant for creating rollovers and navigational menus small enough for online use, just happens to be perfect for creating single player and multi-player online games of many varieties. Even Flash and Java, for all their interactivity capabilities, are only just starting to reach the capabilities that Director has had for quite some time.

Since the inception of Shockwave, a lot of people have gotten very excited about Director and what it can do. For a while, Flash took the spotlight, but with the advent of some of the newer and more powerful Shockwave features, I believe that we will see a steady flow of web designers to Director: those who want to be able to do the things they can only dream of in Flash (or any of the other popular interactive web technologies that exist today).

Educational Developer: The Educational Developer is likely to be an ambitious faculty member or someone involved in a support role for an institution. Trust me on this, if you can get one of these roles in life... Do it! You will never have a more relaxing or rewarding job.

The joy of working for an institution is that you generally get to escape the problems usually associated with interactive development: the timeline and the personality conflicts that inevitably arise when the demands placed on people are too high.

The downfall is that although you get to play all or most of the roles in creating a project, if you hit a brick wall, you have to work it out all by yourself, either by learning to do it yourself, or by locating some genius student intern that happens to be smart enough to figure it out for you.

There are many, many more roles besides, and chances are you're using Director for something different. There's a huge scope of work for Director designers and developers!

Is this the book for you?

We wrote this book to help more experienced Director users take their skills to a new and exciting level; to help you absorb the new features of Director 8.5, and consolidate your working knowledge of the program.

We don't mind if you live in the score or the message window, or if you believe in one–frame, Lingo driven movies or multiple casts, but it *is* important that you know what these concepts are about as you are reading this book. If you've been around Director enough, you should also be aware of the problems that never seem to get fixed... like the frustration of videos that will not play, files that won't link correctly and graphics that chug along as if they were created to run in slow motion. These problems exist *because* Director allows you to assemble projects in many different ways, and you get to know about them as a direct result of the learning curve that Director imposes upon you. So we should warn you now – if you're going to be expending a lot of effort figuring out which dialog box does what, then you will have something of an uphill battle when you get to the chapters on 3D Lingo.

So we recommend that, to get the most out of this book, you should have, or acquire, some understanding of what it takes to assemble a project in Director, and some working experience with Lingo. If you've already completed one or more projects in Director, (either by yourself or on the development side of a team), and you've already experimented with some of the different capabilities of Director, then you'll be just fine.

If you feel you could do with a bit more preparation though, try Foundation Director, which should give you the grounding you need to understand how Director works as a development tool.

The organization of Director Studio

We have organized this book into four main areas. Each of these sections covers a certain aspect of working with Director, so feel free to open, browse through, and select areas that are particularly pertinent to you. If you haven't been working with Lingo extensively, though, we would recommend that you work through the **Working with Lingo** section progressively, to ensure that your understanding of the programming language is solid before tackling the more involved chapters. If you skip ahead you can always come back for what you missed later on. You'll find all the effects that we've made in the book on the CD, so browse through those first if you like, and follow up the ones that grab your interest.

Working in Lingo: Lingo has long been the reason that Director didn't catch on with designers as thoroughly as Flash. In order to produce a really stunning interactive piece, you need to involve a little scripting. This section covers some of the more essential aspects of Lingo, such as Lists and Object Oriented Lingo Programming, as well as the more innovative aspects like Imaging Lingo. By using these powerful concepts and tools, you can take your work in director to a completely new level before you've even begun thinking about 3D! We've even tied it all up with a game created using OOP, where you can see all the theories in action, because, well, what Director book would be complete without a game?

3D in Director 8.5: This section contains chapters that cover the most revolutionary advancement to Director that has happened in years, the inclusion of 3D!

We'll start you off with a basic understanding of 3D worlds and the concepts that you will need to master if you expect to be successful creating them. Then we'll move onto Director's 3D engine and how that works, drawing in a comparison with how 3D could be faked in previous iterations of Director. The increase in the amount of Lingo available in Director 8.5 is due almost entirely to the addition of 3D functions. We'll try to build up your understanding of what these are and how they work gradually through the section, culminating in a dense chapter about 3D modifiers. With a firm understanding of these few chapters, you can begin the trek to understanding all there is to know, not just about 3D, but about building *Interactive* 3D worlds!

Integrating with Director: These chapters cover the areas in Director that have been fairly well perfected over the years, the things that every Digital Media creator should have a good handle on before they get going on any complex projects, like Xtras, Sound, Video, Flash and the Multiuser Server, (a technology that has been around for a while, but can be hard for Director users to get comfortable with.)

We have also covered the integration of XML with Director, and what that means for your projects. XML is a powerful and extensible markup language that allows you to place a lot of the functionality of a project in simple documents that are both small and easily updateable.

Director in the Real World: There's not much point learning to ride a bike if you don't actually go out and do it, so this section covers all you really need to know to get started, producing your director content so that the rest of the world can enjoy it too. We'll cover what you should watch out for when placing Shockwave content on the web, and the tricks of making projectors so that you can distribute on CD–ROM and other offline media.

An important addition to this section is the inclusion of a chapter on planning and process. Yes, process isn't the world's most exiting innovation, but the truth is, it's bad process, or the complete absence of process, that will get you into the most trouble, so I recommend that you read this chapter instead of skipping it.

The final chapter of the book is a walkthrough of some extremely innovative Director projects by their creators, who will talk about the approaches they took, and the tricks and techniques that they used to get their pieces working.

Appendix: Chances are that you might be reading this book having come to Director from Macromedia Flash. Rejoice, then, for this chapter is for you!

Today, the biggest reason that Designers have for staying away from Director is the interface. The interface looks almost identical to Flash, yet functions pretty differently. So, in this chapter we'll cover the areas of instant confusion that many Flash developers experience when they open up Director, and show how your Flash skills are, in some instances, really very transferable.

Getting Started

Whether you have high hopes of creating your own personal version of Doom or whether you are just interested in exploring the new capabilities that Director has to offer, we are glad to have been able to help ease you into this book and would love to see examples of the things that you work on as you become more proficient with Director. We hope that this introduction has covered some of the things you need to consider on your route to a thorough understanding of Director.

Just before you launch into the first chapter, there are a few layout conventions that you should know about.

Layout Conventions

We've tried to keep this book as simple as possible so we've used only a few layout styles to avoid confusion. Please keep in mind, however, that each section has been written by one, and in some cases more, of the different authors that have contributed to Director Studio, so each section will have its own voice.

The styles that you will find are as follows...

Practical exercises begin with headlines like this one

And they'll have numbered steps like this...

1. Do this first

2. Do this second

3. Do this third etc...

When we show Lingo code that needs to be typed into the script or message window, we have styled it like this:

```
on hFormatLingoText
            global gTextSyle, gCodeFont
      gTextStyle = gCodeFont
            hUpdateAllText
end hFormatLingoText
```

Where a line of Lingo is too wide to fit on a page, we'll indicate that it is a single line by using a code continuation mark, like this:

```
repeat with i = 1 to pMatchBox.count
    if intersect(rect(the mouseLoc[1], the mouseLoc[2], the
    ➡ mouseLoc[1] + 10, the mouseLoc[2] + 10),
    ➡ (sprite(pMatchBox[i]).rect)) ⑧> rect(0,0,0,0) then
    puppetSound 1, "Double Click"
    pMatched = 1
end repeat
```

When we refer to Lingo inside a block of text, we will stylize any code, such as `halt` or `on InsertText` so that it appears as code.

If we need to change an existing block of code to show modifications or additions, we will highlight the additions to reflect the change:

```
on hFormatLingoText
    global gTextSyle, gCodeFontHighlight

        gTextStyle = gCodeFontHighlight
        hUpdateAllText
end hFormatLingoText
```

Pseudo Code will appear like this:

```
On FormatLingoText
Global gTextSyle, gCodeFont, gWeAreJustDiscussingCode

gTextStyle = gWeAreJustDiscussingCode
End FormatLingoText
```

Important points that you should really pay attention to will be formatted like this:

> ***And if you ignore them, something very bad will happen!***

Web addresses will be formatted like this one www.friendsofed.com

New or significant words and phrases will appear **like this** so that they stand out from the text

Code Files

All the support files are on the CD that accompanies this book. You will also find a dedicated Director Studio discussion on the Message Boards in the D2D area at www.friendsofED.com.

Support

If you have any questions about this book, or indeed any friends of Ed book, please visit our website at www.friendsofed.com There are several contact email addresses located there and almost everything that you might need to know about us. You can also simply send email to our generic email address: feedback@friendsofed.com.

Chapter 2
Lists

Lingo lists allow you to store sets of pieces of related information. You can, of course store pieces of information in variables, but if you don't know exactly how much information you're going to need to store in advance, then you can run into trouble. Lists allow you to store data in a much more flexible way than variables can, making complex work much easier to develop and saving you having to maintain repetitious code. A good understanding of lists will also come in very useful when you're approaching object oriented programming, and when you need to control aspects of the new 3D environment in Director 8.5.

The complexity of lists can vary greatly, from something much like a shopping list to a structure that holds all the points that make up a three-dimensional object. In this chapter I hope to demonstrate the potential of lists, and how they can help you produce the kind of work you're hoping to make, by showing examples of the work I have created using them.

I have no formal programming training, so my explanations will be from a personal rather than a theoretical perspective. I hope that some of what I have learnt from my eight years experience with Director will empower the less technically confident, with whom I regularly feel a great affinity!

We'll start the chapter by looking at the basic lists operations, move on to some more complex lists, and conclude with some examples that use text file data coming in from outside Director.

List basics

Linear lists are the most basic form of list. They are single lists of data, although this data doesn't have to be of the same type. You can have numeric and string data in the same linear list, for example.

Open up your copy of Director so you can follow some of the Lingo syntax I'm going to go through here. We'll just be working in the message window. To test a line of code in the message window you simply write it and then press return, and the script runs, bringing up an alert box if it can't be executed. The word put makes Lingo output the result.

```
beep

put "test"

put 10 + 5
```

So, let's start by creating a linear list. A linear list begins with '[' and ends with ']', and the pieces of data it contains are separated with commas. So, in the message window first type the following, and then press return:

```
demolist = []
```

Let's see what this produces:

```
put demolist
```

The output in the message window should be:

```
- - []
```

We've created a variable called demolist holding an empty linear list. We could have created a linear list that contains data:

```
demolist = [1,4,5,6,7]
```

Or we might have created it like this:

```
demolist = list(1,4,5,6,7)
```

If you use the put command on demolist, you'll get the five values, rather than the empty string that we saw when the variable was unpopulated:

```
- - [1, 4, 5, 6, 7]
```

Now that we have some data in a list, let's look at how we can make changes to it.

Manipulating linear lists

You can perform all sorts of useful operations on a list by using Director's inbuilt list functions. Let's take a look at the most commonly used functions:

Adding data to a list
add, as its name suggests, adds data to a list. Type the following code into the message window:

```
add demolist 12
```

Your new output should be:

```
- - [1, 4, 5, 6, 7, 12]
```

Or you could use dot notation, like this:

```
demolist.add(12)
```

In most cases, the new data will be added at the end of your list. The exception is with sorted lists, which we'll come to later in the chapter. If you need to ensure that the new item is added to the end of a list, even if it is sorted, use the append function:

```
append demolist 12
```

Or, in dot notation:

```
demolist.append(12)
```

Adding data at a specific position

addAt does the same as add but places the new piece of data at a certain position. It requires a list name, a numeric value for the position of the new data, and then the data itself:

```
addAt demolist  3,66
```

Or:

```
demolist.addAt(3,66)
```

Your output should look like this:

```
- - [1, 4, 66, 5, 6, 7, 12]
```

If you add an item to a position higher than the length of the list, Director will add make the list up to the necessary length using zeros:

```
addAt demolist 10,22
put demolist
- - [1, 4, 66, 5, 6, 7, 12, 0, 0, 22]
```

Changing a value

setAt allows you to change data at a certain position in the list.

```
setAt demolist  2,22
```

Or:

```
demolist.setAt(2,22)
```

demolist is now:

```
- - [1, 22, 66, 5, 6, 7, 12, 0, 0, 22]
```

As with addAt, if you specify a position higher than the number of items in the list, Director will fill the additional items with zeros.

Deleting a value

deleteaAt deletes a piece of data:

```
deleteAt demolist,1
```

So now demolist looks like this:

```
- - [22, 66, 5, 6, 7, 12, 0, 0, 22]
```

If you ask Director to delete a position in the list that does not exist, by supplying a position greater than the number of elements, you'll get an error.

Deleting all values
deleteAll deletes all the content in the list. Don't do this now, because we'll have to make a new list!

The syntax is:

```
deleteAll listName
```

Or
```
listName.deleteAll()
```

Delete one value
deleteOne will delete a piece of data only if the data exists in the list. We pass it a value rather than a position.

```
deleteOne demolist,44
```

This line will leave the list untouched, because the value 44 doesn't exist. But if we try 6, the list will get smaller:

```
deleteOne demolist,6
put demolist
-- [22, 66, 5, 7, 12, 0, 0, 22]
```

So, we can put data into a list, and delete it again, but what about retrieving it? (Other than outputting the whole list using put.)

Getting data from linear lists

Along with the functions for manipulating lists, Director has a variety of functions for extracting data from them. We will look at some of the ones you'll find yourself using most often.

Getting a value from a list
getAt allows you to get a piece of data out of a list, by specifying its position.

```
put getAt(demolist,2)
-- 66
```

However, there is an older and easier way of getting at one piece of data from the list:

```
put demolist[2]
-- 66
```

(You'll get an error if you specify a position that is not valid.)

Getting the last value in the list
getLast returns the last piece of data in a list.

```
put getLast(demolist)
-- 12
```

Or:

```
put demolist.getLast()
```

Getting the position of a value

getOne returns either the position of a particular piece of data, or returns a 0 if the stated data doesn't exists.

```
put getOne(demolist,5)
-- 3

put getOne(demolist,100)
-- 0
```

Getting the maximum or minimum value

max() returns the largest value. It only works if you have a list of numbers.

```
put demolist.max()
-- 66
```

We can get the smallest value in the list by using the min() function.

```
put min(demolist)
-- 0
```

Getting the number of items

count() is an extremely useful function, as it returns the number of pieces of data in a list.

```
put count(demolist)
-- 8
```

You might be wondering *how* knowing the number of data items in a list is useful. Don't worry, it'll all become clear as you progress through the chapter. All you need to know for now is that it allows you to know exactly how many instances are within a list. Using repeat loops you can use count to repeat through every instance within a list. For instance, you could use the following code in a script:

```
repeat with a = 1 to demolist.count()
   put demolist[a]
end repeat
```

This would output each item of the list separately. (This example can't be tested in the message window because it uses more than one line of code.)

You can also retrieve a random item from the list, using the random() function along with count()

```
put demolist[random(count(demolist))]
```

Repeat this a few times and see the different values that random brings out.

There are plenty more list functions, such as ilk(), findpos, findposnear, but we won't run through them here, as they're fairly intuitive. Check out the Director Lingo Dictionary for information on these as you need them.

Data types in linear lists

So far we have only dealt with numeric data, but linear lists can contain all types of data, including strings, symbols, and objects:

```
Textlist = ["apples", pears","grapes"]
Symbollist = [#time,#money]
Objectlist = [<offspring "classy" 1 c0b45c0>, <offspring
➡ "classy" 1 c0fadac>]
```

Data types can also be mixed, but I can't for the life of me think of a situation when this would be useful!

Linear lists are great for representing sequences of values, but for more structured data we need something more flexible. That's where property lists come in.

Property lists

Property lists allow properties to be associated with pieces of data. As with the data itself, this property can be of any type, though you'll probably find it most useful for symbols. Symbols are self-contained units that can be used as flags, and are defined with a # prefix.

Let's start as we did with the linear list by making an empty property list.

```
DemoPropList = [:]
```

So what's new here? Well, the colon. The colon makes DemoPropList a property list rather than a linear list. We'll begin this section by adding symbol properties, rather than any other data type.

Manipulating property lists

Property lists can use some of the functions we've already looked at for linear lists, and they also have their own set of functions. The functions that can be used by both sorts of lists include:

```
count()
getAt()
getLast()
getOne()
deleteAll()
deletAt()
deleteOne()
getPos()
```

The best thing to do, though, is check the Lingo Dictionary when you need to do something specific. Let's take a look at some of the functions specific to property lists next.

Adding a property
You can add a property in various ways:

```
addProp DemoPropList, #prop , "data"
```

Or

```
DemoPropList [#prop] = "data"
```

Or

```
DemoPropList.addProp (#prop, "data")
```

Setting the value of a property
The function setProp will change an existing property and produce an error if the property doesn't exist. A similar command, setaProp, will create the property if it doesn't exist rather than producing an error.

```
setProp DemoPropList, #prop , "newdata"

setaProp DemoPropList, #newprop , "additionaldata"
```

So now if you take a look at your list using the put command, you should get the following:

```
- - [#prop: "newdata", #newprop: "additionaldata"]
```

Getting the data from a property
The getprop function returns the data associated with a property. We'll retrieve the data that we've just added for #newprop:

```
put getProp (DemoPropList, #newprop)
- - "additionaldata"
```

Or, using Director 8's dot notation, which makes property lists a lot clearer, we could access the data like this:

```
put DemoPropList.newprop
- - "additionaldata"
```

> *Note that this only works with property lists. You'll need to use getProp when your properties are not also symbols.*

Similar in nature to getProp, getaProp will return the data associated with a property as long as it exists and return 0 if it doesn't. This is allows you to check whether a property exists before you address it, and avoid any property not found alerts.

Getting a property
This command returns the property (rather than the data) at a particular position in the list. For example:

```
put getPropAt(DemoPropList,2)
- - #newprop
```

You won't find that you need to use it that often, though, because the chief advantage of property lists over linear lists is that you can access the data by using the property name rather than the numerical position. Occasionally, though, it is useful to 'work backwards' and retrieve the property.

deleteProp
deleteProp, as you might have guessed, deletes a specified property from the list. We wont do an example for this because we don't want to lose any of our properties.

Mixing data types in property lists

Mixing data types within a property list makes a lot more sense than in linear lists. I might use a list that looks like this, for example:

```
mylist = [#sp:sprite 11,
➤ #hincrement:3,#vincrement:12,#text:"hello",#mode:#walk]
```

This allows me to access a mix of information associated with this list instance.

```
put mylist.sp
- - (sprite 11)

put mylist.hincrement
- - 3

put mylist.text
- - "hello"

put mylist.mode
- - #walk
```

We've only looked at using symbols as properties here, but there are circumstances where using other media types can be useful. If you were making a piece of work driven by key downs, for example, you could use a property list to contain the different sets of data associated with each key. We'll return to this concept later in the chapter in the video key toy example.

Duplicating lists

Something you need to know about lists is that if you set an existing list to a new variable, and then change the new list, the original list will change too. Try this simple exercise in the Message window:

```
a = [1,2,3,4]

c = a

deleteAt c,1

put a

-- [2, 3, 4]
```

This is because all you're actually doing by setting a new variable to a list is making a pointer to the original list – the variable does not hold the list itself. Any changes made to the new variable will ripple down to the original.

So if you need to make a copy of a list and then manipulate it independently you'll need to duplicate it. For example:

```
a = [1,2,3,4]

c = duplicate(a)

deleteAt c,1

put a

-- [1, 2, 3, 4]
```

Sorting lists

We've covered how we can control the position of our data in a list, but in many cases I find I want a list to be sorted alphanumerically. This can be achieved by making the list a sorted list. Let's take a look at an example with a linear list:

```
mylist = [33,512,13,34,8,99]
mylist.sort()
put mylist
-- [8, 13, 33, 34, 99, 512]
```

Sorting is not exclusive to linear lists. The following example demonstrates how property lists can be sorted alphanumerically:

```
mylist = ["tom":1,"joel":44,"ant":33]
mylist.sort()
put mylist
— — ["ant": 33, "joel": 44, "tom": 1]
```

While the most obvious use of this ability is to create traditional databases, we've had to use sorted lists for other purposes. An example of such an occasion was when Andy Allenson and myself were building 3D models in Director before the Z position was integrated in Lingo. By creating a sorted property list we were able to store, and therefore draw, the sprites in the correct order. Every time the model was calculated, a list was created and each sprite's Z location put into the list as a property. As the list was sorted, entries at the beginning of the list were further away from the screen than those at the end. By then repeating through the list, allocating a successive sprite channel to each instance, we were able to create a convincing Z queued model.

Working with more advanced lists

So, now you've seen how the list basics work, we'll move on to look at how lists can actually be used in our Lingo scripts to achieve some advanced effects.

A structure for Lingo scripting

Over the years, working with members of **antirom** and then **tomato interactive,** we have developed a common mode of working so we could understand each other's code structure. We are going to use this structure in all of the examples in this chapter. You may want to use this structure on your own projects, or you might want to use some other system. The important thing is to find a system that works for you and stick to it.

The simple rules are:

- We have a handler called `hinit`, which is called on the first exit frame script of the movie; this is called once at the beginning of the movie to initialize everything needed in the movie. We use an h before the name init (standing for initialize) to indicate that it is a handler.

- On the second exit frame we have a handler called `hupdate` and then a `go to frame`. `hupdate` is the handler that is called on every exit frame and controls the updating of the movie. (Again, we use h to indicate that it's a handler.)

So there are the rules; let's put them into practice and make a basic structure to use in the examples.

Creating the development framework

1. Create the first exit frame script. In this frame we call the `hinit` handler.

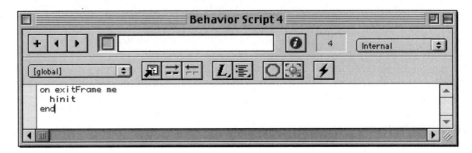

2. Now make another exit frame, this one to call the `hupdate` handler, and follow it with a `go the frame` action.

3. And now we need to set it up:

```
on hinit
end

on hupdate
end
```

We've defined the basic structure, so for the rest of our examples we'll just add additional handlers into the movie script where we need them.

Checking for key downs

Let's work with the idea of a piece of work driven by key downs, with a property list containing strings as properties. If I was writing this script for my own purposes it would be littered with comments, but I wont include them here because the information will be in the numbered instructions.

1. Open up the movie script we've just set up. We'll define a list that we can use between handlers, so we'll declare it global. Note that, as with the h prefix for handlers, we've got a g prefix to designate a global.

```
Global gKeydownList

on hinit
end

on hupdate
end
```

Next, we want to add the properties. We'll do this one at a time to keep the code clean and understandable. For this example the data associated with the character string denotes a hypothetical sound cast member reference.

```
Global gKeydownList

on hinit
gKeydownList = [:]
gKeydownList   ["a"]  = 12
gKeydownList   ["b"]  = 44
gKeydownList   ["c"]  = 66
gKeydownList   ["d"]  = 77
gKeydownList   ["e"]  = 55
end

on hupdate
end
```

2. We'll add a key down command to the basic structure, so that we can keep track of the keys being pressed.

```
Global gKeydownList

on hinit
gKeydownList = [:]
gKeydownList   ["a"]  = 12
gKeydownList   ["b"]  = 44
gKeydownList   ["c"]  = 66
gKeydownList   ["d"]  = 77
gKeydownList   ["e"]  = 55
end

on hupdate
end

on keydown
```

3. We have to safeguard the code from a key being pressed that we haven't accounted for in our property list; attempting to retrieve a property from a list that doesn't exist will cause an error. The next line of code achieves this by leaving the on keydown handler if no properties are found.

```
Global gKeydownList

on hinit
gKeydownList = [:]
gKeydownList   ["a"]  =  12
gKeydownList   ["b"]  =  44
gKeydownList   ["c"]  =  66
gKeydownList   ["d"]  =  77
gKeydownList   ["e"]  =  55
end

on hupdate
end

on keydown

if not(getaProp(gKeydownList, the key)) then return
```

4. We'll now add one final line of code that will play the sound associated with key pressed in channel one.

```
Global gKeydownList

on hinit
gKeydownList = [:]
gKeydownList   ["a"]  =  12
gKeydownList   ["b"]  =  44
gKeydownList   ["c"]  =  66
gKeydownList   ["d"]  =  77
gKeydownList   ["e"]  =  55
end

on hupdate
end

on keydown

if not(getaProp(gKeydownList, the key)) then return

puppetsound 1,getProp(gKeydownList,the key)

end
```

Unfortunately, we can't use dot syntax here because we're not using symbols. It would be so much easier just to write `gKeydownList.the key`.

You can see by this example that we could add another 50 keys and the same key down script would apply.

Lists of objects

Although I don't overuse objects, I do use them now and again and, as with the rest of my code, I pass lists to my objects when they're birthed, as well as retaining them in lists to manage their updates.

At this point I'll introduce the idea of using repeat loops in conjunction with lists. Putting multiple pieces of data in a repeat loop allows you to clarify and condense your code, and to scale it up and down later on.

In the next example we'll make a number of objects that control multiple sprite's horizontal and vertical trajectory.

Using a repeat loop to populate a list

1. Let's return to our original movie script for this exercise:

    ```
    on hinit
    end

    on hupdate
    end
    ```

    We'll make a new linear global list:

    ```
    global gPlayerList
    on hinit
      gPlayerList = []
    end

    on hupdate
    end
    ```

2. We'll define a repeat loop that creates ten instances of the object. (We can change the number of objects created easily enough later on, should we need to.)

    ```
    global gPlayerList
    on hinit
      gPlayerList = []
      repeat with a = 1 to 10
      end repeat
    ```

```
      end

      on hupdate
      end
```

3.   We'll loop from 1 to 10, and on each iteration create a property list containing random horizontal and vertical increments. These will be passed to the parent script called class. The new objects are stored in the property list gPlayerList.

```
global gPlayerList
on hinit
  gPlayerList = []
  props = [:]
  repeat with a = 1 to 10
    props[#sp] = sprite a
    props[#hinc] = random(10) - 5
    props[#vinc] = random(10) - 5
    add gPlayerList, (script "class").new(props)
  end repeat
end

on hupdate
end
```

4.   And that's the hinit handler finished. For this example we're also going to add to the hupdate handler at the end of the script. Again we're going to add a repeat loop. You'll see that we've used the count function to set the loop to the same value as in the hinit handler.

```
on hupdate
  repeat with a = 1 to count(gPlayerList)
  end repeat
end
```

5.   We'll use the loop to go through the list and call the mupdate method for each object that we have created in gPlayList. The mupdate method will be defined at the end of the script.

```
on hupdate
  repeat with a = 1 to count(gPlayerList)
    gPlayerList[a].mupdate()
  end repeat
end
```

So, that's it for the hupdate handler. Now we need to add the Lingo that will define the parent script that we referenced in the hinit handler.

6.   Create a new parent script called class. We'll start by defining some properties. (We're using a p prefix to indicate properties.)

```
property psp
property phinc
property pvinc
```

7. The properties of each object are now set from the property list passed from the `hinit` handler:

```
property psp
property phinc
property pvinc

on new me, props
  psp = props.sp
  phinc = props.hinc
  pvinc = props.vinc
  return me
end
```

To finish off the script, we need to define the `mupdate` function that we called in the `hupdate` handler. This function controls the movement of the sprites.

```
property psp
property phinc
property pvinc

on new me, props
  psp = props.sp
  phinc = props.hinc
  pvinc = props.vinc
  return me
end

on mupdate me
  psp.loch = psp.loch + phinc
  psp.locv = psp.locv + pvinc
end
```

And that's it. A repeat loop that populates a list with objects.

Earlier in the chapter we briefly mentioned sorted lists, so let's take a closer look at those next.

Applying calculations to a list

Another great thing about lists is that you can apply a calculation to everything contained within a list, rather than having to apply it to every instance within the list. I frequently use lists like this to control smooth color transitions. (Before we begin, you need to know that an RGB value only contains whole numbers, but a floating-point number is needed to create the subtle transition.) So let's start.

Creating a smooth color transition

The following script shows how we can apply calculations to a list to achieve the smooth color transition we're looking for.

1. Start by populating two global lists with current and target values for red, green, and blue:

```
global gcurrentcolorlist
global gtargetcolorlist
on hinit
gcurrentcolorlist = [#red:100.0,#green:44.0,#blue:120.0]
gtargetcolorlist = [#red:255.0,#green:22.0,#blue:11.0]
end

on hupdate
end
```

By making all the values .0 we've automatically created a floating-point number.

2. Our next line will set the color to its start position. Because of the order the list is in, gcurrentcolorlist[1] translates to red, gcurrentcolorlist[2] to green, and so on.

```
global gcurrentcolorlist
global gtargetcolorlist
on hinit
gcurrentcolorlist = [#red:100.0,#green:44.0,#blue:120.0]
gtargetcolorlist = [#red:255.0,#green:22.0,#blue:11.0]
(sprite 1).color = rgb(gcurrentcolorlist[1],gcurrentcolorlist[2],
➥ gcurrentcolorlist [3])
end

on hupdate
end
```

3. We've defined our start color as an RGB color, and we know what our destination color is (see gtargetcolorlist). We'll use the hupdate handler to move a percentage value from the current color towards the values defined in gtargetcolorlist.

```
global gcurrentcolorlist
global gtargetcolorlist
on hinit
gcurrentcolorlist = [#red:100.0,#green:44.0,#blue:120.0]
gtargetcolorlist = [#red:255.0,#green:22.0,#blue:11.0]
➥ (sprite 1).color = rgb(gcurrentcolorlist[1],
➥ gcurrentcolorlist[2],gcurrentcolorlist [3])
end
```

```
on hupdate
gcurrentcolorlist = gcurrentcolorlist + ((gtargetcolorlist -
➡ gcurrentcolorlist)/10.0)
end
```

4.   We've now got new values in gcurrentcolorlist that are closer to our target color. Our final line of code sets the new value of sprite 1 to the new values of gcurrentcolorlist.

```
global gcurrentcolorlist
global gtargetcolorlist
on hinit
gcurrentcolorlist = [#red:100.0,#green:44.0,#blue:120.0]
gtargetcolorlist = [#red:255.0,#green:22.0,#blue:11.0]
(sprite 1).color = rgb(gcurrentcolorlist[1],
➡ gcurrentcolorlist[2],gcurrentcolorlist [3])
end

on hupdate
gcurrentcolorlist = gcurrentcolorlist + ((gtargetcolorlist -
➡ gcurrentcolorlist)/10.0)
(sprite 1).color = rgb(gcurrentcolorlist[1],
➡ gcurrentcolorlist[2],gcurrentcolorlist\ [3])
end
```

And that's how you can perform calculations on a list as a whole to achieve something that is extremely useful.

I've already mentioned that lists can contain any type of data, and we've looked at a few such as numeric and string data. Let's now examine a further possibility...

Lists of Lists

As I've explained, lists can contain any type of data type, and as a list is a data type, it's possible, as well as extremely powerful, to put a list inside another list. It allows you retain all relevant information of an instance. Rather than attempting to describe this abstractly, I'll explain it using examples of my own work.

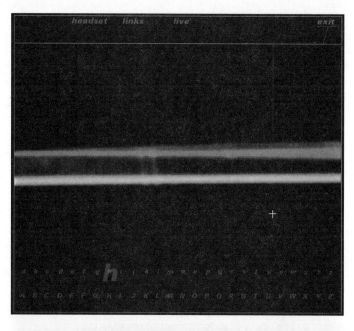

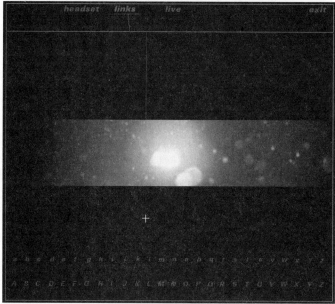

One of the pieces I produced for the underworld DVD *everything_everything* is a piece that allowed the user to trigger 52 video loops (52 because it was using all the alphabetical keys in upper and lower case). The user could either trigger the loop by pressing the key, or by clicking on a sprite that was the keys character.

With our experience of video, we've found that it's far faster to skip around a single QuickTime movie than loading multiple video files from the disk, so we built a single video containing all the separate loops and noted the start and stop time of the movies.

So, we need to store a number of pieces of data for each key: the key, the in point of the loop, and the end point of the loop.

Video key toy

1. We'll start by defining the list, the in point of the loop, and the end point of the loop as globals:

    ```
    global gvideolist
    global gInloop
    global gOutloop

    on hinit
    end

    on hupdate
    end
    ```

2. Then we need to define gvideolist as a property list, and build a list of data for each key with in another new property list, templist:

    ```
    global gvideolist
    global gInloop
    global gOutloop

    on hinit

    gvideolist = [:]

    templist = [:]
    templist[#sprite] = 1
    templist[#inloop] = 1
    templist[#outloop] = 2000

    end

    on hupdate
    end
    ```

3. Now we add the list itself to gvideolist, with its associated key character as its property name.

    ```
    global gvideolist
    ```

```
        global gInloop
        global gOutloop

        on hinit

        gvideolist = [:]

        templist = [:]
        templist[#sprite] = 1
        templist[#inloop] = 1
        templist[#outloop] = 2000

        addprop gvideolist,"a",templist

        end

        on hupdate
        end
```

4. We can add additional data by repeating the process for different characters. I'm going to add the data for the character "b":

```
        global gvideolist
        global gInloop
        global gOutloop

        on hinit

        gvideolist = [:]

        templist = [:]
        templist[#sprite] = 1
        templist[#inloop] = 1
        templist[#outloop] = 2000

        addProp gvideolist,"a",templist

        templist = [:]
        templist[#inloop] = 2200
        templist[#outloop] = 4000

        addProp gvideolist,"b",templist

        end

        on hupdate
        end
```

> *Remember, you should comment your code as you go through, just to keep track of what you're doing. We're not only doing it here because we'd be repeating the information contained in the instructions.*

5. The final part of the hinit section pauses the video, which is in member 11. We do this to stop the video playing until the user selects a video loop:

```
global gvideolist
global gInloop
global gOutloop

on hinit

gvideolist = [:]

templist = [:]
templist[#sprite] = 1
templist[#inloop] = 1
templist[#outloop] = 2000

addProp gvideolist,"a",templist

templist = [:]
templist[#inloop] = 2200
templist[#outloop] = 4000

addProp gvideolist,"b",templist

(member 11).pausedAtStart = 1

end

on hupdate
end
```

This isn't actually the way I constructed the multidimensional list, as it means repeating almost exactly the same piece of code for each character added. The later section on creating lists from cast text files shows how you can create the whole list structure in a repeat loop. We're adding the data the 'hard way' here, just to show you how this technique works.

6. So to the hupdate section of the script. First we'll add a line to make sure that we don't continue through the update handler if there isn't a current loop selected. We do this by checking whether gInloop has been assigned a value.

```
on hupdate

if voidp(gInloop) then return

end
```

7. We now check whether the movies current time is greater than the point defined by `gOutloop`. If it is, the movie time is reset to the point defined by `gInloop`.

```
on hupdate

if voidp(gInloop) then return

  if (sprite 1).movietime >= gOutloop then
    (sprite 1).movietime = gInloop
  end if

end
```

So, we've finished the `hinit` and `hupdate` sections. Now we need to append some more Lingo. Firstly, we're going to add the `keyDown` script.

8. When a key is pressed, we check whether it exists in our list. If it does exist, we call a handler, `hkey` (we'll define this in a moment).

```
on keyDown

  if not(getaProp(gvideolist,the key)) then return

  hkey(the key)

end
```

We now define the `hkey` handler. The first thing it does is to extract the data for the key from the `gvideolist` list.

```
on keyDown

  if not(getaProp(gvideolist,the key)) then return

  hkey(the key)

end

on hkey key

  keylist = getProp(gvideolist, key)

end
```

Then it sets the in and out global variables to the values associated with the key that has been pressed.

```
on keyDown

    if not(getaProp(gvideolist,the key)) then return

    hkey(the key)

end

on hkey key

    keylist = getProp(gvideolist, key)

    gInloop = keylist.inloop
    gOutloop = keylist.outloop

end
```

Finally, it moves the video clip to the in frame and sets the movie rate to 1 to ensure the movie is playing.

```
on keyDown

    if not(getaProp(gvideolist,the key)) then return

    hkey(the key)

end

on hkey key

    keylist = getProp(gvideolist, key)

    gInloop = keylist.inloop
    gOutloop = keylist.outloop

    (sprite 1).movietime = gInloop
    (sprite 1).movierate = 1

end
```

The reason for making two handlers will become apparent as we add the sprite click. The way I got this to work was to make all the sprite buttons out of text fields. This allowed me to use the following exit frame script to reuse the hkey handler:

```
on mouseDown me

 mem = (sprite(the spritenum of me)).member

  hkey mem.text

end
```

It gets the cast member associated with the sprite and then sends the text from the cast member to the hkey handler.

Both the keyDown and mouseDown scripts are generic, so you can add more by simply adding a new list, for c for example, and putting a text member with the character c in it to integrate the new instance.

Using multiple multidimensional lists

All the list actually did in the last example was retain all the static data we need to make the system work. I tend to have at least two lists: one that retains the static data, and one that I use to hold the dynamic data. I'll try to explain the differences in the next example.

For a long time we've been playing with dot matrix fonts, because they are easily described as a list.

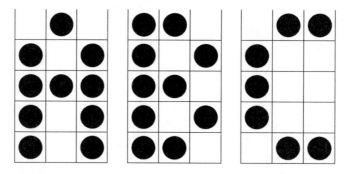

We can make a list for each character. We'll only need to remember which grid reference each dot is on and give their coordinates.

```
a = [[2,1],[1,2] ,[3,2], [1,3],[2,3] ,[3,3],[1,4],
➡ [3, 4],[1,5],[3,5]]
b = [[1,1],[2,1] ,[1,2], [3,2],[1,3],
➡ [2,3],[1,4],[3,4],[1,5],[2,5]]
c = [[2,1],[3,1] ,[1,2], [1,3],[1,4] ,[2,5],[3,5]]
```

Each sub list represents one dot and contains two numbers. The first number in the sub list is its row reference and the second is its column reference.

Dot matrix tweening

We'll make a project that tweens between these characters. We will need a static list, the grid descriptions of the letter forms, and a list that retains the data associated with every sprite instance.

1. So let's start by building a list that contains the character descriptions

```
global gLetterdata

on hinit

  gLetterdata = [:]

  addProp gLetterdata ,"a",[[2,1],[1,2] ,[3,2], [1,3],[2,3],
  ➡ [3,3],[1,4],[3,4],[1,5],[3,5]]
  addProp gLetterdata ,"b",[[1,1],[2,1] ,[1,2], [3,2],[1,3],
  ➡ [2,3],[1,4],[3,4],[1,5],[2,5]]
  addProp gLetterdata ,"c",[[2,1],[3,1] ,[1,2], [1,3],[1,4],
  ➡ [2,5],[3,5]]

end
```

We now need to define variables for the scale of the character gdotspacing, as well as the horizontal and vertical positions (gstarth, and gstartv)

```
global gLetterdata
global gdotspacing
global gstarth
global gstartv

on hinit

  gLetterdata = [:]

  addProp gLetterdata ,"a",[[2,1],[1,2] ,[3,2], [1,3],[2,3],
  ➡ [3,3],[1,4],[3,4],[1,5],[3,5]]
  addProp gLetterdata ,"b",[[1,1],[2,1] ,[1,2], [3,2],[1,3],
  ➡ [2,3],[1,4],[3,4],[1,5],[2,5]]
  addProp gLetterdata ,"c",[[2,1],[3,1] ,[1,2], [1,3],[1,4],
  ➡ [2,5],[3,5]]

  gdotspacing = 60.0

  gstarth = 200
  gstartv  = 40

end
```

We have now created the static list of character descriptions and defined scale and position. We now need to start dealing with the sprites that describe the character (gPlayerlist).

I am going to define a current and target position for each sprite, as well as a current and target blend. These will be used to create the animation as the hupdate handler will then increment the current position toward the target position, creating a the morphing quality.

I will also define the range of sprites to be updated in gOutsprite. I need to do this because the number of sprites varies from character to character that is letter a contains 10 dots and the character c only contains 7. So if we are changing from the letter c to a, we need to get rid of 3 redundant sprites. This will become clearer when we go through the hupdate handler.

```
gdotspacing = 60.0

gstarth = 200
gstartv  = 40

gOutsprite  = 10

gPlayerlist = []


repeat with a = 1 to gOutsprite
  templist = [:]
  templist[#sp] = sprite a

          templist[#currenth]  =  gstarth + (2 *  gdotspacing)
  templist[#currentv] = gstarth + (3 *  gdotspacing)
  templist[#targeth]  =  gstarth + (2 *  gdotspacing)
  templist[#targetv]  =  gstartv + (3 *  gdotspacing)
  templist[#currentblend]  =  0
  templist[#targetblend]  =  0


  add gPlayerlist,templist


end repeat

end
```

We loop through the sprite numbers we want to use with a repeat and set their current and destination coordinates to a point near the center of the character.

2. We've completed the `hinit` handler, so let's start on the keyDown. As before, we'll begin by checking whether the key exists in the `gLetterdata` list and `return` if it doesn't:

```
on keyDown
    if not(getaProp(gLetterdata,the key)) then return
end
```

3. Now we need to get out the character description of the pressed key and set the sprites target positions and blends to form the character, based on the scale and position defined in the `hinit` handler.

```
on keyDown

  if not(getaProp(,the key)) then return
  characterlist = getProp(gLetterdata,the key)

    repeat with a = 1 to count(characterlist)
    gotposreflist = characterlist[a]
    templist = gPlayerlist[a]
    templist.targeth = gstarth + (gotposreflist[1] *
    ➥ gdotspacing)
    templist.targetv = gstartv + (gotposreflist[2] *
    ➥ gdotspacing)
    templist.targetblend =  100
    end repeat

end
```

4. Finally, we'll clean up the unused sprites by setting their target position and target blend to off. This is done by using the result of a from the first repeat loop, which will indicate the number of dots in the character, and the repeating up to the range of sprites we defined in the `hinit` handler as `gOutsprite`.

```
on keyDown

  if not(getaProp(,the key)) then return
  characterlist = getProp(gLetterdata,the key)



  repeat with a = 1 to count(characterlist)
    gotposreflist = characterlist[a]
    templist = gPlayerlist[a]
    templist.targeth = gstarth + (gotposreflist[1] *
    ➥ gdotspacing)
    templist.targetv = gstartv + (gotposreflist[2] *
    ➥ gdotspacing)
    templist.targetblend =  100
```

```
            end repeat

        repeat with b = a to gOutsprite
          templist = gPlayerlist[b]
          templist.targeth = gstarth + (2 *  gdotspacing)
          templist.targetv = gstartv + (3 *  gdotspacing)
          templist.targetblend =  0

        end repeat

     end
```

And all that is left to do is to write the hupdate handler that will control the movement of the sprites in gPlayerlist. All the hupdate needs to do is increment the current data towards the target, and then reset the sprite's position and blend to the new current values. As in the previous example, positions and blends are kept as floating point numbers to create smooth and accurate transitions

```
     on hupdate
        repeat with a = 1 to count(gPlayerlist)
           templist = gPlayerlist[a]

            templist.currenth = templist.currenth + ((templist.targeth
           ➡ – templist.currenth) / 4.0)
            templist.currentv = templist.currentv + ((templist.targetv
           ➡ - templist.currentv) / 4.0)
           templist.currentblend = templist.currentblend +
           ➡ ((templist.targetblend - templist.currentblend) / 2.0)

            templist.sp.loch = templist.currenth
            templist.sp.locv = templist.currentv
            templist.sp.blend =  templist.currentblend
        end repeat

     end
```

If you create the sprites to be controlled by the script, you should end up with something like this:

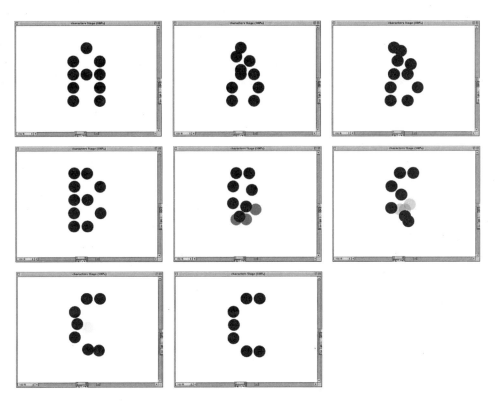

Using the watcher window to monitor lists

If you want to see how the list is changing over time, use the watcher, which is under the window menu item. Type in gPlayerlist and then press return. When you now run the movie you will be able to watch the data changing.

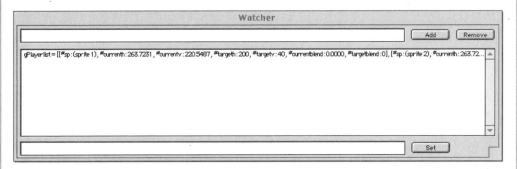

This window is extremely useful for tracking your data as well as debugging.

Lists of lists can be of any configuration of linear lists and property lists. It means you will need to use a mix of approaches to get data out from the sub levels. Try the following in the watcher:

```
GPlayerlist[1].currenth
```

In the dot matrix example we were updating all the instances in every frame update. Often it's a lot more efficient to only update the active instances. This requires us to remove instances from the player list. This will optimize the speed of the animation as you are only updating the instances that are active. I'll use the example of the drip toy that I produced for an exhibition at the barbican in 1996 to illustrate this point. It's a simple exercise of triggering animations where the mouse is clicked.

Drip toy exercise

1. Each animation consists of a series of cast members that are shown in sequence. The hinit handler contains a static list (gdriplist) of the cast numbers of the in and out references of the bitmap animations I have created. We also then create a player list, which is empty until someone mouse downs on the stage. We also have a starting sprite channel (gCurrentChan), which we increment up later in the movie.

```
global gdriplist
global gplayerlist
global gCurrentChan

on hinit

gdriplist = []
   add gdriplist,[11,64]
   add gdriplist,[65,112]
   add gdriplist,[113,158]

gplayerlist = []


gCurrentChan = 1


end
```

2. The next stage is to create the generic mouseDown script. First we increment up the current channel the animation is going to play in. We then check it's not above twenty. I have added this check so we do not end up with a huge amount of animations updating.

```
on mouseDown
     gCurrentChan = gCurrentChan + 1
     if gCurrentChan > 20 then gCurrentChan = 1
end
```

3. To this we then have to add the animation data to the gplayerlist. We first make an empty property list and then set a local variable to a random list from the gdriplist

```
on mouseDown

    gCurrentChan = gCurrentChan + 1
    if gCurrentChan > 20 then gCurrentChan = 1
    templist = [:]
    whichdrip = gdriplist[random(count(gdriplist))]
end
```

4. We then add all the data for the instance of the animation. The sprite and the in and out cast member references are put into the local list and then added to gplayerlist.

```
on mouseDown

    gCurrentChan = gCurrentChan + 1
    if gCurrentChan > 20 then gCurrentChan = 1
    templist = [:]
    whichdrip = gdriplist[random(count(gdriplist))]

    templist[#sp] = sprite gCurrentChan
    templist[#in] =whichdrip[1]
    templist[#out] =whichdrip[2]
    add gplayerlist,templist

end
```

5. And finally we set the location of the lists sprite to the member defined in its list, as well as setting its location to the mouse location.

```
on mouseDown

    gCurrentChan = gCurrentChan + 1
    if gCurrentChan > 20 then gCurrentChan = 1
    templist = [:]
    whichdrip = gdriplist[random(count(gdriplist))]

    templist[#sp] = sprite gCurrentChan
    templist[#in] =whichdrip[1]
    templist[#out] =whichdrip[2]
    add gplayerlist,templist

    templist.sp.loc = the mouseloc
    templist.sp.membernum = templist.in

end
```

6. And lastly we need to `hupdate` the movie. The first thing to do is to repeat through the `gplayerlist` and increment the cast number of every sprite up by one. This will create the animation.

```
on hupdate
repeat with a = 1 to count(gplayerlist)
    templist = gplayerlist[a]
    templist.sp.membernum = templist.sp.membernum + 1
end repeat

end
```

7. Finally we check if every sprite has reached its final cast member. If it has, move the sprite off the screen, and then remove the animations list out of `gplayerlist`

```
on hupdate

    repeat with a = 1 to count(gplayerlist)
    templist = gplayerlist[a]
 ➥ templist.sp.membernum = templist.sp.membernum + 1

    if templist.sp.membernum >= templist.out then
      templist.sp.loch = -2000
      deleteat gplayerlist, a
    end if

  end repeat

end
```

Play the movie and try clicking on the stage. You'll see the animations playing wherever you click.

Lists and files

As lists and files are both ways of storing data, it seems natural to use them together; lists allow you to store data fast while the movie is playing, and files can store data for longer periods of time. There are a number of ways that we can use files and lists together to great effect.

Creating lists from cast text files

When I worked at **Antirom**, half the people were unable to program, so we had to develop a way that these people could integrate their own content into our Lingo engines. The method we devised was to use text field cast members that people could edit to correspond with their requirements.

1. Make a text field, call it data, and write in the following:

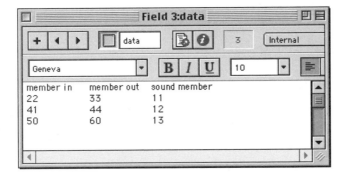

This is a simple hypothetical example, where the member in and member out of an animation, and a sound, are written as numbers.

2. To create the list out of the data we start with our `hinit` handler. We start by creating an empty list. We then repeat through the lines in the text field. We start at line 2 as the first line in the text field is a text description I have put in to indicate what each number means.

```
global ganimationlist

on hinit
  ganimationlist = []

  repeat with a = 2 to the number of lines in field "data"
    end repeat

end
```

3. After this I add a line of code I always put in to avoid errors. This line checks whether there is any data in the current line and exits the repeat loop if there isn't. This is done because it is easy for myself, or anyone else to accidentally leave some returns in at the bottom of the text field, which would effectively mess up the data structure.

```
global ganimationlist

on hinit
  ganimationlist = []

  repeat with a = 2 to the number of lines in field "data"
    if the number of words in line a of field "data" < 1 then
    ➡ exit repeat
  end repeat

end
```

And finally we can pull out the data. As the data in the text field is a string, and we want numbers, we use the phrase value to convert the string into a value.

```
global ganimationlist

on hinit
    ganimationlist = []
    repeat with a = 2 to the number of lines in field "data"

  if the number of words in line a of field "data" < 1 then exit
  repeat
      templist = [:]
      templist[#in] = the value of word 1 of line a of field
      ➡ "data"
      templist[#out] = the value of word 2 of line a of field
      ➡ "data"
      templist[#sound] = the value of word 3 of line a of field
      ➡ "data"

  add ganimationlist,templist

  end repeat

  end
```

This was an extremely useful approach. As we started to use more complex types of data we began to experience problems, because we were simply separating the pieces of data with spaces, so as soon as we used a string that contained spaces, problems arose.

Addressing the text fields as items rather than words solved this problem. Items are a more complex way of separating data. The default way of separating the data is using a comma; as this is regularly used in string data I would normally set the separator to a character that is extremely unlikely to be used. The character used is set through setting the itemDelimeter.

I have decided to use the ~ character to separate my data, and have dropped the description line. Here is the new example of my text data. The ~ defines the end of one piece of data and the next.

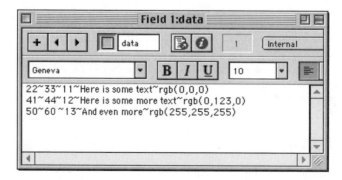

Whenever I change the item delimiter, I always remember what it was before I changed it and change it back to what it was when I've finished. This is because many of my fellow programmers use it, so I play it safe. It is often used to retain what path name delimiter should be used between Mac (:) and PC (/).

```
global ganimationlist

on hinit
  ganimationlist = []
  the itemDelimiter = "~"
  the itemDelimiter = initemdelimiter

end
```

4.   We can now do what we did in the previous example but use an item rather than word.

```
on hinit
  ganimationlist = []

  the itemDelimiter = "~"

  repeat with a = 1 to the number of lines in field "data"
     if the number of items in line a of field "data" < 1 then
     ➡ exit repeat
     templist = [:]

     templist[#in] = the value of item 1 of line a of field
     ➡ "data"
     templist[#out] = the value of item 2 of line a of field
     ➡"data"
     templist[#sound] = the value of item 3 of line a of field
     ➡ "data"
     templist[#text] = item 4 of line a of field "data"
     templist[#colour] = the value of item 5 of line a of field
     ➡ "data"
     add ganimationlist,templist
  end repeat

  the itemDelimiter = initemdelimiter

end
```

Creating lists from an external text files

The internal text field approach is useful for authoring, but we found that we needed a system that allowed us to change the input data externally from Director. This would allow for someone without Director to change the content of a piece. To do this we use the FileIO Xtra, which is included with Director 8.5

1.   Firstly make an instance of the Xtra

```
io = new(Xtra "fileio")
```

We then set the path of where the text field exists and its name. In this example it is in the same folder as the movie.

```
path = the pathname & "text.txt"
```

Then we open the file:

```
io.openFile(path,0)
```

Read the file:

```
Inputtext = io.readFile()
```

And finally close the open file.

```
Inputtext = io.readFile()   io.closeFile()
```

2.   You can now convert `Inputtext` into a list (as in the **Creating lists from cast text files** section), by substituting field `data` with `Inputtext`. For example:

```
templist[#colour] = the value of item 5 of line a of Inputtext
```

Obviously, this is most appropriate when building a projector-based project. The same can be done for Shockwave, we'll find out how to do this in the **Creating lists from text file on the Internet** section later in this chapter.

Retaining a list between sessions

In many cases you will want to retain data between a user's sessions. A nice way of doing this is to read a list when the movie starts and write the new list when the user quits. This can be done in 2 ways. The first is by using the fileIO Xtra that method we created in our last example. We've covered reading a string, and the only difference would be that you would have to convert the string back into list. This is simply done by:

```
mylist  = the value of io.readFile()
```

To write the list at the end of the users session we'll need a `stopMovie` handler. `stopMovie` is a handler name that Lingo will execute when the movie stops. Let's look at the code that makes this work:

```
on stopMovie
  io = new(Xtra "fileio")
  file = the pathname & "test.txt"

  io.openfile(file,0)
```

```
        io.delete()

        io.createFile(file)
        io.openFile(file,0)

        io.writeString(string(mylist))
        io.closeFile()
    end
```

Let's break this down and look at what each part is doing. First it creates an instance of the fileIO Xtra, in the same way as we did when reading from a file:

```
    io = new(Xtra "fileio")
    file = the pathname & "test.txt"
```

Then it deletes the file if it exists already, by trying to open and delete the file:

```
    io.openFile(file,0)
    io.delete()
```

This is important because if the file exists already and our new data is not at least as long as the old data, some of the old data will be left at the end of the file to cause problems.

Then a new file is created and opened:

```
    io.createFile(file)
    io.openFile(file,0)
```

Finally, we convert the list into a string and write it to the file, closing the file once we are done.

```
    io.writeString(string(mylist))
    io.closeFile()
```

If you are producing something that is not rewritable, such as a CD, you'll need to write and read your file from the users hard drive. A useful path to know is that of the system folder – a good place to store and retrieve data from. The path can be found by writing:

```
    Path =  baSysFolder ("System")
```

This is all fine for non-web based applications as the Xtra can be put in with the projector. When we want to do this in Shockwave we use the getPref() setPref() commands. For all forms of Director output there is a preference folder. For Shockwave this is contained in the browsers folder, for a projector it is placed in the same folder as the projector, and when your movie is running in director it uses the folder called prefs in the folder that the Director application is in.

Try the following in the message window:

```
    setPref "text.txt", string([3,45,6,7,7,8])
    put getPref("text.txt").value
```

You might have to be a little careful with your naming, as you don't want to start overwriting other people's preferences. It's also a good idea to check that the data is in the correct form when you import it, and ignore it by creating a blank list if it isn't. This can happen if someone has written another file of the same name as yours, or the file has become corrupt in some way.

1.   Firstly let's get any existing preferences.

```
global gPrefList


on hinit

inputdata = getPref("text.txt")


end
```

2.   We then check if the variable we created with the getPref function is a list. We use listp to test whether it is a list.

```
global gPrefList

on hinit
inputdata = getPref("text.txt")

        if listp((inputdata).value) then
        else
        gPrefList = [0,0,0,0,0,0]
        end if

end
```

3.   And finally we check the list is in the right format in case the imported data was a list but was in the wrong format.

```
on hinit

inputdata = getPref("text.txt")

        if listp((inputdata).value) then
                if count((inputdata).value) = 6 then
          gPrefList =  (inputdata).value
        else
                gPrefList = [0,0,0,0,0,0]
        end if

        else
                gPrefList = [0,0,0,0,0,0]
    end if
end
```

There's one last area that we're going to look at in this chapter, and that is how to create a list when the text file has come from the Internet.

Creating a list from a text file on the Internet

Something we've been doing a lot in our work is retrieving text fields from the Internet, both from projectors and Shockwave. It has been particularly useful for making CDs with updateable content, as well as producing navigation systems that clients can update by modifying text fields. In more complex executions, we've used CGI scripts to return a text field that it has produced on a server after the Shockwave piece has made an enquiry to the server.

1. Unlike the previous methods of importing data, retrieving data from the Internet is not instantaneous. You have to request the data and then wait for it to arrive. I have put a small text field online for you to try. On the first frame we need to request the data. I set the data request to a variable so I can track its progress:

```
global gnetID

on hRequestNetData

path = "http://www.tomato.co.uk/studio/data.txt"
 gnetID = getNetText(path)
end
```

2. Wait until the data is downloaded. netDone will return a value when the data defined by gnetid is downloaded. In my example, when this is done it will put the result into the message window. If it is not downloaded the movie will loop on this frame.

```
on hwaitdata

if netDone(gnetID) then
            put netTextResult (gnetID)
   else
            go the frame
   end if
end
```

Summary

I hope you now have an understanding of the potential that lists have. Lists are a key component in Director – a large component of Directors 8.5 syntax is based on property lists. For example

```
world.model[1].radius = random(200)
```

This sets the radius of the first model in the 3D environment to a random number between 1 and 200. I'll go no further than this at this point, as the 3D syntax will be elaborated on later in the book!

I hope I have sufficiently illustrated how the simplicity of lists can be built upon to create complex solutions. They are still the backbone of my coding strategy and I am sure you will find them as useful as I do.

Chapter 3
Object
Oriented Lingo
Programming

Object Oriented Programming (OOP) is an approach to programming. It's not so much about Lingo in particular, as an approach to your Lingo programming; and you'll find adhering to the principles of OOP will improve the power and flexibility of your Lingo programming no end.

In fact, there are some things that you can do in Lingo that strictly speaking, in OOP terms, you shouldn't be able to do at all – more about this as we go through the chapter. As long as you understand what these things are, and avoid them, you'll find that OOP really is the way forward. In this chapter, we'll thoroughly investigate the principles of OOP, how they apply to your Lingo code, and how you can reap the benefits from them.

The Lingo we'll be dealing with here won't be overly complex: it's the way you do what you do that matters. If you've written custom handlers and worked with lists, then you've already covered most of the Lingo necessary for this chapter. There will be some new Lingo terms, but they'll be thoroughly explained and explored as we go. So, without further ado, let's begin with the all–important question:

What's Object Oriented Programming, why's it important?

What makes OOP so different is not the code, but the concepts behind the code.

Suppose you're using a custom handler; you may have just one handler, but many different sprites can call that single handler for instructions. Each time a sprite asks for instructions, it receives instructions, and you can instruct that handler to send different instructions back to different sprites.

Now imagine that the first time the sprite asks, it not only receives instructions on what to do at that time, but also receives instructions on how to deal with similar situations in the future. The sprite is not just being told what to do, but being taught how to make *decisions* for itself.

Well, that's the basic concept behind Object Oriented Programming. Instructions and variables are **encapsulated** into self-contained **classes**. These classes are used as templates to create **objects**. The objects can have innumerable variations, each based on what goes in and how it gets used. As each object holds its own information, each works independently of the others. And since each object is encapsulated, it is entirely self-contained.

To use a common metaphor for OOP, the parent (**class**) makes the child (**object**), by providing the information that forms the basis for the child. Although the child is created from the parent information, that child is distinct both from the parent, and from any subsequent child objects. Each child object may use the parent's information in different ways, but the parent never changes; it is the stable element in the program.

Director takes this metaphor to heart in its handling of OOP. In Lingo, **Classes**, the basic templates from which objects are created, are **Parent Scripts**. The objects these parent scripts create are called **Child Objects**. A parent script can have a parent, too – an **Ancestor Script**. This is a type of parent that passes information down to another parent script, which then mixes that information to its own and passes it down to the child.

So parent scripts can be thought of as the building blocks for a family of very diverse children. These building blocks become tools that you can assemble and utilize in any number of ways.

As you'll see in this chapter, writing your code in modular chunks means that it can be reused throughout your project. Not only do you save yourself having to recreate certain pieces of functionality over and over again, but you also dramatically lower the size of your projects. What's more, if you turn these modular chunks of code into behaviors, you can reuse your objects in other Director movies, and streamline the process of sharing code in collaborative projects.

For me though, the most interesting aspect of Object Oriented Programming isn't efficiency; it is that you create independent objects that *learn* from their parents; you can create projects with a 'life' of their own. Outline some rules, identify your parents, get them all talking to each other, then zap 'em with that bolt of lightning and you've created a Director movie that is different every time. Not just the random differences we've all played with in the past, but meaningful differences caused by how you interact with the piece, and how the objects in the piece interact with each other.

As such, Object Oriented Programming enables us to approach another level of interactivity, and this chapter will examine the concepts and the Lingo needed to use Object Oriented Programming to create this kind of modularity, efficiency and life in your Director projects.

Thinking in OOP

OOP is all about simplicity. This may seem a little strange after all this talk of life and complex systems, but what it really means is this:

> *If you simplify every concept to its most basic elements, then you can re-use and re-assemble those elements in many, many diverse patterns.*

The basic totem of OOP is just that: **specify and abstract**. Break down every aspect of your project into specifics, and then **abstract** each out to its most general state. If at any point in your project you see that you can simplify what you are working on to another level, do it!

So let's look at how you could implement this idea. **Imagine that you needed to create a** walking machine. The machine will get its walking instructions from a specific instance (a child object) of a parent class. The parent class exists to create child walking objects. It does this by giving each child object a copy of its own information. The child object then applies that information to its own specific situation. The machines themselves reference the instructions contained within the child walking objects.

Now, suppose those machines were sprites (though they don't have to be); physical constructs that need to be told what to do. All we need to do is tell the parent walking class to make a child walking object to give the machine his instructions. But there's another layer of abstraction in there: the parent walking class is **inheriting** information that allows it to do this from its ancestor, the motion class.

The parent walking class talks to its ancestor, the motion class, to get the basics of direction and speed down. Then it applies some specifics to those general constructs in order to build a child walking object. The child walking object hooks itself up to the machine, and the machine walks! The machine is merely the vessel that the child walking object inhabits – give a child walking object to another machine and it will walk too.

But life's never really that simple, is it? Suppose that for some reason machines that walk aren't able to walk because of the conditions that surround them. They're surrounded by water, and they need to swim instead.

To create these, we'd need a parent swimming class to create child swimming objects. But not everything need change: the topmost level of abstraction, the motion class, ancestor to the parent walking class, has information about motion that's just as useful for the new parent swimming class. The child swimming object applies the specifics of the machine's situation to the general constructs it has inherited from its parent, and in turn the ancestor motion class hooks itself up to that machine, and the machine swims.

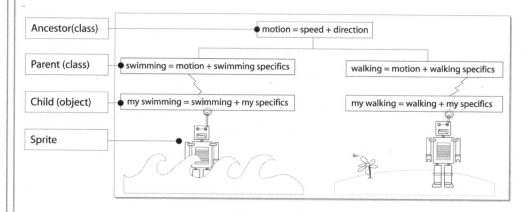

So, while there's more than one way to assemble objects, the same rules always apply: specify and abstract.

Specify all the different elements of your scenario, and then abstract them into rules that can be applied in various ways. Begin with the very general rules (in this case, motion), and get gradually more specific (walking, swimming) and then more specific still (a new machine needs to know how to swim) until you get where you need to be.

Try this on another concept, if you like; pollination, for example. You've got the bees and the flowers. Each has their role. There's a motion class in there, but there are also some classes that we need to define. When a bee moves from one flower to the next, that bee drops a little pollen onto that new flower, and picks up some in the process. When that flower's seeds fall, the new flower it creates depends on the mix of pollen it ended up with. What are the primary elements for pollination? What are the most abstract classes of those elements? A bit later on in the chapter we'll be working with an example very similar to this one in Lingo.

> *There is no wrong or right way to break up this process. Some may be more modular than others, but the point here is to get thinking about breaking processes into objects.*

OOP in Lingo

Now that we've broken down a walking machine, all the way up to a motion class ancestor, conceptually, let's use those pieces to build the motion class in Lingo. We'll begin by just focusing on the motion class itself, and once we've got the motion class working on its own, we'll make some changes so that our Director movie better represents the example we've examined.

Building a Motion Object in Lingo

1. Create a new Director movie. The stage size and color don't matter because all the action in this exercise will be taking place in the script and message windows.

   Now, refer back to that little diagram of how the objects interact.

   $$\boxed{\text{motion} = \text{speed} + \text{direction}}$$

   So, we're going to set up a motion class with the properties of _speed and _direction. We'll use a directionList property to hold the possible directions that can be inserted into the _direction property.

2. Make a new script and name it parentMotion. Now open the property inspector and select Parent from the type drop down-list. Now we're ready to script, so type this code into the script window:

```
property _speed, _direction, directionList

on new me, mySpeed
  me._speed = mySpeed
  me.directionList = list("towards","away from")
  me._direction = directionList[random(2)]
  return me
end
```

You'll already be familiar with the property declarations from other work with Lingo, but let me explain the underscores that I've used. I prefix all the variables that I use to refer to properties with an underscore, to help me understand my code at a glance; so the speed property is _speed, and the direction property _direction. It helps me differentiate at a glance between the list (directionList) and the variables that serve as "physical" properties in the script (speed and direction).

So, what about new me and return me? Well, we'll be calling this script in order to create child objects based upon it. In essence, we'll be making new versions of this parent script. on new me means, '*whenever you make a new version of me, do this*'. In OOP practice, this sort of handler is known as a **constructor function**, as its purpose is to set up the building blocks for the script, *constructing* the initial building blocks we will need to assemble the rest of this script.

As we make these new versions we'll pass a parameter to mySpeed for the new script, to set the speed of the new object. For example:

```
new (script"parentMotion", 12)- -  sets the speed of the new
➥ script to 12
```

So using me cements everything to the specific child being created. me._speed is the version of _speed specific to the particular instance of the parent script that we have created. We could create global variables _speed and _direction that were accessible from anywhere in the movie, but then if we changed one version of those variables, we'd be changing every version. By tying the properties to the specific object being created with me, we give each object its own entity, with its own set of properties, existing independently of the other child objects.

If you are comfortable with lists, you should already know what we are doing with directionList and _direction. We've set up directionList as a list with two entries, "towards" and "away from", and we're setting the _direction of the new child script to be randomly selected from that list.

I like to think of the return me as the return key on your keyboard. It confirms the information and ensures that it is all attached to the new child object sprung from the parent. me is a property that is built into the object on creation; the return me sends that script reference into memory.

3.   Now, we'll allow the child objects to tell us the value of their speed and direction properties, so add this script to the end of your script:

```
on getSpeed me
  put "My speed = " &&  me._speed
end

on getDirection me
  put "My direction =" && me._direction && "you."
end
```

These two handlers put the properties of our new child into the message window.

Altogether, the parentMotion script should look like this:

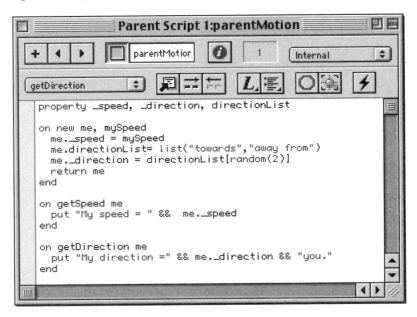

```
Parent Script 1:parentMotion
parentMotion          1          Internal
getDirection

property _speed, _direction, directionList

on new me, mySpeed
  me._speed = mySpeed
  me.directionList= list("towards","away from")
  me._direction = directionList[random(2)]
  return me
end

on getSpeed me
  put "My speed = " &&  me._speed
end

on getDirection me
  put "My direction =" && me._direction && "you."
end
```

If your script window matches, save your work (or just compile the script), and let's start creating some motion objects.

> *Incidentally, just in case you hadn't come across it before, the* '&' *operator concatenates. Concatenation is addition for strings. So* "hello"&"Cleveland" = helloCleveland.
>
> If you need to **concatenate two strings and have a space between them, you need** '&&':
> "hello"&&" Cleveland" = hello Cleveland.

4. Open up the message window and type in:

```
myTest = new(script"parentMotion", 32)
```

We're invoking a new child named myTest, which is based on the parentMotion script. It sets mySpeed to 32 for this specific child, the child named myTest. This child now has its own copy of everything that its parent has access to, including the functionality sitting within the on getSpeed me and on getDirection me handlers.

5. Try it out. Find out what the new child's speed is, by typing this into the message window:

```
myTest.getSpeed()
```

You should get this back:

```
-- "My speed =   32"
```

What we've just done is call the getSpeed() handler that resides within the child we just created. We need to preface the handler with the name of the child because no other handler exists.

6. Try calling the handler without telling Director that we are calling myTest's own version of the handler. Type the following into the message window:

```
getSpeed()
```

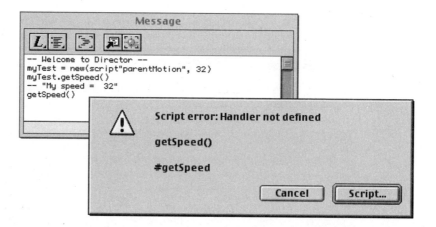

If we had defined a global handler called getSpeed() within the movie script we wouldn't get this error, but then we wouldn't be talking about this specific child's speed. What I'm trying to explain here is that unlike handlers you've probably created in the past, this handler only exists within the child objects we create.

7. Let's slow our tester down a bit. Re-initialize myTest with a speed of 10. Try it yourself before seeing how we do it.

When you type this into the message window:

```
myTest = new(script"parentMotion", 10)
myTest.getSpeed()
```

Director spits back:

```
- - "My speed =  10"
```

We've replaced the original myTest child with a new child of the same name, this time setting mySpeed to 10. The parent script then sets mySpeed to be its own version of _speed, so it can use it within its own handlers.

But this process seems long winded, couldn't we just set _speed to be 10 directly? Well you can bypass the two-step, setting the property directly like this:

```
myTest._speed=15
```

Run the myTest.getSpeed() handler again and you will see:

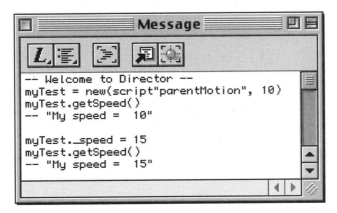

But you should never do this!

> *Setting variables directly in Object Oriented Programming is a severe no-no! The very fact that you can do this in Director is why many people don't consider Lingo a truly Object Oriented Programming language in the strict sense of a language like C++. In order to maintain encapsulation in your objects, changes should be made only by using the tools built into your objects.*

There are good reasons behind this. Suppose that later down the line you enhanced your _speed property to include phenomena like drag and gravity. The value that you set inside mySpeed when you created a new child would likely only be the first step in a more complex process before returning the speed, and if you set _speed directly, you'd be losing all the additional functionality encapsulated within your parentMotion object.

I included this last example, directly setting a variable within a parent from outside of that object, to show you what you should not do, and to introduce the important concept of encapsulation.

Encapsulation

8.   To cleanse ourselves of the OOP sin we've just committed, let's set our child's _speed back to 10 the proper way:

```
myTest = new(script"parentMotion", 10)
```

Now let's give this guy a little competition. Let's name this new child myTest2 and set its speed to 20. Try it on your own before checking how we do it. You should have set it like this:

```
myTest2 = new(script"parentMotion", 20)
```

and then checked it:

```
myTest2.getSpeed()
```

and got this returned:

```
- - "My speed =  20"
```

Check the first child's speed:

```
myTest.getSpeed()
```

you should have:

```
- - "My speed =  10"
```

So, even though we have just run the same handler, getSpeed(), to return a value of 20 for the new child myTest2, the speed of the first child is left as it is, because myTest2 has its own copy of all that information.

9.   Now, try using the handler of a soon to be created child of parentMotion. Type:

```
myTest3.getSpeed()
```

Script error! Since we haven't created this child of parentMotion, myTest3 does not have its own copy of parentMotion's functionality. Director just sees myTest3 as some new variable, and says we are missing an operator because it assumes we are trying to set it in the traditional way.

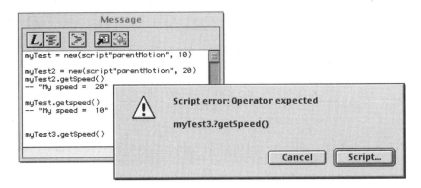

10. Now just to be sure we've got the syntax down, find out the direction for the children we have created. Remember that this is randomly selected from the `directionList` when the new child is created on new me.

Try it yourself before looking how we do it. Experiment with re-initializing the object and then asking for its direction a few times so you can see the random direction generator at work.

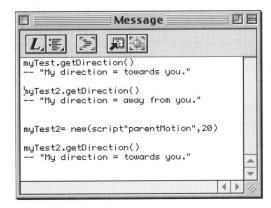

Do we have to re-initialize the entire object every time we want it to change direction? It's not such a big deal now, as all we're doing is setting speed and direction, but if we made this motion object more complex, incorporating gravity and wind-drag and friction and incline for example, it could become a waste of processor energy resetting all these properties every time we want to switch direction.

So let's break the handlers dealing with direction and speed into two separate handlers, one for setting and one for getting. Specify and abstract, even within the object itself.

11. Add the following handlers to your `parentMotion` script:

```
on setSpeed me, mySpeed
  me._speed = mySpeed
```

```
      end

on randomDirection me
  me._direction = directionList[random(2)]
end
```

With these handlers we can now set the _speed and _direction properties individually, so we don't have to recreate the entire child every time we want to change its speed or direction.

However, as we have not initialized any children with these edits, the children we have created still exist with the old functionality, before we broke set and get into separate handlers. We'll have to create new children based on this new code, or reinitialize the children we have already created in order to take advantage of this new code.

So how would encapsulation benefit us in this particular example? Well, if we'd set _direction directly, we might have inadvertently set some other value than towards or away from, either by mistake or by design, and created a bug. By ensuring that we only set _direction through the randomDirection handler, we know that our objects will only have the attributes they are supposed to.

As you design your own objects, keep this all in mind. Specify and abstract, encapsulate your objects, and make it all as modular and flexible as possible.

So now you should be comfortable with the concepts behind parent-child Lingo. You can create children based on parents, use return me, and you've seen the importance of encapsulation.

Next we'll discuss ancestors and inheritance in move detail, and deal with the unmistakable fact that those objects we played around with in the message window don't much resemble the walking and swimming machines we promised at the beginning of the chapter.

Building an Ancestor Script

In this exercise, we are going to alter our script so that we can create a swimming parent script and a walking parent script, both of which use the same parentMotion script as their ancestor, but in different ways.

First we need to make the getSpeed and getDirection handlers more modular, so we'll go in and remove all the strings. While we're at it, let's make speed a little more interesting by adding a random nature to it.

1.   Change the getSpeed and getDirection handlers so they read like this:

```
on getSpeed me
  return me._speed
end
```

```
on getDirection me
  return me._direction
end
```

Then change the me._speed declaration in the on new me handler and setSpeed handler to this:

```
me._speed = random(mySpeed)
```

As a whole, the parentMotion script should look like this:

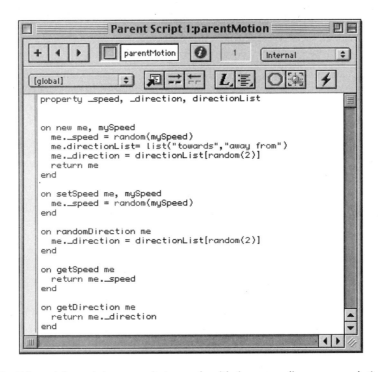

Now we've made this script modular enough to work with in more diverse ways, let's build ourselves a swimming parent script that uses parentMotion as its ancestor.

Inheritance

Note that even though parentMotion will now be serving as an ancestor, we are leaving it named parentMotion, because an ancestor is a parent script just like any other parent. What makes it an ancestor is not the script itself, but how other scripts use it.

2.   Make a new parent script named parentSwim, setting the type to Parent in the property inspector. Now, declare ancestor as a property, the same way we declared

_speed and _direction as properties of parentMotion. Properties don't only have to refer to variables and handlers; properties can be parents in their own right.

```
property ancestor
```

> *The ancestor property is different from other properties in that it can make use of functionality hard-coded into Director. When Director sees that you have declared a particular script as the parent's ancestor property, it shares all the functionality of that ancestor script with the parent, including all of the ancestor's properties and handlers.*

3.   When we create a child of the parentSwim, we'll want to set parentMotion as its ancestor, and then use the ancestor's properties to set a speed and direction for this new swimmingObject child:

```
on new me
   me.ancestor=new(script "parentMotion", 5)
   return me
end
```

You may notice that in parentSwim, we are declaring the ancestor to be an instance of parentMotion the exact same way we declared myTest to be an instance of parentMotion in the message window.

Compare, from parentSwim:

```
me.ancestor=new(script "parentMotion", 5)
```

With the way we created child objects in and from the the message window:

```
myTest = new(script"parentMotion", 10)
```

This makes parentMotion the parent of parentSwim whilst parentSwim itself is a parent. So parentSwim inherits all the capabilities of its ancestor parentMotion, and it can add its own functionality. Since parentSwim inherits the getSpeed and getDirection handlers from its ancestor, parentMotion, we don't have to define these handlers all over again in parentSwim.

Additionally, parentSwim can use the _speed and _direction properties of its parentMotion ancestor itself.

4.   Let's continue with our parentSwim. Type the following after the end of your last handler:

```
on getmyMovement me
```

```
put ("I am swimming" && me._direction &&"you at"&& me._Speed
➡ &&"miles per hour")
end
```

The parentSwim as a whole should look like this:

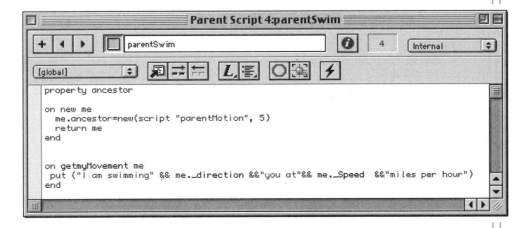

By assigning parentMotion as the ancestor of parentSwim, we have access to all of parentMotion's handlers and variables from within parentSwim. In getmyMovement, we refer to _parentMotion's speed, _direction and directionList without having to repeat any of that within parentSwim. parentSwim has inherited all of that from its ancestor, parentMotion. While these are very simple scripts, you can already see the enormous potential of inheritance. Declare everything in one script, and refer to and manipulate that information from all sorts of places.

5. Now, let's create a child of the parentSwim called mySwim. Make sure you've compiled your new script, and then create a new object through the message window:

```
mySwim= new(script "parentSwim")
```

You've created a child of parentSwim, which declares parentMotion as its ancestor with an argument of 5. The ancestor sets its speed as a random number between 1 and 5, and sets the direction as either towards or away from, selecting at random from the directionList. Then parentSwim will assemble this information from the ancestor into something new, the getmyMovement handler.

Let's see what this child's movement is. Type this in the message window:

```
mySwim.getmyMovement()
```

My child object returned:

```
- - "I am swimming away from you at 2 miles per hour"
```

Although yours may very well return something different!

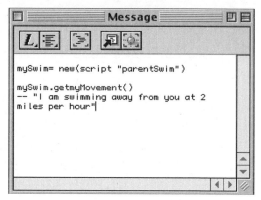

To finish this up, let's create one more parent script: parentWalk. Since machines generally walk faster than they swim (well, those I've met do), set it up so that the argument passed in setParentSpeed is 10. And let's make mySpeed 10 more than whatever getSpeed() returns, so we are assured that these machines always walk faster than they swim. Try it yourself before looking at how we've done it.

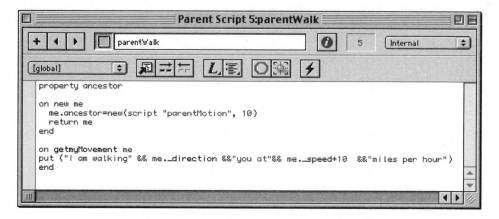

6. Now test the parentWalk script. Create a child of parentWalk and find out his movement.

    ```
    myWalk=new(script"parentWalk ")

    myWalk.getMyMovement()
    ```

    You should get something like this:

    ```
    - - "I am walking away from you at 14 miles per hour"
    ```

    Notice that we used the same handler name, getmyMovement for parentWalk as well as parentSwim. Since these handlers are specific to each parent, they each perform different functions. This brings up one final and important point about ancestor scripts and inheritance.

> *Although parents inherit everything from their ancestor, if the parent and the ancestor ever end up with the same variable name or handler, the parent wins. Priority goes from specific to general, with the more specific instance taking precedence.*

7. Try it, add the following handler to your parentMotion script, the ancestor:

```
on getmyMovement me
   put ("I'm moving you")
end
```

In the message window, make a new child of parentWalk based on this new code (so make sure you've compiled it) and run its getmyMovement() handler.

```
myWalk2= new(script " parentWalk ")

myWalk2.getmyMovement()
```

You'll still get something that you would have been expecting before the changes you made to the ancestor script:

```
- - "I am walking towards you at 11 miles per hour"
```

Since there is still a more specific reference to getmyMovement within parentWalk itself, that takes precedence over the parentMotion ancestor's version of getmyMovement.

8. Test it once more: go back into the parentWalk script you just created, and comment out the getmyMovement handler.

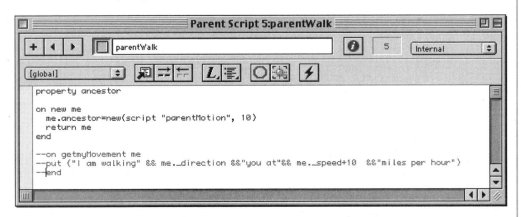

Now, back in the message window, re-initialize myWalk2 and run its getmyMovement.

```
myWalk2= new(script " parentWalk ")

myWalk2.getmyMovement()
- - "I'm moving you"
```

Since there is no longer any specific reference to getmyMovement within parentWalk, Director looks to the ancestor, one step more abstracted.

So, you can set up general rules for whole classes of objects, but allow the child objects to change them for their own use, without affecting the others. The hierarchy for same-named handlers applies to ancestors and parents having the same properties with the same names; priority is assigned in the same way it is assigned with handlers, with the more specific reference taking precedence. For instance, we could define _speed differently in parentSwim from its ancestor parentMotion. Then parentSwim would use its own definition, while parentWalk would still refer to the ancestor's definition.

Keeping Track of Child Objects

1. Remember the first child object we created, myWalk? We created him well before we began working the parentMotion, so even though parentMotion has changed, he is still carrying around that old information, that old functionality. Try him out in the message window:

    ```
    myWalk.getmyMovement()
    - - "I am walking away from you at 14 miles per hour"
    ```

2. While we're remembering old friends, remember good old myTest? Try him out in the message window. If you haven't quit Director since you started this chapter, you should get this:

    ```
    myTest.getSpeed()
    - - "My speed =  10"
    ```

    If you have quit out of Director and restarted, its memory has been purged, so you'll get the Operator expected error, because myTest no longer exists. As long as Director is running, even if you close out of the file in which you created these children, these children still exist in your computer's RAM.

3. Try it, create a new Director file and click Okay to save your changes. Now type into the message window:

    ```
    myWalk2.getmyMovement()
    ```

You should get:

```
- - "I'm moving you"
```

You are no longer in the Director movie in which you created this little guy, yet he is still hanging around! These objects really are their own entities. Once you've created them, they exist independent of the Director movie in which they were born.

While this is extremely powerful, it can also cause you a lot of trouble. For instance, _speed is a pretty generically named property. If you've got animations running in some other Director Movie dependent on a _speed variable, then that Movie's version of _speed could conflict with the Movie that you're working on, and give you some unexpected results. While the persistence of objects in Director's memory can be very valuable, it can also be detrimental, and you need to be careful about keeping track of the children you are creating.

Something else you should bear in mind as you create child objects is that once you start creating more complex parent-child scripts, you could start filling up your RAM with a lot of unnecessary information if you never remove the children you create.

If Director needs RAM to perform some other function, it'll start leaking these children, letting them slip into the cyber–void from which they can never be reclaimed. Director's memory can leak the information stored in the child objects if you let too many amass. Then, when you try to refer to those children that have disappeared later on, you'll get an error. So it's a good idea to keep the amount of children residing in your RAM to a minimum.

Removing child objects

4. Enter the following into your message window:

```
myWalk2 = VOID
```

VOID is a special Director keyword, actually a constant, equal to a value of nothing. VOID is not the same as 0, as 0 is an actual number. Setting something to VOID removes it entirely.

You may have noticed that we have broken one of the rules of OOP; we have forgone handlers and set a value within an object directly. To maintain strict encapsulation, a true OOP implementation would use some sort of destructor function defined within the ancestor or parent itself. For the purposes of this example we'll continue with the VOID, but in practice you can set up your own function to do the same thing, in a manner more appropriate to true OOP.

5. Now, try calling myWalk2 again:

```
myWalk2.getmyMovement()
```

The object has completely disappeared.

So far, you've created an ancestor script, learned how the properties of parent scripts can be parent scripts in their own right, and created and destroyed child objects. We also broke the concept of motion down into an object, and worked with parent-child lingo to use it.

Still, something's missing; it's not been quite as, well, exciting, as you might have hoped. Where's all that power we promised earlier? What about the great power Object Oriented Programming purportedly offers us? How about putting some action to our motion? How about a motion object that actually makes something move?

Beyond The Message Window: Moving objects with the Motion Object

We've been taking it pretty slow so far. We've stopped at every corner, checked out the other possible routes, and made sure we were entirely comfortable with the concepts before moving on. Now that you are familiar with the basics of Object Oriented Programming, we're going to pick up the pace a bit. For this example, we're assuming you already know how to create and manipulate lists in Lingo, and can implement a high-school level of Math into your Director projects. This example is pretty complex, and it is going to call on a large portion of what you have gone over in this book. However, if you've skipped the rest of the book and you only care about OOP, we have set up this example so that it will run fine without that other knowledge, although obviously you'll get more out of it if you understand the other concepts we touch on.

What's important is that you understand how to integrate what you do know (or what someone else has figured out, for that matter) with Object Oriented Programming in Director. Brian has created a set of code for list manipulation, available at http://www.grographics.com/lingo/ . As long as you understand what you are putting in and getting out from these math and list functions, which we will cover, then you'll be able to work through this example with no problems.

One more note before we begin to look at how OOP can be applied to Director to control motion. You'll probably notice the name of the file incrementing each time it appears in the title bar of the score or the stage. This is a simple little trick to get around the fact that Director still doesn't support multiple undos. Not rocket science, just each time you save your project, save it as one number higher than the last. When you are finished for the day, save another copy as the original name without any numbers. That way, if on MyDirectorProject45 you realize that you really need that script you deleted back in MyDirectorProject15, you can go back and get it. And you've always got two copies of the latest version should Director decide to corrupt on you.

Using OOP to control real objects

We're going to create something close to a pollination scenario: a few flowers and some bees flying from one to the other, selecting at random which one they want to nestle on next. If we followed up and strictly implemented the objects we've been working with so far, we'd have objects that went either towards or away from you at different speeds, depending on whether they are swimming or walking – not a terribly visual example. I hope that with the skills and tips you pick up from this example, you'll be able to turn the example we'll work with next into a movie with objects that really affect each other, taking full advantage of the possibilities of inheritance.

1. Create a new Director movie. Size and color doesn't really matter, but in this example we've used 512 x 342 (one of Director's default sizes) with a black background. Just be sure that you can fit a couple flowers on it, with plenty of room for bees to fly around.

2. Now draw yourself a few flowers, and a circle to denote a bee, or a whole bee if you're feeling artistic. We've drawn white flowers on a black background in Illustrator, exported them as Flash .swf, and imported it into Director. You can just draw your flowers in Director's own Vector Shape or Paint windows. If you do decide to import a Flash movie, make sure you set the properties for that Flash file (and all others you bring in) as paused, without sound, and not direct to stage. Check the chapter on importing Flash for more details. We drew the bee in Director's paint window, as a simple circle with a yellow border around a black fill.

3. Now, lay four flowers out in channels 5-8, and three bees in channels 15-17. The first few channels are for you to fill up with stems, a horizon line, or whatever else you think should form the backdrop for this little world. Since all the action will be going on in one frame, it doesn't matter how many frames these sprites take up. I usually make sprites 8 frames long anyway, so I can read the names of the cast members filling each sprite.

    If you draw the stem in Director's vector shape window or as a Flash .swf, you needn't make more than one, because you can twist, warp and contort that stem into all sorts of shapes once it's on the stage. We don't want the bounding boxes to interfere with the other shapes flying around, so set everything to Matte or Background Transparent ink, depending on the look you want.

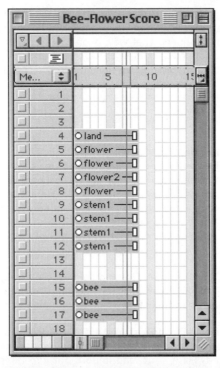

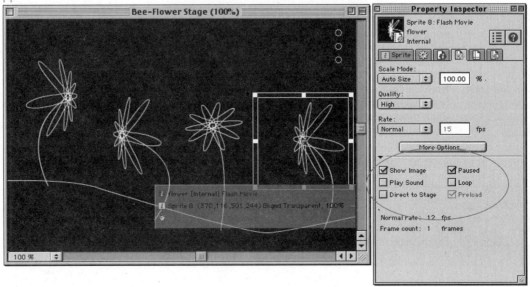

Keeping it all tidy: the house cleaning script

Now, the first thing I always do in a Director movie is create a house cleaning script. The idea is to clear any objects or variables hanging around from previous runs of the movie, which would interfere with subsequent runs.

4.   This is the house cleaning script. Open up the script window, set the type to movie, and type:

```
on prepareMovie
 - - initialize the movie
 the actorList = []
end
```

Call your script HouseCleaning.

This clears the actorList. The actorList is a special list Director has to hold all the children you create. Remember how we had to track down each child and remove it in the last example? Well, in this movie we'll add an entry into the actorList every time we create a new child. This helps us keep track of our children as we run them through their various tasks.

Another nice feature of the actorList is that it gives us a stepFrame handler. Every child in the actorList has a stepFrame handler that is called for each child every time the Director playback head hits the frame. As you'll see later, this can be very helpful for creating animations based on your lingo, and allows us to activate each object in turn to carry out our actions.

The house cleaning script is also where you could clear any global variables you had hanging around with the clearGlobals command. This isn't always a good idea, though. If you were working on a project that involved multiple movies, for example, then clearGlobals would wipe out all of the global variables set by any Director movie; which wouldn't be very helpful to you. For instance, you might have a different bee and flower scenario with its own global variables, and should someone dally off into this other movie, you may not want to sacrifice all the values you've set previously.   When you are working with multiple movies, you'll have to clear the specific variables you want to clear, unless the movies are set up such that it doesn't matter if all the global variables are removed.

At any rate, clearGlobals isn't really necessary in this movie, but it can be a handy clean up script where appropriate.   Now that we've initialized the actorList, let's put some children in it.

Building an actorList

5.   In the first frame, double-click the Script channel in the score to create a new script, and make sure the type is set to Behavior in the property inspector. Name this script BuildActorList, because that is exactly what it will do.

```
on exitFrame me
   - - set the objects in the actorList
   repeat with i = 5 to 8
            add the actorList, new(script"Flower Script",i)
   end repeat
```

Although we haven't yet built the **Flower Script**, you can probably guess what we are doing. Passing an argument that increments from 5 to 8 to a **Flower Script**, creating a new child and adding a new entry in the actorList at each pass. These correspond to the channels in which the associated sprites are sitting, so this script will tie the **Flower Script** to the sprites in channels 5 through 8, which are our little flower drawings.

An aside: in general, it is not good practice to hard-code your sprites into specific channels. There is a more elegant way to build an actorList that finds sprites fluidly, rather than tying the script irrevocably to a set of specific channel numbers. By keeping channel numbers out of your code, you do have much more flexibility. You can move things around without updating your code, and generally enjoy more modular scripts.

I've chosen to do it this way because this a rigorous example, and I'm trying to keep it as simple as possible so that we can focus as much on strictly OOP-related concepts as possible. So, we've hard-coded the channel numbers into the code at first. But you should be aware that you should avoid this practice whenever possible, and we will go back once we've got this script working and do it the right way.

Creating the parent Flower Script

6.   Make a new script, set its type to parent, and name it Flower Script. As you've seen, we'll be passing a number to it as we create child objects from this script, and tying the new child to the appropriate sprite. We'll call the number flowerSprite and we'll tie it to this specific child of Flower Script by making it a property of that child with the familiar syntax me.property.

First declare the property:

```
property mySprite
```

Then tie the number to that property and return me when an object is created.

```
on new me , flowerSprite
  me.mySprite = flowerSprite
  return me

end
```

We did the same thing earlier, tying parentMotion's _speed property to mySpeed when we were playing with myTest. Check back and compare, if you like.

So, now each child object that is created will know the channel number of the sprite it should be controlling. But we need a way for other scripts to interact with this sprite. How is a bee going to approach a flower if it doesn't know where that flower is? So we need a way for other objects to find out that sprite number, and we don't want them digging around inside the properties directly.

7.   We'll keep everything encapsulated by providing a handler that gives other objects the information they need.

```
on getSpriteNum me
  return me.mySprite
end
```

To finish off this script, we'll need a way for others to tell if this is a flower or a bee.

```
on getParentType me
  return "Flower"
end
```

So, in its entirety, the Flower Script looks like this:

```
property mySprite

on new me , flowerSprite
  me.mySprite = flowerSprite
  return me

end

on getSpriteNum me
  return me.mySprite
end

on getParentType me
  return "Flower"
end
```

Planning The Bee

The Bee Script is a lot more complex than the flower. All the flower has to do is know which sprite it's on and that it is a flower. Each bee, on the other hand, needs to know which flower he wants to head towards, how to get there, when he's landed so he can pick a new flower, and on top of all this he needs to know which of the other objects are bees and flowers. Just to make this a bit more interesting, we'll also have two types of bee, that the user can create by pressing a button: lazy bees and crazy bees. The lazy bees move slowly and languish on each flower a long time before taking off again.

Before we get into the specifics of the code, let's examine what exactly the bee will have to do, logically, and set up a framework of handlers and properties to cover these requirements. Remember: specify and abstract.

Well, the bee needs to fly. In order to fly, he'll need to know where he's going (his target) and how fast he's going. Once he reaches a flower, he'll have to wait around a bit to grab the pollen or whatever, then choose a new flower and fly towards it.

What the bee needs to know

To specify that down into properties, in order to fly he needs a target (myTargetFlower), a speed (mySpeed), and some way to wait around for a bit once he's reached a flower. We're going to create a movie in which the user can make lazy bees and crazy bees. The lazy bees move slowly and languish on that flower a long time before taking off again. The crazy bees flit from flower to flower, barely pausing for pollen before they dash off again. Since the amount of time the bees wait on a flower will be different from bee to bee, we'll need a variable to cover how long he waits as well (myWaitDiff).

So, before we've really begun, we know the bee will need at least these three properties:

1. MyTargetFlower

2. myWaitDiff

3. mySpeed

Just thinking about bees and flowers logically, I can't think of any other properties that are needed. But let's start thinking about how we'd make it work in Director to see if we've left anything out (we have).

What the bee needs to do

The primary actions the bee will need to accomplish are:

1. Picking a new target

2. Waiting

3. Flying

Picking a target

How does this bee pick his target? Well, the target needs to be a flower, so first he needs to find a target that is a flower. How does he know if it's flower or not? Well, we can use the getParentType handler in the Flower Script, which is designed to tell whoever needs to know that the script is attached to a flower. But in order to get the bee talking to the flower in the first place, we'll need to use the actorList. (Remember, the actorList is a Director list for holding all the child objects we create with our parent classes. So if the bee runs through the ActorList, asking each child if it's a flower or not, he's bound to find a flower).

Now, we don't want this bee to fly back to the same flower he's just left (bees aren't stupid, you know. In fact this is the beginning of what is known as an *intelligent* system). So, before the bee flies off happily towards the flower target he's just discovered, he needs to make sure the target is not the flower he is currently on. How does he know what flower he is currently on? The flower he is currently sitting on would be his previous target, yes? So we'll compare the flower he wants to go to with the flower he is currently on. Once he ascertains that the new target flower he is contemplating is not his current target flower, that new flower will become his target flower. Once he lands on that new flower, he just checks the next flower against that target again. And so on and so on.

By running through the actions the elements in this system need to take, and then specifying each of those actions until we can't specify them any more, we start to build the framework for our objects.

To specify these steps, in order to pick a target, the bee will need to:

- Ask each child in the `actorList` if it is a flower

- If it is a flower, make sure it's not the flower he is currently on

- If that flower is not the flower he is currently on, then that flower is his new target!

So now our bee has the framework for a handler to find his target, and he needs to fly towards that target. But first, we want him to wait for a bit. Remember, the lazy ones wait around a long time, and the crazy ones lift off immediately. So, let's specify and abstract the waiting part of the bee's actions.

Waiting

What have we got to start with? Well, when we create lazy or crazy bees, we'll be assigning a property called `myWaitDiff`. Essentially, this is a variable that tells the bee how long to wait. Let's specify that a bit more. How exactly will that variable accomplish this?

To answer that, let's step back a moment and consider how we set up timers for ourselves. If I tell you to wait behind the tree for exactly fifteen seconds, and then come out and try to catch me, how will you do it? You'll count to fifteen. You start with zero, and at each increment you compare the amount of time you are supposed to wait with the time you have waited. Well, yes, it does sound incredibly basic. Everyone knows how to count to fifteen, and everyone knows how to set up a timer. But your problems won't always be this easy, and by playing with the techniques of abstraction and specification with these simple examples, we'll be preparing ourselves for tackling much more complex ones on our own. So, what exactly are we doing as we count to fifteen:

- Start at zero

- Each time I count up one number

- Check if that number is the same as the time I am supposed to wait

- If it is the same amount of time, then GO

- Otherwise, keep standing behind the tree and counting

How can we do that in Director? Well, Director has a special incrementing counter, `the ticks`, which in fact a system property that returns the current time in ticks. Your movie starts, the `ticks` are ticking, and all the while `myWaitDiff` holds a static number. So, we can compare `myWaitDiff` to the `ticks`.

So, we just set our `ticks` to zero, let them increment, then once the `ticks` are equal to `myWaitDiff` we know it's time to go. Right?

Wrong. First, you can't set the `ticks` to zero. The ticks can only be read. And we don't want to use the timer because that is a global counter, so any child object making changes with `startTimer` would be affecting all the children dependent on that number. Remember, we want to keep everything encapsulated within each object.

Also, the `ticks` increment regularly, and we'll need to be checking regularly so that we can see when it is time to go.

So, we've specified and abstracted our problem down to the need for a way to check things regularly. And Director allows us to check events in the child objects regularly: on `stepFrame me`. As we mentioned earlier, every child in the `Actor List` can use the `stepFrame me` event handler. This event handler is called every time the playback head enters a frame or the Stage is updated.

So there's our spark. Now, we know how to keep checking (just call it on `stepFrame me`,) and we just have to figure out how to make a localized counter, without getting involved in setting lots of unnecessary variables.

So, how can we make the `ticks` be zero without actually changing them? How can we use this global counter in a way that keeps the numbers distinct to each child object? How do we keep it encapsulated? We're going to have to set another property.

We just set that property equal to the `ticks`, subtract it from the `ticks`, and we have set our counter to 0. Then we compare it to `myWaitDiff` on `stepFrame me`, and we're golden! I'll save the actual equation writing until we get down into the nitty grity of the Lingo itself, but for now we know that the waiting handler needs:

1. To be called on `stepFrame`,

2. To reference the `myWaitDiff` that we set when we create the lazy or crazy bee

3. To utilize a property we hadn't though of earlier, which we'll call `myTimer`

4. To use `myTimer` in tandem with the ticks and `myWaitDiff` to figure out when to fly

Now that we know we need another property (`myTimer`), we'll need to add that to the list of properties we outlined under *What the bee needs to know*.

I know this must seem rather excruciating. Several pages and we haven't even started coding! Over a page to describe something as simple as a timer! But in coding in general, and Object Oriented Programming particularly, it's important to flesh out the concepts of your code before you dive into the application. OOP needs to be modular; it needs to be flexible. OOP isn't just about parents and children and ancestors and on `stepFrame me`; it's about specifying and abstracting all the elements of your system until you've come up with the most elegant solution possible. A good design will go far. Much farther than you'd probably guess.

So, bear with me. This degree of analysis may seem laborious now, but running through these simple exercises in this manner will help you absorb the good habits that will make your code fly.

Speaking of flying.

Flying

Let's specify and abstract the flying part now. Flying, as we saw with walking and swimming, entails a direction and a speed. In this case the direction is his target, and the speed is decided when you click the button that assigns the bee his personality.

To control the bee's motion, we're going to use Zeno's paradox: if you are headed towards a destination and each step you take brings you half of the way there, you will never reach your destination. So if you're a hundred feet away, your first step takes you 50 feet, your second step takes you 25 feet, then 12.5 feet away, 6.25, 3.125, 0.5625, 0.78125, 0.390625... Each step is equal to the distance you will be from the destination after your step: you just never get there. It will get closer and closer, excruciating close, but mathematically, it will never reach zero.

So, what good is an equation that never brings us to our destination? Well, we can cheat in Director. We can say that once we've reached a certain distance from our target, let's just snap to the target. This just gives us a simple way to approach our target.

We'll go into the equation itself when we get into the Lingo of this example. For now, examining this equation has helped us figure out the other sections of the bees flying script.

In order to fly, he needs to know:

1.   His current location

2.   His target location

3.   The distance between him and his target

4.   The point at which he should snap to that destination

For this to animate, we'll call this handler on stepFrame me. Each time it is called, it performs the equation again, coming closer and closer to the flower until it snaps to the flower.

So, what are we still missing from the Bee Script? Well, how does the bee know if he's flying or not? We'll set a variable that tells the bee if he is flying. If he is flying, then on stepFrame he runs through the flying handler. If he has landed, and isn't flying, then he runs through the waiting handler.

We'll call this variable myFlying, and we'll give it to the bee as a property. So, there's another entry into our list of properties: myFlying. We now have five properties for the bee. That does it for the flying part of the bee's duties. Is there anything else he'll need to do his thing?

Setting the sprite and parent type

Well, just like the flower, this bee will need a way to attach himself to the sprite, so we'll need a mySprite property just like the flower. That makes six properties for the bee. We'll need to set up a getParentType handler, just like the flower, which tells whoever asks that he is a bee.

The way this code is set up, we only really have to know if something is a flower or not. As the bee never flies towards bees, and the flower doesn't know what's going on in this scenario, the getParentType handler isn't used for anything other than preventing errors.

You see, when the bee runs through the actorList, he asks each child object in that list what type his parent is. If the bee doesn't have a handler to, um, handle that request, we'll get an error. So, we'll need a getParentType handler for the bee as well.

Now the last thing before we get into the code itself. We've gone into some detail on all the functionality of the bee, and we know that we'll be creating bees that are either lazy or crazy, depending on how the parent script is applied to create the child object that controls the bee sprites. But we haven't yet discussed how we are going to birth our actual lazy and crazy bees.

Creating the bees

Creating the bees is pretty easy. In fact, we've already done most of that process in the message window examples. Remember how we created myTest?

```
myTest = new(script"parentMotion", 10)
```

This invoked a child object called myTest, which was based on the parent class parentMotion, passing a parameter of 10, which parentMotion used to determine its speed.

We'll essentially be doing the same thing when we make the crazy and lazy bees. We'll write a script that we'll attach to a button. When you click on the button, it will invoke a child object based on the parent bee class. As we have discussed already, that child's speed and waiting time will be dependent on the arguments passed in the parameters. The values determined by our choice of lazy or crazy bee will become properties of the bee child object.

We'll enter that bee child object into the actor list, much as we did with the BuildActorList we put in frame 1 of the Movie, and we'll also pass a property that tells the child object which sprite it will be controlling.

It's a step further than what we've done so far, but is all based on the very same concepts and code.

Let's quickly summarize the chain of events for the bee to function:

1. The user selects a lazy bee or crazy bee, using a button, and this sends the proper values to the bee parent class, which in turn creates a bee child object based on this information on new me.

2. The properties we pass to the bee from the lazy bee and crazy bee button refer to the bee's sprite, speed, and waiting time.

3. The bee parent class will have the following properties:

- mySprite

- myWaitDiff

- mySpeed

- myTargetFlower

- myTimer

- myFlying

4. The bee will check whether it should start flying towards a flower in its on stepFrame event. This calls a handler that deals with waiting (goYet), which is dependent on waitDiff, (the amount of time it should wait). We'll set this property when we create a bee using the crazy bee or lazy bee buttons. It is also dependent on myTimer, another property we set in the list of properties, and the ticks.

5. Then the bee checks if it is currently flying. The property that holds this information is initially set up in the list of properties for the bee (myFlying).

6. If the bee is not flying, it will run a handler to find its target. The property that holds this information is initially set up in the list of properties for the bee (myTargetFlower). Once it has found a target, it will run the handler that deals with flying.

7. If the bee is flying, it will continue to run the flying handler on each stepFrame.

8. Once the bee is close enough to its target flower, it will snap to the flower and set myFlying to FALSE so the bee knows it is not flying when it asks again next stepFrame. It will also set myTimer = the ticks, so the bee can start the waiting period properly.

9. The bee then returns to step 4, and checks if it is flying. It's not flying, it calls the handler that deals with waiting, using the new value the bee just set for myTimer in the equation. And so on, over and over.

As we get into the meat of the example, you'll see that it is a bit more complex than this. We add some random variables into the mix to make things more interesting, and will discuss several ways of handling the sprites to which the bee child objects are attached. But, in a nutshell, that is the framework for the bee scripts we are about to write.

Coding the Bee Script

1. Create a new script, call it Bee Script, and set its type to parent.

We know that the bee needs six properties, so set them next:

```
property mySprite, myWaitDiff, mySpeed, myTargetFlower, myTimer,
myFlying
```

We'll send the values for mySprite, myWaitDiff, and mySpeed to the bee when a new bee child object is created, from the buttons. Just to remind you, this is what each property will do:

mySprite	Tells the bee child object which sprite it should control
myWaitDiff	Determines how long the bee waits on a flower,
mySpeed	Will control the speed of the bee mySprite. As you'll see when we get into the handler for waiting, the higher the number the longer it waits. The handler that deals with flying will utilize this property. As you'll see when we build the handler that deals with flying, the higher this number, the *slower* the bee flies.
myTargetFlower	Used by the handler that deals with finding the target to determine the next target flower in the bee's series of hops.
myTimer	The property we use in tandem with myWaitDiff and the ticks to make the bee wait
myFlying	A Boolean that tells the bee whether it is flying or not. (A Boolean is a variable than can only be on or off, 0 or 1, TRUE or FALSE).

Now that we've discussed what each of these properties are going to do, let's do something with them!

We'll be using the crazy bee or lazy bee button to create a child of the parent Bee Script, and we'll be passing three parameters: the sprite the child should be attached to (beeSprite), a number that determines how long the bee waits on a flower (howLong), and a number that determines how quickly the bee will fly (howFast). Let's set that up now:

2. Type the following into the Bee Script after the list of properties we just entered:

```
on new me, beeSprite, howLong, howFast
```

So, we're capturing the three parameters that are passed in the on new me event handler, and turning them into something we can use within the Bee Script itself, along with the other properties that we need. Type this in next:

```
   me.mySprite = beeSprite - - the spriteNumber of each bee
     me.myWaitDiff = howLong - - how long the bee waits between
     ➡ flights
     me.mySpeed = howFast
     me.myTargetFlower = 5 - - the target of the flightpath
     me.myTimer = 0 - - used in timer
     me.myFlying = FALSE - - boolean variable to test whether the
     ➡ bee is in flight
     return me
  end
```

The properties we are given at the beginning (mySprite, myWaitDiff, mySpeed, myTargetFlower, myTimer, myFlying) are general properties. In this piece of code we're making each property specific to each child object created from the parent script, using the syntax me.*MyPropertyName*.

This construct is already familiar to you from the message object examples, but you've probably been using this type of construct in Lingo all along, even before you started experimenting with OOP. For example, how would you set the locH for sprite 5?

sprite(5).locH = whatever

We are using the same syntax here. Just as locH is a property of sprite(5) when we refer to it sprite(5).locH, myTargetFlower is a property of me when we refer to it as me.myTargetFlower. It is not a property of the parent, nor is it the property of another child object. me.myTargetFlower is the property of this specific child, this specific instance of the parent Bee Script.

We'll be changing most of these properties when we run the Bee Script, but this is where we set their initial values. Let's look at each property we are assigning to the new child to see why we have set it is as we have.

The first three lines of this new code are simply assigning the parameters held by beeSprite, howLong, and howFast, (passed in from the lazy and crazy bee buttons) to me.mySprite, me.myWaitDiff, me.mySpeed respectively. They will hold the parameters specific to each child object, setting them as properties of me. As you'll see from the earlier list, *me.mySprite* is the glue that enables us to attach the child object to movement on the screen. We will be using *me.mySprite* to tell the bee which sprite it should control with the child object. me.myWaitDiff = howLong determines how long the bee will wait around on a flower, and howFast the speed of the bee.

As you'll see when we build the findTarget handler, myTargetFlower refers to the sprite that the flower the bee is heading towards occupies. So we're setting that initial value as a sprite a flower actually occupies. Take a look at your score: 5, 6, 7 or 8 will do fine.

We'll be running a randomizer before we actually pick the target, but it is a good idea to set the initial value as something it should be. Setting the initial value to a number other than 5,6,7 or 8 will sometimes cause a bug, sending the bee off the stage.

me.myTimer will be used by goYet, the handler that deals with making the bee wait around on the flower before taking off again. We'll go over it in more detail later when we build that handler, so for now it is enough to know that setting the initial value of me.myTimer to 0 will make the bee take off immediately.

As we mentioned earlier, me.myFlying is a Boolean; it can only ever be TRUE or FALSE, 0 or 1. In fact, this script would work just as well if you set me.myFlying = 0.

TRUE and FALSE are Director keywords, and as far as Director is concerned, 0 and FALSE are the same thing in these circumstances. TRUE and FALSE are not strings. "TRUE" (a string) is not the same thing as TRUE, a director keyword. When we set me.myFlying to TRUE when we work on the flying handler in a few minutes, we could achieve the same results by setting it to 1. For clarity's sake, I'm using the Director keywords TRUE and FALSE, instead of 1 and 0.

It is not necessary to capitalize TRUE and FALSE when we use them as keywords, but it is a good convention to adopt, simply because they're more noticeable like that, and in some other languages, differences in case DO make a difference.

Now we have defined all of our properties as properties specific to the particular child object the parent script is birthing. We finish up by initializing this child and sending it into Director's memory with the return me command.

```
return me
```

We have finished the constructor, set up all the building blocks we will need to assemble with the handlers. Now it is time to take all these properties and use them in our handlers to get this bee working.

Checking and more checking: The stepFrame handler

As we discussed, every child object in the actorList has access to the stepFrame handler. The Director handler on stepFrame is triggered for each object in the actorList every time the playback head enters the frame. This happens just before the on prepareFrame handler.

Take a look at the code and discuss it before you type it in. The goYet() handler is the handler that deals with waiting. Essentially that handler performs a function to determine whether or not the bee should fly. If the bee should fly, goFly() returns TRUE. If it shouldn't fly, it returns FALSE.

me.goYet() is another way of asking 'did goYet() return TRUE?' Should this script return TRUE, then the bee should fly, and so we progress to the next if statement: if not me.myFlying.

So, if the bee is not flying, since goYet has told us it is now time to fly, the bee needs to run the flying handler to make him fly. But first, he needs to find a target. He does this with the findTarget handler. We will code that handler shortly. Once the findTarget handler has told the bee where he should fly to, he will run the flying handler and start flying. That is the next handler we will build, but first let's type in the stepFrame handler we just discussed.

3. So this is how all that looks in code. Type the following into your Bee Script after the end of the `on new me` handler:

```
on stepFrame me
    if me.goYet() then -- if goYet returns true, (if it is time to
  ➡ fly).
        if not me.myFlying then -- if the bee is not flying
            me.findTarget()
            me.flying()
```

If `goYet` tells us it is time to fly, then if we are not currently flying, find the target and start flying. The first time around we set `me.myFlying` to FALSE on `new me`, so the bee will see that he is not flying and will run through the series of handlers.

4. Now to finish up the `on stepFrame` handler jump back to the first `if` statement. If `goYet` tells us it is time to fly, and `not me.myFlying` is FALSE, that means the bee is flying (a double negative being a positive). So we should call the `flying` handler to keep us flying on this `stepFrame`.

Type the following into your bee script to finish up the `on stepFrame` handler:

```
        else
            me.flying() -- call the flight function
        end if
    end if
end
```

In its entirety, the `on stepFrame` handler should look like this:

```
on stepFrame me
    if me.goYet() then -- if goYet returns true, (if it is time to
  ➡ fly).
        if not me.myFlying then -- if the bee is not flying
            me.findTarget()
            me.flying()
        else
            me.flying() -- call the flight function
        end if
    end if
end
```

I like to approach my scripts from the inside out. I start with the center, and spiral my way to the things I'll need to do to achieve my goal, by specifying and abstracting. If you want to go to Timbuktu, you don't say, "Okay, I need to fly there so I'll go to an airport." You figure out which airlines go between Timbuktu and the airport by your home, then you figure out the dates you can go that match with dates they fly, book a ticket and **then** you go to the airport.

When we broke down the script conceptually earlier on, we didn't start by thinking, "Okay, how can we figure out if it is time for the bee to fly or not?" We started logically, at the meat of the action, the flying. How do we get the bee to fly? As we specify and abstract every element of that action, our tree starts to branch out a bit, and we discover circumstances and properties we never could have thought of at the beginning.

Looking at the `stepFrame` handler above, `flying` is buried all the way in the middle of those `if` statements. So, it would be tempting to follow chronologically along with the in depth explanations, running through `goYet`, then `findTarget` and then `flying`.

I don't want this just to be a case study. The goal of this chapter is to practice the concepts of breaking ideas into Object Oriented Programming as much as it is learning the Lingo to apply OOP in Director. While we can see the tree of if statements in order in retrospect, we didn't build this script conceptually in that fashion. I am going to explain the other handlers of this script the way we conceived of it, from the inside out, starting with our goal and working our way out to the elements we need to support that goal.

That way, you won't come out of this chapter just knowing how to make a bee fly to a flower with OOP, you'll know how to approach whatever goals you set for yourself with OOP. So, let's start with the centre of the action: flying.

Making the bee fly: on flying me

As we have already established, the flying handler gets called in two cases. If the bee is not flying, the bee will find a target and then call the flying handler. If the bee is flying, it will just call the flying handler. This handler needs to be written so that it can handle both circumstances. This doesn't mean we need to set up `if` statements for the two cases, it just means we have to make sure the code is modular enough to handle both circumstances elegantly. Put another way, we can keep the code simplest if we set it up so that the flying handler doesn't need to know its circumstances.

> *If you find yourself getting into complex if statements to handle every particular circumstance, take a step back and see if another approach will work.*

So, the bee needs to know several things to fly: he needs to know where he is and where he is going, so that he can calculate how to get from that one point to the other.

5. Type the following into your Bee Script after the last end of the last handler:

    ```
    on flying me
      me.myFlying = TRUE
      myLoc = sprite(me.mySprite).loc
      targetLoc = sprite(me.myTargetFlower).loc
    ```

    Setting `me.myFlying = TRUE` makes this one script handle both circumstances in which it is called without having to know a thing about its circumstances. If the bee is not flying and the `flying` handler is called, now the bee is flying, so we set `myFlying`

= TRUE. If the bee is flying and the `flying` handler is called, it doesn't hurt anything to reiterate that he is flying by setting `myFlying` = `TRUE` again, even though `myFlying` already = `TRUE`. It is a shred of unnecessary code to set a variable to the value it already is, but it is much simpler than the alternative, parsing based on circumstance.

Now the bee needs to know where he currently is. Here we introduce a local variable, `myLoc`, which is only ever used within this handler. When we create a new bee by pressing the crazy bee or lazy bee button (don't worry, we'll get to that script soon enough), one of the parameters we pass is `beeSprite`, the sprite number the child should control. Then we turn that number into a property of this particular child by setting `me.mySprite` equal to it.

That number is the glue that cements our script to the action on the screen. Wherever the bee is on the screen, we can access his current location through `sprite(me.mySprite).loc`.

Now that the bee knows where he currently is, he needs to figure out where he is going. We will build a `getTarget` handler to pick the flower the bee should head towards. The end result we'll need from the `getTarget` handler is the sprite of the flower the bee should head towards. The bee then uses that sprite number to determine the location of his target with `sprite(me.myTargetFlower).loc`. `targetLoc` is a local variable we're creating to hold that information within this handler.

The bee knows where he is and where he should be heading. Now he has to figure out how to get there. In order to get to his destination, he'll get the distance between him and his target, and divide it by two, and then that distance by two, so on and so on.

Now, we can vary the bee's speed by changing the number that he divides the distance he needs to cover by. If he divides the distance between him and his goal by 10, then that first step, and all subsequent steps will be much smaller. If he divides the distance by 100, his step will be smaller still.

Of course, if we adhered too strictly to our paradox, the bee would never get to his pollen, so we'll need to cheat by and decide a distance away from the flower at which we'll snap the bee to the flower and give him some nourishment.

Our script is now almost entirely worked out, except for one thing. In the real world, we can never be −100 feet from our destination. If we're 100 feet away, we're 100 feet away. But in Director, our position is based on a grid. If the Bee is at 50 and the flower is at 0, then the bee will eventually add 50 to his current location to get to 50, where the flower is sitting. But if the bee is at 100 and the flower is at 50, then the bee will need to subtract 50 from his current location to get to that flower. The next part of our flying handler deals with his problem.

6. Add the following to your flying handler:

```
if myLoc < targetLoc then
    totalDistance= targetLoc - myLoc
    posneg= 1
else
    totalDistance= myLoc - targetLoc
```

```
        posneg= -1
    end if
```

So, what's going on here? Well, first we check that the value of the bee's location is less than that of the flower's location:

```
if myLoc < targetLoc then
```

So, then we subtract the lower from the greater, and set the difference equal to a local variable called `totalDistance`:

```
totalDistance= targetLoc - myLoc
```

We're using a local variable, `posneg` to determine whether the bee's step will be positive or negative. If it is positive, as it is if we've arrived at this point in the code, then a step will be added to the bee's current location:

```
posneg= 1
```

If, on the other hand, the bee is at a location higher than the flower's, then we'll subtract the flower's location from the bee's:

```
else
    totalDistance= myLoc - targetLoc
```

And since the bee is at a higher set of numbers than the flower, we'll need to subtract each step from the bee's current location. If the bee were at 100, we'd have to subtract 50 to get to 50. So in this case we set `posneg` = -1.

```
    posneg= -1
end if
```

And we close out the `if` statement.

Now we need to snap the bee to the flower. Since Director has only a finite number of decimal places to work with, our bee wouldn't actually get caught in the same infinitely smaller progression as the paradox dictates. Once his steps got close enough to zero that Director ran out of decimal places to keep making the steps smaller, the size of his steps would round out to zero, so he'd actually stop before he reached his destination.

To make it absolutely clear what is going on here, we've set that snap number to be a pretty large number. Once we get this script up and running, you'll be able to see the bee approach the flower and then see him snap once he gets 12 pixels away. You can experiment with different numbers for the kind of effect you want. But remember, if the snap distance is too small, and the bee's divider number (`me.mySpeed`) is too big, the bee's steps will round out to zero well before he reaches his destination.

Before we look at this part of the script, think back to `me.mySpeed`, a property based on a parameter passed in from the crazy or lazy bee buttons. The larger the number, the smaller the steps, and the slower the bee will approach his target, and the higher `me.mySpeed`, the slower the bee moves.

7. Add the following to your flying handler:

```
if totalDistance> 12 then
    myLoc = myLoc + posneg*(totalDistance/me.mySpeed)
```

As long as the bee is farther away from the flower than the snap distance we have specified, the bee can calculate the equation dictated by the paradox at each step. Remember that this handler is called every `stepFrame`, so as long as the distance is greater than 12, and the bee is flying, this equation will be run every `stepFrame`.

Let's look at the equation itself in detail.

```
myLoc = myLoc + posneg*(totalDistance/me.mySpeed)
```

Remember that `myLoc` is the local variable in which we are holding the bee's current location, and that `totalDistance` is the distance between him and the flower. Dividing the total distance by the speed will set how big or small each step is. We've said it a few times, and we'll say it once more, the higher the `me.mySpeed` (which we will set with the lazy and crazy bee buttons), the smaller each step is and the slower the bee flies . This is the equation that shows you why this is true.

We multiply the size of the step by the local variable `posneg`, which is either –1 or 1. This turns the size of the step into a positive or negative number. And then we add that number to the bee's current location to find out what his new location will be. So, if the bee were at 0 and the flower were at 50, `totalDistance` would be 50 and `posneg` would be 1, so the step would be added to the current location.

Discussing a loc as number like 50, 0 and 100 is somewhat deceiving. It illustrates the general principles, but this is not how Director deals with loc. As you are probably aware, `loc` is a set of 2 coordinates: x and y.

For instance, `sprite (2).loc = point(50,100)`

So the equation going on is more complex than simply subtracting one number from another.

Anyway, we've gone over the equation that gets called on each `stepFrame` as long as the bee is farther away than the snap distance from the flower. Let's look at what happens once the bee has gotten close enough to the flower to snap.

8. Add the following to your flying handler:

```
else

    - - SNAP IF CLOSE ENOUGH
    myLoc = targetLoc
    me.myFlying = FALSE - - set boolean to false, the bee is no
```

```
➥ longer flying
   me.myTimer = the ticks — - reset the counter for checkTimer
```

The if statement that ran the equation happened as long as the bee was farther than 12 pixels away from the flower. Now, the else statement sets myLoc = targetLoc. We haven't yet set the bee's sprite's loc to be equal to this position, so he is still somewhere less than 12 pixels away from the flower. All we have done so far is set myLoc, the local variable that holds the bee's current location, equal to targetLoc, the local variable that holds the flower's position.

Now, what do we have to do once the bee has reached its target flower? We need to stop the bee and make him wait, so we set me.myFlying = FALSE, and me.myTimer = the ticks.

Setting me.myTimer = the ticks will make sense when we build the goYet handler, which handles waiting. For now, trust me that this will start the process that makes the bee wait as long as his me.myWaitDiff tells him to wait.

9.   Now we have to close out the if statement, and set the bee sprite's location equal to the new location, which is the location of the flower.

       Add the following to your flying handler:

```
end if
   sprite(me.mySprite).loc = myLoc
end
```

And that's it for the flying handler. You should have this:

We concluded the script by initializing me.myTimer so that the goYet handler can make the bee wait a specified amount of time on that flower. Let's see how that works.

Making the bee wait with goYet

Remember that me.myWaitDiff was derived from the howLong property that we pass from the crazy bee or lazy bee button. me.myTimer is another property used to make the bee wait. Initially, we set that property to 0, but after the bee flew to a flower, me.myTimer was set equal to the ticks, (a counter that starts as soon as the computer is started. 1 tick = 1/60 of a second.)

10. We will use these three elements to make our bee wait on the flower. Type the following into your Bee Script after the end of the **flying** handler:

```
on goYet me
   if the ticks - me.myTimer > me.myWaitDiff  then
      return TRUE
   else
      return FALSE
   end if
end
```

After the bee had finished flying, we set me.myTimer = the ticks. So the first time goYet is called after landing on a flower, the ticks - me.myTimer = 0.

This handler is called every stepFrame, so by the second time it is called the ticks will have incremented slightly. me.myTimer will remain static. Therefore, the ticks - me.myTimer will be greater than 0. Each time goYet is called, the ticks will be slightly higher, but it will not return TRUE until the ticks has grown to be larger than me.myTimer by an amount equal to me.myWaitDiff.

Let's say we set me.myWaitDiff = 240 by passing a value of 240 in the howLong property. Then the bee will wait on the flower for 240 ticks, which is 240/60 = 3 seconds. This means the bee will wait 3 seconds before lifting off for another flower.

What's great about this script is that it uses a global value (the ticks) without having to set up a new global variable. Plus, it uses it against a property specific to each child (me.myWaitDiff), so that each bee can use the ticks to wait for its own amount of time. An elegant way to give each bee his own characteristics.

That was a pretty simple script. As long as the bee hasn't waited the amount of time he was supposed to wait, goYet returns FALSE. As soon as he has waited long enough, goYet returns TRUE, which tells the waiting bee that it is time to fly.

If you refer back to the on stepFrame handler (3.), you'll see that once goYet returns TRUE, the bee has to run the findTarget handler to figure out which flower he will be heading towards before he can start flying.

Let's see how the findTarget handler works.

Sending the bee to his destination, with the findTarget handler

Let's think though the requirements of the script before we code it. The bee should only fly towards flowers, and he should never fly towards the flower he is currently on. So the bee needs to find a flower and check that that flower is not the flower he is currently on before electing that flower as his target. But how do we get the bee talking to the flowers in the first place?

Well, as you may remember, he'll need the actorList. In the first frame of the movie we built a buildActorList script, which adds each flower to the actorList. When we build the Lazy and Crazy bee buttons, we will be adding each bee to the actorList. Remember that we're adding the bees to the actorList purely so that we can take advantage of the on stepFrame event handler. Only children within the actorList have access to this handler, and everything, from our goYet to our flying handler, depends on that event handler.

Let's take a look at how we are going to wrangle an appropriate target flower out of that actor list for the bee to approach.

Type the following into you Bee Script after the last end of your last handler:

```
on findTarget me
i = random(the actorList.count)- - set i to a random entry in
➡ the list
whichType =  the actorList[i].getParentType() - - get the
➡ Object's type
if whichType = "Flower" then   - - if it's a flower. . .
    tempTarget = the actorList[i].getSpriteNum() - - get its
    ➡ sprite number
if  tempTarget <> me.myTargetFlower then   - - check it's not the
➡ current - - flower
                me.myTargetFlower = tempTarget - - and update
                ➡ myTargetFlower
        end if
    end if
end
```

```
whichType =  the actorList[i].getParentType()
```

If you're happy with lists and how they work, this code should be pretty straightforward for you. We'll just run through it here though, just in case. As we only want the bee to fly towards flowers, we check whether the child we are querying (randomly, from the actorlist) is a flower, using the getParentType handler that we entered in the flower script. (We will shortly set up a getParentType handler in the bee to return 'Bee' similarly.)

As you may have noticed, we're accessing the Flower Script's getParentType handler the same way we accessed the getSpeed handler in myTest, using MyTest.getSpeed(). We created the myTest object by declaring it as a new instance of its parent script in the message window:

```
myTest = new(script"parentMotion", 20)
```

And we created the flower objects with a repeat loop in the frame 1 script, buildActorList:

```
repeat with i = 5 to 8
    add the actorList, new(script "Flower Script ",i)
  end repeat
```

So, back to the findTarget handler in the Bee Script. We're allocating the results of the test on the getParentType handler to a local variable, whichType, and if that result is 'Flower', then we set up a local variable, tempTarget to hold the sprite number of that child.

Remember that we tied each flower to its sprite when we created it in the buildActorList? In order to keep the flower properly encapsulated, we can only access that property by using the getSpriteNum handler on the parent.

```
if whichType = "Flower" then
    tempTarget = the actorList[i].getSpriteNum()
```

Now is a good time to reiterate the concept of handlers with children.

> *Although we are using the same-named handler to query both bees and flowers in the* actorList*, each handler is specific to that particular child. Running* getParentType *on a bee will return 'Bee', and running it on a flower will return 'Flower'. What's important here is that the child objects are properly encapsulated; we are accessing their* parentType *and* spriteNum *through a handler rather than snagging it directly. Although their handlers are all based on the same parent class, each child has its own version of that handler, so each handler is unique to that child.*

This may seem very obvious to you at this point. I'm making the reference here to really hammer down the concepts. If it is blatantly obvious to you, then you've already come an incredibly long way to understanding OOP!

So, at this point in the findTarget handler we have found a flower object from the actorList and we have found the sprite that the flower object controls, which we store in tempTarget. Now all we need to do is make sure the tempTarget is not the flower we are currently on:

```
if   tempTarget <> me.myTargetFlower then
    me.myTargetFlower = tempTarget
```

And if it isn't, then set me.myTargetFlower equal to the sprite number stored in tempTarget. Finally, we closed off the if statements and the script.

Getting the ParentType
We built an almost identical handler for the Flower Script, and we've just seen why it is necessary, so you can figure out this one on your own. Type the following into your Bee Script after the last end of your last handler:

```
on getParentType  me — — used when looking through the actorList
for object type
   return "Bee"
end
```

Whew! We've finished the Bee Script. In it's entirety, the Bee Script should look like this:

```
property mySprite, myWaitDiff, mySpeed, myTargetFlower, myTimer,
myFlying

on new me, beeSprite, howLong, howFast
   me.mySprite = beeSprite — — the spriteNUmber of each bee
   me.myWaitDiff = howLong — — how long the bee waits between
   ➡ flights
   me.mySpeed = howFast
   me.myTargetFlower = 5 — — the target of the flightpath
   me.myTimer = 0 — — used in timer
   me.myFlying = FALSE — — boolean variable to test whether the
   ➡ bee is in flight
   return me
end

on stepFrame me
   if me.goYet() then — — if goYet returns true, (if it is time to
   ➡ fly).
     if not me.myFlying then — — if the bee is not flying
        me.findTarget()
        me.flying()
     else
        me.flying() — — call the flight function
     end if
   end if
end

— — the script to make it fly

on flying me
   me.myFlying = TRUE
   myLoc = sprite(me.mySprite).loc
   targetLoc = sprite(me.myTargetFlower).loc
   if myLoc < targetLoc then
```

```
      totalDistance= targetLoc - myLoc
      posneg= 1
    else
      totalDistance= myLoc - targetLoc
      posneg= -1
    end if



    if totalDistance> 12 then
      myLoc = myLoc + posneg*(totalDistance/me.mySpeed)
    else
      - -SNAP IF CLOSE ENOUGH
      myLoc = targetLoc
      me.myFlying = FALSE - - set Boolean to false, the bee is no
      ➡ longer flying
      me.myTimer = the ticks - - reset the counter for checkTimer
      end if
    sprite(me.mySprite).loc = myLoc
end

- - checks the time to see if  the bee can move

on goYet me
  if the ticks - me.myTimer > me.myWaitDiff  then
    return TRUE
  else
    return FALSE
  end if
end

end

- - find the next flower

on findTarget me
i = random(the actorList.count)
whichType =  the actorList[i].getParentType() - - make a call to
➡ each of the
- - objects and get their type
    if whichType = "Flower" then —if it is a flower...
            tempTarget = the actorList[i].getSpriteNum() - -get
            ➡ that paricular flowers
            - - spriteNumber
                if  tempTarget <> me.myTargetFlower then - -
                ➡ if it does not match the
                - - current myTargetFlower
                me.myTargetFlower = tempTarget —update
                ➡ mytargetFlower
            end if
```

```
        end if
end

on getParentType  me - - used when looking through the actorList
➥ for object type
  return "Bee"
end
```

But we haven't created any bees; we haven't yet called that all important new ("Script Name", property). And we haven't yet added any bee children to the actorList.

We'll set up the crazy bee and lazy bee buttons that will create our bee child objects from the bee script parent class next, and then we'll do a quick review of the bee's functionality, to make sure the concepts are absolutely clear before playing with the system.

Creating two types of bee from the parent bee script

The CrazyBee Script
The CrazyBee script will need to:

- Assign a sprite number for the bee child to attach itself to

- Add this new bee child into the actor list

- Pass the properties that determine the speed of the bee, and the length of time he waits on a flower

In the movie we have set up so far, the bees occupy sprites 15, 16, and 17, so we need to tell the bee child which of these sprites he controls. Because we are using more than one button setting this property, we need to allow the button to communicate which sprites are left for assignation to a child (so that the second bee will display the right characteristics, not replace the first bees characteristics.) Each time we assign a new child bee script to a sprite, we need to increment that number by 1 so that the next bee child affects a different sprite. And since we have only set up three bees, we need to stop assigning new children once we have fulfilled our quota.

There are some serious limitations to this paradigm. We have to hard-code the sprites the bees will be in, and we have limited the number of bees we can have set in sprite channels before running the movie. As I mentioned earlier, it is bad practice to hard code, and whenever possible, you should always look for other alternatives. We'll right this wrong later on, after we've run through the hard-coded example, to get all the concepts across and make sure our objects are behaving properly.

First thing we need to do is set a global variable that tells the crazy and lazy bee buttons which sprite they should be assigning the child's actions to.

1.   Go into your HouseCleaning movie script, and change it so that it looks like this:

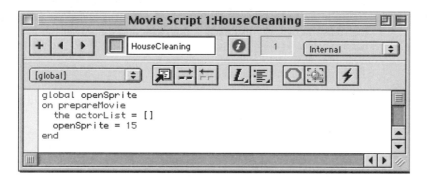

We've set the global variable openSprite to 15, the first channel in which a bee appears, and we'll increment that number each time we create a new bee, stopping after we've created three new bees.

So, now we need to create a behavior that assigns characteristics to new bees while openSprite is 15, 16, or 17 bees, and stops once the it reaches 18.

2.   The CrazyBee script will be applied to a button, so create a new script named CrazyBee, set its type to **behavior**, and type in the following:

```
global openSprite
on mouseUp
   if openSprite < 18 then
     add the actorList, new(script "Bee Script", openSprite, 2,
     ➡ 2)
     openSprite = openSprite + 1
   end if
end
```

Remember that the properties passed to the Bee Script parent class in order to make a new child object are the sprite the child object will control (beeSprite), how long the bee will wait on a flower before taking off again (howLong) and the number that will be used to divide the equation by in the flying handler, which controls how fast the bee flies (howFast). So, the line add the actorList, new(script "Bee Script", openSprite, 2, 2) tells the parent class 'Bee Script' to create a child object with its sprite number set to whatever openSprite is (the first time it is run, 15, then 16, then 17 and then the button won't do anything anymore). The button passes an argument of 2 for howLong and 2 for howFast. The parent class then turns these properties into properties specific to the child object it is creating.

openSprite, which is passed as beeSprite, is assigned to me.mySprite. howLong is assigned to me.myWaitDiff, with a value of 2. And howFast is assigned to me.mySpeed, also with a value of 2.

Remember that me.myWaitDiff is the number of ticks the bee will wait before flying off a flower, so this bee will only wait 2 ticks (2/60 = 1/30th of a second) before taking off again! And as we saw in the `flying` handler, the higher `me.mySpeed`, the smaller the steps the bee will take each `stepFrame`, and the slower the bee will fly. This bee has a very low number, so this bee will take very large steps and will move very quickly.

```
openSprite = openSprite + 1
```

We then increment `openSprite` so the next time we assign a child object to a sprite, it will be the next sprite in the score.

This should be clear, so let's build our `LazyBee` script.

Creating the LazyBee
The Lazy Bee functions the same way as the Crazy Bee, except that his numbers are different. We'll create that now.

3. Create a new script and set it to type: behavior. Name it `LazyBee`:

We'll add some randomness into the lazy bee. Make `howLong` a random number between 100 and 200. This will make the bee wait on a flower anywhere between 1.67 seconds and 3.33 seconds. Then set `howFast` to 12, so it goes pretty slowly. Try it yourself before seeing how we did it.

When you're done, your LazyBee script should look something like this:

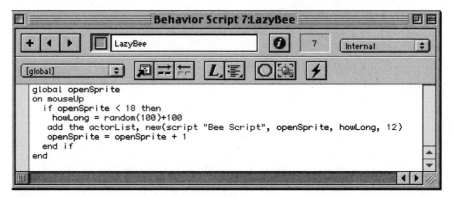

As it really is the same script as the CrazyBeescript, just with different parameters, this should all make sense.

Now we need to attach these behaviors to their buttons, and we're ready to go.

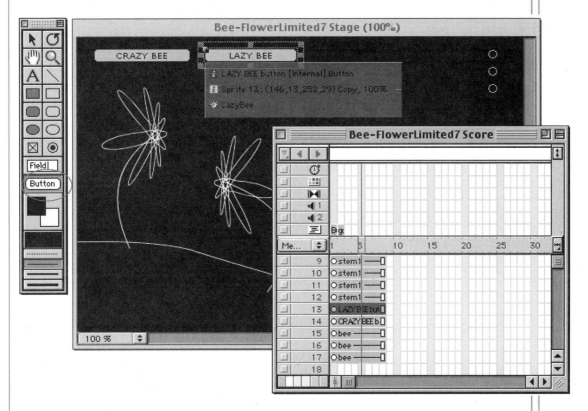

4. Select frame 1 of channel 13 and use the button tool to draw a button. Type LAZY BEE into the button and name it accordingly. Do the same in channel 14 for the Crazy Bee button. Drag the **LazyBee** and CrazyBee behaviors to their respective buttons.

There's just one last touch to add, and then our bees are ready to fly.

Since all the animation is based on Lingo and the on stepFrame handler called by the children in the actorList, all of the action of this piece will occur in one frame. After building the actorList with flowers in frame 1, we need to keep the play back head at frame 2 for the rest of the movie.

5. Go into the second frame of the movie, double click the frame script channel just above the score, and write the following script in the script window that appears:

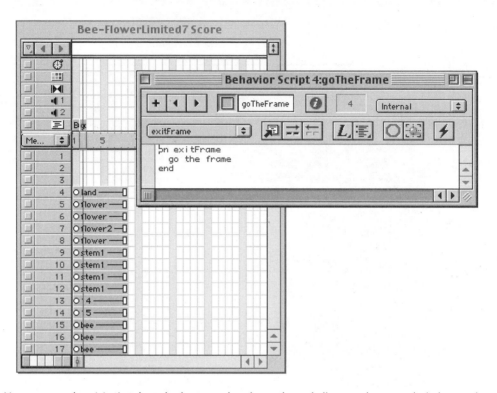

Now we are done! Let's take a look at our handy work, and discuss what exactly is happening behind the scenes.

6. Save your movie, make sure the playback head is at frame 1, and hit play.

We don't see this happen, but we know that as the playback head reaches frame 1 of the movie, it creates four child flower objects from the parent template Flower Script and adds them into the `actorList`. The repeat loop within the `Build ActorList` script passes a value of 5 to the first child, 6 to the second child, 7 to the third child, and 8 to the fourth. This refers to the sprite the flower child will be controlling. Really, all it does is tell the flower to tell its sprite number and parent type when queried.

But it could hold much more information. We could give each flower its own color, and just as bees pick up pollen from one flower and carry it to another, we could have the bees pick up this color and pass it to another. Then this system would start to represent some of the more complex interactions that go on between flowers and bees. It's extremely easy to change well crafted object oriented designs, as everything is encapsulated within classes. Unlike traditional Lingo programming, where we would have to hunt down different handlers and variables, we know where everything is located, and by changing it in one place we can affect numerous objects.

At this point you are staring at four flowers, three bees and two buttons. Not very exciting. Now click either the lazy bee or crazy bee button. You'll create a child of the Bee Script, passing the values for `beeSprite`, `howLong` and `howFast` to the parent class. The child object attaches itself to the appropriate sprite (15 the first click, then 16 and then 17), and the bee in the respective sprite channel flies into action.

The first time around, the bee is not flying so it will run the `getTarget` handler to select a flower and head towards the flower at a speed dependent on the `howFast` parameter you passed when you clicked the button. As soon as the bee gets within 12 pixels of the flower, you'll see it snap to the flower. The bee then sets `me.myTimer = the ticks`, so that the `goYet` will tell it that it is not yet time to fly. Once its time is up, the bee calls the `getTarget` handler to choose its next target and calls the flying handler, which sets `me.myFlying` to TRUE to tell the bee he is currently flying so he doesn't choose another target. And the process continues again.

The whole time it is the `stepFrame` handler that drives all the action. Every `stepFrame` the bee asks if it should go yet. Then it asks it if is flying, and if it's not flying, finds a target and flies. The `goYet`, `findTarget`, and `flying` handlers within each child respond to the `stepFrame`'s call, but it is the `stepFrame` handler that drives that whip, making sure every handler continues to work.

So, now you've taken that motion object we started with conceptually and integrated it into a simple system that mimics nature. Although bees darting from flower to flower aren't particularly spellbinding, I hope that it has introduced you to the concepts and code you can use to build much more complex systems.

Think about how easy it would be to add more bees or flowers to this movie. You just add a few more onto the stage and update the scripts that build the actor lists so that these new sprites are attached to the children that we birth. The bee and flower parent scripts are written modularly, so they will be able to handle as many sprites as we throw at them. Or is that the best way? Just throwing a few more bit and pieces onto the stage *and* updating the scripts that build the `actorLists`, well, it doesn't seem very elegant or modular really. Despite all this talk of Object Oriented Programming, specifying and abstracting, we're still hard-coding our sprites into the score and using an unnecessary global variable (`openSprite`). I mentioned earlier that there is a better way to this – and there is.

We have broken a few rules along the way: in the first place, it's best to avoid hard-coding whenever possible. Tying ourselves to specific channels in the score puts certain limitations on our work, and as extensible as OOP is, we could get a lot more out of our scripts if we give ourselves more freedom. Furthermore, global variables should only be used as a last result. Since they sit around in memory for all to use, it generally a good idea to keep them to an absolute minimum, especially when they're not in constant use. Often, the capability that the global variable provides can be carried out by passing parameters to handlers, and it's not unusual for a global variable to be easily replaced as a property. In many cases, putting a little more thought into your code can specify that global variable all the way down into the oh so transient local variables.

So, let's go back into the system we just created and make it a bit more modular. We are going to remove all the bee sprites from our movie and engage in a little spriteless scripting. While we're at it, we're going to replace that global `openSprite` variable with a nifty little code trick.

We left the global variable and the hard-coded sprites in the first example so that we could focus exclusively on the OOP aspects of the piece. But hard-coding and global variables are generally bad practice, and the last thing I should be teaching here are sloppy Lingo habits. So let's put that right now

Sprite-less Scripting: building the score on the fly

1. Save this first part of your work, and then open the movie and save it by another name. We are going to make some edits to the parent Bee Script, and the CrazyBee and LazyBee scripts so that we can place a seemingly limitless number of bees in the score while the Director movie is playing.

The new Lingo we'll be covering here isn't specific to OOP, but used in tandem with OOP it can be the spark for a whole new realm of possibilities. We'll be using the puppet sprite, which allows you to place cast members into sprite channels that are empty. It lets you animate those sprites, controlling them like you would sprites you had placed in the score prior to playtime.

Making it modular: removing the hard-coding and global variables

2. First, delete all of the bee sprites from the movie (residing in channels 15 through 17.) We don't need them anymore.

3. Now go into the HouseCleaning movie script and remove all references to that global variable openSprite.

When you're done, your HouseCleaning script should look like this:

```
on prepareMovie
  the actorList = []
end
```

We're going to set up a handler in the bee script that automatically scans the score for an empty channel. Then we'll use the puppet command to place a sprite of the bee member into that empty channel, attach the bee script child to that sprite, and we're on our way to infinite beedom!

Since we'll be locating the sprite for the Bee Script's child to attach itself to within the Bee Script, we only need to pass the howLong and howFast parameters from the crazy bee and lazy bee buttons to the parent Bee Script. We don't need the beeSprite property anymore, nor do we need the openSprite global variable.

4. So, go into the CrazyBee script, and change it so it looks like this:

```
on mouseUp
    add the actorList, new(script "Bee Script", 2, 2)
end
```

Now all the crazy bee button will do is create a new child of the parent Bee Script, set howLong to 2, howFast to 2, and add that new child object to the actorList.

5. Let's wield that same surgeon's hatchet on the LazyBee script. Wipe out all references to `openSprite` and `beeSprite` within the LazyBee script. It should look like this when you are done:

```
on mouseUp
  howLong = random(100)+100
  add the actorList, new(script "Bee Script", howLong, 12)
end
```

Scanning the score for an empty channel

Now we need to amend the Bee Script. Each Bee is now responsible for figuring out which sprite he should attach himself to. He also needs to puppet a sprite of the bee member into that channel so he has a bee graphic to control.

6. First let's add the handler that scans the score for an open channel. After the end of the `on new me` handler, enter the following:

```
on getChannel me, start
  repeat with i = start to the maxInteger
    temp =  string(sprite(i).member)
    if temp = "(member 0 of castLib 0)" then
       return i
       exit repeat
    end if
  end repeat
end
```

This probably already makes sense to you. When the `getChannel` handler is called, we pass a parameter for the first open channel we want to put a bee into.

In our example, we left the first few channels empty, in case we want to add more scenery later on. It is generally a good idea to leave those first few channels free. I always start out with the first five channels empty, and then fill them as needed later on. Depending on how your scripts are coded, it can sometimes be a terrible pain to have to move every single sprite up a few channels to accommodate some last minute additions to the scenery.

The problem this could cause here is that `getChannel` would figure out that the first few channels are free, and would put a bee into those channels. Then we'd have bees sliding behind mountains and flowers out of our view, which is not something we want. When we actually call this handler we'll pass a value of 15 through the `start` parameter, as you'll see later on. This will eventually put the first bee above everything else in the score, at the 15th channel.

This handler will then repeat from 15 to the `maxInteger`, checking each sprite for its member. The `maxInteger` is the highest number your computer can count to. On most personal computers it is 2,147,483,647. That's a whole lotta bees!

```
repeat with i = start to the maxInteger
  temp =  string(sprite(i).member)
```

It takes the member of each sprite it queries, converts it to a string, and sets it to the `temp` variable, a local variable.

```
if temp = "(member 0 of castLib 0)" then
      return i
      exit repeat
```

When we ask director for the member of a sprite that doesn't exist, it returns the string `(member 0 of castLib 0)`. Try it: type the following into the message window:

```
put string(sprite(50).member)
```

Director returns:

```
- - "(member 0 of castLib 0)"
```

When this happens, `getChannel` will return that sprite number to whoever has run the handler and exit the repeat loop. The exit repeat is extremely important. Without that, `getChannel` will continue returning the string `(member 0 of castLib 0)` two billion, one hundred forty-seven million, four hundred eighty three thousand, six hundred thirty two times (2,147,483,632)! That'll hang your computer for quite some time. By exiting the repeat, we only ever query as many sprites as a re already there, plus one. So if we have 15 bees in our movie, it would repeat from 15 to 30 until it found an open channel and exited.

Then we close the repeat and end the handler.

Putting a member into an empty channel, using puppet

`puppet` allows you to place members onto empty channels and control various properties of the sprite, such as `loc`, `width`, `rect`, etc. Here we will announce that we are making the channel `getChannel` has told us is empty into a `puppet`. Then we'll place the bee there and adjust his properties until he looks right.

7.   Type the following into your Bee Script after the end of the getChannel handler:

```
on setSprite me
   sprite(me.mySprite).puppet = TRUE - - puppet the sprite
   sprite(me.mySprite).member = member("bee") - - give the sprite a
   ➥ member
   sprite(me.mySprite).ink = 36
end
```

We just explained the first two lines. Let's look at the next one

```
sprite(me.mySprite).ink = 36
```

Since we haven't set the sprite's `ink` manually, (because it's not in the score during authoring), we need to set it with Lingo. Each `ink` has a number that refers to it. You can make a sprite `reverse`, `matte`, `mask`, and so on by setting its `ink` property to the proper number. Look up ink in the Lingo Dictionary for the full list. 36, which we used here, is for Background Transparent, so we have just set the bee we placed in the score to Background Transparent.

8.   Now that we've built the handlers, we need to call them on new me to construct our bee child properly. First, remove the beeSprite property from the on new me line:

```
on new me, howLong, howFast
```

We won't be passing it from the crazy and lazy bee buttons, so we shouldn't try to capture it here.

9.   Now, change me.mySprite to set it equal to the result of calling the getChannel handler with an argument of 15.

```
me.mySprite = me.getChannel(15)
```

Remember, the first empty channel in the score in which we want to place a bee is 15. The getChannel handler starts at this number and counts up until it finds an empty channel.

10. Finally, call the setSprite handler to put the bee member in that free channel and set its ink to Background Transparent.

```
me.setSprite()
```

And we're done. The portions of the Bee Script that we have changed or added now look like this:

```
property mySprite, myWaitDiff, mySpeed, myTargetFlower, myTimer,
➡ myFlying

on new me, howLong, howFast
   me.mySprite = me.getChannel(15) - - the spriteNUmber of each
   ➡ bee
   me.setSprite()
   me.myWaitDiff = howLong - - how long the bee waits between
   ➡ flights
   me.mySpeed = howFast
   me.myTargetFlower = 5 - - the target of the flightpath
   me.myTimer = 0 - - used in timer
   me.myFlying = FALSE - - boolean variable to test whether the
   ➡ bee is in flight
   return me
end


on getChannel me, start
   repeat with i = start to the maxInteger
     temp =  string(sprite(i).member)
```

```
            if temp = "(member 0 of castLib 0)" then
              return i
              exit repeat
            end if
          end repeat
        end

        on setSprite me
          sprite(me.mySprite).puppet = TRUE -- puppet the sprite
          sprite(me.mySprite).member = member("bee") -- give the sprite
          ➥ a member
          sprite(me.mySprite).ink = 36
          -- sprite(me.mySprite).rect = rect(-1,-1,0,0)
          -- sprite(me.mySprite).width =
          ➥sprite(me.mySprite).member.width
          -- sprite(me.mySprite).height = sprite(me.mySprite).member.
          ➥height
        end
```

Save your work, rewind the movie and hit play, and see what's different when you tap the crazy and lazy bee buttons. Although not specific to OOP in Director, the techniques we just added will help you extend your OOP way beyond those a hard-coded sprite allowed you. And we also reiterated the importance of avoiding global variables whenever possible, showing that a little Lingo ingenuity can replace cumbersome global variables.

Taking These Objects Further

OOP is a great technique for making your code more efficient, as it requires that you create compact building blocks to be reused in many circumstances. By integrating OOP with other Director capabilities, you can start to push your Director movies further and further without that much extra effort.

A very intriguing part of OOP is its potential for building pseudo-intelligent systems. What we now have in this Flower Bee movie is the beginning of one such system. Bees do a lot more than just fly from flower to flower. When a bee lands on a flower, it sucks the nectar, and as it does so picks up a little pollen from that flower. When the bee then lands on another flower, that pollen mixes with the pollen of the new flower. By the time that flower is fertilized its pollen has become a hodge-podge of many different flowers. The offspring it creates are different from the parent because that mixed-up pollen is the genetic make-up of the new flower. Sound familiar?

To take these concepts further on your own, why don't you extend the simple system we built into one that better embraces the nature of a true bee-flower system? You might try adding a color property to the bee and flower. When a bee lands on a flower, their color properties mix so that they both come away with a new color. And this goes on and on and on, the movie becoming a different bouquet each time (actually, if you just used an average of the two colors to create the new color you'd always eventually end up with a bunch of gray flowers, but with a little math you can skew the results into something more beautiful). You can tie the color property to the sprite through the color property using:

```
sprite(me.mySprite).color = rgb(200, 150, 75)
```

Of course you wouldn't be hard-coding the color, but deriving it from a function that combined the color the bee was carrying with the color of the flower.

This is just one way to approach it, of course. You could play with imaging Lingo to make the flowers inherit more substantial properties, or make some bees only like certain colors. With some math, you could make the path the bees follow to the flowers more interesting. You could make them swoop to the flowers following a curved path, or add some randomness into the bee's flight path so they buzzed erratically around more like real bees. Go ahead and develop the system we've started on your own. We've put the source for one possible approach up at http://www.grographics.com/lingo, and commented it up thoroughly, so if you get confused as you develop your system that source code might help you along.

Object Oriented systems don't just have to be games of course. Most of our weather forecasting is based on computer models using OOP, updated with variables from our real-world environment. Programmers at the University of Pennsylvania have developed a pseudo-intelligent system for the study of social conflict. Of course, such models are unlikely to ever accurately recreate all the varying conditions that cause these sorts of social catastrophes, but that doesn't negate the fact that OOP has applications in many aspects of life, way beyond sprites and the `actorList`.

Creating Custom Behaviors

Back to Director though. Just as an object can be applied in many different ways to different elements within a Director movie, it can also be turned into a custom behavior. This allows you to quickly apply that functionality anywhere within your Director movies, taking a lot of coding out of future Director projects, and making it easy to streamline and share your work with other coders.

Although the designer usually defines a behavior's parameters and properties prior to runtime, they can also be modified on the fly. Both custom behaviors and parent scripts are used to create new instances of their own script, each of which can contain different values and be applied differently.

To create a behavior, you simply define all the functions and properties very generally, and then add the `getPropertyDescription` handler to give the developer a dialog box interface through which to apply the behavior. So, instead of creating an object from the parent by clicking a button, or typing into the message window, you create it by dragging the behavior to a sprite in the score, or double clicking on the behavior. This prompts a dialog box, where you can enter all the properties that we have been passing with `new ("script name", property)` in the previous examples.

The dialog box is where the developer defines the arguments for this application of the script. For instance, rather than typing `new(script "parentMotion", 5)` to assign a value of 5 to the _speed property, we would pop-up a window asking the designer to enter the speed he or she wants the script to use.

This way, lots of people can apply complex scripts without ever being required to get under the hood and mess with the script itself. We'll do that now.

Remember we started this entire process with the goal of creating a motion object. So let's take the `flying` handler, the handler that deals with motion in the Bee Script, and turn it into a custom behavior.

The goal of this custom behavior will be to make the bee fly towards the sprite the user chooses at the speed the user chooses. So we'll be using the same properties (`mySprite`, `myTarget`, and `mySpeed`) that we used in the Bee Script. This time, though, we will set them by dragging the behavior onto the sprite we want to act as a bee.

There are a few other differences. Although we are creating an instance of this behavior, like we created instances of the parent when we created new child objects, we aren't using `new("script name", property)` or adding the new object to the `actorList`, so we don't have access to the Bee Script's `stepFrame` handler.

We'll be attaching the instance of this script to particular sprites by dragging the script to the sprite and entering the values for the `mySpeed` and `myTarget` properties manually. We'll mix and match which sprites act as bees and which sprites act as flowers as we go. In fact, because each sprite carries its own version of this system, we can make a bee act as a flower for another bee. We can also introduce moving targets into the scenario, by setting one bee's target as another bee,

After all, these are just scripts; they aren't in anyway restricted to bees and flowers. With a few tweaks we can apply these same scripts to many other systems. That is another benefit of coding in a modular style. Since we approached this problem by constantly specifying and abstracting, we came up with code that can be easily applied to other situations. This script has become a building block for other ideas.

Back to the `flying` handler; the motion part of this behavior is almost identical to the `flying` handler in the bee script. We'll be introducing a few new bits of Lingo for dealing with custom behaviors, but the concept behind the motion is essentially the same.

Controlling Motion with a Custom Behavior

1. Create a new movie, and make a new script, with the setting type Behavior, and call it Movement Behavior

Describing your custom behavior to people who will be using it

There are only a few new Lingo terms that we'll need here, so let's go over those first.

We'll be using `getBehaviorDescription` and `getBehaviorTooltip`, which simply dictate the description we give to the user about this behavior.

getBehaviorDescription	used to describe the behavior. Appears in the description pane of the behavior inspector
GetBehaviorTooltip	used· to describe the behavior. Appears when the developer rolls over the behavior
RETURN	inserts a carriage return (like a <br> tag in HTML) is Director's code continuation character

Other than these terms, we'll just be using strings to provide the descriptions you want the developer to see.

2. Type the following into your new script:

```
on getBehaviorDescription me
  RETURN
    "MOVEMENT BEHAVIOR" & RETURN & RETURN &
    ➥ "Sprite will move towards the target at the speed you
    ➥ choose"
end getBehaviorDescription

on getBehaviorTooltip me
  RETURN
    "Moves a sprite towards a target at the speed you choose"
end getBehaviorTooltip
```

To see it in action, compile your script, find it in your cast, and double click. The behavior inspector will pop up.

Select the Movement Behavior (Internal) Score Behavior line and you'll see the behavior's description in the pane below.

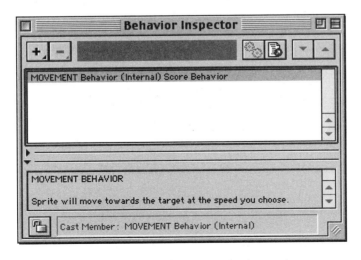

So we've described what our behavior will do to the people who will be applying it. However, since we are counting on a person to attach this behavior, they might well try to attach the behavior to a type of sprite it was not designed to control.

Checking that the script can works with certain types of sprite

The next bit of new Lingo is `isOKToAttach`. As the name suggests, this handler checks to make sure the user is trying to attach this script to an appropriate sprite. We wouldn't want the user to attach this script to the script channel of the score, for example. This handler is used to specify which kinds of sprites the script can work with, by returning TRUE for all acceptable sprites, and FALSE for those that aren't. You can be more specific about it too, if you want. If you didn't want people to use your carefully crafted behavior to make text fly around the screen, for example, then you'd return FALSE in `isOKToAttach me` to prevent the user from attaching it to some text. Personally, I think flying text is just great, especially bitmapped flying text that scales so you can see all the anti-aliasing. But for the sake of example, we'll set up our behavior so it cannot be attached to text. We'll also set it so that it cannot be attached to the script channel.

We'll be using `case`, because it's a nice, clean way to write your `if` statements. You might already have run into situations where your code gets rather tangled if you're writing a slew of nested `if` statements.

The basic format of `case` is

```
case expression of
        expression1 : Statement
        expression2 :
                multipleStatements .
                .
                .
                .
        expression3, expression4 :
                Statement
end case
```

3.   Add the following to your custom behavior:

```
on isOKToAttach me, spriteType, spriteNum
  case spriteType of
    #graphic: return sprite(spriteNum).member.type <> #text
    #script: return FALSE
  end case
end
```

Let's run through it. `case spriteType of` is simple enough. It means *if our spriteType is...*

The next line is a bit more convoluted:

```
#graphic: return sprite(spriteNum).member.type <> #text
```

If the sprite is a graphic, then return the result of '*is the member of this sprite NOT text?*' If the member of the sprite *is* text, then the result will be FALSE. Is text not text? No, so it returns FALSE. If the member of the sprite is not text, then this will return TRUE. Is a non-text graphic not text? Yes.

This may seem counter-intuitive. After all, text isn't a graphic, so it should never call this statement if it were text. Actually, Director thinks of all graphic elements as #graphic, including buttons, movies, text, and so on. The two spriteTypes Director can test directly in isOkayToAttach me are #graphic and #script. That's why we need this two step process to ascertain that the sprite is not text.

Then we simply instruct that FALSE is returned if spriteType is a script.

```
#script: return FALSE
```

So, our behavior can be attached to any graphic except text, and it cannot be attached to a script.

There is another way of writing this same case statement. Just as if has the else clause, case has the otherwise clause.

4. Amend your isOkayToAttach handler so that it looks like this:

```
on isOKToAttach me, spriteType, spriteNum
  case spriteType of
    #graphic: return sprite(spriteNum).member.type <> #text
    otherwise: return FALSE
  end case
end
```

Although we didn't need to use it here particularly, otherwise can be very useful if your behavior can only be attached in very specific circumstances. Let's say you've got a custom behavior that controls movies, and only movies. It won't work on shapes or text or buttons, but you don't want to name every specific case. Then you'd set isOkayToAttach me to return TRUE for graphics that are movies, otherwise return FALSE.

Allowing the user to enter the behavior's properties

One final piece of new Lingo: getPropertyDescriptionList. This handler is triggered whenever you drag a behavior to a sprite. The information contained within this handler determines which properties the user can apply him or herself.

We'll use this handler to create a property list in which we save all the information the user enters, so that we can access it when we run the script. (Just a quick reminder from the last chapter: a property list is a list in which each entry consists of two parts, name and value, in the format #name: value).

Director has a number of inbuilt properties for creating behaviors. The ones we'll be using here are: #default, #format, #integer, #comment and #range. Just as we counted on the Crazy Bee and Lazy Bee buttons to provide the parent with speed, waiting time and sprite properties for the child it was to create, here we count on the user to supply the script with the target and speed properties it will need to apply an instance of itself to the sprite the user dragged the behavior onto.

5. Type the following after the end of your last handler:

```
on getPropertyDescriptionList me
  vPDList = [:] -- a temporary property list
    setaProp vPDList, #myTarget, [#default: "",#format:#integer,
    ➡ #comment:
    ➡ "Which sprite number should the bee head towards?:"]
```

So we define vPDList as a blank property list, and then set some properties for that list using the setaProp command. The first entry is #myTarget, and the properties that follow within the brackets define how that property is presented to the user, and how the information the user enters is accepted.

There are over 20 properties Director has created to identify the kinds of information received through getPropertyDescriptionList, including #bitmap, #filmloop and #field. Take a look at Director's Lingo Dictionary for the full list; they are all pretty much self-explanatory. These properties exist only to help Director parse the information received; they are not passed as properties into the script. Their only purpose is to ensure that the two properties we do care about, #myTarget and #mySpeed, are described and handled properly.

I like to think of these as helper-properties. #default, as you've probably worked out, specifies the default value for the property. Here it is empty. Setting #format to #integer tells Director that the information entered should be an integer. And #comment specifies the text that sits to the left of the user's entry field.

6. Now, add the following to finish up this handler:

```
    setaProp vPDList, #mySpeed, [#default: 10, #format:#integer,
    ➡ #comment: "At what speed (2 is fast, 12 is slow):", #range:
    ➡ [#min:2, #max:12]]
      return vPDList
end
```

Here we define all the helper-properties for #mySpeed, which does exactly the same thing it did in the Bee Script; sets the number to divide the distance by, in order to calculate the size of each step. The higher the number for mySpeed, the smaller the individual steps, and the slower the bee will fly.

You'll recognize the first four properties that follow, #default, #format, #integer and #comment. #range tells Director the range of values that are acceptable for this entry. Here we've set the minimum to 2 and the maximum to 12. It will default to 10.

We've now created everything that is needed for the part of this script that is client facing. Although we haven't defined any functionality for this behavior, we can test it out to see how what we just entered is reflected within Director.

7. Save your work. Use the Director shape tool to draw a graphic sprite in channel 1 of your score, and put some text on the stage in channel 2. Open up the cast window and double-click the behavior we just created.

Now drag the behavior from the cast window onto the sprite in channel 1. You'll get the following dialog box:

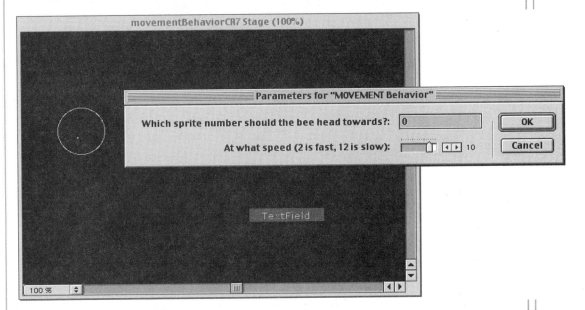

As you can see, the entry for #myTarget is set to the default of 0, and # mySpeed is set to the default we specified of 10. Cancel out of this as we haven't yet made this script functional. We just applied the behavior so you could see what we've built so far in action.

8. Now drag the same behavior to the text field in sprite 2. You get a hand with a bar through it to indicate that you cannot apply this script here. There's no way you'll be able to apply this behavior to text, because of the specifications we made in isOkayToAttach.

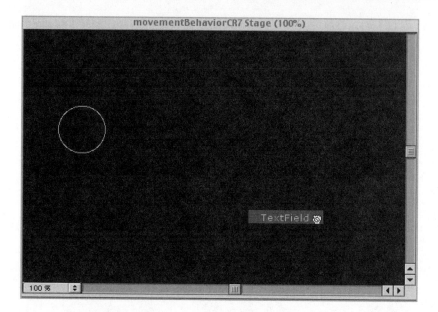

Declaring the properties

So far, we've seen how the user will pass `mySpeed` and `myTarget` to the behavior so that it can fashion an instance to apply to the sprite. This is just like crazy bee or lazy ee button sending the properties of `howFast`, `howLong`, and `beeSprite` to the parent Bee Script so that it could create a child object based on those properties.

Now we need to declare those properties so that the script can use them to create a new instance.

9.   Type the following after the end of your last handler:

```
property myTarget - - the target sprite
property mySpeed - - higher the number the smaller the steps the
➡ slower the bee
property mySprite - -  to the sprite the behavior is placed on
```

After the property declaration in parent-child Lingo, we use the `on new me` handler to construct all the properties in a way the child can use them. The child springs to life `on new me`. But the new instance of this behavior script truly springs to life when the sprite it will be controlling is created. We've already sent `mySpeed` and `myTarget` on `getPropertyDescriptionList`, and declared them as properties so that we can use them in other parts of this script. We still need to tell this instance of the script which sprite it will be controlling

10. Add the following code after the property declaration:

```
on beginSprite me
  me.mySprite = the currentSpriteNum - - set mySprite to the
```

```
➥current Sprite.
end beginSprite
```

This behavior has been attached to a particular sprite before the Movie has started. Once the Movie begins, each sprite calls its own on beginSprite me handler, and this is when the sprite information is passed to this instance of the behavior.

So now we have all the information we need to make this sprite start moving.

Making the sprite move
The movement portion of the script is almost identical to the flying handler from the Bee Script we built earlier.

11. Save your work, open up the Bee Flower movie you created earlier, copy the flying handler from the Bee Script, and paste it into this behavior.

Here's the flying handler:

```
on flying me
   me.myFlying = TRUE
   myLoc = sprite(me.mySprite).loc
   targetLoc = sprite(me.myTargetFlower).loc
   if myLoc < targetLoc then
     totalDistance= targetLoc - myLoc
     posneg= 1
   else
     totalDistance- myLoc - targetLoc
     posneg= -1
   end if

   if totalDistance> 12 then
     myLoc = myLoc + posneg*(totalDistance/me.mySpeed)
   else
     —SNAP IF CLOSE ENOUGH
     myLoc = targetLoc
     me.myFlying = FALSE — - set boolean to false, the bee is no
     ➥ longer flying
     me.myTimer = the ticks — - reset the counter for checkTimer
   end if
   sprite(me.mySprite).loc = myLoc
end
```

The major differences between the flying handler and the motion portion of the behavior we are building are:

- We call the movement on prepareFrame me, not on flying me

If you recall, we called the flying handler on every stepFrame of the Bee Script because it had to work with a waiting time and a findTarget handler to function properly. Here, we already know our target, and this is a one-shot deal, so, we can just call our motion directly from the on prepareFrame me handler. If we did need to work with several handlers, this on prepareFrame me handler would take the place of the on stepFrame me. This would be where we would work out which handlers to call in which circumstances.

- We don't need the me.myFlying property.

Again, as this is a one shot deal, we don't have to check if we are flying or not, we just go, and then stop when we reach our target, and we're done. You can come back into this script when we are done and start adding some other handlers in if you like, adapting them to their new circumstances so that a user could apply them in many different scenarios. But for the purposes of learning how to create a custom behavior, we are going to keep it simple, so you can remove all references to me.myFlying.

- We don't need myTimer.

The reasons for this should be clear by now. We never wait, so we never need me.myTimer.

12. So, go back into the flying handler we just pasted, change on flying me to on beginSprite me. Then delete all references to me.myFlying and me.myTimer. (There are two references to me.myFlying: the second line from the top and the fourth from the bottom. There is only one reference to me.myTimer, third from the bottom)

The handler formerly known as flying should now look like this:

```
on prepareFrame me
  myLoc = sprite(me.mySprite).loc
  targetLoc = sprite(me.myTarget).loc
  if myLoc < targetLoc then
    totalDistance= targetLoc - myLoc
    posneg= 1
  else
    totalDistance= myLoc - targetLoc
    posneg= -1
  end if
  if totalDistance> 12 then
    myLoc = myLoc + posneg*(totalDistance/me.mySpeed)

  else
    --SNAP IF CLOSE ENOUGH
    myLoc = targetLoc
  end if
  sprite(me.mySprite).loc = myLoc
end
```

Aside from the new Lingo we needed to learn to work with behaviors in general, the functionality of a custom behavior is very similar to that of a parent-child script. In parent-child Lingo we create a child object based on a parent class and apply it to something on the stage. With custom behaviors, we create an instance of our behavior and let the user provide the necessary information to apply it to something on the stage. Encapsulation is important in both cases, and we have seen how the same concepts run through both processes.

In it's entirety, the Movement behavior should look like this:

```
on getBehaviorDescription me  - - allowing the author's
➥ description
  RETURN \
    "MOVEMENT BEHAVIOR" & RETURN & RETURN & \
    "Sprite will move towards the target at the speed you
    ➥ choose."
end getBehaviorDescription

on getBehaviorTooltip me - - allowing the author to create text
➥ for tool tip
  RETURN \
    "Moves a sprite towards a target at the speed you choose"
end getBehaviorTooltip

on isOKToAttach me, spriteType, spriteNum
  case spriteType of
    #graphic: return sprite(spriteNum).member.type <> #text
    otherwise: return FALSE
  end case
end

on getPropertyDescriptionList me
  vPDList = [:] - - a temporary property list
    setaProp vPDList, #myTarget, [#default: "",#format:#integer,
  ➥ #comment:"Which sprite number should the bee head towards?:"]
    setaProp vPDList, #mySpeed, [#default: 10, #format:#integer,
  ➥ #comment:"At what speed (2 is fast, 12 is slow):", #range:
  ➥ [#min:2, #max:12]]
    return vPDList
end


property myTarget - - the target sprite
property mySpeed - - higher the number the smaller the stepsthe
➥ slower the bee
property mySprite - - reference to the sprite the behavior is
➥ placed on

on beginSprite me
  me.mySprite = the currentSpriteNum - - set mySprite to the
  ➥ current Sprite
end beginSprite


- - MOVEMENT SCRIPT
on prepareFrame me
  myLoc = sprite(me.mySprite).loc
```

```
targetLoc = sprite(me.myTarget).loc
if myLoc < targetLoc then
  totalDistance= targetLoc - myLoc
  posneg= 1
else
  totalDistance= myLoc - targetLoc
  posneg= -1
end if
if totalDistance> 12 then
  myLoc = myLoc + posneg*(totalDistance/me.mySpeed)

else
  - - SNAP IF CLOSE ENOUGH
  myLoc = targetLoc
end if
sprite(me.mySprite).loc = myLoc
end
- - MOVEMENT SCRIPT
```

13. We're all done. Save your work, drag the behavior script onto sprite 1 (the shape), and fill out the dialog box that pops up. When you're asked 'Which sprite number should the bee head towards?' enter 2, as that is the channel in which the text field sits. We can't apply this script to a text member, but there is no reason we can't use this script to tell a shape member to head towards a text member. Chose whatever speed you like using the slider.

Parameters for "MOVEMENT Behavior"		
Which sprite number should the bee head towards?: 2		**OK**
At what speed (2 is fast, 12 is slow): [slider] ◄ ► 10		**Cancel**

Now hit play, and watch the circle fly towards the text. Just as with the bees, it will snap to its target once it gets within 12 pixels.

A circle flying across the screen to hit a text field is not particularly exciting in its own right, but the fact that it was so easy to turn a parent class into a custom behavior is rather exciting. Creating new instances of a template script is very similar in parent-child Lingo and in custom behavior Lingo. The difference is that instead of defining parameters on new me by sending arguments in the scripting environment, we define them on getPropertyDescriptionList when the user enters values into the dialog box.

Without changing the code any more, we can already start using this behavior for more than it was originally intended. Draw a whole slew of bees on the stage. While you're at it, throw some radio buttons in there too. Now start dragging the custom behavior to the different sprites. And don't just set static sprites that act like flowers as the target. Redefine this system, set sprites that will be moving as the target. Play around with different speeds. Wreak a little havoc.

Now hit play and watch the mayhem ensue!

All right, so a bunch of random shapes and buttons smashing into each other is not exactly ground breaking work. You won't get into New Masters of Director with this script ;–). But you've acquired the building blocks you'll need to take these ideas much further. We've covered all of the Lingo you'll need to know to work with Object Oriented Programming in Director, and we've really hammered in the concepts of OOP. We've gone over good working methods for making the most out of your scripts, and we've seen how, by coding in a modular fashion, your scripts can be flexible enough to be applied to a myriad of possibilities.

Summary

We've covered a lot in this chapter. We started from the general concepts of OOP, and developed that all the way to a motion script and into a custom behavior. We've shown you how you can take your knowledge of OOP beyond the confines of this chapter. So, let's take a moment to review what we've covered here. Most importantly:

> *Object Oriented Programming is an approach, and is not specific to Lingo. As such, there are certain principles that apply across the board.*

More specifically:

Specify and abstract	Approaching a project from an OOP perspective begins by breaking it down into elements: simple, self-sufficient chunks.
Objects are encapsulated	Lingo is not an Object Oriented Programming language in the strict sense of a language like C++, so it is important that we are diligent in mimicking the properties of true OOP languages by keeping our objects encapsulated. Never access a variable or property directly from outside the object; use handlers within that object to return the needed results. By keeping all the action protected within these shells, objects are more portable and flexible than if they are hard–coded.
Objects live on in RAM	The objects you create exist independent of a specific Director movie. This makes them very powerful, as they can have wide-ranging effects in diverse situations if properly coded, but it can also make them dangerous. Memory can leak, and lingering objects can have unintended consequences in other scenarios.
Objects are building blocks	Parent scripts, if written in an abstract and modular fashion, can be assembled by other scripts to perform a diverse set of functions. Child objects can have other objects as properties. They can be assembled like building blocks in a myriad of

formations. Furthermore, parent scripts can be crafted into custom behaviors for use in other Director movies. You can create your own tools out of objects.

Terms specific to OOP in Director

- **Parent scripts** are the templates for **child scripts**.
  When you invoke a new instance of that parent script with the `on new me handler`, you are creating a copy of that script that exists in its own right. The child's properties can vary from those of the parent, and changes to one child will not affect the parent, or the other children.

- **Ancestor scripts** are one more step up in the hierarchy.
  While parent scripts inherit properties from the ancestor, the parent can have entirely new properties and handlers of its own. We connect an ancestor to a parent script by declaring it as a property of that parent and setting the name of the ancestor script as the value of that property in the `on new me` handler. We do this the same way we declare other handlers, functions, lists, etc. as properties within any parent script.

```
property ancestor, property2, property3

on new me
me.ancestor=new(script "ancestorScript")
me.property2.property2Handler()
me.property3=property3List[k]
return me
end
```

- **`return me`** enters the script into RAM

- The **`actorList`** is a special list reserved by Director for the purpose of holding the children we birth from our parent scripts. We must specifically set the child as an entry into this list for it to appear in the `actorList`.

- **`on stepFrame`** is a handler available only to members of the `actorList`. This handler occurs before every `prepareFrame` handler, and so is extremely useful for animation and checking variables. Since it does happen so frequently, be careful what you put in it. Excessive `if-then` statements or `repeat` loops called every frame can quickly bog down Director.

So there you have it. You've gotten some fertile ground to build on. The examples we covered here may be basic, but the concepts and Lingo covered is all you'll need to know to get started in the wonderful world of OOP. We've given you some ideas on where you can take these scripts from here, and you can download some extrapolations from these scripts at http://www.grographics.com/lingo. Check out the CD for more OOP resources.

chapter 2

chapter 3

chapter 5

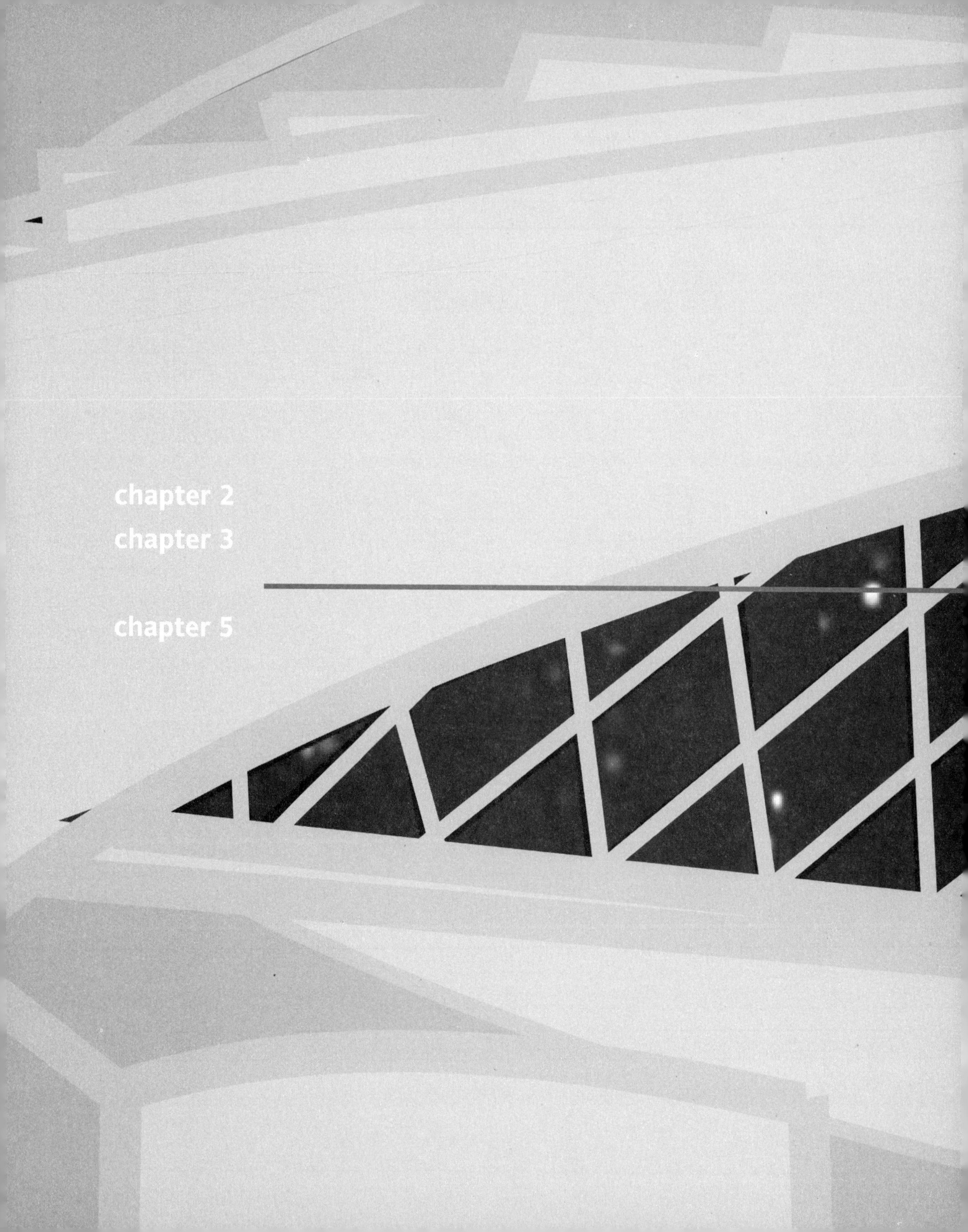

Chapter 4
Gaming with OOP

In this chapter we undertake the task of producing a non-trivial game using the object oriented methodologies we learned previously. Get ready to go step-by-step through each of the sections as we guide you through the complex, but understandable, process of creating a flexible, easily reusable, and debuggable Director game! The game we'll use for this example will be a simple shoot-em-up involving a variety of backgrounds and enemies that possess and display rudimentary intelligence. In order to do this we'll make good use of Director 8.5's improved 3D and on-the-fly media creation abilities.

First we'll talk about games from a developer's point of view, giving a very simple classification of the types of computer games which we could write. We use that classification to label the game we're writing. Then we'll give an overview of some of the design and development strategies we'll use. This will include a description of the object oriented concepts that we'll make use of in the early design phase of the game. Then we'll roll up our sleeves and get to work on implementing our design by writing our game. As we're writing our game we'll talk through the code that we use (all of which is available in the 'UsAndThem.dir file on the CD-ROM accompanying this book) and tell you why we use it, to highlight pertinent points to help your understanding.

This section will start with the idea of rapid prototyping the general form of the game, including the creation of placeholder media, then talk about the creation of placeholder code. It'll then show you how to flesh-out that code and get right into the coding. After the development of the game we'll talk about troubleshooting the game and how you might expand it in the future.

It's a good idea to read the chapter from start to finish before even touching Director, then you'll have an idea of the breadth of the task before you get into the depth. On your marks, get set, read!

An Introduction to Gaming

It's worth discussing the various genres of games that exist, and which of these are 'Director-friendly'. Just about anything that one could do in C++ can be done in Director, the main factor is speed. Hey, you could even write a first-person shooter, but in general don't expect it to run at 90 frames per second! One way to classify games is by the view the user is exposed to: there are three main groups of game according to this classification:

Two-dimensional
The simplest to implement, this type of game presents the user with a two-dimensional view of the game environment, as though they were either looking down at the ground from far above, or from a side-on view. An additional feature is that the backgrounds may be layered, creating a parallax effect. Most classic shoot-em-ups have used this type.

Isometric
Imagine a top-down version of the above, then imagine rotating it so that now the third dimension creeps in, and is represented as height. This is achieved by taking x, y and z coordinates and 'mapping' them (via a simple function) to screen coordinates of h and v. Many adventure games use this type.

First-person
Did someone mention "Quake" or "Doom"? Arguably the most popular of the genres listed here, the first-person shooter immerses the user in a three dimensional space, and presents it to them from their perspective. Computationally intensive, this type of game produces a realistic experience, sometimes exciting, and often scary!

For the sake of simplicity, our game will be of the first type, the two-dimensional type, although we will make use of Director 8.5's 3D in a number of areas.

Design and Development Strategies

You've all heard the term hacker, but what does it mean to 'hack' in a computer programming context? To 'hack something together' is to assemble it in a rough and ready fashion, putting things together in order to get a quick result. It can happen when you're showing an idea to someone, a "proof of concept" as it's known, or it can occur when you fix a problem in an inelegant way - "a quick hack". It's okay to hack, but what's more important is being aware of advantages and disadvantages of such an approach. Whilst hacking something together requires a small amount of effort for a quick result, the disadvantages will make themselves apparent when you try to expand the system by making it more complex, or adding new features. Never allow yourself to be bullied into taking a hack and trying to convert it into a final product - you will only be giving yourself unnecessary grief! It is false economy to think that the time saved in hacking outweighs the problems it creates further down the track.

As we've said, hacking has its legitimate place in rapidly prototyping ideas, but is inappropriate for completed work. So what're the alternatives? Methodologies! This has been a buzzword for a number of years, so let's clarify what we mean by it in this chapter. A software development methodology is a set of philosophies and procedures that prescribe a course of action for the development of elegant, expandable, reliable, and reusable software. There are several available, and many are geared at large scale projects involving hundreds of people, but that is not to say that we can't make use of one for our humble (presumably single person) project!

Actually, we'll be using an assorted selection of techniques in this chapter; the first one that must be mentioned is the top-down approach. This means that we will be designing in a breadth-first fashion; that is, tying down the project in rough strokes first, and completing the detail only when we are satisfied with how the rough strokes are looking. Doing something breadth-first means that at any one time you have a version of the entire project. Doing something depth-first means at any one time you have finished versions of only parts of the project.

The ideas presented here are intended to be as general as possible, so that you can apply them to your own projects, but of course it is difficult to understand such ideas without seeing them applied to a real-world example. So, we'll build a simple game ("Us and Them"), in the section "Implementing Our Design", in order for you to see for yourself how we turn design process and methodology into the finished product. Up until that point we will keep things general enough to apply to any game of the player/enemy variety. Keeping this in mind, read this section carefully and try and consider the game that you want to develop, as well as seeing how the concepts we present relate to the game that we're developing in this chapter.

Let's begin. The first thing to do is define an overall framework that describes the possible situations we might wish to be represented in our game. The framework we'll be using here can be expressed in a few lines:

> *The Game will consist of a number of Environments that are inhabited by the Player and a number of Enemies, which are both a type of Entity. When the Player has satisfied a certain Goal that is specific to an Environment that Environment is completed, and the Player advances to the next Environment. The Game is finished when the last Environment's Goal is satisfied.*

Let's look a bit more closely at what the terms in this definition mean:

User   The final, (generally human!) recipient of the Game. The person who plays the game.

Game   The outcome of efforts, the Director movie that we produce. Also refers to the abstract idea of the game itself.

Environment   A space that is occupied by the Player and Enemies. In our example this is two-dimensional and has boundaries.

Entity   A generic inhabitant of an Environment. The parent type of Player and Enemy.

Player   A representation of the User that is under that User's control. It is through the Player that the User plays the Game.

Enemy   An autonomous, artificially intelligent Entity that occupies the environment. The goal of these Enemies is to prevent the Player from completing the Goals of the Environment.

Goal   A set of conditions, specific to an Environment, which need to be met by the Player in order to progress to the next Environment.

Using Classes to Provide Required Functionality

Once we establish our framework, our task is to create a design that actualizes that framework. Specifically, this involves designing a number of classes and layers that capture and partition the desired functionality of the framework. Another way of saying capture in this context is represent, and another way of saying partition is to say structure and organize.

Initially it is enough to know that we will need one class per significant concept outlined in the framework, i.e. Game, Environment, Player, Enemy and Goal. Although, as you will see, Director's Stage suffices for the environment and the goals of each environment can be represented simply as a yes/no question, so there's no need to have classes for those elements.

Let's look at an overview of how the game will work. It can be helpful to draw a diagram of what modules (in our case classes) will be required in order to make the game work. At this early stage we can settle on at least this much: our game class will manage/contain a player and a number of enemies, and both of these can be considered a type of entity. Let's represent that in a pair of diagrams:

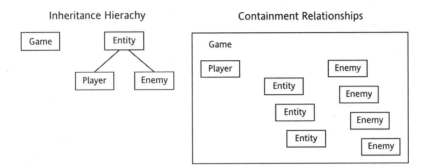

Note that we have not included Environment or Goal. The functionality of these items can be included within the game class and sprite behaviors.

The Game Class

This is undoubtedly the most important class and which is true for virtually any game. We'll use it to manage all the other classes and ultimately all user input will be processed by it. For our game, this class jobs are to allow the movement of entities within the boundaries of Director's stage, to keep the player's score, and to have the responsibility of allowing the player to continue to the next environment or not. In our game this class is intended to have only one instance, in more complex applications of this framework this might not be the case - for example, in the case of savable and loadable games.

When the user runs the game, this instance is created and initialized. This instance has the task of managing the other instances, namely the current environment, the player, and any enemies. This instance is also charged with the task of interfacing with the various layers of the system, for example the Input/Output layer. The parameters for the initialization of this instance include:

- The starting score (i.e. zero);

- The starting environment;

- The player;

- Any enemies.

Additional handlers we will define within this class:

- An 'Idle' routine: the idea behind such a handler is that each class (or more accurately instances of classes) should be given a slice of time in which to do their thing, whatever that is. In the case of the game class, its 'thing' is to accept the user's input, move the player and have it fire if requested, move the enemies, update the score, etc.

The Entity Class

This class is to be the ancestor of both the player and enemy classes. It defines variables that are shared by both of these classes - for example, position, velocity, life, and functions (such as 'beHit', 'Init', and so forth).

The Player Class

In our game this class is intended to have a single instance. A more complex game might involve multiple simultaneous players, but for our example, we will allow only one. It is a child of the entity class. The parameters for the initialization of this instance include:

- The amount of 'life' possessed by the player.

- The set of graphics that are to be used for the player.

The Enemy Class

This class will be instantiated by the game instance as many times as there are enemies for the current environment. As an enemy is destroyed, so is its instance. It is a child of the entity class. The parameters for the initialization of these instances include:

- The amount of 'life' possessed by the enemy.

- The set of graphics that are to be used for the enemy

- Layering the project

Using Layers to Partition Functionality

Software layers are a good way of partitioning the functionality of any program, and so we make good use of them here in developing our game. The idea behind a layer is simply to group functionality of a similar level. For example, we will create an 'Engine Layer' that deals with certain often-used Director functions, i.e. the management of sprites and sound channels. Layers are not to be confused with classes and instances - it is quite possible to create a project without one class or instance, but still make use of layers. This is akin to 'Modular Programming'. Generally layers are a convention maintained by the programmer. Practically speaking in Director this involves using one or more code cast members per layer, in addition to naming them 'Something Layer'. In our project we will use two, an 'Engine Layer' and an 'Input/Output Layer'.

The 'Engine Layer'

Director's sprites are both a useful and problematic feature. By now you will have used the score extensively and you know that you use sprites to put something on the stage. You should also be aware that the order of these sprites is fixed: a graphic in channel 10 will appear in front of a graphic in channel 9, for example. This is a convention that we can break if we need to, using clever code. More specifically, we'll write a 'sprite manager' – that means we don't have to place things in the score manually, but rather via code that serves the needs of the game at any particular moment.

Many people are blissfully unaware of Director's sound capabilities, and only make use of sound in the score. We will write a simple 'sound manager' that handles the effective and flexible playing of sound for us.

The 'Input/Output Layer'
Rather than just haphazardly checking for keyboard and mouse input at various times, it's always a good idea to bundle these functions into a single layer. This layer will have functions that relate to the kinds of input the user can generate. It will also provide handlers that deal with output, such as displaying the player's score.

The Containment Relationship

You've learned about the incredibly important object oriented concept of classes and instances, but there is a similarly important idea that relates to the way that certain instances relate to other instances. This is known as 'Containment' or 'Management'.

In our framework, the game instance (at a single moment in time) will manage player and enemy instances. This means it is the game's responsibility to call the handlers of these instances, as well as receive feedback from them, in the form of returned values from these handlers.

Let's discuss a toy example of this idea before we proceed any further. Imagine we are writing a simple simulation of a number of balls bouncing around in a room. We would use a room class and a ball class, and create a single instance of the room class, and many instances of the ball class. The room instance would manage all of the ball instances. Pragmatically, this would involve the room instance iterating through each ball instance, and calling its 'idle' function. An idle function is one that you would expect to call when you wish for an instance to 'do its thing' within a slice of time. OK, what do balls do? They move due to their velocity, are acted on by exterior forces, check for collision, and so on. So, the room might tell the ball where the walls are, what gravity is doing, and then idle it. Each ball could then return a simple binary value: FALSE if no collision occurred, and TRUE if it did hit a wall.

One final important note before we get on to creating our game: there is a wide continuum between hacking an idea together, and writing the most elegant, object oriented code possible. A good rule of thumb is to only hack something when you do not intend to reuse that code - reuse of design is another matter altogether. So, if you want to cobble together a 'proof of concept' by all means do it the quick and dirty way. Resist at all costs the temptation to try and expand this design into the final product. Start again! You will save much time and frustration by doing so. Learn from the issues you encountered in the hack, and try to think more abstractly.

Anyhow, along this line of discussion, let us quickly examine a 'containment rule' that can help keep our code elegant.

Imagine if you had the task of designing an alarm clock. You decide that you will make two classes, an 'Alarm' class and a 'Clock' class. An alarm instance will contain a clock instance and manage it, waiting for the alarm time, and acting when it comes around. The point we're trying to make here is that in order to make the Clock class as reusable as possible, it shouldn't need to know about the Alarm class. If it did have to know, then we wouldn't be able to reuse it in another application, for example a 'World Clock'. Keep this rule in mind and if you have to break it just be aware of the consequences!

Creating a Game

Now that you've digested all of that theory, it's time to put it into practice. Don't worry if you didn't quite absorb all of the concepts; hopefully, as we put them to work in the actual game, you will see the light.

1.   To get us started on our game, gently, we'll be creating some graphics.

2.   Then we'll write stubs for our code. This means defining the structure of the code without writing any actual functions.

3.   Once we've done that, and only then, will we complete the code.

4.   Following this, we'll create a working prototype of the game, using a single environment, player and enemy.

5.   Then we will be able to use some media, and finally test and modify the game.

So, why have we broken the preceding sentences over many lines? Because they're phases in our game design and build. These phases are listed below:

■   Phase 1: Rapid Prototyping using Placeholder Media

■   Phase 2: Writing Code Stubs

■   Phase 3: Writing the Code

■   Phase 4: The 'One of Everything' version

■   Phase 5: Replacement of Placeholder Media

■   Phase 6: Testing and Reiteration

To give you an idea of where we're heading with this game, here are a few screenshots and a description of how the game will work. You will find it easier, especially where screen effects and colors are discussed, to refer to the graphics on the CD-ROM that accompanies this book.

The above screenshot shows the title screen for the game. We used Director 8.5's new 3D text feature, and wrote some Lingo to subtly rotate that text. We've also added a particle effect per word: red sparks for 'Us' and green for 'Them'. Here's a shot of the options that were used:

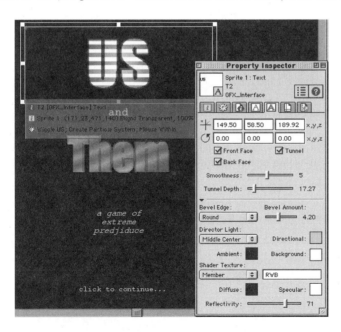

To achieve the red white and blue stripes on the word 'Us', we've used a 'Shader Texture', namely 'RWB'. Have a look at this texture and you will see that we've used the smallest number of pixels possible. Also, check out the behaviors we've attached to this sprite, the last two are part of Director 8.5's library, but the first one is our very own. Here's the listing:

```
property theMember
property theCenterPointAndRadius
property theCenter


- - ===========
on beginSprite me

- - Cache our Variables
 theMember = the member of sprite (the spriteNum of me)

 theCenterPointAndRadius = theMember.model[1].boundingSphere
 theCenter = theCenterPointAndRadius[1]
 theMember.model[1].rotate(theCenter, vector(0,0,0), 0,#world)

end


- - =========
on exitFrame me

- - Set up an oscillator
 theSpeed = 1 * cos(0.01 * the ticks)

 theCenterPointAndRadius = theMember.model[1].boundingSphere
 theCenter = theCenterPointAndRadius[1]
 theMember.model[1].rotate(theCenter, vector(1,0,1)
 ➥ theSpeed,#world)

end
```

The main code to be aware of here is the 'Set up an oscillator' step. Using sine and cosine functions can be a great way to produce smooth oscillations. We've simply set a variable, 'theSpeed', to be the value of this function, and then used this value to set the rotation of the text.

The game proper is to be a classic horizontal scrolling shoot-em-up. On the following page is a screenshot of a typical moment in the game:

In this shot you can see the player's "Mighty Rocket of Justice", plus a number of (at this stage) similarly colored aliens. Note too the layered background and foreground, there are separate parts for the sky, sun, clouds, trees, and two levels of mountains. There is also a score panel, showing the current level (environment), the player's score and number of ships. Here we've used simple text fields, but we could quite easily replace these with an iconic representation. There are a number of enemies onscreen, that simply fly out and seek the player.

OK, enough talk, let's get developing!

Phase 1: Rapid Prototyping Using Placeholder Media

In order to give ourselves the raw materials we need media-wise, we will quickly create the media we require. The specification for what this media is to be is driven by the brief for the game. Instead of waiting for the entire media to be available in a finished version, either from a client or yourself, we shall make it ourselves.

This is where we most often hear the excuse "But I can't draw!". Sorry, in this context, this excuse is not valid! You will agree with us when you see how easy it is to use Director's Paint window. A good idea is to write out a 'Media List' that lists, and names, every single piece of media that we will require. Organize it by type, as shown after.

Graphics
Interface
Scoreboard
Score
Lives Remaining
Level
Player
Player Normal
Player Dying

Player's Energy Bolt

Enemies
Enemy Level 1 Normal
Enemy Level 1 Dying
Enemy Level 2 Normal
Enemy Level 2 Dying
etc.

Sound
Start of Game
End of Environment
Player fires
Player hit
Enemy hit
Player dies
End of Game

Go through the list and quickly and roughly create the media. Graphics are easier to create than sounds, so let's make those first. If you're keen to get started with the programming side of things, then you can simply use the media we've provided on the CD.

For the sake of simplicity we are depicting a minimum of elements; the media required for animation of any kind calls for dozens, if not hundreds, of elements! Luckily though, Director 8.5 can provide us with some three dimensional tools that will make our development a wonderful dream. In the interests of file size, we can use Director's vector shapes. The placeholder graphics shown here are pretty rough, but could be a lot rougher! Consider using the most basic of shapes – a rectangle for the player, and ovals for the enemies, for example. There is a reason for this: spending any more time on this task can serve to distract you from the greater task at hand. Also, when clients are involved they have a tendency to take what they see as the final product – the "Legacy Effect".

The creation of backgrounds using vector shapes can be straightforward and painless too. Keep in mind though, that whilst they are lightweight in terms of number of bytes used, they can be slower to display than bitmap shapes, as they are actively rendered rather than passively copied. When it comes to the creation of sounds, just use your voice. Seriously! If you need an explosion, make that sound...and if you're really self-conscious, you can always just say "Boom!". Make as many sounds as you need, and name them with the entry from the media list. Notice how we have created a number of casts to partition the media. Shown here are three casts: the player's, one for enemies, and one for environments.

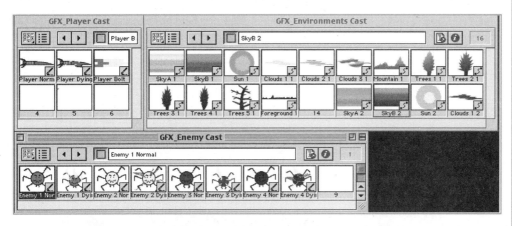

Don't worry about any animation yet, even though it's quite quick to produce in Director. Just make some still images and we'll move on to the next phase. Be aware also that each of these elements will need to be named appropriately, but we'll leave that until Phase 3.

The final part of this phase is the setup of the score. There will be some interplay between the development of the code and the arrangement of the score, but it's good to at least sketch out how the score is arranged. Here's a cropped picture of how we set out our (final) Score - the full picture is available on the CD-ROM and should be referred to to set up your game exactly as we have:

Why not set your score up as shown, and write the frame scripts as we present them. Only the order of the sprites is important, with the exception that the Player's ship needs to be in a sprite that the code references, as do the sprites that we'll use for the Sprite Manager - all will become apparent as you read on. Notice also how the sprites are set out in groups. There are only five markers in our score, so let's explain them and the layout of our score by working left to right, looking at each in turn.

The first, Intro, simply contains the 3D and 2D text proclaiming the mission statement of the game, so to speak. We've seen this screen already, it says "Us and Them". The frame script for this frame is simply:

```
on exitFrame me
  go "Intro"
end

on mouseDown
  go "GameStart"
end
```

The second, GameStart, contains the funky 'Level x' graphic:

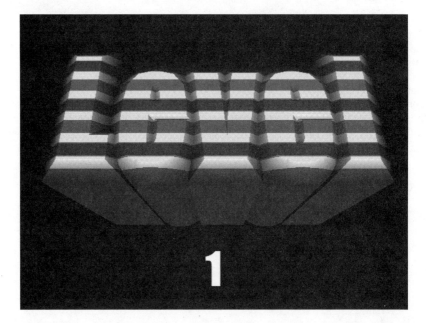

Here's the frame script. Its job is to animate the bevel depth of the 3D text, while checking for the end of that animation, for example when the bevel depth reaches less than one. The purpose of the following code is to initialize the bevel depth of the word 'Level' to a starting value of 100.

```
on beginSprite me

  member("Fat Level").bevelDepth = 100

end
```

Into the following we've thrown in a little 'undocumented feature' that lets us, the developer, skip this level animation if we wish to. It's undocumented in that we wouldn't tell the user about it - it's only for our benefit as developers.

```
on exitFrame me

- - Allow us to skip this when developing
 if the optionDown then
  go "GameIdle"
 end if

 go the frame
- - Decrease the bevel of the text

bd = member("Fat Level").bevelDepth
 bd = bd * .75
 if bd < 1 then
  go "GameIdle"
 end if

 member("Fat Level").bevelDepth = bd
  end
```

The third, GameStep, is the heart of the game. You've already seen a preview of this screen, it's the one with the player battling the enemies. You'll notice the proliferation of cells in this frame, let's take it from the top. (You should refer to the graphic of the score on the CD-ROM or open the UsAndThem.dir and look at the score there to follow the instructions.) The first two blue colored cells are for the sky graphic. Next, we have the sun, not surprisingly colored yellow. The aqua sprites are for clouds. The next two orange sprites are for the background mountains. The nine green ones are for trees. Then there is a long row of yellow sprites that will be used by the sprite manager that we have yet to write. In the middle of these is the player's sprite, marked as blue. The reason it's here is so there is an even chance of an enemy appearing behind or in front of the player, just for variety. The next two orange sprites are for the foreground mountains, and finally, the rest of the sprites are for the score panel. Here's that frame script:

```
on exitFrame me

Game_Step()
 go the frame

end
```

The fourth, Game Over, is (not surprisingly) the place we go when the user has finally messed up. Here's the frame script:

```
on exitFrame me
 go the frame
end
```

```
on mouseDown
  go "Intro"
  Game_Init()
end
```

The final marker, Finished, is visited when the last Level is passed. It has the same frame script as the Game Over frame.

Phase 2: Writing Code Stubs

Here's where we really start coding, we will write 'code stubs' which are essentially empty husks to later be filled with the actual code. You may wonder what use there is in writing code that doesn't do anything. The idea here is again to work 'breadth-first'. That is, to at least settle on what classes and functions will be required as well as how they interface with each other, without having to worry about exactly what code will be written in order to achieve this. Thus, we simply write the most rudimentary definition of our classes, and write plenty of comments to clearly signal our intentions. If you are unable to see the difference between a specification of how a function will do its job and the actual code, then you need to meditate on this point for a bit longer.

It is also a good idea to write some pseudocode to best get our heads around how the game will work. Pseudocode is a nice way of sketching out how a piece of code will work, without having to write actual code. Another term for pseudocode is 'Structured English'.

- *STEP: Initialise the Game*

- *STEP: Set up an Environment*

- *STEP: Place the Player in the Environment*

- *LOOP: Give the Game a slice of time*

- *STEP: Deal with User Input*

- *STEP: Check for Player collision with any Enemies*

- *STEP: Check for Player's weapons hitting any Enemies*

- *STEP: Check if any goals have been met*

The first script you should always write in a Director movie is the main movie script. Its job is to initialize the movie, and in our case, create the game instance. You can open this by pressing SHIFT+COMMAND+U on a Mac, or SHIFT+CTRL+U under Windows

This code creates an instance of the game class and assigns it to the variable gGame. The use of the letter 'g' at the start of the variable name is simply a matter of convention, it reminds us that this is a global variable. Now let's quickly create our classes and layers. Below is a diagram that shows the main scripts in our movie.

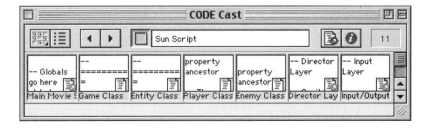

Creating the Classes

Make as many scripts as we have shown here, you need to tell Director that a script cast member is a certain type, for example a class; Director calls them 'parent scripts' by making sure that the type of the script is set to 'parent'. Just select the script in the cast window and press the 'information' button. Here are the classes we will need. We've shown the 'Game' Class in the most detail and just described the remaining classes.

Game

Firstly, we name our properties starting with a 'p', as a matter or convention. (Parameters also start with a 'p'.) So, let's look at each property in turn:

- pEnvironmentNum - the number of the current environment.

- pPlayer - this will contain the player instance.

- pEnemyList - a list, initially empty, which will contain instances of the enemy class

- pBoltList - a list, initially empty, which will contain instances of the entity class, used for the player's energy bolts.

- pScore- the user's score.

- pShips - the number of ships remaining.

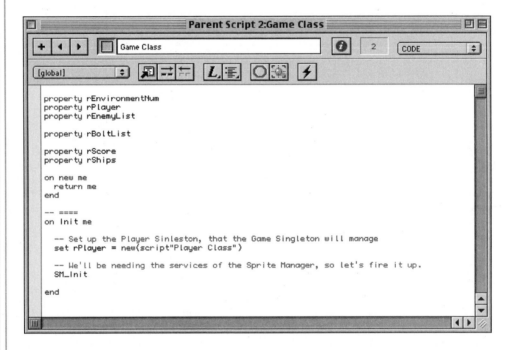

```
Parent Script 2:Game Class

Game Class                              2    CODE

[global]

property rEnvironmentNum
property rPlayer
property rEnemyList

property rBoltList

property rScore
property rShips

on new me
  return me
end

-- ====
on Init me

  -- Set up the Player Sinleston, that the Game Singleton will manage
  set rPlayer = new(script"Player Class")

  -- We'll be needing the services of the Sprite Manager, so let's fire it up.
  SM_Init

end
```

Entity
This class gives us the functionality we need to have an object whiz around on the screen!

Player
We've made a subclass of 'entity' called 'player'. Specific to the player are handlers that cope with the rendering of its media, plus special versions of handlers found in 'entity'.

Enemy
Another subclass of 'Entity', the enemy class needs to provide us with enemy-specific functionality, such as the ability to be 'shooed' - that is, being told to leave the Stage.

Bolt
We could make the player's energy bolt a class of its own, but at this stage there is no real need. We'll just make it an instance of the entity class.

Layers

We'll have two layers, the Engine layer and the Input/Output layer. In the engine layer we will provide two main features, a sprite manager and a sound manager. So, for now, we'll just write the definitions for those handlers. In the input/output layer we will also provide two main features, an input manager and an output manager. Again, we'll just write the definitions for those handlers.

First, the engine layer:

```
- - Engine Layer

- - Sprite Manager and Sound Manager

- - Sprite Manager

- - The need to dynamically allocate sprites is derived from:
- - * Enemies - there could be any number at one time.
- - * Bolts from the Player's ship


- - =======
on SM_Init

- - Initialise the Sprite Manager.

end

- - ===============
on SM_SpritePlease

- - No harm in asking nicely! ;)

- - Return a sprite from the list.

- - If we're out of sprites, return -1. Any calling function needs to
- - check for this.

- - We do it randomly so there are no obvious effects from channel
- - ordering.

- - Get that sprite

- - Remove it from the list

- - return it

end

- - ===============
on SM_ReturnSprite vSprite
```

```
      - - return the sprite to the list so it can be given again.

    end

    - - =============
    - - Sound Manager

    - - ==========
    on Snd_PlayBG vSnd

      - - Get the sound name

      - - By convention, background sounds are played in channel 1, and are
      - - looped.

    end

    - - ===========
    on Snd_PlaySFX vSnd

      - - This handler allows us to use a 'stack' of sound channels
      - - that allow us to play up to 7 channels at once.

      - - Get the sound name

      - - By convention, sound effects are played in channela 2-n, and are
      - - not looped.

      - - Find a free channel and play the sound.

    end

    - - ===========
    on Snd_GetName vSnd

      - - To prevent name confusion, we can prefix our sounds with "snd_"

    end
```

And, finally, the input/output layer:

```
      - - Input Layer

      - - ==========
    on Input_Idle

      - - Trap appropriate keystrokes

      - - Check that there is actually a key held down
```

```
    end


    - - Output Layer

    - - Displays
    - - ==========
    on DisplaySet vDisplay, vText

    end
```

Phase 3: Writing the Code

Now we've established our code stubs, it's time to fill them in with code, in addition to connecting that code to the media it will use.

Here's the listing for our game class. It is by far the most complex of the classes listed here, so read the comments carefully and try to follow what's happening at each stage. What is expected of this class? A number of things, so let's look at them each quickly before we get into the code.

Firstly, containment: it's the game's job to have variable names assigned to created instances of classes, namely the player, enemy, and entity classes. We'll use the variable names 'pPlayer', 'pEnemyList', and 'pBoltList' respectively. It's also the game's job to maintain the user's score, this is done partly with the variable 'pScore'. The game also takes care of the main gaming loop - remember it from our pseudocode earlier? The gaming loop consists of dealing with the user's input, checking for the player colliding with any enemies, checking if any of the player's bolts collided with any enemies, and checking if any goals have been met.

```
    - - ==========
    - - Properties
    - - ==========

    - - A number, signifying the Level the Player has reached.
    - - Initially this will be 1
    property pEnvironmentNum

    - - The maximum Level- make as many as you have media for!!
    property pMaxEnvironment

    - - The Player Instance.
    property pPlayer

    - - A list of Enemy Instances.
    property pEnemyList

    - - A list of Player's bolts.
    property pBoltList
```

```
            - - A number, signifying the Player's points score.
            property pScore

            - - A number, signifying the number of Player's ships.
            property pShips

            - - ===
            on new me

            - - Constructor: no parameters required.
             return me

            end
```

Nothing amazing or new so far, the listing of properties and the provision of a 'new' handler is common to any class script. It's also a good idea to provide an 'Init' handler which, unlike the new handler, may be called more that once if the need arises to reset the instance to initial values.

```
            - - ====
            on Init me

            - - Init handler: called when we wish to reform a new Game.

            - - Initialise variables to the values described above.
            pEnvironmentNum = 1
            pMaxEnvironment = 3
            pEnemyList = []
            pBoltList = []
            pscore= 0
            pShips = 3
```

This is the first use of one of our layers, namely the input/output layer. Here we are making the scoreboard read as it should.

```
            - - Set up displays
            DisplaySet #level, rEnvironmentNum
            DisplaySet #score, rScore
            DisplaySet #ships, rShips
```

Remember what we said about instances containing other instances? Here's where we put that into practice for the first time, in the creation of an instance of the class "player" which is assigned to a variable 'pPlayer'. It's then initialized.

```
            - - Set up the Player Singleton, that the Game Singleton will manage
            rPlayer = new(script"Player Class")

            - - Initialise the Player
             rPlayer.Init()

            end
```

On reading the following, "Frame Step? Why don't we use the word 'idle'?" you scream. Well, in the great lucky dip of word reservation, Director got there first. The word 'idle' is reserved, and using it as a handler name (that you intend to call from another piece of code) will get you into all sorts of strife. You see, the 'idle' handler is a bit like a keyDown handler in that it is executed by Director's event handling system. A keyDown event is generated by Director whenever the user presses a key, and an idle event is generated whenever it gets a moment, which is often. By all means define a single 'on idle' handler, but remember that it will be executed far more often than, for example, an on exitFrame frame script, so code sparingly.

```
- - Frame Step the Game
- - =====
on fStep me

    - - Give a slice of time to the various Instances and Layers under
    - - the control of the Game Instance
```

Recall the pseudocode listing of how the game would work? There was a step "Deal with User Input". Here is where we do just that.

```
    - - The Input Layer
    Input_Step
```

The player's fStep handler is designed to return a value, to inform whatever script is calling it the result of idling it.

```
    - - The Player
    PlayerStatus = pPlayer.fStep(90,620,40,460)
    if PlayerStatus = #dead then
    - - Kill The Player (take one ship away)
```

A #dead result is a serious result indeed! This means that not only was the player hit by an enemy, but has now reached the bottom of the screen, so it's time to start again. If there are no ships remaining, the computer game constitution demands that it is 'Game Over'.

```
        if pShips > 1 then
         pShips = pShips - 1
         DisplaySet #ships, pShips
    - - Reposition the Player
         pPlayer.Init()
        else
    - - Ahhh! Last Ship, so Game Over
         go "Game Over"
        end if

        end if
```

Now it's time to iterate through our list of enemies, which could be empty at any given stage. Note that a loop that goes from 1 to 0 will not be executed. This is convenient for our purposes.

Throughout this repeat loop the temporary variable 'enemy' will be a reference to each of the enemy instances within the list rEnemyList.

```
- - Any Enemies
 repeat with e = 1 to count(pEnemyList)
  enemy = getAt(pEnemyList,e)
  EnemyStatus = enemy.fStep(-20,660,20,500,0,pPlayer.pX,pPlayer.pY)

- - Check what the Enemy reported
  case EnemyStatus of

- - It's hit the deck
   #dead:
    destroy enemy
    deleteAt pEnemyList, e

- - Check if the Enemy has hit the Player
   otherwise:

- - Also, a dying or shoo-ing enemy is no threat at all..
      if sprite pPlayer.pSprite intersects enemy.pSprite and
      ➡ enemy.pMode <> #Dying and enemy.pMode <> #Shoo then

- - Kill The Player (take one ship away)
       pPlayer.Kill()

- - To be fair to the Player, tell the Enemies to go away
       ShooEnemies me

- - No need to go through the Enemy List anymore
       exit repeat

      end if

    end case

  end repeat
```

Now we give each of the bolts (if there are any) some attention and give them a bit of a 'fIdle'.

```
- - Idle the bolts
 repeat with b = 1 to count(pBoltList)
  bolt = getAt(pBoltList,b)
  BoltStatus = bolt.fStep(0,680,0,480,1)
  if BoltStatus = #offscreen then
   destroy bolt
   deleteAt pBoltList, b
  end if
```

At this stage we need to check if the bolt has hit any of the enemies. This involves looking at every enemy in the list. Remember that we're already within the loop that's checking each bolt, so if there are b bolts and e enemies, this will involve b*e steps. This is okay for small values of b and e, but be aware that this is a potential area of low (and variable) performance.

```
- - Check if a bolt has hit an Enemy
  repeat with e = 1 to count(pEnemyList)
    enemy = getAt(pEnemyList,e)
    if sprite bolt.pSprite intersects enemy.pSprite and
➡ enemy.pMode <> #Dying then
```

If a bolt has hit its mark, we award the player points that are directly related to the level that has been reached.

```
      pScore= pScore + 5 * pEnvironmentNum

      DisplaySet #score, pScore
- - Destroy the Enemy
      Kill enemy
      Snd_PlaySFX "Blast"

    end if

  end repeat

end repeat
```

After all of this, we need to check if the goals for this environment have been met. In this case, the goal is to score a certain number of points.

```
  - - Go to Next Level?
  CheckGoals me
```

Here we ask if it's time to add an enemy. Note how this is dependent on the number of the environment we're in.

```
  - - Decide whether or not to make a new Enemy
  if random (1000) < 15 * pEnvironmentNum and pPlayer.pMode =
  ➡ #Normal then
  AddEnemy me
  end if

  - - Or a blitz
  if random(1000) < 3 then
  AddEnemies me
  end if

end
```

```
- - ===========
on AddEnemy me

    - - Spawn an Enemy.

    - - We'll need to give it a sprite
     theSprite = SM_SpritePlease()

     if theSprite = -1 then exit

    - - And the position, offscreen
     tX = 630
     tY = 460

    - - Make an instance of our Entity class
     theEnemy = new(script"Enemy Class",theSprite,tX,tY,
     ➥ pEnvironmentNum,0.1*pEnvironmentNum, "Enemy", "Normal","Dying")

    - - And its member
     theEnemy.setMember()

    - - add it to the Enemy List
     add pEnemyList, theEnemy

end
```

Nothing to this handler, except to tell each of the enemies in the list pEnemyList to 'shoo'. Consult that class for what it really means to be shooed!

```
- - ==========
on AddEnemies me

    - - Give 'em a real challange and release THE SWARM!!
     repeat with e = 1 to 3 + random(6)
       AddEnemy me
     end repeat

end
```

```
- - =========
on ShooEnemies me

     repeat with enemy in pEnemyList
       enemy.Shoo()
     end repeat

end
```

This is an example of a public interface to this class. Nowhere in the rest of the code do we access the game's variable pEnvironmentNum. We instead call a globally accessible function Game_GetEnv() which in turn calls this handler below.

```
- - ==============
on getEnvironment me

  - - If it's unset, then assume 1
  if voidP(pEnvironmentNum) then
    pEnvironmentNum = 1
  end if

  return pEnvironmentNum

end
```

The purpose of this handler is to partially parse (read and interpret) the input generated by the user. Movement input is passed on directly to the player instance, and a #fire input is dealt with by the next handler.

```
- - =====
on Input me, vInput

  - - Sort out the input from the keyboard

  case vInput of

    #up, #down, #left, #right:
- - #up,#down,#left and #right are sent to the Player Instance
      pPlayer.Steer(vInput)

    #fire:
      PlayerFire me

  end case

end
```

This handler is similar in respects to the AddEnemy handler; a new instance is created, is allocated a sprite, and is added to a list designed to hold it. First we check that the player isn't dying - you could remove this check if you wanted that 'going down guns blazing' kind of vibe!

```
- - ==========
on PlayerFire me

  - - Spawn a bolt.

  - - A dying ship cannot fire.
  if pPlayer.pMode = #dying then exit
```

```
- - We'll need to give it a sprite
theSprite = SM_SpritePlease()

if theSprite = -1 then exit

- - And its member
the member of sprite theSprite = member "Player bolt"

- - And the same position as the Player
tX = pPlayer.rX
tY = pPlayer.rY
```

Note the last two parameters in the next 'new' function call: they say the maximum speed of the bolt is 50.0, and its acceleration is 30.0. See in the next line how we set its initial velocity to be the same as the player's?

```
- - Make an instance of our Entity class
theBolt = new(script"Entity Class",theSprite,tX,tY,50.0,30.0)

- - Make it go right
theBolt.pH = pPlayer.pH
theBolt.pV = pPlayer.pV
theBolt.Steer(#right)

- - add it to the Bolt List
add pBoltList, theBolt

- - Make a noise!
Snd_PlaySFX "Fire"

end
```

This handler simply checks whether the player's score is above the amount required to enter the next environment. Note how we've made fiendishly cunning use of a mathematical function to set the bar ever higher:

```
- - ==========
on CheckGoals me

- - Check if our goals have been met
if pScore>= 100 * pEnvironmentNum * pEnvironmentNum *
➡ pEnvironmentNum then
```

If the goal has been met, then it's time to go to the next level. We flush our lists so that the next time we come back to the environment, there aren't enemies and bolts still hanging about.

```
pEnvironmentNum = pEnvironmentNum + 1

if pEnvironmentNum > pMaxEnvironment then
```

```
      set pEnvironmentNum = pMaxEnvironment
      go "Finished"
      exit
    end if

    DisplaySet #level, pEnvironmentNum

- - Flush our lists
    repeat with e in pEnemyList
     Destroy e
    end repeat
    pEnemyList = []
    repeat with b in pBoltList
     Destroy b
    end repeat

    pBoltList = []

    go "GameStart"

  end if

end
```

Not even the most superhuman of coders can get everything 100% right 100% of the time, that's why we've included this debugging handler to print out the pertinent variables of this class. Note that's not every variable.

```
- - ========
- - Debug / Troubleshooting

- - Troubleshooter
on Print me

- - Print out our variables to the message window

  put "pEnvironmentNum" && pEnvironmentNum
  put "pMaxEnvironment" && pMaxEnvironment
  put "pPlayer:" && pPlayer
  put "pEnemyList:" && pEnemyList
  put "pBoltList:" && pBoltList
  put "pScore:" && pScore
  put "pShips:" && pShips

  put "My Enemy List:"
  repeat with e in pEnemyList
   print e
  end repeat

  put "My Bolt List:"
```

```
       repeat with b in pBoltList
        print b
       end repeat

       put RETURN
       put RETURN
       put RETURN

      end
```

The Entity Class

As we're on a roll, let's get on with the listing for the entity class:

```
      - - ==========
      - - Properties
      - - ==========

      - - The Sprite that has been assigned to this Entity
      property pSprite

      - - The Position of the Entity
      property pX,pY

      - - The Velocity of the Entity
      property pH,pV

      - - Acceleration
      property pAcc

      - - The maximum Speed at which the Entity moves
      property pSpeed

      - - The Mode of the Entity
      property pMode
```

These variables will be used to generate names of existing media, which will be used for instances of this class.

```
      - - And, we'll define a number of variables relating to the graphics
      - - for this Entity
      property pBaseName
      property pNormalName
      property pDyingName
```

This 'new' handler (also known as a constructor) will take a few parameters, namely the sprite it will use, its position, maximum speed, acceleration, and media naming variables.

```
      - - New
```

```
on new me, vSprite, vX, vY, vSpeed, vAcc, vBaseName, vNormalName,
➡ vDyingName

- - Assign attributes of this Instance
pSprite = vSprite

pX = vX
pY = vY

pH = 0.0
pV = 0.0

pAcc = vAcc
pSpeed = vSpeed

pBaseName = vBaseName
pNormalName = vNormalName
pDyingName = vDyingName

pMode = #Normal

return me

end
```

It shouldn't surprise you to learn that we define a 'Frame Step' handler here. It does? This handler returns a value (specifically a # symbol) that describes what this entity is up to - did it bounce off the walls? Are you bouncing off the walls, after all this coding? Most of the comments in this class are fairly self-explanatory.

```
- - =====
on fIdle me, vLeft, vRight, vTop, vBottom, vBounceOnCollision

- - A Generic Entity is simply moved
- - and, if 'pBounceOnCollision' is TRUE, is checked against the
- - boundary defined by 'vLeft', 'vRight', 'vTop' and 'vBottom'

- - Move its position
pX = pX + vH
pY = pY + vV

- - By default, all is well with this entity, until detected
- - otherwise
returnmessage = #ok

- - Check the Entity's position against the left hand side of the
- - boundary
if pX < vLeft then
 pX = vLeft
- - Bounce if appropriate
```

```
     if vBounceOnCollision then pH = - 0.5 * pH
     returnMessage = #offscreen
    end if

    - - Check the Entity's position against the right hand side of the
    - - boundary
    if pX > vRight then
     pX = vRight
    - - Bounce if appropriate
     if vBounceOnCollision then pH = - 0.5 * pH
     returnMessage = #offscreen
    end if

    - - Check the Entity's position against the top of the boundary
    if pY < vTop then
     pY = vTop
    - - Bounce if appropriate
     if vBounceOnCollision then pV = - 0.5 * pV
     returnMessage = #offscreen
    end if

    - - Check the Entity's position against the bottom of the boundary
    if pY > vBottom then
     pY = vBottom
    - - Bounce if appropriate
     if vBounceOnCollision then pV = - 0.5 * pV
     returnMessage = #offscreen
    end if

    - - Update the position of the sprite to reflect the Entity's
    - - position variables.
    the loc of sprite pSprite = point(rX,rY)

    - - Tell whatever called this handler what the result of idling it
    - - was
    return returnMessage

  end

  - - =====
  on Steer me, vDirection

    - - This Entity can be instructed to accelerate in one of four
    - - directions.
    case vDirection of

     #left:
    - - Alter horizontal velocity by a function of the Entity's
    - - acceleration and current velocity
      pH = pH - (pAcc + 0.1 * abs(pH))
```

```
- - Make sure the velocity does not exceed the maximum
   if pH < -pSpeed then pH = -pSpeed

   #right:
- - Alter horizontal velocity by a function of the Entity's
- - acceleration and current velocity
   pH = pH + (pAcc + 0.1 * abs(pH))
- - Make sure the velocity does not exceed the maximum
   if pH > pSpeed then pH = pSpeed

   #up:
- - Alter vertical velocity by a function of the Entity's      -
- acceleration and current velocity
   pV = pV - (pAcc + 0.1 * abs(pV))
- - Make sure the velocity does not exceed the maximum
   if pV < -pSpeed then pV = -pSpeed

   #down:
- - Alter vertical velocity by a function of the Entity's      -
- acceleration and current velocity
   pV = pV + (pAcc + 0.1 * abs(pV))
- - Make sure the velocity does not exceed the maximum
   if pV > pSpeed then pV = pSpeed

 end case

end
```

The following handler is very important; it's akin to 'Garbage Collection' in other forms of programming, such as C++. Director takes care of the cleanup of the instance, but we have other chores: remember in the game class an entity is - through its child class, enemy or player - assigned a sprite? Well, we need to give back that sprite so it can be allocated again. Firstly though, we move the graphic that's in that sprite off the stage. Try viewing the stage at 50% so you can see the surrounding area and you'll see it in action.

```
- - =======
on destroy me

- - Move offstage
 the locH of sprite pSprite = - 250

- - Give back the sprite
 SM_ReturnSprite pSprite

end
```

We implement a `print` handler here to help debug this class. Note that this `print` handler is called by the game class' 'print' handler.

```
- - =========
- - Debug
on print me

    - - print

    - - The Sprite that has been assigned to this Entity
    put me && "pSprite:" && pSprite
    put me && "pMode:" && pMode


end
```

The Player Class
Listing is:

```
property ancestor

    - - The main purpose for subclassing Entity for this Player class is
    - - special intantiation variables

    - - Also the Player has a mode and we check for this in the overriden
    - - handlers fStep and Steer

    - - ===
on new me

    ancestor = new(script"Entity Class", 42, 100, 400, 15.0,
    ➡ 2.5,"Player","Normal","Dying")

    return me

end
```

In this `Init` handler we set up the player's position and default mode. Note that we need this handler because a player has more than one ship.

```
    - - ======
on Init me

    - - Reposition the Player
    me.pX = 100
    me.pY = 480
    me.pV = -10.0
    me.pH = 5.0

    me.rMode = #Normal

    setMember ancestor

end
```

This handler is an overridden version of the entity class `fStep` handler. This is a common occurrence when using inheritance. We add the functionality we desire, and call our ancestor's `fStep` method to retain that functionality.

```
- - =====
on fStep me, vLeft, vRight, vTop, vBottom


  case ancestor.vMode of

    #normal:
- - Friction- the bane of the non-Hamiltonian Universe!
      ancestor.pH = 0.99 * ancestor.pH
      ancestor.pV = 0.99 * ancestor.pH

      return fIdle(ancestor, vLeft, vRight, vTop, vBottom, 1)


    #dying:
- - Fall groundward.
      ancestor.pH = 0.5 * ancestor.pH
      ancestor.pV = ancestor.pV + .25

      fStep(ancestor, vLeft, vRight, vTop, vBottom, 1)

      if ancestor.pY >= vBottom then
- - Player has hit the ground
        return #dead
      else
        return #ok
      end if

  end case

end
```

Another overridden handler, this time `Steer` simply checks that the player isn't dying because steering it in that state wouldn't be right! Note that we've used a case statement where a simple `if...then` would have sufficed, because we want to make it easy to add other states in the future.

```
- - =====
on Steer me, vDirection

  case ancestor.pMode of

    #normal:
      Steer ancestor, vDirection
```

```
        #dying:


     end case

   end
```

You'll notice with this class, as well as the enemy class, that there is a period after something hits us, where we fall towards the ground. This is achieved by using the pMode variable.

```
   - - ====
   on Kill me

     - - You cannot kill that which does not live!
     if ancestor.pMode = #dying then exit

     ancestor.pMode = #dying
     setMember me

     - - Make a noise!
     Snd_PlaySFX "Hit"

   end
```

This handler is interesting in that it is using variables from its ancestor, but not overriding any of its handlers. The idea is that the variables prBaseName, pNormalName, and pDyingName are (within the entity class) abstract; that is, they are declared as properties, but there is no handler that uses them. By defining such a handler in this class, we are making it less abstract.

```
   - - ========
   on setMember me

     theEnv = Game_getEnv()

     case ancestor.pMode of
      #Normal:
        theMember = ancestor.pBaseName && ancestor.pNormalName

      #Dying:
        theMember = ancestor.pBaseName && ancestor.pDyingName

     end case

     the member of sprite ancestor.pSprite = member theMember

   end
```

And the Enemy Class

This is the second class we have defined as a subclass of entity. It provides us with the functionality we require to make our enemies do their thing.

```
property ancestor

- - ===
on new me, vSprite, vX, vY, vSpeed, vAcc

  ancestor = new(script"Entity Class", vSprite, vX, vY, vSpeed,
➡ vAcc, "Enemy", "Normal", "Dying")

- - Give the Enemy a random velocity
  ancestor.pH = -3.0*random(3)
  ancestor.pV = -5.0*random(5)

  ancestor.pMode = #Normal

  return me

end
```

You can see here that what makes an enemy different from an entity is the passing of the player's position, as vPlayerX and vPlayerY. This allows an enemy to move towards the player.

```
- - =====
on fIdle me, vLeft, vRight, vTop, vBottom, vBounce, vPlayerX, \
vPlayerY

  case ancestor.pMode of

    #Normal:
- - Decide to attack at random
    if random(100) < 5 then pMode = #Attacking
    return fStep(ancestor, vLeft, vRight, vTop, vBottom, 1)

    #Attacking:
- - Seek the Player!
- - put me, "Attacking"
    if ancestor.pX < vPlayerX then ancestor.pH = ancestor.pH +
➡ Game_GetEnv() * ancestor.pAcc
    if ancestor.pX > vPlayerX then ancestor.pH = ancestor.pH -
➡ Game_GetEnv() * ancestor.pAcc
    if ancestor.pY < vPlayerY then ancestor.pV = ancestor.pV +
➡ Game_GetEnv() * ancestor.pAcc
    if ancestor.pY > vPlayerY then ancestor.pV = ancestor.pV -
➡ Game_GetEnv() * ancestor.pAcc
    return fIdle(ancestor, vLeft, vRight, vTop, vBottom, 1)
```

We can very conveniently use this state to tell an enemy to move off the screen, in its own time.

```
#Shoo:
  ancestor.pH = ancestor.pH + 1.0
  if ancestor.pY >= vBottom or ancestor.pY <= vTop or
  ➡ ancestor.pX >= vRight or ancestor.pX <= vLeft then
  ➡ return #dead
  end if
  return fStep(ancestor, vLeft, vRight, vTop, vBottom, 0)

#Dying:
  ancestor.pH = ancestor.pH - 1.0
  ancestor.pV = ancestor.pV + 1.0
  if ancestor.pY >= vBottom or ancestor.pY <= vTop or
  ➡ ancestor.pX >= vRight or ancestor.pX <= vLeft then
  ➡ return #dead
  end if
  return fStep(ancestor, vLeft, vRight, vTop, vBottom, 0)

otherwise:


end case


end
```

Here's the public handler that does the shooing.

```
- - ====
on Shoo me

- - Exit the Stage!
  ancestor.pMode = #Shoo

end

- - =====
on Kill me

- - the mode
  ancestor.pMode = #Dying
  ancestor.pH = 0.0
  ancestor.pV = 1.0

  setMember me

end
```

Again, this handler uses the abstract naming variables of the entity class. In this case, the difference from the `setMember` handler found in the player class is the expression `string(theEnv)`, which keys the enemy's graphic member to the game's environment.

```
- - ========
on setMember me

  theEnv = Game_getEnv()

  case ancestor.pMode of
    #Normal:
      theMember = ancestor.pBaseName && string(theEnv) &&
      ➡ ancestor.pNormalName

    #Dying:
      theMember = ancestor.pBaseName && string(theEnv) &&
      ➡ ancestor.pDyingName

  end case

  the member of sprite ancestor.pSprite = member theMember

end
```

Environment Behaviors

In order to produce the lovely scrolling backgrounds in the game, we decided to write behaviors for each of the layers:

Sky and Sun

The behavior for these simply sets the appropriate static graphic, which is related to the level that the player has reached. Here's the code for the Sky script, the sun script is the same apart from the different graphic referenced.

```
- - Sky Script- provides a method to set up media on the basis of
the - - current Level/Environment

- - ===========
on beginSprite me

  Init me

end

- - ====
on Init me

  - - Set the media up on the basis of the current Level/Environment
  theEnv = Game_getEnv()
```

```
         theAMember = "Sky A" && theEnv
         the member of sprite me.spriteNum = member theAMember
         theBMember = "Sky B" && theEnv
         the member of sprite me.spriteNum+1 = member theBMember

     end
```

Clouds and Trees

Their behavior is a little more complex. These elements are set up off-screen, and are put in a 'waiting' state. Whilst in this state, these elements simply stay put. After a random period of time, they change state, and begin to move from right to left. Upon reaching the left hand side of the screen, they are recycled, and begin life again in the 'waiting' state. The code for the clouds is different only in the name of the media references. Check out the code for the Tree script:

```
     - - A tree has a mode- either waiting or scrolling
     property pMode


     - - ===========
     on beginSprite me

      Init me

     end

     - - ====
     on Init me

       - - Setup the right Tree for this Environment

       - - Call the Game's getEnvironment handler
       theEnv = Game_GetEnv()

       theMember = "Trees" && random(5) && theEnv
       the member of sprite me.spriteNum = member theMember

       pMode = #waiting
```

The next line sets the tree's position, not only off-screen to the right, but also at a random position, so that the trees don't all come out at once. Note too in the `exitFrame` handler a random factor in the decision for the tree to start scrolling.

```
       the locH of sprite the spriteNum of me = 700 + random(100)

     end

     - - =========
     on exitFrame me

      case pMode of
```

```
     #waiting:
- - 5% of the time, change to scrolling.
  if random(100) <= random(5) then
    rMode = #scrolling
  end if

  #scrolling:
- - Move to the left
  xPos = the locH of sprite the spriteNum of me
  xPos = xPos - 7 * Game_GetEnv()
  the locH of sprite the spriteNum of me = xPos

  if xPos < - 100 then
    Init me
  end if


  end case

end
```

Mountains

A mountain's behavior tells it to start scrolling immediately, whilst simultaneously scrolling the graphic in the next highest sprite. When the horizontal position is such that the right hand side of the graphic is aligned with the right hand side of the stage, both graphics are moved to the right by the exact width of a single graphic. If you think about this, you will see that an illusion is achieved of a continuous scroll. Here's how we did it:

```
- - ===========
on beginSprite me

- - Setup the right Mountain for this Environment

- - Call the Game's getEnvironment handler
 theEnv = Game_GetEnv()

 theMember = "Mountain" && theEnv
 the member of sprite me.spriteNum = member theMember
 the member of sprite me.spriteNum+1 = member theMember

end

- - =========
on exitFrame me

 kS = the spriteNum of me

 xPos = the locH of sprite kS
```

```
xPos = xPos - 3 * Game_GetEnv()

if xPos < - the width of the member of sprite kS then xPos = 0

the locH of sprite kS = xPos
the locH of sprite kS+1 = xPos + the width of sprite kS

end
```

In all of the behaviors above, there is a direct relationship between the environment/level number, and the speed of the scroll. For example, the trees move at seven times the environment/level number.

Layers

Let's have a look at the code that gives us our software layers, namely the engine and input/output layers. First the engine layer.

Engine Layer

```
- - Engine Layer

- - Sprite Manager and Sound Manager
```

Just like the comments say, this layer provides us with sprite and sound managers, two things that no self-respecting Director project should be without.

```
- - Sprite Manager

- - The need to dynamically allocate sprites is derived from:
- - * Enemies - there could be any number at one time.
- - * Bolts from the Player's ship
```

A good programming rule of thumb is to use as few global variables as possible. One reason for this is that it becomes rather messy to have to include them at the top of every script we wish to use them with. Another is that they violate one of the object oriented commandments - that we must encapsulate. With global variables, it's possible for any process to alter their values, and that is frowned upon in OOP. Our game has two globals, gGame, and gSM_SpriteList. Both of these variables are only accessed from within the classes and layers that are responsible for them, so we can sleep well at night.

```
- - Variables from this Layer are simply globals
global gSM_SpriteList


- - =======
on SM_Init

- - Hardwire this list with the sprites you want to use.
- - Note that they need not be contigous
```

```
- - We could do this more elegantly, but this way is quick and easily
- - editable.
 gSM_SpriteList =
➡ [25,26,27,28,29,30,31,32,33,34,35,36,37,38,39,40,41,43,
➡ 44,45,46,47,48,49,50,51,52,53,54,55]
```

Notice how the number '42' is missing from this list, because it's the sprite that we have specially reserved for the Player.

```
 end
```

Here's the handler that doles out the sprites. It is reasonably straightforward, but notice how we return one at random:

```
- - ===============
 on SM_SpritePlease

- - No harm in asking nicely! ;)

- - Return a sprite from the list.

- - If we're out of sprites, return -1. Any calling function needs to
- - check for this.
 if count(gSM_SpriteList) < 1 then return -1

- - We do it randomly so there are no obvious effects from channel
- - ordering.
 theIndex = random(count(gSM_SpriteList))

- - Get that sprite
 theSprite = getAt(gSM_SpriteList,theIndex)

- - Remove it from the list
 deleteAt gSM_SpriteList, theIndex

- - return it
 return theSprite

 end
```

What goes out, must come back, spinning sprite...oh, ahem...yes, that's right, this wee handler deals with the return division of the sprite manager. Note where it says 'check in case, for some reason, it's already in the list'. There's no reason to suspect that it is, but if you did encounter problems with wayward sprites, you could add an else to that if...then and put a breakpoint there. Then, whenever such a malady occurred, you could simply use the debugger to see what was going on.

```
- - ===============
 on SM_ReturnSprite vSprite
```

```
- - return the sprite to the list so it can be given again.

- - check in case, for some reason, it's already in the list
  if getPos(gSM_SpriteList, vSprite) = 0 then
    add gSM_SpriteList, vSprite
```

SM_ReturnSprite is here for a reason - you see, a sprite was passed back to me that I already had in my list. You might want to put a debug point here to catch it the next time it happens!

```
    end if

  end
```

As far as sound managers go, this one is pretty simple, but it does perform one useful task in playing more than one sound at once, without having to know which channel they're being played in.

```
- - =============
- - Sound Manager
- - ==========
on Snd_PlayBG vSnd

- - Get the sound name
  theSnd = Snd_GetName(vSnd)

- - By convention, background sounds are played in channel 1.

  puppetSound 1, theSnd


end


- - ===========
on Snd_PlaySFX vSnd

- - This handler allows us to use a 'stack' of sound channels
- - that allow us to play up to 7 channels at once.

- - Get the sound name
  theSnd = Snd_GetName(vSnd)

- - By convention, sound effects are played in channela 2-n, and are
- - not looped.
  the loop of member theSnd = FALSE

- - Find a free channel
  repeat with s = 2 to 8

    if not(soundBusy(s)) then
```

```
- - Found one!
  puppetSound s, theSnd
  exit repeat
end if

end repeat

end
```

One of the most common problems Lingo newcomers get with sound is attempting to play a sound called "bang" when there's a graphic called "bang" earlier in the cast library. We can banish this bug by using this simple handler and the appropriate naming of media. That way, snd_ can prefix all sounds.

```
- - ===========
on Snd_GetName vSnd

- - To prevent name confusion, we can prefix our sounds with "snd_"
  theSnd = "snd_" & vSnd

  return theSnd

end
```

Input/Output Layers
There's not too much to this layer, just one handler; but in larger and more complex projects this would be the place to put such code.

```
- - Input Layer

- - ==========
on Input_Idle

- - Trap appropriate keystrokes

- - Check that there is actually a key held down
  if the keyPressed <> "" then
```

No clue what's happening in the next line? Don't be afraid to use the watcher window, just highlight an expression, for example charToNum(the Key) or just the Key, and watch what happens when you press various keys. Using codes is more elegant than trying to type the character for 'right arrow'.

```
    case charToNum(the Key) of

- - Up
  30:
    Game_Input #up

- - Down
```

```
        31:
        Game_Input #down

- - Left
    28:
        Game_Input #left

- - Right
    29:
        Game_Input #right

- - Space
    32:
        Game_Input #fire

    end case


  end if

end
```

This too is a pretty simple layer, we only have need to send stuff to our little scoreboard, and we achieve that with this single handler. Note that it also is reliant on naming, not to mention the media that is being named should exist.

```
        - - Output Layer

        - - Displays
        - - ==========
        on DisplaySet vDisplay, vText

        - - construct the member name
         theDisplay = "display_" & string(vDisplay)
         the text of member theDisplay = string(vText)


        end
```

Phase 4: The 'One of Everything' Version

In this phase, it is our task to get the game working with our placeholder media, and create a working prototype of the game, using a single environment, a player and type of enemy.

If you had a good look at the entity, player and enemy classes, you would have noticed that we established a simple convention for the media required by these classes. For example, the player class forms the name of the media it needs by concatenating two strings: "Player" and whatever mode it is in (for example "Normal"). In the enemy's case, we do the same, except that the environment number is wedged in the middle there; for example "Enemy 1 Normal". So, simply name each element appropriately, on the basis of this convention. Together with the code we wrote in the previous phase, you shouldn't have any problems.

We have made three levels worth of placeholder graphics; the number of levels in the final game is entirely up to you.

Phase 5: Replacement of Placeholder Media

In this phase, we start to introduce what will be the final media into the game. This phase can be straightforward, however problems can arise if you rushed through phase 1, and didn't completely specify the important aspects of the placeholder media, for example its size and aspect ratio.

An issue worth noting here is that of file size. A useful consequence of using mostly vector shape placeholder media is its low size footprint. At this stage we could decide to use this version for Shockwave. If however the client has provided specific media then now is the time to use it. Needless to say you've been saving many versions of your Director file as you've been working, now save another one giving it a different base name, as it is such a big step.

There's not too much more to be said about this stage, except that it will take longer the more media you have. That's a cool aspect of making a 'One of Everything' version, once the client says it's okay and the final graphics are supplied, there's not too much to replace.

Phase 6: Testing and Reiteration

Wait! You haven't finished yet. This is an all too often neglected phase of the development process, even though it has the potential to cause you to repeat some, or all, of the previous phases.

Firstly, the requirements for how the game is to function will be driven by your client, even if that client is you! It is helpful to get someone other than yourself to look at your creation, to give you feedback from a fresh point of view.

Look at the final product: does it satisfy the requirements of the brief? Was the brief detailed enough to cope with every potential ambiguity? This is a fairly common cause of having to reiterate the project in game development. It may not be that you didn't follow the brief, but it turns out that the brief itself didn't adequately capture the desires of the client or resolve the ambiguities that inevitably arose.

See the 'Troubleshooting Your Game' section for more advice on how to debug your code.

As far as practical testing is concerned, a good idea is to think of all of the possible (types of) paths through the game, and test for those explicitly. Obviously a game of reasonable complexity has an inordinate number of possible paths through it, so we identify the types of paths. Here are some for our game:

- The player dies three times in a row on the first level. Do we go to the 'Game Over' screen with no problems?

- The player kills all the enemies for level one. Do we go to the next level without any hiccups?

- The player makes it through all the levels. Do we see the infamous 'End of Quest' screen?

- In all of the above three cases, can we click and restart the game?

Conclusions

We'll conclude this chapter by discussing what we could do to improve on the game we've made, and indeed the methodology and paradigm we used.

Abstraction

Of course, when you find yourself frantically trying to meet a deadline, you might in those circumstances be forgiven for, well, hacking a bit. That is, not honoring the lofty object oriented principles you told yourself you'd follow. Don't fret, the middle of a project is not always the best time to have inspired visions on how you could have done it in a more consistent, cogent, and reusable fashion. As you complete projects you will have time for the debrief in which you will certainly be able to pinpoint places where a different strategy or design would have been more elegant. The real issue is whether you document those revelations or not. Do so.

All of this is leading up to the matter at hand, abstraction. Abstraction, in a software engineering sense, is the very important process of looking at a number of classes, and trying to distill the essence of those classes in a way that can be expressed by simpler classes. For example, starting with an 'Apple' Class and a separate 'Orange' Class, and deciding instead to make a 'Fruit' Class, with apples and oranges made possible by instances with different attributes.

Expansion

What can we add to the game in the way of additional features? As far as games go, 'Us and Them' is pretty basic, the enemies have no energy bolts of their own and there's no 'End of Level Boss'. Let's look at how we might go about adding those features! Bolts for the enemies first of all, each enemy currently returns either #ok or #offscreen.

We could easily add the ability for it to return say, a #fire event, which tells the game to generate a bolt for that enemy, in much the same way that the player has bolts generated for it. The decision to have the enemy tell the game what is going on is one in keeping with our philosophy of having the game manage the enemies, and not the other way around. It would be a needless complication to add another 'EnemyBoltList' to the game class; instead we could simply add any enemy bolts to the game's 'pEnemyList'. This way, they are checked for collision with the player like any enemy would be.

Troubleshooting Your Game

Use this section as a guide to fixing those little bugs that can creep into a project.

Message Window

Don't be afraid to use the message window to test the classes and handlers you write, so that you can test code as you write it, and not later when it's part of a much more complex system. Just be aware that when this window is active, any keystrokes that are made will appear there, in addition to being processed by our input layer. To give you an example of what can be done with this little marvel, the next time the game is running, try typing:

```
gGame.AddEnemies()
```

You will see a deadly swarm of aliens appear. You can really push our sprite manager to the limit here, if you type the above line a few times in a row, there will be a load of aliens out there. It's good to do this to test how well our sprite manager copes with running out of sprites. It should cope with that eventuality gracefully, as should any process that made use of its services. But we're getting distracted, let's see what else we can do with the message window.

In some of our classes we have debugging statements. Although these slow Director down when in authoring mode, they can be invaluable when debugging this, or any other project. The classic form of these debugging statements is:

```
put "The value of some variable is:" && aVariable
```

Check your Lingo dictionary for 'put' and '&&' if you're not familiar with their use, but basically what's happening here is the output of a string of text to the message window along with the value of a variable. It's a good idea to do this rather than just, for example:

```
put aVariable
```

That's because in the hurly-burly world of the message window, there'd be no way of knowing which variable was having its value output there.

The Watcher
Director's variable watcher is invaluable when debugging your projects, especially games, where there is not always a predetermined path through the program. Here are some variables that you would do well to watch in this game.

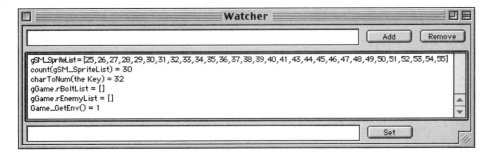

The Debugger

The debugger can be activated in a number of ways. You can select 'Debugger' from the 'Window' menu; you can hit the Debug... button that appears whenever a Lingo error occurs, or you can set breakpoints in your code to tell Director that whenever a line of code is reached it's time to stop and wait for the user to do something. A cool way to use it is whenever you're having a problem with a particular piece of code place a breakpoint there. When the breakpoint is hit, you can stroll through the values of variables. This is hard to explain without pictures, so here's one that does the job:

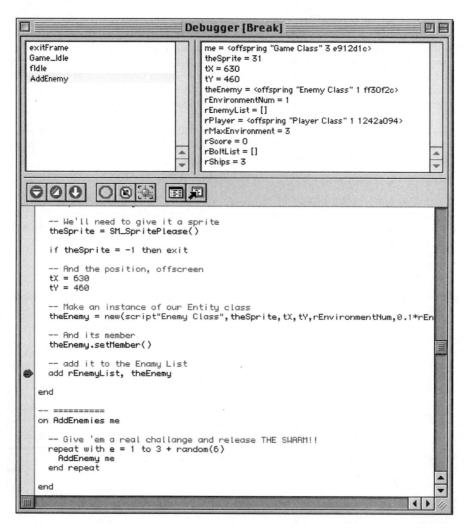

Summary

So, there we have it. If this is your first time of reading this chapter then you're probably quite worried. Don't be. Get yourself a cup of tea (or whatever tipple floats your boat), go back to the beginning of the chapter and work your way through to the end. This time, though, copy the UsAndThem.dir file to your machine and have it open in Director. Follow what we do and, gradually, the constructs and logic will become self-apparent.

If this is your second time of reading, and you've looked at the code as you've been reading through, then at least some of what we've done will make sense. But no one became a Lingo (or any other language) expert by reading one chapter of any book twice! Keep reading, and analyze all the code constructs you can get your hands on.

In order to help you here's a little challenge. If you can build a game, based upon what we've taught you here, and using your own skills, we'll display the ones we consider to be the best on the friendsofED website (www.friendsofed.com).

There are just a few rules for you:

- Your submission must be a DIR file no larger than 2Mb - any bigger and it won't be considered.

- You should show some originality in your game - just changing the sprites isn't original!

- We don't want to offend anyone (intentionally), so your game shouldn't.

- And, naturally, as the game is intended for all of us to learn from and enjoy, we want to be able to see and play with the code.

Well, that's enough rules. Submit your games to games@friendsofED.com before 1st of January 2003 and, who knows, the world may be playing your games!

Chapter 5
Imaging Lingo

Imaging Lingo is very powerful. You can work with an image at pixel level, change the entire content of image cast members, and create and manipulate images on the fly. Moreover, Imaging Lingo allows you to draw graphics directly onto the stage without using any sprites. Understanding how Imaging Lingo works can bring precision and flexibility to your work with quite a speed enhancement.

This chapter is devoted to Imaging Lingo because it remains a hugely significant part of the upgrade from Director 8, and because you can use it to great effect in your 3D work. We'll conclude this chapter with an example that uses 3D Lingo together with Imaging Lingo. 3D Lingo is thoroughly explained later on in the book, so if it all looks a bit mysterious, don't worry; come back to it when you've read the chapters about 3D in Director.

We'll begin by investigating the object that makes Imaging Lingo possible, the image object. This object enables you to duplicate, copy, crop, draw, and manipulate entire images, specific areas of those images, or the individual pixels of an image. Once you're comfortable with these basic mechanisms we'll move on to building some effects that take full advantage of them:

- Superimposing one image on top of another

- An on-the-fly blurring effect

- Ripple effects (a real-time animation)

- A simple drawing system

- A dynamic drawing system

- Using a grayscale bitmap image as a Z–axis database for a 3D grid model.

So let's begin with the image object that makes all this possible.

The essential Imaging Lingo commands

You can create a new image object and access the image object of something already existent. Many Director elements have an image property: a bitmap, a Flash asset, text members and even the stage.

Creating, accessing and manipulating image objects

This script makes an image object called myimage 100 pixels wide by 50 pixels high with a 32-bit color depth:

```
myimage = image(100,50,32)
```

You can also set the alpha and palette properties of the new object. For example, this script creates a myimage image object, 100 by 50 pixels, 8-bit and Grayscale:

```
myimage  = image(100,50,8,#Grayscale)
```

You access an image object in various ways. This script is accessing the image object of the cast member membername:

```
member("membername").image
```

Once you've accessed your image object, there are various things you might want to do with it. Duplicate it, for example.

Duplicating images

You have to be careful when you're duplicating images – you can duplicate an image but still amend the original through that new image, or duplicate the image and keep it independent from the original. This script duplicates the image while keeping a reference to originalImage inside myNewImage:

```
myNewImage = member(originalImage).image
```

Any changes you make to myNewImage will affect the originalImage cast member.

You can use originalImage to create an entirely independent new object, but you need to specifically declare it an independent object:

```
myNewImage = member("originalImage").image.duplicate()
```

The new image myNewImage is the duplicate of the image object of member("originalImage") but independent of any cast members. This function is especially useful when you want to modify the image of bitmap cast members, but you need to be able to revert to the original.

Copying Pixels

As you'd expect, the copyPixels function copies the selected area of an mage object and places it into an area of the same size elsewhere, either in the same or another image object (although it's recommended that you don't copy immediately onto the same image, but though another.) It takes the form:

```
copyPixels (source image object, destination rect/quad, source
➡ rect/quad, {optional params})
```

So this script, for example, copies a 50 pixel square, from top-left corner of member(1)'s image to the bottom-right corner of member(2)'s image:

```
member(2).image.copyPixels(member(1).image,rect(150,150,200,
➡ 200 ),rect(0,0,50,50))
```

Let's try it out. I'll be showing you quick examples of the functions I'm introducing as we go. You can try these all out on the same movie.

Working with the Imaging Lingo essentials

1. Prepare two 200 pixel square 32bit `.pict` files, import one into `member(1)` and the other into `member(2)` of your cast, and place them on the stage next to each other. My stage is 400 by 200; the dimensions will be significant later. You should have something like this:

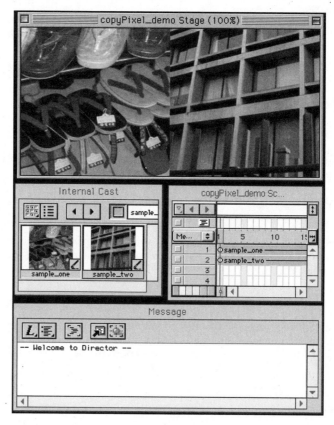

2. We'll copy a 50 pixel square from top-left corner of `member(1)`'s image to the bottom right corner of `member(2)`'s image. Type this script into the message window:

```
member(2).image.copyPixels(member(1).image,rect
➥ (150,150,200,200),rect(0,0,50,50))
```

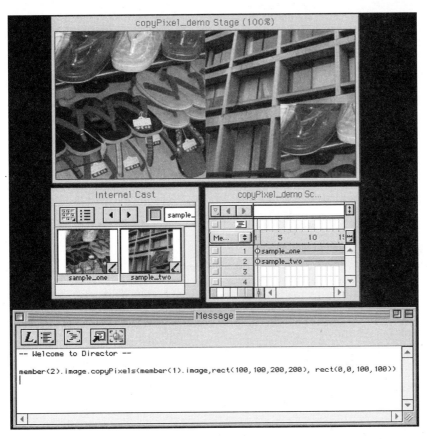

Check out your cast: the function will copy and modify the image in the cast member as well as the image on the stage. The original image data of member(2) has been lost from memory in this example; to get that picture back we would have to import it again.

You can set various effects when you're copying pixels using any or all of the optional parameters. These are the properties that we'll be using in our worked examples in this chapter. Check the entry in the Lingo help file for the complete list:

#color   sets the foreground color of copied pixels (RGB or index value); black by default.

#bgcolor   sets the background color of copied pixels (RGB or index value); white by default.

#ink   sets the ink value of the copied pixels, an ink symbol or corresponding numeric ink value. #copy by default. We'll be using this effect in the superimpose example.

#blendLevel   sets the blend level of copied pixel between 0 to 255. (You can use #blend, to set values from 0 to 100.) We'll be using it to blur an image.

#maskImage   specifies a mask object to be used as a mask for the pixels being copied. We'll be using it in the superimpose example.

#maskOffset   used in conjunction with a mask, as specified by #maskImage, to an x and y offset relative to the upper left corner of the source image.

You can also use copyPixel to do bit depth conversion. This script, for example, converts a image FullcolorImage into 8bit grayscale image, GrayImage.

```
GrayImage = Image(32,32,8,#grayscale)
FullcolorImage = Image(32,32,32)
GrayImage.copyPixels(FullcolorImage, FullcolorImage.rect,
➡ GrayImage.rect)
```

Cropping an image
This function returns a new image object made from a copy of the given image object, cropped to the given rect, while leaving the original image intact. This script, for example, crops a 100 pixel square (rect) from the top left of member(1), and sets it to an image of member(2):

```
member(2).image = member(1).image.crop(rect(0,0,100,100))
```

3.   Try it out in the message window of the movie you created for the previous example. I deleted member(2) and used a black square instead so that the effect would show up better:

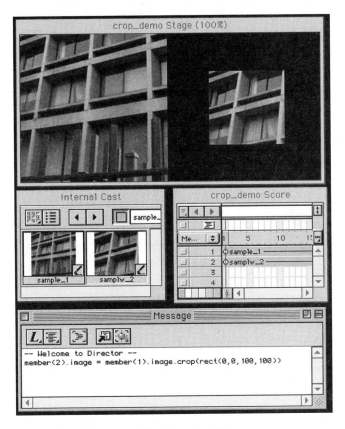

Working with areas of an image: getPixel and setPixel

These two functions get and set color values. The getPixel function returns an indexed or RGB color object from the specified pixel. If you'd rather have the raw value, which makes for marginally faster processing, then you can use the #integer property:

```
getPixel(x,y,#integer)
```

This line returns a color value taken from pixel at the x, y location of an image. Let's try it out:

4. Delete member(2) from your movie and create a field member named colorvalue in its place.

   It will display the color value of the center point of member(1)'s image in the field colorvalue (try it with #integer as well, if you like).

```
put member(1).image.getPixel(100,100) into field "colorvalue"
```

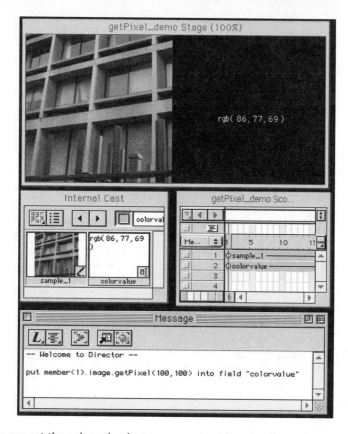

You can set the color value just as you can get it, using the syntax:

```
setPixel (x,y,color)
```

This sets the color of pixel at the specified (X,Y) location in the specified image. You can also use integervalue if you want to pass the raw number.

5. In this script, the color of center point of member(1)'s image is set to red. You'll probably need to zoom into your stage to see it because we're only setting one pixel.

```
member(1).image.setPixel(100,100,rgb(255,0,0))
```

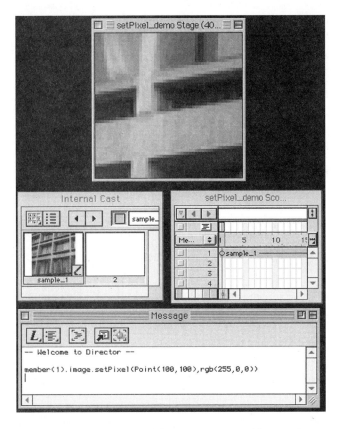

While working with individual pixels can create good interactive or morphing effects, you'll probably want to be able to fill a set area with color as well. For this, you need the `fill` function, which will draw a filled rectangle at given area with specified color:

```
fill (left,top,bottom,right,color)
```

6.   This sample script draws a filled red rectangle in the middle of `member(1)`'s image.

```
member(1).image.fill(50,50,150,150,rgb(255,0,0))
```

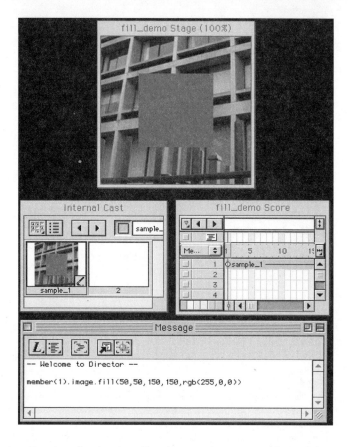

You can also `fill` the stage by drawing directly onto the `image` object of the `the stage`:

```
(the stage).image.fill(50,50,150,150,rgb(255,0,0))
```

The draw function
You can also draw using Imaging Lingo. The `draw` function draws an unfilled shape of the line width and color you specify (if you don't specifically set them, it will revert to the default values), and returns 1 if it is successful:

```
draw(location, [#parameters])
```

The three parameters you can set are:

#shapeType	#oval, #rect, #roundrect or #line (#line by default)
#lineSize	width of the line used (1 by default)
#color	color of line of the shape (black by default)

7.   This script draws an unfilled red circle in the middle of `member(1)`'s image:

```
member(1).image.draw(50,50,150,150,[#shapeType:#oval,
➡ #lineSize:1,#color: rgb(255,0,0)])
```

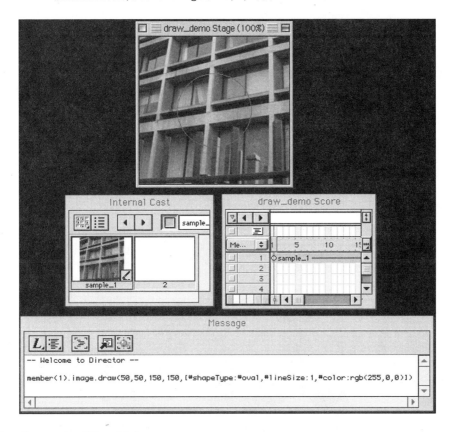

Extracting and setting Alpha

Using extractAlpha and setAlpha you can create a new image from the alpha channel data of an image, set the alpha of a member to an image or an integer, or use one alpha mask for several objects.

> *In order for* extractAlpha *and* setAlpha *to work, the image with an alpha channel has to be 32–bit*

This script, for example, returns an image object, tempimage, created from the alpha data of member(1):

```
tempimage = extractAlpha(member(1).image)
```

This script, on the other hand, sets alpha of member(1) as an image object called tempimage:

```
member(1).image.setAlpha(tempimage)
```

So there are the basic Imaging Lingo commands. Let's start putting them use to create some more interesting effects.

Working with Imaging Lingo

We'll begin with by superimposing an area of one picture onto a specified area of another picture, using the copyPixel command and then using a mask to polish the effect.

Superimposing one image on top of another

Take a look at this image:

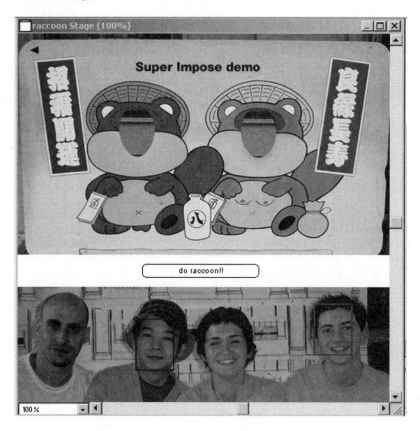

The top section of the stage is a photo I took on the street in Tokyo. It's a couple of raccoons illustrated on a billboard with holes for faces, just waiting for someone to stick their head through. The bottom section is a picture of some people, with heads ripe for sticking through, which I took at a party in Tokyo. You know what's coming next: this movie will copy the faces of those people and paste them into the missing faces of the raccoons, using the `copyPixel` command. We'll select the areas to copy for a male raccoon with a blue rectangular frame and a red frame for our female raccoon face.

1. Import both pictures and place them on the stage. Put the billboard in `member(1)` and the faces in `member(2)`.

2. You will also need a rectangular frame for selecting the area you want to copy, and a button sprite to call the copying function (which we'll create in a bit, alongside the other scripts you can see here). Your rectangle needs to be moveable so that your user can define the area to be copied. Set it to movable on the sprite property window.

I put most of my scripts inside the `main` movie script for convenience, although you may prefer to write them within sprite behaviors.

3. So let's create the main movie script. We'll create a handler, `hInit`, to initialize the variables we'll be using. The `originalimg` variable will store the original image object of `member(1)`, the billboard, before we carry out the Imaging Lingo effect on it.

    We'll use `duplicate` to copy the images, so that we still have the original picture as we manipulate the copy; as we build the movie you'll see why we need to revert back to the original image:

```
global originalimg

on prepareMovie
   hInit
end

on hInit
   originalimg = member(1).image.duplicate()
end
```

4. Now we need another handler to apply `originalimg` back to the image object of `member(1)`. You can simply add a handler named `resetimage` which sets `member(1)`'s image object to the object `originalimg` inside our main movie script.

```
on resetImage
 member(1).image = originalimg
end

on stopMovie
   resetImage
end
```

We're using the `resetImage` handler from `on stopMovie`, so that we can revert to the first picture of `member(1)` every time you stop the movie.

The next step is to make a handler to superimpose the user's selections from the bottom picture (`member(2)`, `sprite2`) onto the top picture (`member(1)`, `sprite2`). We'll use `copyPixels` to make this happen.

5.   We'll create a new handler called `docopyPixel` in the `main` script, to copy the pixels from a defined rectangular area of `member(2)` and paste them to the defined area of `member(1)`.

First we need to declare the handler name, and declare two variables that will hold the location of the rectangle in `script(2)`:

```
on doCopyPixel
    hoffset = sprite(2).rect.left
    voffset = sprite(2).rect.top
```

We'll need two more variables. The first, `sourceRectangle`, will hold the dimensions of the moveable rectangle image by subtracting values `hoffset` and `voffset` from the `rect` of `Sprite(4)` in order to get the position relative to `sprite(2)`. (I'm using `Sprite(4)` in my script to indicate the rectangle that will define the area to be copied from, because that's where my rectangle is. Change the positioning or the script if you need.)

```
    sourceRectangle = sprite(4).rect - \
➥ rect(hoffset,voffset,hoffset,voffset)
```

Then we need one more variable, `targetRectangle`, to hold the area of the rectangle you want to paste to, (around the face area of male raccoon in `member(1)`).

```
    targetRectangle = Rect(131, 95 ,181,163) - - face area
➥ member(1).image.copyPixels(member(2).image,
➥ targetRectangle,sourceRectangle)
end
```

Now all the handlers are ready; you just need to call them. We want to call `doCopyPixel` when the user clicks on to the `sprite(3)`, the button member.

6.   So we need to make a behavior inside `sprite(3)` like this.

```
on mousedown me
 doCopyPixel
end
```

7.   And put a `go the frame` script into the frame you would like to loop at (I used frame of the script channel), or use one of the navigation behaviors from the library palette:

```
on exitFrame me
  go the frame
end
```

Your movie is ready to run.

Drag the frame sprite to any of the faces in bottom picture and click on the button.

It works... but not very well; the image superimposed onto the raccoon's face doesn't really fit into the oval shape.

We'll use the #mask option to make the faces fit properly into this oval shaped hole. I like to use alpha masks, because you get a smoother edge. I made mine in Photoshop. It's a black oval shape 32bit .pict file. You can make your own or use mine.

8. Import this file into your director movie's cast, and call it `oval`.

We'll create a new variable, called `facemask`, from the alpha channel of `member("oval")`. We'll use `image.createMask` to do this, and add the operation to the `hInit` handler we made earlier:

```
facemask = member("oval").image.createMask()
```

We also need to globalize the `facemask` variable, so go into `main` and amend your script so that it looks like this:

```
global originalimg, facemask

on hInit
   originalimg = member(1).image.duplicate()
   facemask = member("oval").image.createMask()
end
```

9. In order to use `copyPixels` with the mask effect, you need to add the `#maskimage` parameter to the script calling `copyPixels`. You also need to set the mask's offset relative to the source picture (in this case `sprite(2)`, the bottom picture). You can give `#maskOffset` as an optional parameter. I've also set `#ink` as background transparent, to help the two images to impose better.

So, altogether, the `doCopyPixel` handler looks like this:

```
on doCopyPixel
      member(1).image = originalimg
      hoffset = sprite(2).rect.left
      voffset = sprite(2).rect.top
      sourceRectangle = sprite(4).rect -
   ➥ rect(hoffset,voffset,hoffset,voffset)
      targetRectangle = Rect(131, 95 ,181,163)
      member(1).image.copyPixels(member(2).image,targetRectangle,
   ➥ sourceRectangle,{#ink:36,#maskimage: facemask,
   ➥ #maskOffset:point(sourceRectangle.left,
   ➥ sourceRectangle.top)})
   end
```

10. Recompile the scripts, play the movie, and you've made the male raccoon.

11. Let's make another one for the female raccoon. We just need to add another sprite for selecting copy area for her face, so I made a red rectangular frame in the sprite(5) channel.

You just need to add another target rect and source rect on to the doCopyPixel handler, like this.

```
on doCopyPixel
     member(1).image = originalimg
     hoffset = sprite(2).rect.left
     voffset = sprite(2).rect.top
     repeat with n = 4 to 5
          sourceRectangle = sprite(n).rect -
          ➥ rect(hoffset,voffset,hoffset,voffset)
          if n = 4 then
            targetRectangle = Rect(131, 95 ,181,163)
          else if n = 5 then
            targetRectangle = Rect(285, 95 ,335,163)
          end if

     member(1).image.copyPixels(member(2).image,targetRectangle,
```

```
        ➥ sourceRectangle,{#ink:36,#maskimage:facemask,
        ➥ #maskOffset:point(sourceRectangle.left,
        ➥ sourceRectangle.top)})
    end repeat
  end
```

12. Try it out again. Everything should work fine.

Blurring with Imaging Lingo

Next we'll use Imaging Lingo function to execute a blur effect, similar to the blur filter you find in paint programs such as Photoshop.

There are two ways of doing this: the correct way, which is a pretty slow process, and by faking blur, which is, well fake, but it is fast.

True blurring and fake blurring

A 'literal' blur works with the color values of each individual pixel. You'd get the color values of a pixel and its neighboring pixels, calculate the mean a color value, and set that back to the relevant pixel. So, if I wanted to blur the 5th pixel of an image, I'd use this algorithm:

```
avcolor = (2's color + 4's color + 5's color + 6's color + 8's
color) / 5
```

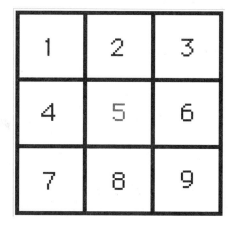

This calculation only checks horizontal and vertical neighbors, but you could check diagonal neighbors too.

It's a simple enough operation, but there are a couple of complications you need to be aware of when you're setting it up. Firstly, you can't simply average the color values by simply adding them up and then dividing them by five. It looks fine in theory, but try this in the message window:

```
put (rgb(255,255,255) + rgb(255,255,255)) /2
```

You'll get:

```
- - rgb( 127, 127, 127)
```

Not doing quite what we'd hope for (rgb(255,255,255)). The way around this is to store the R, G and B values inside a list and do the averaging calculation from there.

Something else you have to watch out for is asking for the color of a pixel that doesn't exist, which will give you a void value – if you tried to get the color value of neighboring pixel on the edge of your image, for example. Try this out in the message window:

```
put member(1).image.getPixel(0,-1)
```

The way around this is to check the value returned by getPixel using an if statement, and where it's a void value, set it to the background color of the movie.

As you'll see from the next example, a literal blur can be quite a drag on processing power, so we'll follow it up with a fake blur. We can create something that is definitely blurred but doesn't use as much processing power, by simply copying the whole area of the picture (using copyPixels), pasting it back offset by a few pixels and incorporating a blend ink effect. If you repeat this between 4 and 8 times in different offset directions, you'll get a pretty blurred image.

Creating a blur effect the proper way

1. I'll be using this 200 by 200 32bit image; either use this one, or import a different image you'd like to try the effect on.

2. Now let's write the blurring script. Declare a global variable to hold the image and then duplicate it:

```
global originalimg

on prepareMovie
  originalimg = member(1).image.duplicate()
end prepareMovie
```

We'll use the `originalimg` image object to manipulate the color data rather than `member(1).image`, because the image object of `member(1)` will be changing as the code runs.

3. We'll carry out the work of the script in a `doBlur` handler. The handler will need to:

- Use `getPixel` to retrieve the color of the pixel in the image.

- Hold the colors of these pixels in variables (`toppixelcolor`, `bttompixelcolor`, `leftpixelcolor` and `rightpixelcolor`).

- Check that each pixel has a value, and where it hasn't, set it to the color of the background. (I'm using `rgb(0,0,0)`, because the background color of the image I'm blurring here is black. Change this to a value that works for your own image if you need to.)

Altogether, the code that retrieves gets the colors of the pixels looks like this:

```
on doBlur
  repeat with y = 0 to 199
    repeat with x = 0 to 199
      if y-1 < 0 then
        toppixelcolor = rgb(0,0,0)
      else
        toppixelcolor = originalimg.getPixel(x,y-1)
      end if

      if y +1 > 199 then
        bttompixelcolor = rgb(0,0,0)
      else
        bttompixelcolor = originalimg.getPixel(x,y+1)
      end if

      if x -1 <0 then
        leftpixelcolor = rgb(0,0,0)
      else
        leftpixelcolor = originalimg.getPixel(x-1,y)
      end if

      if x +1 > 199 then
        rightpixelcolor = rgb(0,0,0)
      else
        rightpixelcolor = originalimg.getPixel(x+1,y)
      end if
```

4. Once we have the colors we need to break them up and put them into a list so that we can run our calculations on them (remember that calculations run on the RGB value don't come out with the result we need). This section code will take keep those RGB values in a list:

```
topcolor =
➡ [toppixelcolor.red,toppixelcolor.green,toppixelcolor.blue]
bottomcolor =
➡ [bttompixelcolor.red,bttompixelcolor.green,bttompixelcolor.blue]
leftcolor =
➡ [leftpixelcolor.red,leftpixelcolor.green,leftpixelcolor.blue]
rightcolor =
➡ [rightpixelcolor.red,rightpixelcolor.green,rightpixelcolor.blue]
```

We'll also call the value of the pixel that we're beginning the calculations with and assign it to the variable middlecolor; it doesn't need to go through the if loop, because we know it won't be outside the area of the picture:

```
middlecolor =
➡ [member(1).image.getpixel(x,y).red,member(1).image.getpixel
➡ (x,y).green,member(1).image.getpixel(x,y).blue]
```

5.   So, now we can work with the values to get the average colors we need using the algorithm we constructed earlier. Here's that algorithm again:

```
avcolor = (2's color + 4's color + 5's color + 6's color + 8s
color) / 5
```

The code that does this work looks like this:

```
avcolor=(topcolor + bottomcolor + leftcolor + rightcolor +
➡ middlecolor)/5.0
```

Then we need to put the new values back into their rightful positions within the RGB code. We'll hold this in the variable newcolor:

```
newcolor =
➡ rgb(integer(avcolor[1]),integer(avcolor[2]),integer(avcolor[3]))
```

So, if you put the second lot of code together, you should have something like this:

```
        topcolor =
➡ [toppixelcolor.red,toppixelcolor.green,toppixelcolor.blue]
        bottomcolor =
➡ [bttompixelcolor.red,bttompixelcolor.green,bttompixelcolor.blue]
        leftcolor =
➡ [leftpixelcolor.red,leftpixelcolor.green,leftpixelcolor.blue]
        rightcolor =
➡ [rightpixelcolor.red,rightpixelcolor.green,rightpixelcolor.blue]
        middlecolor =
➡ [member(1).image.getPixel(x,y).red,member(1).image.getPixel(x,
➡ y).green,member(1).image.getPixel(x,y).blue]
        avcolor=
        ➡ (topcolor + bottomcolor + leftcolor + rightcolor +
        ➡ middlecolor)/5.0
        newcolor =
        ➡ rgb(integer(avcolor[1]),integer(avcolor[2]),
        ➡ integer(avcolor[3] ))
        member(1).image.setPixel(x,y, newcolor)
    end repeat
  end repeat
end
```

Finish off the script by setting the movie back to its original state:

```
on stopMovie
 member(1).image = originalimg
end
```

6.   You can call this doBlur handler from anywhere you like; just attach it to a button like the one you used in the last exercise, with an appropriate behavior attached. I used:

```
on mouseUp
  doBlur
end
```

Use a frame script to loop the movie:

```
on exitFrame me
 go the frame
end
```

7. Run the movie and call `doBlur`. The blur effect will happen, but not particularly quickly.

So, while it works, you might find that you don't have many uses for this approach, simply because it takes so long to generate the blurred image. And it's not so surprising really – this movie is checking and setting 40000 (200*200) pixels every time you ask it to blur. If you wanted to blur more pixels it would be even slower.

You could make it slightly faster by making a list of the 40000 color items in the `on prepareMovie` handler and then referring back to that list, rather than retrieving values using `getPixel` for each pixel. It would still be slow though, because you still have to do `setPixel` for 40000 times.

This sort of list is commonly known as a **lookup table** (because you only use it as a reference), or a **displace map**. The lookup table allows you to do a relatively complex math calculation at reasonable speed. It's a way of using lists that comes in particularly handy if you have plenty of memory space but a slow CPU. We'll be working with lookup tables later on in the chapter.

A better solution in some cases is to find another way to get the effect you want. In this case, we can create a fake blur to get similar results but in much faster processing time.

Creating a fake blur

The Fake blur is actually much simpler. We use copyPixels to copy the whole area of the picture, paste it back offset by a few pixels with blend and ink effects. Repeat this between four and eight times in different offset directions and you'll get a pretty convincing blur.

8. So, let's amend the doBlur handler for this faster effect. Use a loop to run through the script 5 times:

```
on doBlur
    blurvalue =5
    repeat with n = 1 to blurvalue
```

We'll offset the image eight times, copying it and setting the #inktype and #blendlevel of the copied pixels. I'm amending the value of the #blend by the same value as that between the center point of an original image and the offset (n) like this:

```
member(1).image.copyPixels(originalimg,member(1).image.rect -
➡ rect(0,n,0,n),originalimg.rect,{#inktype:32, #blendlevel:5   *
➡ (blurvalue +1- n)})
```

So the further you paste an image from the center, the thinner the value of the blend becomes.

Altogether then, the code inside the loop looks like this:

```
member(1).image.copyPixels(originalimg,member(1)
➡ .image.rect - rect(0,n,0,n),originalimg.rect,
➡ {#inktype:32,#blendlevel:5 *(blurvalue +1 - n)})

member(1).image.copyPixels(originalimg,member(1)
➡ .image.rect + rect(0,n,0,n) ,originalimg.rect,
➡ {#inktype:32, #blendlevel:5 *(blurvalue +1 - n)})

member(1).image.copyPixels(originalimg,member(1)
➡ .image.rect - rect(n,0,n,0) ,originalimg.rect,
➡ {#inktype:32, #blendlevel:5 *(blurvalue+1 - n)})

member(1).image.copyPixels(originalimg,member(1)
➡ .image.rect + rect(n,0,n,0) ,originalimg.rect,
➡ {#inktype:32, #blendlevel:5 * blurvalue+1 - n)})

member(1).image.copyPixels(originalimg,member(1)
➡ .image.rect -rect(n,n,n,n) ,originalimg.rect,
➡ {#inktype:32 ,#blendlevel:5 *(blurvalue - n)})
```

```
member(1).image.copypixels(originalimg,member(1)
➡ .image.rect + rect(n,n,n,n) ,originalimg.rect,
➡ {#inktype:32, #blendlevel:5 * (blurvalue - n)})

member(1).image.copypixels(originalimg,member(1)
➡ .image.rect - rect(-n,n,-n,n) ,originalimg.rect,
➡ {#inktype:32, #blendlevel:5 * (blurvalue - n)})

member(1).image.copypixels(originalimg,member(1)
➡ .image.rect + rect(-n,n,-n,n) ,originalimg.rect,
➡ {#inktype:32, #blendlevel:5 *(blurvalue - n)})
    end repeat
end
```

You should still have the `stopmovie` event form the previous script:

```
on stopMovie
    member(1).image = originalimg
  end
```

9.   Try it out. You should find that it works much faster, and that the final blur is more intense.

If we you wanted to be able to change the level of the blurring, you'd simply globalize `blurvalue`, comment out the line 'blurvalue= 5', and have `blurvalue` set from outside this handler with a slider bar or text field.

As you can see from this example, you can use `getPixel` and `setPixel` to create some effective results at quite a good speed.

Using Imaging Lingo to create a ripple

We'll create a water ripple effect using a slightly more complex algorithm than this one together with a lookup table. The ripple is simply a color value swapping system. It swaps the colors of the pixels according to their angle and distance from the center of ripple.

In this diagram, the color value at point A is going to be swapped with the color value at point B, the points being the same angle from the center of the ripple and a set distance apart:

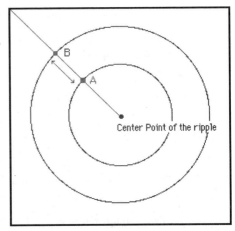

Center Point of the ripple

We'll define the distance between point A and point B according to the distance between the center point and point A using the sin function, which will give us a gently shifting ripple:

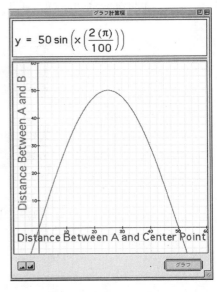

$$y = 50 \sin\left(x\left(\frac{2\,(\pi)}{100}\right)\right)$$

We'll carry out this procedure for every pixel in the area that we want to ripple.

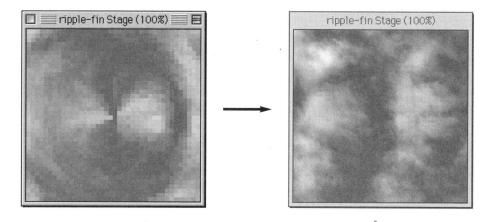

Creating a ripple with a lookup table

1. First you need an image in your cast to collect the color values from. Use your own .pict file or the one I'm using: it's a 16bit image, 256 by 256 pixels.

You don't need to place it on the stage because we only need the image as a color reference; in fact, we'll be using it as a color reference table. We don't need to create an independent copy as we have done in previous examples because we won't be altering the image itself.

We're going to make an image object in memory and apply our swapped color data to it to create the ripple. We'll use a relatively small image, just 40 by 40 pixels, because the image itself will slow the calculation down; we can just stretch it to size when we come to draw it onto the stage.

The script for the ripple effect will have to carry out the following steps:

■ Pick a pixel from the image object, which we'll call bufferimag.

■ Calculate the angle of the pixel from the center point of the ripple.

■ Calculate the distance from the pixel to the center point of the ripple.

■ Pick another pixel (x,y) to swap colors with, according angle, distance, and offset.

■ Get the color value of the new pixel using getPixel.

■ Apply that color value into the first pixel using setPixel.

■ Repeat for the other pixels.

We could write a handler to do all of this but it would be very slow because of the calculations (Director movies start to struggle if they have too many Lingo math functions like `cos` or `sin` to work with), and because you'd be calling `getPixel` and `setPixel` for each of the pixels in real-time.

Instead we'll use a lookup table containing lists storing distance, angle, color value, offset (X,Y) location), and the distance that each pixel should shift. Then we'll simply look up the values as we need them rather than calculating them on the fly:

`colortable[]`	stores all the color value of member, the water image
`distancelist[]`	stores the distances between the pixels and center point of ripple
`anglelist[]`	stores the angles between the pixels and center point of ripple
`distoffsetlist[]`	stores the pixel shift according to the distance (0 – 100)
`distanglist[]`	stores offset point(X,Y) according to the shift and angle

So now we know what we need our script to do, let's start creating it.

2.   Here is a first part of `main` script. We declare the global variables we'll need and initialize them in the `on prepareMovie` handler (notice that my image is `member(3)`, so you'll need to either move yours to that cast member or amend the script):

```
Global originalimg,
➥ imagewidth,imageheight,Rippleeye,gTime,colortable,
➥ RippleEyeinbuffer,distanglist,distoffsetlist,bufferimg,
➥ distancelist,anglelist

on prepareMovie
      originalimg = member(3).image.duplicate()
      imagewidth = 256 – – setting the image width
      imageheight = 256 – – setting the image height
      RippleEye = point(imagewidth/2,imageheight/2)
 – – where the ripple will eminate from
      bufferimg = image(40,40,16)
      RippleEyeinbuffer = point(20,20)– – ripple center
      anglist=[]
      distanglist=[]
      distancelist =[]
      pointlist=[]
      anglelist=[]
      distoffsetlist =[]

   gTime =1  – – an internal handler we'll need later on
   initables  – – the handler that will make the lookup tables
end
```

3.   We need to fill the variables and lists with data using the handler `initables`. We'll create these lists next, calculating the angles and distances we need inside these custom handlers:

```
gedRad(from, where)                    the radian angle between two points
DegToPoint (radius, degree)            point(x,y) according to radius and degree
getDistance (from, where)              the distance between two points
RadToDeg(radian)                       converts radian angle to degree angle

   on iniTables

   colortable = []  - -stores color value for each pixel
     img = member("texture").image
     repeat with y = 0 to 255
       repeat with x = 0 to 255
         colortable[x+y*256+1] = originalimg.getPixel(x,y)
       end repeat
     end repeat

     repeat with x = 1 to 100
     - - returns shift according to distance
       tempoffset = 70* sin(x*((pi()*2)/100))
       add distoffsetlist  tempoffset
     end repeat

     repeat with Pangle = 1 to 360
       repeat with dist = 0 to 100
         temppoint = DegToPoint(dist,Pangle)
         add pointlist temppoint
       end repeat
       add distanglist pointlist
       pointlist = []
     end repeat

     repeat with y = 0 to 39 - -the object in memory is 40, 40
       repeat with x = 0 to 39

         tempdist =
         ➥ integer(getDistance(RippleEyeinbuffer,point(x,y)))
         distancelist[x+y*40+1] = tempdist
       end repeat
     end repeat

     repeat with y =  0 to 39
       repeat with x = 0 to 39
         tempangle = gedRad(RippleEyeinbuffer,point(x,y))
         tempangle = RadToDeg(tempangle)
         anglelist[x+y*40+1] = tempangle
       end repeat
     end repeat

   end
```

```
on gedRad from, where
  xdiff=float(from.locH-where.locH)
  ydiff=float(from.locV-where.locV)
  if xdiff=0 and ydiff >0 then
    rad=pi()*2
  else if xdiff=0 then
    rad=pi()
  else if ydiff=0 then
    rad=pi()/2
  else
    rad=atan(ydiff/xdiff)+pi()/2
  end if

  if xdiff>0 then rad=rad+pi()
  return rad
end

on DegToPoint radius, degree
  rad=degree/(180/pi())
  rad=rad-(pi()/2)
  x=(radius*cos(rad))
  y=(radius*sin(rad))
  return point(x,y)
end

on getDistance from, where
  tempdiff = from-where
  distance=sqrt(power(tempdiff.locH,2)+power(tempdiff.locV,2))
  return distance
end
on RadToDeg rad
  deg=rad*(180/pi())
  return deg
end
```

So by this point in the script, we've made a lookup table ready to be called. Now we need to code the main body of the ripple algorithm.

4. We'll create a doRipple handler to take care of the pixel color conversion by referring to the lookup tables we've made. We're using the variable gTime to shift the look up address of distoffsetlist by one block every time you update doRipple to drive the animation of the ripple. If you don't change the value of gTime, the ripple stays still.

Add this handler to the main movie script.

```
on doRipple
  if gTime >= 100 then
    gTime = 1
  else
```

```
        gTime = gTime+1
    end if
```

gTime will count up to 100, reset to 0, and count up again.

```
repeat with n = 0 to (40*40)-1
    posX = (n mod 40)        - - position x in bufferimg
    posY = n / 40            - - position y in bufferimg
    cposX = (n mod 40) +(128-20)   - - position x in color map
    cposY = n / 40 +(128-20)       - - position y in color map
```

Then we need to get the distance from rippleeye by looking it up in the lookup table. We don't need to swap the pixel color if the distance is 0, but otherwise we need to select a pixel to swap with using gtime (which is cycling from 1 to 100)

```
    distfromcenter = distancelist[posx+posy*40+1]
    if distfromcenter <= 0 then
            myshiftamount= 0
    else
            tempindex = distfromcenter - gTime
            if tempindex < 1 then
                tempindex = tempindex + 100
            end if
```

Next we need to work out how far the shift should be. We're retrieving the angle to RippleEye from the look–up table, setting the offset and the color, setting it all to the bufferimag, and then copying the bufferimage on to the stage. Note that we're scaling bufferimage up as we copyPixel:

```
    myshiftamount = abs(integer(distoffsetlist[tempindex]))
    end if
    myangle = anglelist[posx+posy*40+1]
    myoffset = distanglist[myangle][myshiftamount +1]
    mycolor =
    ➥ colortable[(cposx+integer(myoffset.loch))+(cposy+integer
    ➥ (myoff et.locv))*256 +1 ]
    bufferimg.setpixel(posx,posy,mycolor)
end repeat
(the stage).image.copyPixels(bufferimg,rect(0,0,200,200),
➥ bufferimg.rect)
end
```

5. When you're done with the coding, compile the script and call the doRipple handler from a go the frame script, (I put mine in frame 5 of the script channel):

```
on exitframe me
    doRipple
    go the frame
end
```

You should have a gently rippling effect. The live effect that this ripple creates is part of what makes Imaging Lingo so interesting – and using lists together with the image object makes it really easy to put together sophisticated effects. However, you don't have to have a system that just works away independently of whoever is watching it – you can respond to their input on the fly as well. We'll do that next.

We'll create a dynamic drawing application. This is slightly different to the other drawing programs around, in so far as the drawings will swing on an axis once they've been drawn. Try out the demo version on the CD if that didn't make sense!

This is the kind of thing we'll create:

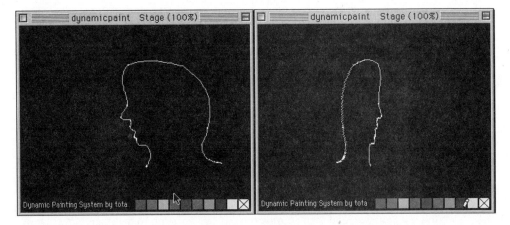

We'll begin by building the static drawing tool, and then add in the swinging movement to it.

Drawing programs in Imaging Lingo

You don't have to use the draw function to create a drawing program; you can use setPixel, or even copyPixel. All you need to do is specify a canvas and detect where the mouse is on that area.

If you want your user to be able to change the color they are drawing in, then you'll need a color picker as well. The easiest way to create a color picker is to create a bitmap member with a selection of the colors and then use getpixel in the onmouseDown event handler to pass the selected color value to the drawing handler.

I'm going to use the draw function in this example (you might remember it from the beginning of the chapter), because it'll be easy to use when we convert the simple painting program into a dynamic one. If you'd rather have a smooth brush, try using copyPixels with a blurred image and alpha mask instead.

Creating a Drawing program in Imaging Lingo

These are the steps that I identified for my normal drawing system:

- Make a color palette bitmap member and place it on to the stage

- Create an image object for the canvas, (I'll call it canvasimg)

- Create a constantly updating handler (hupdate) to check the mouse status, and when the mouse is pressed (another variable, mousepressed), call a drawing handler that draws to canvasimg.

- Create a color picker behavior and drag it onto the color picker sprite. The behavior will return the color value relative to the mouse location when the mouseDown occurs.

So let's begin by setting up the stage and bitmaps:

1. Create a new movie, size your stage 320 by 260 pixels, and set the fps to 60. Then create your a bitmap color palette so that it looks like the one in this image, and call it colorp. Finally, make an image that will give the user an indication of the color that has been selected. Mine is another bitmap cast member.

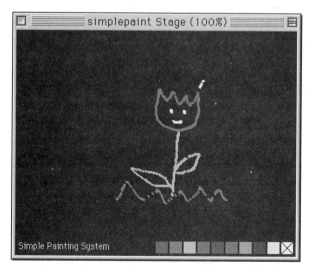

2. Now we need to create the canvas and set up the handlers we'll need in the main movie script...

We'll begin by declaring the global variables to hold the canvas image object, the information we need about whether the mouse has been pressed or not and the color that we'll draw in:

```
global canvasimg,mousepressed,gcolor
```

Then we need to set up a `dotlist` to hold the dots on the canvas that make up the user's drawing, create the canvas object, fill it with color, and initialize the `mousepressed` variable to 0:

```
on prepareMovie
  dotlist = []
  canvasimg = image(320,260,16)
  canvasimg.fill(0,0,320,260,rgb(0,0,0))
  gcolor = rgb(255,255,255)
  mousepressed = 0
end
```

Then we need the `mouseDown` handler. I've created this to prevent users being able to draw on top of the color picker (amend the numbers if your stage has different dimensions to mine):

```
on mouseDown
  if the mouseV < 240 then
    mousepressed = 1
  end if
end
```

```
on mouseUp
  mousepressed = 0
end
```

We need the all important `hupdate` variable to draw a line two pixels wide according to the position of the mouse on `canvasimg`:

```
on hupdate
  if mousepressed =1   then
    canvasimg.draw(the mouseh ,the mouseV,the mouseH +2,the
    ➡ mouseV +2,[#color:gcolor,#shapeType:#line,#lineSize:2])
```

And we'll apply the `canvasimage` to the image object of `the stage`:

```
    (the stage)
    ➡ .image.copypixels(canvasimg,canvasimg.rect,canvasimg.rect)
  end if
end
```

3.   Finally, in order to have the movie update constantly, we need to call the `hupdate` handler from first frame of the script channel:

```
on exitFrame me
  hupdate
  go the frame
end
```

4. Try it out. You should be able to draw onto the stage, but not right down to the bottom of the area because we're disabling the drawing function when the mouse is in the color bitmap area.

That works OK, but it's not quite the colorful drawing program I promised, so let's add the color palette that that users can select their drawing color.

Adding color selection

5. Place the colored bitmap member at the bottom of the stage. You'll also need an image to indicate which color has been selected — either create one of your own or use mine, and put it into your cast. We'll use this to indicate the color that has been selected by the user. Now we're ready to write the behavior for the color palette sprite.

6. Create a new behavior, declare the global variable gcolor, and create a new property for the behavior, mysprite using the property keyword. This makes the mysprite property available outside this behavior script:

```
global gcolor
property mysprite
```

We'll use the beginSprite statement, (an event handler that runs only when the playhead encounters a novel sprite for the first time) to set gcolor to white, and refer to the channel number the sprite is in:

```
on beginSprite me
   gcolor = rgb(255,255,255)
   mysprite = sprite me.spritenum
end
```

Then we change the mouse cursor to a picker while it's over the palette, and to a pen when it's on the canvas:

```
on mouseEnter me
   cursor 281 - -   changing cursor to picker
end
on mouseLeave me
   cursor 256 - - changing cursor to pen
end
```

And then we need to let the user select a color. We'll do this by retrieving the location of the mouse relative to the palette, colorp, on the mouseDown event handler, and using getPixel to ascertain its color:

```
on mouseDown me
   posX = (the mouseH - mysprite.left)
   posy = (the mousev - mysprite.left)
   gcolor = member ("colorp").image.getpixel(posX,posy)
```

In order to put the cross over the relevant section of the palette we have to calculate where on the block the mouse is. We do this by get the width of `colorp`, dividing it by ten (because we have ten colors), and setting the horizontal position of `sprite (2)`'s registration point (using `locH`) to it:

```
imagewidth = member("colorp").image.width +0.0
colorblockwidth = integer(imagewidth/10 )

sprite(2).loch =
➥ colorblockwidth*(integer(posX/colorblockwidth)) +
➥ mysprite.left + sprite(2).width/2
end
```

7. Once you've completed the behavior, drag it onto the sprite, and you should have something that looks like this:

Making it dynamic

We'll use OOP to make this work. Instead of drawing lines to canvas based upon the `mouseDown` status, we'll birth a child object that redraws itself on to the canvas on each update.

The big difference between this application and the last is the parent script we'll be using, `dotparent`. Let's start by looking at what that script will have to do:

- Make an image object for a canvas, using the `image` function

- Make a handler that checks the status of the mouse, and when the mouse is pressed calls a birthing handler to create a dot object

- Store all the objects in a list and keeps the update in a repeat loop

- Use an algorithm to draw a line connecting the dot to its neighbor dot object

- Apply the result of canvas image drawings on to the stage to make it viewable

- Use an algorithm to make the image appear to swing

8. So let's build up the parent `dotparent` (remember to give it the type `Parent`).

First we need to get the current location of the object, and then set a virtual time property, `mytime`.

```
property loc
property mytime
```

Then we'll declare a new property `myid`, which we'll use to store our place within the `dotlist` list we created in the `main` script. I'm also creating a `mate` object, to keep track of the object born before this one. This will allow us to draw a line between the first object and the second (the first born object will simply ignore this property and instruction). We also need a property to store the x and y location of this object's birthplace, and a `mycolor` property to store its color value:

```
property myid   - - my index id inside dotlists
property mate - - keeping track of the previous object
property mycenterv,mycenterh  - X,Y location of this object
property mycolor - - color value of this object
```

Then we need to declare our global variables:

```
global mousepressed
global canvasimg
global gcolor
```

Then we can begin birthing objects and assigning them their properties:

```
on new me, m, id   - - birthing object
  makeObject(me, m, id)
  return me
end

on makeObject me, m, id
  mate = m
  myid = id
  loc = the mouseloc
  mycenterH = loc.loch
  mycenterV = loc.locv
  mytime = 0
  mycolor = gcolor
  return me
end makeObject
```

Now we have our new object we can begin working with it. We'll check for a value in `myid`, which will have a value of less than one as long as a previous object exists, and drawing a line between this object and the last one where there is a previous one:

```
on draw me
     if (myid > 1) then
              canvasimg.draw(mate.loc.loch,mate.loc.locv, loc.loch,
              ➥ loc.locv, mycolor,[#shapeType:#line, #lineSize:1])
     end if
```

The animation (the swinging) won't start until the user releases the mouse. The swinging animation is driven by the incrementing `mytime` variable, which cycles between 0 and `pi()*2` to keep the movement looping nicely.

```
if mousepressed = 0 then   - - hold until the drawing is
➥ finished
  if  mytime >= pi()*2 then
    mytime =0
  else
    mytime = mytime + 0.03
  end if
```

We're using `mytime` for the cosine calculation, defining the `loch` of the dot by `cos(mytime)` * the horizontal distance between the dot object and center of the stage:

```
- - Moving loch of this dot object by the cos wave.
    loc.loch = 160 + ((mycenterH-160) *cos(mytime))
- - 160  is  the center  of the  stage (ie:newloch =
    ➥ centerpoint + radius*cos(angle))

loc.locv = mycenter V

end if
end draw
```

9.   We need to birth these dot objects from the `main` script so we'll need to make a few additions there. They are marked in bold in the following script. This script only draws one line before setting the animation going. This is to make things simpler – users will just have to keep the mouse pressed down if they want to draw a complicated picture in this system!

```
global dotlist, canvasimg, mousepressed,lastmouseloc,gcolor

on prepareMovie
     dotlist = []
     canvasimg = image(320,240,16)
     canvasimg.fill(0,0,320,240,rgb(0,0,0))
     lastmouseloc = point(0,0)
```

```
                mousepressed = 0

    end

    on mouseDown
      if the mouseV < 240 then
        dotlist = []  - - empty the pointlists
        mousepressed = 1 - -  true
      end if

    end

    - - stop adding dots
    on mouseUp
        mousepressed = 0 - - false
    end
```

Every time addDot is called, we'll birth a dot object from the parent script dotparent and store it inside dotlist. If the object is first born, then it births an object without a brother object inside.

```
- - add a new dot object to the list
on addDot

  if(dotlist.count() > 1) then
    dotlist.add(new (script"dotparent", dotlist[dotlist.count()],
    ➡ dotlist.count()+1))
    else
    dotlist.add(new (script"dotparent", 1, 0))
  end if

end
```

We're calling this handler constantly. Each time it's called it checks if the mouse has been pressed or not. If it is pressed, then a new dot object is created by calling the addDot handler. It also updates the draw handler inside all the dot objects that have been born.

```
on hupdate - - called from on prepareFrame of looping frame

if mousepressed then
    if lastmouseloc <>the mouseloc   then
      addDot()    - - new dot object
      lastmouseloc = the mouseloc
    end if
 end if


    - - draw all dots and repeat with object in dotlist
    obj.draw()  - - updating dot object
```

```
        end repeat
- - copy canvasimg to the stage
 (the stage).image.copypixels(canvasimg, canvasimg.rect,
 ➥ canvasimg.rect)
end
```

To avoid a trailing effect you need to clear out the lines you have drawn previously before you draw new lines, using the `on exit frame` handler

```
on flushScreen
      canvasimg.fill(0,0,320,240,rgb(0,0,0))
end
```

You can leave the color picker and its behavior just as in the simple drawing example above.

10. Finally, call `hupdate` and `flushScreen` from your score scripts, like this:

```
on prepareFrame
  hupdate
end
```

```
on exitFrame me
  flushScreen
  go the frame
end
```

And that's it. We made the location of the line keep moving according to the time, but you could develop this painting system by changing the colors and line widths, fills, or something else.

Using Imaging Lingo with 3D Lingo

Just before we end this chapter about Imaging Lingo I would like to show one more experimental piece that uses Imaging Lingo in different way. Take a look at these images:

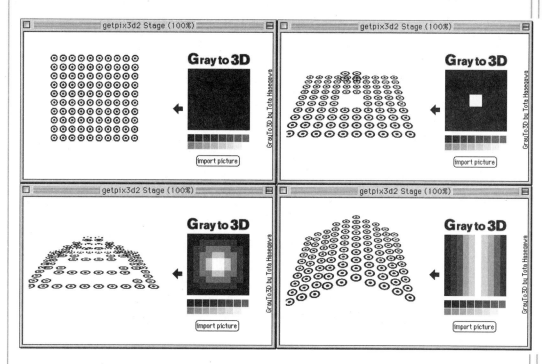

There's a gray scale drawing canvas on the right hand side of the stage, and a grid of a 3D plane on the other side. They are both made of 10 by 10 grids. In this movie, we'll use the gray scale canvas image as a database, and allow the user to change the information it holds visually. The Z–axis position of each plane model is defined by the gray value of its relative pixel in the canvas image. So you can alter the Z-axis of those 3D models by painting in the canvas image. The structure is very simple – use getPixel to retrieve values from the canvas and then apply them to the Z positions of the models.

This example does include some basic 3D, so if you're not yet comfortable with 3D, check out the 'Principles of 3D' chapter further on in the book and then come back to it.

Creating a 3D grid model

1.   First of all, you need to prepare some Shockwave 3D members and bitmap members. You'll need:

   ■   A 220 pixel square Shockwave 3D model member: put it on the stage, in channel 1, and call it world

   ■   A gray scale drawing canvas: a 10 pixel square bitmap placed to the right hand side of stage as sprite 2. Enlarge the sprite size by so it is a 100 pixel square.

- Texture for the 3D model: import a 32bit, 32 by 32 pixel bitmap with alpha mask and name it texture.

- A gray color palette: make a 46bit gray scale palette and place it below the canvas sprite on the stage. This should be sprite 3.

2. The scripts will need to do the following things:

- Make a canvas painting system and color palette system, as we did in the previous example, and ensure that the colors are grayscale only. I've used a sprite behavior, painting, on the canvas sprite (sprite 2), and another behavior, pickcolor, on the palette sprite (sprite 3).

- Create a handler to duplicate and remember the original image of member graybmp in the prepareMovie handler.

- Create a handler to check the current color status of member graybmp to store the value in the list.

- Create a handler to initialize the 3D models inside member 3dworld. I did this using an invisible parent model located at the center point, and a 10 by 10 grid of the plane models with textures related to the first parent model.

- Birth the dot object from parent script dotparent attached to the each plane model

- The parent script dotparent should include a handler called updateZ me to transfer the Z position of the attached model to a given destination.

- Check the color values of member graybmp and store the updated value into the list, colorlist every time a change is made on the canvas.

- Update the 3D models by setting the Z position of each plane model according to the relative color value of colorlist and calling the updateZ handler inside the objects birthed from the dotparent script.

3. So, let's look at the scripts. This first script is the behavior for the canvas sprite, sprite 2, and is the painting behavior.

The script begins by declaring the sprite properties and global variables and then setting them. We're using myMode to capture the mouse downs and setting the mouse cursor accordingly:

```
property mysprite,mymode,colorlist
global color
on beginsprite me
  mymode =0
  mysprite = sprite the spritenum of me
  color = rgb(200,200,200)
```

```
  end

  on mouseDown me
    mymode =1
  end

  on mouseLeave me
    cursor 0
    mymode =0
  end

  on mouseEnter me
    cursor 256
  end
```

Then we'll call a `checkbmp` handler to use to check the canvas image and update `colorlist` each time `painting` ends:

```
on mouseUp me
  set mymode =0
  checkbmp
end
```

We run an `if` loop when the playhead leaves the sprite (`on exitframe me`), to retrieve the location of the mouse in relation to `graybmp` if it is pressed (the value of `mymode` will be 1 if it is):

```
on exitframe me

  if   mymode =1 then

    columndot = (the mouseV -the top of mysprite)/10
    rowdot = (the mouseH -the left of mysprite)/10
    member("graybmp").image.setPixel(rowdot,columndot,gcolor)

  end if

end
```

4.   This is a script for the color palette (sprite 3), the `pickcolor` behavior. Again we're working with the cursor, and setting the value of `gcolor` according to the position of the mouse (using `getPixel`)

```
global gcolor
property mysprite

on beginsprite me
  gcolor =255
  mysprite = sprite the spritenum of me
end
```

```
on mouseenter me
    cursor 281
end

on mouseleave me
    cursor 256
end
on mousedown me
        columndot = (the mouseV - the top of mysprite)
        rowdot = (the mouseH - the left of mysprite)
        gcolor = getPixel(member the membernum of mysprite,
    ➡ rowdot,columndot)
end
```

5.   So, now we come to the parent script, dotparent. We begin by declaring two lists, dotslist to store the object generated by this script, and colorlist to store the colors. We also need a scene global to store the 3D world defined at the beginning of the movie, and some properties to hold the address and dimensions of this particular object:

```
global dotslist, colorlist, scene
property myid   - - index adress of this obj in dotslist
property x
property y
property z
```

Then we create an object with the x,y,z location properties and an index number:

```
on new me  ,xpos,ypos,zpos,id

  initobj (me ,xpos,ypos,zpos,id)
  return me
end

on initobj me ,xpos,ypos,zpos,id
  myid = id
  z = float(zpos)
  x = xpos
  y = ypos
end
```

We'll keep track of the position of the dot in updateZ, which will be called continually from hupdate:

```
on updateZ me
  destz = -abs(colorlist[myid+1].red /10.0)

  if abs(z-destz) <= 0.1 then
    exit
  else
```

```
z = z + (destz -z)/5.0  - - easing out the speed change
  scene.model("plane_"&myid).transform.position = vector(x,y,z)
end if
```

```
end
```

And that's all there is to the `dotparent` script.

6. Finally we come to the `main` script, which initializes the 3D models and analyzes the canvas.

We need to declare all the variables we're using, duplicate the image `graybmp`, and create the lists `colorlist` and `dotslist`:

```
global scene,dotobj,dotslist,colorlist,originalImage
```

```
on prepareMovie
    originalImage = member("graybmp").image.duplicate()
    colorlist=[]
    dotslist=[]
    checkBmp
    initModel
```

```
end
```

Then we create the empty 10 by 10 gray scale image object, and copy the `graybmp` image into it:

```
on checkBmp

    tempimg = image(10,10,8,#Grayscale)
    tempimg.copyPixels(member("graybmp").image,member
    ➥ ("graybmp").image.rect,tempimg.rect)
```

Then check though the pixels inside `tempimg`, and store the color values into the `colorlist`:

```
repeat with n = 0 to 99
  column = (n/10)
  row = (n mod 10)
  tempcolors = value(tempimg.getPixel(row,column))
  colorlist[n+1] = tempcolors
end repeat
end
```

Now we're ready to create the 3D models (planes) with textures. We're using the `scene` object for this. First we make the world empty, then set its background color to white.

```
on initModel
  scene = member("3dworld")
  scene.resetworld()      - - clears the world first
  scene.bgcolor = rgb(255,255,255)
```

Then we make a `plane` model resource, 8 by 8 pixels square

```
pl = scene.newModelResource("plane",#plane,#both)
pl.width = 8
pl.length = 8
```

We create a new `shader` with the texture

```
sh = scene.newShader("sh1",#standard )
tx=scene.newTexture("texture_"&"01", #fromcastmember,
➡ member("texture", 1))
```

and set the texture render format to full color with alpha.

```
tx.renderformat = #rgba8888
```

We also create an invisible parent model, `dad`. The locations of this model is, by default, vector (0,0,0)

```
scene.newmodel("dad")
```

We're actually creating 100 models (`plane`s) with textures. They will all be linked to `dad`, the parent model, and placed in a 10 by 10 grid order:

```
repeat with n = 0 to 99
  ball = scene.newmodel("plane_"&n,pl)
   — texture and shader, more about these later on in the book!
  scene.model("plane_"&n).shaderlist[2] = sh
  scene.model("plane_"&n).shaderlist[2].texture = tx
  scene.model("plane_"&n).shader = scene.shader("sh1")
  column = (n/10 )
  row = (n mod 10)
  tempx = row*10     -50
  tempy = column *10   -50
  tempz =-abs(colorlist[n +1].red /10.0)
  scene.model("plane_"&n).transform.position =
  ➡ vector(tempx,tempy,tempz)
```

Then we set the parent model, `dad`, so that we can spin everything by just spinning the parent, which will give us better performance. We also set the camera angle, and begin generating objects from the `dotparent` script, which will be assigned to each model.

```
scene.model("dad").parent =   scene.model("dad")

      tempobj =
```

```
        ➥ new(script"dotparent",scene.model("plane_"&n).
        ➥ transform.position.x,scene.model("plane_"&n).
        ➥ transform.position.y,scene.model("plane_"&n).
        ➥ transform.position.z,n)
      add dotslist, tempobj
    end repeat

    sprite (1).camera.transform.position = vector(0,0,200)
    scene.model("dad").transform.rotation= vector(300.0,0,0)
    scene.directtostage = 1
  end
```

And we'll rotate the parent plane very slowly, updating the dot objects, and on the stopMovie event, set the graybmp back to the original:

```
on hupdate
    scene.model("dad").rotate(vector(1.0,0,0), #world)
    repeat with n = 1 to 100
    dotslist[n].updatez()
  end repeat

  end

  on stopmovie
    member("graybmp").image = originalImage
  end
```

7. Finally, we need to call hupdate handler using the go the frame in the score script channel.

    Try it out. You could also import an image onto the canvas (which is automatically transformed to be 10px by 10px, and converted to grayscale), and use it as Z-axis data base.

This is a just one small example of the sots of things you can create using Imaging Lingo with 3D Lingo. You could extend the example by dynamically changing the texture image of the 3D models, or create something like real-time video images applied to the 3D model's surface.

Summary

We've covered a lot in this chapter; using Imaging Lingo for a number of different effects, manipulating images on the fly, and working with OOP to make objects that can move themselves on the stage. We also looked at how you can use the image to create a kind of database that the user can access and change for simple image manipulations. You could take this system much further; you might create something like a handwriting or image recognition system, for example. We didn't have time to cover using video for similar effects in this chapter, but you could try working with a video capturing Xtra (like Geoff Smith's QTGrab Xtra) to grab video image in the cast and create some sort of real time video effect.

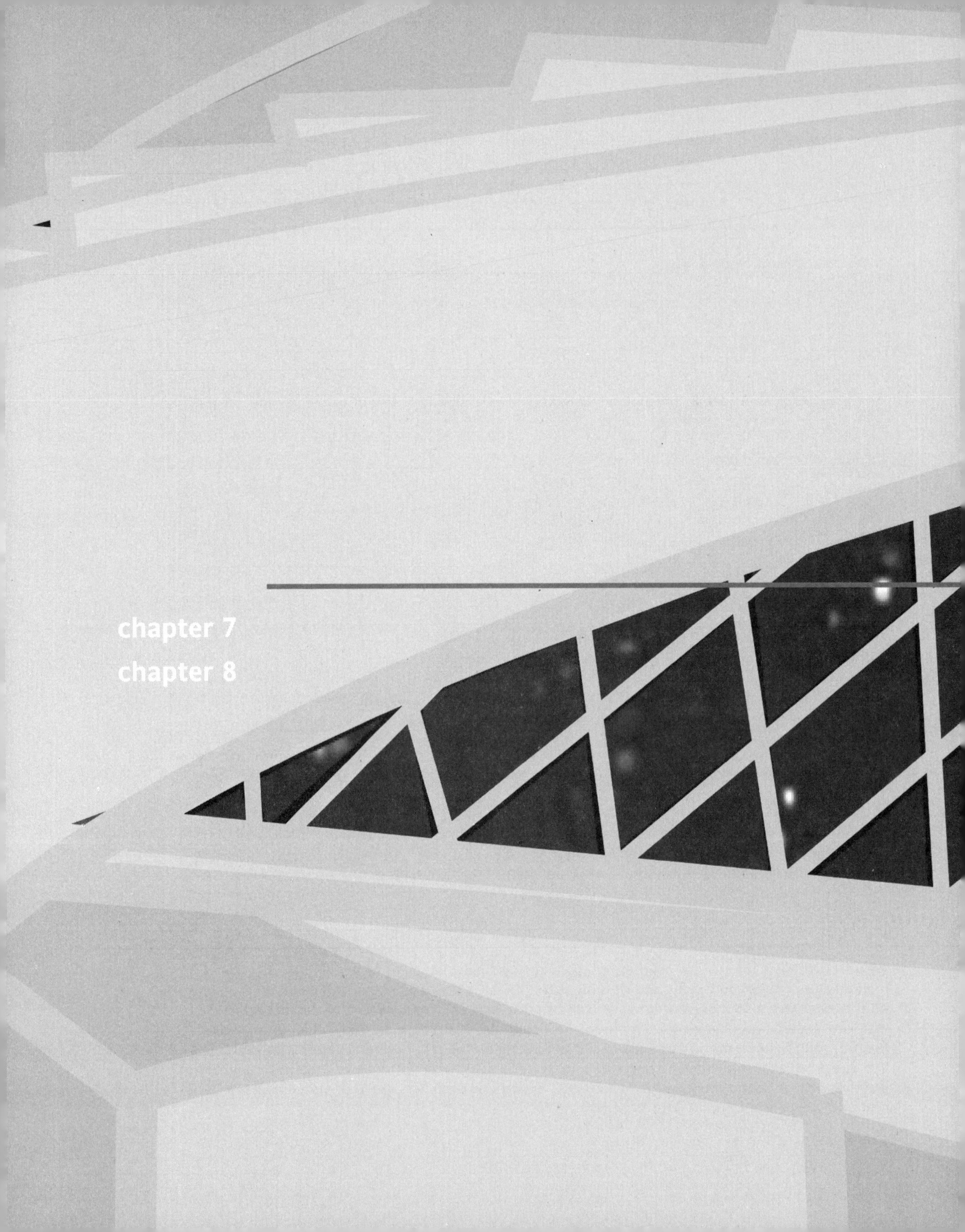

chapter 7

chapter 8

Chapter 6
The Principles
of 3D Worlds

Director 8.5 and Shockwave allow you to create, render and animate real–time 3D. Not so long ago the closest approximation of 3D graphical support we had was being able to import 3D objects, created and pre-rendered in external applications, and convert these into two–dimensional animations. Now we can build fully immersive, highly detailed, animated, and interactive 3D environments. It's an exciting time to be working in Director!

Of course, 3D requires more processing power than 2D does, power that hasn't until recently been available on a wide range of machines. It's not just about hardware either – you'll need to add to your skill set if you're going to be creating and manipulating real 3D. While Director makes this development process easier, and accessible to more people than ever, it's something of a learning curve for those entirely new to the subject. You do need to know something about programming and mathematics, and there are over 300 new Lingo commands for dealing and interacting with these new 3D cast members that you'll need a passing familiarity with if you're going to really get the best out of it. You can, if you really want to, turn your back on these new commands, and you'll get quite a way towards the kind of effects you're looking for from inbuilt behaviors. But if you really want to utilize these capabilities to the full, you'll need to understand what 3D graphics are really all about, and this chapter aims to help you do that by laying the mathematical foundations you'll need.

Although we live our whole lives in three dimensions, somehow thinking in 3D can be quite hard to handle for non–mathematicians, so we'll begin this chapter by trying to bridge that gap. We'll look at the key 3D concepts of models and worlds, examine how Director creates 3D models, and build a model in Studio Max to import into Director (don't worry if you don't have access to that program, you'll find that the same concepts apply to other model creation programs). We'll import the model into Director (it's included on the CD if you want to use my model instead), apply inbuilt interactivity behaviors to it, and finally, create our own custom behavior to generate a background for the 3D world we have created. There's a lot to cover, so let's get started!

3D Basics: back to school and geometry

We couldn't introduce this fascinating world of 3D objects without a brief excursion into mathematics and spatial geometry. Vector math will underpin your three–dimensional work. The good news is, though, that it's really not that hard. If you have used a 3D modeling package before you'll already be familiar with some of the ideas we'll be covering here. You don't need to know all of it in detail if you're only planning to use the new Director 3D engine – most of the real math is kept away from you, so you can just dive in and play around. Be aware, though, if you're going to be developing online projects, that not everyone can see this new Director 8.5 content, and you might need to write your own Lingo 3D engine for older versions of Shockwave in order to reach a wider audience. The following chapter demonstrates how you'd go about doing exactly this.

We'll begin this chapter by going right down to the very basics: vectors, facelists and meshes. While you don't *have* to deal with shapes at this level in Director, you can if you want to, and an understanding of how it all works is going to make your work in 3D Lingo much easier. So let's begin at the very beginning: with vectors.

Vectors

The term 'vector graphic' has been turned into something of buzzword through applications like Flash, Freehand and Illustrator. In essence, vectors can be thought of as little mathematical helpers that describe graphic objects. A vector can be represented as a set of coordinates that describe something within **vector space**.

So what's vector space? Well, a computer screen is a very simple example of a two–dimensional vector space, simple in that the angle between the horizontal and vertical axis is always 90 degrees. We only need two coordinates to address a pixel on the screen, X and Y. The top–left pixel has the coordinates (0,0). This is known as the point of **origin.** A vector specifies the distance of a point from the origin (or from any other point of reference). In terms of the screen, then, the X coordinate specifies the point's distance from the origin in the horizontal direction, and the Y coordinate the distance in the vertical direction.

A vector can describe a direction as well as a location. For example, you might have two location points that define a line, P_1 (100;20) to P_2(20;50). P_1 and P_2 describe the end points of the line relative to the origin. Another way to describe the line would be to introduce directional vector D (-80;30) alongside the initial location vector, P_1, and because vector D is described in relation to point P_1, you no longer need P_2 to describe the line – P_2's information is accounted for in the other two points. Add D to P_1 and you'll get P_2:

$$P_1 + D = (100+(-80) ; 20+30) = (20 ; 50) = P_2$$

We can calculate the length (magnitude) of a vector in 2D using the Pythagorean:

$$V_{length}^2 = v_x^2 + v_y^2 \qquad \text{and therefore: } V_{length} = \sqrt{(v_x^2 + v_y^2)}$$

So to find the magnitude of vector D(-80;30), we'd do this:

$$D_{length}^2 = D_x^2 + D_y^2 = (-80)^2 + 30^2 = 7300$$
$$D_{length} = \sqrt{7300}$$
$$D_{length} = 85.44$$

To translate this into Lingo, you can read and set the location of sprites on the stage in Director like this:

```
put sprite(1).loc
- - point(100,20)
```

point (x, y) can be equal to a 2D location vector, or it can also be used to move an object relative to its current position as in the vector D example above:

```
- - move sprite(1) 80 pixel to the left and 30 down
sprite(1).loc = sprite(1).loc + point(-80,30
```

Vector graphics are usually a lot smaller in file size than their bitmap relatives, essentially because it takes only two vectors to describe a line. In fact, you only need two vectors to describe a circle: one for the center point, the one for the radius. It's really very easy to manipulate these vectors and the resulting graphics.

> *Mathematically, a 2D vector space is called a plane. This will be important later.*

Coordinate systems

In a 3D vector space you need more than the two dimensions we've looked at so far (width and height). You need a third coordinate to express a point's depth value, along what is usually known as the Z–axis.

There are two ways to describe a 3D coordinate system: right–handed and left–handed. The systems differ in the direction of their Z–axis. The coordinate system is right–handed if the positive Z–axis stands perpendicular to the X, Y plane (that would be our screen) and is pointing toward us. Director and in fact most 3D modeling software packages use the right–handed version.

There's an easy way to visualize this. Hold up your right hand with palm facing yourself. Now spread out your thumb to the right, keep the pointing finger straight up and bend your middle finger pointing towards you. Ignore the other fingers, and you have a model of a right–handed coordinate system. Your thumb is pointing along the positive X–axis, your pointing finger the positive Y–axis and your middle finger the positive Z–axis. The emphasis is on 'positive', because this is what indirectly defines the **orientation** of models. It's also possible to form negative coordinates lying on the opposite sides of the Origin – more on this later.

So, vectors within 3D space have three coordinates, X, Y, and Z, and the point of origin becomes (0,0,0). Just think of it as the center of your 3D world.

In Lingo you can create a 3D vector like this:

```
myVector = vector(0,100,0) - - create a vector along the Y-axis
```

Vertices, faces and meshes

There's not a lot of point discussing atoms if you want to build a flourishing universe full of things, and similarly we need a more complex structure for our 3D world. (Although vectors are similar to atoms in that combining them within ever more complex structures will slowly create our world... first things first, though.)

Let's talk about triangles. A triangle is one of the most powerful shapes in math. Triangles are so flexible they can be combined to build any shape or structure you can think of, because the three points of a triangle are the absolute minimum you can use to create a shape in a 3D space. Less is more. It's the holy trinity of mathematics and geometry.

This kind of flexibility is great for 3D modeling, so it should come as no surprise that at a very basic level, all 3D objects are made of triangles of various sizes.

> *In the context of 3D, these triangles are usually called polygons or faces, and the corner points of each polygon are its vertices – which are in fact nothing more than vectors.*

A cube, for example, needs only 8 vertices to define the corner points P_1 to P_8.

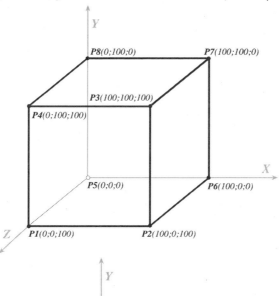

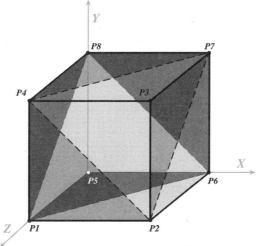

In order to create the cube we need to define the relationship between these points. We can split up the six side squares of the cube into twelve triangles, and specify three points for each of these faces:

```
Face1     ( P1,  P2,  P4 )
Face2     ( P2,  P3,  P4 )
Face3     ( P5,  P1,  P8 )
Face4     ( P1,  P4,  P8 )
Face5     ( P6,  P5,  P8 )
Face6     ( P6,  P8,  P7 )
Face7     ( P2,  P6,  P7 )
Face8     ( P2,  P7,  P3 )
Face9     ( P4,  P3,  P7 )
Face10    ( P4,  P7,  P8 )
Face11    ( P2,  P1,  P6 )
Face12    ( P1,  P5,  P6 )
```

And that's a **facelist** – the assignment of vertices to faces.

A **mesh** just moves the idea on another step; it's a collection of faces and their vertices. A mesh can be a complete 3D object or just the detail of a more complex model. There are a lots of Lingo commands that allow you to manipulate meshes. The chapter on 3D modifiers will tell you much more about them.

> *And it's as simple as that – a facelist is a collection of vertices, and a mesh is a collection of faces and their vertices.*

Normal vectors

A normal vector describes the outward direction of a face. The normal vector is a vector that is perpendicular (at 90 degrees) to the 'surface' of a face. If an outward face of a mesh is away from the camera then that face will be invisible. In this case we need to know the normal vector of the face to know its exact orientation.

Mathematically speaking, any face of a mesh is a plane, as only three points are necessary to fully define a plane in space. Its size and location are irrelevant. This diagram shows a mesh with five visible faces and their normal vectors:

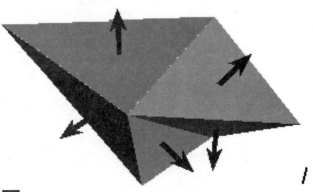

Working with normal vectors

You can calculate the normal vector for any known plane in Lingo. We'll start by defining a plane using two directional vectors, V_1 and V_2. Vector V_1 is parallel to the X–axis and V_2 is parallel to the X–axis.

```
v1 = vector(100, 0, 0)
v2 = vector(0, 100, 0)
```

The plane we have defined by these vectors happens to be parallel to the X, Y plane of the coordinate system, but you can apply the following technique to any plane.

To calculate the normal vector you use the `perpendicularTo` command. This command uses a mathematical function called the **vector cross product** to calculate the components of the normal vector that points perpendicularly away from this V_1V_2 plane. The normal vector in this example is parallel to the world's Z–axis.

```
put v1.perpendicularTo(v2)
- - vector( 0.0000, 0.0000, 1.00000e4 )
```

Another side effect of this function is that the resulting vector is **normalized** too. Normalized just means its magnitude is exactly 1 – don't confuse this with the term 'normal vector'!

There are several potential uses for normal vectors. For example, the normal vector of a face on a polygon can be used to indicate its visibility. If the vector is pointing towards the viewpoint, the polygon is visible. If it points away, then this face of the object will be invisible to the viewer.

Similarly, the 3D engine figures out how to illuminate objects, only in this case it has to compare the face's normal with the direction of an imaginary light source. Normal vectors can be defined for each face in a mesh and then can be used to soften the mesh's surface.

Another useful mathematical function that you can use in Lingo is the **dot product**. The dot product can be used to calculate the angle (?) between two normalized vectors e.g. $v_1(v_x1; v_y1; v_z1)$ and $v_2(v_x2; v_y2; v_z2)$

$$dotProduct = v_x1 * v_x2 + v_y1 * v_y2 + v_z1 * v_z2 = cos\ (?)$$

Without going into further detail, it can be shown *v1* and *v2* are pointing in opposite directions if their dot product is negative.

Vectors and Meshes in Lingo

3D objects are created in Director from a mesh of vectors and faces. You create what's known as the **resource** for the model using the `newMesh` command, giving it vectors and faces using the `vertexlist` and `face` properties. Once the resource holds the information needed for the model, we use the `build` command to create it.

The following example builds a model from the building blocks we've discussed so far.

1.   Create a new Director movie and set the stage color to black. Also create a new 3D cast member by choosing Window>Shockwave 3D and name it MeshWorld.

2.   Create a movie script with the following handlers:

```
on startMovie
   init3DWorld(member("MeshWorld"))
end

on init3DWorld this3Dmember
```

We'll use the init3Dworld function to reset the 3D cast member to its original state before trying to create the model of a cube.

```
this3DMember.resetWorld()
```

We're deleting any Lingo generated models and model resources. If we ran the movie more than once without resetting then we'd be trying to create models that already exist, and we'd get error messages.

Now we can begin building the resource that defines the geometry of our model.

3.   This next line of code creates a mesh resource using the newMesh function. The function takes six arguments, the first being a name for the resource, (I'm calling it boxmesh), the number of faces in the mesh (12) and the number of vertices (8). The final three arguments are used to control color and texture.

```
newBoxRes = this3DMember.newMesh("boxmesh",12,8,0,1,0)
```

4.   Next we create the list of vertices, points P1 to P8.

```
newBoxRes.vertexList = [vector(0,0,100),      vector(100,0,100),
                     ➡ vector(100,100,100), vector(0,100,100),
                     ➡ vector(0,0,0),        vector(100,0,0),
                     ➡ vector(100,100,0),   vector(0,100,0)]
```

5.   From this list we create a facelist defining the vertices used for each face. The numbers in this list correspond to the indices in the newBoxRes.vertexList.

```
- - a list of each face's vertices
newBoxFaceList = [[1, 2, 4], [2, 3, 4], [5, 1, 8], [1, 4, 8],
              ➡ [6, 5, 8], [6, 8, 7], [2, 6, 7], [2, 7, 3],
              ➡ [4, 3, 7], [4, 7, 8], [2, 1, 6], [1, 5, 6]]
```

6.   These faces will have to have color in order for us to see them. The next line of code creates a list of colors that we'll use. In our example we'll only use a light green.

```
newBoxRes.colorList = [rgb(0,255,0)]
```

7. And now we can create each face according to the facelist. We're applying the colors and the values of the facelist to the vertices in the mesh using a repeat loop.

```
repeat with i = 1 to 12
  newBoxRes.face[i].vertices = newBoxFaceList[i]
  newBoxRes.face[i].colors = [1,1,1]
end repeat
```

By accessing the index of the colorList, using [1,1,1], we are setting the color of each face's vertex to the green color defined in colorList.

8. Next we need to calculate the normal vectors for each vertex in our mesh model resource using generateNormals command. We're setting the parameter to #flat to give all three of the vertices of a face the same normal. This will make the faces of the mesh very clear. If we had used #smooth, then the three vertices of a face could be allocated different normals which would create a more rounded appearance to the faces of the mesh – although the outer edges would remain sharp.

```
newBoxRes.generateNormals(#flat)
```

9. None of these mesh manipulations are going to come to anything unless you use the build command to generate the geometric object from the information that you have given:

```
newBoxRes.build()
```

10. Finally, to place the mesh into the world space and make it visible, we have to create a new model based on the mesh resource we have built:

```
newBoxModel = this3DMember.newModel("newboxModel", newBoxRes)
```

11. Now the only things left to do is optimize the view of our cube model. First, move the camera away so that we can see the cube and rotate the cube a little:

```
this3DMember.cameraposition = vector(0, 0, 500 )
newBoxModel.rotate(10,-50,10)
end
```

12. Now close the script window and drag the Shockwave 3D cast member onto the stage. Put a go the frame handler on frame 2 of the script channel:

```
on exitframe
  go the frame
end
```

And test your movie. If you now rewind and play the movie you should see the final 3D cube. Change the #flat parameter of generateNormals to #smooth, and you'll see that the cube is actually made of triangles:

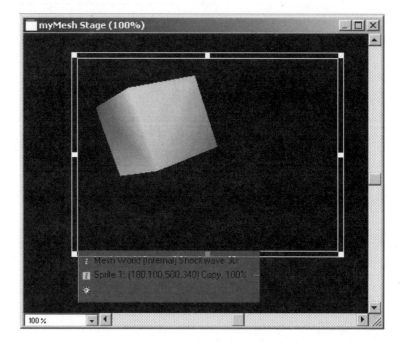

We'll be doing more work with Director and modeling, but first there's a little more theory we should cover.

Viewing 3D worlds

Unfortunately, we can't use screen coordinates as a reference system for modeling because the resolution and dimension are too low. Instead, we have three different coordinate systems for working with 3D worlds: world space, viewport and projection.

World space
A world space contains all models and any other objects. We can select the scale of our world without having to worry about screen resolutions and display sizes.

Imagine you want to build a game along the lines of Star Wars. You'd need to keep the correct scale between the space ships and planets, maybe by using miles as your basic measuring unit. Although most 3D modeling tools let you choose your measuring units, you'll find that meters are the best bet for most applications. If, for example you were planning to incorporate the Havok physics engine, you'll find that most of the physical variables are based upon the metric system. Forces are measured in m/s, so if you'd decided to model in miles then you'd need to convert these values into your own system in order to get the calculations to work.

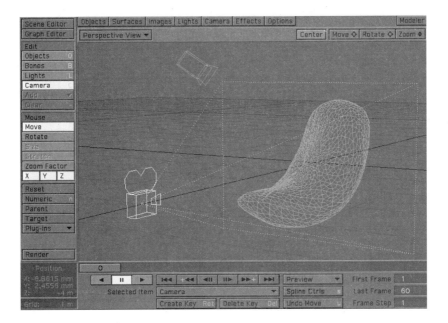

Cameras and viewports

The **viewport** coordinate system represents a certain view of the world. It acts like an imaginary camera or a window into the world space, defining a position and direction from which the world is seen. Theoretically you can define an infinite number of these cameras (viewports) for each 3D cast member and switch between them.

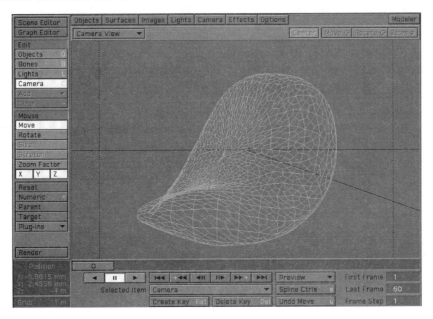

Projection

A **projection** displays the contents of the viewport (our screen). To actually see something on screen we have to transform the content of the viewport onto the screen. As you've probably already found with 3D rendering packages this can be very time consuming and CPU intensive. It still has to be done though, because our world space is three–dimensional and the screen has only two dimensions. Although Director's 3D engine also has a feature that dynamically reduces the Level of Detail (LOD) in a model, and this helps to increase performance on slower machines, you need to know that, in the end, the only way to keep the speed of this projection down in real–time is to keep to a minimum the number of polygons and vertices in your world. Always bear this in mind during the modeling process.

How perspective works

Simulating the third dimension (Z–coordinate) is the main task of doing a 3D to 2D transformation. Let's stay with our camera analogy for just a bit longer. If you're taking a picture with a camera, the rays of light must first go through a lens. This pulls them into a focal point. Before they reach the actual focal point they're projected onto film, which is, mathematically, a projection plane. The distance between lens and focal point, which varies according to the type of lens you're using, also defines the view angle. A longer distance creates a telescopic effect, while shorter ones create a wide–angle view. The focal point also makes objects closer to the camera appear bigger in the projection image than the ones further away. Objects too close to the camera will be warped and distorted.

Of course, there aren't any lenses involved when you view 3D objects on a screen, but the same mathematical concepts still apply. Each vertex's 3D coordinate first has to be transformed from its world space definition into view coordinates and from there into 2D screen coordinates via simple parametric linear equations.

Once we have all vertices transformed into screen coordinates we can start drawing all the visible objects and their faces. Scenes and objects can consist of several thousand polygons, and eliminating the hidden ones is very important for reducing the time the rendering process takes, and to save expensive CPU cycles. We also have to determine its fill colour (or texture), which again is dependant on the position and direction of lights in the scene.

World space and object space

At the beginning of the chapter we talked about vectors being thought of as distances relative to reference point. In some cases that point is the origin of the world space, but in most cases it isn't. The reason for this is that most 3D modelers, as well as Director's 3D engine, are object–oriented, and based on simple parent–child relations. This allows you to group and manipulate your objects relatively easily.

When a new Shockwave 3D cast member is created it is a blank world space, and the parent of all objects that will be created or imported into it later on. As you saw earlier, **model** resources are used to create them. They are a kind of an object repository from which you take the parts you need to assemble complete models and scenes. And if that sounds similar to the relationship between cast members and their sprite instances in Director, that's good: it is!

What's important to this discussion is that each model and model resource within a 3D cast member's world space has its own coordinate system, called **object space**. Object space has its own origin. When a new model is created it uses certain model resources but within its own object space. This object grouping allows the process to go on, and on, and on.

Vector transformations: scaling and rotation

The significance of the relationship between object and world space comes to the fore when you're transforming objects. As we have already seen, you can translate objects in space through simple vector additions. So, for example, to move an object in the opposite direction you simply use negative components in the translation vector. Now, while you can move objects around easily enough without worrying too much about the origin of the coordinate system, the same is not true for scaling and rotation.

> *Scaling and rotation are always relative to the origin.*

Mathematically, scaling is nothing more the simple multiplication of each vector's components by a scaling factor. Think about the definition of our cube model. Let's say we want to scale it up by factor 2 to double its size. In this case point P2(100,0,100) would move to P2'(200,0,200), because our reference point for scaling is the cube's local origin at P5 (0,0,0).

However, if the cube is placed within a world space, say at position A (30,60,-30), you'd have a different calculation. Scaling the cube by factor 2 would include the location offset A in the world space as well, and would automatically move the cube further away from the world's origin, to A'(60,120,-60). Not necessarily what we had in mind.

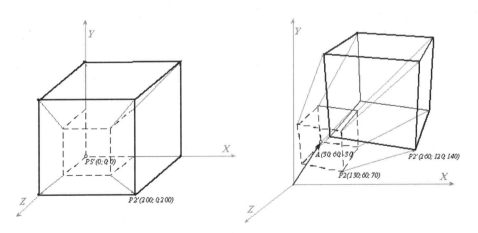

Rotation behaves in a very similar way: an object's position in the world space will be changed by any rotation performed upon it, while rotations performed relative to the object's own space will leave its position in the 3D world unchanged.

> *It is crucial to understand the order in which vector transformations are executed. This order of scaling, rotating and re-positioning is not fixed; it's down to context and application.*

Later, when you start writing your own 3D Lingo to manipulate models you'll see that Director bundles position, scaling and rotation together into transform objects. A transform is a very elegant way of doing compound vector calculations and is nothing else but a mathematical matrix. However, that's a topic for another chapter. Let's start working with some more generic modeling techniques.

3D modeling techniques

3D scenery is usually built from many different models. In the following section we will have a brief look at some 3D modeling techniques common to most Mac and PC packages.

Primitives

Modeling tools provide you with a selection of several basic 2D and 3D objects: cubes, spheres, cylinders, cones, planes, even text primitives are available on click. You do the modeling by deforming these primitives. We'll look at some of these techniques a little further on.

Lights and cameras are also primitives. Although you don't 'model' them as you would your 3D objects, they do play a very important part in the rendering process. To make the models you've labored long and hard over visible you need at least one light source and one camera within a world, and in some situations, much like a photo shoot, you'll need many more lights and cameras. Most applications allow you to add several. You usually select between:

Directional light A simulation of daylight. You can't position or define the light source but you can work with its general direction, color and intensity.

Point light Like a simulation of a bulb, point lights have a defined position but emit light in all directions. You can usually specify color, intensity (brightness) and a fall off value to indicate at what distance the light will be effective.

Spot light A simulation of a spotlight. The light is positioned and has direction. Common light parameters are: intensity, color, angle and a percentage value that can be used to specify soft edges.

Ambient light Usually there's only one ambient light source available. It defines overall brightness and contrast between light and shadows within a world. The brighter this light source, the milder the impact of other light sources (including the casting of shadows) on objects.

Each light will slow down the rendering process. Director doesn't support visible lights, so you'll only see the illumination and shadows thrown by a light.

Adding additional cameras to a scene is like specifying different points of view. This is very different to having several lights, as only one camera can be active at any time. Having several fixed points of view can be very helpful during the modeling process.

Creating primitives in Director

Each 3D modeling application offers a selection of primitives, some more, some less. Director lets you create spheres, boxes, planes and cylinders. We'll look at the basic structure for building these primitive models in Director, using a sphere for our example.

Creating a sphere

Spheres are very simple models, so we'll start with a sphere. As before we'll create a model resource for the 3D world and then use it to create the object.

1. Open a new Director movie and select File>Media Element>Shockwave 3D as we did before to create your empty Shockwave 3D cast member. Give it a name and drag the cast member to your stage.

2. Create a new behavior script and start by adding the following properties:

    ```
    property thisMember
    property thisSprite
    ```

3. Now we'll write the handler that will create the sphere. We begin by setting the sprite that will hold the 3D cast member instance, and assigning the 3D world you will be building in to the cast member:

    ```
    on beginSprite me

      -- the sprite number that holds the 3D cast member instance
      thisSprite = me.spriteNum

      -- the 3D cast member, the 3D world you will be building in
      thisMember = sprite(thisSprite).member
    ```

    Then we create a new model resource for the sphere:

    ```
    thisSphereResource = thisMember.newModelResource
    ```

➡ ("SphereResource", #sphere)

And set the radius of our sphere resource:

```
thisSphereResource.radius = 50
```

Finally we create an instance of the model resource:

```
newSphere = thisMember.newModel ("Sphere",thisSphereResource)
end
```

4.   Attach the behavior to the Shockwave 3D asset, play the movie. There's your sphere.

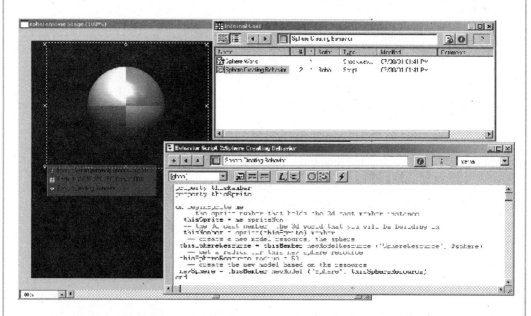

You create the other Director primitives much the same way, but with the different properties they need — boxes need width, height and depth properties, a plane only height and width, and a cylinder needs a height property along with top and bottom radii. (Setting either the top radius or the bottom radius to 0 creates a cone shape.)

There are other ways to create your models. We'll look at some of these next.

Splines and NURBs

Most people know splines as Bezier curves, and in fact a Bezier curve is an example of a spline. Broadly speaking, a spline is an interpolated, parametric curve controlled by a number of points specified by an algorithm. They can also be defined within three–dimensional space, and are used by 3D applications in several ways.

You can use splines as an alternative to triangles in your modeling. Verticies are used in spline–based modeling as control points, rather the corners points of a triangle as we used them earlier. Curves are combined in order to describe what are known as **free–form** surfaces.

Splines are the ideal tools for creating very smooth and exact surfaces, and they're often used in engineering. The main advantage of using splines is the low number of control vertices that are needed. Splines usually only have about four control points, with the curve going through the first and last point, and the points in between used to influence the shape of the surface – although they don't have to be actually on it. To create a similar shape using a triangle–based system would require an extremely complex mesh, and that makes it very difficult to pick out and modify individual points.

The principal difficulty you'll come across if you're working with splines is creating adjoining surfaces while keeping the overall smoothness and accuracy of the rest of these surfaces. Spline–based models also take considerably longer to render than polygon–based ones, which is why they aren't often used for real–time 3D graphics. This is where **NURBS** (Non Uniform Rational B–Spline), come in. These are a kind of 'hyper spline'. They are completely interpolated, so the resulting surface doesn't touch any of the control vertices at all. In most cases NURBS are easier to use than splines, and they're particularly popular for character modeling and for creating organic looking shapes. Most Spline/NURBS modelers control NURBS using a mesh of control points around the surface. It's also possible to convert NURBS models into polygon–based geometry for use in other applications – for use in Director, for example.

Splines can also be used as motion paths for animated objects in most 3D applications. It's common practice to assign a camera to a spline object and have it follow along this curve through world space, automatically changing its view direction relative to the spline's curvature. As smooth as a steady–cam!

Extruding

The transformation of a two dimensional shape into a 3D object is called **extrusion**. A duplicate of the original 2D shape is created and shifted a certain distance along its Z–axis to create the depth of the resulting 3D object. Creating 3D text from standard TrueType fonts is a typical form of extrusion. Most programs will let you create a custom bevel along the objects edges when extruding too.

Lathing

This is another process of building 3D objects based on two–dimensional shapes. Lathing is one of the oldest modeling techniques and you can find it on virtually any 3D modeling package. Objects are formed by rotating a 2D spline (or any other 2D outline) around a freely chosen axis in 3D space. You'll find that lathe objects always look very symmetrical.

Director 8.5 Studio

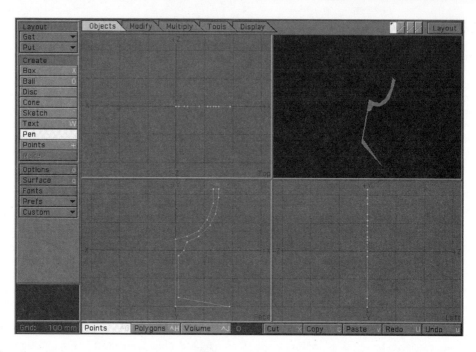

First the shape is defined in two dimensions, and then the lathe tool is applied creating a 3D object.

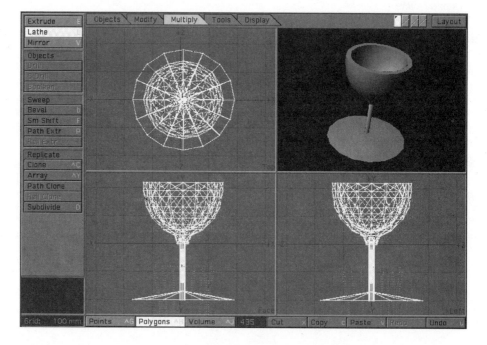

Bones

Working with complex meshes can be quite tricky, and doing it well is something that takes time and experience. This is especially true if, for example, you're doing character modeling and want to change the geometry of a mesh to make a character move naturally. If you've got access to expensive equipment you could use a motion capturing system to transform the movements of a real person into animation data for your 3D character.

The technology that underpins such equipment is known as **bones**. Bones are a 3D geometry based on the parent–child relationships stored within the mesh. If a bone is moved, it causes the surrounding mesh to deform according to the new position.

Bones usually behave according to the laws of Inverse Kinematics. For example, a mesh is the model of a human body and has individual bone definitions for shoulder, upper arm, lower arm and hand. Rotating the shoulder bone would also cause the rest of the arm to change position accordingly, according to the based on the parent–child relationship between the bones. This makes animation easy and efficient.

Bones are an excellent solution if you're planning to develop animated 3D characters for the Web. You only need one mesh definition for all the phases of a mesh's animation, and so it saves you file size without sacrificing the appearance of the animations. Director's 3D engine fully supports the playback of bones.

From design to Director

There are a wealth of 3D objects and models all over the Internet ripe for download. You're likely to find, though, that the novelty of using existing models and objects soon wears off as your knowledge of Director's 3D functions grows. So, to fuel your thirst for more, we're going to step through the process of creating a model using 3DStudio MAX and exporting it for use with Director.

All in the planning

Stop right there. While your newly discovered enthusiasm for all things 3D may send you diving for 3DStudio MAX, it's very important that you stop and think, plan what exactly it is you want to do, and think about the medium and your intended audience.

Having a 350Mb animation is all very well if your intended medium is a CD but you wouldn't want people to try and watch it over the Internet on a 56k modem. You may laugh, but trust me, in a bid to create the latest and greatest hi–tech robot complete with missile launchers and laser sights, the last thing you'll be thinking about is file size and polygon count.

Always begin by sketching out your design, just a simple outline scribbled on the back of a napkin will become invaluable during the design/modeling stage of your project. Without a clear objective your design will drift, hours will pass and you'll have achieved little.

So let's begin. In the following exercise, we'll be creating a simple low polygon jet fighter to use in Director. The technique we'll be using is **polygon modeling** or **mesh modeling**. This is the oldest form of 3D modeling but it's still the most widely used and the most efficient way of modeling for real–time applications such as games and web content, the low polygon count ensures smaller file sizes ideal for use with Director. *And* you've already got a firm grounding on how this works.

Creating a Low Polygon Jet Figher in 3D Studio Max

I used 3DS MAX 4 for this tutorial but the techniques used are equally applicable for most 3D applications.

1. We'll start by creating a rectangular box in the Top viewport (approximately length=200, width=90, height 30). Set the number of length and width segments to 3 and leave the height at 1. Since we're not working to any particular scale the dimensions shown are only approximations as accuracy is not important.

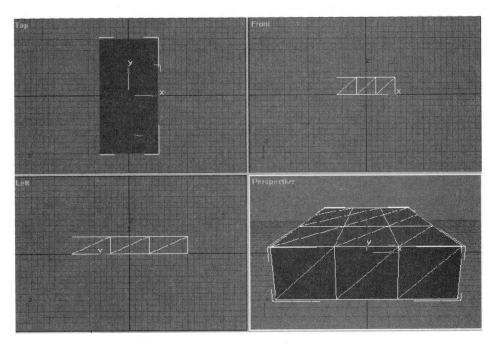

2.   We'll work manipulate the box at vertex level, so we can bend and stretch the box into a jet shape. Go to the Modify panel and select the Edit Mesh modifier from the list.

We'll start by shaping the nose cone of the aircraft, so select the center polygon on the front of the box.

3.   Use the Extrude command to stretch the selected polygon out from the rest of the box as shown.

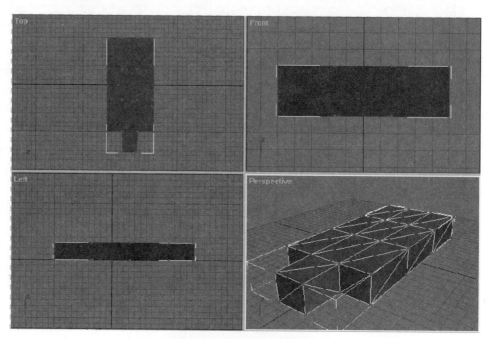

We can shape the nose cone by scaling the polygon face we created with the Extrude command.

4. Select the face and then using the scale command, reduce the face size down to 0, forming a nose cone shape.

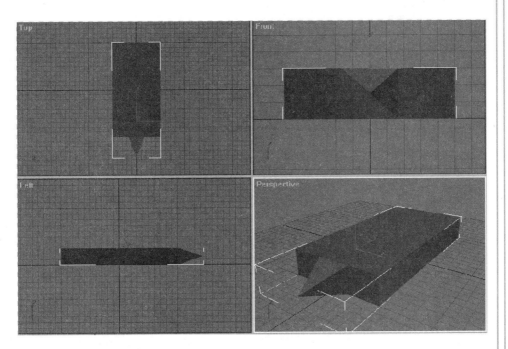

5. I know it doesn't look much like a jet just yet but trust me; we're ready to add the cockpit of the aircraft. Select two faces from the top surface of the box and use the Extrude command to stretch both faces out and away from the main body of the aircraft.

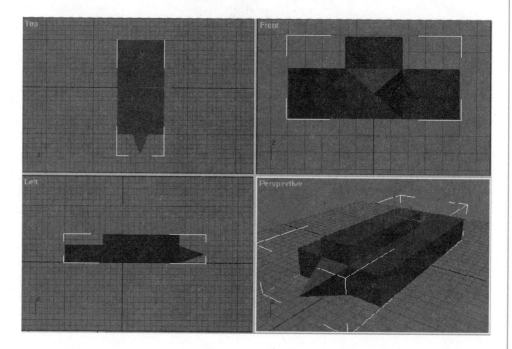

6. Select the four outer vertex points and drag them down towards the main body of the aircraft as shown, to add some shape to the cockpit. You'll notice I've also added some engine detail to the side of the fuselage. I used exactly as we used for the cockpit was used, simply extruded the faces, but this time I added a Bevel command to create the engine edges.

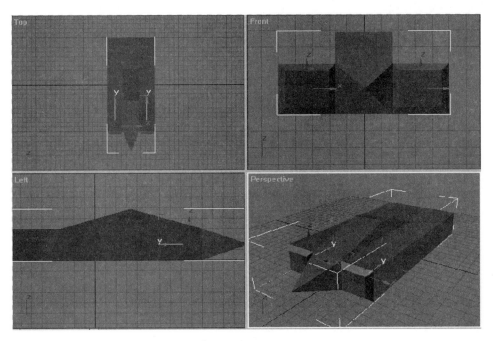

Using these simple Select, Extrude and Bevel commands virtually anything is possible. By extruding the faces of your model you can create ever–increasing detail.

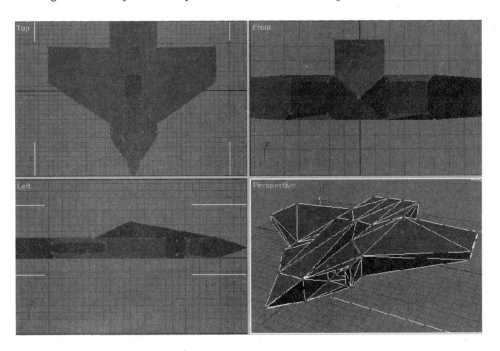

7.   Not bad, we're nearly there. The jet is, however, short of a few crucial components. Time and the Extrude command will have us airborne in no time.

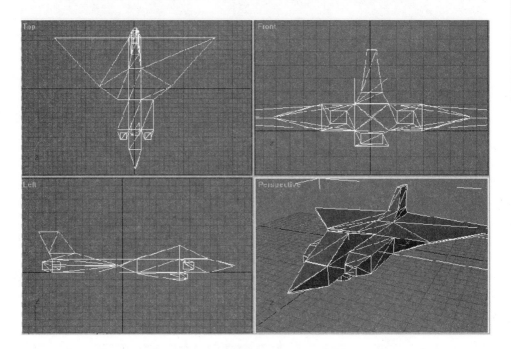

Finally, if you'd like something a little smoother, try adding the Mesh Smooth modifier to the model.

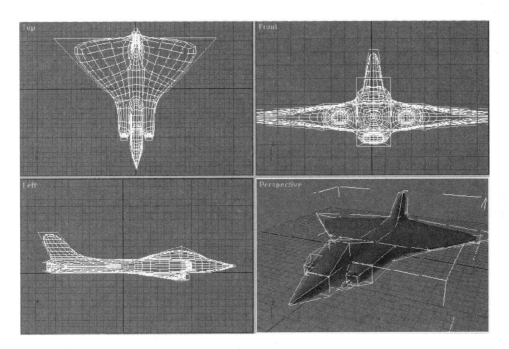

There we have it, a simple low polygon jet fighter ready for use with Director. Its low polygon count makes it ideal for the Internet, or for games.

8.   Before you can use the jet in Director you need to convert it into a suitable format (W3D). To do this in 3DS MAX you'll need the exporter plug–in, which you can download from the macromedia website at:

www.macromedia.com/software/director/3d/exporters/discreet/

Once the plug–in has been installed you can simply export your jet as a W3D Shockwave object for use with Director. As you can see, it's not hard to create a basic 3D model to begin working with. However, the surface of this model isn't particularly convincing – what it needs is a convincing look for the surface, and some lighting effects. In other words, it needs texture.

Textures and shaders

Objects in the real world are made from a combination of materials: stone, glass, metal, plastics, gas, water and so on. In order to create realistic looking images out of virtual models we have to create and specify parameters that define the look of the models' surfaces and the behavior of the light when it hits a surface.

Bitmap images can be 'wrapped' around models as textures. This is a basic but effective way to fake the appearance of materials. Of course there are plenty of other variables that play an important role in defining and simulating the look of a material: transparency, reflectivity, refraction, and specularity (shininess) and so on and so forth. The real fun starts when you begin combining parameters of different materials to create completely new ones – transparent metals, for example, or increasing the specularity of wood so that it's super–polished. In most applications you can stack textures on several layers to create real complex looking materials.

Understanding of the various wrapping modes is important when you're dealing with textures. Just as you'd need to use different approaches to wrap up a football, a shoebox or a bottle of wine, so the 3D renderer needs to know which technique to use for each object. Here're the most common ones supported by Director:

Wrap Planar

Commonly used for objects with large flat areas/planes. The texture is wrapped on the model surface as though it was being projected from an overhead projector.

Wrap Cylindrical

How you'd wrap a bottle of wine. The texture is wrapped around the surface as though the surface has been placed in the middle and the texture rolled around it to form a cylinder.

Wrap Spherical

Wraps the texture around the surface as though the surface was placed in the middle of it and then all four corners of the texture were pulled up to meet at the top. You'd choose this wrapping mode if you wanted to apply an image of the world map as an earth texture onto a sphere to form a globe.

There are special textures 'fake' wraps that you can use for real–time 3D engines to create effects that would take a long time to calculate and render if you'd used one of the methods above.

Reflection

The texture is continuously re–projected onto the surface from a fixed orientation, and doesn't rotate with the model rotates. This is good for simulating light reflected on an object by its environment

**Diffuse Light
or Specular Light**

Generates light mapping textures, simulating a soft light pointing at an area of the model without actually using an additional light source. These forms of light maps are commonly used in computer games to simulate lights or candles hanging on walls.

Textures are usually scaled to fit the whole of the object they're applied to, but if you're dealing with very large objects, or even objects of infinite size, scale–to–fit won't be too helpful. In such circumstances you can simply switch on texture repeat or tiling mode for the texture.

The definition of texture, wrapping mode, transparency setting and other light behaviors of a material, taken altogether, is called a **shader**.

Size, format and performance

As you know, Director's 3D engine is hardware accelerated. As a result, each texture used for 3D objects in Director demands a lot of memory in the VRAM of your graphics card. Textures stored there can be accessed much faster than from the normal memory. This also relieves the CPU load as the actual drawing is done by the DSP chip on the card.

A lot of today's graphics cards have 32Mb or more, but you should always develop for a lower spec machine if you want the largest possible audience for your work. Many laptops and quite a few recent Macintosh models, for example, still only have graphic cards with 8Mb or 16Mb of VRAM. A lot of this memory is used for the normal screen display, so you're left with something between 4Mb and 8Mb to store textures in. It's crucial to keep texture sizes as small as possible. Processors work with the binary system, so to increase performance make sure that your bitmap sizes are powers of 2 only: 2x2, 4x4, 8x8, 16x16, 32x32, 64x64, 128x128, 256x256, and 512x512 pixels.

> *If you're trying to use more textures in a scene than you can store in the VRAM, Director automatically goes into software rendering mode, which disables some 3D features and results in a major speed hit.*

Be careful when you're using large textures, and plan your scene beforehand. Always ask yourself if it really is necessary to, for example, use a 256x256 texture if the model it's applied to always stays far away from the camera and is very small on the screen.

Director supports textures of different bit depths. Usually you'll get the best performance with 16 bit displays and textures. While you can't easily influence the display setting of a user's machine from within Director, you can change the rendering format of textures. Here's a list of these modes supported by director:

#rgba4444	4bit red, 4bit green, 4bit blue, 4bit alpha
#rgba5550	5bit red, 5bit green, 5bit blue, 0bit alpha (alpha channel is ignored)
#rgba5551	5bit red, 5bit green, 5bit blue, 1bit alpha
#rgba5650	5bit red, 6bit green, 5bit blue, 0bit alpha (alpha channel is ignored)
#rgba8880	8bit red, 8bit green, 8bit blue, 0bit alpha (alpha channel is ignored)
#rgba8888	8bit red, 8bit green, 8bit blue, 8bit alpha

This setting can be set individually for each texture, or you can use the global rendering setting (getRendererServices().textureRenderFormat) to define the overall rendering possibilities.

Importing and controlling a 3D world in Director

If you have decided to create your 3D world outside of Director's limited primitives, and you've finished modeling, then you're ready to import it into Director. First, you have to make sure that your model has been saved in the W3D format supported by Director. The decision to create a new file format was probably not an easy one and certainly has its clear advantages, but it is also quite limiting as at the moment W3D is only supported by high-end 3D programs. This situation is changing though, and the good news is most other 3D software houses are currently working on exporters for their tools or even already have them in beta stage. For an up to date list see www.macromedia.com.

So, let's get going on a step–by–step example of importing and using our modelled fighter jet in Director. We will investigate the general structure of a 3D cast member, and work with some of Lingo's default behaviors.

Importing a 3D model

1. In your new movie select File > Import, and select the file `lowpoly_jet_final_smooth.w3d` from the CD or import your own jet.

2. Double-click the new 3D cast member to open the Shockwave 3D window. Our example world only contains the model of a fighter jet. Use the camera controls on the left to play around with the view of the 3D model.

3. At the moment the jet only has a uniform light blue tint, which doesn't look too impressive, so we'll import a bitmap to add texture the plane. Select the file jet_texture.pct from the Import dialog box.

4. We'll need to use some scripting to initialize the world to its original state and apply the imported texture. This code uses some of the new 3D Lingo statements. We'll begin by declaring a global for the plane, creating a startMovie handler, creating the reference to the 3D cast member, and resetting the world:

```
global gW3D - - reference to the 3D cast member
on startmovie
    gW3D=member("lowpoly_jet_final_smooth")
    gW3D.resetWorld()
```

We'll define the rendering format globally:

```
- - set renderformat to 16bits (5+5+5 for RGB + 1bit alpha)
getRendererServices().textureRenderFormat = #rgba5551
```

Create a new texture object and assign it our imported bitmap texture:

```
tTexture=gW3D.newtexture("metal",#fromCastmember,member
➡ ("jet_texture"))
tTexture.quality=#high
```

And then apply the texture to a shader, rather than using the default shader:

```
tShader=gW3D.newShader("sFighter",#standard)
tShader.texture=tTexture
```

We'll use the wrapPlaner wrapping:

```
- - set the correct texture wrapping
tShader.textureMode=#wrapPlanar
```

And finish up by assigning the new shader to the fighter jet model:

```
tModel=gW3D.model[1]
    tModel.shader=tShader
end
```

5. When you've finished scripting, close the script window and drag the 3D cast member into frame 2 of the channel 1 in the score.

6. Open the library palette from the window menu and drag the Hold on Current Frame behavior from the Navigation section into frame 3 of the script channel in the score window. This keeps the playback head looping at frame 3.

Time for a test run. It works all right, but all we have so far is a still image of the plane with the new texture, in the default camera angle. Not much interactivity there.

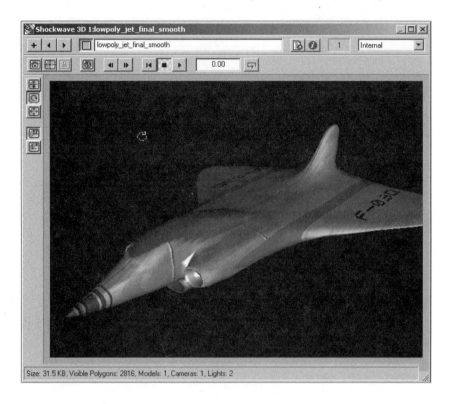

Working with inbuilt 3D behaviors

Let's use some more of Director's inbuilt behaviors to let users control the fighter's position, rotation, and zoom interactively. You'll see that the 3D behaviors in the library palette are divided into Actions and Triggers. This separation is unusual for Director, but necessary, because technically speaking behaviors can only be attached to 3D worlds and not to individual models within those worlds.

When a 3D cast member appears on stage it only occupies one sprite and you can assign as many behaviors as you wish to it. Under normal circumstances, however, you'll have more than one object within a 3D sprite and you probably want to assign different behaviors to different objects instead of having behaviors with equal impact on all models. This is where triggers and actions come in. Triggers capture certain types of events and send them on to their respective action partner. Actions themselves are separated into local, public and independent actions:

■   A **Local action** is a behavior that is attached to a particular 3D sprite and will only accept triggers attached to that same sprite.

- **Public actions** can be triggered by any sprite. You could, for example, have a button sprite to control camera rotation.

- **Independent actions** are behaviors that need no trigger at all.

Using library palette behaviors

All we need for this example are local actions and a few triggers all attached to the same 3D sprite. So, let's get back to the fighter plane movie.

1. Select the Drag Model behavior from the Actions area of the 3D behavior library palette, drag it onto the 3D sprite on the stage, and confirm that the model is not assigned to any group in the dialog box. Repeat with the Drag Model to Rotate behavior.

    We need to assign some triggers to get the behaviors to react to user interactions. Triggers wait for certain user events to occur – a mouse click on a certain model, for example, and then calls the assigned action behavior for that type of event. This gives you much greater flexibility than using preset action behaviors because you can allocate certain type of events, rather than have them hard-coded as they are in conventional Director behaviors.

2. We'll use the Mouse Left trigger and assign it to the 3D sprite. Change the last option in the dialog box that pops up, Select a Group and its Action, to Unassigned! -> Drag Model horizontal and vertical.

    > *When you attach a preset behavior from the Library, the script also appears as new cast member in the cast window. If you're going to reuse a behavior, use the behavior inspector to attach multiple instances to a sprite.*

3. Apply a couple more Mouse Left behaviors. Choose Shift Key as the modifier key and Rotate on X and Y for the first, and Drag model front to back together with the Control Key for the third.

4. Rewind the movie and press play. You can click and drag the fighter jet to move, rotate and zoom around all 3 axes.

You can also find this tutorial file on the book's CD: `fighter_nosky.dir`.

Writing your own 3D behaviors

I hope you agree, it's easy to get basic 3D action and interaction running in your own Director projects just by using a few of the preset behaviors. I really recommend that you spend some time playing with the different 3D behaviors, and looking at the code inside them to get a good feel for interactive 3D before diving into the more advanced 3D Lingo.

Without much more effort we can create a tiny handcrafted independent 3D action behavior to create a sky background for our fighter jet. In order to keep down the amount of Lingo involved, we're not going to create a terribly flexible behavior, and you won't be able to use it with any given 3D world. However, it should be more than sufficient for this tutorial.

The behavior will do two things:

- Create a very basic sky sphere for the background using a cloud texture

- Update its own position, rotation and scaling according to the settings of the fighter jet – so if the user rotates the plane, our background will rotate too. This will give us an impressive depth effect because we're working with a sphere.

Writing a 3D behavior

1. Open your fighter plane movie and import a bitmap for the cloud texture first. There's one on the CD waiting for you – file `sky_texture.pct`.

2. Select the 3D sprite, click on the plus symbol in the behavior inspector and choose New Behavior. Call it `Sky Background`. Click the script window icon to open up the script window.

3. So to the script. First we need to define a few properties for the cast member, for the sky sphere and a reference that we'll copy the transform from:

```
property pW3D
property pBackground - - model reference to the sky sphere
property pOriginal - - to copy the transform from
```

Then we'll need two handlers, the first to initialize the sky and the second to update it as we move around the plane model.

```
on beginSprite me
   createBackground(me)
   updateBackground(me)
end

on prepareFrame me
   updateBackground (me)
end
```

Next we'll set up the sky shader in the `createBackground` handler. We'll create the reference to the 3D cast member the behavior will be attached to, and set up a resource for the new model:

```
on createBackground me
    pW3D=member(sprite(me.spritenum).membernum)
    tSphere=pW3D.newModelResource("rSphere",#sphere,#back)
    tSphere.radius=500.0
```

Then we'll create the new texture using the sky image:

```
tTexture=pW3D.newtexture("sky",#fromCastmember,member
➡ ("sky_texture"))
tShader=pW3D.newShader("sSky",#standard)
tShader.texture=tTexture
```

We won't use any lighting effects on the background:

```
    tShader.ambient = rgb(0, 0, 0)
```

```
tShader.diffuse = rgb(0, 0, 0)
tShader.specular = rgb(0, 0, 0)
```

But we will use the `emissive` property. This allows us to add a light effect to the shader without affecting the lighting of the rest of the scene. We'll finish up by creating the new model and assigning the texture to it.

```
tShader.emissive = rgb(255, 0,153)
pBackground=pW3D.newModel("mSky",tSphere)
pBackground.shader=tShader
end
```

4. The `updateBackground` handler contains one line: the behavior itself. In each frame we copy the size, position and rotation of the original object, and store them within the transform property of a 3D model.

```
on updateBackground me
  pBackground.transform = pW3D.model[pOriginal].transform
end
```

5. We finish off the script by adding the standard behavior handler. This allows users to set parameters.

```
on getPropertyDescriptionList
    description = [:]
    addProp description,#pOriginal, [#default:1, #format:
    ➥ #integer, #comment:"Index of model to copy transform
    ➥ from:"]
    return description
end
```

6. Close the script window and choose Use Defaults from the dialog box that appears. Rewind the movie and press play. You should have everything working as before but this time against a dramatic sky background that moves according to the fighter jet.

If you zoom out far enough you can see how this background is working. The jet is located within the sky sphere and Director is only rendering the backside of the sphere. You can find this tutorial file on the CD as well: `fighter_sky_finished.dir`.

Summary

We've covered a lot of ground here. Hopefully you have a better idea of how 3D graphics work in general, as well as how 3D in Director 'sees' and works with models you create. There's nothing particularly difficult about it, once you understand the mechanisms that are going on behind the scenes. We've also done a little work with some of Director's inbuilt behaviors. If you've some time on your hands, check out the code inside these – they should help you create your own behaviors with the minimum effort. Finally, we created a little behavior to use with the model we've worked with in the chapter. I hope you've seen how relatively easy working with 3D in Director is!

I'd like to leave you with some of the books I've found most useful in understanding the mathematics behind 3D graphics and animation.

Mathematics for Computer Graphics Applications: An Introduction to the Mathematics and Geometry of Cad/Cam, Geometric Modeling, Scientific visualization
by Michael E. Mortenson

3D Graphics Programming: Games and Beyond
by Sergei Savchenko

Geometric Modeling
by Michael E. Mortenson

chapter 6

chapter 8

Chapter 7
Director's
3D Engine

For some time now the Director community has been developing and working with 'fake' 3D using all sorts of ingenious methods. We'll begin this chapter by looking at some of the approaches people have used, and we'll build a simple 3D engine that creates an idea of depth. We'll go on to investigate the intricacies of Director's 3D engine, and then rework our initial example using it. As any Director developer will tell you reworking code is a daily experience for the multimedia developer, so revisiting the first project and rewriting sections of it will demonstrate an approach to this common procedure, but more importantly, illustrate the simplicity of the new 3D engine.

By the end of this chapter you should be familiar with the workings of the 3D engine and have seen what many of the 3D Lingo commands can do. Although we will discuss some math along the way, I hope you'll find that it's more important to be precise in the way you use commands than it is to have an in–depth knowledge of complex math.

3D in Director before 8.5

After working in Director for a while, shifting sprites from left to right, scrolling them up and down, and bouncing them off the edges, most Lingo addicts will start to yearn for a little perspective and depth. They'll start making sprites vanish into fake distance by reducing their size, blurring them into oblivion, and fading them into a washout melting pot, while picking their brains for that long gone math lesson. After weeks of trawling through books and across the Internet, and getting excited about a few good resources they've found, the intrepid developer will begin to ask the unnerving question: "What will I do with all this?"

> *It's truer with 3D than with anything else in Director: only good ideas combined with good technical skill produce great work.*

Up until Director 8.5 all 3D work done in Director relied on Lingo engines using the Director architecture. Most of the early work used a simple sine / cosine function to position and scale cast members in sprites in Director. You did run into problems if sprites with lower numbers passed in front of sprites with higher numbers, because there was no `locZ` (Z location of sprite) available. There were two ways around this. The more true to life version went through a tedious process of checking the depth of each asset on the stage, depth–queuing everything visible, and rearranging it in a front to back order in the sprites of the score. The 'lazy' version was to adapt the interface so that depth–queuing didn't become an issue, using similarly colored assets and transfer controls to fade the back sprites and create an illusion of distance. Some even used multiple versions of a sprite asset with crisp and blurred effects, increasing the blur according to the distance the asset was supposed to be from the viewer. Developers were prepared to go through a lot in order to prevent depth–queuing because it demanded a lot from the processor, and was tough to figure out.

Problems and solutions

These early engines still only allowed the developer to produce 2D sprites that floated around in a 3D space. Nowadays these are called 'billboards' or 'face–forward planes' and you often have to fiddle around to get the effect in modern 3D engines. In those days it was the closest you could get to 3D until quads appeared in Lingo. With the quad Lingo property the sides of a sprite's bounding box didn't need to run parallel anymore, so it was suddenly possible to distort them into polygons or 'fake' triangles where two of the four corners of the sprite's bounding box were the same.

This created all sorts of mayhem in the Director community and soon new Lingo 3D engines began to appear in the open source community. As 3D engines use triangles to create 3D models, wise coders started porting the complicated math of such engines to Lingo. These new engines still suffered from the strain such math put on the processing power. It was possible to create 3D models with a very low polygon count and move them around in Director, but that was about all that the engine could handle.

Another distinction between two different approaches to creating 3D engines in Lingo for Director is the use of matrixes – or lack of it. Matrix math is complex and most developers without a scientific or math background will shy away from it, but engines that don't use matrixes suffer limitations. First of all, although the math seems more complex, calculating many different points and their movement in 3D first often reduces the amount of processing involved later on. Furthermore, a certain sequence of pivoting movements becomes impossible without the use of matrix math because of gimble lock.

With the arrival of both the `locZ` sprite property and the quad sprite property in Director 7 new Lingo 3D systems started to appear on the Internet. Some were free and others were shareware. These systems used primitives like planes, spheres and doughnuts, (also know as toroids) rather than just forward facing sprites, and because they were built from polygons, and each polygon needed its sprite, they were made up of hundreds of sprites. The accomplishment was amazing, even if the resulting 3D engine was slower than a hardware accelerated one will ever be. T3D (www.theburrow.co.uk/t3Dtesters/) and Dave's 3D engine (www.dubbus.com/devnull/3D/) are just two such examples.

Che Tamahori (www.sfx.co.nz/tamahori/home/) is one of the first open source developers I encountered on the Internet. He lead by example when he published his early Shockwave work with accompanying explanations and code. One of the sections of his website, 'How to cook 3D in Director', describes in detail how to recreate one of his 3D Shockwave pieces.

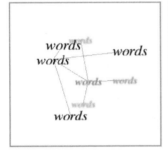 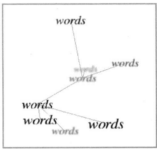 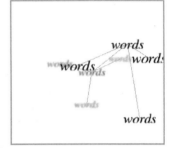

The code Tamahori writes essentially goes through four stages. First he describes a set of points and registers them in the 'mind space' three–dimensional coordinate system. Then he checks for any change that should be applied to the system. He uses the mouse location to move the coordinates, so he checks the mouse location and deduces the change that needs to be applied to the entire coordinate system, and applies it to the 'mind space', transforming all the coordinates to their new locations. Only then does he calculate the way any assets related to these coordinates should be represented on the stage. This is what I describe as translating from the 'mind space' to the 'screen space'.

Tamahori creates the illusion of distance by reducing the size of assets that are at a further depth in his mind space coordinate system. He also sets the blend of the sprites attached to coordinates further down the Z–axis to strengthen the illusion. Using this method to visualize his coordinate system allows him to bypass the complex Z–queuing system (at the time he published this code, Director did not incorporate the sprite property `locZ`.) He also uses a set of graphics that vary from sharp to blurred and assigns them to a sprite depending on how far along the Z–axis the sprite is in the mind space coordinate system. Clever!

Lingo 3D engines: an example

Here is some code I developed after playing around with the code examples Che has on his site. The bits of code I will show are different to the ones on his site because I added in my own stuff, and because Director has introduced more Lingo commands since then. We'll be delving deeply into this example, and after we have looked at the new Shockwave 3D engine, we'll rebuild it with new 3D Lingo. You'll be amazed at how much better it is.

The project I will describe here is based upon a Shockwave navigation system. It was developed for www.vaionet100.com and can still be seen in their archive at www.vaionet100.com/en/topics/006.

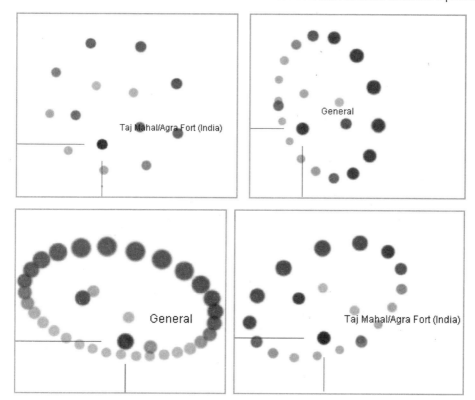

The main bits of Che's engine are here. Instead of setting the mind space coordinates from a text cast member as he does on his site, I calculate the positions using the number of points needed and a radius to spread them in a circle around a midpoint. Once they are there I check the influence from the mouse position and then pass this data to the 3D calculator and transforming method. After changing all the positions I use a method to translate all mind space coordinates into screen space coordinates, and finish off with a loop that checks for changes, transforming the points in mind space into screen space coordinates. That is basically it.

Creating our own 3D engine

1. So, let's begin setting everything up. Start up a new movie and set your stage to 300 by 300. Double–click frame 4 of the script channel in the score and call hInit between the on exitframe and end lines.

```
on exitFrame me
  hInit()
end
```

2. Now open frame 5 of the same channel and enter the following:

```
on exitFrame me
  hRun()
  go the frame
end
```

3. Next you'll need an asset. You can either create it in an outside application and import it, or just make it in Director. I'm using a fuzzy ball made out of a 32–bit Photoshop graphic. The Photoshop asset uses an alpha channel, which allows clean, anti–aliased overlay of gradient edged assets. Name the cast member you use ball to stay coherent with my program.

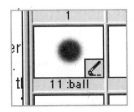

4. We'll add four text fields to the stage, two of which need to be editable, and a button. Put them up at the top of the stage as the balls will be flying around the center.

    Call the first editable field radius and the second editable field balls. Add field member radius into sprite channel 1 and field member balls into sprite channel 2. The text of the non editable text fields should read radius: and balls: Add them into sprite channels 3 and 4 and align them.

    The button should have the text go on it, or something similar, and should be in sprite channel 5. Don't worry about the fact that my screen shows '10' and '100' in field members 'radius' and 'balls'.

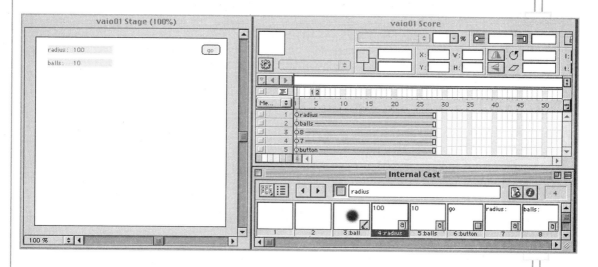

5. Finally, you need a 1–pixel placeholder. Create this in the paint window by making a dot with the pencil tool, and making sure that its registration point is off the visible part of our stage. The placeholders are only there to hold the places of our flying balls – we don't want them to be seen.

6. Open the movie properties in the property inspector and set the score channels field to 320. Now drop the placeholder in all sprite channels from 10 to 310.

7. Open the control panel (shortcut CTRL-2 or APPLE-2) and set the tempo to 999. That's it; we are ready to write some code.

The main movie script

8. Open a new movie script window from the window menu (CTRL-0 or APPLE-0) and call it main. This is where our main two handlers, hInit and hRun, will live. A few more handlers and functions will reside here as well, because they will be needed to help these two main handlers.

Start out by declaring the global variables we need for this program. We will need a list to hold our point objects, gPointList, and a center point to offset all the points from in our screen space coordinate system. To determine this point we will use an X and a Y coordinate, gXoff and gYoff.

In modern 3D terms the position and perspective of the users view is usually described and set as a camera. We will use values gDepth and gZoom to control the perspective and the distance from the center point of our world.

The center point of our mind space is (0,0,0): 0 in the X–axis, the Y–axis and the Z–axis. While our center point in the screen space is determined by gXoff and gYoff, Z is missing. You can already see that some translating will be needed.

We'll need another global variable to keep track of the sprite number of the sprite that we are assigning, so we know which sprites are still available. This will be gUseSprite. We'll use gSpeed to determine the sensitivity of our interface, to allow us to adjust how fast the model spins according to how far the cursor is from the center of our screen space. So, altogether we have:

```
global gPointList
global gXoff
global gYoff
global gDepth
global gZoom
global gUseSprite
global gSpeed
```

9. Now let's initialize these globals with values and instantiate our objects. (We have not defined our classes or parent scripts yet, but we can start thinking about what we'll need them to do and the arguments we should pass to them).

    To do this we need to start coding the hInit handler. We'll set up our variables and objects and prepare our program to enter a constant 'run' loop. The hInit handler is only called once, while the hrun handler is called on every frame update.

    ```
    on hInit

    end
    ```

10. Declare the gPointList global variable as a list, gPointList = []. Because we set the stage to 300 by 300, gXoff and gYoff global variables will be 150 and 150; they represent the center of the intended screen space. Through fiddling with the system I've found that a good set of initial values for gDepth and gZoom is gDepth = 750 and gZoom = 250:

    ```
    gPointList = []
    gXoff = 150
    gYoff = 150
    gDepth = 750
    gZoom = 250
    ```

    > *Try your own values once the program works: you can get some quite interesting results.* gDepth *and* gZoom *control the distance of our viewport to the objects and the distortion of the lens we use to view them. Lens, in this case, is used to describe a distortion through perspective.*

11. Set the global variable gUseSprite to equal 0 as we haven't used any sprites for the model yet. We have used some for the interface, but they are static so they won't be assigned and reassigned during the running of this program – we're using gUseSprite

for this. I suggest you start by setting the global variable gSpeed to 0.0005. This makes the interaction tangible without making the entire interface sluggish. Again, try different values once you've got it all working:

```
gUseSprite = 0
gSpeed = 0.0005
```

12. We want the interface to reflect the initial values we're using to start the program, the default values. Set up two local variables lStartRadius = 100 and lStartBallCount = 10.

```
lStartRadius = 100
 lStartBallCount = 10
```

We'll pass them to the entry fields by converting their values to strings and setting the field members' text to those strings:

```
sprite(1).member.text = string(lStartRadius)
sprite(2).member.text = string(lStartBallCount
```

Finally initiate the instantiation process by passing these values as arguments to a handler called hSpread. This handler takes two arguments, the first being the number of balls you are going to use, and the second being the radius you would like the circle of balls to use. Your hInit handler should look like this:

```
on hInit

   gPointList = []
   gXoff = 150
   gYoff = 150
   gDepth = 750
   gZoom = 250
   gUseSprite = 0
   gSpeed = 0.0005


   lStartRadius = 100
   lStartBallCount = 10

   sprite(1).member.text = string(lStartRadius)
   sprite(2).member.text = string(lStartBallCount)

   hSpread(lStartBallCount,lStartRadius)

end
```

Placing the balls

1. Now we need the hSpread handler, so add this to our script:

    ```
    on hSpread passBallCount, passRadius

    end
    ```

    This handler will use a function to help it calculate the offsets of coordinates in the mind space so that all the points we get are spread around a central point equally. It receives a radius and an angle and returns a Cartesian coordinate. It is a useful little function that transforms polar coordinates to Cartesian coordinates.

2. Let us create this function:

    ```
    on hCalcPos   passRadius, passAngle

    end
    ```

3. The function receives two arguments and uses these to calculate the coordinate it returns. The main calculation is done in the following lines of code:

    ```
    Xnew = integer((passRadius*cos(passAngle)-
    ➦ passRadius*sin(passAngle)))
    Ynew =
    ➦ integer((passRadius*sin(passAngle)+passRadius*cos(passAngle)))
    ```

4. All we need to do now is make a point object out of the two local variables Xnew and Ynew, and return it to line of code initiated the function:

    ```
    return(point(Xnew, Ynew))
    ```

    The finished function should look like this:

    ```
    on hCalcPos   passRadius, passAngle
      Xnew = integer((passRadius*cos(passAngle)-
      ➦ passRadius*sin(passAngle)))
      Ynew = integer((passRadius*sin(passAngle)+
      ➦ passRadius*cos(passAngle)))
      return(point(Xnew, Ynew))
    end
    ```

5. Let's go back to the hSpread handler. We need to find the average angle between the balls for the number amount of balls in the circle. For this we'll use a local variable, Ang, equal to two *pi* divided by the number of balls.

    ```
    Ang = ((2*pi)/passBallCount)
    ```

6. Since we are going to use the `hSpread` handler more than once we must make sure that every time it is used the sprites are reset to our initial placeholder asset member, and all the objects that have been birthed are eliminated. Once we are sure all the objects have been disposed of we can reset our list to empty. We'll go through the list, resetting every object's sprite member back to the placeholder. By setting the value of a position in a list of instances to 0 the object is disposed of. As we are repeating through a list of instances we just need to set the current position's value to 0. Once we exit this repeat loop and are sure all objects are eliminated, we reset the list to be empty.

```
repeat with X in gPointList
    sprite(X.mysprite).member=  member("placeholder")
    X = 0
  end repeat

  gPointList = []
```

7. The next step is to carry on instantiating instances of the parent script (we'll create this later) for the number of balls we want to spread around a central point. These instances are placed in `gPointList`. We will pass the birthing handler of each instance of the parent script the arguments that will customize each one of them.

Start by setting up the repeat loop.

```
repeat with X = 1 to passBallCount
end repeat
```

8. Create a local variable inside this repeat loop called `tempAng` to multiply the `Ang` variable we defined earlier by the current X value (representing the current ball in the list of balls). Get a value for a local variable called `temp` by passing the radius `hSpread` received as an argument and `tempAng` to the function `hCalcPos`.

```
tempAng = Ang * X
temp = hCalcPos(passRadius,tempAng)
```

9. Now we can set up some of the variables we will pass onto the handler birthing instances of our parent script. Create a local variable called `passSprite`. By checking how many objects already exist in `gPointlist` and adding 10 to that amount we will get the next usable sprite number, (remember the balls will be in channels starting from 10.)

```
passSprite = gPointList.count + 10
```

10. Set up a local variable called `passMem`. Give this local variable the `membernum` of our `ball` cast member.

```
passMem = member("ball").membernum
```

11. Set up three local variables, calling them passX, passY, passZ. Give passX the X coordinate you received from the hCalcPos function, and give passY the Y coordinate you received from the hCalcPos function. Set passZ to 0 because we want to spread the coordinated in the XY plane first:

```
passX =    temp[1]
passY =    temp[2]
passZ =  0
```

12. Now create an instance of a parent script called point and add it to gPointList. Pass it all the following variables as arguments: passSprite, passMem, passX, passY, passZ, gXoff, gYoff, gDepth, gZoom, passRadius. Make sure you pass the arguments in the order you want to receive them later on in the birthing handler of your parent script.

```
gPointList.add(new(script"point", passSprite, passMem,
➡ assx, passy, passz, gXoff, gYoff, gDepth ,gZoom, passRadius))
```

Your hSpread handler should look like this:

```
on hSpread passBallCount, passRadius

  Ang = ((2*pi)/passBallCount)

  repeat with X in gPointList
    sprite(X.mysprite).membernum = member("placeholder")
    X = 0
  end repeat

  gPointList = []

  repeat with X = 1 to passBallCount
    tempAng = Ang * X
    temp = hcalcPos(passRadius,tempAng)
    passSprite = gPointList.count + 10
    passMem = member("ball").membernum
    passX =    temp[1]
    passY =    temp[2]
    passZ =  0
    gPointList.add(new(script"point", passSprite, passMem,
      ➡ passX, passY, passZ, gXoff, gYoff, gDepth ,gZoom,
      ➡ passRadius))
  end repeat
end
```

Controlling the balls

Let's write the point parent script that this handler will create instances from next.

1. Open a new script window, change its cast member properties to a parent script, and call the script `point`.

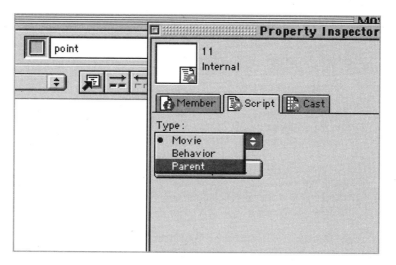

2. First of all declare the properties we will need our instance to have: `mySprite` to hold the instance's sprite number, `myMem` to hold the instance's cast member number, `myX`, `myY`, and `myZ` to hold the instances mind space X, Y, and Z coordinates, and `myRad` for using the radius to determine the max depth so that we can get a good blending effect:

```
property mySprite
property myMem
property myX
property myY
property myZ
property myRad
```

These properties are initialized in the birthing handler of the parent script. Every time an instance of the script is created, it is birthed using the birthing handler. The difference between the instances is created by the difference in arguments passed to each instance. A simple birthing handler looks like this:

```
on new me, arg01, arg02, etc
    return me
end
```

The birthing handler is similar to our `hInit` handler in that it is called on only once during the existence of an instance of an object. It is the handler that initializes the object.

4. We need to receive the arguments passed to our birthing handler in the same sequence they are sent to us in so that we can make sense of the incoming values.

```
on new me, passSprite, passMem, passX, passY, passZ, passRad
```

Once we have received the values we use them to set up our properties. We will be using these properties in more than one method.

```
myMem = passMem
myX = passX
myY = passY
myZ = passZ
myRad = passRad
```

Finally we initialize our sprite, but we send it off stage because we have not yet calculated a proper screen space coordinate for it. The birthing handler should look like this:

```
on new me, passSprite, passMem, passX, passY, passZ, passRad
  mySprite = passSprite
  myMem = passMem
  myX = passX
  myY = passY
  myZ = passZ
  myRad = passRad
  sprite(mySprite).locH = -200
  sprite(mySprite).locV = -200
  sprite(mySprite).membernum = myMem
  return me
end
```

The two important things that point needs to be able to do are move in mind space and represent itself in screen space. We will create two methods for this purpose.

5. Since we are moving by rotating around a central point, let's call this method mRotate me. We will pass the method an argument for it to use to calculate the change of position in mind space. In the parent script you need:

```
on mRotate me, passPoint

end
```

This is where we start using some of the code inspired by Che Tamahori. It's a simple variation on the math he first published, but the influence his open source has on this project goes much further than just introducing me to this equation. It really is the structure of code that helped me on more than anything. Thanks, Che.

Given an xAngle, and yAngle of change, and a position in space from an X, Y, Z coordinate, the following calculation changes the position accordingly. It's true that as this deformation leaves the model lost in space the initial position cannot be regained, but that is not of importance in this routine.

```
tempzpos = Z * cos(xAngle) - X * sin(xAngle)
X = Z * sin(xAngle) + X * cos(xAngle)
Z = Y * sin(yAngle) + tempzpos * cos(yAngle)
Y = Y * cos(yAngle) - tempzpos * sin(yAngle)
```

6. Let's add this to our method to complete it:

```
on mRotate me, passPoint
  xAngle = passPoint[1]
  yAngle = passPoint[2]
  tempZpos = myZ * cos(xAngle) - myX * sin(xAngle)
  myX = myZ * sin(xAngle) + myX * cos(xAngle)
  myZ = myY * sin(yAngle) + tempZpos * cos(yAngle)
  myY = myY * cos(yAngle) - tempZpos * sin(yAngle)
end
```

7. The second method we need will set our sprite on the stage, translating our mind space coordinates to screen space. Let's call the method mDraw me. We need to pass it four arguments from the main movie script; gDepth, gZoom, gXoff, and gYoff.

```
on mDraw me, passDepth, passZoom, passXoff, passYoff

end
```

8. We use these arguments to translate mind space coordinates to screen space. First of all we need a scalar, defined by dividing the zoom by the sum of the instance's Z position and gDepth (in this case passDepth, because that is the name of the argument used to receive gDepth). We need the resulting value to be a floating point number, not an integer.

```
scalar =  float(passZoom/ (myZ+passDepth))
```

9. Now we use this scalar on our mind space X and Y coordinates. Since the center of the mind space system is 0,0,0 we need to apply the resulting X and Y coordinates to our screen space center point (gXoff, gYoff). Having passed those values as arguments, we create these four lines of code:

```
xp = myX * scalar
yp = myY * scalar
sprite(mySprite).loch = xp + passXoff
sprite(mySprite).locv = yp + passYoff
```

10. We need to use the scalar again to modify the width and height of the sprite we use to represent our ball asset. Sprites further away in the distance will become smaller, to increase the impression of depth.

```
sprite(mySprite).width = member(myMem).width * scalar
sprite(mySprite).height = member(myMem).height * scalar
```

11. We will also use the blend of sprite (sprite(spritenum).blend) to increase the impression of depth. The range of the blend is from 0 to 100, and we will use the percentage of depth of a point's Z coordinate from the overall maximum depth, using the radius supplied to us. We will use the same procedure to determine the locZ of the sprite.

Use a local variable named toblend to determine the percentage of the Z coordinate from the total depth possible. To be sure that the blend doesn't make the sprite too transparent we set the lowest value to 30, and to make sure sure it doesn't exceed 100 we set it to 100 if it exceeds 99.

```
toblend = (((myRad - myZ)/(myRad * 2)) * 100 )

if toblend < 30 then
   toblend = 30
else if toblend > 99 then
   toblend = 100
end if

sprite(mysprite).blend = toblend
sprite(mysprite).locz =   myRad*2 - myZ
```

The final mDraw me method should look like this:

```
on mDraw me, passDepth, passZoom, passXoff, passYoff
  scalar =   float(passZoom/ (myZ+passDepth))
  xp = myX * scalar
  yp = myY * scalar
  sprite(mySprite).loch = xp + passXoff
  sprite(mySprite).locv = yp + passYoff
  sprite(mySprite).width = member(myMem).width * scalar
  sprite(mySprite).height = member(myMem).height * scalar

  toblend = ( ((myRad - myZ)/(myRad * 2)) * 100 )

  if toblend < 30 then
     toblend = 30
  else if toblend > 99 then
     toblend = 100
  end if

  sprite(mysprite).blend = toblend
  sprite(mysprite).locz =   myRad*2 - myZ
end
```

User interaction

1. Now we've finished the `point` parent script we can finish off the `main` movie script. There are two things missing: the `hRun` handler and a function to take care of checking the mouse position in respect to the central point of our screen space. We need to add the factor `gSpeed` to the equation to give the mouse checking procedure some scalability.

Let's start by creating the function and calling it `hCheckMouse`.

```
on hCheckMouse

end
```

2. We need two local variables to calculate the distance from the mouse position to our center point in X and Y. They should also be influenced by our `gSpeed` variable. Our mind model is inverted, so we need to reverse the values we get from checking the distance on the Y-axis by multiplying by −1. Then all we need to do is return these values, so we'll store them in a point object that we'll return to the line of code that initiated the function. So our handler becomes:

```
on hCheckMouse

    localX =  float((the mouseh - gXoff)*gSpeed)
    localY =  -float((the mousev - gYoff)*gSpeed)

    return point(localX, localY)

end
```

3. So finally we come to the `hRun` handler. Start by creating the handler itself.

```
on hRun

end
```

Remember the principles of Tamahori's code. All we need to do is check for influence, and then use the result of that check to calculate change and translate the current state from mind space to screen space. We have set everything up that will enable this procedure.

4. To check for influence we set a local variable `tempDisplace` to the result of our `hCheckMouse` function.

```
    tempDisPlace = hCheckMouse()
```

5. Now we need to pass that influence to the calculating code of each instance of `point`. To do this we use the `call` Lingo command to call on the `mRotate` method in each instance in the list and pass it `tempDisplace`:

```
call(#mRotate, gPointList,tempDisPlace)
```

6. We'll use the same procedure to call on the mDraw method for all instances of the point parent script in gPointList. We will pass it gDepth, gZoom, gXoff and gYoff as arguments so that it can use these values to calculate the points screen coordinates.

```
call(#mDraw,gPointList,gDepth, gZoom, gXoff, gYoff)
```

The hrun handler looks like this:

```
on hRun
   tempDisplace = hCheckMouse()
   call(#mRotate, gPointList,tempDisplace)
   call(#mDraw,gPointList,gDepth, gZoom, gXoff, gYoff)
end
```

Finally, remember the go button you created right at the start? That button needs coding so that you can change the ring of balls according to the input you type into the fields.

8. Open the cast window from the window menu and select the go button cast member. Open the cast member script window by clicking on the cast member script icon at the top right of the cast window. If the mouseUp handler is missing, write it in:

```
on mouseUp

end
```

9. We need to check that the input in the fields can be used. If it is useless we need to ignore it, but if it is useful we need to respond. We'll begin by checking to see if it is useful. Let's check that the content of the radius and the balls fields is numeric rather than text or symbols. If it is something we can't use then we'll return without it:

```
if voidp(sprite(1).member.text.value) then return
if voidp(sprite(2).member.text.value) then return
```

10. Now let's make an integer out of the input of the balls field so that we're not trying to work with fractions. (We can't use fractions of balls.) We also check out the local variable lRadius.

```
lRadius = sprite(1).member.text.value
lBalls = integer(sprite(2).member.text.value)
```

11. We must also check that the text in the balls field does not exceed the number of sprites we have allocated for it (300) and that it is not less than 1. lRadius cannot be less than 1 either.

```
if lBalls < 1 or lBalls > 300 then return
if lRadius < 1 then return
```

12. If all these conditions are fulfilled then we can call the hSpread handler with lBalls and lRadius as arguments:

```
hspread(lBalls,lRadius)
```

13. The final cast member script for the go button cast member should look like this:

```
on mouseUp

    if voidp(sprite(1).member.text.value) then return
    if voidp(sprite(2).member.text.value) then return

    lRadius = sprite(1).member.text.value
    lBalls = integer(sprite(2).member.text.value)

    if lBalls < 1 or lBalls > 300 then return
    if lRadius < 1 then return

    hspread(lBalls,lRadius)

end
```

That should be it. Your program should work fine now. If you are experiencing problems, please have a look at the vaio01.dir on the CD that comes with this book. Save your completed movie, because we'll be returning to it and upgrading it later on the chapter. First, though, we'll have a look at Director 8.5's new 3D engine.

3D in Director 8.5

As you'll be only too aware by now, Director 8.5 has been fitted with a full 3D engine that makes it possible for users to develop and engage in three–dimensional space within their projects *without* the need to figure out tedious mathematical equations.

The preceding exercise should have given you some idea of how much of the 3D code we used to create actually concentrated on getting an engine to work, never mind the project itself. With the arrival of 8.5 developers don't need to occupy themselves with the interior workings of the engine; in theory, all you need to figure out is how to use the engine with the commands available to create the results you want. However, you'll find it much easier to implement the flexibility that some of these commands bring with them for manipulating an entire 3D scene if you do understand something of what's going on. So let's take a look at how this addition has been implemented in Director 8.5.

The Shockwave 3D world

While Director 8.5 is a big step forward for the Director developer community, it's not a drastic change in terms of the program as whole. The other features of the environment and its workings have remained intact, so all movies made in earlier versions should still function correctly in 8.5.

> *This is important: it means that Director's principle functionality has not been altered to accommodate working in 3D space, but that the functionality needed has been implemented on top.*

The 3D engine is an extra, and a Shockwave 3D cast member is just another asset format that can be used in Director. To use the asset in a project it must be brought into the score either by hand or by Lingo. Every sprite that you place the Shockwave 3D cast member into becomes an instance of that 3D scene. You can view the same scene from different cameras in the different sprites. So let us have a look at a Shockwave 3D asset.

The model

1. Open the cast window and select an empty cast member. Open the Shockwave 3D asset window from the windows menu. If you look at your cast now you will see the Shockwave 3D cast member. If you close the Shockwave 3D asset window, the cast member disappears. To stop this from happening, give the member a name before closing the Shockwave 3D asset window.

2. Let's create a Shockwave 3D cast member using Lingo. Open the message window, type in following code and hit return:

    ```
    temp = new(#Shockwave3D, member(10))
    ```

    If you've still got your cast window open you'll see that you have a new Shockwave 3D cast member in what was an empty window at member 10. (If your cast window was closed, open it. The new cast member should be there.)

    > *Use the message window to test Lingo commands. Use it a lot! You will learn a lot and save valuable time.*

3. Let's give the cast member a name. Try this our in the message window:

    ```
    temp.name = "3Dscene"
    ```

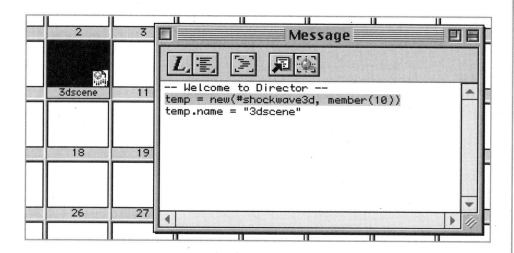

4. Let us examine our new member 3Dscene. We can use the Shockwave 3D window, the message window and the property inspector. Open the Shockwave 3D window for member 3Dscene by double–clicking on the cast member. At the bottom of the window you can see that the scene is quite empty. There are 0 visible polygons and 0 models, but we do have a camera and two lights. Not much to look at there.

5. Let's use Lingo to create a simple shape. Open the message window and write:

   ```
   put temp
   ```

   If put returns a void then you have lost the link between the variable temp and the Shockwave asset, so you need to write

   ```
   temp = member("3Dscene")
   ```

   And hit return. Then try again. The put statement should return the following:

   ```
   - - (member 10 of castLib 1)
   ```

   The message window tells you that the variable temp is currently set to store member 10 of castLib 1.

6. On a new line in the message window type in res = . Leave the right side of the equation blank for the moment. You'll seen the icon for categorized Lingo at the top of the message window:

Click on it to access Lingo commands by category. Let's use it now. Select 3D>3D Member Palettes>newModelResource(). This will come up in your message window:

```
res = member(whichMember).
➥ newModelResource("resourceName", modelType)
```

> *Use the categorized Lingo menu as much as possible when you're learning new Lingo commands, to check how exactly a command should be written and what arguments it expects.*

All we need to do is fill in the blanks and hit return. Put `temp` instead of `member(whichMember)`. Now replace `"resourceName"` with `"ball"` and `modelType` with `#sphere`. The line should now look like this:

```
res = temp.newModelResource("ball", #sphere)
```

Once your line is correct hit return.

8. There isn't anything to see yet because we might haven't actually added a sphere to our scene yet, merely the possibility of a sphere. Let's refine it a bit. Type `res.radius = 30`. Our 3D scene now has a model resource to call on.

> *Model resources are raw 3D shapes that can be used on their own or in combination to create 3D models. A 3D scene can harbor a multitude of model resources, but they are only visible when a model is using them. They are resources that a model uses to take form, so they can be used by a multitude of models, over and over again.*

9. Let's create a simple model. Type `mdl = temp.newModel("ball")`. Still nothing. This is because we need to give the model a model resource for it to know what it actually is.

So let's do that. Write:

```
mdl.resource = res.
```

Now, if you look at the 3Dscene in the Shockwave 3D asset window, you'll see a sphere in the center. The window also tells us that 874 visible polygons and one model are present in the scene.

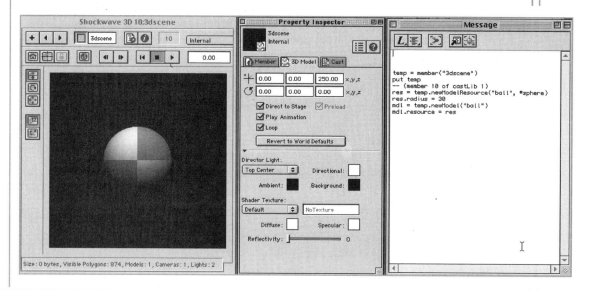

Surface issues

1. Let's texture the sphere. Import an image (bitmap) or if you want to use mine, use
joelsface.pct (this example is 3DMovemenet.dir on the CD). If you're using your
own image, you'll need to call it joelsface for the purpose of this exercise.

2. Type in:

```
tex =
```

Leaving the right side of the equation blank again, go to the categorized Lingo pull
down menu and chose 3D>3D Member Palettes again. This time select newTexture().

The line looks like this:

```
tex = member(whichMember).newTexture("whichTexture", type, source)
```

3. Again, we need to fill in the appropriate data. Replace member(whichMember) with
temp, "whichTexture" with "joelsface", type with #fromCastMember, and
source with member("joelsface"):

```
tex = temp.newTexture("joelsface", #fromCastMember,
➥ member("joelsface"))
```

Having a texture is not enough. We still have work to do. We need a shader to add this
texture to. A shader describes the quality of the surface of a model that the texture is
applied to; it determines if the surface is dull or reflective, rough or smooth.

4. Type `shd =` and use the categorized Lingo menu again to collect `newShader` from the 3D>3D Member Palettes category:

    ```
    shd = member(whichMember).newShader("whichShader", shaderType)
    ```

5. By filling in `temp` for `member(whichMember)`, `"faceShader"` for `"whichShader"` and `#standard` for `shaderType` we transform the line to:

    ```
    shd = temp.newShader("faceShader", #standard)
    ```

    Hit return.

6. Now all we need to do is hand the texture to the shader and attribute the shader to the model. This should do the trick:

    ```
    shd.texture = tex
    ```

    Hit return and then:

    ```
    mdl.shader = shd
    ```

    The sphere in the Shockwave 3D asset window should now be textured with the image of cast member `joelsface`. If it isn't, and the window was open during your coding in the message window, it might not have been updated so close the Shockwave 3D window and open it up again.

    The sphere should be textured with the image. Here are all the lines that we used, including Director's responses, in the message window:

    ```
    temp=new(#Shockwave3D,member(10))
    temp.name="3DScene"
    temp=member("3DScene")
    put temp
    - - (member 10 of castLib 1)
    res = temp.newModelResource("ball", #sphere)
    res.radius = 30
    mdl = temp.newModel("ball")
    mdl.resource = res
    tex = temp.newTexture("joelsface", #fromCastMember,
    ➥ member("joelsface"))
    shd = temp.newShader("faceShader", #standard)
    shd.texture = tex
    mdl.shader = shd
    ```

Exploring our world

Now we've got something to work with in the 3D scene, let's have a closer look at what's going on.

1. Open the Shockwave 3D asset window for member 3Dscene if it's not already open, the property inspector, and then the message window. Now explore the 3D scene by using the Dolly Camera, Rotate Camera and Pan Camera options on the left hand side of the Shockwave 3D window. You can select any of the options and by clicking and dragging on the scene.

    It might look like you're moving the object, but you're really moving the camera. You can tell because the shades on the object don't change, so it's actually staying in the same position with regard to the light.

    Let's check out the other buttons. Check the values for the camera position and camera rotation in the property inspector before doing the following.

2. Rotate the camera so it is looking at the model from badly illuminated angle and press the Set Camera Transform button.

    The face of the object is suddenly illuminated. Note that the values for camera position and rotation in the property inspector have changed.

3. Now move the camera around a bit more using pan, dolly and rotate. This time hit Reset Camera Transform.

    The camera scene jumps back to the position you last pressed Set Camera Transform in. Now if you hit Revert to World Defaults in the property inspector the camera position goes back to 0,0,255 and the camera rotation goes back to 0,0,0, but the scene stays the same. You need to hit Reset Camera Transform again to get the camera to jump to these values. You should have the scene set as it was at the very beginning.

    By playing around like this you can familiarize yourself with the 3D features of a Shockwave 3D scene. One thing you've probably noticed is the changes in lighting. Let's examine them a bit. We will use the message window for this.

4. Our camera should be at its original position. If not, press Revert to World Defaults in the property inspector and then the Reset Camera Transform button in the Shockwave 3D window. Let us find out what lights we have in the scene and where they are positioned.

    Type this into the message window and hit return:

    ```
    temp = member("3Dscene")
    ```

Now type this:

```
put temp.light[1]
```

You get the response:

```
- - light("UIAmbient")
```

6. Now try:

```
put temp.light[1].type
```

You get the message - - #ambient back. Do the same for light [2]. The second light is called "UIDirectional" and its type is #directional.

7. Now let us ask for the positions of the two lights. Try this out:

```
put temp.light[1].transform.position
```

Do the same for light [2]. Light one is positioned in the center of the world, vector (0,0,0) whereas light two, the directional light, is positioned at vector (0.0000, 176.7767, 176.7767).

8. If we test our model's position in the scene by writing:

```
put temp.model[1].transform.position
```

We get the same position as the ambient light, light [1].

Remember that if we moved the camera to an angle that obscured the model and hit Set Camera Transform the model suddenly seemed to be lit up again. Let us try that and see if the directional light, light [2], moves.

9. In the Shockwave 3D window, move the camera with dolly, rotate and pan so that the model is seen from an angle that nearly covers it with darkness.

Write put temp.light[2].transform.position in the message window.

Now hit Set Camera Transform in the Shockwave 3D window. Try:

```
put temp.light[2].transform.position
```

Compare the returned vectors. The light has changed position, hence the lighting up of the model. Your text in the message window, before and after hitting Set Camera Transform, should look something like this:

```
put temp.light[2].transform.position
- - vector( 0.0000, 176.7767, 176.7767 )

put temp.light[2].transform.position
- - vector( -202.6008, -272.2190, 103.6426 )
```

We have done all this without even running a movie, without writing a handler and without using a behavior. Working with the interface like this is a great way to explore the huge number of new Lingo commands pertaining to the 3D features in Director. You don't have to launch yourself into complex projects to learn the fundamentals of how a Director 3D scene works and behaves.

How the Shockwave 3D asset works

What have we learned so far about the Shockwave 3D asset? We have seen that most of the process of creating and changing values takes place inside the Shockwave 3D cast member. It gets stocked up with model resources, models, textures, shaders, lights and cameras. They need to be assembled in a specific order. Let's look at the order and hierarchy of the elements that makeup the use of the 3D engine in Director. You'll have seen some of this at work in the previous chapter, but running over it here should help clarify what you were doing there, and solidify the concepts you need to handle 3D in Director confidently.

We need at least one **camera**, as a **viewport**, inside a Shockwave 3D member so that when we bring the scene onto the stage using a sprite we can see it through the camera. We can have multiple instances of the same scene in different sprites on the stage and they can all be looking at the scene through different cameras, or we can use the different viewports of different cameras set in a scene to jump in between views inside the single sprite.

We need lights in the scene so that we can see the models that we place into the scene. The lights determine the visibility and mood of the scene, and without them we can't see the models. Good lighting design can be very important to the atmosphere of a scene in 3D.

A model is a container for a **model resource**. It's one instance of a model resource, stored in the member. The model resource determines the shape of the model. For example, imagine we load a model resource into a member that is a juggling ball. We want three juggling balls in the scene, so we create three models and assign as their resource our juggling ball resource.

The resource determines the shape of the model, but not the surface. The surface of a model is determined by its **shader**. The shader determines how the surface reflects light. The default shader is photorealistic. A shader helps make a model look like it is made of a certain material, plastic, clay or brass for example.

Textures are assigned to a shader. The textures are 2D images that are drawn onto the surface of a 3D model using a shader. You can combine up to eight textures to create the surface of a model.

Models, lights and cameras can be assigned into **groups**. Groups can even be reassigned to other groups. This creates a hierarchy that allows for objects to animate *on their own and in a group* at the same time. The highest level group is called group("world"). Group("world") is another way of expressing the entire scene, or even the member itself.

Rendering methods

Finally let's have a look at the engine itself. One of the main advantages of the Director 3D engine over former Lingo based engines is its capability to access hardware and modulate its rendering method accordingly. This allows the processing of the 3D scene to go much faster and therefore gives us higher quality 3D renditions at greater frame rates. The rendering methods are:

Auto rendering

The #auto rendering method leaves it up to Director to determine the best method according to the hardware and drivers information available on the client machine. Although #auto is accurate most of the time, sometimes it will find it difficult to determine the presence of a driver or device, particularly when drivers or software have been faultily installed. Wherever possible you should try to determine the render method in advance.

OpenGL

The #openGL method should be used when openGL drivers are used to access a hardware accelerator device. OpenGL acceleration is common on both Windows and Macintosh computers.

DirectX7_0

The #directX&7_0 method should be used when DirectX7_0 drivers are being used to access a hardware accelerator device. DirectX acceleration is only available on Windows computers.

DirectX5_2

The #directX&5_2 method should be used when DirectX5_2 drivers are used to access a hardware accelerator device, again DirectX acceleration is only available on Windows computers.

Software rendering

The #software method should be used if you need to render without hardware acceleration. The #software renderer is built into Director, so no driver or hardware detection needs to take place.

Creating a model and moving it with Lingo

Now we've had a look at some of the workings of Director 8.5 3D, let's go back to our first example. We created a simple 3D engine and used it to create a simple immerse toy. Since then we have tested a few ways of communicating with the Director 3D engine and created a simple 3D scene.

So, we'll learn how to use the 3D engine with simple models created inside it and animated using Lingo. Let's go back to the toy we built with our simple engine and recreate it using Director 3D.

Remaking the model in 8.5 Lingo

1. Open the vaio01.dir movie from the CD, save it under a new name. Consider for a moment what we will need to change to use the Director 3D engine instead of its custom Lingo one.

2. Since we are going to use real spheres instead of the blurred dot, you can begin by deleting the ball cast member first. Replace it with a member called ball that you will use as a texture for your spheres. Any image will do; if you don't have one to import, just make one in Director in the paint window.

3. Since the mDraw and the mRotate methods of the point class are the major components of our custom 3D engine we might as well scrap the entire class. Delete the point parent script from the cast.

Let's start by commenting out the bits of code we won't need anymore. As the global variables are declared right at the beginning of main, we'll start with them.

4. We won't need gPointList any more, since we will not be birthing instances of the parent script point ever again. Variables gDepth and gZoom can go as well, because we have binned the engine that used these variables to render to screen. Finally we can comment out gUseSprite, since our scene is going to be contained in one sprite. We will need to add a global variable called g3D. This variable will be used to refer to our 3D scene or Shockwave 3D cast member.

5. Let's doctor the hInit handler. We can comment out all the initialization lines for gPointList, gDepth, gZoom and gUseSprite. Let's change gYoff just a bit, so that our Shockwave 3D asset doesn't cover our interface. Set gYoff to equal 180. You also want to set gSpeed to 0.05 since 0.0005 will be to slow in this interface.

6. Now we can create our Shockwave3D scene. First of all we need to create a new Shockwave 3D cast member by adding the code:

```
g3D = new(#Shockwave3D)
```

We should set the background of our new cast member to the color of the stage, which is white:

```
g3D.bgcolor = rgb(255,255,255)
```

7. We'll use sprite channel 10 to host our 3D scene. Let's prepare its location before introducing the scene to prevent a nasty jump at the beginning of the movie:

```
sprite(10).loc = point(gXoff,gYoff)
```

Now that the sprite is set to the right position, we can insert the 3D scene:

```
sprite(10).member = g3D
```

Leave the rest as it is. We'll make some more changes further down the line.

Your global variable declaration and your hInit handler should look like this:

```
- - global gPointList
global gXoff
global gYoff
- - global gDepth
- - global gZoom
- - global gUseSprite
global gSpeed
global g3D
```

continues overleaf

```
on hInit

    - - gPointList = []
    gXoff = 150
    gYoff = 180
    - - gDepth = 750
    - - gZoom = 250
    - - gUseSprite = 0
    gSpeed = 0.05

    lStartRadius = 100
    lStartBallCount = 10

    sprite(1).member.text = string(lStartRadius)
    sprite(2).member.text = string(lStartBallCount)

    g3D = new(#Shockwave3D)
    g3D.bgcolor = rgb(255,255,255)
    sprite(10).loc = point(gXoff,gYoff)
    sprite(10).member = g3D

    hspread(lStartBallCount,lStartRadius)

end
```

As we are using the hSpread handler in conjunction with the hCalcPos handler to create the circle of spheres, we should have a look there next. The hCalcPos handler is not changed at all, since it is only used to return values that are then required to create the even circle of spheres. First, though, we'll make some amendments to hSpread.

8. Let's start by commenting out the redundant code. We can lose the loop used to clear the objects in gPointList. Comment out the following lines:

```
    - - repeat with X in gPointList
    - -     sprite(X.mysprite).membernum = member("placeholder")
    - -     X = 0
    - - end repeat
    - - gPointList = []
```

9. We can also get rid of the entire instantiation process used to fill the gPointList with instances of the point parent script. We need to hang onto this repeat loop because we still want to spread the given amount of balls around a central point using the given radius. You can comment out the following lines:

```
    - -     passSprite = gPointList.count + 10
    - -     passMem = member("ball").membernum
    - -     passX = temp[1]
    - -     passY = temp[2]
    - -     passZ = 0
```

```
- -    gPointList.add(new(script"point", passSprite, passMem, passX,
- -    passY, passZ, passRadius))
```

10. Now we can start adding the lines that will create our circle of balls in the g3D Shockwave cast member. First of all let us reset the g3D cast member's values to default, just in case something has slipped. Add g3D.resetworld() to the top of the hSpread handler.

> To create a full textured model in a 3D scene in Director we need a model resource that determines the model's shape, a shader that determines a model's way of reflecting light, at least one texture to that determines the models surface appearance and a model to contain all of these.

Creating the model resource

1. Create a model resource in our 3D scene by adding:

   ```
   res = g3D.newModelResource("ball", #sphere)
   ```

   Create the new texture:

   ```
   tex = g3D.newTexture("alpha", #fromCastMember, member("ball"))
   ```

   Then the new shader:

   ```
   shd = g3D. newShader("phot",#standard)
   ```

   And add the texture to the shader:

   ```
   shd.texture = tex
   ```

   We still need to specify the radius of the spheres that our model resource will create.

   ```
   res.radius = 30
   ```

   We leave Ang =((2* pi) / passBallCount) the way it is, because it produces the angle needed for our calculations in the hCalcPos function.

   We need to do a bit of tweaking to the camera to make sure it is set up to see our scene. We need to pull the camera back from the scene and perform a translation on it with a positive value in the Z–axis.

   > In Director 3D the X–axis goes from left to right the Y–axis from bottom to top and the Z–axis from far away to nearer to us. This is also the positive direction of the axis.

So, if I translate the camera with a positive value in the Z–axis, it will move in the direction toward me, moving itself further away from the center of the world, which is vector(0,0,0).

2.   Set the camera to look at vector(0,0,0). The camera is now looking at the center of the world of our 3D scene:

```
g3D.camera[1].translate(0,0,700)
g3D.camera[1].pointat(0,0,0)
```

Now we can rewrite the loop that calculates positions for the spheres and sets them up.

3.   We will need the temp value returned to us from the hCalcPos function, as we did before, so we leave the two first lines in the loop as they are. Every time round the loop we receive a new position from the hCalcPos function, so we need to create a new model each time and place it at this position in the scene (above the functions we commented out in there earlier).

```
it = g3D.newModel("ball" & X)
```

We should also apply a model resource and a shader to this new model.

```
it.resource = res
it.shader = shd
```

4.   A new model is always placed in the center of the world when it is created, by default, so we need to move it to the position we want:

```
it.translate(temp[1], temp[2],0).
```

So finally, the hSpread handler should look like this:

```
on hSpread passBallCount, passRadius

    g3D.resetworld()
    res = g3D.newModelResource("ball", #sphere)
    tex = g3D.newTexture("myText", #fromcastmember, member("ball"))
    shd = g3D.newShader("phot", #standard)
    shd.texture = tex
    res.radius = 30
    Ang = ((2*pi)/passBallCount)
    g3D.camera[1].translate(0, 0, 700)
    g3D.camera[1].pointat(0,0,0)

    -- repeat with X in gPointList
    -- sprite(X.mysprite).membernum = member("placeholder")
    -- X = 0
    -- end repeat

    -- gPointList = []
```

```
repeat with X = 1 to passBallCount
  tempAng = Ang * X
  temp = hcalcPos(passRadius,tempAng)
  it = g3D.newModel("ball" & X)
  it.resource = res
  it.shader = shd
  it.translate(temp[1], temp[2], 0)

  - -      passSprite = gPointList.count + 10
  - -      passMem = member("ball").membernum
  - -      passX =    temp[1]
  - -      passY =    temp[2]
  - -      passZ =  0
  - -      gPointList.add(new(script"point", passSprite,
  - - passMem, passX, passY, passZ, passRadius))
end repeat
```

```
end
```

Let's move onto the two remaining handlers, hRun and hCheckMouse. The hCheckMouse handler is not useful to us anymore because we don't need to retrieve the difference in position of the cursor to the center of the screen to pass it on to a complex handler that calculates rotation. All we need to do is check the difference in position and ask the camera to move appropriately. Spinning the camera is simpler than moving the model in this case.

5. So, let's comment out everything in the hRun handler, since we don't want to use hCheckMouse, and gPointList doesn't exist anymore.

```
on hRun
  - -      tempDisplace = hCheckMouse()
  - -      call(#mRotate, gPointList,tempDisplace)
  - -      call(#mDraw,gPointList,gDepth, gZoom, gXoff, gYoff)
end
```

Since we are not calling hCheckMouse anymore, we might as well leave it as it is.

6. Now let's write some new code for the hRun handler.

We need to check the difference between the position of the cursor and the center we describe by gXoff and gYoff. The values that we get should be multiplied by the scaling value of gSpeed, so that we can tweak the sensitivity of the interface later on.

```
localXmov = (the mouseh - gXoff) * gSpeed
localYmov = (the mousev - gYoff) * gSpeed
```

7. These local variables need to be passed to the camera in our 3D scene for it to move accordingly. There's something a bit surprising about this. The syntax to send to the

camera would be: *member.object.translate(X,Y,Z)* so logically we should write g3D.camera[1].translate(localXmov, localYmov, 0).

Instead, though, we need to write:

```
g3D.camera[1].translate(localYmov, localXmov, 0,\
g3D.group("world"))
```

> *The X and the Y values are inversed because a move on the X–axis in screen terms is in fact a move on the Y plane in the 3D engine. You should refer back to the chapter on the principles of 3D worlds for more this. Again we see an example of the difference between mind and screen space.*

Using the final 0 for Z makes sure we are mapping our circle of balls on a flat plane, since all the coordinates are Z for the Z–depth. You need to make sure the camera is translating relative to the world, and not itself. If you do not add g3D.group("world") at the end you'll see that the camera starts spinning on itself as the circle of balls flies past your view. Try it for a laugh! The final hRun handler should look like this:

```
on hRun
    localXmov = (the mouseh -gXoff) * gSpeed
    localYmov = (the mousev -gYoff) * gSpeed
    g3D.camera[1].rotate(localYmov,localXmov,0,g3D.group\
    ("world"))
- -    tempDisplace = hCheckMouse()
- -    call(#mRotate, gPointList,tempDisplace)
- -    call(#mDraw,gPointList,gDepth, gZoom, gXoff, gYoff
end
```

To finish off your movie, run through it and delete the redundant code – but be careful! Once your scripts are cleaned up, save the movie and then try some more stuff out. Add different textures, or try different movements to the camera, the lights, the objects and the groups.

More Essential 3D Lingo

Let's look at some more of the 3D Lingo commands you can use to manipulate 3D scenes:

Translation

A translation is a movement of the specified object in the direction determined by the passed values. If you translate an object by the vector [0,0,1] by writing

```
member.object.transform.translate(0,0,1)
```

The object will move 0 units on its X, 0 units on its Y–axis and 1 unit on its Z–axis.

This means the movement is relative to its own rotation in the world, as long as no other `relativeTo` node is supplied. If you wrote:

```
member.object.transform.translate(0,0,1, member.group("world"))
```

Then the object will move 0 units on the world X–axis, 0 units on the worlds Y– axis and 1 unit on the worlds Z–axis.

Note: You can omit referring to the transform of the object and just write

```
member.object.translate(xIncrement, yIncrement,
 ➡ zIncrement, relativetoNode)
```

But since the `transform` of an object is the *accumulation* of changes, position, scale and rotation, it actually helps for the sake of clarity to refer to the transform of a node.

The `pretranslate` command adds the incremental movement of a node to the beginning of the stack of translations, rotations and scaling to be executed on the node. Other than that it is the same as the `translate` command.

We refer to the stack when we are speaking about a sequence of translations and rotations. The sequence in which changes are executed on a node is extremely important. Just stand up for a moment and take a big step forward. Now turn around 180 degrees. Remember your position and orientation. Go back to the exact position you begun and carry out the exercise again, but this time inverting the order of execution. Rotate 180 degrees on take a big step forward. Do you see the difference?

Rotation

The `rotate` command performs a rotation of the specified object in the angle determined by the passed values. If you rotate an object by the vector [0,0,1] by writing:

```
member.object.transform.rotate(0,0,1)
```

Then the object will rotate 0 units about its X–axis, 0 units about its Y–axis and 1 unit about its Z–axis.

In terms of rotation, units refer directly to degrees, where 360 degrees make up one revolution. This means the rotation is relative to its own position and rotation in the world, as long as no `relativeTo` node is supplied.

If you write

```
member.object.transform.rotate(0,0,1,member.group("world"))
```

Then the object will rotate 0 units about the world's X–axis, 0 units about the worlds Y–axis and 1 unit about the worlds Z–axis.

You can omit referring to the `transform` of the object by just writing:

```
member.object.rotate(xIncrement, yIncrement, zIncrement,
➡ relativetoNode)
```

The `prerotate` command adds the incremental rotation of a node to the beginning of the stack of translations, rotations and scaling to be executed on the node. Other than that it is the same as the `rotate` command.

You can get, as well as set, the position property of:

```
transform (member.object.transform.position)
```

By setting it, the vector you specify becomes the position of the object in relation to its parent.

Similarly you can get as well as set the rotation property:

```
transform (member.object.transform.rotation)
```

Setting it, the vector you specify becomes the rotation of the object in relation to its parent.

You can also get and set the `transform` of an object. The default transform is the identity matrix. We'll talk a bit more about matrix math below. All the changes applied to the position, scale and rotation of an object are calculated through this matrix. This is how you would go about setting an object's matrix:

```
t= transform()

t[1]  =value
t[2]  =value
t[3]  =value
t[4]  =value
t[5]  =value
t[6]  =value
t[7]  =value
t[8]  =value
t[9]  =value
t[10] =value
t[11] =value
t[12] =value
t[13] =value
t[14] =value
t[15] =value
t[16] =value

member.object.transform() = t
```

The Matrix

So what's the effect of a matrix then? Well, good question. Let's talk about math. It's helpful to understand matrices, but you don't have to understand them to code for the Director 3D engine. (Although it'll help when your work starts getting really complex.)

In actual fact, all a matrix really represents is a two–dimensional array. Imagine a list of lists, something like this:

```
myMatrix = [[1,2,3],[4,5,6],[7,8,9]]
```

It's a two–dimensional array. To write this list of lists as a matrix we would write:

```
myMatrix = | 1 2 3 |
           | 4 5 6 |
           | 7 8 9 |
```

It is important to be consistent about the order of the lists. The lists inside the bigger list should represent rows, because convention has it that a position in a matrix is addressed first by its row position and then by its column position. For example, if we refer to the integer 6 in the above matrix, it would be addressed as *myMatrix[2][3]*. Let's try it out:

Matrices in the message window

1. Open the message window from the window menu, and create a variable, m, to hold a linear list:

    ```
    m= []
    ```

2. Create three more variables holding linear lists filled with integers, called X, Y and Z:

    ```
    X = [1,2,3]
    Y = [4,5,6]
    Z = [7,8,9]
    ```

3. Add the lists X, Y and Z to m:

    ```
    m[1] =x
    m[2] =y
    m[3] =z
    ```

4. Check out the two–dimensional array m, using put m.

    Now, to test that the rows precede columns in our notation, try out put m[2][3]. The position we are looking for is in row 2 and in column 3. As we can see from our matrix above, this position should be filled with the value '6'. The put m[2][3] command should return 6.

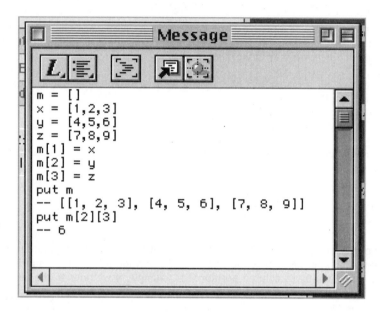

Being able to access positions is important for calculations being performed on a two –dimensional array. Matrices are useful for exactly that: performing operations like addition, subtraction, multiplication and division.

> *In terms of 3D graphics, it is common to use either 3x3 or 4x4 matrices. A 3x3 matrix has 3 rows and 3 columns, whereas a 4x4 matrix has 4 rows and 4 columns. The difference is really the processing intensity and the possible manipulations. Director 8.5 uses 4x4 matrices.*

We use matrices to express changes we want to perform on coordinates in our 3D world, and as containers for combining such expressions. There are set matrices for translating and rotating coordinate vectors, and these matrices can be concatenated, in order of transformations, by multiplication. When you've finished working with them, you apply the result to the coordinate you want to be transformed.

Another advantage is that you can apply such a container matrix to a set of coordinate vectors, then add more rotations and translations to the container matrix and apply it to another set of coordinate vectors. Sound pretty complicated, I know. Let's step back and explain slowly.

Remember what an identity element is in math? The identity element of a multiplication or division is 1, whereas the identity element of an addition or subtraction is 0. If you add 0 to 2 the result stays at 2, and if you divide 2 by 1 the result stays 2. The identity element is defined as a value used in an operation on an operand that results in the operand itself. The same can be said about the identity matrix. It is a matrix that, when another matrix M is multiplied by it, results in matrix M.

> *It is important to remember that matrix multiplication is not commutative, so matrix m multiplied by matrix m2 is NOT equal to matrix m2 multiplied by matrix m.*

The identity matrix for a 3x3 matrix system looks like this:

```
im = | 1 0 0 |
     | 0 1 0 |
     | 0 0 1 |
```

5. Let's create our identity matrix in the message window:

```
im = [[1,0,0],[0,1,0],[0,0,1]]
```

The rule of thumb used to multiply matrices is *multiply row into column and sum the result*.

We'll fill a new two–dimensional array, nM using our 3x3 matrix m and multiplying it by the identity matrix im.

```
nM = | 1 2 3 |              | 1 0 0 |
     | 4 5 6 |        X     | 0 1 0 |
     | 7 8 9 |              | 0 0 1 |
```

6. We'll create a function, mConcat(m, im) in a movie script, where m is the matrix to be multiplied by im:

```
on mConcat m,im

  NewMatrix = []
  NMRowOne = []
  NMRowOne[1] = (m[1][1] * im[1][1]) + (m[1][2] * im[2][1])
  ➥ + (m[1][3] * im[3][1])
  NMRowOne[2] = (m[1][1] * im[1][2]) + (m[1][2] * im[2][2])
  ➥ + (m[1][3] * im[3][2])
  NMRowOne[3] = (m[1][1] * im[1][3]) + (m[1][2] * im[2][3])
  ➥ + (m[1][3] * im[3][3])

  NMRowTwo = []
  NMRowTwo[1] = (m[2][1] * im[1][1]) + (m[2][2] * im[2][1])
```

continues overleaf

```
➡ + (m[2][3] * im[3][1])
NMRowTwo[2] = (m[2][1] * im[1][2]) + (m[2][2] * im[2][2])
➡ + (m[2][3] * im[3][2])
NMRowTwo[3] = (m[2][1] * im[1][3]) + (m[2][2] * im[2][3])
➡ + (m[2][3] * im[3][3])

NMRowThree = []
NMRowThree[1] = (m[3][1] * im[1][1]) + (m[3][2] * im[2][1])
➡ + (m[3][3] * im[3][1])
NMRowThree[2] = (m[3][1] * im[1][2]) + (m[3][2] * im[2][2])
➡ + (m[3][3] * im[3][2])
NMRowThree[3] = (m[3][1] * im[1][3]) + (m[3][2] * im[2][3])
➡ + (m[3][3] * im[3][3])

NewMatrix[1] = NMRowOne
NewMatrix[2] = NMRowTwo
NewMatrix[3] = NMRowThree

return NewMatrix
end
```

7.   Compile your script. If you now pass this function our matrix m and the identity matrix im it should return the same matrix as m. Try this out in the message window :

```
nM= mConcat(m,im)

put nM
```

It's getting complex again, but hang in there. If we now use the Identity matrix as a basis and perform concatenations (multiplications) of rotation or translation matrices on it, we get a matrix to use on a coordinate vector that will change its position and rotation according to our series of instructions. It's even more important to understand that you can use the matrix at any given point and still add changes to it for a further set of coordinates. This is the hierarchical element in 3D that is aided by matrix math.

On top of this all elements in a 3D world can use their own matrix that can then be used in combination with other objects matrices. As an example, objects in a scene will move and rotate, but the camera can move and rotate as well. When combining the matrix of an objects world space and the cameras matrix the resulting matrix describes the view that should be used to render the scene from that camera.

> *The order in which manipulations are performed on a matrix is of importance. As mentioned earlier multiplication of matrices is not commutative. That means given a matrix mA and a matrix mB, mA X mB is NOT equal to mB X mA. It is also important to understand that the order of rotations and translations is important for the outcome. This order is referred to as the stack, as mentioned earlier.*

The line of lingo code `t = transform()` initializes our variable `t` with an identity matrix. If we apply this identity matrix to a coordinate vector, the coordinates will not change. But if we concatenate the identity matrix `t` with translation and rotation matrices, the resulting matrix represents an entire set of instructions to perform on one or many coordinate vectors.

8. We can check on the matrix `t` above in our message window:

```
t = transform()

put t
```

You should get:

```
- - transform(1.00000,0.00000,0.00000,0.00000,
➡ 0.00000,1.00000,0.00000,0.00000,  0.00000,0.00000,
➡ 1.00000,0.00000,  0.00000,0.00000,0.00000,1.00000)
```

So you can see that this is the identity matrix:

```
| 1  0  0  0 |
| 0  1  0  0 |
| 0  0  1  0 |
| 0  0  0  1 |
```

Instead of being a list of lists, it's represented by a linear list with 16 positions. This is possible as long as the engine used to calculate the concatenations of matrices takes into account that position 5 in the list is actually position [2][1], and so on. This is possible if all matrices used in the system are 4 X 4 matrices.

Hey, stack

Let us just try to illustrate the idea of a stack.

1.   Put this in the message window:

```
t = transform()

t.rotate(0.3, 0, 0)

put t
```

This is what you should get:

```
- - transform(1.00000,0.00000,0.00000,0.00000,
  0.00000,0.99999,0.00524,0.00000, 0.00000,
  -0.00524,0.99999,0.00000, 0.00000,0.00000,0.00000,1.00000)
```

It's a transformed matrix.

2.   Now write:
```
t.translate(0,20,0)

put t
```

We get:

```
- - transform(1.00000,0.00000,0.00000,0.00000,
  0.00000,0.99999,0.00524,0.00000, 0.00000,
  -0.00524,0.99999,0.00000, 0.00000,20.00000,0.00000,1.00000)
```

3.   If you now try the two in the opposite order, first translating and then rotating, you get:

```
- - transform(1.00000,0.00000,0.00000,0.00000,
  0.00000,0.99999,0.00524,0.00000, 0.00000,
  -0.00524,0.99999,0.00000, 0.00000,39.99945,0.20944,1.00000)
```

Quite a different matrix. If you applied these two different matrices to a model in a scene with Lingo, you would get a different outcome each time.

That's as far as we will go with matrix math in this chapter.

Transformations

Let's create a little exercise movie to test these movement commands. We will race through this section because you've seen it all before:

1. Import the `joelsface.pct` file from the CD (or use your own, just call it `joelsface` in the cast).

2. Make a 1–pixel placeholder asset and offset its registration point. Put this placeholder cast member into sprite channel 1.

3. Double–click on frame 5 of the script channel in the score and call `hInit` in the `exitframe` event

   ```
   on exitframe me
               hInit()
   end
   ```

4. Double–click on frame 6 in the same channel and call `hRun` and `go the frame` between the `on exitframe me` and `end` lines.

   ```
   on exitframe me
               hRun()
               go the frame
   end
   ```

5. Create a movie script and declare global variables `gPosTest` and `gSwitch`. As you may have gathered from these global variables names, we are going to use them to test and set the position of a model. We will use the `gSwitch` variable to switch between adding or subtracting from `gPosTest` to achieve a movement backwards and forwards along a path.

6. Now create our initializing handler:

   ```
   on hInit

   end
   ```

7. Initialize `gPosTest` to 100. This is just a value we are going to use to move our mode. Initialize `gSwitch = -1`. You will see what `gSwitch` is doing when we come to implement it in the handler.

8. Create a new Shockwave 3D scene in cast member 11 and cast the new 3D scene onto the stage.

   ```
   it = new(#Shockwave3D,member(11))
   sprite(1).member = it
   ```

9. We'll create a sphere, so we need a resource first, and then we can set its size.

```
rez = it.newModelResource("ball", #sphere)
rez.radius = 30
```

10. We'll create a box as well, and set its size.

```
rez02 = it.newModelResource("box", #box)
rez02.height = 30
rez02.width = 30
rez02.length = 30
```

11. Now we need a texture, tex, and a shader, shd, for our objects, and to attribute our texture to our shader:

```
tex = it.newTexture( "joelsface", #FromCastMember,
➡ member("joelsface"))
shd = it.newShader("phot", #standard)
shd.texture = tex
```

12. Now we can create our models. First create the sphere and apply the shader.

```
mdl = it.newModel("ball")
mdl.resource = rez
mdl.shader = shd
```

And then the box:

```
mdl02 =it.newModel("box")
mdl02.resource = rez02
```

13. Now we need to attribute our shader to each one of the six sides of the box by using the shaderList.

Create a repeat loop with x = 1 to 6. Inside the loop we'll fill each position in the shaderList corresponding to a side of the box with our shader, shd.

```
repeat with X = 1 to 6
  mdl02.shaderlist[X] = shd
end repeat
```

Your script window should look like this:

```
global gPosTest
global gSwitch


on hInit
  gPosTest = 100
```

```
gSwitch = -1
it = new(#Shockwave3D, member(11))
sprite(1).member = it

rez = it.newModelResource("ball", #sphere)
rez.radius = 30

rez02 = it.newModelResource("box", #box)
rez02.height = 30
rez02.width = 30
rez02.length = 30

tex = it.newTexture("joelsface", #FromCastMember,
➡ member("joelsface"))
shd = it.newShader("phot", #standard)
shd.texture = tex
mdl = it.newModel("ball")
mdl.resource = rez
mdl.shader =shd
mdl02 = it.newModel("box")
mdl02.resource = rez02
repeat with X = 1 to 6
  mdl02.shaderlist[X] = shd
end repeat

end
```

Moving the objects

1. Let's create our hRun handler and start moving these objects around.

```
on hRun

end
```

We'll just add some movement commands to switch around and comment out so we can get familiar with all the things happening in the scene. Let's try to move an object's absolute positions first of all by using the global variables gPosTest and gSwitch.

2. Write an if statement that tests the value of gPosTest. If it is smaller than –100 set gSwitch to 1, but if it is higher than 100 set gSwitch to –1.

```
if  gPosTest < -100 then
    gSwitch = 1
else if gPosTest > 100 then
    gSwitch = -1
end if
```

Then increment gPosTest by gSwitch. This statement will bounce an object back and forth along a path using a positive or negative increment. I am going to apply gPosTest to the X,Y, Z values of a transform command on a model. So that the model doesn't move too far to be seen I'm using 100, which is not too big, but not so small that it can't be seen on the screen.

```
if  gPosTest < -100 then
    gSwitch = 1
else if gPosTest > 100 then
    gSwitch = -1
end if
gPosTest = gPosTest + gSwitch
```

3. Now set the sphere's position to gPosTest on the X–axis, Y–axis and Z–axis:

```
member(11).model[1].transform.position =
➥ vector(gPostest,gPostest,gPostest)
```

If you run the movie, the sphere should be traveling away from the camera and then coming back to a position behind and on top of the camera, and the box staying steady in the center of the stage.

4. Now add these in, and experiment with the values, commenting individual lines out and seeing how the movie is affected:

```
member(11).model[2].rotate(0,2,0, #self)
member(11).model[2].rotate(0,0,10, #world)
member(11).model[2].translate(0,0.3,0, #self)
```

We'll add some movement to the camera and the lights.

5. Add this line to the hRun handler:

```
member(11).camera[1].rotate(1,0,0, member(11).group("world"))
```

Since this line uses *relativetonode*, the object that the rotation is being performed on should revolve around it rather than spinning around its own center point. So the camera will rotate one degree around the X–axis of the world center point of member 11.

6. Now add:

```
member(11).light[2].transform.position =
➥ member(11).camera[1].transform.position + vector(10,10,0)
```

This result of this command can be obtained in one of two ways. We could use the hierarchy and set the camera to be the light's parent, but we have chosen to calculate the light's position relative to the camera. We set the light's position to be offset from the camera's position by a adding a vector to the camera's position. Wherever the camera moves, the light will be right next to it.

7. Finally, we'll add a central light:

```
member(11).light[2].pointat(0,0,0)
```

This line makes sure the light is shining at the center of the world.

Altogether, our hRun handler should look something like this:

```
on hRun

    if  gPosTest < -100 then
    gSwitch = 1
    else if gPosTest > 100 then
    gSwitch = -1
    end if
    gPosTest = gPosTest + gSwitch

member(11).model[1].transform.position =
➥ vector(gPostest,gPostest,gPostest)

    member(11).model[2].rotate(0,2,0, #self)
    member(11).model[2].rotate(0,0,10, #world)
    member(11).model[2].translate(0,0.3,0, #self)
    member(11).camera[1].rotate(1,0,0, member
    ➥ (11).group("world"))

    member(11).camera[1].rotate(1,0,0,
    ➥ member(11).group("world"))
    member(11).light[2].transform.position =
    ➥ member(11).camera[1].transform.position + vector(10,10,0)
    member(11).light[2].pointat(0,0,0)
    end
```

Try commenting out and adding bits to test the movement. As you can see movement using the Director 8.5 engine has less to do with calculating complicated math, but it is giving precise directions.

Modifiers

One final element of this new engine I would like to discuss is the notion of modifiers. A modifier is there to control the way a model animates or how it is rendered. A modifier is attached to a model using the addModifier command. Once it has been added, the program can interact with it via Lingo. Let us explore this feature a little by using the collision modifier.

Collision course

Let us modify the example above to implement collision detection and reaction.

1. To the bottom of the hInit handler add:

```
mdl.addmodifier(#collision)
mdl02.addModifier(#collision)
```

These are our two collision modifiers for the models in our scene. Now we can use Lingo to interact with them.

2. You need to set the modifiers up with a few lines of code. We want the models to allow collisions to be detected, so we need to add the lines:

```
mdl.collision.enabled = true
mdl02.collision.enabled = true
```

If we set the collision.enabled to false the modifier would ignore any collision involving this model, regardless of whether was its own modifier or one attached to another model.

3. We want the models to stand still if they collide so that they don't melt into each other and interlock. To do this we'll need to let the modifier resolve the collision event. This means that when a collision is detected, the objects that collide will stop any movement, whether it's rotation or translation:

```
mdl.collision.resolve = true
mdl02.collision.resolve = true
```

If we left these as false then the collision between the objects would be detected but the would go on passing through each other regardless.

4. Now all we need to decide what the modifier should do when a collision is detected. We'll invoke the hCollide handler from within the main script, when a collision is detected (if you haven't called your script main, now would be a good time to do that!):

```
mdl.collision.setCollisionCallBack(#hCollide, script("main"))
```

The hInit handler should now look like this (I've ordered by collision detection code according to model):

```
on hInit
  Postest = 100
  gSwitch = -1
    it = new(#Shockwave3D, member(11))
```

```
sprite(1).member = it

rez = it.newModelResource("ball", #sphere)
rez.radius = 30

rez02 = it.newModelResource("box", #box)
rez02.height = 30
rez02.width = 30
rez02.length = 30

tex = it.newTexture("joelface", #FromCastMember,
➥ member("joelsface"))
shd = it.newShader("phot", #standard)
shd.texture = tex
mdl = it.newModel("ball")
mdl.resource = rez
mdl.shader =shd
mdl02 = it.newModel("box")
mdl02.resource = rez02
repeat with X = 1 to 6
  mdl02.shaderlist[X] = shd
end repeat

mdl.addModifier(#collision)
mdl.collision.enabled = true
mdl.collision.resolve = true
mdl.collision.setCollisionCallback(#hCollide,
➥ script("main"))
mdl02.addModifier(#collision)
mdl02.collision.enabled = true
mdl02.collision.resolve = true
```

```
end
```

5. All that is left to do is to write the hCollide handler:

```
on hCollide coldata
end
```

coldata is a collisionData object. This object is passed onto the handler specified in the setCollisionCallback command, and the handler receives it as an argument. It tells us a bit about what exactly happened in our collision event. The collisionData object has four properties: modelA, modelB, pointOfContact and collisionNormal properties.

6 . Add put colData.modelA into the handler:

```
on hCollide me, colData
  put colData.modelA
end
```

If you run the movie now you'll see lots of callbacks being written into the message window telling you which model detected the collision. The two objects will stop when a collision is detected.

Let's create a simple reaction to this collision. We'll get both objects to invert the movement, rotation or translation that led to the collision, add a crash and some sparks. It won't be terribly realistic, but it'll make the point, and it's simple to build.

Feel free to create your own, more complex reaction. You could use collisionNormal together with the transformation and rotation of both colliding objects to calculate the resulting trajectories of the colliding objects. There is quite a bit of math involved.

7.   Back to our example. Import a sound file (AIF) of an explosion or crash. I recorded myself making crash noises earlier, so you can use mine if you like. Its called bang.aif Make sure your sound cast member is called bang and then add:

```
puppetsound 1, "bang"
```

To your hCollide handler.

If you run your movie now, you'll only get a lot of clicking. This is because the movie keeps detecting collision and reacting with the sound before the previous sound has finished playing. We need to react to the collision by moving the models away from each other, so that no more but one collision is detected.

8.   Let's use another switch to invert the rotation and translation of our box model. Declare another global called gColSwitch at the top of the main script, and set it to false inside the hInit handler

```
gColSwitch = false
```

9.   Now we'll change the hRun handler so that we can invert the rotation and translation of the models. Use the variable gColSwitch in a conditional statement, testing to see if the switch is false before the lines that set the rotation of model 2 of member 11.

```
if gColSwitch = false then
   member(11).model[2].rotate(0,2,0, #self)
   member(11).model[2].rotate(0,0,10, #world)
   member(11).model[2].translate(0,0.3,0, #self)
```

After the rotation is set, use the else statement to create the opposite rotation and close the end if statement

```
else
        member(11).model[2].rotate(0,-2,0, #self)
        member(11).model[2].rotate(0,0,-10, #world)
        member(11).model[2].translate(0,-0.3,0, #self)
```

```
    end if
```

So, altogether the hRun handler should look like this:

```
on hRun
  if   gPostest < -100 then
    gSwitch = 1
  else if gPosTest > 100 then
    gSwitch = -1
  end if
  gPostest = gPostest + gSwitch
  member(11).model[1].transform.position =
➡ vector(gPostest,gPostest,gPostest)

  if gColSwitch = false then
    member(11).model[2].rotate(0,2,0, #self)
    member(11).model[2].rotate(0,0,10, #world)
    member(11).model[2].translate(0,0.3,0, #self)
  else
    member(11).model[2].rotate(0,-2,0, #self)
    member(11).model[2].rotate(0,0,-10, #world)
    member(11).model[2].translate(0,-0.3,0, #self)
  end if


member(11).camera[1].rotate(1,0,0, member(11).group("world"))
member(11).light[2].transform.position =
➡ member(11).camera[1].transform.position + vector(10,10,0)
member(11).light[2].pointat(0,0,0)

end
```

10. Since we've accommodated the switch in the hRun handler, let's set it in our hCollide collision callback handler as well. Create a conditional that checks whether the switch is false or true and sets it to the opposite Boolean value.

```
if  gColSwitch = true then
    gColSwitch = false
  else
    gColSwitch = true
  end if
```

11. We'll also invert the movement of our ball model when the models collide. This is very easy to arrange, because we've already created a switch that we can use: gSwitch. All we need to do is multiply gSwitch by –1:

```
gSwitch = gSwitch * -1
```

If you run the movie now, the collision should invoke the sound cast member "bang" to play and make the two models reverse their movement.

12. All we need now is the sparks. We'll pass a new handler, `hSparks`, the `collisionData` object `ColData`

```
hSparks(Coldata)
```

The final `hCollide` handler should look like this:

```
on hCollide me, colData
  puppetsound 1, "bang"
  if  gColSwitch = true then
    gColSwitch = false
  else
    gColSwitch = true
  end if
  gSwitch = gSwitch * -1
  hSparks(colData)

end
```

Now we need to create the `hSparks` handler.

Making sparks fly

1. The `hSparks` handler will receieve the `collisionData` object as an argument:

```
on hSparks, collisionData

end
```

To create sparks we will use the particle `emitter` element of the `#particle` model resource. As we need this to happen every time two models collide, we'll need to check that a previous collision has not already created the resource, or we'll clutter the scene with rogue models and model resources.

We know that we are meant to have just one box model and one ball model, so we'll check the scene to find out if there are more than two models. If there is a third we'll delete it before we create a new model.

2. First we need the conditional that will find out if we need to delete a model from the scene:

```
if member(11).model.count > 2 then
    member(11).deletemodel(3)
end if
```

3. Now we're sure there aren't any rogue models around, we'll check for a model resource with the same name. If that exists we'll delete it, and if not, we'll make it. We need to arrange things like this because we can't reuse the old one. An `emitter` model resource has temporal properties that can't be reset:

```
if voidp(member(11).modelResource("Sparks")) then
    nmr = member(11).newModelResource("Sparks", #particle)
else
    member(11).deletemodelresource("Sparks")
    nmr = member(11).newModelResource("Sparks", #particle)
end if
```

4. Now that we are sure to have a local variable that represents our model resource `Sparks`, we'll set some properties for it:

```
nmr.emitter.mode = #burst
```

This line simply sets the `emitter` of our model resource to burst out particles. We could have used `#stream`, but we didn't because burst makes all the particles burst out at once, while stream lets groups of particles stream out of the `emitter` in consecutive frames.

5. Setting the emitters `loop` property to `false` simply makes sure that the particle emitting is a one off thing, and that the emitter ceases to emit particles at the end of its set lifetime. Setting it to true would cause the particles to keep going:

```
nmr.emitter.loop = false
```

6. Now we set the range that each will randomly allocate a velocity to each particle:

```
nmr.emitter.minSpeed = 30
nmr.emitter.maxSpeed = 50
```

7. We'll make sure that the emitter is not set to emit particles in a specific direction – the particles should burst out in all directions. By setting the angle of the emitter to 180 I can make sure that the particles burst out into all 360 degrees. The angles set here actually represent the spreading to the left and right of the directional vector set in the emitter direction property, so 180 actually equals 360.

```
nmr.emitter.direction = vector(0,0,0)
nmr.emitter.angle = 180
```

8. By setting the `start` and end `colorRange` properties of the resource, we control the colors the particles cycle through during their lifetime.

```
nmr.colorRange.start = rgb(230, 220, 0)
nmr.colorRange.end = rgb(10, 10, 0)
```

9. The lifetime of the resource determines the duration of the visibility of the particles emitted and the duration of their cycling through from `colorRange.start` property to `colorRange.end`. The lifetime value corresponds to milliseconds.

```
nmr.lifetime = 5000
```

10. Finally, we need to create a new model to associate the resource with, and to position this new model at the point of collision of our box and ball model. This is where the collisionData comes in handy.

```
nm = member(11).newModel("SparksModel", nmr)
nm.transform.position = collisionData.pointOfContact
```

The final hSparks handler should look like this:

```
on hSparks collisionData
  if member(11).model.count > 2 then
    member(11).deletemodel(3)
  end if
  if voidp(member(11).modelResource("Sparks")) then
    nmr = member(11).newModelResource("Sparks", #particle)
  else
    member(11).deletemodelresource("Sparks")
    nmr = member(11).newModelResource("Sparks", #particle)
  end if

  nmr.emitter.mode = #burst
  nmr.emitter.loop = false
  nmr.emitter.minSpeed = 30
  nmr.emitter.maxSpeed = 50
  nmr.emitter.direction = vector(0,0,0)
  nmr.emitter.angle = 180
  nmr.colorRange.start = rgb(230, 220, 0)
  nmr.colorRange.end = rgb(10, 10, 0)
  nmr.lifetime = 5000

  nm = member(11).newModel("SparksModel", nmr)
  nm.transform.position = collisionData.pointOfContact
end
```

If you run the movie now you should hear the bang sound file play every time the two models collide, and see the models inversing their direction and rotation and yellow sparks flying from the point of contact. Simple collision detection followed by a reaction to collision. As I hope this example has demonstrated, the effects you use for collisions will usually look much more realistic than they actually are – working out a way to do things that doesn't try to emulate the way they work in the real world, but rather concentrates on the effects, will usually require less processing than trying to emulate the effect more realistically.

Summary

Think back to how you anticipated 3D would be when you first came to it, and how you think about think about the 3D effects you want now. I hope it's less mysterious to you now, and that you're ready to explore the 3D commands further. Use the different 3D methods mentioned in this chapter freely, so that you create your own ideas about what works and what doesn't.

> *Remember – the math you need has already been written down somewhere, and the tools you end up using are just tools. It's the way you use it that makes the difference.*

We created a simple 3D engine in this chapter and saw that although it is useful to be able to create perspective without the help of a powerful inbuilt engine, there are some drawbacks to such homemade tools. I hope you found reworking that code a good way into the intricacies of the powerful Macromedia 3D engine.

Although we've finished up with collision detection and reaction, this is really where the real quest begins. I hope you enjoy experimenting with this exciting new environment, and find some great effects!

Chapter 8
3D Modifiers

Modifiers overview

As you've just seen in the previous chapter, the 3D engine incorporated into Director 8.5 offers a broad toolset for the complete manipulation of 3D objects contained within a given "world". Many of these tools are familiar to those who work routinely within standard 3D modeling and animation applications. Within those applications, the goal is to create a 3D environment that matches a targeted objective for the given project at hand. Typically that translates into using the given toolset to create a model (or series of models), apply textures to those models, add lighting and set up cameras to produce a final rendered image. In many cases it is also desirable to add animation to bring the scene to life. The end result may be photorealistic, cartoonish, or have a final visual character that is as unique as the artist responsible for creating it. This process can be a very time consuming one to say the least and is therefore not conducive to the creation of interactive applications. The toolset offered through Lingo in Director 8.5 not only contains the tools for setting up 3D worlds (build models, position them, add and adjust lights and cameras, etc.), but it also contains tools for realtime alterations of model meshes, rendering appearance, and model interaction detection. These capabilities are lumped into a group of properties called **modifiers**.

A modifier is essentially a set of parameters that can be attached to any model within a scene or 3D member and they can be broken down into three main categories:

- Rendering modifiers. These are "toon" and "inker" and have the effect of altering the way a model is displayed so they look more "cartoonish" or "technical" and less "photorealistic". Each has a number of properties that we'll discuss later.

- Model modifiers have the effect of altering the model to which they are attached in some way. This can include realtime polygon count modification and/or vertex level mesh modifications.

- Interaction modifiers are attached to models that we anticipate will be part of an interaction either with other models (as in a collision), or with time and Lingo (as in an animation sequence controlled by Lingo).

Modifier Lingo

To begin working with modifiers we must first understand how to determine their availability, test for their association with a model, apply them, and remove them from models. First off, specific modifiers may or may not be available using your current rendering engine. To test for available modifiers use the message window and the `getRendererServices` command with `modifiers` as the parameter:

```
myModifiersList = getRendererServices().modifiers
```

`myModifiersList` now contains a linear list that can be tested for the availability of a specific modifier. Using the `put` command will write that list to the message window:

```
put myModifiersList
```

```
- -[#collision, #bonesPlayer, #keyframePlayer, #toon, #lod,
➡ #meshDeform, #sds, #inker]
```

To test within a script we can use the `findPos` list command, which will return an integer value for the position of a given modifier in the list if it's present, and 0 if it's not.

```
isModPresent=findPos(myModifiersList, #toon)
```

Then, as you'll probably know by now, to get the output:

```
put isModPresent
```

Once we determine that our renderer supports a given modifier then we can apply it to a model, but before we do that it's good practice to determine if it has already been added. To test for a given modifier we use the following Lingo:

```
member(my3Dmember).model(modelname).modifier.count
```

If this returns 0 then there are no modifiers attached to your model. A value other then 0 indicates the presence of a modifier whose type we can determine as follows:

```
member(my3Dmember).model(modelname).modifier[indexValue]
```

As an example if we had a cast member named "3DModel" containing one model named *Ball* which had the toon modifier attached we would get the following when typing in the message window.

```
put member("3Dmodel").model("Ball").modifier.count
- -1

put member("3Dmodel").model("Ball").modifier[1]
- -#toon
```

If the modifier is already associated with the model then we can skip ahead and alter the properties that are available to that modifier. If it's not present we can add it with a single line of Lingo:

```
member(my3Dmember).model(modelName).addModifier(modifierToAdd)
```

Where `modifierToAdd` is one of the modifiers that we determined to be available from the `getRenderServices`. Therefore, to add the collision modifier to our model above we would use:

```
member("3Dmodel").model("Ball").addModifier(#collision)
```

Finally, if a modifier is no longer necessary it can be removed using the `removeModifier` command.

```
member(my3Dmember).model(modelName).removeModifier(modifierToremove)
```

Rendering modifiers

The first type of modifiers we will examine alter the appearance of the rendered image on the fly, therefore we'll refer to them as **rendering modifiers**. Prior to application of these modifiers the renderer will display textures and shaders in the standard photorealistic mode. The term **photorealistic** is a bit of a misnomer, or a piece of wishful thinking on the developers part, as the Shockwave 3D rendering engine does not really render with true photorealistic qualities. Since the intention of the engine is to deliver rendered images in realtime (or as fast as possible) there are several properties that would be present in a true photorealistic image that cannot be generated natively by the renderer. Some of these include true shadows, refraction (the bending of light by objects with a refractive index that doesn't equal one, such as water or glass), and anti-aliased edges on the models. The rendering capabilities of the Shockwave 3D engine as it relates to image maps is nonetheless impressive and realistic, while accomplishing the main task of rendering several frames per second as opposed to the several seconds per frame of a typical true photorealistic renderer.

With that said, if we "join the club" and refer to the standard rendering mode of Shockwave 3D as photorealistic we can examine the toon and inker modifiers as additions to individual models that will result in the models being rendered in a non-photorealistic mode. We will examine the use of toon modifier first.

Toon

The toon modifier alters rendering of the model to which it is attached to look more "cartoonish" or hand drawn. The effect is essentially accomplished by rendering the model with a limited number of colors, the number of which can be predefined using the colorSteps property. The toon modifier is applied to a specific model and its properties are set uniquely for each model that it's applied to. This application is accomplished with the following Lingo:

```
member(my3Dmember).model(modelname).addModifier(#toon)
```

This will apply the toon modifier to the model modelname of cast member my3Dmember. Once applied, other properties of that model including all shaders, textures, and their related properties are ignored. There are several properties specific to the toon modifier that can be adjusted to get a specific final rendering appearance. The first one to consider (which has the greatest overall effect) is the style property.

The style property dictates the overall rendering appearance. Depending on the style assigned to your model, the remaining properties we will discuss will have different or no effect on the models appearance when rendered. The style type available are #toon, #gradient (the default) and #blackAndWhite.

The simplest of these to understand is #blackAndWhite which causes the model to be rendered in black and white (if only it were all that simple!). The effect is not dithered but rather a threshold rendering between the threshold values for the shadow and highlight. Therefore parameters which have the largest effect on the appearance are the shadowPercentage and highlightPercentage values. The transition between black and white is hard (aliased) and it gives the model a very harsh appearance.

A simple testbed movie can be utilized to test various settings for the model of your choice. In this chapter we have built such a testbed movie for and it contains the graphics and code that will be built here and used for a number of the examples in this chapter. It's available for you to download from the friends of ED web site. If you'd prefer to build it yourself, simply import a model into a blank Director movie, drag and drop it into sprite channel 1. Add a new movie script to the cast. To that movie script add the following Lingo:

```
on addtoon tStyle, tSteps, tShadowp, tHighp, tSS, tHS, tSil,
➡ tCrease, tCA, tB, tLO

  mycast=sprite(1).member.name
  repeat with counter=1 to member(mycast).model.count

    set myname=member("mouse4").model[counter].name
    member(mycast).Model(myname).addmodifier(#toon)
    member(mycast).Model(myname).toon.style=tStyle
    member(mycast).Model(myname).toon.colorSteps=tSteps
    member(mycast).Model(myname).toon.shadowPercentage=tShadowp
    member(mycast).Model(myname).toon.highlightPercentage=tHighp
    member(mycast).Model(myname).toon.shadowStrength=tSS
    member(mycast).Model(myname).toon.highlightStrength=tHS
    member(mycast).Model(myname).toon.lineColor=rgb(0,0,255)
    member(mycast).Model(myname).toon.silhouettes=tSil
    member(mycast).Model(myname).toon.creases=tCrease
    member(mycast).Model(myname).toon.creaseAngle=tCA
    member(mycast).Model(myname).toon.boundary=tB
    member(mycast).Model(myname).toon.lineOffset=tLO

  end repeat

end addtoon

on addinker iSil, iCrease, iCA, iB, iLO

  mycast=sprite(1).member.name
  repeat with counter=1 to member(mycast).model.count

    set myname=member("mouse4").model[counter].name
    member(mycast).Model(myname).addmodifier(#inker)
    member(mycast).Model(myname).inker.lineColor=rgb(0,0,255)
    member(mycast).Model(myname).inker.silhouettes=iSil
    member(mycast).Model(myname).inker.creases=iCrease
    member(mycast).Model(myname).inker.creaseAngle=iCA
    member(mycast).Model(myname).inker.boundary=iB
    member(mycast).Model(myname).toon.lineOffset=iLO
  end repeat

end addinker
```

This allows the application of either the toon or inker modifiers by entering values into a call from the message window as in the following example:

```
addtoon #gradient, 16, 50, 50, .5, .5, FALSE, FALSE, 0.1, FALSE, -1
```

After pressing RETURN, click on the stage to update the model to see how the settings affect it. Changing values and reapplying them can be done without removing previous settings for the same modifier. If you want to switch from toon to inker or vise versa you will need to reset your world or remove the modifier by adding the following script to your movie script:

```
on delmod whichmod

    mycast=sprite(1).member.name
    repeat with counter=1 to member(mycast).model.count


        member(mycast).Model[counter].removemodifier(whichmod)

    end repeat

end delmod
```

This would then also be called from the message window. To remove the toon modifier from your model before applying inker you would enter:

```
delmod #toon
```

Then you would need to press RETURN and click on the stage to update the rendered model.

The example images in the following sections were generated using this method. The key elements of what is being achieved are identified and the complete call is stated above each image.

Unmodified Image:

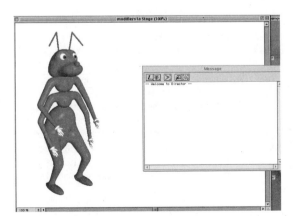

To achieve: *Toon (Style=#blackAndWhite, shadowPercentage=50, highlightPercentage=50)* we type the following into the message window:

```
addtoon #blackandwhite, 16, 50, 50, .5, .5, FALSE, FALSE, .01, FALSE, -2
```

And the effect on our model is:

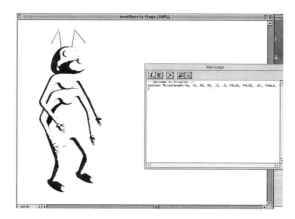

To achieve: *Toon (Style=#blackAndWhite, shadowPercentage=90, highlightPercentage=10)*.

```
addtoon #blackandwhite, 16, 90, 10, .5, .5, FALSE, FALSE, .01, FALSE, -2
```

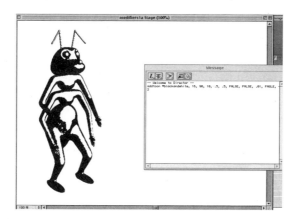

To achieve: *Toon (Style=#blackAndWhite, shadowpercentage=10, highlightPercentage=90)*

`addtoon #blackandwhite, 16, 10, 90, .5, .5, FALSE, FALSE, .01, FALSE, -2`

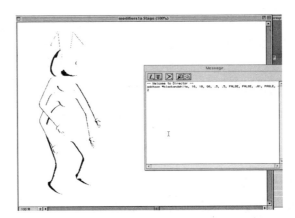

`#toon` is very similar to `#blackAndWhite` in that it results in a harsh, very contrast-centric rendering. However, unlike `#blackAndWhite`, the use of `#toon` retains the color definitions of the underlying shader. It is also affected by the `colorSteps`, `shadowStrength` and `highlightStrength` properties. Therefore, a red model will render in harsh highlight/shadow variations of the base red color (light and dark) when the `#toon` style is applied as demonstrated by the following examples:

Unmodified model:

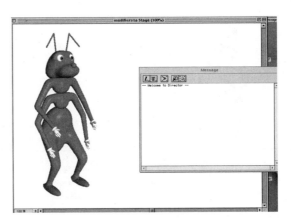

Toon (Style=#toon, colorSteps=16, shadowPercentage=50, highlightPercentage=50,
➥ shadowStrength=.1, highlightStrength=.9)

```
addtoon #toon, 16, 50, 50, .1, .9, FALSE, FALSE, .01, FALSE, -2
```

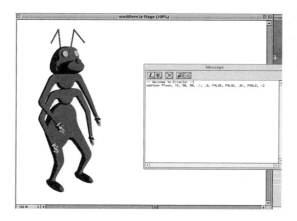

Toon (Style=#toon, colorSteps=16, shadowPercentage=50,
➥ highlightPercentage=50, shadowStrength=.9, highlightStrength=.1)

```
addtoon #toon, 16, 50, 50, .9, .1, FALSE, FALSE, .01, FALSE, -2
```

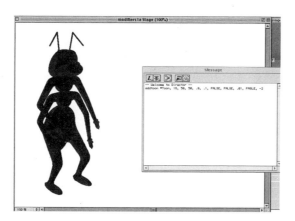

When using the #gradient style the number of colors actually used to render the model is governed by the colorSteps property. The value assigned to colorSteps is an integer rounded to the nearest power of two between 2 and 16. Obviously, the larger the number the more colors that are used to render or image. As more colors are available, the model will gain more dynamic range between highlight and shadow resulting in better appearance of the 3D characteristics of the model. Although only slight, as it's in black and white here, you can still see how smoothly the colors blend on the first image which has a colorSteps value of 16, whereas there is a sharp contrast (especially around the torso area) where colors meet on the second image, which has a colorSteps value of 4.

Toon Modifier (style=gradient, colorSteps=16)

```
addtoon #gradient, 16, 20, 80, .2, .8, FALSE, FALSE, .01, FALSE, -2
```

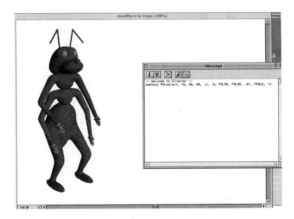

Toon Modifier (style=gradient, colorSteps=4)

```
addtoon #gradient, 4, 20, 80, .2, .8, FALSE, FALSE, .01, FALSE, -2
```

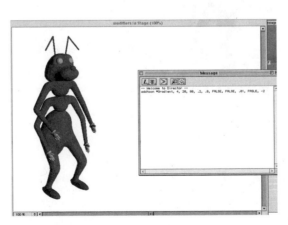

The number of colors actually dedicated to highlight and shadow portions of the model are controlled using the shadowPercentage and highlightPercentage properties. These properties are percentage values between 0 and 100, which define the number of assigned colorSteps that are used to render shadows and highlights respectively. The default values are 50 for both, so if the colorSteps property is set to 16 then 8 colors will be used to render the highlight and 8 will be used to render the shadows. Offsetting the percentages to favor either highlights or shadows will result in smoother transitions in the favored areas and more posterization (less dynamic range) being applied to the opposite area. As an example, a shadowPercentage of 10 and highlightPercentage of 90 with a colorSteps of 16 would result in 2 colors being applied to shadows and 14 to the highlights.

The values given to the shadowPercentage and highlightPercentage should, but do not have to, total 100 when added together. If the total is greater then 100 then precedence is given to the highlightPercentage. For example, setting the highlightPercentage to 100 will always result in the maximum colors being devoted to the highlight areas, regardless of the setting for the shadowPercentage. If the shadowPercentage if set to 100, any value greater then 0 for the highlightPercentage will result in some colors being assigned to the highlighted areas of the model.

Adjusting the depth of shadow or highlight - the equivalent of setting the shadow darkness or specular brightness in an external 3D application - will dictate how different the colors assigned to the highlight and shadow will be. This is accomplished by setting the shadowStrength and highlightStrength properties. These are both floating point values between 0.0 and 1.0. The default is 1.0 and results in the maximum strength or the darkest shadows and brightest highlights.

The remaining properties deal with drawing lines on the model in various situations. The first property is lineColor, which is an RGB value - default RGB (0,0,0) is black - that simply defines the color of lines that will be used when certain criteria are met. Lines can be added to the model at the silhouette of the model, at creases in the mesh and at the joints of the mesh. Each line type adds a different appearance to the model. The properties of silhouettes, boundary, and creases are all Boolean values (set to TRUE as default), which cause lines to be drawn in the lineColor value at their respective positions.

> silhouettes *and* boundary *may seem intuitively identical, but their effect can be quite different. Lines applied to the silhouette always follow the outline of model as the camera sees it. This, unlike the boundary line designation, adds lines that are always drawn on the boundary of the model's mesh. The mesh boundary may or may not be the outer boundary of the model as the camera sees it.*

Crease lines are drawn on the mesh surface when the angle between adjoining faces of the mesh is greater then the predefined creaseAngle property. This property is a float value between -1.0 and 1.0 (default = .01) which defines the threshold angle at which two faces can be adjoined before a crease line is drawn. The larger the number, the larger the acceptable angle and the more crease lines that will be added. Therefore, at a setting of 1 all faces will be outlined, and at a value of -1 none will be. The lines drawn by these parameters can also be offset using the lineOffset parameter. This value is a float between -100.00 and 100.00 (default = -2) which causes the lines to be drawn the specified world units from their original location.

Inker

The inker modifier adds crease, boundary, and silhouette lines to models without distorting their color properties as the toon modifier does. It also allows the retention of shader properties that the toon modifer will ignore. The properties of lineColor, silhouttes, creases, and creaseAngle are applied in the same fashion with the same values and results as with the toon modifier. (Remember to type delmod #toon to get rid of the toon modifier before moving on to use the inker.)

```
Inker applied [linecolor=rgb(0,0,255)], silhouettes=TRUE, creases=TRUE,
creaseAngle, boundary=TRUE, lineoffset=-2)

addinker TRUE, TRUE, .9, TRUE, -2
```

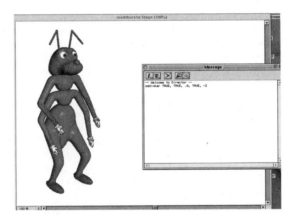

In practice, toon and inker are applied in a trial and error process until the desired effect is reached for the model you are applying it to. Using the scripts provided above should make that process much more efficient. Experience has shown that even if the getRendererServices returns the availability of these two modifiers, the final results may be somewhat unpredictable!

> *Different video cards may not display boundary, crease, or silhouette lines, making the #inker modifier useless. As with any production project it's best to test these effects on as many machines a possible to determine if the results are reproducible for your target audience.*

Model Modifiers

Model modifiers act on the actual mesh of the model to which they are attached. They can be further subcategorized into those which modify the polygon count of a given model, and those which affect mesh geometry. Level of detail (LOD) and subdivision (SDS) modify the number of polygons while mesh deform must is used to alter mesh geometry. We will examine LOD and subdivision first.

To understand the use of these modifiers we must analyze some important facts, which can be used to our advantage. First, the development of interactive 3D (or any interactive application for that matter) is often a compromise between performance and complexity. The ultimate objective is to get the performance we want with all the exciting features as well. In days gone by that would mean making certain optimizations during the development process so that the project played as well as possible but still had all the bells and whistles to keep things interesting. Some examples of such optimizations may include reducing images from 24bit to 8bit, using 15fps video instead of 30fps, or using Lingo instead of the score to control animations.

These types of techniques are effective in a 2D world but they don't always translate effectively to 3D. To illustrate this point let's consider the most common method of improving rendering speed in a 3D application. This technique is to reduce the polygon count of the models structure. Fewer computations allow the final image to be generated faster.

When developing any project it's always imperative to analyze and understand the target audience with respect to what you're attempting to accomplish. In the case of 3D we need to get the best performance and have the audience not realize that we're cheating a little to get there. Since this is a visual problem we first look at the human eye to find its limitations. The first major limitation is that the human eye is designed to work best on objects that are close by. Our eyes actually have fairly poor resolution at best and for those of use plagued by near sightedness it only gets worse. To exploit this in a standard 3D application we would model objects that are far away from the camera with fewer polygons then those which are closer to the camera. Objects that move in an animation would have a polygon count necessary to produce a smooth rendering at the closest position we would expect it to be to the camera. Using this technique, we minimize the polygon count and thereby minimize rendering time or increase rendering performance. Now, in an interactive 3D application, we may not know how close the camera will get to a given object, but it's all the more important that we minimize polygon count used in the rendering process since we're attempting to render in real time. This is a job for the level of detail modifier.

LOD

The level of detail modifier doesn't modify the number of polygons in the model, instead it dynamically alters the number of polygons used in the rendering process relative to the model's distance from the camera. As the camera gets closer the polygon count used to render goes up, and as the camera moves away the polygon count used to render automatically goes down.

To add the modifer to a specific model use:

```
member(my3Dmember).model(newmodel).addModifier(#lod)
```

The LOD modifier has 3 basic properties, `auto`, `bias`, and `level`, which control its effect on the target model. The `auto` property, which is a Boolean value (default=True), is set with the following Lingo:

```
member(my3Dmember).model(newmodel).lod.auto=true
```

If set to true (the default value) then the polygon count is automatically adjusted according to the distance from the camera and the `bias` property value for that model. If set to false then the polygon count of the model will be adjusted to the percentage given by the the `level` property.

The `lod.bias` property is used when the `auto` property is **true**. It must be a float value between 0.0 and 100.0 (100.0 is the default). This number represents the amount of polygon reduction that takes place as you move away from the camera: the larger the number, the **less** reduction that will occur. Therefore, at the default of 100 there should be no visible reduction in polygon count as an object moves away from the camera. At 0, all the polygons will eventually disappear. When using this option I find it is best to start with a number between 50 and 75 and experiment a little to find the optimum setting. Since it's dependent on the number of polygons you are starting off with, each model will appear to react differently depending on its starting mesh density. To alter the value use a command of the format:

```
member(my3Dmember).model(newmodel).lod.bias=50.0
```

When the `auto` property is **false**, the polygon count is altered with reference to the `level` property. This must be a float value between 0.0 and 100.0 (100.0 is the default). This number represents the percentage of polygons from the original mesh to use and it's independent of distance from the camera. The larger the number, the **less** reduction that will occur; again at the default of 100 there should be no visible reduction in polygon count as an object moves away from the camera, whereas at 0, all the polygons will disappear. To alter the value use a command like:

```
member(my3Dmember).model(newmodel).lod.level=50.0
```

Following are some example images demonstrating the effect of the LOD modifier. The images are shown in both wireframe and filled rendering modes. This allows us to see the effect of the modifier on models mesh and how that translates into the final rendered image.

Unmodified model:

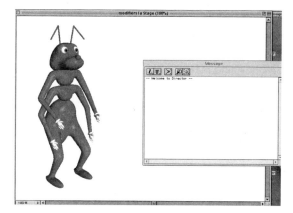

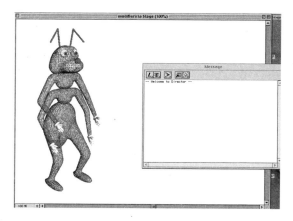

LOD Modifier (auto=FALSE, bias=100, depth=1)

```
addLOD False, 100, 1
```

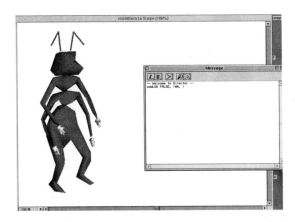

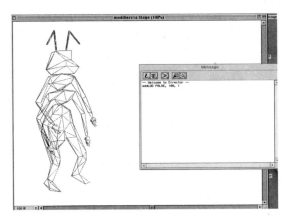

```
LOD Modifier (auto=FALSE, bias=100, depth=10)

addLOD False, 100, 10
```

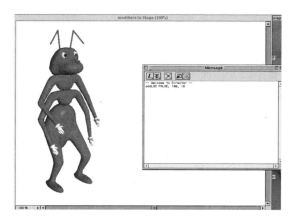

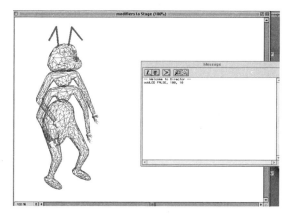

SDS

While the LOD modifier is useful for dynamically reducing polygon count in relation to camera distance, it may be desirable in many cases to dynamically increase the polygon count in relation to the camera position. This is where the subdivision modifier comes into play. When you export a model from your 3D application you may be asked for a "Mesh quality" or "Mesh resolution" value. Typically this is a percentage between 0 and 100 (100 being no change in the mesh). This value allows you to essentially define the "default" mesh resolution your model will render with when brought into Director. That default value is the starting point at which the LOD modifier removes geometry and, more interestingly though, the point from which the subdivision modifier can add it back. To clarify this idea, if you were to export a model with 10,000 polygons and a mesh quality of 50 then when imported into Director that model may only use 5,000 polygons as the default when it is rendered. The LOD modifier allows you to decrease that number based on camera position.

However, while only 5,000 polygons are used to render the model, all 10,000 are still present in the file and the subdivision modifier allows us to dynamically put them back into the render calculations based on the camera position relative to the model we are modifying.

This modifier must be added to each model you would like to apply it to and it can only be added to models created outside of Director. The additional modeling detail must be added in the external modeling application and included with the W3D model when it is exported - W3D format was discussed in **Chapter 6**. To add this modifier use:

```
member(my3Dmember).model(newmodel).addModifier(#sds)
```

Once the modifier is added to a given model it can be activated or deactivated at runtime using the modifier's `enabled` property. By setting it to true (the default value) the SDS modifier is activated:

```
member(my3Dmember).model(newmodel).sds.enabled=true
```

Setting it to false disables the effect of the modifer without removing it from the model

```
member(my3Dmember).model(newmodel).sds.enabled=false
```

Unlike the LOD modifier, which always affects the mesh uniformly, the SDS modifier can add geometric data in a controlled non-uniform fashion. The method in which the data is added back to the model is controlled with the `subdivision` property which can have two values: `#uniform` and `#adaptive`. Uniform subdivision forces all the visible surfaces to be subdivided in the same way. With adaptive subdivision, only those surfaces at major orientation changes (joints and curves, or bevels, for example) are subjected to subdivision. The joint areas are typically those which require more polygons to render smoothly. Therefore, `#adaptive` will result in fewer polygons being added in comparison to `#uniform`, but they are located in critical areas which will likely result in the best compromise between model quality and render speed. Also, using the `#adaptive` setting results in only the visible areas of the mesh being modified. Off-camera mesh areas and models which have the SDS modifier applied are not included in the polygon increase. By leaving their polygon counts low, overall program performance will be increased. You can set this property with the following command:

```
member(my3Dmember).model(newmodel).sds.subdivision=#uniform
```

Three additional properties are available in the SDS modifier, which can be adjusted to fine tune its effect on the model. They are `depth`, `tension` and `error`. Let's look at each of them:

- `depth` is a value from 0 to 5 (default is 1) that defines the degree to which surfaces are subdivided. A value of 0 results in no subdivision while 5 results in the maximum amount. As subdivision increases performance will decrease, so it's advisable to use the smallest number possible to get the detail you require.

- `tension` is a percentage value (0-100; default=65) which defines how closely the subdivided mesh matches the original mesh. A value of 100% means the subdivided mesh will be identical to the original. This is generally undesirable since you're taking a performance hit and will see no difference from the original.

■ error is applicable only when using a subdivision property set to #adaptive. It's set in the form of a float from 0.0 to 1.0 (default=0.0). The larger the number the less error tolerance there is.

Application of these three properties is accomplished with the following commands:

```
member(my3Dmember).model(newmodel).sds.depth=2
member(my3Dmember).model(newmodel).sds.tension=75
member(my3Dmember).model(newmodel).sds.subdivision=#adaptive
```

The SDS modifier cannot be used with the toon or inker modifiers. You can use it with the LOD modifier, but the auto property should be set to false and the level property should be set to a specific value.

In the following examples, the effect of the SDS modifier is most pronounced in the head as best seen by comparing the wireframe views.

Unmodified model:

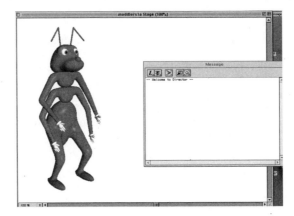

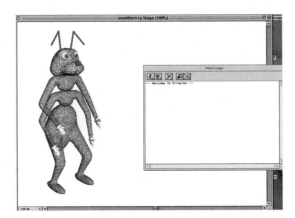

```
SDS  modifier  (enabled=True,  subdivision=#adaptive,  depth=3,  tension=65,
error=0)
```

```
addSDS TRUE, #adaptive, 2, 65, 0
```

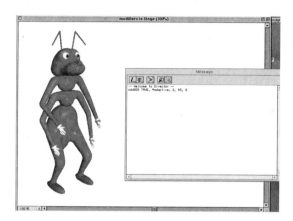

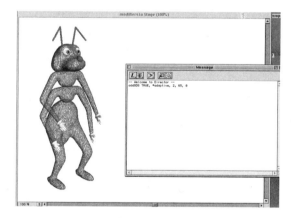

Mesh deform

The last model-based modifier we will examine is the mesh deform modifier. This is perhaps the most complicated aspect of Shockwave 3D and it brings with it complete vertex level control over any mesh in your scene. In doing so, it gives us the ability to dynamically alter a model on the fly using Lingo. While it doesn't allow us to add geometry to a model, it does allow us to move specific points in a model. This can be used to bend, twist, morph, and add other effects to models, which would be difficult to accomplish interactively using any other technique.

To understand and use the mesh deform modifier effectively, we not only need to understand its parameters, but we also need to understand basic vector math and how mesh geometry is defined in Shockwave 3D.

To define a face Director stores three index values from the cast member's vertexList in a particular order to define the three corners of the triangle in 3D space. This list is called the facelist. The order of the vertices define the direction of the face. Face direction determines how the face will reflect light when rendered. A "forward" face is always defined in a counterclockwise direction, as shown in the figure below, and will reflect light as you would expect. A "reversed" face will be defined in a clockwise direction and will reflect light reversed from what you would expect. The illustration shows a typical #front face with its vertex definition list.

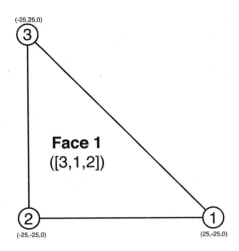

The rendering process uses "vertex normals" to give the model its final rendered appearance. A vertex normal is a vector which defines the direction light should reflect from a given point on your model. The normals can be altered in a given model to give the appearance of texture without altering the model's physical geometry. A technique common to most 3D artists which exploits this feature is bumpmapping. This technique uses greyscale images to alter the surface normals of a model at render time to add fine textures, like wood grain, which would be difficult or resource prohibitive to recreate using surface geometry alone. Director uses surface normals too, they are stored in the normalList. When updating the position of vertices during a mesh deform operation it is imperative to update the corresponding surface normal. Failure to do so will result in a moved vertex that is shaded as it was before it was moved. As an example, if you move a point away from the surface of a plane it will still render flat, as if it were still in the plane, until by updating the corresponding normals it is shaded smoothly into the surface it came from.

The final item that's important for the mesh deform modifier is the texture properties for a given model. The texture coordinates are stored in the textureCoordinateList which can be referenced and modified using mesh deform. This allows the modification and placement of the textures as the model changes.

To use the mesh deform modifier we have 8 primary properties at our disposal. These can be get and set and are the ones responsible for actually changing the model mesh properties:

```
member(my3Dmember).model(modelname).mesh[index].vertexList
member(my3Dmember).model(modelname).mesh[index].normalList
```

```
member(my3Dmember).model(modelname).mesh[index].
➥textureCoordinateList
```

These are used to gather information to manipulate the lists in an efficient fashion.

```
member(my3Dmember).model(modelname).mesh.count
member(my3Dmember).model(modelname).mesh[index].face.count
member(my3Dmember).model(modelname).mesh[index].face.[index]
member(my3Dmember).model(modelname).mesh[index].face.[index]
➥ neighbor[index]
member(my3Dmember).model(modelname).face.count
```

All these properties, with the exception of mesh.count and face.count that simply provide the number of meshes and faces in a specific model respectively, are lists which can be fairly complex in their makeup. In order to use them effectively I would recommend brushing up on Lingo's lists and list handling functions.

Viewing the meshDeform data

The primary business end of the meshDeform modifier are the three lists containing the vertex, normal, and texture coordinate data for your model. These items can be viewed with a simple Lingo script in a movie with an empty 3D cast member.

1. In Director, create a new movie and add a new Shockwave 3D cast member (Insert > Media Element > Shockwave 3D). Name that member 3Dmember, and drag and drop it onto the stage.

2. Create a new movie script and start by adding the following handler, which will build a front facing plane, myX polygons wide by myY polygons high, in our 3D cast member.

```
on buildplane whichmember, myX, myY

  member(whichmember).resetworld()

  myplane = member(whichmember).newModelResource("plane1", #plane,
  ➥ #front)
  myplane.width = 50
  myplane.length = 50
  myplane.widthVertices=myX
  myplane.lengthVertices=myY

  newPlane= member(whichmember).newModel("myplane", myplane)
   newplane.rotate(0,180,0)

member(whichmember).bgcolor=rgb(255,255,255)
```

3. We'll now add the `meshDeform` modifier.

```
member(whichmember).Model("myplane").addmodifier(#meshDeform)
```

4. Then add this section, which displays the `meshDeform` data in the message window.

```
put "Mesh Count: " &
➡ member(whichmember).Model("myplane").meshDeform.mesh.count
put "Face Count: " &
➡ member(whichmember).Model("myplane").meshDeform.face.count

repeat with counter=1 to
➡ member(whichmember).Model("myplane").meshDeform.mesh.count
  put "Face Count for mesh "& counter & ": " & member
  ➡ (whichmember).Model("myplane").meshDeform.mesh[counter].face
  ➡ .count
  put "Vertexlist for mesh "& counter & ": " & member
  ➡ (whichmember).Model("myplane").meshDeform.mesh
  ➡ [counter].vertexlist
  put "Normallist for mesh "& counter & ": " & member
  ➡ (whichmember).Model("myplane").meshDeform.mesh
  ➡ [counter].Normallist
  put "TextureCoordinatelist for mesh " & counter & ": " &
  ➡ member (whichmember).Model("myplane").meshDeform.mesh
  ➡ [counter].TextureCoordinatelist

  repeat with facecounter=1 to member(whichmember).Model
  ➡ ("myplane").meshDeform.mesh[counter].face.count
    put "List references for face "& facecounter & ": " &
    ➡ member (whichmember).Model("myplane").meshDeform.mesh
    ➡ [counter].
  face[facecounter]
    repeat with neighborcounter=1 to 3
    put "List for neighbor "& neighborcounter & " of face "&
    ➡ facecounter & ": " & member(whichmember).Model("myplane")
    ➡ .meshDeform.mesh[counter].face[facecounter].neighbor
    ➡ [neighborcounter]
    end repeat
  end repeat

  put return
end repeat

end buildplane
```

5. Close the script window or select from the main menu Control > Recompile All Scripts. Then enter the following in the message window.

```
buildplane "3Dmember" 2,2
```

You will get the following:

```
- - "Mesh Count: 1"
- - "Face Count: 2"
- - "Face Count for mesh 1: 2"
- - "Vertexlist for mesh 1: [vector( 25.0000, -25.0000, 0.0000 ),
➥ vector( -25.0000, -25.0000, 0.0000 ), vector( 25.0000, 25.0000,
➥ 0.0000 ), vector( -25.0000, 25.0000, 0.0000 )]"
- - "Normallist for mesh 1: [vector( 0.0000, 0.0000, -1.0000 ),
➥ vector( 0.0000, 0.0000, -1.0000 ), vector( 0.0000, 0.0000,
➥ -1.0000 ), vector( 0.0000, 0.0000, -1.0000 )]"
- - "TextureCoordinatelist for mesh 1: [[0.0001, 0.0001],
➥ [0.9999, 0.0001], [0.0001, 0.9999], [0.9999, 0.9999]]"
- - "List references for face 1: [4, 1, 2]"
- - "List for neighbor 1 of face 1: []"
- - "List for neighbor 2 of face 1: []"
- - "List for neighbor 3 of face 1: [[1, 2, 1, 1]]"
- - "List references for face 2: [3, 1, 4]"
- - "List for neighbor 1 of face 2: [[1, 1, 3, 1]]"
- - "List for neighbor 2 of face 2: []"
- - "List for neighbor 3 of face 2: []"
```

Let's examine the output, as it's very important for demonstrating the principles of mesh deform.

```
- - "Mesh Count: 1"
- - "Face Count: 2"
- - "Face Count for mesh 1: 2"
```

The first three lines tell us that we created a single mesh with two faces and that the first mesh contains two faces. That makes sense since we only created one mesh so lines two and three should always be the same number under these circumstances. So far this is pretty simple, but hang on to your seats because each of the following lines is a little more difficult to follow.

```
- - "Vertexlist for mesh 1: [vector( 25.0000, -25.0000, 0.0000 ),
➥ vector( -25.0000, -25.0000, 0.0000 ), vector( 25.0000, 25.0000,
➥ 0.0000 ), vector( -25.0000, 25.0000, 0.0000 )]"
```

Line 4 is the vector list for the mesh we just created. If you recall, the vector list defines each vertex in the mesh we are examining. Given that, please note that there are only four vectors given for two triangular faces. In order to define two triangles we should have six vectors, but in order to make a plane from two triangles we need to share a common side. By sharing that side we in turn share two vertices, which means we only need to define four vectors to define the two faces as illustrated.

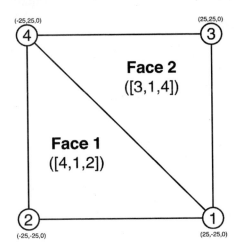

It also means that if we move or alter one of the shared points we alter or move both faces, since they both reference those vectors. That may not always be the case as you could have independent entries in the vector list for the same point with different faces referencing their own independent vectors for the same point. Having independently referenced vectors for points could be useful in some cases, but it will generally be the exception rather then the rule. The extra references waste memory, slow down performance and should be avoided when building meshes on the fly.

```
- - "Normallist for mesh 1: [vector( 0.0000, 0.0000, -1.0000 ),
➡ vector( 0.0000, 0.0000, -1.0000 ), vector( 0.0000, 0.0000, -
➡ 1.0000 ), vector( 0.0000, 0.0000, -1.0000 )]"
- - "TextureCoordinatelist for mesh 1: [[0.0001, 0.0001],
➡ [0.9999, 0.0001], [0.0001, 0.9999], [0.9999, 0.9999]]"
```

The next two lines give the `normalList` and `textureCoordinateList`. They will contain the same number of entries as the vector list as they provide coordinates corresponding to each vector. They are also in the same order as the vector list, so the normals and texture coordinates in position 1 of their respective lists are the values for the vector in position 1 of the vector list. That in itself is not particularly useful since the model is defined as faces which are assembled and rendered using the values in these lists. The values in those lists are not referenced by the faces in a linear order, therefore we have to go on the next line to get to the glue that hold this all together.

```
- - "List references for face 1: [4, 1, 2]"
```

This face reference list, is accessed by:

```
member(my3Dmember).model(modelname).meshDeform.mesh[index].face[index]
```

It returns three integer values corresponding to the list positions of the respective vector, normal, and texture coordinates for the three vertices of the face. So, given a face index number, we can determine the position of the modeling data in its respective list, which we can then alter and reset to update the model with new coordinate information.

The next three lines contain reference information for the faces next to (neighbors) the specified face:

```
- - "List for neighbor 1 of face 1:  []"
- - "List for neighbor 2 of face 1:  []"
- - "List for neighbor 3 of face 1:  [[1, 2, 1, 1]]"
```

It is accessed with the following Lingo command:

```
Member(my3Dmember).model(modelname).meshDeform.mesh[index].
➥ face[index].neighbor[neighborIndex]
```

neighborIndex is an integer value between 1 and 3 that corresponds to one of the three neighboring polygons. If there is no neighbor in that direction then an empty list is returned. When a neighbor is present, this property generally returns a list with four values. The first value is the index value for the mesh the face belongs to. The second value is the neighbor face index. In this example, the value for this position in the only neighbor is 2 and for face 2 the value is 1. This makes sense since we only have two faces and 1 is 2's neighbor and vice versa. The third position of the list holds the vertex index of the vertex in the neighboring face that isn't shared by the two faces. The last entry defines if the neighboring face is pointing in the same direction (0) or if it is reversed (1). Neighbors are defined by the vertex designations in the facelist as shown.

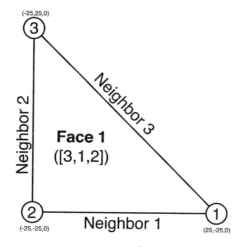

As an interesting side note, if we changed the definition of our plane to be two sided (#both) by changing the line of the on buildplane handler in the above example from:

```
myplane = member(whichmember).newModelResource("plane1", #plane,
➥ #front)
```

to match the following:

```
myplane = member(whichmember).newModelResource("plane1", #plane,
➥ #both)
```

When we call the handler from the message window, again using:

```
buildplane "3Dmember" 2,2
```

the response is quite different:

```
- - "Mesh Count: 2"
- - "Face Count: 4"
- - "Face Count for mesh 1: 2"
- - "Vertexlist for mesh 1: [vector( 25.0000, -25.0000, 0.0000 ),
➥ vector( -25.0000, -25.0000, 0.0000 ), vector ( 25.0000,
➥ 25.0000, 0.0000 ), vector( -25.0000, 25.0000, 0.0000 )]"
- - "Normallist for mesh 1: [vector( 0.0000, 0.0000, -1.0000 ),
➥ vector( 0.0000, 0.0000, -1.0000 ), vector( 0.0000, 0.0000,
➥ -1.0000 ), vector( 0.0000, 0.0000, -1.0000 )]"
- - "TextureCoordinatelist for mesh 1: [[0.0001, 0.0001],
➥ [0.9999, 0.0001], [0.0001, 0.9999], [0.9999, 0.9999]]"
- - "List references for face 1: [4, 1, 2]"
- - "List for neighbor 1 of face 1: [[2, 1, 1, 1]]"
- - "List for neighbor 2 of face 1: [[2, 1, 3, 1]]"
- - "List for neighbor 3 of face 1: [[1, 2, 1, 1], [2, 1, 2, 1],
➥ [2, 2, 1, 0]]"
- - "List references for face 2: [3, 1, 4]"
- - "List for neighbor 1 of face 2: [[2, 1, 2, 0], [2, 2, 1, 1],
➥ [1, 1, 3, 1]]"
- - "List for neighbor 2 of face 2: [[2, 2, 3, 1]]"
- - "List for neighbor 3 of face 2: [[2, 2, 2, 1]]"
- - "
"
- - "Face Count for mesh 2: 2"
- - "Vertexlist for mesh 2: [vector( 25.0000, -25.0000, 0.0000 ),
➥ vector( -25.0000, -25.0000, 0.0000 ), vector ( 25.0000,
➥ 25.0000, 0.0000 ), vector( -25.0000, 25.0000, 0.0000 )]"
- - "Normallist for mesh 2: [vector( 0.0000, 0.0000, 1.0000 ),
➥ vector ( 0.0000, 0.0000, 1.0000 ), vector( 0.0000, 0.0000,
➥ 1.0000 ), vector ( 0.0000, 0.0000, 1.0000 )]"
- - "TextureCoordinatelist for mesh 2: [[0.9999, 0.0001],
➥ [0.0001, 0.0001], [0.9999, 0.9999], [0.0001, 0.9999]]"
- - "List references for face 1: [4, 2, 1]"
- - "List for neighbor 1 of face 1: [[1, 1, 1, 1]]"
- - "List for neighbor 2 of face 1: [[2, 2, 1, 1], [1, 1, 3, 1],
➥ [1, 2, 1, 0]]"
- - "List for neighbor 3 of face 1: [[1, 1, 2, 1]]"
- - "List references for face 2: [3, 4, 1]"
```

```
- - "List for neighbor 1 of face 2: [[1, 1, 3, 0], [1, 2, 1, 1],
➡ [2, 1, 2, 1]]:"
- - "List for neighbor 2 of face 2: [[1, 2, 3, 1]]"
- - "List for neighbor 3 of face 2: [[1, 2, 2, 1]]"
```

As this indicates we actually generate two separate planes, one for each side. Upon closer examination we see that the `vector list` and `textureCoordinateList` for both are identical. The differences lie in the `facelist`, `normalList` and the `neighborList`. Two sided faces are generally not used in Director 3D applications, but the differences we see are substantial enough to warrant explanation, as this adds understanding to just how these objects function.

The focus of this examination should be between the two sets of data as defined by their meshes so compare and contrast the results between mesh 1 and mesh 2. The definitions of mesh 1 are identical to the first example, which defined the plane as a single sided `#front` object. Mesh 2, on the other hand, has a facelist, which reverses the direction of the face: [vertex 4, 2, 1] in relation to the forward facing counterpart [vertex 4, 1, 2,]. This ultimately results in reversed normals - normal direction being derived directly from face vertex direction.

> Face 1 of the front plane has normals of vector(0.0000, 0.0000, -1.0000), vector(0.0000, 0.0000, -1.0000), vector(0.0000, 0.0000, -1.0000) or the vectors at positions [4,1,2] in the vector list for mesh 1.

> Face 1 of the back plane has vectors of vector(0.0000, 0.0000, 1.0000), vector(0.0000, 0.0000, 1.0000), and vector(0.0000, 0.0000, 1.0000) as defined by positions 4,2,1 in the vector list.

The faces are clearly reversed as evidenced by the consistency in positions 1 and 2 of each vector and a negative to positive sign change in the third position of each vector (-1 to 1).

The other striking difference in these results in comparison to those generated by a single-sided plane are in the neighbors lists. A double-sided object will return a list of lists for the neighbors, as each face may have more then one neighbor in a particular direction. The ones which had no neighbors now have one neighbor which is in the opposite mesh facing the opposite direction as indicated by positions 1 and 4 respectively in the sublist. The ones which had one neighbor in the previous example now have three neighbors, two in the other mesh (one forward and one reverse) in addition to neighboring face in the same mesh.

> *When performing mesh deforms on two-sided objects, the deformation must be applied equally to the opposite face. Ignoring the opposite face will result in some very unusual effects. Due to the complexity and performance degradation associated with mesh deformations on two-sided objects it would be advisable to avoid them when possible.*

So we now have a good understanding of how Director handles and stores 3D data as well as how we access it efficiently using the mesh deform modifier. So how do we use that to actually deform a mesh? Fortunately, this is the relatively easy portion of the exercise. The process has four steps.

1. Copy the list you wish to alter into a variable (for example, copy the `vertexList` to alter vectors).

2. Use the `face[index]` property to determine the location of the items in their respective lists you would like to alter. The face index could be defined arbitrarily, by a loop, a collision event, through model picking Lingo, by the `neighborList`, or by any combination thereof. Alternatively, if a pattern can be defined (as it can with most primitives) as to the order of vertices in the vertex list, you can use a mathematical approach to alter the vertex list directly. An example of this follows.

3. Use standard list manipulation commands to alter the respective lists in the specified positions.

4. Set the `meshDeform` property back to the new list.

As an example, if we wanted to modify the position of vertex 2 of face 1 of the single-sided plane used in our first example, we would use a script like:

```
on modifyvertex whichmember, whichmodel

    set myVertexlist=[]
    set myNormallist=[]

    set myVertexlist=duplicate(member(whichmember).
    ➥ Model(whichmodel).meshDeform.mesh[1].vertexList)
    set myNormallist=duplicate(member(whichmember).
    ➥ Model(whichmodel).meshDeform.mesh[1].normalList)

    myVertex=getat(myVertexlist, getat(member(whichmember).
    ➥ Model(whichmodel).meshDeform.mesh[1].face[1],2))

    set myVertex.z=25

    setat myNormallist,2, getnormalized(myVertex)

    set member(whichmember).
    ➥ Model(whichmodel).meshDeform.mesh[1].vertexList=myVertexList
    set member(whichmember).
    ➥ Model(whichmodel).meshDeform.mesh[1].normalList=myNormalList

end modifyvertex
```

Calling this with the following line from the end of the original plane generation script.

```
modifyvertex "3Dmember", "myplane"
```

The result is a slightly deformed plane with the vertex at position 2 on face 1 being moved 25 units in the Z direction.

Using the meshDeform modifier

The following exercise is a slightly more complex and repetitive example. In this case we generate a plane to which we add flowing sine waves using the mesh deform modifier. This script is a behavior that can be added to any blank 3D cast member.

1. Open a new movie and add a new 3D member. (Insert > Media Elements > Shockwave3D).

2. Drag and drop that cast member onto the stage.

3. Add a looping script to the frame script of the last frame of the movie that contains the 3D sprite.

4. Open a new behavior script for the sprite. The properties used by this behavior are the current castname (myCast), the width vertices of the plane (pWidth), the height vertices of the plane (pHeight) and a variable pWaveX that allows the sine waves to move along the x-axis. Add:

    ```
    property myCast, pWidth, pHeight, pWaveX
    ```

5. The beginsprite handler sets our properties and calls for the plane to be generated. Alterations to the values of pWidth and pHeight will increase or decrease the polygon count of the plane. Try changing these values to see the effect of polygon count on performance and model appearance (they both must be greater than or equal to 2 or an error will occur).

    ```
    on beginsprite me

        myCast=sprite(me.spritenum).member.name

        pWidth=20
        pHeight=20

        buildplane

        pWaveX=1
    end
    ```

6. The buildplane handler is essentially the same as the one we created earlier, with its parameters supplied through the properties we defined in the beginsprite handler. We have also removed the put commands to prevent writing values to the message window.

```
on buildplane

    - - build a back facing plane pWidth polygons wide and pHeight
    - - polygons high

    member(myCast).resetworld()

    member(myCast).newtexture("blank")

    color_shade=member(myCast).newShader("red_shader", #standard)
    color_shade.diffuse=rgb(200,75,100)
    color_shade.ambient=rgb(200,75,100)
    member(myCast).shader("red_shader").texture=member(myCast).
    ➥ texture("blank")

    myplane = member(myCast).newModelResource("plane1", #plane,
    ➥ #back)
    myplane.width = 75
    myplane.length = 75
    myplane.widthVertices=pWidth
    myplane.lengthVertices=pHeight

    newPlane= member(myCast).newModel("myplane", myplane)

    member(myCast).Model("myplane").shader=color_shade

    - - add the meshDeform modifier

    member(myCast).Model("myplane").addmodifier(#meshDeform)

end buildplane
```

7. Now add an `exitFrame` handler - this is where all the fun happens:

```
on exitFrame me

    planeModel=member(myCast).Model("myplane")
```

8. We next set variables to the `vertexlist` and the `normalList`. Remember, since we alter the `vertexlist` to change the position of the vertices of the mesh, we must also alter the surface normals that are associated with them. If we do not, the vertex will change, but the shading will not and an unnatural looking deformation will occur.

```
    set myVertexlist=planeModel.meshDeform.mesh[1].vertexlist
    set myNormallist=planeModel.meshDeform.mesh[1].normalList
```

9. To actually alter the mesh, we must go through all the positions in the vertexlist. A plane is generated with the first vertex in the bottom right position, and the last vertex

in the list is the in the top left position. A place with four vertices is therefore in the following format:

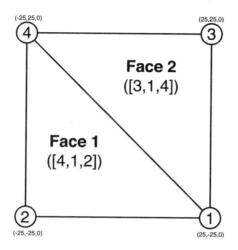

9. So, in the vertexlist, position 1 is the bottom right, position 2 is the bottom left, and so on. To cycle through those based on our vertexwidth and vertexheight we use the following repeat loop:

```
repeat with counterX=1 to pWidth
  repeat with counterY=0 to pHeight-1
```

10. Using these loops, grabbing the vertices in order is done like this:

```
myvertex=getat(myVertexlist, (counterX+(pWidth*counterY)))
```

11. In this next piece of code to add we alter the z position of the vertex by the sine of the x position plus our offset counter variable pWaveX. We then amplify the wave by a fixed value of 2. If you change that value, the waves get deeper accordingly.

```
set myvertex.z=sin(counterX+pWaveX)*2
```

12. After altering the vertex values we set it back into our list at the same position we took it from:

```
setat myVertexlist, (counterX+(pWidth*counterY)), myvertex
```

13. After changing the vertex position we need to reset the normal at that position as well. The correct normal value is calculated using the getnormalized(vector) command with the vector value used being the new vertex vector we just put back into the vertex list. That is the last we have to do in these repeat loops:

```
        setat myNormallist, (counterX+(pWidth*counterY)),
     ➥ getnormalized(myvertex)

    end repeat
  end repeat
```

14. Next we increment pWaveX by one. If it is then greater then the vertex width parameter (pWidth) we set it back 1. This will have the effect of moving the waves of the sine function across our plane in a horizontal direction.

```
set pWaveX=pWaveX+1

if pWaveX>pWidth then pWaveX=1
```

15. Finally, we set the vertexlist and normalList of our model to their respective altered lists.

```
set planeModel.meshDeform.mesh[1].vertexlist=myVertexlist
set planeModel.meshDeform.mesh[1].normalList=myNormallist

end exitframe me
```

16. Adding this behavior to our empty 3D world, and playing the movie, produces a rippling plane effect.

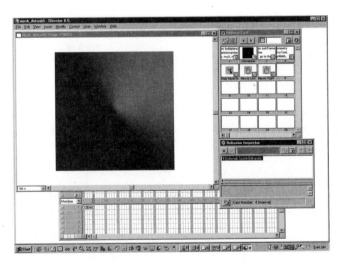

Interaction modifiers: collision

The final modifier we will examine is the collision modifier. This modifier is applied to specific models and it allows us to detect when two models collide as well as to obtain important information about the collision event. That information can be used in additional scripts that control reactions that are specific to those events. In previous versions of Director there were similar functions that operated in a two-dimensional mode, such as `intersect`, which allowed for the testing of intersection between two sprites. The collision detection system built into the 3D engine is significantly more sophisticated then its two dimensional counterpart. Fortunately, it is very easy to implement this feature, which will allow for the rapid development of very sophisticated games, training tools, simulations, and other applications where models need to interact with one another.

To understand collision detection we will first take a look at the chain of events relative to one another, as well as their placement in a typical Director project. The first step is to apply the modifier. In order to have collisions occur at least two models, the ones you expect to collide, must have the modifier attached. For the sake of convention, we will call them modelA and modelB. We add the modifier with the same simple Lingo line:

```
member(my3Dmember).model(modelname).addmodifier(#collision)
```

In this case we will substitute *modelname* with `modelA` and `modelB`. This command can be issued from any script in your movie; however, it is typically included in a behavior that is attached to the 3D sprite we're dealing with.

When applying the collision modifier, there is one parameter of particular importance to the behavior of the collision which may need to be adjusted. The `resolve` parameter (default = TRUE) will reposition models to their point of contact. This is useful since moving objects will rarely meet each other perfectly in 3D space, and when they don't they will appear to overlap each other. Setting the resolve property to true will prevent that from occurring and will result in a more solid appearance for your models by preventing them from passing through each other.

In some instances you may want to detect that two objects have collided while still allowing them to pass through - for example, a fish jumping into water, when it hits the water surface we detect that to play a splash sound, but allow it to enter into the water model. In those cases, you'll need to explicitly set the `resolve` property to false.

After attaching the collision modifier to the models, a collision callback script must be associated with each model. There are a couple ways we can do this. To specify a callback script that executes when any two models collide we can use the following Lingo:

```
member(my3Dmember).registerforevent(#collideany, #handlername,
➡ member "MovieScript")
```

`#handlername` is the name of the handler that will be called in the specified movie script. Replacing member *MovieScript* with 0 will allow the target handler to be located in any moviescript; however, care must be taken not to use the same handler name in more then one moviescript. By altering this slightly to use the `#collidewith` property we can specify a script to be executed only when a specific model registers a collision event.

```
member(my3Dmember).registerforevent(#collidewith, #handlername,
➡ member "MovieScript", SpecifiedModel)
```

The shortcut for this method of defining a callback is as follows:

```
member(my3Dmember).model(modelname).collision.setcollisioncallback
➡ (#handler, scriptname)
```

The `collisioncallback` handler must be located in a moviescript separate from the script containing the Lingo that assigns the callback. This script generally handles the determination of what collision event occurred and what to do next based on that event. A third script must be called from the `collisioncallback` handler to bring the effect of the collision to bear.

To reiterate the process in sequence we:

1. Attach the modifier to two models.

2. Attach a callback script to each model.

3. Write a callback script to determine the specifics of the collision which calls the appropriate handler.

4. Write script(s) to affect a response to the collision.

In its simplest state, collision detection between two objects can be applied with only a few lines of code. However, the detection of collisions between two objects in 3D space can be a processor intensive operation. In the very basic example above, we don't have to worry about that too much since we are simply detecting the collision of two objects in their default modes. In a more sophisticated application, say a simulated aircraft battle game, where there may be several objects that we must track, then optimizations will likely yield significantly improved performance. Fortunately, there are several parameters associated with the collision detection modifier that can be altered just for such optimizations.

The first parameter is `enabled`, a Boolean parameter which is by default true, that allows collision detection to be selectively enabled or disabled as needed while the program executes. When disabled the model is not included in collision detection calculations, so performance is improved.

The next parameter is `immovable`, also a Boolean value, which is false by default. This parameter should be set to true for all the objects in your scene which do not move, but may be involved in a collision. If you recall, the collision modifier must be added to each model that is expected to be involved in a collision. All objects with attached collision modifiers and the `enabled` property set to true are tested to determine if another object has collided with them. Only those with the `immovable` property set to false are also included in the calculation to determine if they have collided with another object. Given those facts, collision-enabled objects with `immovable` set to true undergo half the collision detection calculations that `immovable` set to false objects do. A real-world example of the applications of this would be in a virtual pinball game. The only moveable objects would include the ball, plunger, and paddles, which would all have the `immovable` property set to false. These objects would be greatly outnumbered by the fixed bumper objects which would have `immovable` set to true. By setting up your collisions in this fashion, a noticeable performance gain would likely result over leaving all objects at the default `immovable` value.

The final performance effecting parameter is mode, set in its default state as #sphere. The mode property dictates how collisions are actually detected for each model. As mentioned previously, collision detection can be a very processor intensive operation. Like many other operations used in real-time 3D graphic engines a minimalist approach is used in detecting collisions in Shockwave 3D to get optimal performance. The three possible values for mode are #sphere, #box, and #mesh. From these names we can deduce how the 3D engine can rapidly detect collisions between two objects.

Each model in a scene has a bounding sphere which denotes the "area" that the model occupies. The default mode setting of #sphere uses this bounding sphere to determine if the "area" of two models is intersecting. This is the fastest method of collision detection, however it doesn't use the actual mesh of the model to determine collision, it will likely only appear accurate if your object is a sphere.

For non-spherical objects the next fastest mode is #box. This is slightly slower as it doesn't use the inherent bounding sphere property of your model. However, it's still relying on the area of a bounding box rather then the mesh of the model itself for collision detection.

The last mode is the most processor intensive and has accuracy down to the vertex level. The #mesh mode actually uses the mesh of the model to determine intersections. The use of this mode should be done sparingly with careful consideration to the polygon count in associated models. Clearly, any operation with vertex accuracy must be applied to all vertices in the model. With that in mind, it's fair to expect that performance can be severely affected as polygon count increases.

In most cases, the use of #sphere or #box will yield suitable results. An example use of the #mesh mode may be something like raindrops falling on a plane. Since the modifier can return vertex level accuracy we could determine the exact position of the raindrop/plane intersection and perform a mesh deform operation originating from that point to generate a ripple in the plane.

Camera collisions

One of the most common and interesting applications for collision detection in Shockwave 3D is in the creation of first person games. In a typical first person game, you play from the main character's point of view. This effect is accomplished by driving the camera around your virtual 3D world. Any obstacles you encounter will need to block your path and prevent you from moving forward. This is where collision detection comes in. The problem with doing this in Director is that while collision detection for models is a simple feature built right into the engine, collision detection for cameras is not. In fact, Director has no built-in features for detecting collisions between cameras and other objects.

Fortunately, there is a relatively simple way around this, which involves the use of a couple key features of the 3D engine. The most significant of these features is that a camera can be a child object of any model. One of the basic rules of parent/child objects is that the child will automatically follow the parent, so any translations applied to the parent are automatically duplicated in all the child objects.

The next item of importance is the 3D engine's ability to render an object as invisible. These two key facts allow us to add a "detection" primitive, or a primitive model to a scene, position it at the camera's position, make it invisible, and attach the camera as a child object. When we apply translations to the detection primitive the camera will automatically follow. Furthermore, even though we set the visibility of the detection primitive to #none, it can still detect collisions with other models through the collision modifier. The following is a basic example of this technique.

Collisions with an invisible object

1. Create a new movie and set the stage size to the size you desire.

2. Select member 2 in the cast internal and select Insert > Media Element > Shockwave 3D. Name that member 3Dmember and drag and drop it so it spans frame 1 to 5 in channel 1 of the score. Scale it to fit the entire stage.

3. Next, select the first castmember and open a movie script window. To hold the script's place put a comment on the first line such as:

    ```
    - - first person camera collision example
    ```

4. Name the cast member main movie. Close that window.

5. Double-click in the frame script box of frame 5 and enter the following script in the subsequent script box and close it. This code will keep the playback head on the last frame when the movie is run. It will automatically be placed in member 3.

    ```
    on exitFrame me
       go to the frame
    end
    ```

6. Finally, select the 3D sprite in channel 1 and add a new behavior. The majority of the scripting will occur here, so we will go through it line by line.

7. Our first task is to declare the properties we will need. myCast will contain the name of the member this behavior is attached to. pMouseX and pMouseY will be the mouseH and mouseV values respectively of where the user clicks on the 3D sprite. pMove will be a Boolean toggle, true when the model player is moving, false when he is not.

    ```
    property myCast, pMouseX, pMouseY, pMove
    ```

8. The first major handler of this behavior will be to set up the basic elements of the environment when the sprite begins. That includes setting pMove to false since the player is not yet moving, building an object that we can run into (a box), and then call secondary handlers to add a collision detection object to the camera, and to add the collision modifiers to our objects.

    ```
    on beginsprite me

       - - The player is not moving yet
    ```

```
        set pMove=False

        - - Set the mycast property to the name of this sprites castmember
        set mycast=member(sprite(me.spritenum).membernum).name

        - - clear the castmember of all models before starting
        member(mycast).resetworld()

        - -create a new "blank" texture so our spheres can be a solid
        - - color
        member(mycast).newtexture("blank")

        - -create a green shader
        color_shade=member(mycast).newShader("green_shader", #standard)
        color_shade.diffuse=rgb(100,200,100)
        color_shade.ambient=rgb(100,200,100)
        color_shade.texturemode=#wrapplanar

        - - set the shaders to a blank texture so they appear as a solid
        - - color

        member(mycast).shader("green_shader").texture=member(mycast).
        ➡ texture("blank")

        - - create a new box with a size of 50

        newbox = member(mycast).newModelResource("green_box",
        ➡#box, #both)
        newbox.height = 50
        newbox.width = 50
        newbox.length = 50
        newbox.lengthvertices=4
        newbox.widthvertices=4
        newbox.heightvertices=4

        - - create the box
        aa = member(mycast).newModel("green_box", newbox)

        - - apply the shader
        member(mycast).Model("green_box").shader=color_shade

- - change the background color to white
member(mycast).bgcolor=rgb(255,255,255)

        - - call the routine to add the detection box to the camera
        addcamerabox

        - - call the routine to add the collision modifiers
        addcollisionmodifiers
end
```

9. The `addcamerabox` handler is a straightforward addition of a new model resource to the member in the form of a `#box` primitive. To minimize the effect of this box on playback, we only build the `#front` faces and keep the polygon count to a minimum by setting all the vertices values to the minimum of 2. The size of the box we have set to 10 - the size is arbitrary and essentially dictates the size of your camera. The smaller this box is, the closer you can get to objects before a collision event occurs and vice versa.

```
on addcamerabox me

    newbox = member(mycast).newModelResource("camera_box", #box,
    ➥ #front)
    newbox.height = 10
    newbox.width = 10
    newbox.length = 10
    newbox.lengthvertices=2
    newbox.widthvertices=2
    newbox.heightvertices=2

    - - create the box
    aa = member(mycast).newModel("camera_box", newbox)
```

10. Now that we have defined the detection box, we need to make it invisible and position it at the same location as the camera (in this case we're using the default camera at position 1). Assigning the objects to variables allows for the application of a simple and constant naming convention throughout the script. In this case, we always refer to the detection box as "camerabox" and the camera itself as "mycamera".

```
    set camerabox=member(mycast).model("camera_box")
    set mycamera=member(mycast).camera[1]

    - - set the detection box to be invisible
    camerabox.visibility=#none

    - - set the position of the detection box to the camera position
    camerabox.worldposition=mycamera.worldposition
```

11. Now that everything has the proper visibility and is in the proper position, we make the camera a child object of the box. After this point, we never alter the camera position directly with Lingo. All transformations are applied to the `camerabox` object only. The camera itself will update automatically to match the parent box.

```
    camerabox.addchild(mycamera)

end addcamerabox me
```

12. The `addcollisionmodifiers` handler applies collision detection modifiers to both the `camerabox` and the `box` we built in the `beginsprite` script, which we will use at runtime as an obstacle to run into. We refer to that box here as `targetbox`. The script

is very basic with the following points to note: First, we have `resolve` set to true for the camera box only.

```
on addcollisionmodifiers

  set camerabox=member(mycast).model("camera_box")
  set targetbox=member(mycast).Model("green_box")

  camerabox.addmodifier(#collision)
  camerabox.collision.enabled=true
  camerabox.collision.resolve=true
  camerabox.collision.mode=#mesh
```

13. The `targetbox` doesn't move so we set the `immovable` property to true. The `resolve` property can also be set to false since this object doesn't move.

```
  targetbox.addmodifier(#collision)
  targetbox.collision.enabled=true
  targetbox.collision.resolve=false
  targetbox.collision.immovable=true
  targetbox.collision.mode=#mesh
```

14. We set the `collisioncallback` only for those objects that need to respond to the collision. Since we're only dealing with the camera here, we have added the callback for it only.

```
  camerabox.collision.setcollisioncallback
  ➥ (#bounce, member "Main Movie")

end addcollisionmodifiers
```

15. The `on mouseDown` handler within this behavior sets our mouse location property values to the mouse location at mousedown. It also sets a third property that lets the behavior know that the camera should be in motion. We could accomplish the same thing with a `do while the stilldown` loop, however that technique will lock us into this script until mouse up. This would prevent other scripts and events from occurring while we are navigating our scene. To avoid that we use this flag property which can be accessed in the `on exitFrame` script below.

```
on mouseDown me

  set pMouseX=the mouseH
  set pMouseY=the mouseV

  set pMove=True

end mouseDown me
```

16. In the `on exitframe` handler we want to move our box/camera if the mouse is down. We use the pMove flag in the `if` statement to prevent attempting calculation based on the mouse position until the mouseDown event has been processed in which we set the initial values needed for the calculation. If we don't do this there is the risk of runtime errors, or unexpected results for these calculations. The idea here is that if we move the mouse right from its original mouseDown location while holding the mouse down the camera will pan right. Move the mouse left, the camera will pan left. Moving the mouse up transforms the camera forward, while down transforms it backward. The speed of motion is governed by how far the mouse moves from the original mousedown location (further is faster). Note that both pMove and the stillDown must be true for the camera motion to occur. If either is false it checks the value of pMove and sets it to false if its true.

```
on exitframe me

  if pMove and the stilldown then
    set camerabox=member(mycast).model("camera_box")

    set stepX=(the mouseV-pMouseY)/25
    set stepY=(pMouseX-the mouseH)/25

    camerabox.translate(0,0, stepX)
    camerabox.rotate(0, stepY, 0)

  else

    if pmove then
      pMove=false
    end if

  end if

end exitframe me
```

17. In the moviescript "main movie" we add the following collision callback handler. The collisioncallback handler is always passed the collisiondata variable. That variable contains several properties which include the models involved in the collision (modelA and modelB), collisionnormal (the direction of the collision) and the pointofcontact (the vector when the two models meet). The last two items (collisionnormal and pointofcontact) only contain useable data if the collision mode specified for both models is #mesh. In this example we did specify #mesh mode for both objects so the following script will return results for all variables. Finally, we calculate the angle between the objects at the time of contact, which would be useful for determining a bounce angle to bounce the camera off the target object.

```
on bounce me, collisiondata

  put "Model A: " & collisiondata.modela
  put "Model B: " & collisiondata.modelb
```

```
put "Collision Normal: " & collisiondata.collisionnormal
put "Point of Contact: " & collisiondata.pointofcontact
put "Angle between objects: " &
➡ collisiondata.collisionnormal.anglebetween
➡ (collisiondata.pointofcontact)

end bounce me
```

Summary

Director 8.5's built in 3D technology provides a very powerful array of tools that are useful for modifying the models in a 3D scene. While toon and inker can provide for some interesting appearing models the powerful features are those provided by meshDeform, SDS, LOD and collision. These modifiers are almost limitless in their applications in realtime interactive 3D applications. The explanations, Lingo and examples provided here should establish a good base to explore.

We would strongly recommend that you play - *yes, play* - with these modifiers. They can provide some very powerful effects to your presentations, but can also cause you a lot of headaches if you have to have them present in your Director applications. The best way to get to know their limitations is by trial and error, by adjusting parameters and settings, and from spending a lot of time with them. The examples used in this chapter go a long way towards getting you accustomed to the capabilities of the 3D engine, but only time spent *playing* will get you there.

In the next chapter we look at the use of sound in Director and combine it with the capabilities of the 3D engine. Why not see if you can create a collision handler that generates a sound effect...?

Chapter 9
Sound

This chapter will give you a broad grasp of how to use Lingo to handle audio in Director 8.5. Hopefully, it will tempt you to go beyond the usual backing track to a presentation, and inspire the creation of interactive work that uses sound as an intrinsic element. More specifically, this chapter will show how the newer Lingo sound commands allow us to build compelling online experiences that use relatively small file sizes.

Media created for the computer has undervalued the potential impact of sound. Visual concerns dominate the design process with sound often only considered towards the end of production. With the development of the web, new media became increasingly silent. It is game designers who value the audio-visual over the purely visual: effects and the sound track are blended in creative ways to enhance the gaming atmosphere. Increasingly the musical score for a game is programmed to subtly shift mood and tempo to match the player's progress.

Although new media developers have been slow to respond to the challenges of designing audio for interactivity, there has been interesting experimental work that suggest some of the possibilities. Toshio Iwai, Golan Levin, and my own group, Antirom, have all explored new forms that combine sound, interaction, and graphics. To see what's out there and what's possible have a look at the URLs at the end of this chapter.

Throughout this chapter we're going to learn how to use Lingo to play sounds. We are first going to look at a number of different Lingo commands and structures available to the Director developer when using sound. Then we'll attempt to apply some of this knowledge to create Director movies that respond to user interaction according to some simple rules of music creation - sound toys.

Matters of import

How do we make noise in Director? Since Director is an environment for playing back different media, we'll need to import an audio file. This will create a sound cast member that we then play in Director. We use the standard Import to do this. If you don't have your own sounds you can find some on the CD relating to this chapter.

Internal or linked?

The only option you have when you import the sound files is whether the sound cast member's data is written into the Director movie itself (internal), or just referenced (linked) from a separate file. If the sound is internal we can load the whole sound into memory so that we have better timing. These internal sounds are imported from AIFF, WAV, AU, Shockwave Audio, and MP3 formats, and from Macintosh System 7 sounds. I advise that you use 16-bit sounds and choose a sample rate of 44.1 or 22.050 kHz.

If the sound is linked we don't use as much memory because Director will be streaming the audio as it plays. Generally we use internal sounds for short single notes, loops, or effects, and we use external sounds for longer sound tracks. The examples in this chapter will use internal sounds because we'll be playing short sounds, hopefully with more accurate timing.

Importing sound

OK, let's get a sound into Director to work with.

1.   Choose the File > Import menu item.

2.   Select the sound file you wish to import. For our examples we're going to use piano.aif, which is included on the CD.

3.   The next step is to decide if you want the sound to be internal or linked. The bottom pull down menu allows you to select Standard Import to make an internal sound, or Link to External File to make a linked sound. Choose the Standard Import option.

4.   Click the Import button.

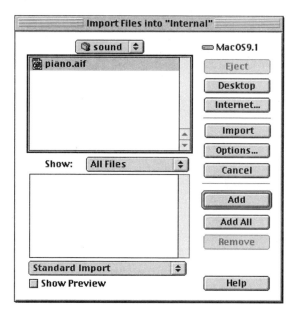

5.   The newly created sound cast member will now be in the cast window. Don't close the file, we'll use it straight away.

Inspecting the sound

Now that we have imported a sound we can use the **Property Inspector** to play it, view its properties, and change those properties that are editable.

6. Select the `piano` sound cast member.

7. Choose Window > Inspectors > Property to open the property inspector.

8. Click Member to access the member tab. The name of the sound cast member can be edited in the member tab. The size of member can also be viewed in this tab.

9. Click Sound to access the sound tab. The Loop property can then be edited, and the sound played in the sound pane here. The duration of the sound, the sample rate, the sample size and the channels non-editable properties can be viewed from this tab. The channels property tells you whether the sound is mono or stereo. A mono sound has one channel, and a stereo channel has two. I usually use mono sounds as stereo sounds take twice the space. If you have imported the piano sound from the CDROM it will look like this:

Keep this file open, as we'll come back to it again, in just a minute.

Musical scores

Although we're going to concentrate on using Lingo to control sound, we'll quickly cover sounds in the score first, as this will help us to understand the way Director plays sounds. Just as bitmap cast members are displayed as sprites in channels in the score, sounds are also played in channels.

There are eight channels for sounds in Director, but only two of these are accessible from the score. These channels can play one sound at a time each.

When using the score to control sounds, the sound cast member will play as long as it's in a sound channel for the current frame. Unlike the way a bitmap will display, a sound in the score may not play if its sprite is too short. This can be remedied by setting the sound cast member to loop. A gap between sounds in the score will cause the sound to start again. There is no way in the score to control where to play from in a sound cast member or at what speed the sound cast member plays. The score can only **trigger** sounds, which is fine for most presentations and other simple linear work.

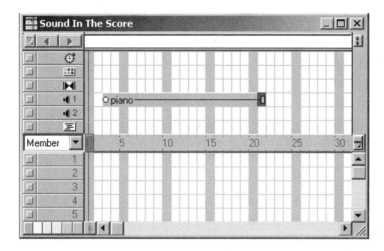

Adding the sound to the score

Have you still got your piano cast member waiting?

10.　If you cannot see the two sound channels, show them by clicking the Hide/Show Effects Channels button in the top right of the score - it's the button with the icon that has two vertical arrows pointing together.

11.　Drag the piano sound cast member from the cast window to the score window and then drop the sound onto one of the sound channels. In the above screenshot I have dropped the sound onto frame 3

12.　Drag the sound sprite out to span the desired length in frames. In the above screenshot I have dragged the end of sound sprite to frame 21.

13.　Save your file as playsound.dir, we'll make use of it again.

Now you can rewind and play your movie. You should hear the sound play again and again as the playhead loops round the movie. Try making the sound span less or more frames, and listen to how this makes the sound cut out before it has finished, or pause before the movie loops again.

The sound of Lingo

The score is fine for adding sounds to animations and presentations, but to leave it at that is really wasting the potential of Director: we want interactivity, and to get interactivity we need to use Lingo.

Lingo has far more control over a sound than the score and allows us to play up to eight sounds at once, ignoring what is already set in the score, and allowing us to decide exactly when to start and stop them. We can access sounds outside of the Director cast - even remote sounds on the Internet - and can control the exact timing of sound playback, which is so important for creating musical experiences. This timing control extends to being able to start playing and looping any part of a sound cast member. We can also change the pan, pitch, and volume of sounds with Lingo.

As we've seen in earlier chapters, the best place to learn Lingo is the message window, so that is where we will start.

Message window music

The very simplest way to use Lingo to make sound is the command:

```
beep
```

Try it in the message window. The command gets Director to play the computer's system alert sound. We can pass it an argument that is the number of times the beep repeats:

```
beep(2)
```

If we want to change the volume of this beep we have to use the Director system property called the soundLevel, which we can set like this:

```
the soundLevel = 4
```

soundLevel values go from 0 (silent) to 7, which is the maximum volume. Note that the soundLevel sets the global sound level of the entire computer system. I think it's quite rude to adjust the soundLevel in Director as users may have turned their volume down for a good reason. So, we now know beep and the soundLevel, which don't use the Director sound system at all and aren't much use for making music, but are very simple. We're going to have to get a little deeper into Lingo before we can truly control Director's sound system. We access sounds inside Director using the syntax:

```
sound(whichchannel).function(arguments)
```

You'll notice here that we're using dot syntax to access the functions of a sound object. There is one sound object for each channel, each with properties and functions that you access using dot syntax. Lets find the sound object that controls channel one in the message window:

```
put sound(1)
- - <Prop Ref 2 c897cf0>
```

There it is. It's got a funny name, I'll grant you that, but it and seven of its friends control all our access to sound, so be nice to it. (Don't worry if you get a different value to the above, but it should look at least slightly similar.)

What about sound cast members? Well they are objects too, and they behave much like other cast members. We can use the cast member name, so open `playsound.dir` and try typing the following:

```
put member("piano")
- - (member 1 of castLib 1)
```

Or you can try their number:

```
put member(1)
- -(member 1 of castLib 1)
```

We can access their properties with Lingo too:

```
put member("piano").duration
- - 5818
```

And we can set some of their properties too. If you open the property inspector and select the sound cast member, you will be able to see your message window Lingo changing the tick of the loop property when you type the following:

```
member("piano").loop = true
```

The first thing we need to do to play a sound cast member is to load it into Director's RAM buffer. We do that with the following function that allows us to pass the sound cast member to the sound channel object. Try it in the message window.

```
sound(1).queue(member("piano"))
```

Now we've definitely loaded the sound, but we still can't hear it. Make sure you have unchecked the loop property of the sound in the inspector (otherwise the sound will loop forever), before playing it with:

```
sound(1).play()
```

The `queue()` and `play()` functions also give control over the way the sound is played beyond the properties of the sound channel object. For example we can queue two sounds and then play them as a sequence. So, let's queue each sound, one at time, in the message window and then play them:

```
sound(1).queue(member("piano"))
sound(1).queue(member("piano"))
sound(1).play()
```

So, we can use queue to play sounds one at a time with no pauses between them. This feature is perfect for making shockwave jukeboxes and radios, but we are going to make something a little more interactive: a Lingo synthesizer!

Pitching it up

A 'synthesizer' is so called because it plays sounds as a musical instrument. This means that it needs to be able to play sounds at different pitches. In order, therefore, to make a synthesizer we need to be able to control the pitch of the sound that we output.

The queue function only accepts a single argument, which is normally the sound cast member that we want to play. We can, however, gain extra control over the sound object using the queue function: instead of sending it a sound cast member we can send a property list. That property list always contains the sound cast member we want to play, but it can also contain lots of other properties, including one that allows us to set the pitch of the sound. This use of Lingo is of particular interest when developing for the Internet, as final file sizes can often be drastically reduced by reducing the number of sounds that need to be sent to achieve the same audio range. Instead of making separate sound cast members for different pitches, we can play differently pitched notes using a single sound file.

With playsound.dir open, make a property list for the queue function in the message window:

```
a = [#member:member("piano")]
```

And let's send it through a queue function to a sound channel:

```
sound(1).queue(a)
```

Now, we'll play it:

```
sound(1).play()
```

We can also make the property list and then call the queue function in one line of Lingo:

```
sound(1).queue([#member:member("piano")])
sound(1).play()
```

That sounded much the same as before, but now we've got the power to add other properties to that list that affect the way the sound is played:

```
sound(1).queue([#member:member("piano"), #rateShift:8])
sound(1).play()
```

Listen to the last two examples. Can you hear the difference? The #rateShift property of the queue function argument list sets the pitch of the sound. It does this by playing the sound faster or slower. When #rateShift is zero, the sound plays as usual. If we set #rateShift to a positive integer Director plays the sound faster. This means the sound will be higher in pitch and the duration of sound will be decreased from normal. If we set #rateShift to a negative integer Director will play the sound slower. This means the sound will be lower in pitch and the duration of the sound will be increased.

We can also check the rateShift property of a currently playing sound channel with:

```
put sound(1).rateShift
```

OK, let's start pitching the curve!

Creating a mouse piano

We've already imported sound to our movie, so we're ready to move beyond the message window and to find out what these units of #rateShift are. We're going write a behavior to help. Make sure you delete the sound sprite from the score sound channel if you want to continue to use playsound.dir, or you could just open a new movie and import piano.aif as we did earlier in "Importing a Sound". Now, double-click on a script channel frame to automatically create a new behavior script, as shown:

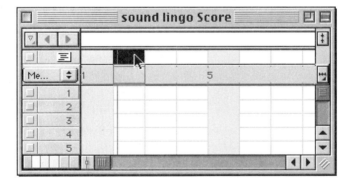

This should open the script window and automatically create our first event handler for us. We type one line of Lingo into this exitFrame handler to make this:

```
on exitFrame me

    go the frame

end exitFrame
```

Close the script window. Now when we rewind and play the movie, if we're looking at the score, we'll be able to see the playhead looping on the single frame. Director generates the exitFrame event every time we leave a frame. Our behavior's exitFrame handler has handled that event by telling Director to move the playhead back to the start of the current frame. This is a crucial trick in Lingo programming used to effectively stop the score playing, whilst still getting updates to our script. *You knew that already?* Just checking.

Now stop the movie, open the cast window and open the behavior again. You can do this in one of two ways:

- You can double-click on the behavior script cast member. This will open the behavior inspector. Now click on the behavior inspector's script button. This will open the behavior's script.

- You can select the behavior script cast member. Now choose Window > Script. This will also open the behavior's script.

We're going to add another event handler. This time we are going to handle a user-generated event: a mouseDown event. Type the following below the exitFrame handler:

```
on mouseDown me

    sound(1).queue([#member: member("piano")])
    sound(1).play()

end mouseDown
```

Play the movie. Now when you first click the mouse on the stage the sound plays; if you let the sound finish, a subsequent click will play the sound again. If you click before the sound stops, then the sound will start to queue up in the buffer and play again only when the sound has completed playing. So we need to stop the old sound before we start the new one by modifying our mouseDown event - simply adding one line to our handler can do this:

```
on mouseDown me

    sound(1).stop()
    sound(1).queue([#member: member("piano")])
    sound(1).play()

end mouseDown
```

Once again, play the movie. Now the sound should re-trigger every time you click the mouse on the stage. Let's add #rateShift. We could just add a fixed #rateShift like:

```
sound(1).queue([#member:member("piano"), #rateShift:10])
```

But let's try and change with a dynamic #rateShift value instead. Our script is going to remember the rate we want using a custom property we will call pPitch. The 'p' in front of the name reminds us that it's a property.

Add the following to the very **top** of the behavior:

```
property pPitch
```

Underneath this line, we'll initialize the value of the property when the behavior is created with a handler:

```
on beginSprite me

    pPitch = 0

end
```

We can now modify the mouseDown handler to use this property:

```
on mouseDown me

    pPitch = pPitch + 1
    sound(1).stop()
    sound(1).queue([#member:member("piano"), #rateShift:pPitch])
    sound(1).play()

end mouseDown
```

With this new handler each time we click the mouse, the property pPitch is incremented by one. pPitch is used as the value for #rateShift when we queue the next sound. Try it, what does it sound like? It sounds like a cat walking up a piano keyboard. So what are the units of #rateShift? A single key on a piano, which is an interval called the semitone. You're playing a chromatic scale: each and every key on the piano, one at a time. We will return to scales in a moment, but first let's consider the closeness of our little synthesized piano to a real piano.

Polyphonic funk

When you trigger two sounds close together using our mouse piano behavior, what do you hear? *One note.* You may even notice a slight click when the first note is cut off by the second. When you play the same thing on a real piano we still hear the remains of the first note whilst the second note is playing. This is because a real piano is polyphonic: it can play many keys (notes) at once. Our mouse piano behavior is monophonic: it can play only one note at a time. And we can only play one note at a time because we're using one sound channel and, as you know, a sound channel can only play one note at a time.

You've probably guessed that the way around this problem is to use more than one sound channel. With a real piano we theoretically have eighty-eight sound channels: we can play all the keys at once. With our mouse piano behavior we have only eight possible channels. To get around this we'll use a technique called 'voice stealing'. Every time we need a new note, we'll use a new channel. When we run out of channels we'll steal the oldest note. Even if this oldest note is still playing we'll already be playing seven other notes, so stopping it won't sound nearly as dramatic as when we were using just one sound channel for the whole mouse piano behavior.

Let's add to our existing behavior to make it polyphonic. First we need to keep track of the last sound channel that we used. Make another property in our behavior by adding to the top of the script:

```
        property pSoundChannel
```

We'll need to set the initial value of this property as we did with pPitch. So, add as the first line of the beginSprite handler:

```
        on beginSprite me

          pSoundChannel = 1
          pPitch = 0

        end
```

Now comes the real action! We add the following code to the beginning of the mouseDown handler:

```
        on mouseDown me

          pSoundChannel = pSoundChannel + 1

          if pSoundChannel > 8 then
            pSoundChannel = 1
          end if

          pPitch = pPitch + 1
          ...
```

The purpose of these lines is to make sure that the sound channel allocation goes round in a loop: 1, 2, 3, 4, 5, 6, 7, 8, 1, 2, 3, 4, 5, 6, 7, 8, 1, 2, 3, 4, 5, 6, 7... and so on. This makes sure that we never run out of sound channels and only reuse the oldest sound.

To make use of the pSoundChannel property when we ask for a sound to be played, we need to change the three lines that start:

```
        sound(1)
```

We change them to lines that start:

```
        ...
        pPitch = pPitch + 1

          sound(pSoundChannel).stop()
          sound(pSoundChannel).queue([#member:member("piano"),
          ➥ #rateShift:pPitch])
          sound(pSoundChannel).play()

        end mouseDown
```

That's it. Try it out. Run the movie and click on the stage. It's pretty good - the notes hang on and overlap nicely. However, with some sounds, it all gets a little distorted. This is because we're playing eight sounds at once, all at full volume. We need to turn down each sound channel sound so that they don't overload Director's sound system and distort. To do this we make use of another property of the sound channel object. This time, you've guessed it: it's volume. We can set the volume of channel like this:

```
sound(whichChannel).volume = whichVolume
```

The volume property can be set between a minimum of 0 and a maximum of 255.
I want to set all the sound channels to 50. You can choose your own value, depending on the sound you are using. We're going to be do this with a repeat loop in the beginSprite handler:

```
on beginSprite me

  repeat with channel = 1 to 8
    sound(channel).volume = 50
  end repeat

  pSoundChannel = 1
  pPitch = 0

end
```

This should now sound less distorted and all the clicking should have disappeared. We've made a simple polyphonic synthesizer.

Your behavior should now look something like the following script. Notice that I've added some comments to make the lingo easier to read.

Mouse piano frame behavior

```
- - - - - - - - - - - - - - - - - - - - - - - - - - - -
- - mouse piano : frame behavior
- - - - - - - - - - - - - - - - - - - - - - - - - - - -


    property pSoundChannel
    property pPitch


- - - - - - - - - - - - - - - - - - - - - - - - - - - -
- - beginSprite : initialize properties
- - - - - - - - - - - - - - - - - - - - - - - - - - - -
on beginSprite me

  repeat with channel = 1 to 8
    sound(channel).volume = 50
  end repeat

  pSoundChannel = 1
  pPitch = 0

end
```

```
- - - - - - - - - - - - - - - - - - - - - - - - - - - -
- - exitFrame : loop on the current frame
- - - - - - - - - - - - - - - - - - - - - - - - - - - -
on exitFrame me

    go the frame

end exitFrame

- - - - - - - - - - - - - - - - - - - - - - - - - - - -
- - mouseDown : play a new note in a new channel
- - - - - - - - - - - - - - - - - - - - - - - - - - - -
on mouseDown me

  pSoundChannel = pSoundChannel + 1
  if pSoundChannel > 8 then
    pSoundChannel = 1
  end if

  pPitch = pPitch + 1

  sound(pSoundChannel).stop()
  sound(pSoundChannel).queue([ #member: member("piano"),
➡ #rateShift:pPitch ])
  sound(pSoundChannel).play()

end mouseDown


- - - - - - - - - - - - - - - - - - - - - - - - - - - -
```

We can make an interesting variation to this behavior by changing just one line of Lingo in the mouseDown handler. Instead of making the pitch rise forever, we're going to map the vertical mouse position to the pitch of the note. The height of the stage is given by:

```
the stagebottom - the stagetop
```

Therefore we can get a value for the pitch using the calculation:

```
pPitch = the mouseV * 12 / (the stagebottom - the stagetop)
```

Write this over the old line:

```
pPitch = pPitch + 1
```

Now run the movie and click in different places. Save this move as my mouse piano.dir, as we'll be using it again very soon. If you've had any problems building the mouse piano refer to the mouse piano.dir file on the CD.

For another version, why not see if you can work out how to make the pitch rise as you click higher up the stage.

Scales as lists

Although you don't need to be a music aficionado, in order to create funky, flowing sounds it helps if you have at least a basic understanding of musical scales. So, here's your crash course...with a Lingo slant. Let's start by taking a look at a piano keyboard:

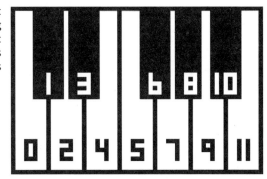

It's a rather short piano keyboard - it only covers one octave - but since the notes repeat in each octave, it will be fine for our purposes. As you can see there are 12 keys numbered from 0 to 11. I've done this because the number can be used to represent the #rateShift of the key. Since the first key can be played at normal speed it's value is zero. As we discovered earlier, each #rateShift unit is a semitone and, therefore, the series of whole numbers makes the chromatic scale. Using a linear list we can now define the scale in Lingo. The chromatic scale would be:

```
[0, 1, 2, 3, 4, 5, 6, 7, 8, 9, 10, 11]
```

Let's try and write a simple handler to play this list as a musical scale from the message window. First make a movie script by selecting an empty slot in the cast (of either your mouse piano or by opening mouse piano.dir from the CD), and choosing Window > Script. This will open the script window with a new movie script. Now write in the handler:

```
on playPitchList(pitchList)

  sound(1).stop()

  repeat with note in pitchList
    sound(1).queue([#member:member("piano"),#rateShift:note,
    ➡ #endTime:300])
  end repeat

  sound(1).play()

end playPitchList
```

You may have noticed that we're using a new queue property called #endTime. This lets us decide when we want a particular sound in the queue to stop. In this handler we add every note in the scale to a single sound object's queue and then leave it to play them all. Close the script window and now try calling it from the message window with our first scale:

```
playPitchList([0, 1, 2, 3, 4, 5, 6, 7, 8, 9, 10, 11])
```

Because octaves repeat themselves just twelve semitones up, we can calculate the octave above this in the message window as:

```
put [0, 1, 2, 3, 4, 5, 6, 7, 8, 9, 10, 11] + 12
```

And we can be sure to get returned:

```
-- [12, 13, 14, 15, 16, 17, 18, 19, 20, 21, 22, 23]
```

We can also calculate the octave below, thus:

```
put [0, 1, 2, 3, 4, 5, 6, 7, 8, 9, 10, 11] - 12
```

Returning:

```
-- [-12, -11, -10, -9, -8, -7, -6, -5, -4, -3, -2, -1]
```

If we were to use all these pitch values, the far extremes of 23 and -12 would sound pretty strange and unmusical. Generally pitching down is a bad idea because the sound becomes grainy and distorted quite quickly. Pitching the sound up a large distance is a bad idea because the sound becomes too short and sounds less and less like the original instrument. Sometimes pitching the sound a long way results in creative and interesting effects, but most of the time it doesn't. Try these transposed scales for yourself using the playPitchList handler.

White keys and modes

We can make different scales from this keyboard as well as the chromatic scale; we just need to leave some notes out. One of the most common scales is the diatonic, or major, scale. We can derive this from our keyboard by just using the white keys and leaving out the black keys. This gives us the list:

```
[0, 2, 4, 5, 7, 9, 11]
```

As you can see it's a scale with seven notes in. By just changing which note we start with, we get seven different variants of this scale. These variants are called modes. For instance if we started on the second note, we get a mode called the Dorian mode:

```
[2, 4, 5, 7, 9, 11, 12]
```

Notice how I've added the first note of the scale an octave up at the end of the list by adding 12 onto its 0 value.

We can get the third mode, the Phrygian mode, in a similar way:

```
[4, 5, 7, 9, 11, 12, 14]
```

You can work out the other diatonic modes for yourselves. Remember that if the pitch distance gets too big you might want to subtract or add some value onto the whole list to get a set of values nearer to zero center.

For instance, the last mode, on the seventh degree of the scale would work out as:

```
[11, 12, 14, 16, 17, 19, 21]
```

We get a better sounding scale if we do this in the message window:

```
put [11, 12, 14, 16, 17, 19, 21] - 15
- - [-4, -3, -1, 1, 2, 4, 6]
```

The sound of a scale is created more by the number of notes left out between the two notes in scale rather that the actual pitch that scale starts on. This space between two notes is called an interval. So feel free to choose different numbers to subtract and add to your lists. Try out these scales for yourself using the playPitchList handler.

Black key blues

Another really fun set of scales that work very well with interactive music are those with only five notes in. These are called pentatonic scales. We can make one very easily by choosing all the notes from the keyboard that we didn't use before: the black keys. This pentatonic scale makes the list:

```
[1, 3, 6, 8, 10]
```

Because there are not as many notes in these scales they are generally a lot more forgiving when the user tries out different combinations of notes. Pretty much any combination of five notes will make a reasonable pentatonic scale, as long as some of the intervals between pitches are greater than one. Another very common scale is called the major pentatonic scale; notice that it is made out of some the notes of white key scale we looked at earlier:

```
[0, 2, 4, 5, 7]
```

Just as we did with modes earlier we can rotate pentatonic scales to get different versions. If we start on the second position of the major pentatonic we get the minor pentatonic, which some people call the blues scale:

```
[2, 4, 5, 7, 12]
```

Try making up your own pentatonic scales and playing them using the playPitchList handler.

Key Piano

We've now played with quite a few different scales and are about ready to build our first toy that uses these musical lists. The Director movie we're going to build still needs just one sound, but actually has a bitmap graphic and two scripts! It's going to use the number keys on the top of the keyboard to trigger notes and a simple animation. The easiest starting point will be to save the mouse piano movie, then save the movie again (using Save As...) calling it my key piano.dir, so you can use it here.

First, we're going to modify the frame behavior. This behavior is pretty similar to the old mouse piano behavior. So double-click on it in the cast to open up the script window and we can type the changes in. There is a new property, called pPitchList, whose purpose (after the last section) I'm sure you can all grasp. Below the existing pPitch declaration we add:

```
property pSoundChannel
property pPitch
property pPitchList
```

Now add to the beginSprite handler:

```
...
repeat with channel = 1 to 8
    sound(channel).volume = 50
end repeat

pPitchList = [-5, -4, -2, 0, 2, 3, 5, 7, 8, 10]
pSoundChannel = 1
...
```

Notice that this list has ten notes in it. That's because the toy we're making plays ten different pitches from the keyboard number keys. You can use any scale that you want here, as long as it has ten entries in the list. To get my pPitchList I started from the major scale:

```
- - [0, 2, 4, 5, 7, 9, 11]
```

I found the octave above:

```
put [0, 2, 4, 5, 7, 9, 11] + 12
- - [12, 14, 16, 17, 19, 21, 23]
```

Starting from the third note I added five notes from each octave to get:

```
[4, 5, 7, 9, 11, 12, 14, 16, 17, 19]
```

I then moved the scale down to keep the #rateShift numbers small:

```
put [4, 5, 7, 9, 11, 12, 14, 16, 17, 19] - 9
```

```
-- [-5, -4, -2, 0, 2, 3, 5, 7, 8, 10]
```

The next block of code, the `exitFrame` handler stays exactly the same.

Notable keys

The biggest change comes, not surprisingly, in what was the `mouseDown` handler. We change the event that we are handling from `mouseDown` to `KeyDown`. So instead of:

```
on mouseDown me
...
end mouseDown
```

We have:

```
on keyDown me
...
end keyDown
```

Now we need to add some lines of Lingo to find out what number key is being pressed. We know what the last key was from `the key` system property. This is given to us as a string. By turning it into a whole number using the `integer` command we should get either a number or a nothing (`void` in Lingo). So, insert the following:

```
on keyDown me
note = (the key).integer
...
```

We'll get a `void` if the user presses a letter key by mistake. The next line checks if we have indeed got a `void` value. If so, we give up here and stop the handler execution using the `return` command:

```
if note.voidP then return
```

Now we need to check if the number key was zero. If it is we set it to ten, so that the sequence of keys on the keyboard correlates to the sequence of notes in our `pPitchList`.

```
if note = 0 then note = 10
```

This is because the number 0 comes after the number 9 on the keyboard, never mind that we can't get the zero-eth position from a list in Lingo anyway. So, if we've got this far, the user has probably pressed the right key: a keyboard number between 1 and 0.

The next four lines remain as in the mouse piano behavior. They are still needed to set `pSoundChannel` to the oldest sound channel. After this we need to change the Lingo that sets `pPitch`. Rather than using an incrementing property or the mouse position, we're going to use the `note` variable to tell us which position to get from the `pPitchList` property:

```
...
```

```
pSoundChannel = 1
  end if

pPitch = pPitchList[note]

sound(pSoundChannel).stop()
...
```

The next four lines remain the same as before, we're making good use of our existing code. We queue and play the sound just as the mouse piano behavior did. We're halfway there now. You can now run the movie. Press the number keys to play notes from our scale. Try changing the scale to something more to your taste.

Visual feedback

All that remains is to add the animations. The last line we need to add to our new KeyDown handler calls the relevant sprite to tell it to start animating:

```
...
sound(pSoundChannel).play()

sprite(note).startAnim()

end keyDown
```

We'll define the startAnim function later when we write the sprite's behavior.

We now need to make our bitmap graphic:

1. Open the paint window by choosing Window > Paint.

2. Draw in a simple shape with the pencil tool. I drew a simple square made up of four pixels.

3. Close the paint window.

4. Drag the bitmap cast member you have just created from the cast window to the stage.

5. Repeat this dragging process ten times to create ten sprites.

6. Make sure that the sprites are in the first ten channels of the score.

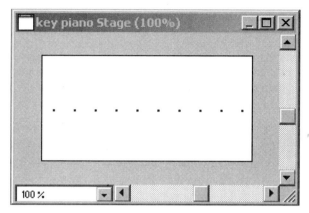

Once you have arranged these sprites to your satisfaction on the stage, we'll create the animation behavior for them:

7. Select all ten sprites

8. Open the behavior inspector by choosing Window > Inspectors > Behavior.

9. Click on the behavior inspector's Behavior pop-up button (the button with the '+' icon).

10. Choose the New Behavior... menu item.

11. The Name Behavior dialog box will appear. Name our new behavior key anim

12. Now click on the behavior inspector's script window button, and the script we have just created will appear.

Now we can start writing the Lingo that will make our sprite behavior animate. When the sprite isn't animating it's going to be scaled down to be a tiny dot. We are going to make the sprite scale up suddenly at the start of the animation, and then each frame gently get smaller and smaller until it's a dot again. This will visually reflect the sudden attack and slow decay of a piano note. The only properties we need to use in this simple behavior deal with the size of the bitmap. Firstly we'll need to remember the current size, which we'll call pCurrentSize. Add this line to the top of the script:

```
property pCurrentSize
```

Apart from the current size, we need to know the extremes of the animation. When the key is pressed the bitmap is instantly scaled to its maximum size, so we'll call this number pMaxSize. Add this Lingo underneath the first line:

```
property pMaxSize
```

The last number we need to remember is the size of the bitmap when the toy starts and when there is no animation playing. This is its minimum size. Add the last property for this behavior:

```
property pMinSize
```

Now that we have defined our properties, let's write the handlers. The first handler that gets called by Director, and therefore the first one we shall write, is our behavior beginSprite. We'll set the starting values of our three properties. You can change the numbers in pMaxSize and pMinSize to get different effects later on. Notice that pCurrentSize is set to pMinSize so that the sprite does not start the movie by animating. After this, we call a custom handler, draw, that we'll write later. For now, let's just accept that the draw handler will use pCurrentSize to scale the sprite's bitmap.

```
on beginSprite(me)

  pMaxSize = 50
  pMinSize = 2
  pCurrentSize = pMinSize
  me.draw()

end beginSprite
```

That was pretty simple. The next handler that we need to deal with is prepareFrame. This is the handler that is called in every single frame, so it's placed where the animation code is going to go. We want the sprite's bitmap to get slowly smaller as the animation plays. Since pCurrentSize represents the size of the bitmap, we can start with the line:

```
pCurrentSize = pCurrentSize - 1
```

This decreases the property by one every frame of the animation. Of course, to act on it we'll have to call our custom drawing handler:

```
me.draw()
```

But these two lines are not enough. If left at this the sprite would always be animating, and pCurrentSize would end up in the negative numbers very quickly. We need to check if the pCurrentSize is still big enough to continue scaling down. We do this by adding the following condition:

```
on prepareFrame(me)

  if pCurrentSize > pMinSize then
    pCurrentSize = pCurrentSize - 1
    me.draw()
  end if

end prepareFrame
```

Whenever we want to change the size of the bitmap we change pCurrentSize, but to make anything happen on stage we need to use this to affect some real sprite properties. We do this dirty work in our custom handler draw. To scale a bitmap we must set the sprite's height and width properties.

But the Lingo is not quite that simple. How do we know which sprite we're talking about? This behavior is attached to ten different sprites so we can't fix the sprite number in the Lingo. We need to access the sprite the behavior is attached to dynamically. We do this by using the me object. This is a reference that is passed to every handler in every behavior by Director. In fact, the object passed by the me argument of a handler is the instance of the behavior that is attached to a particular sprite. There is a separate instance of the behavior for each sprite that the behavior is attached to. This me object has one, and only one, default property: spriteNum. We access spriteNum using:

```
me.spriteNum
```

We can use this to get the sprite object itself with the following Lingo:

```
sprite(me.spriteNum)
```

This finally allows us to access the height and width properties for different sprites with the same behavior:

```
on draw(me)

  sprite(me.spriteNum).width = pCurrentSize
  sprite(me.spriteNum).height = pCurrentSize

end draw
```

The last handler we're going to add is another custom one and, arguably, the most important. You may remember that we finished the last frame behavior by adding the line:

```
sprite(note).startAnim()
```

This call generates an event that is sent to the relevant sprite. The sprite looks at its behaviors and tries to find a handler with the same name to handle the event. If there is no appropriately named handler an error is generated. So we had better write the handler! We start the animation by scaling the bitmap up to its maximum size. From there, the prepareFrame handler will continue the animation process by scaling the sprite back down to its original, minimum size.

```
on startAnim(me)

  pCurrentSize = pMaxSize
  me.draw()

end startAnim
```

That's it. Run the movie. Hit the number keys. We should now have sound and vision. Here's the complete listing of both behaviors:

Key piano frame behavior

```
- - - - - - - - - - - - - - - - - - - - - - - - -
- - key piano : frame behavior
- - - - - - - - - - - - - - - - - - - - - - - - -
property pSoundChannel
property pPitch
property pPitchList


- - - - - - - - - - - - - - - - - - - - - - - - -
- - beginSprite :
- - - - - - - - - - - - - - - - - - - - - - - - -
on beginSprite(me)

  repeat with channel = 1 to 8
    sound(channel).volume = 50
  end repeat

  pPitchList = [-5, -4, -2, 0, 2, 3, 5, 7, 8, 10]
    pPitch = 0
  pSoundChannel = 1

end beginSprite


- - - - - - - - - - - - - - - - - - - - - - - - -
- - exitFrame :
- - - - - - - - - - - - - - - - - - - - - - - - -
on exitFrame(me)

  go the frame

end exitFrame


- - - - - - - - - - - - - - - - - - - - - - - - -
- - keyDown :
- - - - - - - - - - - - - - - - - - - - - - - - -
on keyDown(me)

  note = (the key).integer
    if note.voidP then return
  if note = 0 then note = 10

  pSoundChannel = pSoundChannel + 1
  if pSoundChannel > 8 then
    pSoundChannel = 1
  end if

  pPitch = pPitchList[note]
```

```
        sound(pSoundChannel).stop()
        sound(pSoundChannel).queue([#member:member("piano"),
➥ #rateShift:pPitch])
        sound(pSoundChannel).volume = volume
        sound(pSoundChannel).play()

        sprite(note).startAnim()

    end keyDown
```
- -

Key piano sprite behavior

```
    - - - - - - - - - - - - - - - - - - - - - - - - - -
    - - key piano : sprite behavior:
    - - - - - - - - - - - - - - - - - - - - - - - - - -
    property pCurrentSize
    property pMinSize
    property pMaxSize


    - - - - - - - - - - - - - - - - - - - - - - - - - -
    - - beginSprite : initialise the size properties
    - - - - - - - - - - - - - - - - - - - - - - - - - -
    on beginSprite(me)

        pMinSize = 2
        pMaxSize = 50
        pCurrentSize = pMinSize
        me.draw()

    end beginSprite


    - - - - - - - - - - - - - - - - - - - - - - - - - -
    - - prepareFrame : scale the sprite down
    - - - - - - - - - - - - - - - - - - - - - - - - - -
    on prepareFrame(me)

      if pCurrentSize > pMinSize then
          pCurrentSize = pCurrentSize - 1
          me.draw()
      end if

    end prepareFrame


    - - - - - - - - - - - - - - - - - - - - - - - - - -
    - - draw : make the sprite scale to pCurrentSize
    - - - - - - - - - - - - - - - - - - - - - - - - - -
    on draw(me)
```

```
          sprite(me.spriteNum).width = pCurrentSize
          sprite(me.spriteNum).height = pCurrentSize

      end draw

      - - - - - - - - - - - - - - - - - - - - - - - - - - - - -
      - - startAnim : called by the frame script
      - - - - - - - - - - - - - - - - - - - - - - - - - - - - -
      on startAnim(me)

        pCurrentSize = pMaxSize
        me.draw()

      end startAnim


      - - - - - - - - - - - - - - - - - - - - - - - - - - -
```

Are you impressed? Amazing what you can do with a single note 5-second sound clip when you put your mind to it, isn't it?

OK, let's crank it up a notch and make our sound interact with Directors new 3D capabilities.

Cubic panorama - a sound in space

The biggest aspect of this release of Director is the addition of 3D capabilities. In fact, the 3D engine pretty much the biggest ever change in Director. Sadly, there isn't a way to put sounds directly into a Shockwave 3D world. We can, however, quite easily write Lingo handlers to spatialize the audio ourselves. There are two properties of the sound channel object that help us to give the illusion of a sound source moving in 3-dimensional space. The first we have met before:

```
      sound(channel).volume
```

By setting the volume of a sound we make it appear to be moving nearer to or further away from the camera. Remember that volume has a range of 0 (minimum) to 255 (maximum). The second property that we're going to use, pan, is one we haven't seen before:

```
      sound(channel).pan
```

Pan controls the spread of the sound between the stereo outputs. pan has a range of -100 (hard left) to +100 (hard right). To center a sound with pan we give it a value of zero. We can set and get both of these properties. For example:

```
      sound(channel).volume = 23
      put sound(1).volume
```

And:

```
      sound(channel).pan = 23
```

```
put sound(1).pan
```

We're now going to try and make a sound using volume and pan to do some simple sound spatialization. We'll write a behavior that adds a model to a 3D world, with a sound source that appears to come from that model. We'll also add some Lingo that will allow us to move the model about in space.

Casting our movie

First let's get together the assets we'll need to make our little sound toy. Create a new movie and then go through the following steps:

1.   We need a Shockwave 3D cast member. We can add one of these to the cast by choosing Window > Shockwave 3D. When the Shockwave 3D window appears, name the cast member. Close the Shockwave 3D Window, and drag the new 3D cast member from the cast window into sprite channel 1 of the score. Scale the sprite to fill the stage.

2.   Import a sound loop to the cast. I've used the one called organ loop, which you can also use by copying from the CD.

3.   Create a bitmap cast member that we can use as texture for our model. You can do this by choosing Window > Paint and drawing something. Name this cast member texture.

Now we're ready to add the Lingo. This movie uses two behaviors. The first is a simple frame behavior that holds on the current frame. The second is a sprite behavior that we add to the 3D sprite to do everything else.

Double-click in the frame script channel and type the following in the script window:

```
on exitFrame me

    go the frame

end exitframe
```

Close the script window and select the Shockwave 3D sprite on the stage. As we did in the last exercise, open the behavior inspector. Click on the behavior inspector's behavior pop-up button and choose the New Behavior menu item. The name behavior dialog box will appear. Name our new behavior pan 3d. Now click on the behavior inspector's script window button, and the script we have just created will appear.

Creation of the world

First we are going to add the 3D model. The only property we need to remember is the cast member that contains our 3D world. Write at the top of the script:

```
property p3d
```

Now write the custom handler that will initialize the 3D world, camera, and model. We start by setting the p3d property to the 3D Shockwave cast member that is used by our sprite. Then we reset the world, so that it doesn't fill up with models every time we run the movie. We complete our world initialization by moving the camera away from the center to look back at where our model will be rotating.

```
on init3d(me)

    p3d = sprite(me.spriteNum).member
    p3d.member.resetWorld()
    p3d.camera[1].transform.position = vector(0,0,600)

end init3d
```

We still have more to add within this handler - creating and adding an actual model to the world requires quite a few more lines of Lingo. First we make a resource, the template for the model, using a box primitive and add the following Lingo before the end init3d statement:

```
boxResource = p3d.newModelResource("boxResource", #box)
```

Next, make a texture from the bitmap cast member you drew earlier:

```
boxTexture =
➥ p3d.newTexture("texture",#fromCastmember,member("texture"))
```

Then the model itself is created from the resource we just made:

```
boxModel = p3d.newModel("boxModel", boxResource)
```

We place the box model just off the center of the world so it will be easy to rotate around the center later:

```
boxModel.transform.position = vector(100, 0, 0)
```

Now we make a shader from the texture and use it to texture the box:

```
boxShader = p3d.newShader("boxShader",#standard)
boxShader.texture = boxTexture
boxModel.shaderlist = boxShader
```

Lastly we add our box model to the world, so we can see it:

```
boxModel.addToWorld()
```

That's one handler done. We need to call it when the frame starts, with:

```
on beginSprite(me)

    me.init3d()

end beginSprite
```

You can try running the movie now and you should see a static cube sitting on the right hand side of the screen, something like below:

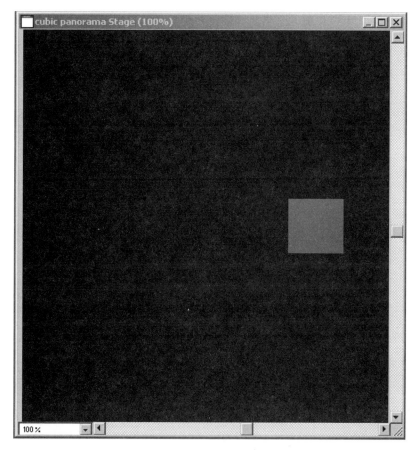

Now let's try to make the cube spin around the center of the world using the mouse. This will be done by another custom handler, which will be called in every frame from the prepareFrame handler written into our sprite behavior.

```
on prepareFrame(me)
```

```
        me.update3d()

end prepareFrame


on update3d(me)

    v = vector(0,2,0)
    p3d.model[1].rotate(v,#world)

end update3d
```

This first line of Lingo in the update3d handler makes a vector that is then used in the second line to rotate our model. The vector I've used here rotates the model around the X-axis, that is, left to right and front to back. Play the movie and then try out different value for the vector. You should see it rotating around the center of the world, whatever numbers you put in.

Moving sound

Now we can add the handlers for sound. Firstly, we need to set our sound loop playing when the behavior begins. Again, we are going to write a custom handler that will be called from the beginSprite handler.

```
on initSound(me)

    sound(1).queue([#member:member("organ loop"), #loopCount:0])
    sound(1).play()

end initSound
```

The scripting in this handler is pretty straightforward. The only new thing is the #loopCount property used when we queue the sound. This property tells the sound object how many times to play the sound before moving onto the next item in the queue. If the property is set to zero then it will loop forever, and that's what we are using it for. After adding the initSound handler, call it from the beginSprite handler by inserting the line of code:

```
on beginSprite(me)

    me.init3d()
    me.initSound()

end beginSprite
```

When you play the movie now you'll hear the loop playing. All we need to do now is change the pan and volume properties of the sound with the movement of the cube. We've left the camera looking at the center of world, which means that the X-axis travels from left to right across the screen, matching the way the pan control moves a sound across the stereo image. In other words the X position of an object in the world will map onto a sound's `pan` property without any vector mathematics.

With the camera in its current position, the Z-axis travels directly into the screen, and this matches the way we want to map distance to volume. The Z position of an object in the world will map onto a sound's `volume` property, again without any complex calculations.

Because of the starting position of our box, and because it's rotating around the center of the world, its X position in the world is always moving between -100 and 100. That means we can use this value as we find it to set the `pan` of the sound:

```
sound(1).pan = p3d.model[1].worldPosition.x
```

The volume is almost as easy to set. The Z position of the model travels around the center axis, just as with the X, between the values of -100 and 100. However, unlike `pan`, `volume` works between 0 and 255. So we need to map these maximum and minimum values. To get from -100 to 0, we add 100.

```
sound(1).volume = p3d.model[1].worldPosition.z + 100
```

But this means that the maximum will be 100+100 = 200. To make the maximum reach 255 we need to multiply the value by a fraction. This fraction is given by the desired maximum divided by the current maximum:

```
sound(1).volume = (p3d.model[1].worldPosition.z + 100)*(255.0/200)
```

So that's it - just two lines! Let's add them to the behavior to make a custom handler:

```
on updateSound(me)

  sound(1).pan = p3d.model[1].worldPosition.x
  sound(1).volume = (p3d.model[1].worldPosition.z +
  ➥ 100)*(255.0/200)

end updateSound
```

Because the sound will be changing constantly, add a call to this handler from the `prepareFrame` handler:

```
on prepareFrame(me)

  me.update3d()
  me.updateSound()

end prepareFrame
```

When you watch this movie running, watch the position of the cube as it rotates. As it moves to the left you should hear the sound coming from the left speaker. Move it to the right, the sound source should appear to be coming from the right speaker. If the cube is roughly in the middle, then the volume of both speakers should be the same. As the cube moves off into the distance, the sound should become fainter.

Interactivity

Finally, let's modify the `update3d` handler to rotate the cube according to the location of the mouse, rather than a fixed value. At present we're rotating the cube using `vector(0,2,0)`. We need to create a similar vector from the Director system properties, `the mouseH` and, `the mouseV`.

The mouse properties start at the top left of the screen and get larger as they move right and down. We want our values to increase the rotation as we move away from the center of the stage. The width of the stage is given by the subtraction of two other system properties:

```
the stageRight - the stageLeft
```

To map the mouse coordinates so that they are zero at the center of the stage, we subtract half the width (or height) of the stage from them:

```
the mouseH - ((the stageRight - the stageLeft)/2)
```

We're going to use the vertical mouse position to control the X rotation and the horizontal mouse position to control the Y rotation. Z is left as zero, because the mouse has only two dimensions on the screen. We can now make a vector from these values to rotate the cube. Change the definition of `update3d` by deleting the old:

```
v = vector(0,2,0)
```

Replace it with the following lines:

```
on update3d(me)

    x = the mouseV - ((the stageBottom - the stageTop)/2)
    y = the mouseH - ((the stageRight - the stageLeft)/2)
    z = 0
    v = vector(x,y,z)
    v = v/20.0
    p3d.model[1].rotate(v,#world)

end update3d
```

Note that the last line scales the vector so that it doesn't rotate too fast. You can change the value here to get different speeds of rotation and hence different sounds. When you run the movie, move the mouse and watch how it affects the position of the cube. Notice how the x and y rotation interact with each other to produce unexpected twists and turns. See how the change in volume and pan can make musical rhythms. You could try adding further sounds and models that all respond to the mouse in different ways.

Cubic panorama sprite behavior

Here's the complete listing of the sprite behavior.

```
- - - - - - - - - - - - - - - - - - - - - - - - - - -
- - Cubic panorama: sprite behavior
- - - - - - - - - - - - - - - - - - - - - - - - - - -
property p3d


- - - - - - - - - - - - - - - - - - - - - - - - - - -
- - beginSprite :
- - - - - - - - - - - - - - - - - - - - - - - - - - -
on beginSprite(me)

  me.init3d()
  me.initSound()

end beginSprite


- - - - - - - - - - - - - - - - - - - - - - - - - - -
- - prepareFrame :
- - - - - - - - - - - - - - - - - - - - - - - - - - -
on prepareFrame(me)

  me.update3d()
  me.updateSound()

end prepareFrame


- - - - - - - - - - - - - - - - - - - - - - - - - - - - -
- - init3d :
- - - - - - - - - - - - - - - - - - - - - - - - - - - - -
on init3d(me)

  p3d = sprite(me.spriteNum).member
  p3d.member.resetWorld()
  p3d.camera[1].transform.position = vector(0,0,600)

  boxResource = p3d.newModelResource("boxResource", #box)

  boxTexture = p3d.newTexture("texture",#fromCastmember,
  ➥ member("texture"))

  boxModel = p3d.newModel("boxModel", boxResource)
  boxModel.transform.position = vector(100, 0, 0)

  boxShader = p3d.newShader("boxShader",#standard)
  boxShader.texture = boxTexture
```

```
            boxModel.shaderlist = boxShader

            boxModel.addToWorld()

        end init3d

        - - - - - - - - - - - - - - - - - - - - - - - - - - - -
        - - update3d :
        - - - - - - - - - - - - - - - - - - - - - - - - - - - -
        on update3d(me)

          x = the mouseV - ((the stageBottom - the stageTop)/2)
          y = the mouseH - ((the stageRight - the stageLeft)/2)
          z = 0
          v = vector(x,y,z)
          v = v/20.0
          p3d.model[1].rotate(v,#world)

        end update3d

        - - - - - - - - - - - - - - - - - - - - - - - - - - - -
        - - initSound :
        - - - - - - - - - - - - - - - - - - - - - - - - - - - -
        on initSound(me)

          sound(1).queue([#member:member("organ loop"), #loopCount:0])
          sound(1).play()

        end initSound

        - - - - - - - - - - - - - - - - - - - - - - - - - - - -
        - - updateSound :
        - - - - - - - - - - - - - - - - - - - - - - - - - - - -
        on updateSound(me)

          sound(1).pan = p3d.model[1].worldPosition.x
          sound(1).volume = (p3d.model[1].worldPosition.z +
          ➡ 100)*(255.0/200)

        end updateSound

        - - - - - - - - - - - - - - - - - - - - - - - - - - - -
```

Musical boxes - a 3D pattern sequencer

The last example in this chapter introduces a new concept: **sequencing**. Sequencing is a sort of recording where we remember the notes and not the audio. We're making a very simple sequencer called a pattern sequencer. This is a software version of the old mechanical pianolas and music boxes that used long punch cards to represent musical sequences - remember them from the classic Western movies? As notes are played into our sound toy the system remembers them as a pattern and repeats them after a certain loop period. We're using objects orbiting around in a 3D world to represent that musical loop or pattern. In our example the notes gradually fade out as they repeat, and then disappear after about three repeats. You can, therefore, think of the toy not just as a simple sequencer, but also as an audio-visual echo - it's a lot like a tape-loop or tape-delay system.

We'll combine Lingo elements introduced in our previous examples: the note stealing from mouse piano, the keyboard interaction from key piano, the 3D world and model from cubic panorama.

Assembling our assets

As with our other examples, musical boxes require assets to work with. In fact musical boxes use pretty much the same set of assets that cubic panorama required. The only difference is that this time our sound isn't a loop but a single hit or note, such as the piano sound. So assemble for yourself:

1. A sound cast member, that the code will refer to as piano

2. A bitmap cast member called texture to use as a texture map.

3. A 3D Shockwave cast member placed at frame 1, channel 1 in the Score.

4. The usual go the frame frame behavior on frame 1.

Another box, another world

Follow the instructions in the last example to create and attach a behavior to the 3D sprite in the score. Now we can get on and write that 3D sprite behavior. First the properties, we've used this one before in cubic panorama to hold the 3D Shockwave member:

```
property p3d
```

These two both came up in key piano to handle channel allocation and scales respectively:

```
property pSoundChannel
property pPitchList
```

Let's carry on by initializing the 3D code:

```
on beginSprite(me)

  me.init3d()

end beginSprite
```

```
on init3d(me)

    p3d = sprite(me.spritenum).member
    p3d.member.resetworld()
    p3d.camera[1].transform.position = vector(0,0,2300)

    boxResource = p3d.newModelResource("boxResource", #box)
    size = 220
    boxResource.height = size
    boxResource.width = size
    boxResource.length = size

    p3d.newTexture("texture",#fromCastmember,member("texture"))

end init3d
```

This code was nearly all introduced in the last example. The only addition is that there are some lines to increase the size properties of the box primitive for our model resource. Now we can write a custom handler that will create the actual model for us. In the last example this code was all placed in the handler above, but since we're going to make models dynamically and place them in the world according to user interaction, we need to separate out this Lingo.

```
on addBox(me, pos)

    boxModel = p3d.newModel("b"&the milliseconds,
    ➥ p3d.modelResource("boxResource"))
    boxModel.transform.position = pos

    boxshader = p3d.newShader("s"&the milliseconds,#standard)
    boxshader.texture = p3d.texture("texture")
    boxshader.transparent = true
    boxModel.shaderlist = boxshader

    boxModel.addToWorld()

    if p3d.model.count > 20 then
      me.deleteBox(p3d.model[1])
    end if

end addBox
```

The last three lines just check if there are too many models, and kills the oldest one if there are. You can bump this number up if you have a good 3D card. The middle line calls this handler that you can write in now:

```
on deleteBox(me, boxModel)

    p3d.deleteShader(boxModel.shaderList[1].name)
    p3d.deleteModel(boxModel.name)
```

```
      end deleteBox
```

Let's try running our movie. Nothing! We can't see anything because no one is creating a model. Let's create a model in the message window.

```
      sprite(1).addBox(vector(0,0,400))
```

You should see a model appear, much as we did in the last example. Now let's add the code that makes the model move through the world.

```
      on prepareFrame(me)

        if p3d.model.count then

          repeat with i = 1 to p3d.model.count

            boxModel = p3d.model[i]
            boxModel.rotate(0,2,0,#world)

          end repeat

        end if

      end prepareFrame
```

This again is straightforward after the last example. The only difference is that we're using a repeat and a condition to rotate any number of boxes. Run the movie and this time add a few models from the message window. They will all go around and around! Pretty soon we end up with a complete jam of boxes. If you remember, we want this toy to gradually fade out the boxes so it acts like a gentle echo.

Fade out

We're going to do this by giving each model a property called energy that will gradually diminish. We'll fade the box by setting its blend to its energy. When the box has no energy we'll delete it. Director allows us to add our own properties to models using a property list that is built-in to all models, called userData. Let's create the energy property at the bottom of the addBox handler

```
      if p3d.model.count > 20 then
        me.deleteBox(p3d.model[1])
      end if

      boxModel.userData.addProp(#energy,40)
      ...
```

Now let's use it in a new custom handler:

```
      on setEnergy(me, boxModel)
```

```
energy = boxModel.userData.energy
energy = energy - .21
boxModel.shaderList[1].blend = energy
boxModel.userData.energy = energy

if energy <= 0 then
  me.deleteBox(boxModel)
end if

end
```

This handler gets the energy, reduces itself by a little, and then sets the model's blend to its new value. The last three lines of Lingo check it to see if the model has run out of juice, and if it has it deletes the model by calling the handler we wrote earlier. We call the setEnergy from the prepareFrame handler after the rotate Lingo:

```
...
repeat with i = 1 to p3d.model.count

  boxModel = p3d.model[i]
  boxModel.rotate(0,2,0,#world)
  me.setEnergy(boxModel)

end repeat
...
```

Let's play the movie again and add boxes from the message window. Now we can see them fading out and disappearing as they rotate.

Playhead

In any music box or cassette recorder, there has to be a line where the notes are played across. This is often called the playhead. In our 3D loop we're going to put this playhead right in the middle at the front, looking back down the Z-axis from the camera to the origin. We can easily check to see if a box has crossed this line by checking if its worldPosition has passed the X and Z axes. The only problem with this approach is that the double check will return true all the time while the box is in the (X>0, Z>0) quadrant. We can remedy this problem by adding another property to each box called latch, which we'll set to false as soon as the box enters the quadrant, and set to true as soon as the box leaves the quadrant. We'll therefore know that box has just crossed our mathematical playhead, because it will be in the quadrant and the latch will be true. This condition will only test true once per cycle. This test will be used to trigger the sound. We'll also animate the cube by giving it back a little energy. Let's add the check and the animation before the music. First, let's add the latch property at the bottom of addBox:

```
...
if p3d.model.count > 20 then
  me.deleteBox(p3d.model[1])
end if
```

```
        boxModel.userData.addProp(#energy,40)
        boxModel.userData.addProp(#latch,true)

    end addBox
```

Now, let's add a handler to perform the checks and the animation:

```
    on checkHit(me, boxModel)

      pos = boxModel.worldPosition

      if pos.x >= 0 then
        if pos.z >= 0 then

          if boxModel.userData.latch = true then
            boxModel.userData.energy = boxModel.userData.energy + 25
            boxModel.userData.latch = false
          end if

        else

          if boxModel.userData.latch = false then
            boxModel.userData.latch = true
          end if

        end if
      end if

    end
```

Although it looks complex, this handler is not really that bad. It tests for two states: one is crossing the playhead and the other resetting the latch. The first test does three checks outlined above with three if statements. If the model passes the test we give it some extra energy. Let's call CheckHit from the prepareFrame handler just before the setEnergy call:

```
    ...
        repeat with i = 1 to p3d.model.count

          boxModel = p3d.model[i]
          boxModel.rotate(0,2,0,#world)
          me.checkHit(boxModel)
          me.setEnergy(boxModel)

        end repeat
    ...
```

Try the movie again, adding boxes from the message window. They will become more solid as they cross the playhead at the front.

Click through the screen

The main interaction with this toy is by using mouse clicks to add new boxes into the world. This Lingo is a little more involved than you would first expect as the mouse is a 2D device and our toy is in a 3D world. There's no fixed position in the 3D world for where a mouse click is, because there is no Z information for the mouse click. We have to decide which Z-depth we want to project the mouse click onto. Luckily, Lingo has a function to convert screen coordinates into 3D world coordinates: spriteSpaceToWorldSpace. All we have to do is move this position back or forth to the depth we require. Add the following handler to the bottom of script:

```
on clickPosition(me, loc, zt)

    centre=(sprite(1).loc-point(sprite(1).width,sprite(1).height)/2)
    pos = p3d.camera[1].spriteSpaceToWorldSpace(loc-centre)

    zc = p3d.camera[1].transform.position[3]
    zo = pos[3]-zc
    zt = zt-zc
    ratio = zt/zo

    pos[1] = pos[1] * ratio
    pos[2] = pos[2] * ratio
    pos[3] = pos[3] + (zo * (ratio-1))

    return pos

end clickPosition
```

This handler returns a 3D vector position when it's passed a point and Z-position. We use spriteSpaceToWorldSpace as one possible position in the 3D world. A click of the stage represents a point in 2D, but in 3D a line through the world. We must pass a point to decide how deep into the world our point is positioned. We then scale the position according to the Z-position. We make use of the clickPosition handler in the mouseDown event handler that you can add now:

```
on mouseDown(me)

    pos = me.clickPosition(the clickloc,0)
    me.addBox(pos)

end mouseDown
```

Notice that we ask clickPosition to project the screen coordinates onto a Z-depth of zero. When you run the movie now you no longer need to make use of the message window. You can just click anywhere on the stage and the boxes will appear.

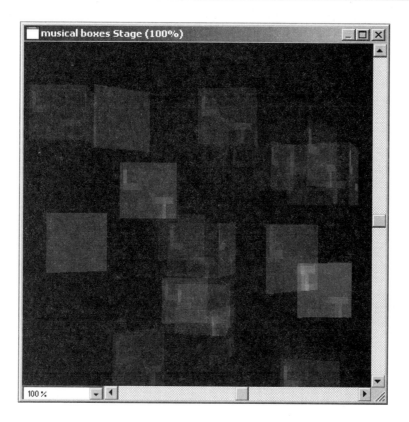

And finally ...the music

Now that the system is working we can add the sound handling. Although this toy uses a 3D model, like cubic panorama, the sound handling uses a lot of the same code as the key piano toy. First we initialize the sound properties. Both of these properties are recycled from key piano:

```
on initSound(me)

  pSoundChannel = 1
  pPitchList = [-3, -1, 0, 2, 4, 6, 7, 9, 11,12]

end initSound
```

We call initSound from beginSprite:

```
on beginSprite(me)

  me.init3d()
  me.initSound()
```

```
    end beginSprite
```

The next block of Lingo was not in key piano. We add it to the bottom of addBox:

```
boxModel.userData.addProp(#latch,true)
  note = ((pos[2]/140)+5).integer
  note = max(1,min(10,note))
  boxModel.userData.addProp(#note, note)

end addBox
```

This calculates a note number depending on the vertical position of the new box. As with key piano, it is a number between 1 and 10 that will be used as a position in pPitchList. The higher the box is, the higher the note. We store this number in a userData property of the model called note.

Because this toy is more complex than key piano, we can't leave the queue function calls inside the prepareFrame handler. Instead we write a new custom handler, but essentially it has the same code in. The only extra functionality is the ability to set the volume of each note using the last argument to the handler. We use this to link the volume of each note to the boxes energy. This allows us to create the fading echo effect of the sequencer.

```
on playSound(me, note, volume)

  pSoundChannel = pSoundChannel + 1
  if pSoundChannel > 8 then
    pSoundChannel = 1
  end if

  pitch = pPitchList[note]

  sound(pSoundChannel).stop()
  sound(pSoundChannel).queue([#member:member("piano"),
➥ #rateShift:pitch])
  sound(pSoundChannel).volume = volume
  sound(pSoundChannel).play()

end playSound
```

We call the playSound handler from the checkHit handler underneath the third if statement, which tells us that we have just crossed the playhead:

```
if boxModel.userData.latch = true then
  me.playSound(boxModel.userData.note,boxModel.
➥ userData.energy)
  boxModel.userData.energy = boxModel.userData.energy + 25
  boxModel.userData.latch = false
```

Play the movie, click in a string of boxes, and you will be able to see and hear your click sequence fading away gracefully.

Musical boxes sprite behavior

Here's the last listing of the chapter, and there's a surprise handler add the end. See if you can work out what it does!

```
- - - - - - - - - - - - - - - - - - - - - - - - - - - -
- - musical boxes : 3d sprite behavior
- - - - - - - - - - - - - - - - - - - - - - - - - - - -
property p3d
property pSoundChannel
property pPitchList


- - - - - - - - - - - - - - - - - - - - - - - - - - - -
- - beginSprite :
- - - - - - - - - - - - - - - - - - - - - - - - - - - -
on beginSprite(me)

  me.init3d()
  me.initSound()

end beginSprite


- - - - - - - - - - - - - - - - - - - - - - - - - - - -
- - init3d :
- - - - - - - - - - - - - - - - - - - - - - - - - - - -
on init3d(me)

  p3d = sprite(me.spritenum).member
  p3d.member.resetworld()
  p3d.camera[1].transform.position = vector(0,0,2300)

  boxResource = p3d.newModelResource("boxResource", #box)
  size = 220
  boxResource.height = size
  boxResource.width = size
  boxResource.length = size

  p3d.newTexture("texture",#fromCastmember,member("texture"))

end init3d


- - - - - - - - - - - - - - - - - - - - - - - - - - - -
- - addBox :
- - - - - - - - - - - - - - - - - - - - - - - - - - - -
on addBox(me, pos)
```

```
          boxModel = p3d.newModel("b"&the milliseconds ,
       ➡ p3d.modelResource("boxResource"))
          boxModel.transform.position = pos

          boxshader = p3d.newShader("s"&the milliseconds,#standard)
          boxshader.texture = p3d.texture("texture")
          boxshader.transparent = true
          boxModel.shaderlist = boxshader

          boxModel.addToWorld()

          if p3d.model.count > 20 then
            me.deleteBox(p3d.model[1])
          end if

          boxModel.userData.addProp(#energy,40)
          boxModel.userData.addProp(#latch,true)

          note = ((pos[2]/140)+5).integer
          note = max(1,min(10,note))
          boxModel.userData.addProp(#note, note)

        end addBox

- - - - - - - - - - - - - - - - - - - - - - - - - - - - -
- - deleteBox :
- - - - - - - - - - - - - - - - - - - - - - - - - - - - -
on deleteBox(me, boxModel)

  p3d.deleteShader(boxModel.shaderList[1].name)
  p3d.deleteModel(boxModel.name)

end deleteBox

- - - - - - - - - - - - - - - - - - - - - - - - - - - - -
- - prepareFrame :
- - - - - - - - - - - - - - - - - - - - - - - - - - - - -
on prepareFrame(me)

  if p3d.model.count then

    repeat with i = 1 to p3d.model.count

      boxModel = p3d.model[i]
      boxModel.rotate(0,2,0,#world)

      me.checkHit(boxModel)
      me.setEnergy(boxModel)

    end repeat
```

```
      end if

   end prepareFrame

- - - - - - - - - - - - - - - - - - - - - - - - - - -
- - setEnergy :
- - - - - - - - - - - - - - - - - - - - - - - - - - -
on setEnergy(me, boxModel)

   energy = boxModel.userData.energy
   energy = energy - .21
   boxModel.shaderList[1].blend = energy
   boxModel.userData.energy = energy

   if energy <= 0 then
     me.deleteBox(boxModel)
   end if

end

- - - - - - - - - - - - - - - - - - - - - - - - - - -
- - checkHit :
- - - - - - - - - - - - - - - - - - - - - - - - - - -
on checkHit(me, boxModel)

   pos = boxModel.worldPosition

   if pos.x >= 0 then
     if pos.z >= 0 then

        if boxModel.userData.latch = true then
          me.playSound(boxModel.userData.note,boxModel.
          ➥ userData.energy)
          boxModel.userData.energy = boxModel.userData.energy + 25
          boxModel.userData.latch = false
        end if

     else

        if boxModel.userData.latch = false then
          boxModel.userData.latch = true
        end if

     end if
   end if

end
```

```
- - - - - - - - - - - - - - - - - - - - - - - - - - - - - - -
- - clickPosition :
- - - - - - - - - - - - - - - - - - - - - - - - - - - - - - -
on clickPosition(me, loc, zt)

  center=(sprite(1).loc-point(sprite(1).width,sprite(1).height)/2)
  pos = p3d.camera[1].spriteSpaceToWorldSpace(loc-center)

  zc = p3d.camera[1].transform.position[3]
  zo = pos[3]-zc
  zt = zt-zc
  ratio = zt/zo

  pos[1] = pos[1] * ratio
  pos[2] = pos[2] * ratio
  pos[3] = pos[3] + (zo * (ratio-1))

  return pos

end clickPosition

- - - - - - - - - - - - - - - - - - - - - - - - - - - - - - -
- - mouseDown :
- - - - - - - - - - - - - - - - - - - - - - - - - - - - - - -
on mouseDown(me)

  pos = me. clickPosition (the clickloc,0)
  me.addBox(pos)

end mouseDown

- - - - - - - - - - - - - - - - - - - - - - - - - - - - - - -
- - initSound :
- - - - - - - - - - - - - - - - - - - - - - - - - - - - - - -
on initSound(me)

  pSoundChannel = 1
  pPitchList = [-3, -1, 0, 2, 4, 6, 7, 9, 11,12]

end initSound

- - - - - - - - - - - - - - - - - - - - - - - - - - - - - - -
- - playSound :
- - - - - - - - - - - - - - - - - - - - - - - - - - - - - - -
on playSound(me, note, volume)

  pSoundChannel = pSoundChannel + 1
  if pSoundChannel > 8 then
    pSoundChannel = 1
  end if
```

```
        pitch = pPitchList[note]

        sound(pSoundChannel).stop()
        sound(pSoundChannel).queue([#member:member("piano"),
        ➥ #rateShift:pitch])
        sound(pSoundChannel).volume = volume
        sound(pSoundChannel).play()

    end playSound

    - - - - - - - - - - - - - - - - - - - - - - - - -
    - - keyDown :
    - - - - - - - - - - - - - - - - - - - - - - - - -
    on keyDown(me)

      noteKey = (the key).integer
      if noteKey.voidP then return
      if noteKey = 0 then noteKey = 10
      ypos = (noteKey - 5.5) * 140
      pos = vector(0, ypos, 350)
      me.addBox(pos)

    end keyDown
```

We're there!

Summary

Director's sound capabilities, on the surface, would seem to be fairly limited: only 2 channels of sound on the score and even then they may not play if circumstances conspire against you!

But we know otherwise... Lingo provides us the functionality to play eight simultaneous sounds, to stop and start them anywhere in their playback, and even to manipulate those sounds to such a degree that a 5 second audio clip of one piano note can be made to replicate scales played on a Steinway! And, that manipulative functionality means that only small snippets of sound are needed to create awesome multimedia experiences when combined with the visual presentation that Director, with added 3D capabilities, now possesses.

Using just the paint window and 2 audio clips, totalling 6 seconds of sound (!), you've created a synthesizer, a piano keyboard capable of accurately representing diatonic and pentatonic scales, a spatially aware 3D object capable of interacting with the user and producing a stereo output in relation to its ...had enough? We haven't even got to Musical Boxes yet.

We covered a lot of ground in this chapter. Beyond the use of sound you will have seen how you can build reusable and efficient code, how powerful applications can be built - if you put thought and good design to effect - with the minimum of resources, and how an effective interactive experience doesn't need to be a hard-drive eating beast - the Musical Boxes DIR is about half a megabyte.

So, onward and forward to "Video", but first the URLs of some sites you may want to experience, as promised earlier.

www.pickledonion.com
www.antirom.com
www.iamas.ac.jp/~iwai/iwai_main.html
www.romandson.com
www.modifyme.com
www.singlecell.org
acg.media.mit.edu/people/golan/
www.thesquarerootof-1.com/
www.tokitoki.com/
www.mushimushi.net/

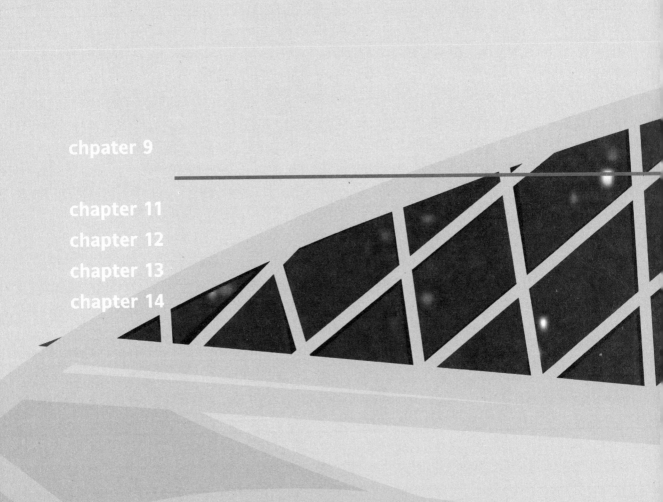

Chapter 10
Video

This chapter concentrates on the use of video in an interactive manner, rather than just for full screen playback purposes. I have yet to come across a project that involves the playback of full screen video on a computer that can compete with a video presented from a VHS tape, or DVD, on a TV screen. To me, the use of video on a PC (or Mac) is justified by the possibility of interacting with it, but never by the quality it achieves in simple playback.

In this chapter you'll find references to some projects that have used video in Director in the past, tips on how to integrate and optimize the use of video assets in Director, how to control video assets in Director via Lingo, and how to create video assets for Director projects.

You'll probably notice, throughout this chapter, that my personal preference in using video in Director tends towards using QuickTime. This is not due to the fact that I use a Macintosh (I have two PC's as well), but rather due to the quality of video, the possibility of interaction, and the ease of cross-platform development that QuickTime allows for. My examples are all written using QuickTime, but in some cases the digital video assets can be substituted with AVIs. The best way to find out is by trial and error...and it's that experience that has persuaded me to use QuickTime in most of my projects.

Video in Director projects

Let's have a quick look at some projects that use video in Director. An early project was the original *Antirom* CD-ROM, created by a collective of students at the University of Westminster, and their tutor, in 1995. The CD-ROM combined a variety of 'toys'. Some of them used digital video in combination with simple Lingo. The video was compressed with Cinepak - a compression standard frequently used at that time. The interaction was limited to playing a video asset forward or backwards, leaving trails on the stage, and overlaying video assets that weren't "direct to stage" using ink effects. I'll explain the Director specific terms, and the digital video specific terms, in more detail later on in the chapter. The strength of the project, in this case, wasn't the technical use of video in multimedia, but rather the ideas behind the toys. Simplicity is often a wise choice for the technical design of a Director project that involves video.

We'll discuss later how to make a video toy like these. The sound in these video loops is also a key element of the toy. By controlling the playback speed of the video you also control the playback speed of the sound. If you then allow the user to play the video backwards, the sound gets distorted in an interesting way.

Antirom later used the video loop idea in a totally different, yet simple way, in a kiosk they made for Levi's Europe. The only interaction in the toy was a simple click on the trackball button, which would switch the current loop playing for another. Its beauty really lived *between* the video loops, not *in* the loops themselves. Again, simplicity and good ideas make affective use of video in Director.

Another project worth mentioning is *tomato3*, the CD. Although this CD was by no means a conventional multimedia piece, the use of video on it seems straightforward. The CD showcases the work done by *tomato*, *tomato films*, and *tomato interactive*, in one accessible common interface. But the use of video here is more complex. The interface doesn't surround the video like we are used to, but it sits in the middle of all its possible sections.

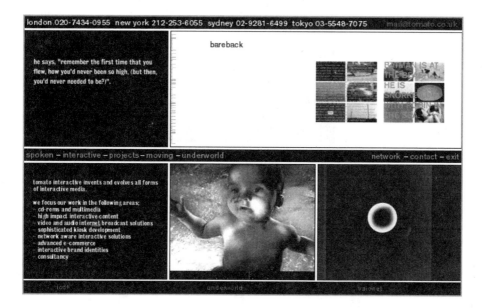

You can download the *tomato3* CD-Rom at www.tomato.co.uk.

Sometimes it's wise to use another animation device to create the illusion of a moving image, rather than using video.

I would like to mention two of the alternative possibilities. One of these is the scrolling movie strip. This is a long image strip of a segment of film, or a sequence of images pasted together at equal distances in one long image file. When scrolled by the user at a variety of speeds the illusion of a moving image is created. This device has been used in many projects and is usually very effective. One of the early versions I saw was part of the Jam exhibition in London in 1997.

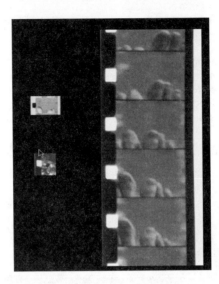

The other possibility is to use a sequence of images that are then imported as individual cast members and animated inside Director using Lingo. Sometimes this method gives the developer far greater control over the sequence. This method is recommendable if the sequence is not played in sync with sound. An example of this can be seen in the 'Jam' project. A drop of ink diluting in water was filmed on video, made into an image sequence, and used in Director as an animation. One reason for not using the original video file was the impossibility of superimposing direct to stage video.

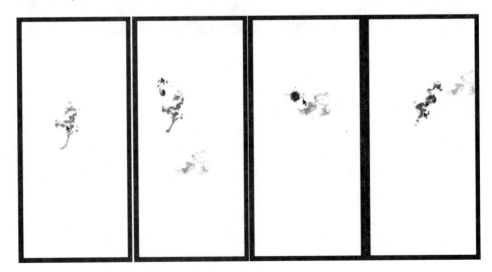

Video is a great asset to start with. It's often important to remember that it can be quite sufficient in itself as an engaging device. If one simple command's influence on a video sequence engages you while messing around with video in Director, it is often a useful experience to remember that when working on projects. After all, if it amused you it will most likely amuse others as well.

Creating out a video asset

Let us start with a simple example. If you don't have a video file stored on your computer, get one from the CD-ROM that accompanies this book. I've supplied video files joelsVideo.mov and joelsVideo.avi for this purpose. If you have QuickTime installed, I suggest using the MOV file (note that a minimum of version 5 is required for some of the examples in this chapter). The AVI file is provided for those who don't have, and don't wish to install, QuickTime. If you're on a computer without QuickTime, but you would like to install it, the latest version can be downloaded from: www.apple.com/QuickTime/

Once you have loaded the file onto your computer, open Director and save a new movie into a new folder. We'll call the folder videoProj, and the movie Video01.dir. We also need to move the downloaded video file into the same folder. Open the Director cast window (CTRL-3 or APPLE-3) and select member 1 (using the Thumbnail view). Next select Import (CTRL-R or APPLE-R) and import the digital video file. Once the video asset appears in your cast, save the movie again.

If you're on a Windows computer that has QuickTime installed and you are opening an AVI, a dialog window appears allowing you to choose whether QuickTime or AVI drivers should handle the video asset. The difference is quite significant, but for the moment I recommend you play with it and try out both solutions. If the video is handled by AVI, you will see that it has no control bar, nor does it give you the option to use one.

Once imported you can inspect the new video cast member and its properties. This is what a video window looks like on a Macintosh computer that has QuickTime installed. A QuickTime asset on a Windows computer will look similar, but an AVI one will look different. It won't appear with a control bar, as this one has. To play the QuickTime movie you can hit the space bar or press the start arrow. To play an AVI, just click on the movie. To stop the QuickTime click the stop icon that replaced the arrow on start, or just hit the spacebar again. To stop an AVI just click the movie again.

Let's have a closer look at the properties of this video asset, the screenshot shows the member, QuickTime, and cast properties in list view mode:

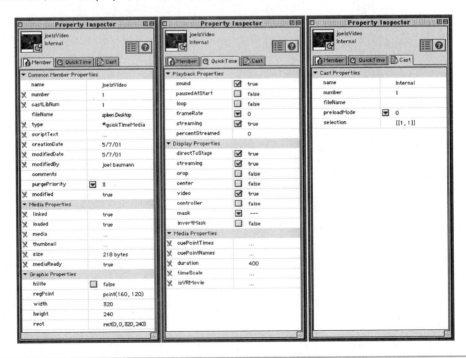

The little pencil on the left with the red line through it marks properties that are not editable, as you can see there are quite a few.

There are some important properties and settings in the property inspector that we need to take note of. Let's take a look at these now.

Properties in the inspector

1. In the Common Member Properties section of the properties window, the property name, in combination with the property fileName, create the link to the digital video asset.

> *All digital video assets are linked files. They are not imported into the project, so the files have to be provided along with a projector. The path to the file combined with the file name determines the file used. As you can see in the* Media Properties *section of the properties inspector, the linked property is set to true and it's not editable.*

So, in our example, if you save and close the video01.dir, then move your video file out of the folder videoProj and reopen the video01.dir, it will prompt you to locate a replacement movie for the missing file at the location it expected the video to be at. This is why you always need to keep your folder structure intact when delivering projects with video involved.

2. The purgePriority property in the same section specifies how Director removes the asset from memory, depending on whether memory is low or not.

- 3 (Normal). This asset will be removed from memory after all priority 2 assets are removed when memory gets low.

- 2 (Next). This asset is amongst the first to be removed from memory.

- 1 (Last). This asset will be removed as one of the last providing memory gets low.

- 0 (Never). This asset is never removed from memory, at least not as long as the projector, Shockwave movie or DIR is still running.

3. All the properties in the Graphics Properties section determine how the asset is handled in its sprite.

4. The properties in the Playback Properties section determine the way a video asset performs once it is put on stage.

- The sound property can be set to true or false, and it determines whether the video assets soundtracks are played as well as its video tracks when the asset is used on stage.

- The pausedAtStart property determines whether or not a video cast member that is put onto the stage plays once the playback head enters the frame it's in.

- The loop property determines whether a video asset loops once it has reached its end, or if it stops playing.

- The frameRate property determines the frames per second rate at which the video member will try to play at. There are some special settings.

- If you set the frameRate to 0 it will synchronize the video with the soundtracks frame rate.

- If you set the frameRate to -1 the video asset will play at its default frameRate.

- If you set the frameRate to -2, the video asset will play as fast as it possibly can.

- You can set the frameRate to other figures via Lingo as well.

- The streaming property will allow the video asset to play while it is being loaded into memory, either from the Internet or off a hard disk. The property can be set to true or false. Streaming is only available to QuickTime video assets.

5. The Display Properties define how the asset is displayed on stage.

- If the directToStage property is set to true, the video assets playback is entirely handled by the corresponding QuickTime or AVI drivers installed on your computer, which increases the stability of its playback. directToStage does have its drawbacks. A video asset set to be directToStage always overlays any other asset on stage, regardless of z-location or sprite number. Likewise, no ink effects will work on an asset that is set directToStage.

- If the crop property is set to true the video will playback at its original size. If the sprite's bounding rectangle is smaller than the video itself, the portion of the video outside of the bounding rectangle won't show.

- The center property sets the video to playback in the center of the sprite's bounding box, providing that the crop property is set to true as well. If it is set to false, the video plays back in the top left corner of the sprite's bounding box.

- If the video property is set to false only sounds from the video will play.

- The controller property is specific to QuickTime. If QuickTime is installed on your system, and the controller property is set to true, the video on stage will appear with a control bar at the bottom.

- The mask property allows the user to select a bitmap cast member to be used as a mask on a video asset. The video's directToStage property must be set to true. The bitmap is mapped onto the video at the top left corner using its regPoint.

- If the invertMask property is set to true, the video plays through the white areas of the bitmap used as a mask.

6. The Cast Properties are common to all asset types.

Checking out video assets using Lingo

We've just used the property inspector display to look at the assets and properties of our video, but to control the movie in runtime we'd probably want to use Lingo.

Getting info from the message window

Open your video01.dir, and resize the stage to be 640x480 in the movie properties window (note though that the movie tab won't appear if you have anything selected within the stage or the score). Delete the video cast member out of any score channels you might have placed it in and apply it to sprite channel 2. Now, let's open the message window. We're ready to check and set some of the properties of a video cast member and a video sprite.

Let's work through an exercise in the message window. Type the following code:

```
put the type of member(1)
```

This line will produce the following output. Note that we're showing the value for the MOV file (with the AVI file results in brackets):

```
- - #quickTimeMedia
(- -#digitalVideo)
```

Our next line will enquire about the video type:

```
put member(1).digitalVideoType
```

Which results in:

```
- - #quickTime
(- -#videoForWindows)
```

So, we're communicating with the video cast member and retrieving information about it. Let's try setting something:

```
put sprite(2).movieTime

-- 0
```

The value this produces is 0. Let's try and set the value:

```
sprite(2).movieTime = 100
put sprite(2).movieTime

-- 100
```

Not only does it tell you that setting it worked, if you look at the video on the stage you will notice that it has changed to another frame further along in the video.

One of the fundamentals of working with video in Director is to understand that time in a video cast member is calculated in ticks, not in frames, as you would expect of video. To access the ticks of a video member, you need to refer to its movieTime and its movieRate.

You should really try most of the video Lingo commands here from the message window. Some of these commands control the member while others control the sprite. You need to understand the difference. If you place the video onto the stage twice using two different score channels, any command you send the member will have an impact on both occurrences. By changing sprite properties, you influence only one of the two.

Let's have a quick look back at our Director movie before we start testing more commands. Make sure your video asset is in member 1 of the internal cast, and check that member 1 has been assigned to sprite channel two in your score. Now, double-click on frame 5 of the script channel in your score. Between the on exitFrame me and end lines, write go the frame. This will keep the movie looping in frame five, giving our video time to play.

In the message window, write:

```
mem = member(1)
spr = sprite(2)
mem.controller = true
```

(The controller command will only work if your video is being handled by QuickTime.)

We now have two variables holding our sprite and member, making it easier for us because we have less to type. We have set the controller property of our digital video member to true. On stage, our video has now got a controller at the bottom. As you can see, I haven't even started playing my movie to manipulate it with Lingo commands. This works for commands that set up properties of members. However, a lot of commands only work when the movie is playing.

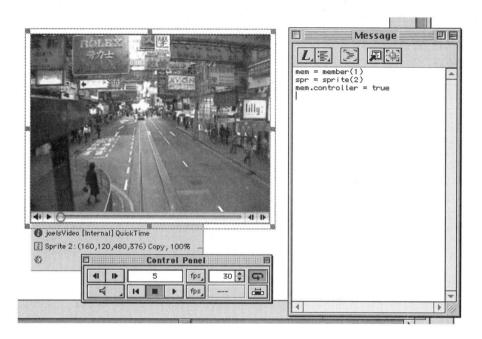

Let's try to control playback. Write the following code in the message window:

```
mem.loop = true
mem.pausedAtStart = true
```

Now start the movie. The video shouldn't start playing. To start it you can press the little play button on the controller beneath the movie (if you are using QuickTime), but to start it with Lingo you need to write:

```
spr.movieRate = 1
```

The movie plays at normal speed, you can see its video track playing, and you can hear its soundtrack playing. When it comes to its end, it loops around and starts from the beginning again. Let's stop the Director movie and write:

```
mem.frameRate = 2
```

Now restart the movie, and once more type our Lingo to get the movie to play:

```
spr.movieRate = 1
```

The video runs at twice the speed, but the soundtrack does not play anymore. Now stop the Director movie and write:

```
mem.frameRate = 0
```

Once again restart the movie and let's type our code to start playback:

```
spr.movieRate = 1
```

The video runs at normal speed again and the soundtrack can be heard again. Let's try changing the movieRate value as opposed to the frameRate:

```
spr.movieRate = 2
```

This time the video runs faster and you can hear an accelerated soundtrack as well. Let's try one more thing:

```
spr.movieRate = -1
```

On slower computers the video runs backwards for a moment, but then the video track stops playing back properly while the soundtrack still plays back sound that is running backwards. The video track stopping is because of the compression used on this bit of video. Since there is temporal compression involved, the video builds on keyframes to interpret in-between frames. When we run backwards this process is impossible. Here we see that how we want to use video in our project bares some consequence on how we prepare the assets. We'll come back to this when we talk about video compression.

One other feature we want to check out is the directToStage property of a video member. For this exercise please use the joelsVideoV.mov asset (or one of your own digital video files that is not compressed to the video codec or the animations codec if you are using QuickTime). For those of you using an AVI file you can continue using the same clip as before, but you may not experience the full effect by using the AVI format.

Stop the Director movie and delete the joelsVideo member from your cast. Import the joelsVideoV.mov file into cast member 1 in your cast, and drag it into channel 2 of the score. Write:

```
mem = member(1)
```

Open the paint window from the window menu and paint a big cross. Let's name this member cross. Find the member in your cast window and drag it into channel 3 of the score. You'll not see it, because it's hidden behind the video member, even though it should be in front according to its channel number. This is because the video members directToStage property is set to true. In the message window, write:

```
mem.directToStage = false
```

The cross should now appear on top of the video. Write:

```
mem.loop = true
```

Next start the Director movie and type the following code in the message window:

```
sprite(3).ink = 36
```

The sprite property ink allows you to apply different kinds of ink effects to a sprite. In Lingo the ink effect equal to 36 is called background transparent. The cross's bounding box disappears, but the cross stays above the video. The sprite(whichsprite).ink command wouldn't work if the movie wasn't running. Stop the Director movie. Open the paint window again and create a new image member with a squiggle. Call it squiggle and drop it into channel 1. We'll now run the movie and type the following lines in the message window:

```
sprite(2).blend = 90
sprite(3).ink = 36
sprite(3).blend = 80
```

You can see the overlaying sprites though the transparency of each other. (Note that if you're using an AVI you may not see the squiggle, although the red cross should be visible. I strongly recommend using QuickTime in these examples.)

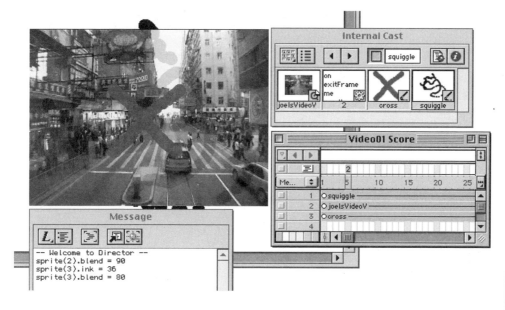

When a video member's directToStage property is set to false, you're able to apply the background transparent ink (or any others) and the blend sprite property to it. The downside of directToStage being set to false is that the video asset playback sometimes isn't as good as when directToStage is set to true.

Using Lingo to create a simple toy

Let's use our video asset and the commands we've learned, along with a few new ones, to create a simple video toy. You'll see that it doesn't take a lot to produce something interesting, because video in itself is quite a complex device.

The toy we're about to recreate goes way back to the original Antirom CD-ROM. It uses simple playback controlling Lingo. There are a few screenshots of such video toys from the Antirom at the beginning of this chapter.

A video asset is draggable on stage. Its playback depends on the horizontal position of the cursor. If it's moved, it paints trails of itself on the stage. That's it, colorful and easy.

1. Open Director and save a new movie called `video02.dir` into your `VideoProj` folder. Import our `joelsVideoV.mov` file into cast member 1. You'll need to create a QuickTime movie with just a soundtrack for this exercise. The track should be 44.1 kHz and 16 bits if possible. If you don't have the facilities, just load `mySoundLoop.mov` from the CD. Import this file into member 2 of your internal cast.

2. Open the score of the new movie and double-click frame 3 of the script channel. In between the `on exitFrame me` and `end`, write `hRun()`. Double-click on frame 4 of the same channel and write `hRun()`, and `go to the frame` in between the `on exitFrame me` and `end` lines. Your two script channel frame behaviors should look like this:

   Frame 3:

   ```
   on exitFrame me
    hInit()
   end
   ```

   Frame 4:

   ```
   on exitFrame me
    hRun()
     go the frame
   end
   ```

3. Drop member 1 onto the sprite channel 2 in the score, and member 2 onto channel 6.

4. In the cast choose an empty member and open the script window. We'll need a global variable to store a value that is needed throughout the movie - the duration of the video clip. So, at the top of the script add `global gDur`.

5. Let's use the `hInit` handler to initialize our digital video members and their sprites. Write `on hInit` and `end`, and in between these lines we'll initialize all the properties

of our video members and their corresponding sprites. Write `gDur =` `member(1).duration` to set our global variable equal to the length of the video in member 1. Let's setup member 1 now. Write `member(1).loop = true` to make sure the member's video will loop if it comes to its end.

Next write `member(1).controller = false` because we don't want to use a controller to control the movie, we want to use the mouse position. Our next line will be `member(1).pausedAtStart = true`, because we don't want the video to play on its own, we want to make it playback via Lingo. Since we want to be able to jump quite far forward in the video, we don't want the movie to start before the entire video is loaded into memory. That's why we set its streaming property to false by writing:

```
member(1).streaming = false.
```

We're going to use the sound in member 2 for our project, so we actually don't need a QuickTime movie which has a soundtrack. Since our QuickTime movie has a soundtrack, we need to disable the sound from playing. Write `member(1).sound = false`. All of this should result in the following block of code:

```
gDur = member(1).duration
member(1).loop = true
member(1).controller = false
member(1).pausedAtStart = true
member(1).streaming = false
member(1).sound = false
```

6. Now let's set up member 2. We need to go through a similar checklist. We want the sound in our project to loop as well, so we write `member(2).loop = true`. We don't have a QuickTime video track in member 2, so we want to disable the video of the member by writing `member(2).video = false`. The controller isn't needed for member 2 either, so we write `member(2).controller = false`.

We're also going to jump around in the soundtrack, so we have to make sure the entire QuickTime is loaded into memory before we start using it, therefore `member(2).streaming = false`. The soundtracks playback will be handled by Lingo, so we don't need it to start playing when loaded, so write `member(2).pausedatStart = true`.

```
member(2).loop = true
member(2).video = false
member(2).controller = false
member(2).streaming = false
member(2).pausedatstart = true
```

7. Now that both members are set up, let's have a quick look at the sprites. For this specific toy, we want to be able to drag the video around and leave trails, so we'll prepare the sprite holding the video for that. Write `sprite(1).moveableSprite = true` and `sprite(1).trails = true`. The global variable declaration and the hInit handler should look like this:

```
global gDur

on hinit
  gDur = member(1).duration
  member(1).loop = true
  member(1).controller = false
  member(1).pausedAtStart = true
  member(1).streaming = false
  member(1).sound = false
  member(2).loop = true
  member(2).video = false
  member(2).controller = false
  member(2).streaming = false
  member(2).pausedAtStart = true
  sprite(1).trails = true
  sprite(1).moveablesprite = true

end
```

Once our members, sprites and variables are all initialized, we need to think through the logic of our project. We need to check the horizontal position of the cursor. If this position is further left than the center of the video sprite, then we need to rewind the video, but if it is further right, we need to play the video forward. The bigger the distance to the center point, the larger the increment at which we shuttle back or forward. Instead of controlling the speed of playback, in other words the *movieRate*, we'll control the exact position in the video to jump to each time - the *movieTime*.

By setting the *movieTime*, we have a greater control over the playback. To keep the video looping instead of incrementing the *movieTime* beyond the movies actual length, we need the length of the video in ticks so that we can check if we exceed it. This is where gDur comes in handy. We've used gDur to store the duration of the video asset in member 1. All we need to do is check if we have jumped beyond gDur or, if we are rewinding, check if we have jumped beyond 0. In the case that we've gone beyond gDur, we simply need to deduct gDur from the exceeding value. The other way around, if we have gone beyond 0 into a negative value for our movie, we just add gDur. By adding or subtracting gDur in this way, we make sure we're looping inside the movieTime of our video asset.

8. Let's have a look at this in code. First create the hRun handler by writing on hRun and end. We'll use a local variable called temp to store the increment that we'll use on the movieTime of the video in member 1. We obtain the increment by checking the distance from the cursors horizontal point to the center of sprite that has the video asset assigned to it. We scale this by 0.05 so that our increment is not to extreme. Write temp = (the mouseH - sprite(2).loch)*0.05. We'll use a local variable called newTime to store the current position incremented by our value in temp, and check whether the result is out of the range of possible movieTime values for our video member. If the newTime value is under 0 we add gDur to it, and if it's over gDur we subtract gDur from it. At the end, we set the movieTime of sprite 2 equal the value of newTime. So, we'll use newTime = sprite(2).movieTime + temp. We need to create a conditional to check if newTime is under 0 or over gDur. Write:

```
if newTime < 0 then
   newTime = newTime + gDur
else if newTime > gDur then
   newTime = newTime - gDur
end if
```

9. At the end set the `movieTime` of sprite 2 to `newTime`. This takes care of the video side of things. Try and run it.

```
on hRun
   temp = (the mouseH - sprite(2).loch)*0.05
   newTime = sprite(2).movieTime + temp
      if newTime < 0 then
    newTime = newTime + gDur
   else if newTime > gDur then
      newTime = newTime - gDur
   end if
sprite(2).movieTime = newTime
end
```

10. If we use the same method to control the soundtrack in sprite 6 we'll get a load of clicking noises as we jump to different bits of the sound sample. We're jumping around in time, not increasing the playback mechanism. This works better for the visual aspect of video, but it doesn't work well at all for soundtracks. To get the speeding up, slowing down, and playing backwards effect in the soundtrack to match the visual behavior of our project, we need to use `movieRate` instead of `movieTime`. Before the end of the `on hRun` handler write: `sprite(6).movieRate = temp`.

    If you run the movie now, it will work, but you get quite a bit of clicking, depending on your sound asset. If you add the conditional `if sprite(6).movieRate = temp then return` before you set the `movieRate` of sprite 6 to `temp`, you avoid unnecessary setting of the movieRate, when it's code already set.

    Run the movie again and you should hear a change, but there is still some clicking if you're using my sound file. If you work on the sound file you should be able to get rid of the clicking. I noticed the clicking happens most when the `movieRate` isn't an integer. I'd rather have less variation in the sound and use only integer values than have clicking, so I slip in `temp = integer(temp)` after `temp` has been used for sprite 2 and before it gets used for sprite 6. Try it out, (if you like but the call is yours). If you can doctor your sound file to get rid of all clicking, then that's the best solution. My final `hRun` handler looks like this:

```
on hRun
   temp = (the mouseH - sprite(2).loch)*0.05

   newTime = sprite(2).movieTime + temp
  temp = integer(temp)
   if newTime < 0 then
     newTime = newTime + gDur
   else if newTime > gDur then
```

```
        newTime = newTime - gDur
    end if
    sprite(2).movieTime = newTime
    if sprite(6).movieRate = temp then return
    sprite(6).movieRate = temp
end
```

The trails and moveable features of the video toy are handled by the sprite itself. So, if you run the movie, the interactivity should be as simple and playful as on the original Antirom CD-ROM.

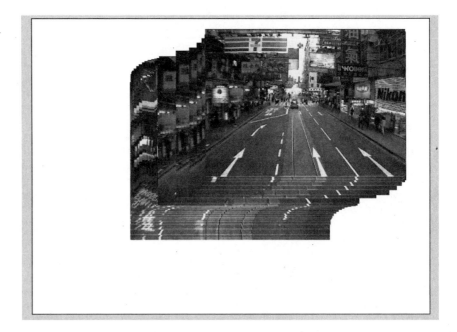

Compression

Compression is defined as a process that reduces a file in size by removing unused or less important information. There are two kinds of compression to take into account when compressing video: temporal and spatial compression.

Temporal compression compares frames in a digital video and only stores the difference between them. As an example of temporal compression, imagine a video sequence of a locked off shot of a person sitting in the center of a room talking. The change in the image will be very minimal, practically only the person's face and maybe his/her hands sometimes will move. Temporal compression will only store the changes made over time to a keyframe image. The surroundings of the person speaking don't change over time, so why store their unchanged pixel data for every frame?

Spatial compression reduces file size by removing redundant information within the image of a frame. As an example, imagine a video of a bird flying through the sky. The sky is blue. In every image in the frames of the video the pixels of the sky are all the same blue. By just storing information about the area of the sky and remembering it is blue for the entire area takes up less memory than remembering blue for each pixel.

Video formats

The preparation of video assets for use in Director is a vital step in creating professional multimedia projects, providing you're using video at all in your project. A lot of thought goes into the way video is used in the project itself, while it's often forgotten that first of all the video needs to be able to perform on the platforms your project is going to run on. As an example, if you're creating a kiosk, then you have the possibility to optimize your video assets for the computer you'll be using for the kiosk. The issues of cross-platform developments won't apply and you can test what format and compression works best for the OS of your computer, and the performance of its hardware. At the other extreme, if you're creating a CD-ROM for the grand public, you'll have to decide what the minimum specification of the computers should be that your CD-ROM will run on. You'll need to choose a format that works on a wide variety of computers, operating systems and versions of operating systems. We'll go into this more specifically later on in the chapter, but let's look at platforms and their variations now. This is important so that I can get all of you with your different computers to be able to do the exercises I will write about. The options I will write about are AVI, QuickTime, and MPEG.

AVI

The most common compressors for AVI are Intel Indeo (version3.2a or 5), Microsoft Video 1, Microsoft RLE (Run Length Encoding), Cinepak, and uncompressed. Uncompressed leaves the video data uncompressed, as the name implies. Microsoft Video 1 works fine on the Windows machine and on the Mac. The different versions of Intel Indeo are fine on a Windows machine, but they simply don't playback on a Macintosh machine when QuickTime tries to handle the AVI file. In fact, QuickTime alerts that a component is missing. The same goes for the RLE codex. It's important to understand that AVI isn't restricted to these codex, but they're the ones widely used. They're also the ones supplied with Video for Windows.

MPEG

MPEG is a compression standard that is optimized for video playback and is currently the preferred broadcast standard for digital video. The compression is, however, very processor heavy, and (due to the compression format) an MPEG video track isn't ideal for interactivity. Since the compression relies heavily on interlacing video, soundtracks, and on temporal compression, it's difficult to access frames of an MPEG track and also its playback speeds.

MGEP stands for Motion Picture Experts Group. This group is a body of ISO/IEC that develops international standards for compression and decompression, and other areas of digital video. Originally, the idea was to create four MPEG standards, but since MPEG 2 has incorporated HDTV, the need for MPEG 3 has subsided.

MPEG 1 is designed to work at 1.2 Mb/s, the approximated data rate of a CD-ROM. The initial intention was to allow for video to be played back from CDs. The image quality of MPEG 1 is very poor.

MPEG 2 allows for a variety of compression ratios, created via the combination of temporal (INTER-FRAMES) and spatial (INTRA-FRAMES) compression. Its data rates go from below 4 to 100 Mb/s. It's used in broadcast to deliver digital TV to our homes and on DVD's. To encode MPEG 2 requires a lengthy procedure. Usually, MPEG 2 uses very high compression rates and is therefore unsuitable for editing, or, in our case, interaction. It is, however, very useful for full screen playback of digital video.

MPEG 4 is itself mostly about interactivity. It is neither implemented in QuickTime, nor is it accessible in Director via Xtras...*yet*.

There are two methods of using MPEG in Director on a PC. You can either use Xtras such as the DirectMedia Xtra, or you can access MPEG video via QuickTime. On a Mac, QuickTime is the standard method used to playback MPEG.

A good source of information about digital video is the "Digital Fact Book" that you can order for free from the Quantel website: www.quantel.com

QuickTime

What is QuickTime? QuickTime is the standard media player on the Macintosh and has been added to the system. It is also a major player on Windows, but it isn't shipped with the current versions of windows. There are methods of detecting that QuickTime isn't installed on a PC for both CD-ROMS and the web. In both cases, the user can be prompted to install QuickTime, either form the internet, or from the CD-ROM.

An example script for the detection of QuickTime from a CD that ships with a QuickTime installer would look like this:

```
on preparemovie
    if the QuickTimePresent = 0 then
            alert("Please install QuickTime before running this
➥movie!")
            quit
    end if
end
```

Alternatively, you could even create a window with two buttons that you go to prompting the user to either install QuickTime, or quit. The install QuickTime buttons script would look like this:

```
on mouseUp
    open the moviepath & "QuickTime Installer"
end
```

The above script will only work if the installer is placed next to the projector on the CD-ROM. I suggest doing this, so that people not using auto install can see it and install QuickTime if they wish to without even running the projector. If you, however, for some reason want to place the installer somewhere else, you must specify the entire path to the installer. Remember that the path delimiter on a Mac is the ":"character, while it is the "/ " on a windows computer.

In a browser you would need to write the detection into the HTML page that holds the Shockwave movie, as the open command in disabled in Shockwave.

QuickTime supports a phenomenal number of formats that can easily be added to it. The current version is QuickTime 5.0.2 and the codex it ships with are:

- H.261
- H.263
- Animation
- Apple BMP
- Apple Video
- Cinepak
- Component video
- DV NTSC and PAL
- Graphics
- Microsoft OLE
- Microsoft Video 1
- Motion JPEG A and B
- Photo JPEG
- Planar RGB
- Sorenson Video 1, 2, and 3

QuickTime can do a lot more than just play video: it can handle sounds, images and other file formats, it can import and export different types of data, and it can even be scripted - that's another issue entirely. What's important is that QuickTime is probably the best cross-platform format to use, although Windows users may need to install QuickTime to view your project. QuickTime 5 can be installed on Windows 95, 98, ME, NT, and 2000 as well as Macintosh OS 7.5.5 or later.

I recommend using QuickTime in conjunction with the Sorenson codex, although I have been known to create cross-platform CD's using AVI. Happily, I can say that those days are over for me, but you should feel free to do so. If you use AVI, QuickTime will handle the videos in your

Director project on a Macintosh providing you use a codec that is supported in QuickTime. Windows users will not have a problem with AVI. If you use QuickTime, Windows users will need to have QuickTime installed or install it, but Macintosh users will have no problem. Director is slightly favorable of QuickTime, my experience has led me to believe. That is one of the reasons I recommend it.

How to compress video

In general when preparing video for a multimedia project you should consider three important factors: the source material, the delivery platform, and the intentions of the project itself.

Source material

One of the common mistakes people make is to compress video media multiple times during the process of preparation. Always try to receive video from a client or create it at the highest quality possible for you to still use. Do all alterations, such as color correction, effects, and editing to the video sequence at the highest quality possible. Calibrate the audio of the source at the highest quality possible.

Once you really have the final version of the source material in your hands, make a copy of it at the highest quality possible and store the copy away in a secure place that you won't forget. This may sound silly, but some of the biggest problems in multimedia arise from dodgy version control and/or lost source material.

Delivery platform

If you're creating a kiosk, test on the computer you'll install the kiosk on as much as you can. Find out how fast the drives are. Make sure you have good amount of RAM installed, so that higher quality video at a greater size can be loaded into it. Test the speed of the CPU. If you're using QuickTime, make multiple renditions of Sorenson compressed video files and test how well they run. If you're using AVI on a Windows computer, you don't need to use Cinepak, since its benefit is cross-platform use, but its downfall is the amount of artifacts it creates in a video image. Use a compressor that works well on the Windows computer you are using.

If you're creating a CD-ROM, consider the audience you're targeting. Decide if your project needs to be cross-platform. Decide if you're willing to demand that your Windows audience install QuickTime, and if you need to deliver to a Macintosh audience at all. You also need to decide how powerful the minimum specification computer will be.

The calculation with CD drives goes somewhat like this. A single speed drive could handle a max transfer rate of 150 Kb per second. Therefore, dual-speed drives are thought to handle a max rate of 300 Kbps, and quad-speed drives should make 600 Kbps. As we all know, it isn't wise to go near the max, so if your bottom spec is a quad-speed CD-ROM drive you should look at a maximum transfer rate of 450 Kbps. You can get very good quality Sorenson compressed video at that rate. With Sorenson, the CPU is another issue. The compression needs the processor to work hard on decompressing, so check that the CPU at your bottom spec can handle your video.

The project's intentions

When you're compressing video for your project you need to keep in mind what you're going to do with it. You must consider the size you want to play back your video at. If you're going to move around in the video a lot, like we did in example video02.dir, you don't want a lot of temporal compression, so keep the key frame rate up high. If you want to jump back and forth between clips, you might want to create one big video clip so that you just need to go to a new movieTime setting, instead of loading in a new clip every time. This is demonstrated in our example video03.dir.

Once you've finished editing and altering your source and it's still at its highest quality, you'll need to digitize it into a computer, providing it isn't stored to disk already. Depending on the setup and drive space you have available, you should digitize the video at the highest quality possible. If you're using QuickTime I would recommend using animations at millions of colors and at the source's original frameRate and size. If you're not going to use QuickTime, I would recommend digitizing your source as an uncompressed AVI, at the source's frameRate and size.

When using QuickTime I recommend getting Media Cleaner 5 and a license of the Sorenson 3 video codec to compress digital video. If you don't want to spend a lot of money, I recommend buying a QuickTime Pro license: it isn't expensive and is well worth the purchase. I'll go through an example process of compressing a movie for use on a CD-ROM.

If you're digitizing via an analog input from analog or digital video, use the highest possible quality that your hardware and software allows, and use what is possible with your available disk space. That way you will lose the least quality on the transfer.

For those who are digitizing DV source via a digital input, keep the DV format of the source on the disk, if possible. That way, your transfer will be without loss.

> *The better the quality of the digitized source material, the better the quality of compression and image of the compressed video.*

Digitizing video used to be difficult because expensive hardware was needed to get decent quality analog to digital conversion, but since DV has invaded the consumer market the issue of price has been eradicated.

Once you have your source file, use the software you prefer to compress it. Testing is always a good idea. For the purpose of testing it's wise to digitize a short bit of your source file as well, so that you can run tests on it without having to create keyframes in a huge source file. Some applications need to load a great amount of the source file into RAM, even if you're just using a little bit of it via keyframes. To have a test file is always useful.

Compress your test source file in various ratios, depending on how your digital video will be used in your project. If you're going to just play it back, and you want to compress its file size and data rate so that it can fit on your CD-ROM and so that even slow computers can play it back, it's wise to use both spatial and temporal compression. Try using a codec that employs temporal compression, such as Sorenson. Using less keyframes compresses the video more, but the quality goes down as well. If you can set keyframes in the application you're using to compress the video, try setting them on crucial edits, or fast moving images.

On the other hand, if you're going to interact a lot with the playback speeds, or if you want to jump to random frames in the movie, temporal compression is not favorable since it depends on the sequence of images. Temporally compressed video builds inter-frames of information obtained from a previous keyframe. If you jump around in the order, this information is missing for the frame to be decoded. Use a codec that relies on spatial compression, such as animations in QuickTime. Animation compresses areas of similar color in each separate frame, so that every frame is independent. Spatial compression isn't as efficient as temporal compression, but that is a burden you need to work with if you want to allow for greater interactivity. You might need to compensate for it by reducing the size of you video in the project.

To digitize and compress video on a Mac without spending lots of money on software and hardware, I recommend using a DV camera, a Mac with firewire ports, a firewire cable (preferably made by Apple), iMovie and QuickTime Pro.

You then need to connect the camera to your Mac using the firewire cable and open iMovie. Make sure your camera is set to 'player' (in my case its 'VCR') instead of 'camera'. Make sure all the settings on the Camera are correct so that it can be seen and controlled via the Mac.

Next, open iMovie and digitize the clip you want. (Digitizing in iMovie is simple. Just play your tape and press 'import' when the bit you would like to digitize is on.)

The digitized clip in iMovie looks like this:

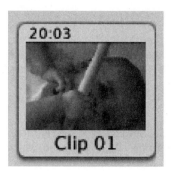

The same clip will be represented in the media folder of your iMovie project folder like this:

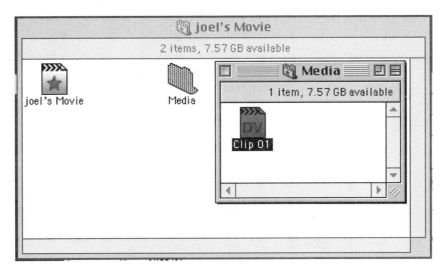

If you drag and drop this media file on the QuickTime Icon, it opens the video file in the QuickTime player. Conversely, you could open the QuickTime player, then select open form the file menu and select the media file in the media folder of your iMovie project.

If you get the movies properties (CTRL + J or APPLE + J) from the movie menu, you get a little window that gives you a load of information about your video file.

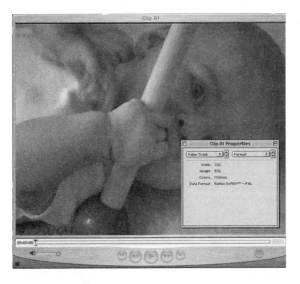

Once the iMovie media file is open in the QuickTime player, you can choose export from the file menu and select the setting you would like to use from the pull down menu at the bottom. In this case we are making a QuickTime movie from the open file, so choose Movie to QuickTime Movie.

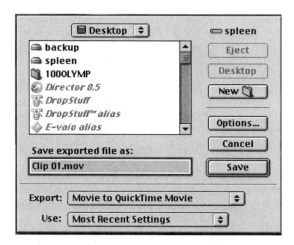

If you now hit Options you get a window that shows the current settings that your video and soundtrack will be compressed to on export. If you want to change these settings, hit the Settings button. You now have a multitude of options.

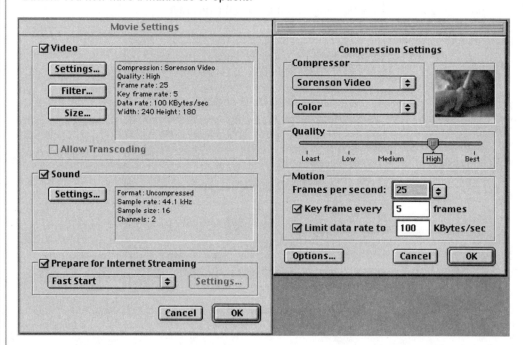

The settings you use really depends on your project, so make a few test versions using different frame rates, codex, and so on. You need not worry about the Prepare for Internet Streaming option, since you're not going to use it.

Remember, the option to export out of QuickTime only exists in the Pro version. A license for the Pro version is easily obtained at www.apple.com/QuickTime.

Video used in commercial Dirctor Projects

The next project we'll recreate is that of a video interface. The main player in this kind of project is the video itself, and the interface around it is there to facilitate access to the asset. We'll create two movies for this purpose, using one to collate information for the other one. The idea is to create a long video asset that is made to appear as if it is separate video clips. The user will be able to watch the entire video from start to finish, but we'll also give them the opportunity to jump from clip to clip. To be able to do this, we'll need each clip's start times in `movieTime` format. Imagine you were programming the interface; while someone else was editing the video. Since you can only integrate the video once he has finished editing, you must create the program before the asset is ready. Therefore we'll create a system into which we can fit the final asset once it's ready. We'll use one movie as a tool to feed the other movie with the info we need. Right now we need to create a video asset with different sections, as a placeholder for our video asset. Let's use Director to create such an asset.

1. Open Director and save your movie as `placeholder.dir`, make it 640 by 480 pixels in size. Create 5 different image members in the paint window. Don't be too precious, remember, this is going to be a placeholder. Now put your assets into one score channel, one after another, and animate them. I gave each of my image members about 50 frames to animate in, ending with a 250 frame long movie. Open the control panel window and make sure your movie's frame rate is set to 30.

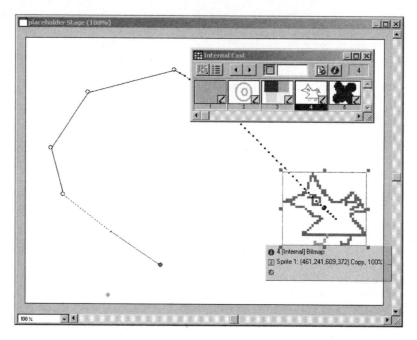

2. Choose Export from the file menu. Select Frame Range from the Export option and enter the range of your frames. Then select QuickTime Movie from the pull-down menu. Now choose All Frames to be exported as a QuickTime movie. Within the Options window, set the Frame Rate to Tempo Settings, the Compressor to Animation, the Quality as high as you can, the Color Depth to Millions, and the Scale to 50%. Make sure that the Sound Channels 1 and 2 are not selected. Hit OK and Export. We'll save the video as `placeholder.mov`.

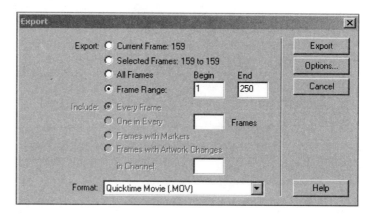

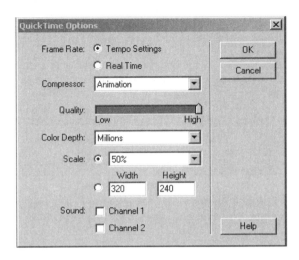

How to get our sections by building the tool

Now that we have our placeholder, let's build our tool. The tool will be used to create a list of different sections in our final video asset corresponding to the start movieTime for each named section.

1. Open Director and save a movie called videoTool.dir into the videoProj folder.

2. Create a long text field on the stage in the top left hand corner. In the cast, select the field member and open its properties window. Call the member sectName and set its editable property to true. We need to make sure its background color is different to the stage's background color. Next create a button in the bottom left corner of the stage and call it enter. Write ENTER into it as well. Import the placeholder.mov file into cast member 3 and drag it into sprite 3. We want to set it to be pausedAtStart, and you should ensure that the controller is visible - bring up the property inspector for your new sprite and, in the QuickTime tab, tick the Show Controller option.

3. Create another field member under the sectName member on stage – this one need not be editable. Name it movieTime. Make two small buttons under the placeholder video on the stage. Write - and + into them and name them minus and plus.

4. Double-click on frame 4 of the script channel in the score and type hInit() in between the lines on exitFrame me and end. Double-click on frame 5 of the same channel and write hRun and go to the Frame between the lines on exitFrame me and end.

5. Add a movie script to the movie by selecting an empty cast member and opening the script window. First of all we need the list we want to populate. It will need to be a global variable so that it is stored throughout the movie. Write global gVideoList.

6. We need to initialize members, sprites, and variables in our `hInit` handler. Write `on hInit` and `end`. Inside this handler, let's declare `gVideoList` to be a property list: `gVideoList = [:]`. Make sure the editable text field cast member, into which we will write the section headers for our video presenter, isn't populated with leftover text from the last time we used the tool. Write `member("sectName").text = ""`. The same is true for our `movieTime` counter. We must make sure the video is at the beginning and that the counter is set to the video's beginning `movieTime`. Write `sprite(3).movieTime = 0` and `member("movieTime").text = string(sprite(3).movieTime)`.

7. Create our next handler, after the `end` of our `hInit` handler, by typing `on hRun` and `end` Since most of the work will be done by us filling in editable text fields, moving the movie controller to set the playhead to the right point and pressing buttons to enter data, the hRun handler really only has little to do. It actually only makes sure the text in member `movieTime` is the actual `movieTime` of sprite 3. Write `member("movieTime").text = string(sprite(3).movieTime)`. The movie and the movie script should look something like this now:

Stage:

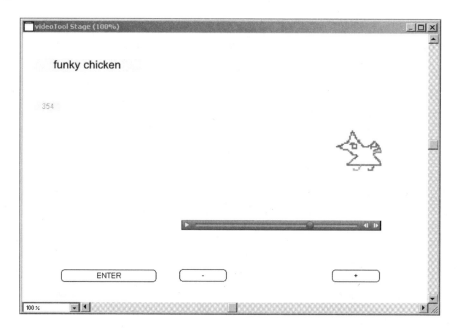

Score:

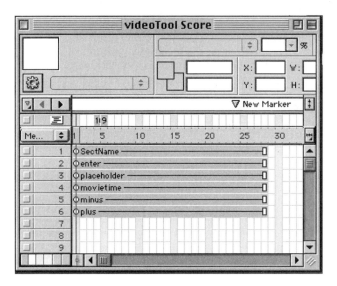

Script:

```
global gVideoList


on hInit
  gVideoList = [:]
  member("sectName").text = ""
  sprite(3).movietime = 0
  member("movietime").text = string(sprite(3).movieTime)
end


- - - -
- - - -


on hRun
  member("movieTime").text = string(sprite(3).movieTime)
end
```

9. The most important button is obviously the enter button. Let's configure its script. We want to use the global variable gVideoList, so we need to declare it at the beginning. Type global gVideoList at the start of the script. We want to add the current movieTime of sprite 3 and the text of member sectName to our list. Use a local variable called tempTime to retrieve the current movieTime of sprite 3. Write, in the on mouseUp handler, tempTime = sprite(3).movieTime. Use a local variable `tempTxt` to hold the text written into the editable field member `sectName`, and write `tempTxt = member("sectName").text`.

9. We need to make sure that some text was entered into the editable field. Check by creating a conditional and an alert, this way we don't corrupt the list we're compiling if no text is present. If `TempTxt` is not empty we'll allow the data to be entered into the list.

    ```
    if tempTxt = "" then
        alert("Section name missing!")
        return
    end if
    ```

10. Next, write `gVideoList.addProp(TempTime, TempTxt)`. We've now used the timestamp `tempTime` as the property for our listed entry. This is useful as, in the video presenter movie, we need to parse the data for all entries by their timestamps. Finally we need to empty the editable text field to show that the entry has gone into the list. Write `member("sectName").text = ""`. The buttons script should look like this:

    ```
    global gVideoList

    on mouseUp

      tempTime = sprite(3).movieTime
      tempTxt = member("sectName").text
      if tempTxt = "" then
        alert("Section name missing!")
        return
      end if

      gVideoList.addProp(tempTime,tempTxt)
      member("sectName").text = ""
    end
    ```

11. We just need to add two little scripts to the plus and the minus buttons for them to be able to function as helpers, moving `movieTime` by just one frame backwards or forwards. All we need to do is check that the `movieTime` isn't at its extremities and add or subtract 1 from sprite 3's `movieTime`. The script for button minus is:

    ```
    on mouseUp
      if sprite(3).movieTime = 0 then return
      sprite(3).movieTime = sprite(3).movieTime - 1
    end
    ```

    The script for button plus is:

    ```
    on mouseUp
      if sprite(3).movieTime = member(3).duration then return
      sprite(3).movieTime = sprite(3).movieTime + 1
    end
    ```

12. If you run the movie, move the video though its frames via the two buttons. Add section headers, and enter the data via the enter button, and end by querying the movie for its list in the message window. Write put gVideoList.

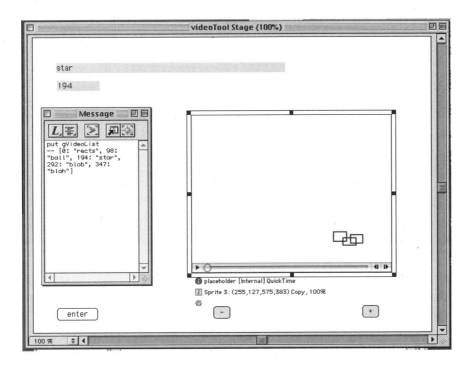

The video presenter movie

1. Now we have the tool and the list of info we want, let's create the video front-end that will use this info. Save the videoTool movie, copy the list, and open a new movie with black background (open the movie properties in list view and enter 255 for bgcolor).

2. Open the text member window and paste the list into that window. Name this member list, and save the new movie as video03.dir into your videoProj folder.

3. In the score window double-click on frame 4 of the script channel and write hInit() between the lines on exitFrame me and end. Double-click on frame 5 of the script channel and write hRun() and go to the frame in between the lines on exitFrame me and end. You've probably noticed that this is the usual way I set up my movies.

4. In the cast window select the next free cast member, member 4, and open the script window. Call this movie script cast member main. We can already add our two usual handlers, hInit and hRun. So, write the lines on hInit and end, and on hRun and end.

5. Select member 5 in the cast window and import our video file called placeholder.mov. Select the next free member in the cast window, member 6, and open the paint window. Make a one pixel dot with the pencil tool, offset the regPoint by more than half the stage height and width to the top left, and call the member dot. Drag this cast member into score channel 5, and channels 10 through to 30.

6. We're now ready to start coding. Go back to the main movie script. We'll need one global variable, global gListPos.

7. In the hInit handler we need to create some local variables that hold values we will need to use to position our video section menu later on. We want the video section menu to start at the same height as the video itself. Since the video is placed at a vertical location of 240 and is 240 high, we want to start 240 minus half the video's height, which equals 120. Write lListTop = 120.

8. The menu should end at the bottom of the video's edge, which is its vertical location plus half its height, 240 + 120, which equals 360. Write lListBottom = 360. We want the menus left edge to be at 100 pixels in from the stages left edge. Write lListLeft = 100. We still haven't declared gListPos to be a list itself, so we'll write gListPos = []. The values held by our local variables need to be added to gListPos. Write gListPos.add(lListTop), then write gListPos.add(lListBottom) and gListPos.add(lListLeft).

9. We need a local property list to set to the list we have brought into this movie from our videoTool movie. We'll achieve this by coding lList = [:]. Now set lList equal to the value of the text in member list by writing lList = value(member("list").text). This is dangerous, if you're not careful, because you might have left spaces or other characters in the text of member list that would prevent Director from not recognizing the text inside it as a property list. Make sure you only copied the property list (the [] square brackets and their contents) into the member's text (and ensure you've not copied the - - comment delimiters).

10. We're using all these local variables instead of just using the values we set them to, so that if we open the movie in two weeks time and need to edit something, we still have indications to what all the values represent. For instance, instead of just adding 100 to the gListPos list, we created a local variable lListLeft, gave it the value of 100, and added it to gListPos. This way we know that the menu was set to 100 pixels from the left of the stage without having to trace the flow of code all the way to the statement that actually sets the value. If we need to edit it, let's say set the list to be only 50 pixels from the left edge of the stage, the local variable is a lot easier to find and remember, rather than knowing that the third position in gListPos equals the left increment of the menu.

11. Let's use another local variable, lStartSprite, to indicate the first sprite we use to create the menu items. We'll set it equal to 10, so write lStartSprite = 10. Now we can pass the list lList and the local variable lStartSprite to another handler to compile the menu. So, continue by adding the line hCompile(lList, lStartSprite).

12. We're going to use sprite 5 for the video member, but let's first prepare the sprite all. Write `sprite(5).loc = point(400,240)` to set it off from the center, a bit to the right. The next line we need to include is `sprite(5).memberNum = 5`.

13. Finally we need to make sure that the video in member 5 will loop, by writing `member(5).loop = true`. The entire hInit handler should look like this:

```
on hInit
  lListtop = 120
  lListBottom = 360
  lListLeft = 100
  gListPos = []
  gListPos.add(lListtop)
  gListPos.add(lListBottom)
  gListPos.add(lListLeft)

  lList = [:]
  lList = value(member("list").text)
  lStartSprite = 10
  hCompile(lList, lStartSpirte)

  sprite(5).loc = point(400,240)
  sprite(5).memberNum = 5

  member(5).loop = true

end
```

Setting up the menu

1. We now have to deal with the hCompile handler mentioned earlier. The hCompile handler takes two arguments that we need to be ready to receive. Type `on hCompile passList, passSpr` and end. Inside the hCompile handler create a local variable tempSpr and set it to the passed value of passSpr by typing `tempSpr = passSpr`.

2. Now we need to calculate the vertical increment we'll use to spread the menu items in the menu. We have the start and end vertical positions stored in a global variable and we know how many items there are to be from the list that has been passed to us. We'll now create a local variable to hold the value of this increment. This can be achieved by the following code:

```
listVInc = float((gListPos[2] - gListPos[1] - 10)
➡ (passList.count -1))
```

a. Here we take the bottom of the list and subtract the top from it to get the list's height.

b. We subtract 10 from that because the text is set to be font size 10 and we don't want it to extend beyond the bottom of the menu value. Remember, the `regPoint` of a text member is top left, not center.

c. We divide this by the amount of items there will be, minus one, so that we fill both top and bottom slots.

d. We also need to turn the value into a floating point number. Although the result of using the increment will be a screen coordinate and screen coordinates are integers, when we use the increment in a multiplication, the floating point value will give us a more accurate approximation of the correct integer to use. If we rounded up or down to an integer before multiplying the increment, the multiplied increment would be further off from the actual value we wanted.

3. The next step is to repeat through our list and to create text members for our video menu. So, next we write `repeat with x = 1 to passList.count` and `end repeat`. Inside this repeat loop, use a local variable to store newly created text members by writing `it = new(#text, member(x + (tempSpr-1)))`.

4. We'll give these new members the `movieTime` we used as properties in our property list as their names, so that we can access the `movieTime` easily. Write `it.name = string(passList.getPropAt(x))`.

5. Set the text member's font, font size, color and width by adding the following line to your handler `it.font = "arial", it.fontsize = 10, it.color = rgb(255,0,0)` and `it.width = 40`.

6. The next step is to set the text of the new text member equal to the text in our property list for the `movieTime` we used to name the member. To achieve this we'll type:

`it.text = passList.getat(x).`

We'll use a local variable to prepare a sprite for the menu item:

`spr = sprite(x+(tempSpr-1)).`

7. We now need to prepare the sprites position by using our increment. We do this by writing:

`spr.loc = point(gListPos[3], gListPos[1] + (x-1)*listVInc)).`

8. Set the sprites ink to background transparent and blend to 70. This is done by entering the lines:

`spr.ink = 36` and `spr.blend = 70.`

9. Finally, we'll set the sprites member to be our newly created text member. Write `spr.member = it`. The complete `hCompile` handler should look like this:

```
on hCompile passList, passSpr
  tempSpr = passSpr
  listVInc = float((gListPos[2] - gListPos[1]-10)
  ➥ (passList.count-1))
  repeat with x = 1 to passList.count
    it = new(#text, member(x + (tempSpr-1)))
    it.name = string(passList.getPropAt(x))
    it.font = "arial"
    it.fontsize = 10
    it.color = rgb(255,0,0)
    it.width = 40
    it.text = passList.getat(x)
    spr = sprite(x+(tempSpr-1))
    spr.loc = point(gListPos[3],gListPos[1] + ((x-1)*listVInc))
    spr.ink = 36
    spr.blend = 70
    spr.member = it
  end repeat

end
```

10. All that is left to do is to create a behavior for the menu items that we apply to all the possible menu item channels. Create a new behavior in Channel 10. Make three event handlers in the script window for the events `mouseUp`, `mouseEnter`, and `mouseLeave`. To know which sprite has actually been activated, write `target = me.spritenum` into each of the event handlers

11. In the `mouseUp` handler, we want to set the `movieTime` of sprite 5 to the value of the name of the member in the activated sprite. Use a local variable to get the value of the member of the target sprite's name. Write `tempMovTime = value(sprite(target).member.name)` to do this. Finally, set the `movieTime` of sprite 5 to this local variable by writing `sprite(5).movieTime = tempMovTime`. The event handler should look like this:

```
on mouseUp me
  target = me.spritenum
  tempMovTime = value(sprite(target).member.name)
  sprite(5).movieTime = tempMovTime
end
```

12. In the `mouseEnter` and `mouseLeave` handlers, all we want to do is change the blend of the sprite.

```
on mouseEnter me
  target = me.spritenum
  sprite(target).blend = 100
end


on mouseLeave me
  target = me.spritenum
  sprite(target).blend = 50
end
```

Now apply this behavior to all channels in the score from 10 to 30. As you see, we didn't need the hRun handler at all, but you'll probably do some refining of this movie, in which case it might come in handy. Try to add the functionality of shuttling through the video if you roll on it, like you have in our example video02.dir.

You obviously don't need to make a vertical list of headers for your cue points. This is just the beginning. We've used this kind of an interface to map cue points onto a timeline representing our video track, adding the possibility to jump forward and backward in the entire track. The interface I am talking about is on *tomato3*, a CD-ROM created by Tom Roope (author of Chapter 2, "Lists"), which won a D&AD silver in 1999.

The tool is used to create a list of cue points that are mapped on the little timeline at the bottom of the window. The user can jump to the different little lines to see separate clips from their beginning, or he/she can just sit back and watch the *tomato* showreel loop through from beginning to end.

Summary

I've attempted to involve you in the use of interactivity and video in Director. You might use this chapter as a basis from which to take the simple examples explained further, so that you can create your personal style of using video in Director.

I hope you understand that I haven't attempted to explain how to get a video to run full screen at a high frame rate and to leave it at that, but to involve video in interactive projects, because it's my belief that the use of video in Director makes sense through interaction, not just playback.

The chapter should be used as a starting point and the examples are a basic building block, not a finished product. From here, it is up to you.

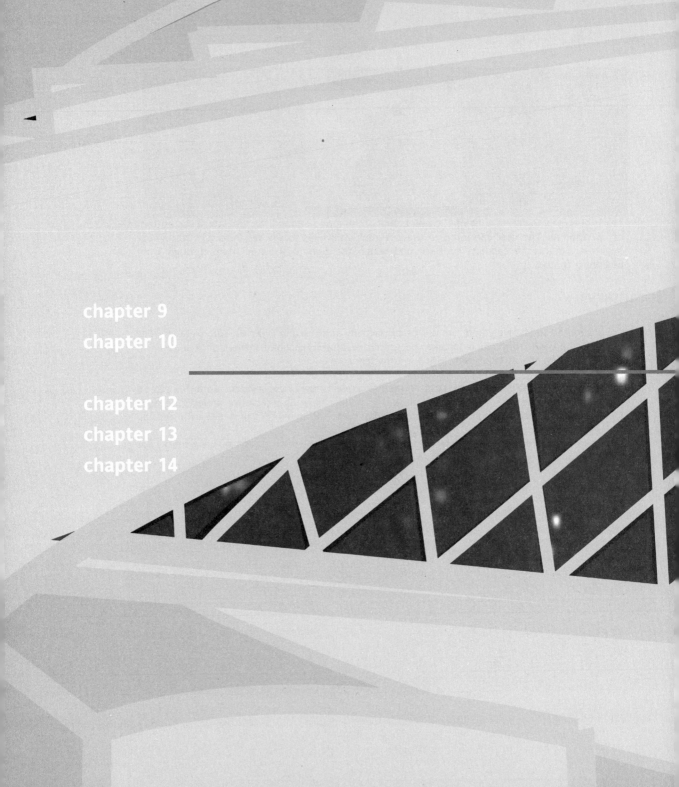

Chapter 11
Xtras

These days, everyone's familiar with how functionality is added to applications by sticking a file in a folder. In the same way that Adobe Photoshop has plug-ins, features can be added to Macromedia Director through the use of Xtras (pronounced *extras*).

The use of Xtras is a feature that was added to Director in version 5 of the program, way back in 1996. As the multimedia market evolved, the Macromedia engineering team saw a growing need for the ability to change how Director worked without entirely rewriting it.

There was already a way to add new features to Director movies: XObjects were the precursor to Xtras, but were a bit more difficult to use. They couldn't be used to modify the abilities of the Director application itself, only movies and projectors made with the application. Xtras changed all of that.

This chapter will look at the types of Xtras that exist and which of these are essential. We'll progress to look at how to install Xtras, how to use the Xtras folder, and what you need to do to use Xtras in your movies. Then we'll look at how to use some of the most popular Xtras and how you may go about making your own Xtras.

What is an Xtra?

An Xtra is a file that adds some additional functionality to the Director application, a Director projector, or a Shockwave movie. If an Xtra file is in the right place it is detected at startup time by the application, projector, or the Shockwave player, which then has the ability to do something it couldn't otherwise do.

Xtras provide some of the basic functions of Director, as well as the ability to do things that the engineers would never have time to put into the application. They also allow Director to be modified without replacing or reinstalling the entire application.

Some Xtras are automatically installed with the Director application and some come on the CD-ROM that's in the Director box, but don't get automatically installed. Others can be downloaded from developer sites on the Web. Some cost money, some are free.

Most of the Xtras mentioned in this chapter are written in the C programming language, but some types of Xtras can be created in Director itself.

Types of Xtras

Xtras are so well integrated into Director that they can affect many different aspects of the application. Their functions fall into a number of general categories with some Xtras belonging in two or more of the following categories:

- **Asset Xtras** are used to support different types of media within the Director application as well as in projectors and the Shockwave player. Text, digital video, Flash, Animated GIF, and many other types of media are supported through the use of Xtras in Director.

- **Import / Export Xtras** are used by the application, projectors, and the Shockwave player to convert external files such as bitmaps, sound files, and other media to Director's own internal format and vice versa. Any time an external media file is linked into a movie, it is translated into data optimized for playback in Director. Some Xtras support only importing files and others are used only for export. Many of those distributed with Director support both.

- **Transition Xtras** add new types of transitions to the Director application, projectors, and the Shockwave player. Instead of the standard wipes and slides, you can have weird patterns, starbursts, and smooth fades.

- **Tool Xtras** are used only in the authoring environment of the Director application to help you build your movie. Tools can be very simple or enormously complex: the ShapeShifter3D Xtra is an entire 3D modeling program. You can build your own simple Tool Xtras with Director.

- **Lingo Xtras** add new Lingo commands and functions (as well as new features) to Director. They can be used in the authoring tool, projectors, and in the Shockwave player. Some Lingo Xtras are just that: Lingo. Others, such as the Flash Asset Xtra, both support playback of Flash movies inside Director and provide Lingo that can control and modify the Flash movie.

Xtras included in Director

Much of the basic functionality of Director is in the Xtras that are installed along with the application. Some are used only in the Director application during the authoring process. Others are needed for playback purposes and must be included in (or with) a projector, or are installed in the Shockwave player.

The included Xtras fall into eight basic categories, and are grouped into folders:

- The **Filter Support Xtra** supports the ability of Macromedia Director's paint window to use certain image processing filters that are compatible with Adobe Photoshop and other imaging programs.

- The **Flash Xtras** include the **Flash Asset Xtra** (needed in both authoring and playback) and the **Flash Asset Options Xtra**, which provides the code needed to set Flash support in the Property Inspector.

- The **Havok Xtra** supplies a 3D physics engine for Shockwave 3D.

- The many **Media Support Xtras** include import, export, and playback support for animated GIFs, fonts, text files, text cast members, RealMedia, and other media.

- The **MIX Xtras** are another set of files that provide access to outside media types, including many bitmap image formats, audio formats, and digital video. These tend to be older formats, and rely on the MIX Services Xtra.

- The **Multiuser Xtra** can be used to connect to the Shockwave Multiuser Server and other types of network servers.

- The **Net Support Xtras** includes files that contain Lingo commands used for connections to HTTP and FTP servers, as well as code making it possible to import and link to files on remote servers.

- The **QT Xtras** support playback and export of QuickTime movies, as well as the ability to modify cast member properties of QuickTime members.

Windows has a couple of other specialized Xtra types:

- The **ActiveX Xtras** support the use of ActiveX controls within Director movies.

- The **Devices Xtras** provide different sound-mixing controls on the Windows platform.

Third-party Xtras

Macromedia provides information to developers interested in creating their own Xtras for custom uses or for sale to other Director users. A number of individuals have created Xtras and released them to the general community as well. These Xtras cover an extremely wide range of uses: everything from printing to databases to graphics. We'll look at a number of them a little later, but there are hundreds of commercial, shareware, and freeware Xtras available, as well as many more that have been developed for in-house use.

Where can you go to find out if there's an Xtra that can add some capability that you need to Director?

- The official **Macromedia - Xtra Extensions: Director** page taps into their database of information about Xtras, with links available to the companies or pages where you can order or download them.
  www.macromedia.com/software/xtras/director/main.html

- The **updateStage** site is a source of commercial Xtras, but they also maintain the Mile High Table o' Products. Most of this is the same material as on the Macromedia list, but each site is somewhat unique. At updateStage, there's a searchable database version of the site implemented with a Shockwave movie. updateStage also distributes and supports nearly twenty Xtras, most of them from individual developers. They have a number of tools that provide access to the computer system, control the interface, and manipulate data.
  www.updatestage.com/products.html

- At **MediaMacros** you'll find another useful database of Director-related products along with, for example, Xtras that can import a file from the user's hard drive into a Shockwave movie.
  www.mediamacros.com/

In addition to dozens of companies that offer one or two Xtras there are several long-time purveyors of note where you can find an assortment of Xtras available. They're usually a good place to begin looking for that additional functionality you require.

- **DirectXtras** is a company with a wide range of tools. Their Xtras provide communications, transitions, and file export capabilities among others.
  www.directxtras.com/

- Australian developer **Paul Farry** has a number of Xtras that can do everything from play MOD music files to capture the screen.
  www.powerup.com.au/~farryp/director/xtras/

- **Integration New Media** has Xtras that function as databases and display PDF files inside Director applications.
  www.integrationnewmedia.com/

- Penworks has an Xtra that can control audio CDs, one that can display live video, and more.
  www.penworks.com/xtras/index.cgi

- Brazil-based **Tabuleiro** provides a number of Windows-only Xtras allowing browsers within Director movies and MPEG video, amongst others. Their latest cross-platform tool is an Xtra that's a Shockwave3D modeling tool.
  http://xtras.tabuleiro.com/

- Some of the Xtras **RavWare** makes are distributed by updateStage, but there are some for creating custom window shapes and controlling the PowerPoint viewer that they make available on their own site exclusively.
  www.ravware.com/xtras.htm

- At **MediaLab**, you'll find image-related Xtras that aid in importing complex native Photoshop files and real-time image manipulation.
  www.medialab.com/

- **Electronic Ink** provides tools for printing and text-to-speech.
  www.printomatic.com/products.cfm

- The Netherlands-based developers at **PegHole** have Xtras that perform useful tasks, as well as a programming aid you can't miss.
  www.peghole.com/xtras/index.html

There are many other third-party suppliers of Xtras (and other tools) not mentioned in this list, but this should give you some idea of the scope of what's available. Check with the sites listed at the beginning of this section to continue your search.

Using Xtras

Now that you've got a basic understanding of what Xtras can do, let's look at how to get ready to work with them.

Where Xtras go

Xtras must be in the correct place for you to use them. You either won't be able to use them, or you'll get an error when a movie assumes that the Xtra is there but can't find it, if they're not where Director, a projector, or Shockwave expects to find them.

Xtras in Authoring mode

When the Director application starts up, it looks for a subfolder called **Xtras** in the folder where the application file is. Any files in the folder (or any files in subfolders within the Xtras folder) that meet the specifications of a Director Xtra are then referenced by the application. Files that can't be used as Xtras (PDF files, text files, etc.) are ignored.

Xtras outside of the Xtras folder (in the same folder as the application, for instance) are ignored by the application.

Installing and using Photoshop Filters in the Xtras folder

To get to know our way around the Xtras folder, we'll start with an easy task designed for the Mac, like installing some bitmap filters from Adobe Photoshop. If you don't have any Photoshop filters (which are in Photoshop's Plug-Ins folder) you can use the Eye Candy 4000LE filters that are installed with the copy of Fireworks 4 that comes with the Director 8.5 Shockwave Studio. (Look in the Xtras folder in the Fireworks Configuration folder.)

1. Make sure the Director application is closed, then locate the Director 8.5 application folder and find the Xtras folder inside of it.

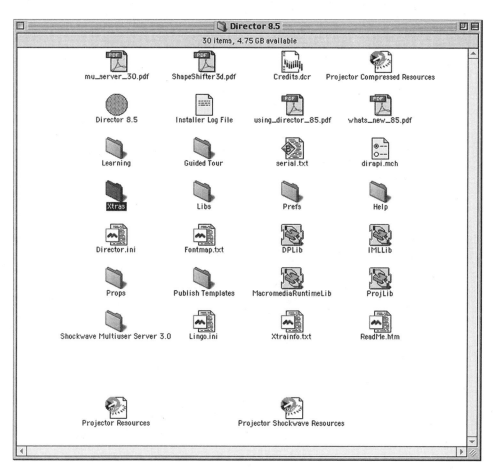

2.   Find the Photoshop-compatible plug-ins you want to use in Director.

Psychoderma

3.   Copy the plugins from their folder to the Xtras folder. You can put them anywhere in the folder: at the top level of the Xtras folder, in the Filter Support folder, or in their own folder. As long as they're somewhere in the Xtras folder, Director will find them.

4.   Open the Director application and import an image as a bitmap cast member.

5.   Open the paint window and find your newly imported bitmap image.

7. Select the portion of the image you want to apply the filter to.

8. From the Xtras menu select Filter Bitmap.

8. Choose a filter and hit the Filter button.

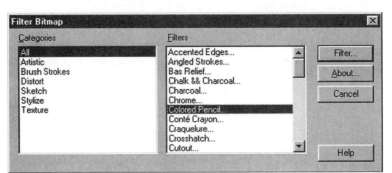

9. Some filters will display a preview image where you can adjust the filter settings. Press OK to apply the settings.

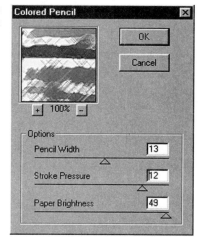

10. Depending upon the filter chosen, you should see some visible difference to your image.

Xtras in Projectors

Director projectors also search for an Xtras folder when they start up. Just like the Director application, a projector searches for an Xtras folder in the same folder as the projector file.

Additionally, projector files can have Xtras included in the projector itself. This is an option you select when making a projector. When a projector with Xtras included is run, a temporary Xtras folder is created and the Xtra files are extracted for playback. For more on this, see **Packaging for Projectors** later in this chapter.

Xtras in Shockwave

The Shockwave player – either a Netscape plug–in or an ActiveX control, depending on which browser you're using – has its own Xtras folder. Many of the standard playback Xtras are installed there with Shockwave. Shockwave can automatically update those files when new versions are available by downloading them from Macromedia.com.

Some Macromedia Xtras aren't included in the basic Shockwave install. The Animated GIF Xtra, for instance, only downloads the first time a Shockwave movie requiring it is encountered.

Third–party Xtra developers can create **Shockwave–safe** versions of their Xtras, which are downloaded when a movie requires them. For more on using Shockwave–safe Xtras see **Packaging for Shockwave**.

Installing third–Party Xtras
Most third–party Xtras are installed by simply placing them into the Director application's Xtras folder. Just follow steps **1** to **4** of the instructions for the **Installing and Using Photoshop Filters in the Xtras Folder** exercise, above. Most of the commercial Xtras require registration of some sort, but the instructions are fairly simple.

Working with Xtras

It can seem like there are almost as many different ways to work with Xtras as there are types of Xtras. Some Xtras are only seen by means of a custom interface in the authoring process. Others work behind the scenes without you needing to do anything. A number of Xtras are only accessed through the use of Lingo commands.

In this section we'll look at some of the different types of Xtras that are available, what they can do, and how to use them. Some of these Xtras are included on the Director 8.5 CD–ROM in the Xtra Partners folder. One of them is a part of the standard Director installation. Others must be purchased to use all of their capabilities.

External files

Lots of Xtras work with external files in one way or another, but the tools in this section deal specifically with manipulating files and the computer's file system.

As you may suspect, file manipulation can be a dangerous proposition. These tools give you the ability to overwrite or delete important data, or even crash the user's (or your own) computer.

> **Due to security concerns, neither FileIO nor FileXtra3 is certified for use in Shockwave.**

FileIO Xtra

The FileIO Xtra is one of the Media Support Xtras installed with Director. It is a Lingo Xtra that adds a number of commands to Director that don't appear in the Lingo documentation. Why not? Director developers have been asking that for years. Nevertheless, it's there. Amongst others, FileIO Xtra provides the functionality to:

- Create file selection and file save dialogs

- Open text files

- Create new text files

- Delete files

- Determine the number of characters in a text file

- Move to a specific position in a text file

- Read characters, words, or lines in a text file

- Write or append data to a text file

> **Most Lingo Xtras have a function that displays the Lingo commands the Xtra adds to the vocabulary. The interface function returns a string containing commands and (usually) brief descriptions. To display the commands of the FileIO Xtra open the Message window and execute the following command:**
> ```
> put interface (xtra "FileIO")
> ```

The FileIO Xtra is one of the most overlooked items in a Director installation. Since it's not explained in the documentation, many new users don't even know it's there until they suddenly find they need to read or write text data.

Creating, writing, and reading a text file with FileIO

One way to get to know what a Lingo Xtra can do is to try out its commands in the message window. To understand how to use the FileIO Xtra, we'll use the message window to create a new text file, add data to it, and read the text from the file.

1. To work with FileIO, you first need to create an **instance** of the Xtra. An instance is a temporary object in the computer's memory. The object can execute commands that the Xtra defines for it, and it operates independently of any other instances of the same Xtra. You can create an Xtra instance by assigning the results of a new function call to a variable. Open the message window in Director. Type the following into the message window and execute the statement (by hitting ENTER on your keyboard):

   ```
   filecontrol = new (xtra "FileIO")
   ```

2. To use FileIO's commands, address them to the variable containing the Xtra instance. The createFile command tells the computer's file system to make a new, empty file in the location specified by the string within the parentheses. The status function returns a code indicating what happened with the last FileIO command. In the following example, a Windows–style file path is used that points to the top level of the C: drive, using Windows separators (the back slash). A Mac user with a drive named Hard Drive should use the string "Hard Drive:testio.txt". The Mac uses the colon as a file path separator.

   ```
   filecontrol.createFile ("c:\testio.txt")
   put filecontrol.status ()
   ```

   The following is returned:

   ```
   - - 0
   ```

   A text string that explains the status code is returned by the error function. If anything other than a 0 is returned by the status function, you should check the error function to determine what the status code indicates. Execute the following command:

   ```
   put filecontrol.error (0)
   ```

   The function should return:

   ```
   - - "OK"
   ```

3. Once a file has been created, it can be opened in one of three modes: 0 = read/write, 1 = read, 2 = write. We'll open the file in write mode, add some data, and then close the file.

   ```
   filecontrol.openFile ("c:\testio.txt", 2)
   filecontrol.writeString ("Tyger, tyger burning bright")
   filecontrol.closeFile ()
   ```

4. Now that there's some text in the file, we can get data from it by using one of the read functions. Open it in read mode, then use the `readFile` function to read the entire text. Note that since each instance of the Xtra can only have one open file, once the file's been opened, you don't need to specify which file you're reading or writing to. Type and execute the following:

```
filecontrol.openFile ("c:\testio.txt", 1)
put filecontrol.readFile ()
```

Which returns:

```
- - "Tyger, tyger burning bright"
```

When you read or write a file, the Xtra keeps track of what part of the file you're working in. If you try to read in any more data right now, you won't get any text, because a `readFile` leaves you at the end of the file:

```
put filecontrol.readWord ()
```

The empty string that's returned to the message window by the `readWord` function shows that there's no more text:

```
- - ""
```

To get back to the beginning of the file (0 is the position before the first character of the file), use the `setPosition` method of the FileIO Xtra. Then you can read in the first word – words are separated by spaces or end–of–line characters.

```
filecontrol.setPosition (0)
put filecontrol.readWord ()
```

Returns:

```
- - "Tyger,"
```

Now close the file:

```
filecontrol.closeFile ()
```

5. Next, we'll open the file for reading and writing, so that we can add some more text to it.

```
filecontrol.openFile ("c:\testio.txt", 0)
```

When you open the file, the file position is set to the beginning of the file. If you write the next line of the poem there, you'll obliterate the text for the first line. To append something to the file, you need to move to the end of the file.

```
filecontrol.setPosition (filecontrol.getLength ())
```

```
filecontrol.writeString (RETURN & numToChar (10) & "In the
►shadows of the night")
filecontrol.setPosition (0)
put filecontrol.readFile ()
```

Which will return:

```
- - "Tyger, tyger burning bright
In the shadows of the night"
```

> *Most Windows text applications require both a carriage return*
> *(RETURN) and a linefeed (numToChar (10)) character at the end*
> *of a paragraph. If you're writing files that need to be read by*
> *other applications on Windows, use RETURN & numToChar (10)*
> *instead of just RETURN.*

Then we close the file as before:

```
filecontrol.closeFile ()
```

6.   When you're done with the Xtra, be sure to purge its instance from memory. Xtras and
     their data can take up a lot of available RAM that could be used for other purposes.
     You can do this by just setting the variable you're using to some other value:

```
filecontrol = 0
```

There are many other functions and methods for the FileIO Xtra that you should check out with
the interface function. This is a sample line from FileIO's results:

```
error object me, int error - - return the error string of the error
```

It's pretty easy to figure out what this is supposed to do; the text after the double dashes tells
you that. What's the rest saying?

The first word (error) is the name of the method. After the method name come parameters,
expressed as two words: a data type and a description. Usually, the first parameter is the Xtra
object instance, which is data of the type object. The description me is just something you
replace with the instance name, usually a variable. The error method's second parameter is an
integer value (int) that represents an error code, usually a value returned by the status
function as shown at the beginning of the exercise.

If filecontrol is the variable name you use for an instance of the FileIO Xtra, and you're
checking to see what error code 0 means, you could put the text description of the code into
the message window with either of these Lingo commands:

```
put error (filecontrol, 0)
put filecontrol.error (0)
```

> *The FileIO Xtra can only manipulate read and write ASCII text files. To manipulate binary data files (which include most types of documents created by other applications), you need to use an Xtra like BinaryIO from updateStage.*

FileXtra3

Kent Kersten's no–cost FileXtra has been included on the Director CD–ROM for several years, ever since it was used as a part of the Save as Java feature. In 2000, he released a new version that added features to an already incredibly useful tool.

FileXtra can perform many file management tasks, including

- Determining whether a file or folder exists

- Listing all files and folders within a folder

- Testing for and creating alias files

- Moving files to Trash or Recycle Bin

- Setting file protection flags

- Comparing files

- Copying or moving files and folders

- Synchronizing the contents of folders

- Identifying CD–ROM drives

- Ejecting and unmounting drive volumes.

Combined with the FileIO Xtra, the FileXtra gives you an enormous amount of power for manipulating the user's system. Naturally, it isn't Shockwave–safe either.

> *FileXtra3 requires that an instance of the variable must be created (just like the FileIO Xtra), which is a change from earlier versions. The names of the Xtra's methods have changed with this version as well.*

Controls

Director gives you tools to create check boxes, radio buttons, and buttons, but they belie the Macintosh heritage of the program and its emphasis on custom interfaces. If people are going to design their own interfaces, there isn't a whole lot of reasons to provide them with standard operating system controls.

☐ check box
◯ radio button
[button]

As more and more people began using the program, though, it became apparent that it wasn't just a good tool for multimedia, it was also useful as a software prototyping tool, and even as a fast and efficient application development system. One little problem existed though: you really had to jump through hoops if you wanted something that looked and acted like it was just another program. Developers have spent a lot of time refining scripts and techniques to mimic controls that people have come to expect in their programs.

If you want to be able to take advantage of common program elements, try out some of these Xtras.

Popup Xtra

Red Eye Software's Popup Xtra (US$299 from updateStage) is one of the best–established Xtras in this category. It's a Shockwave–safe Lingo and Asset Xtra. To use the Xtra you create a new Popup cast member, assign it a field containing the data for the menu's choices, and create a handler that is executed when a selection is made from the menu.

The Popup cast member has a special interface. You can change a variety of options that can be set through the dialog or through Lingo commands and properties.

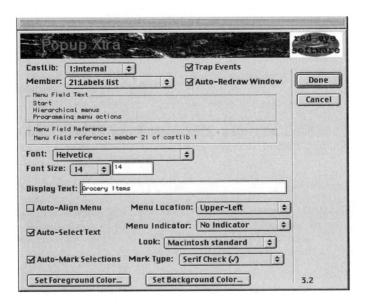

Popup Xtra menus can be made dynamic (meaning that you can change their selections), enable or disable items, and much more while the Director movie is running. It can also create hierarchical menus that contain submenus.

Popup Xtra is cross–platform, and its text and background colors can be customized, but the menus it creates can't mimic the custom appearance of the system the Director movie is running on.

MUI Maker Utility

The MUI (Macromedia User Interface) Xtra is used by the Director application to create (among other things) dialogs for setting the properties of behaviors; it wasn't intended for direct use by developers. Since it's there, though, and developers are an inquisitive lot, people started poking at it to find out what they could use it for.

Two problems with the MUI Xtra are that (since it's intended for internal Macromedia use) documentation is extremely limited, and the complicated property lists used to create even a simple dialog box are hard to build. The code to just display the dialog shown in the MUIMaker application, below, is 160 lines long.

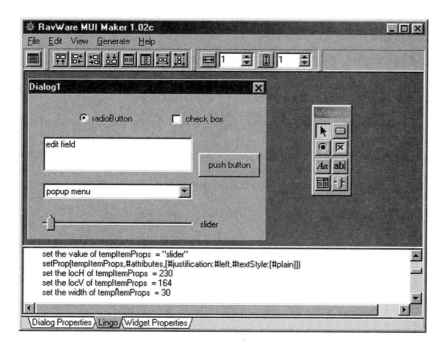

The Windows–only MUI Maker Utility has an interactive design interface that allows you to arrange buttons, check boxes, radio buttons, text blocks, pop–up menus and sliders. MUI Maker generates the basic cross–platform Lingo code needed to display the dialog, which you can then manipulate as you need. Developed by RavWare, MUI Maker is available from updateStage for US$99.

OSControl Xtra

PegHole, which consists of a couple of developers from the Netherlands, offers the OSControl Xtra (US$129), which can make controls that are drawn on the screen using the system's own styles. The picture below shows the exact same Shockwave movie viewed on a Mac and a Windows machine.

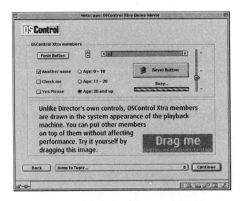 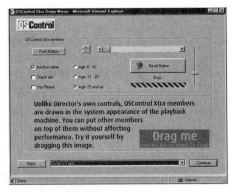

OSControl can create buttons, scrollbars, check boxes, push buttons, sliders, progress bars, and menus among other things. Each item is a separate sprite and appears along with the rest of the sprites in the Score and on the Stage. You still need to write Lingo to react to choices of menus and buttons.

ActiveX Xtra

Microsoft's ActiveX technology is designed to enable different programs to share discrete elements of code, so you can create an ActiveX control, use it in one program, and then insert the same control in another program. Because ActiveX controls have such widespread possibilities and because they can be used in everything from C programs to Visual Basic, there are literally thousands of controls available as freeware, shareware, and commercially.

Many of those controls can be used in Windows-based Director applications through the ActiveX Xtra included with the basic Director install since version 6. Not all will work with Director, and it's best to do extensive testing to ensure that things will run properly, but some of these tools are very powerful.

Embedding a Browser in Director with the ActiveXtra

Displaying web pages inside Director has got to be one of the most requested tasks. With so much content available in HTML form, integrating it into multimedia presentations or kiosks is essential to many applications. One of the standard ActiveX controls is the Microsoft Internet Explorer browser.

1. Create a new Director movie on a Windows machine.

2. Use the Insert > Control > ActiveX menu command to create a new ActiveX control in the movie. Select the Microsoft Web Browser from the list of controls and press OK.

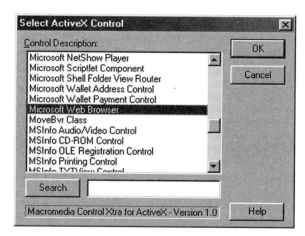

3. The ActiveX Control Properties window displays the properties of the control. Tabs also describe the methods and events the control uses. These allow you to customize the specifics of the control as well as to see what types of commands and messages it generates.

A look at the Methods tab shows the various way to control the browser. Looking through the list, you'll see the Navigate method. If you select it, you'll see a description of what it does at the top of the pane:

Navigate returns nothing
    Parameter 1: URL is a string
    Parameter 2: Flags is a string
    Parameter 3: TargetFrameName is a string
    Parameter 4: PostData is a string
    Parameter 5: Headers is a string

We just need to use parameter 1. Press OK to close the dialog.

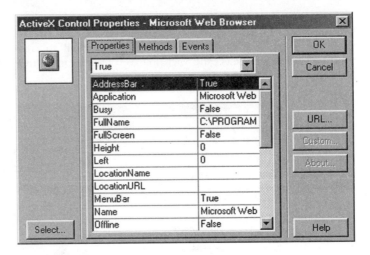

4. The control now appears in the cast window. Drag the control from the cast window onto the stage and size it so that it covers almost all of the stage.

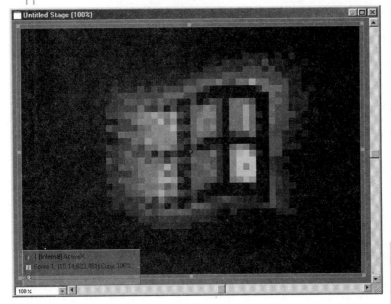

Insert a loop script in one of the frames of the score containing the ActiveX sprite. The following will do:

```
on exitframe
  go the frame
end
```

6. Play the movie from the beginning. Open the message window and use the Microsoft Web Browser ActiveX control sprite's Navigate method to load a page. Execute this line in the message window (the ActiveX sprite should be in sprite channel 1):

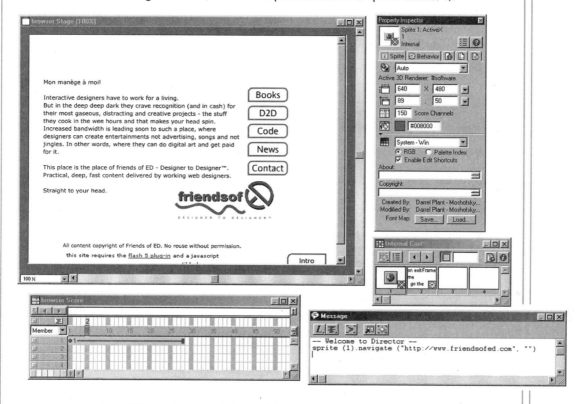

```
sprite (1).navigate    ("http://www.friendsofed.com")
```

The control displays a white box until the page begins to load. The size of the sprite defines the size of the browser window, and the contents are displayed just as if the browser had been sized to the same dimensions.

Controlling the System

We've seen how it's possible to write external files and even make Director applications look like other applications, but what if you actually need Director to interact with the computer's operating system? A number of applications give you the capability to control the system and/or other applications.

BuddyAPI Xtra

With over 100 functions, Buddy API is not only one of the most complete system control Xtras, but it's also been around for a while, so there are a lot of people who can offer advice. It's available for US$160 from Magic Modules in Australia: www.mods.com.au/.

Support is also available from reading the Buddy API forum at: http://bne001w.webcentral.com.au/~wb038.

Originally available only for Windows, even though the Mac version still isn't as full–featured, it is still a very useful tool on either platform. The free version gives you access to any two functions you want for your applications.

Among BuddyAPI's many capabilities, it can:

- Find locations of system folders

- Get drive information

- Determine installed fonts

- Encrypt and decrypt text

- Position the cursor

- Copy, delete, encrypt, and set file info

- Control application windows

- Get version information on OS, QuickTime, Video for Windows

- Determine processor information (Windows only)

- Disable keyboard, task switching, and screensavers (Windows only)

- Install fonts (Windows only)

- Find out whether a previous instance of the Director application is running (Windows only)

- Control Program Manager groups (Windows only)

- Read and write information to registry and INI files (Windows only)

Buddy API is a pure Lingo Xtra; there's no special interface to its features. Because it can cause serious harm to a system, it is not Shockwave–safe.

MasterApp Xtra

Glenn Picher's MasterApp (cross–platform, US$299, available from updateStage) is another stalwart in the system control category. Its specialty – as you might guess from its name – is controlling other applications from a Director projector.

MasterApp can open an application, open a file with an application, and even control the other application while the Director projector is running in the background. It can send keystroke commands to an application and even simulate mouse clicks. It's been an invaluable aid for many people creating software–training tools. Instead of writing a special training version of a program, or attempting to mock up an application in Director or Visual Basic, you can use MasterApp to control the user's interaction with the actual software they're trying to learn,

MasterApp is another Lingo–only Xtra. As with most of the tools in this category, it isn't Shockwave–safe.

CDPro Xtra

This Xtra is much more limited in scope than the previous entries in this category – but then it's free – from Tab Julius's Penworks. With CDPro, you can control audio CDs in the computer's CD–ROM drive and make a projector that acts like a jukebox. It can tell whether a disc is in the drive, get the title from a disc, find out information about the number of tracks and their length, and most importantly, it can play, pause, and jump to any position on the CD.

PrintOMatic Xtra

Electonic Ink's PrintOMatic (cross–platform, US$300) is the most full–featured printing tool for Director. While Director has limited printing capabilities which are augmented by those in the Flash Asset Xtra, it just doesn't hold a candle to PrintOMatic. See **Chapter 18** for more on this Xtra.

Graphics

Working with a wide range of graphics has always been one of Director's strong points. Director 8 introduced a whole new class of Lingo commands that enable you to create and modify bitmap images in a number of ways, and of course, the Director 8.5 has a 300+ 3D Lingo keywords.

There's always something else that people want to do, though, and here are a few things that help.

Fireworks Import Xtra

Macromedia's image editing application, Fireworks, is a great tool for creating screens for Director. Director's Paint window is not, to say the least. Since Fireworks comes with the Director Shockwave Studio, you might want to check it out, even if you're a Photoshop user.

Fireworks was one of the first image editors to introduce **slicing** capabilities. Prior to DHTML there was no allowance for overlapping graphics on web pages, if you wanted to create a single seamless screen with hot spots and rollovers complex tables had to be built. With Fireworks you can define rectangular slices on an image and when the image is exported Fireworks will create an HTML table and individual graphics for each of the cells of the table. It will even export portions of multiple frames in a Fireworks image as rollover and active states, if rollover behaviors have been defined for the slice.

The Fireworks Import Xtra is installed with Director 8.5. It reads HTML generated by Fireworks and imports each of the slices as individual cast members, maintaining their relationship to each other by manipulating their registration points. It automatically applies behaviors for buttons that have been assigned JavaScript rollovers in Fireworks.

Unfortunately, the Fireworks Import Xtra only works with the first two to three frames of the Fireworks document. It won't import the slices of a longer animation as separate bitmap cast members.

AlphaMania, Effector Set, and PhotoCaster Xtras

Back before Director 7 introduced alpha channel import to bitmap images, the folks at MediaLab offered AlphaMania, which let you create a 32–bit image in a program like Photoshop and have portions of the image transparent, opaque, and everything in between. Suddenly, irregularly shaped sprites were possible, without all of the tedious hand editing needed to get them working with the Background Transparent ink.

Then MediaLab came out with Effector Sets I and II, which make it possible to do real–time, Lingo–controlled special effects on bitmaps imported using the AlphaMania Xtra. The Effector Sets can perform colorization, blur, magnification, bevel, rotation, drop shadow, ripple, and swirl effects, among others. They also have a user interface where you can apply effects and effect animations.

> *Any kind of real time image manipulation requires a lot of CPU power. The Effector Set effects are a lot faster than writing your own with Imaging Lingo, but they can still seriously slow your movie.*

PhotoCaster is an Xtra that imports layered Photoshop (PSD) files without having to export each image as a separate, flattened file. Director will import a Photoshop file itself, but all of the layers are composited, and effects are lost. PhotoCaster 3 (released in mid–2001) has an import interface that lets you turn layers on and off, has an option to import layers as separate cast members, can import effects layers, and even imports text layers as text cast members.

PhotoCaster is an Import Xtra and is $199 per platform. AlphaMania, an Import and Asset Xtra, is $249 per platform. Each of the Lingo Xtra Effector Sets are $99 per platform, and require the AlphaMania Xtra. All of MediaLab's Xtras are registered to a specific Director serial number, although you can get new registration keys free when you upgrade Director. If you buy an Xtra for only one platform, you can still distribute it on both Mac and Windows. A number of multi–Xtra, cross–platform bundles are also available.

The AlphaMania and Effector Set Xtras are Shockwave–safe.

Grabber Xtra

Paul Farry's Grabber Xtra (US$50 per platform from powerup.com) is an image tool that can capture part or all of the screen and even make new cast members out of existing cast members.

Commands in this Lingo Xtra let you define what part of the screen to capture. It's as simple as installing the Xtra then typing this in the Message window:

```
GrabScreen (0)
```

This command captures the entire screen and puts it into a new cast member. You can also specify a specific cast member, capture the Stage, or capture any rectangular area on the screen. Other commands (which cannot be used in Shockwave, although the Xtra is Shockwave–safe) let you save the captured image to a file (BMP on Windows, or PICT on Mac).

Grabber can capture Shockwave3D members. The demonstration version places a cross through the captured image.

Audio

Working with audio files can be one of the most complex and frustrating tasks in Director. Everything depends on walking the delicate balance between other processes running on the computer, decompression speed, and the fact that these things rely on not just the system software, but other elements beyond your control, like sound cards for example. Anything that can make it easier is usually welcome.

asFFT Xtra

One task that's just not possible within the many avenues of audio and video playback is sound wave analysis. What if you want to base something in the movie on input from a microphone, or from a CD audio file?

That's what the cross–platform, Shockwave–safe Lingo Xtra asFFT (the FFT is for Fast Fourier Transform) does. It just has a few functions, but it lets you select a sound input source like a microphone, or the CD drive, and will retrieve actual samples of the sound waves, returning a list of data that shows you the waveform of the sound and the frequencies that make up the sound. With this data, you can do things like create equalizer displays and animations that change based on the sound.

```
vas = new (xtra "asFFT")

vas.asFFTInit (64, 1)
```

```
put vas.asFFTGetFFTValues ()
-- [507, 498, 384, 274, 255, 250, 263, 234, 163, 143, 119, 136,
➡108, 69, 29, 85, 88, 77, 38, 52, 40, 21, 59, 30, 46, 35, 16,
➡23, 20, 31, 27, 67, 35, 41, 16, 27, 15, 22, 15, 61, 63, 45, 38,
➡45, 21, 43, 32, 6, 39, 22, 34, 20, 20, 22, 52, 29, 33, 60, 57,
➡21, 53, 44, 60, 58]

vas.asFFTClose ()
```

In this code sample, the variable vas is used to hold an instance of the asFFT Xtra, then the Xtra is initialized with two values defining the number of divisions you want to make within the overall sound bandwidth, and the accuracy you prefer. The asFFTGetValues function returns a linear list containing numbers revealing the prevalence of frequencies within a bandwidth. The asFFTClose function is used to shut down the Xtra's data processing. Unlike some other Xtras, only one instance of the asFFT Xtra can be instantiated at one time.

The asFFT is available from Antoine Schmitt as freeware from: www.as–ci.net/asFFTXtra/)

Audio Xtra

This US$299 Xtra by Red Eye Software (distributed by updateStage) is a Lingo Xtra that can record sounds and save them to memory, cast members, or external files, even in Shockwave. The Xtra can convert files between AIFF, WAVE, and AU formats; can change the sampling and bit rates used for recording; and can create a playlist of recorded sounds.

Communications

Director already has a number of ways to talk to servers of various sorts. The Network Lingo commands can communicate with HTTP and FTP servers from projectors. In Shockwave, you can even use the hosting browser to talk to secure HTTPs servers. Projectors and Shockwave movies can download files from servers. The Multiuser Xtra even lets you create chat rooms and multiplayer games. But there's always something else you want to do.

XtraNet

Back in the early days of the Web, when Shockwave was still a young pup, people already wanted more. At the time, you couldn't use Net Lingo in a projector but, of course, people wanted their projectors to be able to talk to a server. What to do?

The folks at Human Code came up with XtraNet. For a couple of years they sold the Xtra, but now it is available for free from their site: www.humancode.com/xtranet/

XtraNet is unsupported which means that if you use it you're on your own; you also have to get the documentation elsewhere: one place is Warren Ockrassa's Nightwares site: http://nightwares.com/xnet–docs–and–samples.zip

That said, XtraNet is a very powerful tool. One extremely useful feature is its XNetIPAddress function, which will tell you the number assigned to the computer the projector is running on. It can do domain name service (DNS) lookups.

XtraNet has HTTP and FTP capabilities which can talk to the appropriate server types, and it also has a special protocol for communicating movie–to–movie and for creating its own servers and clients.

One of the most powerful features is the XtraNet Raw class. The Raw class can be used to mimic a wide variety of TCP/IP protocols as either client or server. One of the examples linked from the XtraNet download site includes an email client. I actually wrote a specialized HTTP server using XtraNet and Director 5!

XtraNet is not Shockwave–safe.

DirectEmail Xtra

One of the most common types of communication on the Internet is email. While the getNetText command in Network Lingo can be used to open a browser's email client, most of the time you want to do it all within a projector or Shockwave. This tool ($349 for the cross–platform version from DirectXtras) can do that.

The DirectEmail Xtra can send plain or HTML mail – with attachments – from projectors and Shockwave movies. It can use a relaying mail account or even act as its own mail server (each method has some advantages and disadvantages). So there's no need to open up the client's email application or browser.

A Couple More Xtras

There are so many Xtras out there. By the very fact of their existence someone finds them useful. Here are a couple of more that are of particular note.

AutoComplete Xtra

Programming in Director involves a lot of typing the same thing over and over again. The folks at PegHole have made that task a lot easier (for Mac developers at least) with their US$15 AutoComplete Xtra.

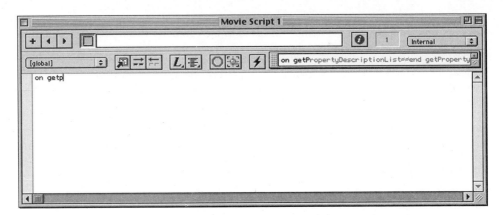

The AutoComplete Xtra displays a small floating palette near the title bar of the Script, Message, and Watcher windows. As you type in any of those windows, the AutoComplete window displays the first match from its library of Lingo keywords. Hitting a key (by default, the TAB key) enters the word AutoComplete is guessing. For instance, instead of typing on getPropertyDescriptionList in a behavior script, all you need to do is type on getp then hit TAB, and AutoComplete will enter not only the entire handler name but also an extra line and the end getPropertyDescriptionList that goes at the end of the handler.

AutoComplete reads the handlers from all of your Lingo Xtras and it's already been updated for the new Director 8.5 Lingo set. It's also very user–customizable.

V12 DataBase Engine Xtra and GoldenGate Database Connector

It's entirely possible to do a complex database system in Director using linear lists, property lists, or even objects. Is it fun to do so? Not always. And, once the database gets fairly large, speed becomes a real issue. The main culprit is sorting, because if you've implemented all of your routines in Lingo, it just isn't going to be as fast as a regular database.

Integration New Media's V12 Database Engine Xtra is a Shockwave–safe database tool that can create, import, and modify databases, as well as search, sort, and index them. The full version can have up to 128 tables open simultaneously. Total database size is limited by the storage media rather than memory, as is the case with most Lingo database implementations. A 1–user license costs US$469.

V12–DBE can store just about anything in its fields: text, numbers, dates, even sounds and bitmaps. It is used extensively for projects like catalogs and educational projects that require quick sorts on thousands of items. V12–DBE even supports multiuser access to a networked database. There's also a limited–function 'Lite' version available for US$199. INM's documentation is generally recognized as excellent.

INM's GoldenGate Database Connector isn't an Xtra by itself, but you use an Xtra to connect to it. GoldenGate is a Windows–only server (starting at US$895) that connects to ODBC–compliant databases. Unlike other middleware products, the scripting of searches with GoldenGate is performed at the client side; the server just executes the instructions by talking to the database, getting the information the client requested, and passing it back to the client. The Xtra can be distributed freely, and is Shockwave–safe.

Distributing Xtras

Knowing how to use Xtras is only a part of the knowledge you need. Installing an Xtra for use in Director doesn't automatically make it available when the movie is played back outside of the authoring application. Once your movie's done, what do you do?

Packaging for Projectors

A projector needs its Xtras just like Director needs them; it just doesn't need all of the same Xtras. Many of the Xtras used by Director are only used in the authoring process – projectors (and Shockwave movies) don't use them. When you send your projector out into the world on a CD–ROM, copied to a hard drive, or distributed on the Web, the Xtras it needs for playback have to go along. You do have a couple of options for that, but first you need to know which Xtras you need, don't you?

Determining which Xtras you need

A new movie in a fresh install of Director 8.5 starts off with a few Xtras associated with the movie by default:

- INetURL
- NetFile
- NetLingo
- SWA Decompression
- MacroMix
- DirectSound
- Sound Control

How can you tell this? If you select Modify > Movie > Xtras from the menu, you'll see the Movie Xtras dialog, which lets you control Xtras for a specific movie. The Xtras you see in the dialog box are the ones that are added when the Add Defaults button is pressed. The first three are those added by the Add Network button, and as you might imagine, they provide the mechanics for the built–in networking in Director. The other four are related to the use of sound.

The SWA Decompression Xtra decompresses Shockwave Audio files. The Sound Control Xtra provides the sound Lingo added in Director 8. Mac users might find the inclusion of the **MacroMix.x32** and **DirectSound.x32** files a bit odd, since **.x32** is the file extension for Xtras in Director 8.5 for Windows. These two Xtras are in the list to support cross–platform playback. Because the same source (DIR) file must be taken to a Windows machine to make a Projector for that platform, rather than require that someone remember to add those Xtras to the required list every single time, they're a part of the default for every movie, even though there aren't any equivalents on the Mac for these Xtras.

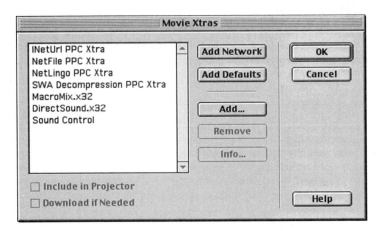

My own first step is usually to clear out all of the Xtras from this list.

As you add media to the movie by importing it, the appropriate Xtras are added to the required list. In this example, I've added an Animated GIF, a bitmap image, a Flash movie, a QuickTime file, and a Popup Xtra cast member. You can see the cast member type in the Cast window and the associated Xtras in the Movie Xtras dialog.

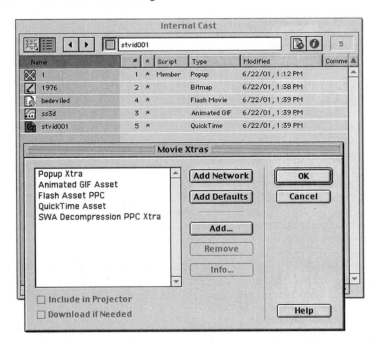

However, this method only informs you about Asset Xtras. For pure Lingo Xtras (like the Net Lingo, Net File, and INetURL Xtras, you need to manually add them to the Movie Xtras list if you want them to show up there. Director doesn't have any way to tell which Lingo Xtras you might call during the course of playback. For Lingo Xtras that are also Asset Xtras like the Popup Xtra, you don't need to worry about adding it manually.

If you want something like FileXtra3 to show up in the list, you must use the Add button. Just click the button and a new dialog with a list of all of your Xtras appears. You just select whichever one should be added to the list and press OK.

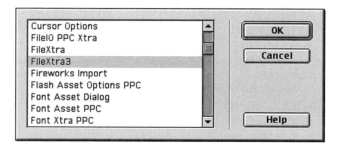

It's a good habit to add Lingo Xtras to the list when you use them in a script. It can save you some time and grief later, even when (as we'll see) it's not always necessary.

> *Something to watch for is that some Xtras have dependencies on the default Xtras. For instance, the Shockwave 3D Asset Xtra requires the Net Lingo Xtras to be available for playback.*

When you're ready to make a projector, you have two basic choices about what to do with the Xtras that are needed for playback.

The simplest option is to let Director handle making sure the Xtras are all there (which is why you add them to the list of required Xtras). Each Xtra in the list has an option for Include in Projector. All Xtras for which this option is checked will be included as a part of the projector file when it's created. The progress bar indicating how much of the projector is completed displays the names of the Xtras as they're added to the file.

A projector made this way only requires a single file to be distributed (apart from any external media), and it makes it easier for you to keep track of the Xtras used by the movie.

The other option is to uncheck the Include in Projector option. This requires you to create an Xtras folder in the same directory and hand–copy the Xtras you need into the folder. This seems like more work, particularly in a complex movie that uses a lot of Xtras, doesn't it?

The advantage is speed. A projector that has its Xtras included must copy and decompress the data for the Xtras into a temporary folder on the user's system before the projector starts playing. If no Xtras are included and they're in an Xtras folder instead, the projector can just get going.

> *Current versions of projectors unpack their included Xtras to a temporary folder. In older versions of Director, included Xtras were unpacked to an Xtras folder in the projector's directory, which meant that you couldn't use included Xtras with projectors on locked media like CD–ROMs.*

For more information on Xtras and projectors, see **Chapter 19**.

Packaging for Shockwave

The basic Shockwave installation includes many of the standard types of Xtras for Net Lingo, Flash, audio, and text, as well as Shockwave3D and multiuser communications. Certain Xtras have been left out of the basic distribution, though, and if you use them or any third–party Shockwave–safe Xtras, you need to know how to include that information in the Shockwave movie you distribute.

For things like the Animated GIF Xtra, it's incredibly easy. Just select the Xtra and choose Download if Needed in the Movie Xtras dialog box. Shockwave 8.5 will download the required files from Macromedia's server, install them into the correct place, and begin playing the movie when it's done; the user won't see anything except perhaps a brief message in the status line of their browser.

When you select the Download if Needed option for the Animated GIF Xtra, you'll see two brief downloads of the package information that is incorporated into the Shockwave movie file, and is used when the movie is downloaded by a Shockwave player that hasn't already downloaded the necessary Xtra.

Third–party Xtra vendors must go through an approval process before their Xtras can be made Shockwave–safe. Their Xtras will display a security dialog requiring user approval before the Xtra will be installed into Shockwave.

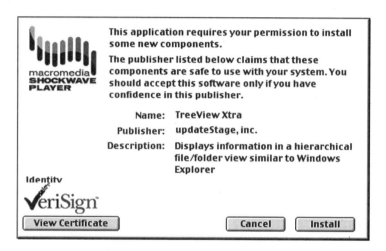

Simply installing an Xtra isn't enough to make it possible to download in Shockwave. If you install a third–party Xtra and look at the Movie Xtras dialog, you'll see that the Download if Needed checkbox is grayed out and unavailable. Director has to know where the files will be downloaded from before it will let you check that box. For Macromedia's own Xtras, that information's already known.

To tell Director the address, you need to edit the xtrainfo.txt file in the Director application folder. This file contains all of the addresses for the downloadable Xtras your copy of Director knows about. You need to check the documentation for your particular Xtra to find out what to add to this file. For Media Lab's AlphaMania and Effector Set Xtras, the text you need to add is:

```
; AlphaMania from MediaLab
[#nameW32:"AlphaMania.x32", #namePPC:"AlphaMania",
➥ #package:"http://www.medialab.com/shockpak/AMES",
➥ #info:"http://www.medialab.com"]
```

The semicolon is a comment character in xtrainfo.txt. The rest of the data is a property list containing the names of the Xtras on the Windows and Mac platforms, the address where the Shockwave packages are located, and the location to go to when the Movie Xtras dialog's Info button is pressed.

> *Some Xtra developers require that you host the package files on your own servers, meaning you must change the address for the* #package *property in the template they provide in their documentation.*

Now you can package the Xtra with your Shockwave movies, just like any of the Macromedia Xtras. This only needs to be done once for each Xtra for each copy of Director. The `xtrainfo.txt` file is shared by any movie you open with that copy of Director.

Making Xtras

Sometimes, even after you've looked at every Xtra you can find, you still can't find one that does what you need. That's when you start thinking about writing your own. What's involved?

There are two approaches to creating Xtras. The types of Xtras we've discussed in this chapter were written in the C language, using Macromedia's XDK (Xtra Development Kit). If you're not a C programmer, though, you can create some types of authoring tools using Director itself.

Using Director to Create an Xtra

If your task is something that could be performed with a Director movie, you can probably turn it into an Xtra. The reason for this is that any Director movie, protected Director movie, or compressed Director movie (Shockwave) that is placed into the Xtras folder of your Director application will appear in the Xtras menu as a selection.

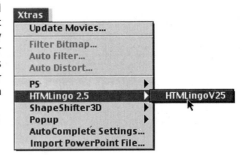

Selecting a Director–created Xtra from the Xtras menu opens the Director movie as a MIAW (Movie in a Window), just like it would be if you used the `open window` command in Lingo. The Xtra has access to all of the other Xtras in the Director application's Xtras folder, so it can perform file access, import graphics, or just about anything else you can do with Lingo.

Director–created Xtras are much more limited in their capabilities than Xtras created using the XDK. They can't be packaged as Xtras with projectors or in Shockwave, and they tend to fall into the category of Tool Xtras, although they can be used for other tasks like importing files during run–time. They are often developed in–house to speed up development by production teams.

One example of this type of Xtra is my own PS2VS tool, a freeware utility which converts simple Adobe Illustrator and EPS (Encapsulated PostScript) files into vector shapes in Director. It uses the FileXtra and FileIO Xtra to read the PostScript information from a file and convert it to vectors line–by–line. The Xtra can create new cast members in the cast of the open movie and assign the vector data to them. PS2VS is available from the Moshplant site at:
http://www.moshplant.com/direct–or/ps2vs/

Dave Mennenoh provides a great utility called HTML–ingo, which converts Lingo into styled HTML code for use in a web page. We use it extensively at Director Online for all of our code samples. It's free, it's up to date, and it's provided as a DIR file, so you can open it up and see what's going on. Oh, and it's available from: www.execpc.com/~ktm/dave/davedir.htm

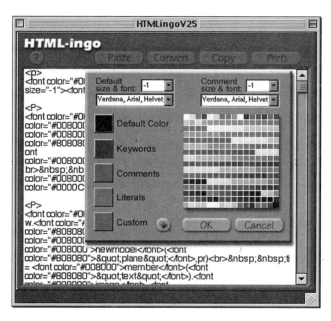

How Do I Make a 'Real' Xtra

Developing an Xtra using the Macromedia XDK isn't – as programmers call it – a 'trivial' task. It requires knowledge of the C programming language, and the mastery of some arcane knowledge called MOA (Macromedia Open Architecture).

Here's where you can get started if you want to make your own XDK Xtras:

- Macromedia's Xtras Support Center has descriptions of the process and the MOA, developer web sites, and mailing lists, as well as tech notes and the XDK itself at: www.macromedia.com/support/xtras/

- Trevi Media operates Xtras–L, a mailing list for Xtras developers. You can find out more information at: www.trevimedia.com/mailinglists/.

- The University of Queensland in Australia maintains a page covering tips about compiling Xtras: www.ems.uq.edu.au/Public/TechNotes/Xtras/.

- Gary Smith, the developer of the Buddy API Xtra, has made XtraBuilder available as a preview release. XtraBuilder generates source code for building Lingo scripting Xtras on the Windows platform. You can find it at the Magic Modules site: www.mods.com.au/.

- Chris Thorman has initiated an open source Xtras site with his PRegEx Xtra, a regular expression text manipulation tool at: http://openxtras.org/.

The important things to remember when writing Xtras with Director are:

- MIAWs share their global variables with the open movie. If your MIAW uses global variables, it may overwrite something that's happening in the movie or other MIAWs. It's a good idea to use unusual names, behavior properties, or as few globals as you can get away with.

- When a MIAW Xtra is closed for good, make sure you use the `forget window` command. When a MIAW window is closed it doesn't actually go away, it's just not being seen, much like minimizing an application. To truly put away the tool, you should clear its global variables by setting them to 0 (`clearglobals` will also clear the globals in the main movie) and `forget` the window to dispose of the movie reference.

- If you distribute your Xtra for use by others, make sure they know where to find any Xtras it depends on.

Custom Xtra Developers

If the idea of making your own Xtra looks a little daunting, but you still need one to do something special, many of the developers listed in this chapter also do custom Xtra programming. As with any software development, the price will probably start in the thousands of dollars and go up from there, but if you've got a definite need it may well be worth your while to talk to someone with experience first. Join one of the developer lists, check web sites, and look for someone who's done something similar. It can save you money and a lot of aggravation!

Summary

You should now know much of the wide and diverse functionality that Xtras in Director can provide as well as where to find and how to use many of the most popular third–party Xtras. We've looked at how to install Xtras and how to package and distribute Xtras in your own movies and projectors.

Throughout this chapter we've had two aims: firstly, to show to you that Xtras in Directors can take Director way beyond the functionality displayed on the cover of the box, to extremes that can even mess with a users hard drive and system files(!); and, secondly, to show you that Xtras really aren't 'extra': they perform many of the basic, vital functions that make Director such a powerful and versatile tool.

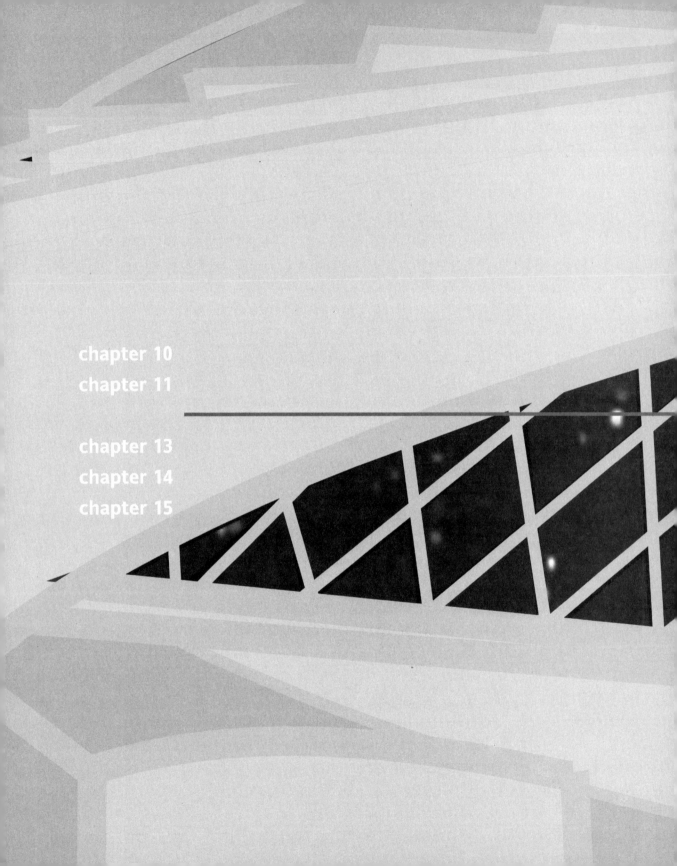

Chapter 12
Flash

It is unlikely there is anyone who is unaware of Flash, (to quote the Macromedia slogan) **"the professional standard for producing high-impact, vector-based Web experiences"**, and its current dominance on the Internet. Flash is now widely acknowledged as 'the' solution for those requiring low-bandwidth, streaming, interactive, animated media on the web.

In this chapter we'll look at how best to make use of the advantages that Flash offers to your Director movies, and we'll look at the common pitfalls associated with the use of Flash - where possible, we'll tell you how to work around these. Then we'll move on to look at the Flash 5 Asset Xtra (and its new features), which continues to increase the interoperability between Flash and Director, before taking a brief look at (and contrasting with Lingo) ActionScript, Flash's native scripting language.

Overview of Flash

One of the greatest factors in the success of The Flash Player has been the small size of its web player (combined with having it included in most browsers), which has led to a very healthy base of potential viewers across multiple platforms. Flash can be viewed on a significantly diverse range of platforms from Sun Solaris and LINUX, to PocketPC, and even Sony PS2.

Possibly the most important factor in the success of Flash was Macromedia opening the SWF (Flash movie) format, allowing anyone with sufficient C++ programming skills to make a program that can generate/export to the SWF format. The SWF (pronounced 'swiff') format is now considered 'standard' for small files size vectors although fans of the SVG (Scalable Vector Graphic) format may disagree.

This has lead to the situation where Flash as an authoring environment has some competition, with Adobe's LiveMotion and Corel's R.A.V.E being the two most notable. Since both applications output SWF intended for browser based viewing and interaction they are directly supporting the SWF format, making it increasingly popular and increasing its chances of long term survival against rivals such as SVG and other vector-based onscreen formats. Also, any future rivals to SWF will not only need to be technologically superior, but will also need to overcome resistance from a large, enthusiastic, entrenched user base.

> *The FLA format (source that opens in Flash, equivalent to Directors DIR) isn't open, so only Flash can open and edit the contents of a FLA.*

For more on Flash – everything from its development history to its availability on the PS2 – have a look at the 'Useful Links' section at the end of this chapter.

Advantages of Flash

Flash has some major advantages over Director and you can use these to enhance your Director movies by adding aspects that the Flash feature set provide, as detailed below.

File Size

Flash, being vector based, produces small files, which makes it great for use on the web - always remember that not everyone has broadband connections. There are many myths of Flash file size versus Shockwave file size: the truth is that (if the content is exactly the same) the Shockwave movie will be smaller than the Flash movie. Director has a more efficient optimization process, which means that even text is reduced to a smaller file size than in Flash.

Vectors Scale Well

This vector nature of the Flash environment led to a situation where scaling of the output movies is encouraged and easy to do for both browser based movies and projectors. Director output can be scaled, but not as well as in Flash (because of its raster nature and its lack of Flash raster graphics smoothing – rasters look less jaggy when scaled or rotated).

Media Goes Anywhere

In Director everything has its place: sound in the sound channel, sprites in the sprite channel, scripts into the script channel, etc. Flash has a more flexible structure: in the Flash timeline not only can any type of media (rasters, vector shapes, sound, scripts, etc) be used in any layer, but they can also be mixed within layers. So, you can put a raster image and a sound into the same layer. Furthermore, you can put the raster and the sound into the same keyframe. For those not used to Flash's timeline this may seem chaotic, but it means that you need much fewer Flash layers than you would need Director channels.

It can lead to some confusion when all of the media is mixed; using a good layer naming convention helps, as does separating the media – not putting sound and raster on the same layer. Note that when tweening the object must be in its own layer.

One Movie, Many Timelines

The biggest advantage that Flash has over Director is the way it handles timelines. In Director it's quite tricky and sometimes impossible to produce interactive animation with multiple timelines. LDMs (Linked Director Movies), MIAW (Movie In A Window), and FilmLoops are all possible solutions, but none have the power, ease of use, and simple scripting of Flash MovieClips (often referred to as MCs). In Flash it's possible to nest multiple MCs within multiple MCs, which allows for very complex animations that are fully scriptable and easy to control.

Streaming

One of the most quoted advantages of Flash is that it can stream, though many web sites and Flash intros seem to be designed with the intention of ignoring this feature in favor of the much hated pre-loader: "Loading, please wait". Of course experienced developers know that Director can also stream.

Disadvantages of Flash

Flash has some downsides, some more significant than others. However, with careful planning, testing early in the process, and being fully aware of the limitations imposed by Director, you can overcome them.

Speed

The rendering of anti-aliased vectors is very CPU intensive (compared to raster animations in Director). This means that using Flash in your Director projects can cause a serious decrease in the frame rate. Director's composition based display engine only needs to layer the images (sprites) on-screen. Flash uses a real-time curve to pixel rendering engine, sometimes compared to a scan line render in 3D applications.

This means that Flash will have a lower frame rate than Director. So, if you design your Director movie for 60fps playback and then import a Flash movie, you won't be able to increase the speed that the Flash animation was designed to play at. Flash designed for modern CPU playback is typically 24fps and only a very few Flash movies are set to play above 30fps.

You may find that Flash playing inside Director is more CPU intensive than Flash in its own player. This is true especially with greater use of scaling, as the increased number of pixels requires more calculations, increasing CPU loads. So, testing a Flash movie immediately on import to check for unwanted frame rate drops, or other nasty surprises, is a very good idea. Don't be shocked to see a Flash movie playing back with a reduced frame rate, maybe a 10% drop on the rate achieved in the Flash Player. You may wish to change the default properties of the Flash member to increase the playback rate of the movie. Setting the Quality to Low will stop the Flash vectors from anti-aliasing, reducing the number of calculations performed per frame, so reducing the CPU load and increasing the rate. Set the rate to Lock-Step (if the Flash movie skipping frames is acceptable), the movie will now drop frames so it can match the rate set for Directors score.

Rasters

Frame rates in both Director and Flash are very much the product of content and size. As the playback engine was designed for vectors, Flash has a problem with rasters (not just the player bug reported below). So, in terms of frame rates, Flash handles rasters poorly, though Flash can produce better quality due to smoothing. You can expect to see identical raster animations in Flash playing at about half the speed (or less) as they would in Director. Using alpha effects (blends in Director) have a much greater effect on frame rates in Flash. So, even though Flash has raster smoothing, if you're alpha tweening and scaling rasters at the same time in a large Flash movie, frame rates can hit single figures quite easily - the smoothing also takes a hit on the CPU as the pixels need to be recalculated. In extreme cases smoothing can half the frame rate. Try to use tint tweening whenever possible as it has a lower hit on the CPU, thereby preserving rates. Tints are normally only possible when graphics don't overlap, or the graphic being tint tweened is on the bottom.

When importing rasters into Flash scale them to 99% or set the alpha value to 99% - that includes tweening rasters using alpha settings; don't tween from 0% to 100%, tween from 1% to 99%. This avoids the much discussed Flash bitmap shift, where some of the pixels in the image appear to move a small amount (like a wave) just as the animation is coming to an end.

Frame Rates

Always bear in mind that as frame rates are set in maximum frames per second that this is a target that can't be exceeded. If your rates drop significantly on older CPUs and you design around them playing slow, you will get unexpected results on faster CPUs. This can result in the strange situation of animations being too fast. You should design such that there is an acceptable viewing experience on the minimum spec **and** the fastest machines (standard desktops) currently available. If in doubt set the frame rate low to prevent 'too fast' animation on new CPUs while retaining good rates on older CPUs.

There is a reported bug in the Mac version of The Flash Player that causes movies to play at 21fps, even when the frame rate is set higher and the design elements would permit higher rates playback. Depending on the situation you may see an increase in frame rates on the Mac. This may be balanced out by reports of much larger decreases in scaled Flash movie frame rates when in Director.

Math Calculations

Math is not a strong point of Flash, so try to keep mathematical functions in Lingo. There have been many brave attempts to produce 3D engines in Flash but all have suffered from being too slow, even on the fastest machines available.

Minimize Potential Problems

The single most important thing to keep in mind when dealing with Flash is not to design in isolation. Don't think you can create a large project in Flash then drop the whole thing into Director and have it work 100% effectively – you'd need a lot of faith and far more luck! Flash in Director can be thought of in much the same way as video: it will work best when small chunks are used, one at a time.

The Flash 5 Asset Xtra

Director hasn't missed out on exploiting the features of its increasingly popular stablemate. Inclusion of The Flash Asset in Director 6.5 gave full support within the native authoring environment and Flash members have become a more important part of Director development with each new version.

Flash 5 and Director

Director 8 didn't have **support** for Flash 5. The word 'support' is highlighted as SWFs exported in Flash 5 format will import into Director 8, but only features common with Flash 4 will work correctly. So something written in the Flash 5 ActionScript will fail, but tweened animation will work fine (as tweening isn't unique to Flash 5).

The more important new features in Flash 5, some of which may come to Director users as a pleasant surprise (as they are features that have been present in Director for some time), are:

- New ActionScript syntax

- XML transfer support

- HTML text support

- Smart Clips

- MP3 audio import support

As most will have noticed, Flash and Director have a greater margin of overlapping features with each new release.

New Lingo Commands

There are five new Lingo commands to accompany the Flash 5 Asset Xtra. They are:

- callFrame

- print

- printAsBitmap

- sendXML

- tellTarget and endTellTarget

Let's take a look at each of these in turn.

callFrame

Flash ActionScripts placed in frames on the main timeline can be run using the `call` function in Lingo. The concept may seem a little odd to Director developers, but with some careful planning it's possible to achieve the required results.

```
sprite(whichSprite).callFrame(frameNumber)
sprite(whichSprite).callFrame(frameLabel)
```

A Flash sprite in channel 1 with a script you wish to call in frame 10 would be:

```
sprite(1).callFrame(10)
```

If the script is in a frame with the label "runningMan" and the sprite identification is pSprite, the syntax is:

```
pSprite.callFrame("runningMan")
```

A typical situation would be where you wanted a complex set of interactions to occur in the Flash movie but wish the Flash main timeline playback head to remain on its current frame. You can put the scripts into frames (using labels to help with identification) and call them without moving the head to the frame containing the required script.

It's not the most elegant of methods, but it must be borne in mind when designing your Flash movies if they are intended to be used in projects involving Director - the 'technical' design of the Flash movie will need to be sacrificed to make the desired characteristic possible. All your graphics (not just animations) should be made into MovieClips; this makes them easily scriptable at a later date and ensures minimal file size.

Ironically, in Flash 5, the `call` action is deprecated. The Flash 5 ActionScript (AS) action `function` now replaces `call`. This doesn't affect its use in Director.

> *In the Director 8.5 documentation,* `callFrame` *is referred to as* `call`*; this is incorrect as explained in the following Macromedia Technote:*
>
> http://www.macromedia.com/support/director/ts/documents/
> flashcall.htm

print

Printing using Flash isn't the easiest of subjects, the fact thats it's very poorly documented in the Director manual doesn't help. Luckily the Flash manual does a better job of explaining the basic concepts. If you don't have the manual to hand, you can download the PDF from:
http://www.macromedia.com/support/flash/documentation/flash5/using_flash_5.html

The method of producing prints from Flash many seem strange for those who haven't encountered it before as, unlike Director, it involves some additional work on the timeline, but does have some advantages over Director. It's much more flexible than the PrintOMatic Lite Xtra that ships on the Director CD-ROM as Flash doesn't rasterize the output at 72dpi and can print elements that aren't on screen.

The Flash printing workflow has four steps:

1. Decide which frames you wish to print.

2. Work out which print area is best for your situation.

3. Separate the frames into those that require transparency (use `printAsBitmap`) and those that don't (use `print`).

4. Switch to Director, write the Lingo print action.

The Lingo syntax for printing from Flash is:

```
sprite (whichSprite).print ("targetName", #printingBounds)
```

"targetName" is used when you aren't printing a frame on the Flash main timeline, so use it when you are printing a frame within a MovieClips timeline. It's best practice to put 0 for the `targetName` if you require a reference to the main timeline.

#printingBounds can have three values:

-   0

-   #bframe

-   #bmax

If #printingBounds is left unspecified or is 0 (zero), the bounds of the Flash movie are used to specify the printing bounds unless you define the print area with #b (see below).

Setting up the Flash movie for printing:

A frame label #p is used to identify each frame within your Flash movie that you wish to print.

Open up Flash, insert a blank keyframe, add the frame label in the frame panel, Window > Panels > Frame (or Ctrl + F),

So if you wanted to print frames 5, 10 and 15:

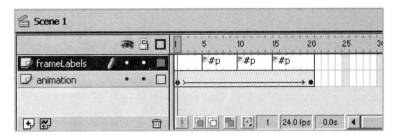

If you don't want to specify a given frame to print, no additional label is required. The !#p frame label (which disables the print option in the Flash context menu) isn't required for use in Director.

> *As you may be defining more that one frame with the #p label, you will get an error when exporting the movie. It will work OK when printing.*
>
> *You can only define one print area #b per timeline, meaning you can't define two or more print areas in the same MC.*

The diagram below (bounds drawn as dashed lines) shows what occurs when no bounds are defined, and would be generated by:

```
sprite (whichSprite).print("targetName", 0)
```

As you can see, the dimensions of the movie are scaled up such that the movie bounds and the printer bounds are coincident:

On-Screen Width

Printed Width

The diagram below shows what is printed when you define a **print area** (the gray rectangle)

If the Flash movie (in channel 1) has a MovieClip with instance name printMe, the graphic shown in the top left would be frame 1 with a frame label of #p and the shape defining the print area on the bottom left would be in frame 2 with a frame label of #b.

```
sprite(1).print("printMe", 0)
```

Note: this is the same syntax as the previous example, it's just that now #p has been defined.

We'll show the #bframe and #bmax options with a worked example.

Simple Example of Flash printing

The source files for this example are circle.fla and flashPrint.dir, which are available on the CD or can be downloaded from the friends of ED website.

1. In Flash draw a simple circle with no fill and turn it into an MC (or graphic if you wish).

2. Make a new MC and put the circle MC into it.

3. Add two keyframes and offset the circle.

4. Add a fourth keyframe and draw a rectangle (using onion skinning to help placement), as shown in the image on the following page .

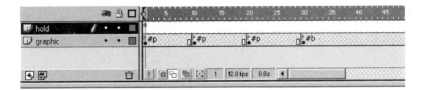

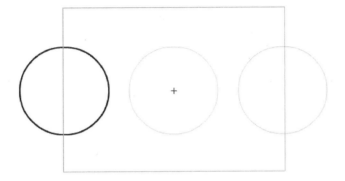

5. Add #p labels to the three frames containing circles.

6. Add a #b to the fourth keyframe, defining the rectangle as the print area.

7. Add a stop frame action on the first frame to prevent the MC from playing.

8. Put the MC on the main timeline and give it an instance name of printMe.

9. Export the movie as circle.swf and import in Director 8.5.

10. Place the Flash member into channel 1 in the score.

11. Write a standard 'go the frame' frame script to cycle the head within the frame.

12. Highlight the Flash member in the cast and set its 'Scale Mode' to 'No Scale' in the property inspector.

13. Make three standard buttons like so:

(bounds)

(frame)

(max)

14. Make three behaviors and drop them onto their respective buttons.

```
— this is the script for the bounds button
on mouseUp me
    sprite(1).print("_root.printMe", 0)
end


— this is the script for the frame button
on mouseUp me
    sprite(1).print("_root.printMe", #bframe)
end


— this is the script for the max button
on mouseUp me
    sprite(1).print("_root.printMe", #bmax)
end
```

Play the movie and press each of the buttons in turn. Every button press will print three pages, as follows:

Bounds Button: Since the print area is defined with #b and the rectangle, the prints will look like:

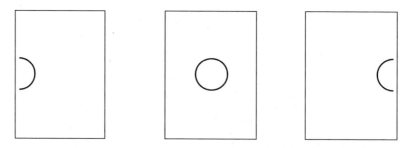

As you can see this looks very much like the onion-skinned view for the MC in Flash. The print area has been scaled to fit the page and remains fixed for all three pages.

Frame Button: When using the #bframe option, each printable frame (the ones with #p labels) are printed in isolation, that is each frame is scaled to fit the page. Note that the line weight is also scaled.

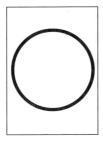 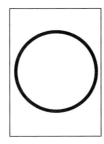 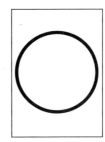

Max Button: The #bmax option is a little like the exact opposite of the #bframe option in that it looks at all the printable #p frames and applies an 'imaginary' print area that encompasses all the elements that will be printed. So, in this example, the left and right circle will define the extents of the print.

 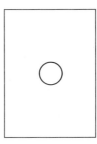 

printAsBitmap
Use printAsBitmap when you have objects containing transparency or colour effects. This is due to printer inability to interpret the vector data within the graphics. In this situation printAsBitmap will give you the correct results. The syntax is:

```
sprite(whichSprite).printAsBitmap({"targetName", #printingBounds})
```

Use printAsBitmap just as you would print (detailed above). The print resolution will be the maximum supported by the printer.

Flash printing: tips and techniques

- Use printAsBitmap if you need to preserve any transparency.

- Use print when you need the very highest quality (transparency and colour effect will be lost).

- All elements (symbols, fields, raster, text) will print.

- The Flash movie's background colour is used to determine the print background colour. If you need to change it dynamically, make a MovieClip with various coloured rectangles that cover the stage in each frame. Control the MovieClip with tellTarget to get the frame you require to show on the stage. As it's in the bottom layer, it will give the effect of changing the background colour.

- The MovieClip must be on the stage, in the main timeline – levels can't be used – and it must have an instance name to be printable.

- If you don't want the viewer to see the MovieClip being printed, set its _visible property to FALSE.

- Changing the physical attributes of the MovieClip using any trasformation techniques has no effect during printing.

- You can't print a frame from the MovieClip until the frame is fully loaded.

- Set the Flash members Scale Mode property to No-Scale, to prevent skewed printing from occuring.

sendXML
Use this command to 'capture' XML data sent from Flash. The command in Flash is used to send (using POST) an encoded XML object to a given URL, and is written as follows:

```
myXML.send(url, window);
```

window identifies the browser window that the server will return the data to, values include:

_self is the current frame in the current window;
_blank is a new window;
_parent is the parent of the current frame;
_top is the top-level frame in the current window;
or you can define the frame's name.

This information is given as background information, as if you want Flash to send the XML to Director the syntax and usage is different. The syntax for sending XML data from Flash to Director is the following:

```
sendXML "sendxmlstring", "window", "postdata"
```

If you are already familiar with the way Flash can send strings to Director using getURL, then sendXML works in a very similar way. As you can see, the objects are passed as arguments:

```
on sendXML me, urlFromFlash, xmlFromFlash
  postNetText (urlFromFlash, xmlFromFlash)
end
```

tellTarget and endTellTarget
Flash 4 users will be immediately at home with this command, as it was (arguably) this command that contributed most to making complicated tasks easier to achieve. tellTarget in Flash is the means of identifying which MovieClip is being controlled by specifying the path to its timeline. If correctly specified, all subsequent commands refer to the MovieClip's timeline, leaving the main

timeline and other MovieClips to act independently. The main timeline is identified as (/) in Flash 4; in Flash 5 it is _root.

Why has reference to Flash 4 been made in the above paragraph when this section is on the Flash 5 Asset Xtra? As with the call function, tellTarget is now obsolete in Flash 5 ActionScript, but that has no effect on how it's used in Director 8.5 as the MovieClips that are being controlled operate the same whether or not tellTarget is used.

The Lingo syntax is as follows (where "targetName" is the path to the target MovieClip's timeline):

```
sprite(whichSprite).tellTarget("targetName")
sprite(whichSprite).endTellTarget()
```

Right is a typical Flash 4 path showing the nested MovieClips expanded. The target shown would control the timeline of MovieClip "finger".

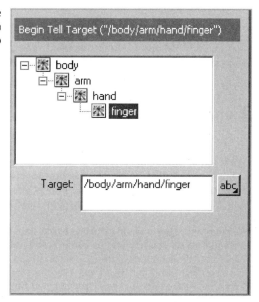

In Flash 4 it would be: /body/arm/hand/finger
In Flash 5: _root.body.arm.hand.finger

endTellTarget() returns the focus of all subsequent commands to the Flash main timeline, just as using (/) in Flash 4 will, or _root in Flash 5.

To stop the playback head in the timeline of MovieClip "myHead" that is on the main timeline with a button behavior you would use:

```
on mouseUp me
  sprite(1).tellTarget ("_root.myHead")
  sprite(1).stop()
end
```

If you wanted to advance the playback head of the MovieClip "leftArm" that is nested in a MovieClip called "myBody" you would use:

```
on mouseUp me
   sprite(1).tellTarget ("_root.myBody.leftArm"))
   sprite(1).play()
end
```

Returning the target to the main timeline with:

```
on mouseUp me
   sprite(1).endTellTarget()
   sprite(1).stop()
end
```

> *In the above examples,* _root *is optional: you can leave it out if you wish but it's good practice to include it.*

Limitations When Using Flash Members

There are plenty of things Director doesn't like about Flash. Even though Macromedia does a great job in producing both Flash and Director, you could be forgiven for thinking that there is a lack of communication during the development of each product! You'll find that not all Flash functions are supported when you import your finished SWF into Director, place it on the stage and press play. The lack of co-operation is what we'll look at here.

Before you begin a Director project that uses Flash members you need to know what problems and limitations you're likely to come across. Although you might expect to be able to create the Flash and then import it into Director this is actually a recipe for disaster. Should one of the unsupported Flash functions be a cornerstone of your Flash movie you'll need to carry out extensive rebuilding to regain that original function.

Poor Playback

As the CPU load increases when using Flash, there may be huge reductions in frame rates. This may cause buttons to 'freeze', video to skip or flicker, and the whole movie to pause or stutter. When using Flash and video overlaid both members must have Direct to Stage unticked, which may cause both the Flash movie and the video to slowdown. Very complex Flash movies can easily reduce frame rates to single figures and even crash the system with excessive loads. Playing more than one Flash movie at a time, or combinations of Director, Flash and video all progressively decrease frame rates.

LoadMovie

MovieClips will still continue to work when played in Director but LoadMovie won't, so any movies that are in other levels won't function. Keystoke capture by Flash will also not work, as it would interfere with Lingo's control over the environment.

Sound Issues

Sound can also cause problems. Often imported Flash movies 'lose' their sound – the Director sounds play fine but there are no Flash sounds. The most common solution is to give Flash the control over sound by setting soundMixMedia to FALSE, releasing Directors control over sound:

```
soundMixMedia = FALSE
```

The disadvantage is that Director and Flash sounds can't be played at the same time when soundMixMedia is FALSE.

If you require Flash and Director sounds at the same time and setting soundMixMedia to TRUE gives you no Flash sounds or they aren't playing as intended, you will need to take the somewhat drastic step of removing the sounds from the Flash movie and adding them to the Director movie, possibly triggering the sounds via calls from Flash.

ActionScript:

```
on (release) {
    getURL ("playSound");
}
```

Lingo:

```
on getURL me, stringFromFlash
  case stringFromFlash of
    "playSound":
      sound(1).queue("mySound")
      sound(1).play()
  end case
end
```

> *Setting soundMixMedia to TRUE increases the CPU load when the movie plays.*

The Problem With Go

There has been a problem with Flash and the Lingo go command since Director 6.5 and the workaround is well documented in the Macromedia Technotes. The string method is used here;

the two other methods, `lingo` and `event` are explained later in this chapter under the heading "How Flash Communicates with Director".

ActionScript:

```
on (release) {
    getURL   ("myFrame");
// where "myFrame" is a marker in Director
}
```

Lingo:

```
property myDestination

on beginSprite me
  myDestination = VOID
end

on getURL me, stringFromFlash
  myDestination = stringFromFlash
end

on exitFrame me
  if NOT voidP(myDestination) then
    go myDestination
    myDestination = VOID
  end if
end
```

The problem is caused because the target frame doesn't have an instance of the embedded Flash movie that issued the command to move the playback head. Setting a variable in Lingo to temporarily store the target destination frame avoids this problem.

Lingo vs. ActionScript

Flash has advanced to the point where it can challenge Director for the title of 'best-tool-for-the-job' for web-based animation. So, with lots of overlapping features, you might expect the scripting language used in both programs to be very similar. You'd be surprised – unpleasantly! Unfortunately, for developers using both applications (and that will probably be the majority of you), they aren't based on the same model.

Lingo

It could be said that the origin of Lingo is that old mainstay BASIC, but (unusual for a programming language) this has changed in format and importance with each new version of Director. As such, the language isn't static and continues to adapt to the needs of the modern Director developer: take, for example, the addition of the dot syntax in Director 7 (making VB and Delphi/Pascal programmers feel more at home), or the raft of new commands in Director 8.5 to deal with Shockwave3D.

ActionScript

In Flash 4 ActionScript was a quite strange affair; although you could write code with it, its main purpose was to allow complex interaction to occur between elements without the need to learn any programming skill or language syntax. The commands could be accessed and selected through pop-up windows and drop-down lists of commands. The instructions could then be modified though a number of option fields, to provide the given instruction with parameters. Flash 5 ActionScript is another country, not based upon the work done with Flash 4 ActionScript but evolving into its own unique 'fully fledged' scripting language.

Flash 5 ActionScript is compliant with the ECMA-262 standard, sometimes referred to as a specification for JavaScript. The syntax will be immediately familiar to anyone who has programmed with C++, Java or JavaScript. This gives the language a very strong potential user base as C++ and Java are seen as 'the professional developers choice for industrial strength application'. JavaScript skills are very commonly found in web development, its ranks of supporters including those self-taught programmers without experience in the languages commonly used by computing science graduates. The 'gamble' to make ActionScript was lessened, as there was a ready-made developers community with experience and resources in the language before the software was released.

Whereas code in Director is a cast member in its own right, scripts in Flash exist only when attached to frames, buttons or MovieClips (smart clips). You can have a Script Clip, which is a 'blank' MovieClip that only contains code, not graphics, which is then executed from elsewhere in the movie.

Comments

Lingo: Comments come after the double dash in Director,

```
- - this is a comment
```

ActionScript: Flash uses a double slash,

```
// this is a comment
```

Variables

Lingo: Variables can be declared using global

```
global gWidth    - - declare the variable gWidth as a global
```

ActionScript: Local variables in Flash must be declared using var, but unlike Director, variables only occupy the level (or timeline) they are declared in,

```
var width.......//declare the variable width as local
```

Operators, Increments and Maths

Many of the operators in Lingo and ActionScript are the same. Some of the differences between the two are listed in the following table:

DESCRIPTION	LINGO	ACTIONSCRIPT
Setting a value	x = 10	x = 10
Equal to	if x = 10 then	if (x == 10) {
Not equal to	if x <> y then	if (x != y) {
Combined operator	x = x + 10	x += 10
Postfix increment by one	x = x + 1	x++
Prefix increment by one	x = x + 1	++x
Postfix increment used in expression	gHeight = gWidth gWidth = gWidth + 1	height = width++
Prefix increment used in expression	gWidth = gWidth + 1 gHeight = gWidth	height = ++width
Postfix decrement by one	x = x - 1	x - -
Prefix decrement by one	x = x - 1	- - x
Postfix decrement used in expression	gHeight = gWidth gWidth = gWidth - 1	height = width - -
Prefix decrement used in expression	gWidth = gWidth - 1 gHeight = gWidth	height = - - width
Logical OR	OR	||
Logical AND	AND	&&
Logical	NOT	NOT !

Conditionals and Loops

DESCRIPTION	LINGO	ACTIONSCRIPT

if...then...else	if x = 10 then
	    go frame
	  else if x = 20 then
	    go frame 2
	  else
	    go frame 3
	  end if
		if (x == 10){
		    gotoAndPlay (1);
		} else if(x == 20) {
		    gotoAndPlay (2);
		} else {
		    gotoAndPlay (3);
		}

while	repeat while x < 10
	  - - do this
	end repeat
		while (x < 10) {
		  // do this
		}

iterate	repeat with i = 1 to 10
	  - - do this
	end repeat for
		(var I = 1; I <= 10; I++) {
		  // do this
		}

Mouse Events

DESCRIPTION	LINGO	ACTIONSCRIPT

Mouse Clicks	on mouseUp me
	  - - do this
	end
		on (release) {
		  // do this
		}

How Flash Communicates with Director

There are three methods that can be used to put Flash and Director into communication:

Event

ActionScript:

```
on (release) {
    getURL ("event: flashMouseUp, \"hello\"");
}
```

Lingo:

```
on flashMouseUp me, stringFromFlash
  alert stringFromFlash
end
```

Importing the Flash movie and dropping the behavior on it, then clicking the button in the Flash movie calls the handler and passes the string. You will see this in Director:

Lingo

ActionScript:

```
on (release) {
    getURL ("lingo: alert \"world\"");
}
```

Lingo: The major advantage of this method is that all the scripting is done in the Flash environment, so you don't need to write any extra Lingo. However, be aware that if you need to make changes you'll need to edit the Flash movie and re-import the SWF into Director.

String

This time there will be three Flash buttons each giving a different message,

ActionScript:

```
on (release) {
    getURL ("welcome");
}

on (release) {
    getURL ("bye");
}

on (release) {
    getURL ("pear");
}
```

Lingo:

```
on getURL me, stringFromFlash
  case stringFromFlash of
    "welcome": alert "hello world"
    "bye": alert "you are the weakest link"
    "pear": alert "you don't get many of them for a pound"
  end case
end
```

As you can see, passing a string via the getURL command is not only easy to use, but also offers much more flexibility than the other two methods. If you call Lingo within Flash and need to modify the instruction you must open up the original .fla, make the edit, export the movie, import the .swf into Director, then swap the sprites.

However, using the getURL method only a string is passed to Director. Since interpretation of the string is done in Lingo, you need only change the action in the case statement to affect the function of the call - no editing outside the native environment as the passing of the string is just an event trigger; the string contents are unimportant.

You will notice that the pointer to finger button visual aid is missing from the buttons in the Flash movie - you need to add them back. First we'll look at a long way round: it isn't a good idea to use this method and is provided only as an example that there are often multiple ways to achieve the same goal.

ActionScript:

```
on (rollOver, dragOver) {
    getURL ("finger");
}
on (rollOut, dragOut) {
```

```
            getURL ("arrow");
    }
    on (release) {
        getURL ("action");
    }
```

Lingo:

```
on GetURL me, stringFromFlash
  case (stringFromFlash) of
    "finger": cursor 280
    "arrow": cursor -1
    "action": —button action
  end case
end
```

Now let's look at a much more efficient method. This method only requires additional coding in Director, so offers speed and flexibility, and doesn't require several lines of ActionScript per Flash button. Drop the following behavior onto the Flash sprite.

Lingo:

```
property pSprite

on beginSprite me
  pSprite = sprite(me.spriteNum)
end

on exitFrame me
  if pSprite.mouseOverButton = TRUE then
    pSprite.cursor = 280
  else
    pSprite.cursor = -1
  end if
end
```

Controlling Flash with Lingo

Basic properties for controlling Flash sprites:

- Play – moves the Flash playback head to the next frame.

- Rewind – moves the head to the first frame in the movie.

- Stop – holds the head on the current frame.

Let's look at investigation properties for interrogating Flash sprites.

Playing

The most commonly used command is the playing property, which checks whether the Flash movie has finished. You can use this to pause the playback head until the Flash animation has completed playing all its frames before advancing the Director playback head:

```
Frame Action:
on exitFrame me
  if sprite(1).playing = TRUE then
    go the frame
  else
    go the frame + 1
  end if
end
```

findLabel

The Flash timeline will be searched for a frame label corresponding to whichLabelName, then return its frame number. If the search is unsuccessful, 0 is returned.

```
sprite(whichFlashSprite).findLabel(whichLabelName)
```

goToFrame

If you need to go to and play from a specific frame number or label use the goToFrame property.

```
on controlFlash whereNext
    sprite(1).goToFrame(whereNext)
end
```

Frame

Use the frame property to determine which frame in the Flash timeline is currently under the playback head. I'll demonstrate with a really simple example. If the Flash sprite is in channel one and pauses on the first frame, type this in the message window.

```
put sprite(1).frame
```

The output will be:

```
-- 1
```

How tellTarget has helped

In Director 8, if your Flash movie had MovieClips and you needed to control them, the scripts had to be in frame scripts in the Flash main timeline. They were executed by moving the playback head to a given frame that contained the ActionScript code, it would then control the MC. As you can see the Flash 5 Xtra (using tellTarget) is a much less agricultural way of controlling MCs in your Flash movies.

Try the following exercise which brings together some of the concepts that we have covered in this chapter.

Controlling a Flash Movie

The source files for this example are bounce.fla and bounce.dir which can be found on the CD accompanying this book, or may be downloaded from the friends of ED website.

When you play the movie, the button will read pause, and the circle will bounce. (Because it's a MovieClip in the Flash timeline, it will continue to loop). When you press the pause, the path to the MovieClip is used in the tellTarget command (after that it's not, so a flag is called) and the MovieClip is paused with the stop() action. The button will now read play. Clicking the button moves the playback head in the MovieClip timeline and changes the button text to pause, waiting form the next click to repeat the process.

1. Open a new Flash movie.

2. Make a circle and turn it into a MovieClip (to make use of the looping benefit described above).

3. Make a new MovieClip, put the circle into it and tween with easing to give the impression of a bouncing ball.

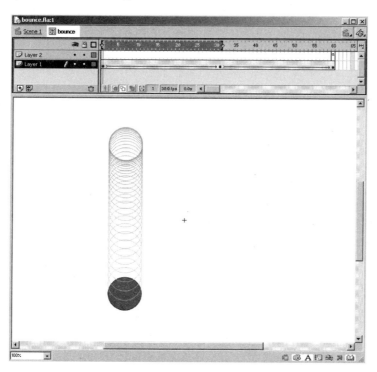

4. Put the MovieClip on the main timeline with a instance name bounce,

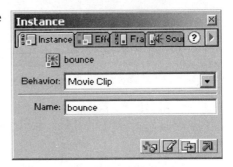

5. Export as Flash 5 SWF and import into Director 8.5. You are now finished with Flash for this exercise.

6. Draw a standard button with text "pause".

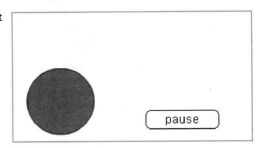

7. Use this movie script:

```
global gState, gNoPath

on startMovie
  gState = #play
  gNoPath = #noPath
  member("myButton").text = "pause"
end
```

8. Then make a behavior with this script and drop in onto the button:

```
global gState --used to store the condition #play or #pause
globalgNoPath -- used to detect if there is a path to the MC

on mouseUp me

  if gNoPath = #noPath then
    sprite(1).tellTarget("bounce")
    gNoPath = #path
  end if

  if gState = #play then
```

```
         gState = #pause
         member("myButton").text = "play"
         sprite(1).stop()
       else
         gState = #play
         member("myButton").text = "pause"
         sprite(1).play()
       end if
     end
```

9.   Play the movie.

Here is a more elaborate worked example using more of the techniques covered in this chapter. It will take you through the process of creating a QT video player with a Flash interface. The source files for this example are interface.fla and gtPlayer.dir which can be found on the CD accompanying this book, or may be downloaded from the friends of ED website.

Flash Interface QT Player

1.   Make an MC called 'base' and a shape to act as a base for the player.

2.   Make four buttons, 'back', 'play', 'pause' and 'forward'.

3.   Make an MC called 'buttonChange'.

4.   Put the 'pause' button on the first frame and add this script:

```
on (release) {
    play ();
    getURL ("pause");
}
```

5.   Put the 'play' button on the second frame and add this script:

```
on (release) {
    play ();
    getURL ("play");
}
```

6.   Make a new layer and put a stop action in each of the two frames.

7.   Make a new layer with two keyframes.

8.   Put this in frame one:

```
butState = "showPause";
```

9. Put this in frame two:

```
butState = "showPlay";
```

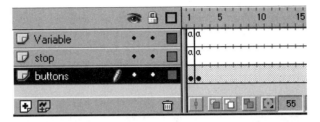

10. Make an MC called 'line' with a dark line in it, to represent the path that the visual indicator will follow.

11. Place the 'line', 'base', 'back' button, 'forward' button, and 'buttonChange' MC in the main timeline.

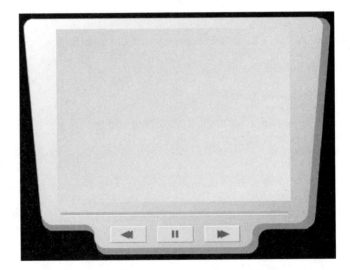

12. Select the 'buttonChange' MC and give it an instance name of 'playPause'.

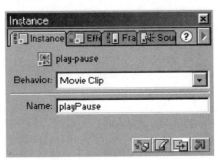

13. Export the movie as Flash 5 (File > Export Movie), give it the name 'interface.swf'.

14. Import the SWF into Director8.5 and place it in the first channel in the score.

15. Make a behaviour called 'flashCode'.

```
— — — — — — — — — — — — — — — — —
— — — — — — — — — — — — — — — — —
—                                 —
—  this script will be used on    —
—  the Flash sprite, it will      —
—  control the QuickTime video    —
—                                 —
— — — — — — — — — — — — — — — — —
— — — — — — — — — — — — — — — — —


property pSprite
property pVidSprite
property pCurRate — -current video rate
property pNewRate — -new video rate


on beginSprite me
  pSprite = sprite(me.spriteNum)

  pVidSprite = sprite(2)
end


on getURL me, stringFromFlash
  pCurRate = pVidSprite.movieRate

  case (stringFromFlash) of
    "back": pNewRate = pCurRate - 1
    "play": pNewRate = 1
    "pause": pNewRate = 0
    "forward": pNewRate = pCurRate + 1
  end case

  pVidSprite.movieRate = pNewRate

  — - get the variable set in the Flash movie
  test = pSprite.getVariable("_root.playPause.butState")

  — - the Flash movie will only show the play button when the
➡ movie is paused
  if (pNewRate = 0 AND test = "showPause") OR (pNewRate <> 0 AND
➡ test = "showPlay") then
    pSprite.telltarget("_root.playPause") — -path to the
```

```
play/pause MC
    pSprite.play() — - move the playback head one frame on the MC
timeline
  end if

end


on exitFrame me — -add the pointer to hand rollover
  if pSprite.mouseOverButton = TRUE then
    pSprite.cursor = 280
  else
    pSprite.cursor = -1
  end if
end
```

16. Drop it on to the Flash sprite.

17. Make a frame script to cycle the head within a frame, call it 'hold'.

```
on exitFrame me
  go the frame
end
```

18. Import a QuickTime movie into the cast and place it in channel 2 of the score.

19. As the QT is above the SWF sprite, you will need to change the QT's properties. Highlight the QT member in the score, untick Direct to Stage in the property inspector.

20. Play the movie.

You will now be about to see if there are any playback problems caused by the video into Flash. If you are still getting flickers, you will need to modify the Flash member such that it doesn't sit under the video, like cutting it into four.

You will see that continuing to press back or forwards increases the rate, pressing the play/pause button cycles the states.

Next we'll add a visual indicator

21. Make a new Flash movie with just a simple small circle and export as 'indicator.swf'.

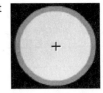

22. Import 'indicator.swf' to Director and place it in channel 3 of the score, at the left position of the line on the interface.

23. Make a new behavior with this script:

```
-------------------
-------------------
-                 -
-  this script will be used to  -
-  move a visual indicator in   -
-  step with QuickTime video    -
-                 -
-------------------
-------------------

property pSprite
property pStartPosn —left most position of the indicator
property pEndPosn —right most position of the indicator
property pMovieLength —duration of the QT video
property pCurTime —current movie time
property pPercent —% calculation
property pNewPosn —new indicator location


on beginSprite me
  the floatPrecision = 3

  pSprite = sprite(me.spriteNum)

  —change these valuses to fit your own movie
  pStartPosn = 67 —fix the left position
  pEndPosn = 377 —fix the right position

  pSprite.locH = pStartPosn —put the indicator at the left
position
end


on exitFrame me
  pMovieLength = sprite(2).duration

  pCurTime = sprite(2).movieTime

  pPercent = pCurTime.float / pMovieLength.float

  pNewPosn = ((pEndPosn - pStartPosn) * pPercent) + pStartPosn

  pSprite.locH = pNewPosn

end
```

24. Drop it onto the 'indicator' Flash sprite.

25. Play the movie.

You will see the sprite move in time with the video.

Summary

In this chapter we've looked at the Flash 5 Asset Xtra and how to use Flash movies to enhance your Director projects by extending its feature set to include all of the supported Flash functionality.

The advantages and disadvantages of using Flash functionality (as opposed to Director) were discussed early on and these should be referred to and considered when you're deciding which package to use to achieve the functionality and desired effects you require.

We've looked at the new features of Flash 5 and covered new Lingo commands in the Flash 5 Xtra - callFrame, print, printAsBitmap, sendXML, and tellTarget and endTellTarget. We've devoted a lot of time to the coverage of Flash printing in Director as this is an area that many users have difficulty with and that can cause considerable headaches!

The differences between the ActionScript and Lingo languages have been highlighted for you along with the methods of communicating from Flash to Director.

As promised earlier in the chapter, some very useful and some very interesting URLs have been collated for you here. Happy surfing.

Useful Links

If you'd like further information on the success of Flash, here are some resources.

Flash on Sun Solaris and LINUX:
http://www.macromedia.com/macromedia/proom/pr/2001/index_fp_linux_solaris.fhtml

Flash on PocketPC:
http://www.macromedia.com/software/flashplayer/pocketpc/

Flash on Sony PS2:
http://www.macromedia.com/macromedia/proom/pr/2001/flash_playstation2.html

A list of Web players:
http://www.macromedia.com/shockwave/download/alternates/

Player penetration stats for:
   Flash:
   http://www.macromedia.com/software/player_census/flashplayer/
   Shockwave:
   http://www.macromedia.com/software/player_census/shockwaveplayer/

A history of the development of Flash:
http://www.macromedia.com/macromedia/events/john_gay/contents.html

SWF software development kit:
http://www.macromedia.com/software/flash/open/licensing/fileformat/

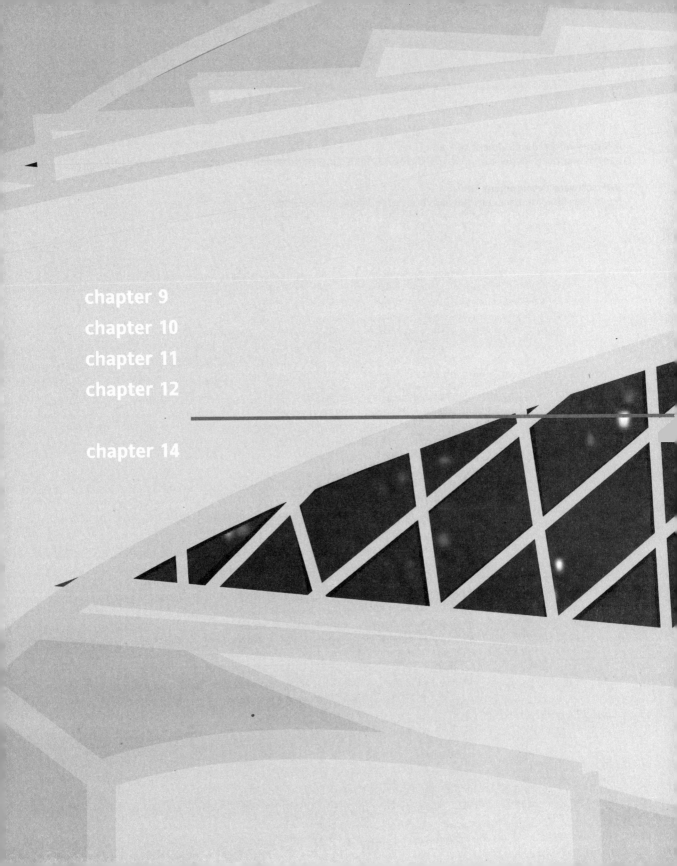

Chapter 13
The Multiuser
Server

One of the most powerful features of Director is the ability to create real—time collaborative applications. Not only can we now create rich 3D worlds, we can also let a number of people to come in and explore these worlds in real—time.

There are many potential applications for this multiuser ability — many areas of business, for example, would benefit from a real—time, collaborative application. Imagine a customer support application that allows a company to control a customer's browser, bring up more information about a product, or to send diagram images directly to the customer to explain a difficult process. Or an interactive graphic design program that enables business partners to arrange page layouts together in real—time. You could give real—time presentations over the Internet with synchronized voice and image data. And, of course, there are digital whiteboards, shared Web browsing, online teaching, learning, testing, and so on and so on.

Gaming is usually the first kind of multiuser application that comes to mind. Director is great for making games, and games can work very well in a multiuser environment. You've probably seen many sites dedicated to multiplayer games: board games, casino games, and action games are everywhere on the Internet. Most of these sites stay very busy, with people from all over the world, playing and chatting together, at all hours of the day and night. Games are a good way to learn multiuser applications in Director, and we'll build a multiuser game later in this tutorial.

The key to any of these applications is the Shockwave Multiuser Server together with the multiuser Xtra. You can even create server—side scripts using Lingo. In this chapter we'll look at how client—server applications can be powers powered by Lingo on both sides, building an application as we go.

Introducing the server application

If you haven't yet installed the server, do that now and we'll start it up and we'll take a look inside.

The first thing you'll notice is that there isn't much in the way of an interface. The server application is intended to route messages to and from clients, process scripts, connect to databases, and read and write files, and as such the interface simply works like a terminal window, indicating what's going on inside the server engine. You can use the interface to monitor several types of information about the server itself, to find out how many users are connected, and as a debugging tool.

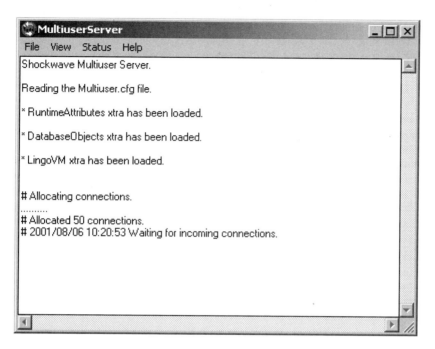

When you start up the server you'll see that it supports 50 simultaneous users by default. You can change this number by editing the `Multiuser.cfg` file located in the directory where the server was installed. Go ahead and find that directory now – we'll be working with it in the course of this chapter. It'll be in the same directory as your Director installation, unless you selected somewhere else for it to go during installation.

To change the number of allocated connections, open the `Multiuser.cfg` file in any text editor, and look for the Director users licensing information section.

```
#==================================================================
# Director  users  licensing  information
#
...
```

You'll find a commented out entry that allows you to change the maximum number of simultaneous users allowed on your system. You can have anything from 50 to 2000:

```
# Number of connections the server will handle (up to the license
limit)
# ConnectionLimit = 50
```

Edit the **ServerOwnerName** entry to include your name, and the **ServerSerialNumber** entry to include the serial number that came with your copy of Director.

```
# ServerOwnerName = "Enter Your Name Here"
# ServerSerialNumber = DRW850-12345-12345-12345
```

While you're here, check out the various configurable settings. You won't need to touch these settings, usually but it's still a good idea to familiarize yourself with the options available. You'll need to restart the server to make any changes you've made take affect.

Configuring the server

You need to know the address of the computer hosting the server in order to connect to it to your Director clients. The easiest way to check this is to use the server itself. Select the Server option from the Status menu. This outputs several pieces of information about your server and its environment to the console. Make a note of your Server IP address for later use:

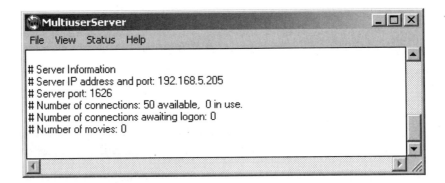

Testing the connection

Before we move on, let's make sure that everything is working properly.

1. First let's tell the server that we want to monitor when users log on and log off. Start the server, making sure that Users Log On And Off is checked, under the View menu.

2. Now open Director, and bring up the message window. We're going to log on to the server with just two lines of code!

   Director communicates with the server through the Multiuser Xtra, so the first thing we need to do is create a new instance of it. Type this into the message window and hit ENTER:

   ```
   gMU = new( xtra "Multiuser" )
   ```

3. Now let's log onto the server. Replace the *username* parameter in this code with a suitable name and *serverAddress* with your server's IP Address and hit ENTER *again*.

   ```
   gMU.connectToNetServer( "username", EMPTY, "serverAddress", 1626,
   ➡ "WatchMeWin" )
   ```

So you'll have something similar to this:

```
gMU.connectToNetServer( "Digidude", EMPTY, "66.56.29.195" ,
➥ 1626,"WatchMeWin" )
```

4. Now check the server console. You should see something like this:

```
+ 2001/07/05 20:04:58 Created movie WatchMeWin.
+ 2001/07/05 20:04:58 Digidude (66.56.29.195) connected to movie
➥ WatchMeWin.
```

When you see this in the console you know you are connected and that the server is functioning properly. You'll find little checks like this invaluable when you're debugging large applications. A great feature of the Multiuser Server is that we don't even need to connect to the Internet to test our applications – we can do it all locally.

Planning the application

We're going to build a multiplayer game called **Watch Me Win**, where players take turns playing a round of Black Jack against a virtual dealer. Players will be able to chat while they're waiting for their turn, and they'll be able to see the progress of other players. You can download the source files for it from the CD.

It's especially important to plan out the architecture carefully before writing a single line of code when you're developing multiuser applications. You need to take into account all the possible scenarios for all the different users. In this application, for example, we need to know before we do anything at all that the active player in our game will see a betting interface while other users won't. Waiting players will see the results but not the actions of the betting player.

Our application will be an ongoing game that players can join and leave at any time. When a player joins a game in progress, they need to be updated on the current status of the game, and when the active player leaves the game, the game must continue on to the next player.

Dividing functionality between server and client

A multiuser application actually consists of two applications. The **client** must react to instructions *from* the server, and transmit player actions *to* the server. The **server** must keep track of players, scores, and game state. In our game, the client application will act as a simple 'display' interface, while the server application will contain all the logic for the game. The server logic won't contain any code specific to the display of information, and the client won't make any game play decisions.

Architecting the code

We can plan out the structure of our client–server application by grouping messages and functions into logical feature sets. This way each set can be developed separately and can operate independently of the others.

Client architecture

We can group the client code architecture into four main objects. These will deal with routing incoming messages from the server to the user interface objects on the screen, and transmitting user actions to the server.

Connection manager   Holds the connection instance and handles making the connection to the server, disconnecting from the server, and dealing with errors related to the connection. It is also responsible for informing the user of the status of the current connection.

Room manager   Tracks the participants in the game, by holding a list of players and receiving messages from the server when a player enters or leaves. It can also request the full list of players currently in the room.

Chat manager   The chat object handles chat messages being sent and received, and requests a chat log when a player enters the room.

Game manager   Sends and receives messages specific to the game play itself, such as submitting a bet, displaying cards, and so on.

Although the Connection Manager will have to be present for all other objects to operate, this architecture allows us to create each object separately, and keeps the code neatly segmented into specific feature sets.

Server architecture

We can also separate the server code into feature sets similar to our client architecture. We'll only be using one server script but we'll segment into four main areas.

Server features   The server sends several messages by default to each custom script. We'll need to work with the messages that relate to script creation, user logon, user logoff, and the custom messages sent from our clients. Remember: there will be one server but more than one client.

Room features   The functions that keep track of user names, when users enter, and when users exit. It will also send messages to clients about the status of users in the room.

Chat features   These features keep a chat log of all chat messages, route chat messages to the appropriate clients, and send the chat log to new users upon request.

Game features   These are the core features of the game. They will handle card dealing, shuffling, and drawing, which player is active currently and which will be up is next, and will determine the winnings of each player.

Writing a server–side script in Director

Our client will need something to communicate with, so let's start by setting up our server–side script. If you go into the directory with the server installed you'll find the Scripts directory, which is where we'll put our scripts. Lingo server scripts are nothing more than standard text files, with an .ls extension.

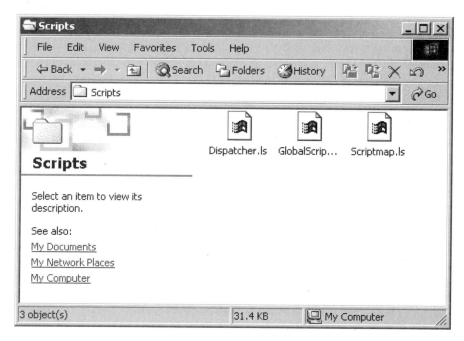

Notice the three files present in the Scripts directory. These files are prewritten scripts used by the server. Open them up in a text editor of your choice and we'll take a look:

Dispatcher.ls

This is the link between the server engine and the Lingo server scripts. It dispatches messages from the server to the appropriate scripts. You won't find that you need to edit this file very often, although you can if you need to.

GlobalScripts.ls

This is where you put handlers that need to be accessible from any other script – much like Director's movie scripts. Any routine that is commonly used across several different applications should be place here.

Scriptmap.ls

This is where we let the server know about our custom script. When the server starts up, Dispatcher.ls will ask the Scriptmap.ls for a list of all scripts that should be instantiated for use within the server. This file is one that we definitely do want to edit. We'll create our own script and include an entry for it in this file.

Creating and installing the server script

1. Create a new Director movie and save it as `WatchMeWin_Server.dir`. Save it in anywhere you like – we won't be using this movie for anything other than writing server–side scripts.

    We can use Director to create our Lingo server scripts because Director supports linked script files.

2. Create a movie script cast member and go into the properties window. Select Link Script As..., name it `WatchMeWin.ls`, and save it in the server's Scripts directory. Save the script as Linked Script in the property inspector tab.

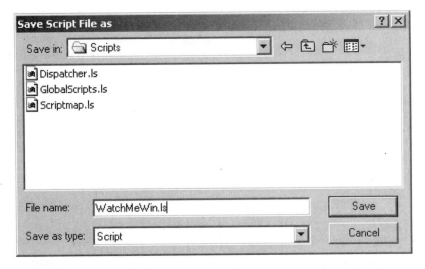

    Now we've got a server–side Lingo script that we can edit from within Director, using Director to compile the script, check for errors, and save the file. Each time you choose Save in Director, the external script file will be saved as well.

3. Now open the `Scriptmap.ls` file from the server's Scripts directory by importing it into Director as a linked file. Find the `Scriptmap` handler.

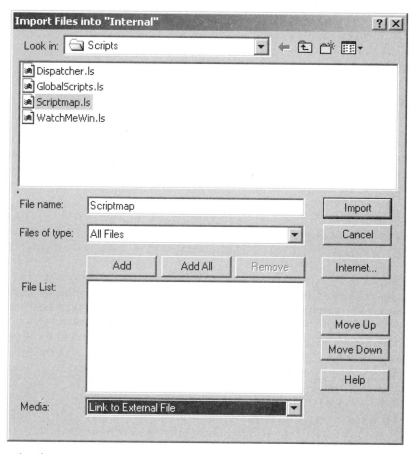

You'll notice that #scriptFileName property from the list must be present, and #movieID, or #groupID, or both– we'll be using #movieID.

#movieID	Tells the server that our custom script is to be used only for users who belong to a specified movie. Our script will be active for all users who belong to the movie WatchMeWin.
#groupID	Tells the server that our custom script is only to be used by users belonging to a specified group.
#scriptFileName	Tells the server what script file we want to be added to the server.

4. Add the following line of code after theMap = []:

```
theMap.append( [ #movieID: "WatchMeWin", #scriptFileName:
➥ "WatchMeWin.ls" ] )
```

5. Restart the server. Now our script is ready to receive messages from the server and from our clients.

Programming for multiuser applications

Let's look at the differences between multiuser application programming and 'normal' programming before we start programming the Director client movie. The code in this section is just for the sake of example – don't try typing it in yet, it'll come in later on.

When you call a handler in Lingo it will usually execute and return a result immediately. Here, for example, a value is assigned to the variable myResult immediately. This is called **synchronous** programming.

```
myResult = getSum( 1, 1 )

on getSum ( firstNum, secondNum )
  return firstNum + secondNum
end getSum
```

Now imagine that the handler definition for getSum exists in a script on another machine connected to the Internet. We can't simply call getSum(1, 1) and expect an immediate result, because we need to send the message to the other machine and receive a result back. And of course, this could take some time depending on the current network traffic and our connection speed.

In other words, we have to program the application so that the program doesn't need to wait for a return message. This is **asynchronous** programming.

Sending messages to the server

The multiuser Xtra delivers every message sent to the server, so before we can send messages we need to create an instance of that Xtra. This gives us a **connection instance**. If we were typing this now (which we're not!) we would type:

```
pConnection = new( xtra "Multiuser" )
```

Connecting
Our first message will usually be a connection message. We connect to the server the ConnectToNetServer method of the Xtra.

```
pConnection.connectToNetServer( userID, password, server, port,
➡ movieID )
```

The parameters are:

userID	Your screen name. There must not be any other user currently on the system with the same userID if you are going to be connected successfully. The userID is used by the server andother clients to route messages to the correct client.
password	You can use this argument to restrict user access to the server. This can be used in conjunction with the inbuilt database features. In our program, we'll leave it EMPTY.
server	The hostname or IP address of the server machine. This can be in the form www.yourdomaim.com or it can be an IP address such as "66.56.29.195".
port	The server and Xtra use the TCP protocol for communication. The protocol requires that communication take place over a specific port, and both client and server must be set to communicate using this port number. The default value for the server is 1626.
movieID	Each client that connects to the server belongs to a specific movieID. The server uses movieID to route messages to the server script. In our application, any clients that are connected with the WatchMeWin movieID will be able to send messages to the WatchMeWin.ls server script.

The connection message we'll use for our game looks like this:

```
pConnection.connectToNetServer("Alan", EMPTY, "66.56.29.195",
➡ 1626, "WatchMeWin")
```

Sending messages

We can send messages to the server by calling the sendNetMessage handler in the connection instance.

```
pConnection.sendNetMessage( [#recipients: stringOrList, #subject:
➡ anyString, #content: StringOrList ] )
```

#recipients	This can be a string or a list and usually contains a user name or a group name. You can send messages to the server and to custom scripts.
#subject	The subject of the message, this can be any string, but make sure you plan out subject titles in advance because you'll use the subject of a message for handling callbacks and processing messages in the server script.
#content	This can be almost any data type Director supports. In our application we'll be using strings and lists.

This message will be directed to the server to indicate that a player has submitted a bet in the game we're creating. We can intercept this message in the server script and react appropriately.

```
sendNetMessage([ #recipients:"system.script",
➡ #subject:"SubmitBet", #content:\ 15 ])
```

Dealing with messages using callbacks

The mechanism that we use for intercepting and handling the messages that the server sends to our client is called a **callback**. We need to define a callback for every message we expect to receive.

A callback is a set of instructions that tells the Multiuser Xtra to look at each incoming message and route it to according to the handlers that we create. We can define a handler to handle each message that we expect to receive from the server individually using the connection instance's setNetMessageHandler method.

Handling callbacks

When a message arrives from the server, the Xtra will first look at the message subject and who it came from and determine if there are any callbacks assigned to it. If there are, it will pass the incoming message as an argument to the handler.

```
pConnection.setNetMessageHandler( whichHandlerToCall,
➡ whichObjectToCall, whatSubjectToLookFor, fromWhatUser,
➡ sendMessageAsArgument )
```

whichHandlerToCall	The name of the handler you create to handle the message. You must prefix the handler name with the hash symbol.
whichObjectToCall	Tells the Xtra where to find the handler. This can be a reference to any object, not just the object you are currently in. In our game we'll always use the current object (me).
whatSubjectToLookFor	This is how the Xtra links the message to the handler. You'll often find that you need to use this subject name in several places, so make sure it is always spelt correctly.
fromWhatUser	In addition to matching the subject, you can also tell the Xtra to look at this variable and only route the message if it comes from the specified user. We'll be setting it to EMPTY in our example.
sendMessageAsArgument	It's useful to have the Xtra send the contents of the message along with the call to the handler. When this argument is set to 1 the Xtra will send the message contents as an argument to the designated handler. On the other hand, if this argument is set to 0 you'll have to call pConnection.getNetMessage, which will return the last message in the message queue. We'll tell the Xtra to send the message as an argument to our handlers in our application.

We also need to instruct the Xtra to route any message with a BetSubmitted subject to the BetSubmitted_Received handler located in the current object (me). This code with do that for us, as well as telling the Xtra to disregard who it was sent from and to provide the full message as an argument to the assigned handler. This message will be sent from our server script that we'll write later:

```
pConnection.setNetMessageHandler( #mBetSubmitted_Received, me,
➥ "BetSubmitted", EMPTY, 1 )
```

Then we can define a handler to handle the message. Notice we provide an argument variable so the Xtra can deliver the message directly to the handler.

```
on mBetSubmitted_Received( me, vMsg )
  - - do something
end mBetSubmitted_Received
```

> *It's important to think about all the messages you can expect to receive before writing your code. Then you can just go down the list and define callbacks for each message.*

Default messages
You'll need to have defined a default callback to deal with it any message that arrives with a subject that doesn't have a callback assigned to it. The Xtra will route any incoming message that doesn't have a callback assigned to the handler we define here.

All we have to do is leave out the *subject*, and *user target* arguments, because the Xtra will call the assigned handler to handle the message if it can't find a callback for it. If you plan all your messages well you shouldn't come up against this scenario, but as always, it's best to prepare for all eventualities.

```
pConnection.setNetMessageHandler( #mDefault_Received, me, 1 )
```

Dealing with disconnection
It's important to clear out all defined callbacks before you disconnect from the server – if you don't, you run the risk of it crashing. You can do this using the setMessageHandler and setting the handler name to 0. This will effectively remove the callback from the connection instance.

```
pConnection.setNetMessageHandler( 0, me, MessageSubject )
```

The following line of code, for example, clears our BetSubmitted callback:

```
pConnection.setNetMessageHandler( 0, me, "BetSubmitted" )
```

> *Be sure to clear out all your defined callbacks before disconnecting.*

Receiving messages

When a message arrives to our callback handler its contents are passed in as the first argument.

```
on mBetSubmitted_Received( me, vMsg )
  - - do something
end mBetSubmitted_Received
```

The message is a property list that contains all the information about the message.

```
[#errorCode: errorCode, #recipients: recipientListOrName,
➡ #senderID: whoSentTheMessage, #subject: messageSubject,
➡ #content: listOrSting, #timeStamp: timeInteger]
```

#errorCode	Besides the actual content of the message, the errorCode is the most important feature. You should always check the errorCode of the message before interrogating the rest of the message. (You can find all the errorCodes listed in the Director Help.) You should only act on a message if the errorCode is 0, which indicates there was no problem with the message. If the errorCode is anything other than 0, you should take appropriate action.
	You can get the actual meaning of the errorCode by calling getNetErrorString(errorCode):
	`errorString = pConnection.getNetErrorString(errorCode)`
#recipients	This will be a group name, a user name, or a list containing the intended recipient.
#senderID	A string representing the sender of the message.
#subject	The subject of the message
#content	This will be a string, a list, or any other Director data type.
#timestamp	This will be a time stamp indicating the time on the server that the message was sent.

Here's an example of a message sent from the server when a player submits a bet. Notice that senderID indicates that the message came from our server script. The content is defined by our server script and consists of a property list indicating who submitted the bet and for what amount.

```
[#errorCode: 0, #recipients: ["Alan"], #senderID: "System.Script",
➡ #subject: "BetSubmitted", #content: [#Player: "Alan",
➡ #BetAmount: 15], #timeStamp: 264481592]
```

So, we first check the error code, and if it's 0, tell the user interface to display the bet amount.
Our message handler would look something like this.

```
on mBetSubmitted_Received( me, vMsg )
  if vMsg.errorCode = 0 then
    member("CurrentBet").text = string(vMsg.content.BetAmount)
  end if
end mBetSubmitted_Received
```

Error handling
It's important to always check for errors on each incoming message. Always make a plan for
handling errors when you're planning your messages, just in case. Make sure you do all these
things for each message you expect to receive:

- Call setNetMesageHandler, to define a callback handler

- Write the handler

- Check for errors when the message arrives

- Handle a message without an error

- Handle a message with an error

- Clear out the callback when you disconnect

Creating the connection for real

We'll start writing the code with the connection itself. This involves both client and server code.
We'll begin with the client.

The client's connection manager

The **connection manager** object is the most important object in our architecture. It holds the
connection instance and handles connecting, disconnecting, and connection problems. All other
objects in the architecture will rely on this object to function properly.

Before we add the code, let's look at what we want this object to do.

When it's first created, the object initializes the internal properties, creates a connection instance,
and then creates any necessary callbacks. When the user clicks the Log In button from the log in
screen, the ConnectToServer handler is called, which attempts to create a connection with the
server. The server responds to the ConnectToServer_Reponse handler, indicating the status of

the connection. If successful, the game is started. If the connection failed, the user is informed, and it all starts over.

If the connection unexpectedly drops, the `ConnectionProblem_Received` handler is called, the user is informed, and the application starts over. If any unknown messages arrive then the `Default_Received` handler is called.

When the application is stopped the `stopMovie` handler will call our `KillCallbacks` handler, which will clear out any callbacks that have been set. Finally it calls `DisconnectFromServer`.

Creating the connection manager object

1. Open the `WatchMeWin.dir` file located in the 1 Connection directory on the CD. Open the cast library named MU OBJECTS and find the `ConnectionManager` script. Note that this script is a **parent script**. Open the script and let's add some code.

2. We'll begin with the properties that we'll use to store information about the connection. We'll create an initialization handler later that will initialize each of these properties. I'm using plenty of comments as I go so that we can easily check back through the scripts and check what's doing what.

```
- - PROPERTIES
property pConnection - - This holds our connection instance
property pUserID - - The chosen screen name
property pPassword - - This will be EMPTY for our game
property pServer - - The server IP address
property pPort - - 1626, the default port used by the server
property pMovieID - - "WatchMeWin"
property pDebug -- Development purposes only
```

3. Each object we create will be a parent script, so add the `new` handler after the properties. When the object is created it will call the initialization handler.

```
- - NEW
on new( me )
  me.mInitialize()
  return me
end new
```

4. Then we're ready to initialize the properties. The `pUserID` and `pServer` properties will be set through the user interface, but we'll also need to set some default values. The debug property is used to output information to the message window. You can set this to TRUE for development. The initialization handler will also connect to the Xtra and set some callbacks, which we'll discuss next.

```
- - INITIALIZE
on mInitialize( me )
  me.pUserID = EMPTY
  me.pPassword = EMPTY
  me.pServer = "66.56.29.195" -- Add the IP address of your
  ➡ computer.
  me.pPort = 1626
  me.pMovieID = "WatchMeWin"
  me.pDebug = TRUE

  me.mConnectToXtra() -- Create the connection instance
  me.mInitCallbacks() -- Define callbacks for incoming messages
end mInitialize
```

5.   Then we need a handler to create the instance of the Multiuser Xtra and store it in our pConnection property. The pConnection property is our sole point of contact with the server.

> *All messages sent to the server, will be sent through this property.*

```
- - CONNECT TO XTRA
on mConnectToXtra( me )
  me.pConnection = new ( xtra "Multiuser" )
end mConnectToXtra
```

6.   Now we'll add a handler that will assign three message handlers to messages coming in from the server related to our connection. We'll create these three handlers later, but for now, we need to tell our connection instance which handlers to call when incoming messages arrive. Note that the two outer callbacks are to intercept messages sent by default from the server and therefore won't be found in the server script.

```
- - INITIALIZE CALLBACKS
on mInitCallbacks( me )
  if NOT( me.pConnection = 0 ) then
    me.pConnection.setNetMessageHandler(
    ➡ #mConnectToServer_Response, me, "connectToNetServer",
    ➡ EMPTY, 1 )
    me.pConnection.setNetMessageHandler( #mDefault_Received, me,
    ➡ 1 )
    me.pConnection.setNetMessageHandler(
    ➡ #mConnectionProblem_Received, me,\ "ConnectionProblem",
    ➡ EMPTY, 1 )
  end if
end mInitCallbacks
```

7. Any callbacks assigned to our connection need to be unassigned before releasing the connection. Let's create a handler that will set each message handler to 0.

```
- - KILL CALLBACKS
on mKillCallbacks( me )
  if NOT( me.pConnection = 0 ) then
    me.pConnection.setNetMessageHandler( 0, me,
    ➥ "connectToNetServer" )
    me.pConnection.setNetMessageHandler( 0, me )
    me.pConnection.setNetMessageHandler( 0, me,
    ➥ "ConnectionProblem" )
  end if
end mKillCallbacks
```

8. We need a handler that will carry out the connection to the server. We'll pass in the user's screen name and save it in the `pUserID` property. The server will call our `ConnectToServer_Response` when this handler is executed, indicating connection failure or success:

```
- - CONNECT TO SERVER
on mConnectToServer( me, vUserID )
  me.pUserID = vUserID
  vError = me.pConnection.connectToNetServer( vUserID,
  ➥ me.pPassword, me.pServer, me.pPort, me.pMovieID)
end mConnectToServer
```

This handler is executed by the user interface by calling (we don't have to type this):

```
gConnectionManager.mConnectToServer("Alan")
```

Please note that in this chapter we're dealing with the multiuser capabilities of our game, and as such we're not concerned with the user interface. When the project is finished, take a look through the completed file to see how the interface actually works.

9. We need a handler to sever our connection to the server. Setting the connection instance to 0 will instruct the Xtra to close the socket and disconnect.

```
- - DISCONNECT FROM SERVER
on mDisconnectFromServer( me )
  me.pConnection = 0
end mDisconnectFromServer
```

10. Earlier we instructed the connection instance to call this handler in response to our server's `connectToNetServer` default message. This is the first message we'll receive from the server. It will contain information about the success or failure of the connection. Let's add the response handler now.

The first thing you need to check for each incoming message handler is the error code. Notice here, that if the connection was successful, it displays a status message and tells the user interface that it is connected. If the connection failed, we have no choice but to disconnect and start over.

Remember to clear out all callbacks before disconnecting.

```
- - CONNECT TO SERVER RESPONSE
on mConnectToServer_Response( me, vMsg )
  if vMsg.errorCode = 0 then
    if me.pDebug then put "CONNECT TO SERVER RESPONSE: CONNECTED:
    ➡ " & vMsg
    member("ServerStatus").text = "Connection Successful"
    sendAllSprites(#mConnected)
  else
    if me.pDebug then put "CONNECT TO SERVER RESPONSE: ERROR: " &
    ➡ vMsg
    member("ServerStatus").text = "Connection Failed"
    me.mKillCallBacks()
    me.mDisconnectFromServer()
    go "Server"
  end if
end mConnectToServer_Response
```

11. If the connection with the server is unexpectedly dropped, or the server crashes, the Xtra will send a ConnectionProblem message. Earlier, when we set our callbacks, we instructed the connection instance to call this handler when it receives a ConnectionProblem message. We'll add that handler now. Notice that we clear out the callbacks, disconnect, and start over when it happens, as well as informing the user that something went wrong with the alert message.

```
- - CONNECTION PROBLEM RECEIVED
on mConnectionProblem_Received( me, vMsg )
  if me.pDebug then put "CONNECTION_PROBLEM_RECEIVED: " & vMsg
  ➡ me.mKillCallBacks()
  me.mDisconnectFromServer()
  alert("There was a problem with the connection to the server.")
  ➡ go "Server"
end mConnectionProblem_Received
```

12. When we set our callbacks earlier, notice that we included an entry with no subject argument. This tells the connection instance to route any message that does not have a callback to this handler. Normally this shouldn't happen, but, as you'll soon find out, when you're creating multiuser applications anything can happen, so always be prepared for unexpected messages. Add this handler now. It doesn't do anything but output the message to the message window, but at least that will give us some way of knowing what's going on:

```
- - DEFAULT RECEIVED
on mDefault_Received( me, vMsg )
  if me.pDebug then put "DEFAULT_RECEIVED: " & vMsg
```

```
end mDefault_Received
```

We've finished with the connection manager object for now, so let's test the code and see what happens.

13. First, make sure the server is up and running. Rewind and start the movie. Keep the message window open so you can see what's happening.

   On the Choose Server screen, enter your server address or accept the current entry, which is set to the IP address we defined earlier. Click the Choose Server button, and let's enter a screen name. Enter any name, and click the Log In button. Watch the message window.

14. If everything went according to plan you should get the following message in the message window, and see that the application has advanced to the game area. The user name will be different of course.

```
- - Welcome to Director - -
- - "CONNECT TO SERVER RESPONSE: CONNECTED: [#errorCode: 0,
➡ #recipients: ["Alan"], #senderID: "System", #subject:
➡ "ConnectToNetServer", #content:\ <Void>, #timeStamp: 0]"
```

15. Now look at the server console. Make sure that User Log On And Off is selected under the View menu. You should see a message something like this:

   + 2001/07/07 12:41:09 Alan (66.56.29.195) connected to movie WatchMeWin.

   So everything's working OK. Good. Go ahead and stop the movie.

   We know that our ConnectToServer_Response handler is functioning properly, but we should really test the ConnectionProblem_Received handler. We can do this by shutting down the server while our movie is connected.

16. Rewind and run the movie again, and get connected. Now shut down the server. In the director movie, you should now see a message in the message window indicating a connection problem. You'll also see an alert message.

```
- - "CONNECTION_PROBLEM_RECEIVED: [#errorCode: -2147216214,
➡ #recipients: [""], #senderID: "System", #subject:
➡ "ConnectionProblem", #content: "Alan",\ #timeStamp: 256431619]"
```

(Note that the time stamp listed here is variable.)

Working with server–side events

Now we've created the client connection manager we're ready to start dealing with server–side events.

The `Dispatcher.ls` script will automatically call certain handlers in our server script that we can use to intercept the messages. There are several standard handlers called by the `Dispatcher.ls` script. For our project we're only concerned about four of them, `movieCreate`, `movieDelete`, `userLogOn`, and `userLogOff`, but have a look at Director's help files for the full list. We intercept these messages through handlers in the script file. For example:

```
on movieCreate(me, movie, group, user, fullMsg)
```

Each server event message handler is sent four parameters by the `Dispatcher.ls` script:

movie	The reference to the server movie object. We save the reference to this object in this handler, because we'll be using it later to send messages back to the client.
group	The reference to a group object. In our case this argument will be empty since we attached our server script to a movie rather than a group in the `.ls` file.
user	The reference to the object that represents the user in the server.
fullMsg	The full content of the message. The format of these messages is very similar to those we receive in the client.

These parameters will not always contain values for every server event. The server will pass arguments as required by each type of message. For the movieCreate *event message only the* movie *parameter will contain a value. The other three parameters will be empty. This is because there is no group, user, or message involved in this event. For the* userLogOn *event, only the movie and user parameters will contain values.*

Writing the server-side script

The `Dispatcher.ls` script will send the `movieCreate` message to our server script the first time a user logs on with a `movieID` that matches the `movieID` we indicated in the `Scriptmap.ls` (`WatchMeWin`). This is the starting point for our server application, and it works much the same way as Director's `startMovie` event.

We'll use this event handler to initialize the game properties and get the game started, and we'll only pass it one value using the `movie` parameter.

1. Open up the Director file you created earlier, `WatchMeWin_Server.dir` and then open the linked Script cast member. We'll start by adding some handlers related to the connection.

2.   We need a couple of properties for the server movie and the client script:

```
property pMovie - - a reference to the server movie the script
➡ belongs to
property pDebug - - As in our client script, we can use this for
➡ debugging
```

3.   Then we'll use the movieCreate handler:

```
on movieCreate(me, movie, group, user, fullMsg)
  me.pDebug = TRUE

  if ( me.pDebug ) then
    put "WatchMeWin.movieCreate
    ➡ ("&movie&","&group&","&user&","&fullMsg&")"
  end if
- - Save the movie reference
  me.pMovie = movie
end movieCreate
```

> *Note that we can output messages to the server console just as we can send output to the message window in Director. In server scripts, the* put *statement will send a message to the console display.*

4.   When the last user of a server movie logs off the server will delete the movie object and send a message to our script. The movieDelete handler acts mush the same way as Director's stopMovie – it's where we can do any clean up necessary, like killing timers and de-referencing objects.

Add the movieDelete handler.

```
on movieDelete(me, movie, group, user, fullMsg)
  if ( me.pDebug ) then
    put "WatchMeWin.movieDelete
    ➡ ("&movie&","&group&","&user&","&fullMsg&")"
  end if
end movieDelete
```

5.   Each time a user logs on the server will send our script a userLogOn event message, with values for the movie and user parameters. Later we'll use this to add the new user to our list of users in the game, and to update the new player on the current game state.

Add the userLogOn handler now:

```
on userLogOn(me, movie, group, user, fullMsg)
    if ( me.pDebug ) then
      put "WatchMeWin.userLogOn
      ➡ ("&movie&","&group&","&user&","&fullMsg& ")"
    end if
end userLogOn
```

6.   And finally, when a user disconnects, the server will send our script a userLogOff event message, which again includes values for the movie, and user parameters. This handler will eventually be used to remove a user from the game's list of users when they log out.

So, add the userLogOff handler:

```
on userLogOff(me, movie, group, user, fullMsg)
     if ( me.pDebug ) then
     put "WatchMeWin.userLogOff
     ➡ ("&movie&","&group&","&user&","&fullMsg&")"
     end if
end userLogOff
```

Managing incoming messages

This is the point of entry for custom messages sent from our client to our server script. A client sending a message directly to our server script will use system.script as the #recipient property of the message, and the server will forward any messages with this entry to the incomingMessage handler in the server script.

It's up to us to handle each message individually. We'll differentiate between messages using the #subject property and a case statement to determine what to do with the message.

7.   Let's add the incomingMessage handler now. We'll add code to this later to handle the custom messages we'll create for our game.

```
on incomingMessage(me, movie, group, user, fullMsg)
    if ( me.pDebug ) then
             put
             ➡ "WatchMeWin.incomingMessage("&movie&","&group&","
             ➡ &user&","&fullMsg&")"
     end if

     case fullMsg.subject of
             - - This is where our code will be added.

     end case
end incomingMessage
```

Now we have a complete script that we can test, so begin by restarting the server.

8. Make sure that Users Log On And Log Off is checked under the View menu in the server application, and make sure that Movie Creation and Deletion is checked under the View menu as well.

9. Now run the Director client movie that we've been working on, `WatchMeWin.dir`. Once you have established a connection, take a look at the server console window. You should get some messages that look similar to these:

```
+ 2001/07/07 14:44:52 Created movie WatchMeWin.
- - "WatchMeWin.movieCreate(<Movie 6 141a04>,,,)"
+ 2001/07/07 14:44:52 Alan (66.56.29.195) connected to movie
➥ WatchMeWin.
- - "WatchMeWin.userLogOn(<Movie 7 141a04>,,<User 6 14184c>,)"
```

Stop the Director client and you should get some messages like this:

```
- 2001/07/07 14:55:48 Alan disconnected from movie WatchMeWin.
- - "WatchMeWin.userLogOff(<Movie 7 141a04>,,<User 6 14184c>,)"
- 2001/07/07 14:55:48 Deleted movie WatchMeWin.
- - "WatchMeWin.movieDelete(<Movie 7 141a04>,,,)"
```

Notice that two of these messages have been output by the server itself, and the other two by our script. You can use the pDebug property in the server script to turn messages from our script off and on.

Sending messages from the server script to the client

Before we move on, we should discuss the process for sending messages from the server script to the client. Remember that in our on movieCreate handler we saved the movie argument in a property so that we could use it elsewhere. We'll use it to send messages to some or all of the clients connected to the movie object on the server.

To do this, we call the sendMessage method of movie:

```
movie.sendMessage( recipients, subject, content )
```

The sendMessage method needs at least three arguments.

Recipients	A name or a list of names of users to send the message to.
Subject	Our server script will send messages with subjects as the message identifier, just as our client scripts do. The subject name will be used by the client to create the callbacks mentioned earlier.
Content	This can be any Director data type. In this game we'll be using strings, integers, linear lists, and property lists.

So, for example, this next line would send a message to a list of users, instructing them to add a new user's name to the user interface. The client will have a callback using the AddUser subject name.

```
movie.sendMessage( [ "Jeff", "John", "Susan" ], "AddUser", "Alan" )
```

Just as we used the movie object argument from the movieCreate handler, we can also use the user object argument from another handler such as the userLogOn handler. The message format is the same, except that we can leave out the recipient argument since we're using the user object to send the message.

This message would send a list of user names to one user:

```
user.sendMessage( "GetUserNames", ["Jeff","John","Susan"] )
```

Keeping track of users in the room

Now that we have both the client and server parts of our connection completed, we can start to add some real code to the project. We'll begin with the aspects that keep track of the users in our game: the client-side Room Manager, and the server-side Room Features we planned earlier.

We'll start with the server-side room features, as we'll need these up and running in order to be able to test our client scripts. The server script will maintain a list of users who are playing the game. Each time a user logs on to the server, the user's name will be added to the list, and an AddUser message will be sent to each client. Each client will receive this message and display the new user's name in the user interface. Each time a user leaves, the user's name will be deleted from the server list, and a DeleteUser message will be sent to each client. Finally, when a new user arrives the client will request a list of all the other users currently connected to the game.

Keeping track of users in the room

1. Return to the Director file you created earlier called WatchMeWin_Server.dir, and open up the cast member script that links to the WatchMeWin.ls.

2. We'll start by adding a new property to hold the current users in and an initialization handler just after the incomingMessage handler. We'll use the pUserNames list to send messages to clients:

```
property pUserNames -- A list of all current user names in our
➡ game

on mInitRoom( me )
    me.pUserNames = []
end mInitRoom
```

3. Now let's add a line to the `movieCreate` handler at the start of the script to call our new `InitRoom` handler.

```
me.mInitRoom()
```

The `movieCreate` handler should now look like this.

```
on movieCreate(me, movie, group, user, fullMsg)
    if ( me.pDebug ) then
    put "WatchMeWin.movieCreate
    ➥ ("&movie&","&group&","&user&","&fullMsg&")"
end if
    - - Save the movie reference
    me.pMovie = movie

    - - INIT the ROOM
    me.mInitRoom()
end movieCreate
```

Adding in users

4. We'll create a handler that will add a new user's name to the list and send a message to all clients. Remember that the `user` argument represents the user on the server. You can get the user's screen name by calling `user.name`.

```
on mAddUser( me, movie, group, user, fullMsg )
    - - Add the user to our user names list.
    (me.pUserNames).add( user.name )

    - - Tell everyone that this new user joined
    movie.sendMessage( me.pUserNames, "AddUser", user.name )
end mAddUser
```

(Notice that we can use our `pUserNames` list for the recipient argument in the `sendMessage` call.)

5. In order for this to work we also need to add a line to the `userLogOn` handler that will call our `AddUser` handler. Add the following line to the `userLogOn` handler. Notice that this line will forward the arguments passed in to the `userLogOn` handler.

```
me.mAddUser( movie, group, user, fullMsg )
```

The `userLogOn` handler should now look like this.

```
on userLogOn(me, movie, group, user, fullMsg)
  if ( me.pDebug ) then
    put "WatchMeWin.userLogOn
    ➥ ("&movie&","&group&","&user&","&fullMsg& ")"
  end if
```

```
          me.mAddUser( movie, group, user, fullMsg )

end userLogOn
```

When a user logs on to the server, their name will be added to our pUserNames list in our server script.

Deleting a user

6. We need to create a handler that will delete the user's name from our pUserNames list when they log off. Add a DeleteUser handler now:

```
on mDeleteUser( me, movie, group, user, fullMsg )

          - - Delete the user from our user names list.
          (me.pUserNames).deleteOne( user.name )

          - - Tell everyone that this user left.
          movie.sendMessage( me.pUserNames, "DeleteUser", user.name )
end mDeleteUser
```

7. We need to add a line to the userLogOff handler to call our DeleteUser handler. Add the following line to the userLogOff handler.

```
me.mDeleteUser( movie, group, user, fullMsg )
```

Now, when a user logs off, their name will be deleted from our pUserNames list.

Getting user names

When a client logs on to the system one of the first requests it will make to the server script is for a list of all current users in the game. The GetUserNames handler will simply send our pUserNames list back to the client.

Let's first discuss how this will work. The client will send a message to the server script, with a subject of GetUserNames. (We're not going to code this here because we're not covering the interface in this chapter.)

```
          pConnection.sendNetMessage( [#recipients:"system.script",
 ➥ #subject:"GetUserNames"]
```

The recipient property of the message will be system.script, so the server will forward the message to our incomingMessage handler in our server script.

The incomingMessage handler uses a case statement to check the subject property of the incoming message. If the subject is GetUserNames, our script will call our new handler, GetUserNames, which will in turn send a message back to the client.

8. So, let's first add the GetUserNames handler, and then a line to the incomingMessage handler to call it. Notice that we'll simply return the same subject property sent by the user.

```
on mGetUserNames( me, movie, group, user, fullMsg )
    user.sendMessage( fullMsg.subject, me.pUserNames )
end mGetUserNames
```

9. Now add a line to the case statement in our incomingMessage handler.

```
on incomingMessage(me, movie, group, user, fullMsg)
  if ( me.pDebug ) then
    put "WatchMeWin.incomingMessage
    ➡ ("&movie&","&group&","&user&","&fullMsg&")"
  end if

    case fullMsg.subject of

            - - ROOM FEATURES
            "GetUserNames": me.mGetUserNames( movie, group, user,
            ➡ fullMsg )

      end case
end incomingMessage
```

10. Finally, make sure the script compiles, save it, and restart the server. We're now ready to add some code to the client that will take advantage of these new features.

    If there are any compile errors in your script, the server will inform you of this on startup.

Building the client-side room manager

Now we can add the room features to the client. We'll do this by adding code to the room manager object in the client. Open the version of the file WatchMeWin.dir located in the 2 RoomManager directory. This file will have a completed ConnectionManager script with the room features in the user interface turned on. Open the MU OBJECTS cast library, and let's edit the code for the RoomManager script.

1. The first thing we need to do is add some properties and a new handler as we did in our connectionManager script:

```
- - PROPERTIES
property pCM
property pDebug

- - NEW
```

```
on new( me, connectionManager )
  me.pCM = connectionManager
  me.mInitCallbacks()
  me.pDebug = TRUE
  return me
end new
```

A reference to our connectionManager object will be passed in as an argument when the script is instantiated. We need to save this reference in a property, called pCM, so that we can make calls to the pConnection instance. And as with our ConnectionManager object, we need to initialize some callbacks for messages related to this object.

> *Remember, the* pConnection *instance is our single point of contact with the server. Therefore it should live in the* connectionManager. *However, we want a modularized code architecture, so we're separating features sets into separate objects.*

The room manager callbacks

We expect the Room Manager object to receive three messages from the server, so we need to set up some callbacks. Remember that the server will send an AddUser, DeleteUser, and GetUserNames message to our clients. We'll set up three handlers to handle these messages later, but first let's add the callback handlers.

2. First, we'll add the InitCallbacks and KillCallbacks handlers. We're actually setting these callbacks in the connection instance located in connectionManager, but the difference here is that the incoming messages will be routed to the RoomManager object. Type the code into the RoomManager script.

```
- - INITIALIZE CALLBACKS
on mInitCallbacks( me )
  me.pCM.pConnection.setNetMessageHandler(
  ➡ #mGetUserNames_Response, me,\ "GetUserNames", EMPTY, 1 )
  me.pCM.pConnection.setNetMessageHandler( #mAddUser_Received, me,
  ➡ "AddUser",EMPTY, 1 )
  me.pCM.pConnection.setNetMessageHandler( #mDeleteUser_Received,
  ➡ me, "DeleteUser", EMPTY, 1 )
end mInitCallbacks

- - KILL CALLBACKS
on mKillCallbacks( me )
  me.pCM.pConnection.setNetMessageHandler( 0, me, "GetUserNames" )
  me.pCM.pConnection.setNetMessageHandler( 0, me, "AddUser" )
  me.pCM.pConnection.setNetMessageHandler( 0, me, "DeleteUser" )
end mKillCallbacks
```

> *Notice the handler names represent the type of message being sent by the server. The* GetUserNames *callback is actually a response to a request the client will make. The other two handlers are messages that are received, and not a response to a client message. It's sometimes helpful to differentiate these types of messages for debugging purposes.*

Now let's add the handlers that will receive these callbacks.

3. We added some code to our server–side script that will send each client an AddUser message when a new client logs on to the server. We'll set a callback for this message that will call an AddUser_Received handler when the message arrives in the client. Let's add this new handler now:

```
- - ADD USER RECEIVED
on mAddUser_Received( me, vMsg )
  if me.pDebug then put "ADD USER RECEIVED: " & vMsg

  if vMsg.errorCode = 0 then
    sendAllSprites(#mAddUser, vMsg.content )
  end if
end mAddUser_Received
```

When this message arrives, it will forward the content on to the user interface which will add the new user's name to a text field that displays all the users' names.

4. Remember that we added some code to the server script that sends all the remaining clients a DeleteUser message when a client logs off? We need to set a callback for this message to call a DeleteUser_Received handler when the message arrives. Add this new handler to your code:

```
on mDeleteUser_Received( me, vMsg )
  if me.pDebug then put "DELETE USER RECEIVED: " & vMsg

  if vMsg.errorCode = 0 then
    sendAllSprites(#mDeleteUser, vMsg.content )
  end if
end mDeleteUser_Received
```

So, now we have enough code to keep track of a user coming and going during the game. We also need to know who's already in the game when our new client arrives. We can get this information by sending a GetUserNames request to our server script. This will require two handlers, one to send the message, and another to handle the response.

5.   First add the request handler:

```
- - GET USER NAMES
on mGetUserNames ( me )
  me.pCM.pConnection.sendNetMessage(
  ➥ [#recipients:"system.script",\ #subject:"GetUserNames"] )
end mGetUserNames
```

This handler is executed by the user interface calling:

```
gRoomManager.mGetUserNames()
```

The server will forward this message to the incomingMessage handler in our server script because we've entered system.script in the #recipients property of the message. The incomingMessage handler in the server script will see the GetUserNames subject and forward the message on to the GetUserNames handler in the server script.

6.   Now we can add the response handler. We assigned this handler earlier, as a callback for the GetUserNames message. When the message arrives, it will be forward to the user interface, which will update its list of current users in the game. Type the following code at the end of our RoomManager script:

```
- - GET USER NAMES RESPONSE
on mGetUserNames_Response ( me, vMsg )
  if me.pDebug then put "GET USER NAMES RESPONSE: " & vMsg

  if vMsg.errorCode = 0 then
    sendAllSprites(#mSetUsers, vMsg.content )
  end if
end mGetUserNames_Response
```

So now we have the room features added, and can now see players coming and going in our game. Let's test the RoomManager by running the client. You can use the file you've just been building up, or use the completed version of WatchMeWin.dir file, from the 2 RoomManager directory (Completed subfolder), for this to work.

7.   Run the Director client, enter a screen name, and log on. Once connected, you should see your name appear in a text field on screen. Check the message window to see the full incoming messages. You should see something like this in the message window.

```
- - "ADD USER RECEIVED: [#errorCode: 0, #recipients: ["Alan"],
➥ #senderID: "System.Script", #subject: "AddUser", #content:
➥ "Alan", #timeStamp: 339809412]"
```

Great, it works! But it's a bit lonely in there isn't it? Let's add more clients to our server to really see things happening. (Well, talking to yourself is fine when there's nobody there to see.)

8. We'll do this by previewing our movie, and then opening multiple browser windows of the same html file. Choose Preview In Browser from the File menu, or just hit F12, on the keyboard. This should open our Director client move in an html page. Go ahead and log on with any screen name. One thing to bear in mind here is that accepting the default MacromediaSecretIPAddressCookie: bd will allow testing with no connection, whereas if the IP address is entered an Internet connection is looked for.

> **PC users: If you have problems connecting in preview mode, you might need to add the** Multiuser.x32 **Xtra to the movie. Do this by choosing** Movie, **then** Xtras, **from the** Modify **menu. Choose** Add... **and add** Multiuser.x32 **to the default Xtras. Save the movie, and preview again.**

9. Now create another browser window with this same file in it. This time, log on with a different screen name – you should see two names when you enter the game. Test the room features by watching both windows as one player enters or leaves. You can run as many browser windows you like. You can also run the client in Director at the same time and watch the message window. You'll need to run through this kind of testing procedure often if you need to really test an application.

Working with chat features

Now let's get our users talking to each other, by adding in some chat features.

We'll let users submit a chat message and use the client to send the messages to the server with Chat indicated as the subject property of the messages and system.script as the recipient property. The server will route the message to the incomingMessage handler in our server script. The incomingMessage handler will check the subject property of the message and route it to a Chat handler in the server script. The Chat handler in the server script will append the message to a ChatLog list and then forward the message on to all clients. The clients will receive this message and display it in the user interface. (If your interested, you can see all the file names for chat the chat by using put in the WatchMeWin.dir file's Main script.) When users first log onto the system they send a request to the server script, asking for the ChatLog so they can see what everyone's been talking about before they got there.

Creating the chat features

Let's start with the server script. Open the Director file you created earlier, WatchMeWin_Server.dir. Once again, open the Linked Script cast member that we've been working in.

1. We'll add some chat properties and an initialization handler at the end of the room features we added earlier:

```
property pChatLog
property pChatLogLength

on mInitChat( me )
    me.pChatLog = []
    me.pChatLogLength = 10
end mInitChat
```

We'll keep a list of chat messages in pChatLog. Each incoming chat message will be appended to this list, and clients will request the ChatLog when they enter the room. The pChatLogLength property is used to keep the pChatLog list down to a reasonable length. New users don't need to see all chat messages ever submitted, just the last few messages, so they can get an idea of what's been discussed recently.

2. Next, we'll add a line to the movieCreate handler (at the start of the script) that will call our chat initialization handler:

```
on movieCreate(me, movie, group, user, fullMsg)
    me.pDebug = TRUE
    if ( me.pDebug ) then
    put "WatchMeWin.movieCreate
    ➥ ("&movie&","&group&","&user&","&fullMsg&")"
    end if
    - - Save the movie reference
    me.pMovie = movie

    - - INIT the ROOM, and CHAT features
    me.mInitRoom()
    me.mInitChat()
end movieCreate
```

3. Now let's create a handler that will receive an incoming chat message, append it to the ChatLog, and forward it to all clients.

```
on mChat(me, movie, group, user, fullMsg )

    - - Chop off the first message if the log is full.
    if (me.pChatLog).count() >= me.pChatLogLength then
    ➥ (me.pChatLog).deleteAt(1)
    - - Append the incoming chat to the end of the log.
    (me.pChatLog).append( user.name & ":" && fullMsg.content )

    - - Send the last message from the log to all users.
    movie.sendMessage( me.pUserNames, fullMsg.subject,
    ➥ me.pChatLog[ (me.pChatLog).count() ] )
end mChat
```

Notice that we are trimming the ChatLog if necessary and then append the new message, including the user's name, to the beginning of the message. Finally, we send only the last message in the ChatLog to all clients, using the same subject as the incoming message. The client will create a callback for this message and display it in the chat output window when it arrives.

4. Now let's add a line to our incomingMessage handler that will route the Chat message to our Chat handler:

```
on incomingMessage(me, movie, group, user, fullMsg)
   if ( me.pDebug ) then
      put WatchMeWin.incomingMessage
      ➥ ("&movie&","&group&","&user&","&fullMsg&")"
   end if

   case fullMsg.subject of

      - - ROOM FEATURES
      "GetUserNames": me.mGetUserNames( movie, group,
      ➥ user, fullMsg )

      - - CHAT FEATURES
      "Chat": me.mChat( movie, group, user, fullMsg )

   end case
end incomingMessage
```

Using a log to keep track of the chat

When clients enter the game, they need to know what everyone's been talking about recently. They'll get this information by sending a request to the server for the ChatLog.

5. We'll add a handler that will send the current ChatLog to a single user upon request. Notice that we can use the user argument to send the message to the client.

```
on mGetChatLog( me, movie, group, user, fullMsg )
    user.sendMessage( "GetChatLog", me.pChatLog )
end mGetChatLog
```

6. And for all incoming messages we'll add a line to the incomingMessage handler that will route the message to this handler, based on the subject name.

```
on incomingMessage(me, movie, group, user, fullMsg)
   if ( me.pDebug ) then
      put "WatchMeWin.incomingMessage
      ➥ ("&movie&","&group&","&user&","&fullMsg&")"
   end if
```

```
            case fullMsg.subject of

                    - - ROOM FEATURES
                    "GetUserNames": me.mGetUserNames( movie, group,
                ➡ user, fullMsg )

                    - - CHAT FEATURES
                    "Chat": me.mChat( movie, group, user, fullMsg )
                    "GetChatLog": me.mGetChatLog( movie, group,
                ➡ user, fullMsg )
            end case
        end incomingMessage
```

7. Finally, make sure the script compiles, save it, and restart the server. We're now ready to add the code to the client that will take advantage of these new features.

Creating the Chat Manager

We're now ready to add the chat features to the chat manager object in the client. Open the version of WatchMeWin.dir located in the 3 ChatManager directory. This file has completed ConnectionManager and RoomManager scripts, with the room features and now the chat features in the user interface turned on. We'll edit the code for the ChatManager script.

8. Just like as we did with the RoomManager script, the first thing we need to do is add some properties, and a new handler:

```
- - PROPERTIES
property pCM
property pDebug

- - NEW
on new( me, connectionManager )
  me.pCM = connectionManager
  me.mInitCallbacks()
  me.pDebug = TRUE
  return me
end new
```

When this script is instantiated, a reference to our ConnectionManager object will be passed in as an argument. We need to save this reference in a property called pCM, so that we can make calls to the pConnection instance. And like our RoomManager object, we need to initialize some callbacks for messages related to this object.

The chat manager callbacks

9. Our callbacks will be initialized and killed in the same way as in the RoomManager. This time we expect to receive only two messages for the server. So let's add the code to respond to these messages:

```
- - INITIALIZE CALLBACKS
on mInitCallbacks ( me )
  me.pCM.pConnection.setNetMessageHandler
  ➥ ( #mChat_Received, me, "Chat",EMPTY, 1 )
  me.pCM.pConnection.setNetMessageHandler ( #mGetChatLog_Response,
  ➥ me, "GetChatLog", EMPTY, 1 )
end mInitCallbacks


- - KILL CALLBACKS
on mKillCallbacks ( me )
  me.pCM.pConnection.setNetMessageHandler ( 0, me, "Chat" )
  me.pCM.pConnection.setNetMessageHandler ( 0, me, "GetChatLog" )
end mKillCallbacks
```

Next we'll create the handlers that will receive these callbacks.

10. When chat messages arrive from the server script, the callback we entered earlier will route the message to this handler. This handler will then display the message in the user interface. Add this handler to the script:

```
on mChat_Received(me, vMsg )
  if me.pDebug then put "CHAT RECEIVED: " & vMsg

  if vMsg.errorCode = 0 then
    sendAllSprites(#mChat, vMsg.content )
  end if
end mChat_Received
```

11. When the server script sends the ChatLog, as per request from the client, the message will arrive here, and the user names will be displayed in the user interface. We'll add this handler now:

```
on mGetChatLog_Response ( me, vMsg )
  if me.pDebug then put "GET CHAT LOG RESPONSE: " & vMsg

  if vMsg.errorCode = 0 then
    sendAllSprites(#mChatLog, vMsg.content )
  end if
end mGetChatLog_Response
```

12. Now let's add the handler that will send chat messages to the server script:

```
on mChat( me, vMsg )
  me.pCM.pConnection.sendNetMessage( [#recipients:
  ➥ "system.script",#subject:"Chat", #content: vMsg ] )
end mChat
```

This handler is executed by the user interface by calling:

```
gChatManager.mSendChat("Hello")
```

13. We also need a handler to request the current chat log from the server script:

```
on mGetChatLog( me )
  me.pCM.pConnection.sendNetMessage( [#recipients:"system.script",
  ➥ #subject:"GetChatLog" ] )
end mGetChatLog
```

Now we have the chat features added and can communicate with other players in our game. Let's test it.

14. First make sure the server is running, and has been restarted since our server script alterations. Then test the `ChatManager` by running the client. (If you're not building up the script, you can working with the version of `WatchMeWin.dir` from the 3 ChatManager>Completed directory.)

Run the Director client, enter a screen name, and log on. Now enter a chat message and click Send Chat. You should see the chat message appear, along with your name, in the chat output window. Also, check the message window. You should see a message similar to this:

```
- - "CHAT RECEIVED: [#errorCode: 0, #recipients: ["Alan"],
➥ #senderID: "System.Script", #subject: "Chat", #content: "Alan:
➥ Hello!", #timeStamp: 344879168]"
```

15. Open up a few more clients again, as you did earlier. Use different screen names, send some messages and watch how the interfaces react.

We've a successful connection, some room features, and a basic chat room running. So now we can start adding in game specific features. The game we're creating allows users to take turns playing a round of Black Jack against a virtual dealer.

Creating the game specific features

The server script will define a list of game states and how much time should be spent on each state. The server script will cycle through the list of game states for the duration of the game. We'll be using a Lingo timeout object in the server script to keep the game moving from state to state.

When the `movieCreate` handler is called, the server script will initialize the game state list and create a new timeout object. The script will determine what the current state should be, send a message to all clients, and then set the period property of the timeout object to the time indicated in our game state list for the current state.

Each time the timeout object expires, the next state in the list will be called. When it's time for a new game state, the server script will send a new state message to all clients. This process will continue until the last user leaves the server and the `movieDelete` handler is called in the server script. We'll begin by planning the game states we need.

Planning the server–side game states

The game states will keep the game synchronized for all users. We'll be sending game state messages from the server script to each client, so first we need to implement each game state on the server.

> The server script will control the flow of the game, and the clients will simply react to game state changes.

New Round	This state will be sent to the current player and next player names when it's time for a new round. The New Round state ends when the timer runs out.
Bet	This state is sent when the timer runs out for the New Round state and it's time for the current player to place a bet. Only the current player will see the bet interface, the other players will see a status message indicating who is betting. The Bet state ends when either the timer runs out or the current player submits a bet. All clients will see the resulting bet amount.

Deal	This state will be sent after a bet has been received, or after the timer runs out for the Bet state. The virtual dealer will draw two cards for both the current player and the dealer. The card data will be sent along with the Deal state message. The Deal state ends when the timer runs out.
Player Turn	The Player Turn state will be sent when it's time for the current player to play out their hand. Only the current player will see the Hit and Stay buttons; other clients will see a status message indicating that the current player is playing their hand. All clients will see new cards appear as the player is dealt additional cards. This state ends when the player chooses to stay, is bust, gets a Black Jack, or when the timer runs out.
Dealer Turn	The dealer takes a turn playing out its hand after the current player. Clients will see new cards appear as the dealer draws new cards. This state ends when the dealer chooses to stay, is bust, gets a Black Jack, or when the timer runs out.
Payout	The server script calculates the winnings for the player based on both hands once the dealer has finished playing its hand, and then the Payout state change is sent to all clients. The current player's winnings will be included in this message. This state ends when the timer runs out.
Wait	This state is only used when the server script first starts up. It gives the server script time to initialize all properties before starting the game state cycle.

The timeout object

The timeout object is a generic timer that we'll use to help move our game along. We create a timeout object by giving it a name, the length of the timer, a handler to call when the timer expires, and an object for the handler to live in.
For example:

```
me.pTimerObject = timeout( "WatchMeWin" ).new
➡ ( 5000, #mNewRound, me )
```

This example creates a timeout object named WatchMeWin that will run for five seconds, and then call the mNewRound handler in the current script.

When the mNewRound handler is called, we'll set the timer's length again, determine the next state, and change the handler that gets called. To change the timer length, we set the period property of the timeout object. We can also, set what handler is called, with the timeOutHandler property.

```
me.pTimerObject.period = 5000
me.pTimerObject.timeOutHandler = #mBet
```

Adding in game features

1. Let's add some code to the server script that will get these game states going. Once again, return to the Director file you created earlier, `WatchMeWin_Server.dir` and Open the linked Script cast member.

We'll add in some properties related to the game features and an initialization handler after the chat features we added earlier,

```
property pGameStates
property pCurrentState
property pTimerObject

on mInitGame( me )
  me.pGameStates = [ #Wait:5000, #NewRound: 5000, #Bet:15000,
  ➡ #Deal:5000, #PlayerTurn:15000, #DealerTurn:5000, #Payout:10000
  ➡ ]

    me.pCurrentState = #Wait
    me.pTimerObject = timeout( "WatchMeWin" ).new(
    ➡ me.pGameStates.Wait, #mNewRound, me )
end mInitGame
```

Notice the `pGameStates` property is a property list with the name of the state as the property, and the time length for the state as the value. The time value is in milliseconds. The timeout object is initialized with the length of the `#Wait` game state. The `NewRound` handler will be called when this timer object expires,

2. Now let's add a line to the `movieCreate` handler that will call our game initialization handler.

```
me.mInitGame()
```

The `movieCreate` handler should now look like this:

```
on movieCreate(me, movie, group, user, fullMsg)
    if ( me.pDebug ) then
    put "WatchMeWin.movieCreate
    ➡ ("&movie&","&group&","&user&","&fullMsg&")"
  end if
    - - Save the movie reference
    me.pMovie = movie

    - - INIT the ROOM, CHAT, and GAME features
    me.mInitRoom()
    me.mInitChat()
    me.mInitGame()
end movieCreate
```

3. We need to clear out the timer object when the server script shuts down, so let's add a line to the `movieDelete` handler:

```
on movieDelete(me, movie, group, user, fullMsg)
  if ( me.pDebug ) then
    put "WatchMeWin.movieDelete
    ➥ ("&movie&","&group&","&user&","&fullMsg&")"
  end if

    me.pTimerObject.forget()
end movieDelete
```

Setting up new rounds

As you can see from the code we entered in the `InitGame` handler, the timer will run for five seconds and then call the `NewRound` handler. The `NewRound` handler will send a game state change to all clients. The message will contain the new player's name, and the next player's name. It will also send the timeout period or length along with the message, so that the client will know how long this state will last.

The `NewRound` handler will eventually determine who the new player should be and who the next player should be, but for now let's just hard code these values as we're really only interested in getting the game states running.

4. Add the `NewRound` handler now:

```
on mNewRound( me )

  vNewPlayerName = "NewPlayer"
  vNextPlayerName = "NextPlayer"

    - - Send the new round message
  (me.pMovie).sendMessage( me.pUserNames, "ChangeState_NewRound",
  ➥ [#NewPlayer:"NewPlayer", #NextPlayer:"vNextPlayerName",
  ➥ #TimeLength:(me.pGameStates).NewRound ] )

    if ( me.pDebug ) then
      put "NEW ROUND"
    end if

    - - Set the current game state and reset timer for next state
    me.pCurrentState = #NewRound
    me.pTimerObject.period = (me.pGameStates).NewRound
    me.pTimerObject.timeOutHandler = #mBet
end mNewRound
```

Notice the last part of the handler. It will save the current game state, set the timeout period, and reset the `timeOutHandler` to `mBet` – the next game state.

Setting up the betting
The timeout object will call the Bet handler once the NewRound state expires. This handler will send a message to all clients indicating the change in game state change and who's betting.

5. Add the Bet handler now:

```
on mBet( me )

    if me.pDebug then
    put "BET"
    end if

    vCurrentPlayer = "CurrentPlayer"

    - - Send the bet message.
    (me.pMovie).sendMessage( me.pUserNames, "ChangeState_Bet", [
    ➡ #Player: vCurrentPlayer, #TimeLength:(me.pGameStates).Bet ] )

    - - Set the current game state and reset timer for next state
    me.pCurrentState = #Bet
    me.pTimerObject.period = me.pGameStates.Bet
    me.pTimerObject.timeOutHandler = #mDeal
end mBet
```

Setting up the dealing
6. The timeout object calls the Deal handler on the expiry of the Bet state. Once again, a message is sent to all clients, informing them of the change in game state. The identity of the current player, the player's cards, the dealer's cards, and the length of the time for this state are once again appended.

7. The Deal handler should look like this be coded as follows:

```
on mDeal( me )

    if me.pDebug then
       put "DEAL"
    end if

        vCurrentPlayer = "CurrentPlayer"
        vPlayerCards = []
        vDealerCards = []

        - - Send the deal message
    (me.pMovie).sendMessage( me.pUserNames, "ChangeState_Deal", [
    ➡ #Player: vCurrentPlayer, #PlayerCards: vPlayerCards,
    ➡ #DealerCards: vDealerCards, #TimeLength:(me.pGameStates).Deal ] )

        - - Set the current game state and reset timer for next
    ➡ state
```

```
     me.pCurrentState = #Deal
     me.pTimerObject.period = me.pGameStates.Deal
     me.pTimerObject.timeOutHandler = #mPlayerTurn
end mDeal
```

Setting up turns

Once the player has been dealt their cards they can play them.

8. We need a PlayerTurn handler to inform each client of this change in state:

```
on mPlayerTurn( me )
  if me.pDebug then
    put "PLAYER TURN"
  end if

  vCurrentPlayer = "CurrentPlayer"

    - - Send the player turn message
  (me.pMovie).sendMessage( me.pUserNames,
➥ "ChangeState_PlayerTurn",
➥ [#Player:vCurrentPlayer,#TimeLength:(me.pGameStates).PlayerTurn ])
    - - Set the current game state and reset timer for next
state
    me.pCurrentState = #PlayerTurn
    me.pTimerObject.period = me.pGameStates.PlayerTurn
    me.pTimerObject.timeOutHandler = #mDealerTurn
end mPlayerTurn
```

The dealer turn

9. The timeOutHandler of the PlayerTurn handler informs us that the next port of call will be the DealerTurn handler. So, let's add that handler:

```
on mDealerTurn( me )
  if me.pDebug then
    put "DEALER TURN"
  end if

  vCurrentPlayer = "CurrentPlayer"

    - - Send the player turn message
  (me.pMovie).sendMessage( me.pUserNames,
➥ "ChangeState_DealerTurn", [#Player:vCurrentPlayer,
➥ #TimeLength:(me.pGameStates).DealerTurn ] )
    - - Set the current game state and reset timer for next
    ➥ state
    me.pCurrentState = #DealerTurn
    me.pTimerObject.period = me.pGameStates.DealerTurn
    me.pTimerObject.timeOutHandler = #mPayout
end mDealerTurn
```

And finally — the Payout state.

Payout

Here we are at the final game state. If you look at the `timeOutHandler` for this handler, you'll see that it returns to the `NewRound` handler.

10. This creates a constant loop through the game states in sequence.

```
on mPayout( me )
   if me.pDebug then
      put "PAYOUT"
   end if

      vCurrentPlayer = "CurrentPlayer"
      vPayoutStatus = "BlackJack"
      vWinnings = "$15"

      - - Send the payout message.
   (me.pMovie).sendMessage( me.pUserNames, "ChangeState_Payout",
➡ [#Player:vCurrentPlayer, #PayoutStatus:vPayoutStatus,
➡ #Winnings:vWinnings, #TimeLength:(me.pGameStates).Payout ] )

      - - Set the current game state and reset timer for next
      ➡ state
      me.pCurrentState = #Payout
      me.pTimerObject.period = me.pGameStates.Payout
      me.pTimerObject.timeOutHandler = #mNewRound
end mPayout
```

11. Save the script now and restart the server so the changes take effect. We're nearly there now — we just need to set up the client side.

Setting up game manager

Now we can add some code to our client to receive each game state change message from the server script.

12. Open the version of `WatchMeWin.dir` in the 4 GameManager directory. You guessed it: we're going to edit the `GameManager` script.

As with the other scripts we've made in this file, we're going to start by adding properties and the `new` handler:

```
- - PROPERTIES
property pCM
property pDebug

- - NEW
```

```
on new( me, connectionManager )
  me.pCM = connectionManager
  me.mInitCallbacks()
  me.pDebug = TRUE
  return me
end new
```

13. Now we need to deal with the callbacks. The initialization and killing of our callbacks will take the form that we've used in the earlier scripts. This time we have six callbacks – one for each of the game states we've just defined handlers for in the server script:

```
- - INITIALIZE CALLBACKS
on mInitCallbacks( me )
  me.pCM.pConnection.setNetMessageHandler(#mChangeState_NewRound_
  ➥ Received,me, "ChangeState_NewRound", EMPTY, 1 )
  me.pCM.pConnection.setNetMessageHandler(#mChangeState_Bet_
  ➥ Received, me, "ChangeState_Bet", EMPTY, 1 )
  me.pCM.pConnection.setNetMessageHandler(#mChangeState_Deal_
  ➥ Received, me, "ChangeState_Deal", EMPTY, 1 )
  me.pCM.pConnection.setNetMessageHandler(#mChangeState_
  ➥ PlayerTurn_Received, me, "ChangeState_PlayerTurn", EMPTY, 1 )
  me.pCM.pConnection.setNetMessageHandler(#mChangeState_
  ➥ DealerTurn_Received, me, "ChangeState_DealerTurn", EMPTY, 1 )
  me.pCM.pConnection.setNetMessageHandler( #mChangeState_Payout_
  ➥ Received, me, "ChangeState_Payout", EMPTY, 1 )
end mInitCallbacks

- - KILL CALLBACKS
on mKillCallbacks( me )
  me.pCM.pConnection.setNetMessageHandler( 0, me,
  ➥ "ChangeState_NewRound" )
  me.pCM.pConnection.setNetMessageHandler( 0, me,
  ➥ "ChangeState_Bet" )
  me.pCM.pConnection.setNetMessageHandler( 0, me,
  ➥ "ChangeState_Deal" )
  me.pCM.pConnection.setNetMessageHandler( 0, me,
  ➥ "ChangeState_PlayerTurn" )
  me.pCM.pConnection.setNetMessageHandler( 0, me,
  ➥ "ChangeState_DealerTurn" )
  me.pCM.pConnection.setNetMessageHandler( 0, me,
  ➥ "ChangeState_Payout" )
end mKillCallbacks
```

14. And now we need the handlers that will deal with the callbacks. For now, we can just output each message to the message window, since we are only interested in making sure the messages arrive at the correct location. Let's put those handlers in our script:

```
on mChangeState_NewRound_Received( me, vMsg )
    if ( me.pDebug ) then put "NEW ROUND RECEIVED: " & vMsg
end mChangeState_NewRound_Received
```

```
on mChangeState_Bet_Received( me, vMsg )
    if ( me.pDebug ) then put "BET RECEIVED: " & vMsg
end mChangeState_Bet_Received

on mChangeState_Deal_Received( me, vMsg )
    if ( me.pDebug ) then put "DEAL RECEIVED: " & vMsg
end mChangeState_Deal_Received

on mChangeState_PlayerTurn_Received( me, vMsg )
    if ( me.pDebug ) then put "PLAYER TURN RECEIVED: " & vMsg
end mChangeState_PlayerTurn_Received

on mChangeState_DealerTurn_Received( me, vMsg )
    if ( me.pDebug ) then put "DEALER TURN RECEIVED: " & vMsg
end mChangeState_DealerTurn_Received

on mChangeState_Payout_Received( me, vMsg )
    if ( me.pDebug ) then put "PAYOUT RECEIVED: " & vMsg
end mChangeState_Payout_Received
```

Testing the game states

15. Now we can test the game states we just implemented for both the server and the client, so restart the server, open up the WatchMeWin.dir version in the 4 GameManager>Completed folder. Now run the Director client, get connected, and open the message window.

As each game state timerObject runs out, you should see new messages appear in the window. After running the server for a while, you should see something like this:

```
- - "NEW ROUND RECEIVED: [#errorCode: 0, #recipients: ["Alan"],
➥ #senderID: "System.Script", #subject: "ChangeState_NewRound",
➥ #content: [#NewPlayer: "Alan", #NextPlayer: "Alan",
➥ #TimeLength: 5000], #timeStamp: 368010842]"

- - "BET RECEIVED: [#errorCode: 0, #recipients: ["Alan"],
➥ #senderID: "System.Script", #subject: "ChangeState_Bet", #content:
➥ [#Player: "Alan", #TimeLength: 15000], #timeStamp: 368015841]"

- - "DEAL RECEIVED: [#errorCode: 0, #recipients: ["Alan"],
➥ #senderID: "System.Script", #subject: "ChangeState_Deal",
➥ #content: [#Player: "Alan", #PlayerCards: [#Total: 10, #Cards:
➥ [[#Suit: "Clubs", #FaceValue: "7", #value: 7], [#Suit:
➥ "Hearts", #FaceValue: "3", #value: 3]]], #DealerCards: [#Total:
➥ 20, #Cards: [[#Suit: "Diamonds", #FaceValue: "10", #value:
➥ 10], [#Suit: "Diamonds", #FaceValue: "10", #value: 10]]],
➥ #TimeLength: 5000], #timeStamp: 368029656]"

- - "PLAYER TURN RECEIVED: [#errorCode: 0, #recipients: ["Alan"],
➥ #senderID: "System.Script", #subject: "ChangeState_PlayerTurn",
➥ #content: [#Player: "Alan", #TimeLength: 15000], #timeStamp:
```

➥ 368034656]"

```
- - "PAYOUT RECEIVED: [#errorCode: 0, #recipients: ["Alan"],
➥ #senderID: "System.Script", #subject: "ChangeState_Payout",
➥ #content: .[#Player: "Alan", #PayoutStatus: "Bust", #Winnings:
➥ "$-10", #TimeLength: 10000], #timeStamp: 368039206]"
```

We included put statements for each game state in each of the server script handlers, so take a look at the server console window. You should see something similar to this:

```
- - "NEW ROUND"
- - "BET"
- - "DEAL"
- - "PLAYER TURN"
- - "DEALER TURN"
- - "PAYOUT"
```

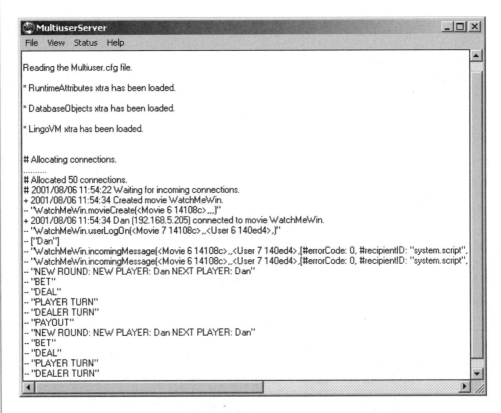

So now you should have an application that supports multiple users, displays user names, allows chat, and receives game state changes. These are the basic building blocks for any multiplayer application. Every multiuser application you build is likely to need at least these basic features.

We won't go into the specifics for completing the game because they are not directly related to multiuser programming in general, but go ahead and install and run the completed version now to see the game in action:

Open the WatchMeWin.dir file from the 5 Completed directory. Copy the WatchMeWin.ls file from this directory to the server scripts directory and restart the server.

Now run the Director client to see the completed version. Try previewing the movie with multiple browser windows.

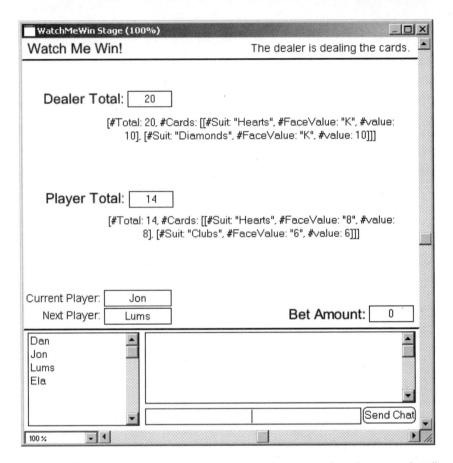

Take a look at the GameManager script in the client. Notice that there are handlers for SubmitBet, Hit, and Stay. Each of these handlers sends messages to the server script, indicating a user action. Also, notice the callbacks and handlers added to receive additional messages from the server script.

Now open the WatchMeWin.ls file that we've just put in the server scripts directory. Notice the incomingMessage handler. Here we've added lines to forward the user actions from the client to the appropriate handlers.

Finally, notice that the userLogOn handler now calls an updateGameState handler. This handler will get a new user up to date on everything that's happened in the current round. Remember that our game supports users joining the round in progress.

A word about testing

As with any application testing is very important in developing multiuser applications.

One of the first things you should do before starting a multiuser application is to determine how many users you expect to be connected to the server at any given time. The server can handle anywhere up to handle 2000 simultaneous users with minimal server scripts. Server scripts will put an additional load on the server, which will bring down the number of users you can support.

Your development process should include **load testing**. This entails writing a separate application that creates several connections and run through each of your messages. Try to write this program so that it simulates a real user on the system.

You can create multiple instances of the Multiuser Xtra in Director. Each one will act as a virtual user. If you expect to have 500 users connected simultaneous, write a program that creates 500 instances of the Multiuser Xtra, and run the program for hours at a time.

Run your test program on a separate machine from the server. As your test program runs, watch the system resources on the server, to find out how the server is handling the load. Increase the amount of users until the server slows to a crawl or crashes. This will give you an idea of how the server will perform with your application.

You will also want to write an administrative program that will monitor the state of your application. This program could perform special functions, such as booting an offensive user.

Summary

I hope I've provided you with a good basis for using Director with the Multiuser Server. You could expand on the start we've made here in all sorts of ways. You might, for example, combine a multiuser game with a database to create high score tables.

We've looked at how a project can be modularized according to the specific features that the end application will have and how the architecture can be divided between the server and client elements. It's always helpful to divide your projects up because it makes debugging easier, your modules re-usable in other projects, and the application as a whole extensible.

Another great thing about the development of multiuser applications is that it isn't expensive. Once you've got Director there is no further cost as applications can be tested on your local machine. Even if you want to test the application over the Internet there is an alternative. For those of you who don't own a running server, Macromedia provide a trial server that you can test your scripts on (www.macromedia.com/support/director/ts/documents/trialserver.htm).

Enjoy the multiuser experience.

chapter 9
chapter 10
chapter 11
chapter 12
chapter 13

Chapter 14
Database and
XML

Data-driven applications, dynamically generated content, portable data; these are all phrases that we may have heard or used at one point in our programming lives. If not, then we've surely come across a situation where we might have benefited from the use of one of these concepts.

Handling, sorting, manipulating, and presenting data is, essentially, the entire reason behind every application ever created. The data may be in any number of formats: audio, visual, textual, or abstract. Indeed, many applications exist solely to handle the data manipulation for the user, and others exist to enable the user to handle the data in a more user-friendly way. In this chapter we'll look at some of the options available to the Director user to collate, store, and present data.

Data-driven applications

Consider a scenario where you have a simple linear presentation. Each screen will have the same basic navigation and one of several possible layouts for content. You are not sure how many pages there will be in this presentation in total, but you have a feeling that it may be more pages than you feel like laying out in Director's score. How would you handle that situation? You could bite the bullet and put a couple more developers on the job, break it down into chapter/movies, and split the work. Unfortunately, aside from the sheer potential for a lot of manual labor, a big concern is the visual and version continuities between these movies. This makes the case for a data-driven shell.

A shell can be thought of as the framework of a presentation/application. There are certain aspects of the application that will remain the same throughout, and certain handlers and behaviors that could be applied globally. This, along with some thoughtfully placed sprites, makes up the shell of any application. Granted that not all situations require this – in some instances the architecture or navigation will be very unique from screen to screen and not well suited for this technique.

If crafted properly, this shell or framework can be fed information from a variety of sources. These sources contain the data that will drive our application. So, we'll look at the variety of ways that Director can interface with different data types. We'll also look at some real-world examples and code that exemplifies what, in my humble opinion, a data-driven application should do. This involves considering the data, formatting it in such a way that it's updatable and portable, and integrating the data into a Director-based framework.

In our main example in this chapter we will be creating a Shockwave movie that will access information from a publicly hosted XML data file. Our application will connect to and read the contents of the file, parse and interpret the data, and use a preset template to display this information in a manner that is visually appealing and technically sound.

First, let's look at some of the options that are available to us.

The options for data-driven applications

Among the many options for integrating databases with Director there are what I consider to be two main categories: I call them the **pseudo-databases** and the **true databases**.

The pseudo-databases refer to Director's internal data types and are probably the most common and easily accessible. These can be broken down into two sub-types: either the basic Director constructs (arrays, lists, fields, the Prefs file), or the use of FileIO with external text files (flat files) that contain information in a format that can be easily understood or parsed by Director. Alternative options in this realm include third-party Director Xtras and the new and improved Multiuser Server.

The other options are the *true* database types, such as Access, SQL, and MySQL. These will allow another level of flexibility in your applications as well as extend the portability of your data. Data housed in databases, or XML documents, are useful not only to your current Director application, but may be used by a variety of standalone, Web, or wireless applications. Though XML is not exactly a database per se, an XML document can be used in a very similar way, so I tend to group XML with the true database types. For a more detailed explanation of XML and its features take a look at the XML portion of the section named "Director Database Types and Pseudo-Types".

In conjunction with these and other database options there is CGI (Common Gateway Interface). In many cases CGI bridges the gap between the database, the Web, and your application. CGI is more of a concept than an actual application; it can be carried out using many, if not all, of the server-side scripting languages available today.

Director database types and pseudo-types

Most of us are relatively familiar with at least some of the database options and solutions to a certain degree. To make sure we're all on the same page, let's take a quick look at each of the data types mentioned above and see how they integrate with Director.

Also keep in mind that, although your data may be coming from any one of these sources, in order to make it useful to Director it may have to be reformatted, parsed, or otherwise interpreted and then placed into one of Director's internal data types. For this reason, a bit more time will be spent introducing the techniques I employ when using fields, lists, and arrays, than with the other introductions.

The Prefs file

The Prefs file is by far the simplest data storage method available to Director. Although it's possible to host a huge database, such as a band's discography, within a Prefs file it's more applicable to storing bits of information on your user's local system. As we'll encounter later, there is a size limitation to the amount of data that can be written to a Prefs file in one session. This information can be easily stored and retrieved by your projector or Shockwave movie and can add another dimension to your application.

The syntax for using a Prefs file is relatively simple:

```
setPref prefFileName, prefValue
getPref(prefFileName)
```

Simple uses of the Prefs file

Include:

1. Storing a user's state. For example, how far they have gotten in a particular presentation, so that they can begin at the same point when they return.

2. Keeping track of local high scores for a video game.

3. Saving a user's preference, their favorite color scheme, or user name.

As mentioned before, the Prefs file is handy, but not quite a database. It's also is local to the user's system. Keep in mind that there are some limitations to the use of the Prefs file as a data source.

Limitations of the Prefs file

Although the Prefs file is a useful tool, there are many things for which it shouldn't be used. You should be aware that:

1. The information stored within the Prefs file can't be easily shared with other users and can't be retrieved by a user when working from a different computer.

2. Using the Prefs file is the only way that Shockwave can write to a local disk, but the information stored within the Prefs file is in no way private or secure. It is recommended that no confidential information be stored within a Prefs file.

3. When used from a projector the Prefs file is read from and written to a folder named "Prefs" that is automatically created in the same directory as the projector. If your projector is running from a CD-Rom or other "read-only" media type you won't be able to write a Prefs file and attempting to do so will cause an error in your application. You can, on the other hand, read in a previously created Prefs on the CD-Rom.

4. The name that a Prefs file is saved should be unique. Using a common name such as "myPrefs" or "prefsFile" may lead to someone else's application overwriting your preferences and causing errors.

5. When writing a Prefs file via Shockwave there is a preset limit of 64K that can be stored by any one instance of a Shockwave movie. This is due to the fact that browsers will only allow a limited amount of data storage per session. The Prefs file can be overwritten with an empty string or a new set of data, but unless the user allows the Shockwave movie to write more that 64K – a dialog box will prompt them for this decision when the limit is reached – this limitation could lead to errors. Keep in mind also that there is no limit to the actual number of Prefs files that can be written.

6. In order to be cross-platform compliant you should keep the filename of a Prefs file to 8 characters or less. Don't use any characters that may be considered offensive by other operating systems. Some of the characters include: #, &, /, \, *, ?, etc.

7. The only valid extensions for a Prefs file are `.txt` and `.htm`, using any other extensions will lead to errors in your application.

Arrays, lists and fields

You will already have covered these in some detail in **Chapter 2**, but let's take a moment to draw the parallels between the standard Director constructs and a more traditional database, since these concepts carry throughout our discussion.

In its most simple form, a database consists of two main components: **fields** and **records**. The fields serve as column headings and the records are the content contained therein. Another common element of a database is the **key field**. The key serves as an index by which we can tell which record we're currently looking at. All of these components are housed in what is known as a **table**. More complex databases can relate one table to another table, or to several other tables, as well as contain stored procedures that speed the execution of certain functions of the database

> *In these examples the ID isn't truly necessary as the data index is just its position in the list. It's a good idea, however, to have this kind of redundant information available when it's time to check the integrity of your data. For example if you miss entering a particular line of data in one field, you can use this ID value to check that the position of the item in the list matches its ID. This is very helpful when you're debugging this kind of Director-based database.*

A **property list** in Director can be clearly compared to one record in a database. Take the following simple table:

id	Name	Year	Label
1	The Grateful Dead	1967	Warner Bros.
2	Anthem of the Sun	1968	Warner Bros.
3	American Beauty	1970	Warner Bros.
4	Wake of the Flood	1973	Grateful Dead
5	The Pretend '68 Album	1968	No Label
...	...	...	...

The definition of a property list containing the first record of this database would look something like this:

```
albumInfo = [#pID: 1, #pName: "The Grateful Dead", #pYear: 1967,
➡ #pLabel: "Warner Bros."]
```

If we wanted to create a pseudo-database of the first three records, we can just create a list of property lists. This list would contain, in order of their ID values, all of the `album info` property lists.

```
albumList = [ [#pID: 1, #pName: "The Grateful Dead", #pYear:
➡ 1967, #pLabel: "Warner Bros."], [#pID: 2, #pName: "Anthem of
➡ the Sun", #pYear: 1968, #pLabel: "Warner Bros."], [#pID: 3,
➡ #pName: "American Beauty", #pYear: 1970, #pLabel: "Warner Bros."] ]
```

The information could be retrieved relatively easily. For example, if we wanted the year that the third album was released, we would write something like this in the message window:

```
put albumList[3].pYear
```

Director would return:

```
- - 1970
```

If you're looking for a specific album name, or albums released by a specific label, you have to loop through all of the items (records) in our list (table), and look for a match. When a match is found, the index value (key) can be stored and used to retrieve the pertinent information.

One of the main drawbacks of this technique is populating the lists and creating the arrays. For a very simple database you could do it as shown above, but most likely if there are more records and fields than in our example, things could get a bit confusing, and the chance for a data error to occur increases.

Text fields are one way to address this concern. We could in fact create a Director text field for each of the possible database fields and insert our data accordingly. The main drawbacks here would be execution time (as fields, generally, read much slower than lists), and brevity of syntax — the Lingo for accessing text fields isn't as clean as that for accessing lists, though the latest versions of Director have made some moves forward in this respect.

The items in these text fields could be separated, or delimited, in any number of ways. Generally, I like to use carriage returns with this kind of field. Spaces and commas are good in some cases, but hitting ENTER at the end of each line of data is usually much more legible.

> *When using text fields in this way it's a good idea to use a mono-spaced font such as Courier. This makes for easier reading and error checking.*

That said, one technique that I use when limited to internal databases is to use the fields to enter and check the data, and a list array to hold the data at runtime. A simple loop and append routine can be written and executed early in the movie. This routine reads through the fields and inserts, or appends, their values into the proper list or array.

Here is one version of such a routine:

```
- - This handler will read through the series of
- - text fields and append the data to an array
- - of property lists that can be used as a simple database.
```

```
global albumList

on createDataBase

  - - Grab the text from the existing fields.

  tIDtext = member("id").text
  tNAMEtext = member("name").text
  tYEARtext = member("year").text
  tLABELtext = member("label").text

  - - Base the total number of records on the number of IDs

  tRecordCount = tIDtext.line.count

  - - Initialize the main list of lists
  albumList = []

  - - Loop through the available records

  repeat with tRecord = 1 to tRecordCount

    - - Initialize the current property list / record
    tThisRecord = [:]

    tThisRecord.addProp(#pID, tIDtext.line[tRecord])
    tThisRecord.addProp(#pName, tNAMEtext.line[tRecord])
    tThisRecord.addProp(#pYear, tYEARtext.line[tRecord])
    tThisRecord.addProp(#pLabel, tLABELtext.line[tRecord])

    - - Append this record to our main list of lists
    albumList.append(tThisRecord)

  end repeat

  - - Output to the message window

  put "Database created." && tRecordCount && "records were added."
end


on albumsByYear tYearInQuestion

  - - Base the total number of records on the number of items in
➨ our
  - -"database"
  tRecordCount = albumList.count
```

```
- - Use a variable to track if any matches were found
tMatches = 0

- - Loop through the available records
repeat with tRecord = 1 to tRecordCount

   - - Look for a match
   tThisRecordYear = albumList[tRecord].pYear

   if tThisRecordYear = tYearInQuestion then

     tMatches = tMatches +1

     - - Output to Message Window
     - - In a real application this information
     - - would be stored or returned.

     put "The album '" & albumList[tRecord].pName &"' was released
     ➥ in "& tThisRecordYear & " by" && albumList[tRecord].pLabel

   end if

  end repeat

  - - If no matches were found in the database...
  if tMatches = 0 then
     put "Sorry, there are no albums in our database that were
     ➥ released in "& tYearInQuestion
  end if

end
```

Since we're reading from text fields in this technique, all of the values inserted into our pseudo-database are strings. Should we want to do any integer-based calculations we would have to remember to change the values from strings to integers before doing so.

The handlers in this exercise are simple examples of a field and list database. They're not part of an actual program, but can be tested in the message window. The sample file (db_field_database_cast.dir) can be found on the CD accompanying this book.

The following code is what building the database and doing a couple of albumsByYear queries would look like:

```
createDataBase
- - "Database created. 5 records were added."
```

```
albumsByYear 1970
- - "The album 'American Beauty' was released in 1970 by Warner
Bros."

albumsByYear 1968
- - "The album 'Anthem of the Sun' was released in 1968 by Warner
➥ Bros."
- - "The album 'The Pretend '68 Album' was released in 1968 by No
➥ Label"
```

Flat Files, FileIO and getNetText

A **flat file** is another name for a plain ASCII text file. These files can be used to store information, and are sometimes easier to handle than a bunch of fields within a cast. In addition, these files are external to Director, and can therefore be read and/or generated by other applications. One method that I've used in the past combines the previous techniques with reading in data from an external data file via FileIO or getNetText.

FileIO is most often used when running a projector, while getNetText is more prevalent on the Web. Both can be used to read text into Director, which is our main concern here.

FileIO adds some additional functionality. With FileIO you can also create, write, append, and delete files. You can also read files incrementally based on a **token** or item delimiter. The finer points of FileIO are beyond the scope of this chapter, but coverage of some of its other uses is covered in **Chapter 11, "Xtras"**. Check, also, the References and Resources section at the end of this chapter for more information.

On the other hand, getNetText is a particularly handy tool to have in Shockwave, and can also be used in web-enabled, projector-based applications. The true beauty of getNetText can only be appreciated once we get into the CGI discussion and start pulling bits of information from a database across the Web.

XML

XML has been called the next big thing for several years now. It's now beginning to come into its own. No longer an industry buzzword, it has proved to be a useful and agile language for describing data and data structures. Though it's not quite a database, an XML document can be used in similar ways. You can also use XML within an actual database environment, thereby increasing the flexibility and portability of the information you store.

As you may already know, an XML file is pretty much a text file with some specific formatting. This fact allows us to edit XML files in any simple text-based editor such as SimpleText on the Mac and NotePad on the PC. The language itself is tag-based, like HTML, but much more flexible in that you can create your own tag sets to describe your data. As we've mentioned earlier, you can read external files through either FileIO or getNetText. In addition, if your data isn't going to be dynamic, that is to say that it won't change within the application itself, you can store your XML data in a Director text field and read it from there.

Once we have an XML file within Director, we can use the built-in XML Xtra to decipher, or parse, the XML data into a form that can be readily understood. We'll go into more detail with regards to parsing and manipulating XML data in the Slashdot.org XML News Reader example towards the end of this chapter.

XML primer

In case you're new to XML, let's take a moment to consider the fundamentals of what it is. Please keep in mind that a complete XML primer is out of the scope of this chapter (as entire tomes have been devoted to its study), but there are links in the resources list that will get you going in the right direction.

Following is a simplified example of an XML file based on our previous examples.

```
<discography>

    <artist name="The Grateful Dead">
      <album year="1967" label="Warner Bros.">The Grateful Dead
      </album>
      <album year="1968" label="Warner Bros.">Anthem of the Sun
      </album>
    </artist>

    <artist name="Blues Traveler">
      <album year="1990" label="A&M.">Blues Traveler
      </album>
      <album year="1991" label="A&M">Travelers and Theives
      </album>
    </artist>

</discography>
```

As you can see, there is an XML tag for each of the data objects defined. The tags are nested to show their relationship to each other. For example, the albums belong to the artist so they are within the artist tag, in turn the artists are part of the discography so they are placed wihin those tags. As with HTML some of these tags, or elements, have attributes which also contain related data.

Just like with HTML, there are some rules that apply to the markup language. An XML document that follows these rules is said to be a "well formed" XML document. Since you can write XML in any text-editing program it is up to you to make sure that you follow the rules. There are some HTML programs that will color code your XML and make it easier to spot problems. There are also some XML editing programs that will check the "wellformedness" of your XML.

Here is a short listing of the most important guidelines you need to follow to make sure that your XML will be valid and well-formed:

1. Any tag that is opened must be followed by a closing tag:

```
< TAG > </ TAG >
```

2. Any attribute of a tag must be within the opening tag and its value must be within quotes:

```
< TAG attribute="value">
```

3. The text data or character data (sometimes known as CDATA) must appear between the opening and closing tags:

```
< TAG > This is some text data. </ TAG >
```

4. Tags cannot overlap, but they can be nested:

   This is **WRONG**:
   ```
   <TAG_A> <TAG_B> </TAG_A> </TAG_B>
   ```

   This is **RIGHT**:
   ```
   <TAG_A> <TAG_B> </TAG_B> </TAG_A>
   ```

5. If the tag has no character data you can close it at the end of the open tag:

```
<TAG attribute="value"> </TAG>
```

is interpreted in exactly the same way as:

```
<TAG attribute="value" />
```

Director has a good few keywords dedicated to the handling of XML data. For reference purposes, here is a quick list of these keywords:

```
getAttributeName
getAttributeValue
getCharacterData
getElementName
getNumberOfAttributes
getNumberOfChildren
isCurrentAnElement
makeList
parseString
visitChild
visitParent
```

For more information about XML, and how Director interprets it check the **References and Resources** page at the end of this section.

MySQL, SQL, and Access

In the previous examples, we saw how we could use a series of field members, and a few dynamically generated lists, to create a simple database. We also saw how we could expand this through the use of external files and XML. This would work well for a limited amount of data, but can become rather slow and unwieldy when it comes to thousands of records and intricate searches. There is also the concern of portability. Once we've devoted a good bit of energy to creating a database it would be nice to be able to re-use, and possibly even share, this data in other environments. This is somewhat addressed with the use of external files and XML, but could be better handled with a more robust, true database.

There are many flavors of database available these days. They vary widely in price, availability, hosting platform, and installed user base. One point that most of them agree on is the use of a **Structured Query Language**, or **SQL**. This is the language used to access and modify the information stored within a database.

MySQL is the least expensive of all of the options – it's free – and can run on a variety of operating systems. It's not as robust as some of the other options and is decidedly more stable on Linux than Windows NT, but it can handle most basic tasks. Microsoft SQL Server is more robust in its feature set and can handle a much greater load than MySQL. The drawbacks of MS-SQL are the cost and the fact that it only runs on Windows server. Another option from Microsoft is Access, which is part of the Office suite of programs (another Windows only application). Other database options, each with their particular needs, limitations, and widely varying costs, include Oracle, dBase, Ingres, Informix, C-ISAM, DB2, Quickbase, and Interbase.

If your database will be locally hosted, say on a CD-ROM, you can use some third-party Xtras to pull information from an Access database file. There are also other Xtra-based options that include their own data formats.

Here is a quick list of the third party database Xtras currently available:

DataGrip and DataGrip Net
DAOTable
EasyBase
FileFlex
V12
Valentina

Links to the developer sites of some of these Xtras are included in the "Database Xtras" section of the References and resources portion of this chapter.

CGI

As alluded to, you can't actually talk to a database directly. There are several components that allow for this communication. One of the most important concepts of this communication is the **Common Gateway Interface**, or **CGI**. Although CGI is specific to executable programs, we're using the term loosely to group any technique or language that will allow for interactivity, or data transfer, between two systems on the Web. Having said that, there are many different languages that can be used to achieve this connectivity. Some are free, and usually available on servers, others carry with them a cost and are less prevalent on the Web.

Director interfaces with CGI languages mainly through the use of postNetText and getNetText. As we discussed earlier, getNetText is a way for Director to read external text files via a GET request to a specific URL. In the same way, postNetText, sends a POST request to a specific URL.

One major difference is that when sending a query string along with the request, a `getNextText` query is limited to 1-4Kb depending on the browser, while a `postNetText` request can have a query string of unlimited size.

Requesting text from a CGI file will cause this file to be executed. The idea is to have a CGI file connect to the database, manage the query, and return its findings to Director in a way that is useful to our application. It's even possible to send information from Director to a CGI file, which can then base its actions on this information. This can be done by either including a URL-encoded string along with the request for a CGI file, or by sending a property list to the CGI file (which Director automatically translates into a URL-encoded string).

So, to show you what your options are, here is a list of the most commonly used CGI languages and a simple example of what the code looks like.

ASP

Microsoft Active Server Pages (ASP) is a server-side scripting language that is part of the default installation of any NT server.

```
<% Response.Write "Hello World!" %>
```

PHP

PHP is a free server-side scripting language that has been ported to several operating systems.

```
<?php echo "Hello World!<p>"; ?>
```

PERL

The classic CGI language, PERL, is also free, and can be used on almost any server. Both PERL and PHP have very large developer bases, which can be handy when you are looking for that tidbit of code to help you through a project.

```
#!/usr/local/bin/perl
print ('Hello World!');
```

ColdFusion

A relative newcomer to the server-side scripting world, ColdFusion is probably one of the easier languages to learn since its syntax is based on familiar tag-based conventions.

```
<CFSET message="Hello World!"> <CFOUTPUT>#message#<CFOUTPUT>
```

Other database options

Among the other options available are the Multiuser Server and third-party database Xtras.

The Multiuser Server that ships with Director 8.5 has expanded capabilities, including its own server-side scripting language and enhanced database commands. In addition to the new database functionality of Director 8.5, any of the techniques described in this chapter can be used in conjunction with the Multiuser Server. For more on this see **Chapter 13**.

There are too many third-party database Xtras to list at this time. You can be sure that whatever your need, there is probably an Xtra out there that will handle it. The main distinction between these Xtras is that some use a data format that is proprietary, and others can be used to connect to and interpret existing database types. Xtras, and where to find them, are covered in **Chapter 11**.

OK, we've covered quite a few concepts, so let's see some of them in action.

Slashdot.org XML news reader

Slashdot is a pretty well known web site among the technically savvy. "News for Nerds. Stuff that matters." is their actual tag line. They offer information, links, and rumors related to the open source movement and other information technology subjects. Members of their online community post these items. A homespun, PERL-based gem of open source code, called Slashcode, runs the entire site. One of the coolest things about Slashdot, and the reason why they are being featured here, is that they make available an XML version of their current news stories. If you're not familiar with Slashdot, you may want to take a look at the site:

The concept

What we want to do, to illustrate a point, is build an application in Director that will work either as a Shockwave movie or a stand-alone projector. This application should read and display the current Slashdot headlines. The point we are illustrating is that XML is a great data format. It can be read and displayed by any variety of applications...including Director.

The concept is simple:

1. Read in the XML file posted on the Slashdot site.

2. Parse it using the XML Parser Xtra.

3. Convert the data in to a format we are familiar with, such as a list of property lists.

4. Use basic Lingo commands to display and link the Slashdot headlines to their respective stories on the Web.

How XML news reader works

In order to understand the process, we should step through the code as it executes, pausing to take note of the important details. Remember, this movie and its code is available on the CD, so it may be a good idea to open it in Director and give it a quick look, then follow through the code as we discuss it here.

The playback head moves directly across the score as the movie is pre-loaded, the variables are initialized, the XML file is read and parsed, and the headlines are displayed. We'll be referring to the markers, and the different points of Director's score at which code is executed.

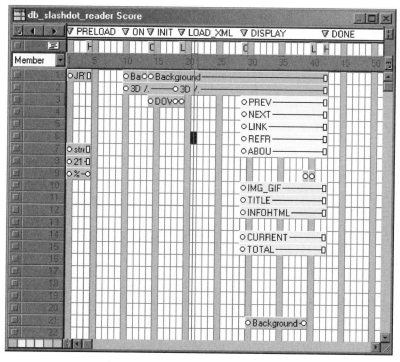

The other item we should be familiar with is the actual XML document we'll be downloading and parsing. The document follows this format and is available from the Slashdot web site: www.slashdot.org/slashdot.xml

```
<?xml version="1.0" encoding="ISO-8859-1" ?>
<backslash xmlns:backslash="http://slashdot.org/backslash.dtd">

<story>
 <title>Supreme Court Sides With Freelancers On Net
 ➥ Copyright</title>
 <url>http://slashdot.org/article.pl?sid=01/06/25/172208</url>
```

```
<time>2001-06-25 17:54:18</time>
<author>Hemos</author>
<department>good-move-by-the-court</department>
<topic>doj</topic>
<comments>117</comments>
<section>articles</section>
<image>topicdoj.jpg</image>
</story>
```

...

The XML format repeats for the 10 stories that are usually featured. As you can see, the syntax is relatively self-explanatory. There are a series of elements, each containing some text data, and the text data describes the particulars of each story. The simple and sensible structure makes this an excellent example of a basic XML document (barring the fact that properties are not used).

Our application will make use of most of these elements and lay them out in such a way that users can quickly see if there are any new stories of interest, and easily link to them. The article described above looks something like this in our final application:

Now that we're familiar with the score and the data that we'll be interpreting, we can step through the execution of the application.

Part 1: The Pre-loader

The pre-loader screen, just after all media elements are loaded:

The first few frames of this movie are dedicated to a pre-loader. This pre-loader displays a logo animation created in Flash, and a progress bar. The progress bar script is taken from Director's built-in Library Palette, and modified slightly to tell the playback head to jump to a particular frame after all of the movie's internal media has loaded. In the event that we're running this movie as a projector, there's a frame script that assures the playback head will continue forward rather than wait for the movie to load. This is very important to success, as it's both a Shockwave movie and a projector. A projector won't recognize the getStreamStatus() function and would wait infinitely for the movie assets to load.

Part 2: The initialization handler

The necessary variables are initialized and XML data loads:

Once the movie is loaded, the playback head jumps to a frame labeled ON. At this point in the movie a score-based animation fades the interface on and reports that the XML data is being downloaded and passed. This message will remain on-screen until the initialization handler has successfully executed.

After the interface has faded on, the playback head passes a frame labeled INIT. At this frame there's a frame script that calls the handler named initSlashRead. This handler contains the following Lingo code:

```
- - - - - - - - - - - - - - - - - - - - - - - - - - - - - -
- - - - - - - - - - - - - - - - - - - - - - - - - - - - - -
- - Init Routine
- - - - - - - - - - - - - - - - - - - - - - - - - - - - - -
- - - - - - - - - - - - - - - - - - - - - - - - - - - - - -
on initSlashRead()

   - - XML Parser Object
   gXMLobj = VOID
   gXMLobj = new (xtra "xmlparser")


   - - This Property List
   - - will hold our global variables
```

```
        gProps = [:]

        - - Paths to /. XML and IMAGES
        gProps.addProp(#pXMLpath, "http://www.slashdot.org/slashdot.xml")
        gProps.addProp(#pIconPath, "http://images.slashdot.org/topics/")

        - - Display Variables
        gProps.addProp(#pCurrHeadline, 0)
        gProps.addProp(#pMaxHeadline, 0)
        gProps.addProp(#pAboutScreen, 0)

        - - XML Variables
        gProps.addProp(#pXMLdata, VOID)
        gProps.addProp(#pXMLerror, VOID)
        gProps.addProp(#pStoryData, [])

        - - Net XML Text
        gProps.addProp(#pNetIDxml, VOID)

        - - Net Image Icon
        gProps.addProp(#pNetIDimg, VOID)

        - - Make sure that if we are running in a projector
        - - the XML document is checked every time and not
        - - read from Director's Cache
        clearCache

        - - Begin Loading XML File
        gProps.pNetIDxml = getNetText (gProps.pXMLpath)

        - - Jump to the Loading Loop
        go "LOAD_XML"

    end
```

As you can see in the comments, this handler basically sets up the global variables that we'll use throughout our movie. The first global that's initialized holds an instance of the XML Parser Xtra. This instance will be the key to parsing the XML data once it has been loaded. The second is a property list that contains a series of properties, pertaining to loading, parsing, and displaying the XML data for the Slashdot headlines.

These property variables include: the path to the XML file we will be reading, as well as the related image icon that is displayed with each story; three display variables that tell the movie which headline is being displayed, how many total headlines there are at this time, and whether the user is on the about "screen" or a regular headline display screen.

There are also two very important properties, pNetIDxml and pNetIDimg, which will hold the unique ID for each of the network operations. The first of these is initialized at the end of this handler by setting its value to the ID returned by the getNetText function.

Finally, this handler sends the playback head forward to the frame labeled LOAD_XML.

Part 3: The XML loading loop

There is a frame script executed at the frame labeled LOAD_XML. This frame script checks the status of the getNetText operation tasked with fetching our XML data. The script itself looks like this:

```
- - Loop While XML Loads

- - Global Property List
global gProps


on exitFrame me

  - - Check to see if the XML file has been loaded
  if netDone(gProps.pNetIDxml) then

    - - Check for errors
    tNetError = netError(gProps.pNetIDxml)
    put tNetError
    if tNetError = "OK" then

      gProps.pXMLdata = netTextResult(gProps.pNetIDxml)
      parseXMLdata()


      go "DISPLAY"
      abort
    else

      - - There has been an error loading the file.
      tErrorText = errorText(tNetError)
      gProps.pXMLerror = "NET ERROR:" & tNetError &RETURN&
      ➡ tErrorText
      go "ERROR"
      abort


    end if


  else

    go the frame -1
```

```
        end if


      end
```

This script first checks, using the `netDone` function, if the file requested has actually been completely loaded. This function returns TRUE once it is complete. Immediately after we check for completion, we do an error check. If the operation is not complete, the playback head loops back to the previous frame.

Houston, we have a problem:

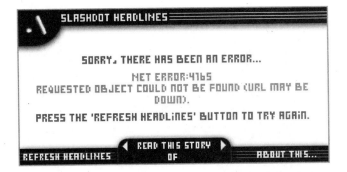

As just mentioned, both an error and a success will signify that this network operation is complete, and will lead to the execution of the next bit of code. Using the `netError` function we can be certain whether or not we have been truly successful in this data transfer. NetError will return either the string OK, or a numeric response that relates to an error. I've written a simple handler which, consisting of a single case statement and a return statement, translates the numeric error value into the error's text-based translation. Should an error occur, the playback head is sent to a frame labeled ERROR, where the error information is displayed and the user is given a chance to try the process again by clicking REFRESH HEADLINES.

Part 4: Parsing the XML document

If the network operation is complete and error free, the resulting text (our XML document) will be stored in one of our global properties using the `netTextResult` function. This function simply makes available to us, via Lingo, the data that has been loaded. Immediately following this storage procedure is a call to one of our handlers (`parseXMLdata`), and a line that sends the playback head to the frame labeled DISPLAY. The `parseXMLdata` handler, however, is executed before the playback head moves on. Here's what this handler looks like.

```
- - - - - - - - - - - - - - - - - - - - - - - - - - - - -
- - - - - - - - - - - - - - - - - - - - - - - - - - - - -
- - XML Data Parsing Routine
- - - - - - - - - - - - - - - - - - - - - - - - - - - - -
- - - - - - - - - - - - - - - - - - - - - - - - - - - - -
```

```
on parseXMLdata()

   - - Check for Parsing Errors
   tErrorCode = gXMLobj.parseString(gProps.pXMLdata)
    tErrorString = gXMLobj.getError()



   if tErrorString then

     gProps.pXMLerror = "XML PARSE ERROR"&RETURN&tErrorString
     go "ERROR"
     abort

   else

     - - No Parsing Errors were encountered...
     - - continue by making a list out of the parsed XML data.

     - - Note: This could also be done using the makeList(gXMLobj)
     - -          command... but doing it this way gives us more
     - -          control over the situation.

     - - Count the number of stories.
     tTotalStories = gXMLobj.child[1].child.count

     - - Initialize a list to contain these stories.
     tStoryData = []

     repeat with tThisStory = 1 to tTotalStories

       - - Clear out the property list for this story
       tThisStoryData = [:]

       - - Pull the text information from each of the XML nodes
       tTitle =
       ➥ gXMLobj.child[1].child[tThisStory].child[1].child[1].text
       tURL =
       ➥ gXMLobj.child[1].child[tThisStory].child[2].child[1].text
       tTime =
       ➥ gXMLobj.child[1].child[tThisStory].child[3].child[1].text
       tAuthor =
       ➥ gXMLobj.child[1].child[tThisStory].child[4].child[1].text
       tDepartment =
       ➥ gXMLobj.child[1].child[tThisStory].child[5].child[1].text
       tTopic =
       ➥ gXMLobj.child[1].child[tThisStory].child[6].child[1].text
       tComments =
```

```
      ➥ gXMLobj.child[1].child[tThisStory].child[7].child[1].text
      tSection =
      ➥ gXMLobj.child[1].child[tThisStory].child[8].child[1].text
      tImage =
      ➥ gXMLobj.child[1].child[tThisStory].child[9].child[1].text


      - - Create properties from each
      tThisStoryData.addProp(#pTitle, tTitle)
      tThisStoryData.addProp(#pURL, tURL)
      tThisStoryData.addProp(#pTime, tTime)
      tThisStoryData.addProp(#pAuthor, tAuthor)
      tThisStoryData.addProp(#pDepartment, tDepartment)
      tThisStoryData.addProp(#pTopic, tTopic)
      tThisStoryData.addProp(#pComments, tComments)
      tThisStoryData.addProp(#pSection, tSection)
      tThisStoryData.addProp(#pImage, tImage)

      - - Add this story's data to a temporary list of lists
      tStoryData.append(tThisStoryData)

    end repeat

      - - Store our List of Lists
      gProps.pStoryData = tStoryData

      - - Prep the Story Display Variables
      gProps.pCurrHeadline = 1
      gProps.pMaxHeadline = tTotalStories

    end if

  end
```

Since this handler is a bit more complex we'll go block-by-block as we break down what it's doing. The first few lines of code attempt to parse the XML data. This is a way to assure that the XML we have received is well formed and available within the XML object instance we created earlier. An XML document that is not well formed won't parse correctly and will, therefore, call up an error.

Should an error be found, the resulting error code is stored in a variable named tErrorCode. The descriptive string associated with this error is then retrieved using getError and stored in one of our global properties, pXMLerror, for display. The playback head is sent to a frame labeled ERROR where the specific error information is displayed.

If the document parses without error, the code continues to execute. The first thing we have to do is check how many headlines we'll be displaying and therefore parsing from our XML document. Once we have this number, we can initialize the temporary list variable, tStoryData, which will be hosting our information.

Following that we'll start a loop that will execute once for each of the stories. There are a few things we have to accomplish within this loop. First we pull each of the bits of information for the current story and store it in temporary variables. This is done to keep the code neat and legible. Then we take these variables and values and use them to populate a property list. Finally, this property list is appended to tStoryData which, when the loop is complete, will contain all of the information for each of the story headlines in the XML document. This temporary list is then stored in our permanent global property list as pStoryData. The portion of pStoryData for the segment of XML shown previously looks something like this:

```
[[#pTitle: "Supreme Court Sides With Freelancers On Net
➥ Copyright", #pURL:
➥ "http://slashdot.org/article.pl?sid=01/06/25/172208", #pTime:
➥ "2001-06-25 17:54:18", #pAuthor: "Hemos", #pDepartment: "good-
➥ move-by-the-court", #pTopic: "doj", #pComments: "196",
➥ #pSection: "articles", #pimage: "topicdoj.jpg"]]
```

The last two lines of code in our script store the current headline number, which at this point is 1, and the total number of headlines in our global property list. Now we're ready to move on to the display portion of our code.

Part 5: Displaying the current headline information

The current headline (1) title and story specific information (2):

Once the playback head reaches the frame labeled DISPLAY the displayCurrentHeadlines handler is called. This handler contains the following Lingo code:

```
- - - - - - - - - - - - - - - - - - - - - - - - - - - - -
- - - - - - - - - - - - - - - - - - - - - - - - - - - - -
- - Headline Display Routine
- - - - - - - - - - - - - - - - - - - - - - - - - - - - -
- - - - - - - - - - - - - - - - - - - - - - - - - - - - -

on displayCurrentHeadlines

   tCurrentStory = gProps.pStoryData[gProps.pCurrHeadline]
```

```
- - Populate the TITLE Field According to our Story Data
member("TITLE").text = tCurrentStory.pTitle

- - Create HTML Text for the rest of the information.
tInfoHTML = "<HTML><BODY bgcolor='#FFFFFF'><TABLE>"&RETURN
tInfoHTML = tInfoHTML & "<TR><TD align='right'
➥ width='100'>Author: </TD><TD><B>" & tCurrentStory.pAuthor &
➥ "</B></TD></TR>"&RETURN
tInfoHTML = tInfoHTML & "<TR><TD align='right' width='100'>Time
➥ Stamp:\ </TD><TD><B>" & tCurrentStory.pTime
➥ "</B></TD></TR>"&RETURN
tInfoHTML = tInfoHTML & "<TR><TD align='right'
➥ width='100'>Topic:\ </TD><TD><B>" & tCurrentStory.pTopic &
➥ "</B></TD></TR>"&RETURN
tInfoHTML = tInfoHTML & "<TR><TD align='right'
➥ width='100'>Section:\ </TD><TD><B>" & tCurrentStory.pSection
➥ & "</B></TD></TR>"&RETURN
tInfoHTML = tInfoHTML & "<TR><TD align='right'
➥ width='100'>Comments:\ </TD><TD><B>" &
➥ tCurrentStory.pComments & "</B></TD></TR>"&RETURN
tInfoHTML = tInfoHTML & "</TABLE></BODY></HTML>"


member("INFOHTML").HTML = tInfoHTML

- - Placing the image requires a bit more work...

- - Hide Image sprite and show placeholder until it is available
sprite(10).visible = FALSE
sprite(9).visible = TRUE

- - Preload The Image Icon from Slashdot
gProps.pNetIDimg = preloadNetThing(gProps.pIconPath &
➥ gProps.pStoryData[gProps.pCurrHeadline].pImage)

- - Display Current and Total Headline Numbers
member("CURRENT").text = string(gProps.pCurrHeadline)
member("TOTAL").text = string(gProps.pMaxHeadline)

end
```

This handler takes the current story, as defined by pCurrHeadline, and pulls its property list into a temporary variable named tCurrentStory. From this temporary variable the particular items we want to display are parsed.

The title of the current headline is placed in a text field of its own. This allows for a specific font and placement for this item. Since Director can now interpret a good deal of HTML code, the remaining information is added to an HTML formatted string. We keep it neat and simple by using a table to align and display most of our data, and a couple of bold tags to separate headings from content. Once the string is complete we set the HTML property of our display field to the value of the string:

```
member("INFOHTML").HTML = tInfoHTML
```

This allows Director to display the code we've written as an actual HTML document within a field. This takes care of displaying our textual information. *Pretty cool stuff, don't you think?*

Slashdot include an image icon with each of their stories. These icons are also available from a Directory on Slashdot's server. The next bit of code assures that the icon graphic is available when we want to display it, and that it displays in the correct format.

First of all, on the stage, we have a placeholder image and a host image. The placeholder simply lets the user know that there is a loading process occurring. The host image is where the final image will be placed when downloaded. The "loading" image is show by setting its visible property to TRUE, and the host image sprite is hidden. This next line begins the loading process.

```
gProps.pNetIDimg = preloadNetThing
  ➡ (gProps.pIconPath &
  ➡ gProps.pStoryData[gProps.pCurrHeadline].pImage)
```

Slightly further along in our score we test to see if this loading is complete and swap in the correct image.

The last bit of code in this handler places the current and total number of stories into a couple of fields on our stage. This lets the user know precisely what story headline they are viewing and how many others there are to see.

Part 6: Displaying the image icon

The image icon (3) for this story is displayed after it has loaded:

In the last section of this deconstruction we set gProps.pNetIDimg to preload the image icon that is related to the current headline being displayed. The next frame script that the playback head runs into completes this process by assuring that the image has indeed loaded, and that there haven't been any transfer errors. This is done using the same technique we saw earlier (Part

3: The XML Loading Loop). If no network errors are detected, the following handler, showImageIcon, is executed:

```
on showImageIcon

    - - Check to see if this is a JPEG or GIF
    - - and swap the onstage member accordingly.

    if gProps.pStoryData[gProps.pCurrHeadline].pImage contains ".GIF"
    ➥ then
        sprite(10).member = "IMG_GIF"
    else
        sprite(10).member = "IMG_JPG"
    end if


    - - Replace our current image with
    - - a piped-in version from the Slashdot Site
    sprite(10).member.fileName = gProps.pIconPath &
    ➥ gProps.pStoryData[gProps.pCurrHeadline].pImage
    sprite(10).visible = TRUE
    sprite(9).visible = FALSE

end
```

There are two image types that are used for displaying this icon. Sometimes the image is in GIF format, and sometimes it is in JPEG format. In order to assure that our image displays properly we have to make sure that the image on the stage is the same type as the image that we are swapping in. We do this by checking to see if the file name actually contains the .GIF extension. If it does then we swap in our placeholder GIF file. If the file name doesn't contain the string .GIF we can be pretty sure that the file is a JPEG, and we swap in that particular place holder. Once we're sure we are displaying the right file format we simply set the fileName property of that member to the filename (using the full path to that file via the Internet). The last thing this handler does is hide our "loading" image and show our placeholder, which now contains the image icon for this particular story.

Part 7: Done – waiting for user input

At this point our playback head should be comfortably looping at the frame labeled DONE. If we've made it this far then we've successfully completed the task of hooking Director into an XML document and displaying the data we found within that document.

The user has a few options now. There are several hotspots or buttons on the stage. Let's take a quick look at these. These buttons (4, 5, and 6) allow users to interact with our movie and XML data:

The REFRESH HEADLINES button (5) will send the playback head to the point in the movie where the XML document is read and parsed. This is handy since Slashdot's content is updated quite often.

The lower center portion of the interface (4) has three active areas. The small arrows pointing to the left and right allow navigation back and forth across the (usually) ten story headlines that will be available at any one time. When the user presses one of these arrow buttons the value of gProps.pCurrHeadline changes, sending the playback head back to the frame labeled DISPLAY. The READ THIS STORY button executes the following bit of code:

```
tStoryURL = gProps.pStoryData[gProps.pCurrHeadline].pURL
gotoNetPage(tStoryURL,"_blank")
```

This opens a new browser window and loads the URL for the current story, based on the data we've culled from the XML document.

At the far right, there is the ABOUT THIS... button. This button displays a screen with some information about this application.

One more item that deserves notice is the spinning /. on the top left corner of our movie (7). This is one of Director 8.5's coolest new features: 3D text. It has nothing to do with databases, but I had to throw it in just to spice this movie up a bit. Clicking on it will launch the Slashdot home page.

Next we will look at how to get this, and other types of information, into Director from other sources, namely a web database.

The following example is more advanced and requires that you have basic knowledge of what a database is and how to create one on the Web. If you need more information on this topic check the resources listing at the end of this chapter.

Slashdot.org database news reader

We've just seen how we can access the XML data posted by Slashdot to build our own little Slashdot headline reader. While we have this fresh in our minds I would like to consider another possible option. What would this process be like if the Slashdot headline data had come from an Internet database rather than an XML document?

The concept

Let's take the following purely fictitious database table as an example:

ID	420	421 - — —		
TITLE	Slackware 8.0	Released Review: A.I.	- -- --	
URL	http://slashdot. org/article.pl?sid= 01/07/01/1316222	http://slashdot.org/ article.pl?sid= 01/06/30/0751239		- -- --
TIME	7/1/2001 13:33	7/1/2001 16:30	- -- --	
AUTHOR	CmdrTaco	michael	- -- --	
COMMENTS	174	71	- -- --	
IMAGE	topiclinux.gif	topicmovies.gif	- -- --	

For the sake of simplicity I have only used five of the elements that were used in the XML example, and two headlines, but you get the picture. This is an imaginary database table that contains the current story headlines and information available on Slashdot's site. The database itself could have been created in any number of ways. For this example we'll imagine that the database has been created and populated with all the information we need and is living on our server as a data source named slashdot. Let's say that the table we're looking at is named headlines.

One thing to keep in mind is that almost all of our existing code will work with minor adjustments. All we are replacing is the source of the information we are going to display. So, rather than loading an XML document, we'll be loading data from a CGI script file that will be accessing our database. As we've mentioned earlier, this CGI script can be written in a variety of languages.

How database news reader works

Let's take a look at what a couple of these scripts might look like, and then at how Director will talk to these scripts.

The CGI script: ColdFusion version

In ColdFusion our CGI file would be named getHeadlines.cfm, and would contain the following bit of code:

```
<cfquery name="headlineQuery"
         datasource="slashdot"
```

```
                username="theUserName"
                password="thePassword">

        SELECT * FROM headlines

    </cfquery>

    <cfoutput query="headlineQuery">
    #TITLE#,#URL#,#TIME#,#AUTHOR#,#COMMENTS#,#IMAGE#^
    </cfoutput>
```

The details of this code are out of the scope of this chapter, but here's a brief of what's going on.

The first tag, CFQUERY, begins a query of the database. A query takes certain parameters, usually written in some form of SQL, and returns all of the records in the database that matches this criteria. Our SQL statement simple says: select everything (*) from the table named `headlines`.

The second tag, CFOUTPUT, will loop through the data returned by our query and execute whatever code is within the tag for each record found.

The code we're executing simply writes out the data in a comma-delimited format and separates each record with a carat (^) character. This will allow us to later distinguish between each of the records returned.

The CGI Script: PHP/MySQL Version

The same script we just saw, translated to PHP would look *something* like this:

```
// Connect to DSN and DB
$mysql_link = mysql_connect
("theLocationOfTheDatabase","theUserName","thePassowrd");
mysql_select_db("slashdot",$mysql_link);

$query = "SELECT * FROM headlines";
$mysql_result = mysql_query($query,$mysql_link);

// GRAB THE VALUES
while ($row = mysql_fetch_array($mysql_result)) {
        $thisline = "";
        $thisline .= $row["title"].",";
        $thisline .= $row["url"].",";
        $thisline .= $row["time"].",";
        $thisline .= $row["author"].",";
        $thisline .= $row["comments"].",";
        $thisline .= $row["image"]."^";

        echo $thisline;
                };
```

```
//close connections;
mysql_close($mysql_link);
```

It takes a little more scripting to do this in PHP and MySQL, but many would argue that it's well worth the effort to use this powerful and inexpensive combination. It's possible that portions of this script are unnecessarily verbose, but the output returned to Director should be the same. For more information about PHP script take a look at the resource list at the end of this chapter.

The CGI script: other versions

A similar CGI script could be written in a variety of server-side scripting languages - take your pick! There are pros and cons to each of the choices. Some have platform limitations and others pose budgetary or technical concerns. The truth is that you should take a look at the options, talk to folks who have experience with these techniques, and come to a decision. The decision can be obvious sometimes. At other times the decision is forced upon you by a client or by a particular hosting scenario. Either way, you now have the means, or at least a push in the right direction!

Enough about that, let's take a look at what these CGI scripts are going to give back to us and how we can make use of it in our Director applications.

Parsing the CGI script

Once the database is set up and our CGI script is in place we tell Director to getNetText from the script files. The script file will access the database and format the information in the way we have set up. It will get the following string in return (based on the two records in our imaginary table):

```
"Slackware 8.0 Released,
http://slashdot.org/article.pl?sid=01/07/01/1316222, 2001-07-01
13:33:49, CmdrTaco, 174, topicmovies.gif ^ Review: A.I,
http://slashdot.org/article.pl?sid=01/06/30/0751239, 2001-07-01
16:30:40, Michael, 71, topiclinux.gif"
```

At first glance this may look like a mess, but in reality it's much like the very first database example in this chapter. It's a list, and using Director's flexible list handling capabilities we're only a couple of steps away from pStoryData, the property list from which we culled the data needed to make our headline display. The main difference is that, rather than pulling child node information like we did in the parseXMLdata handler, we'll be pulling items from a list. There is one trick that you should be aware of before you try this on your own. As you might recall, the carat character separates the records. You will have to change Director's default itemDelimiter from a comma to the carat in order to loop through these records, and then back to a comma to pull the data from each particular record. The code for this would look something like this:

```
on parseCGIdata

    the itemDelimiter = "^"
```

```
      tInputData = netTextResult(gProps.pNetID)

      - - NOTE: If you want to try this on your own just uncomment
   ➡ the next
      - - 5 lines and comment the previous uncommented line.

      - - tInputData ="Slackware 8.0 Released,\
      - - http://slashdot.org/article.pl?sid=01/07/01/1316222, 2001-07-
   ➡ 01
      - - 13:33:49, CmdrTaco, 174, topicmovies.gif ^ Review: A.I, \
      - - http://slashdot.org/article.pl?sid=01/06/30/0751239, 2001-07-
   ➡ 01
      - - 16:30:40, Michael, 71, topiclinux.gif"


      - - Count the number of records in our data
      tRecordCount = tInputData.item.count

      tStoryData = []

      - - Step Through Each Record in Our Data
      repeat with tRecord = 1 to tRecordCount

        tThisRecord = item tRecord of tInputData

        the itemDelimiter = ","

        tThisStoryData = [:]

        - - Create properties from each
        tThisStoryData.addProp(#pTitle, item 1 of tThisRecord)
        tThisStoryData.addProp(#pURL, item 2 of tThisRecord)
        tThisStoryData.addProp(#pTime, item 3 of tThisRecord)
        tThisStoryData.addProp(#pAuthor, item 4 of tThisRecord)
        tThisStoryData.addProp(#pComments, item 5 of tThisRecord)
        tThisStoryData.addProp(#pImage, item 6 of tThisRecord)

        - - Add this story's data to a temporary list of lists
        tStoryData.append(tThisStoryData)

        the itemDelimiter = "^"

      end repeat

      - - Store our List of Lists
      gProps.pStoryData = tStoryData


    end
```

> *You can find this handler in the* `db_slashdot_reader.dir` *file in a movie script cast member named* `EXAMPLE : PARSE CGI SCRIPT`.

Notice that there are many similarities between this script and the script that we used to parse the XML data. Keep in mind, as you follow along the other versions of the CGI script, that this bit of code will remain the same as long as we have our CGI file return the data in the same format.

Also, keep in mind that it's always a good idea to do error and data integrity checks on your data. You should make sure that you get something back from the CGI file, and that it's in the format that your Director code is expecting. Otherwise, you may be stumped by any number of script errors, especially the infamous Index out of range error (which means that Director is looking for a list item that doesn't exist).

Summary

As you can see by these examples, and the other methods theorized in this chapter, there are many ways for Director to interface with data. These methods and techniques vary in execution, but the logic behind them all is the same: locate and read your data, interpret or parse your data, utilize and display your data.

The beauty of these applications is beyond skin deep. They can allow you to do things with Director and Shockwave that may have once seemed beyond reach. The flexibility and portability of data stored external to an application will yield a more useful project. You will have a more efficient work distribution in larger groups and the ability to put new interfaces, graphic or otherwise, to this information.

Hopefully you have come away with enough knowledge to choose for yourself which technique suits your particular job, deadline, skill set, or budget. Don't forget to follow up what you have learned here with a bit of research in the topics that interest you the most. The following list of references and resources is a good starting point.

References and resources

List-based databases

www.macromedia.com/support/Director/how/show/list/complexlist.html
www.Director-online.com/accessArticle.cfm?id=953

FileIO examples and tech notes

www.macromedia.com/support/Director/ts/documents/sample_fileio.htm
www.macromedia.com/support/Director/ts/documents/tn3192.html

XML resources and tech notes

www.xml.com
www.stars.com/Authoring/Languages/XML/
www.xml.com/pub/a/1999/09/expat/index.html
www.macromedia.com/support/Director/internet/using_xml_parser_xtra/
www.macromedia.com/support/Director/internet/xml/xml_Lingo_dict/

Database information and resources

www.stars.com/Authoring/DB/
www.mysql.com/
www.microsoft.com/sql/
www.microsoft.com/office/access/

CGI language resources

PHP
www.php.net
www.phpbuilder.com

ASP
www.asp.net/
www.4guysfromrolla.com
p2p.wrox.com

PERL
www.perl.com/

COLDFUSION
www.coldfusion.com/
www.cfhub.com/

Multiuser server and databases

poppy.macromedia.com/multiuser/
www.macromedia.com/support/director/multiuser/multiuser/ then follow the link titled "Using the Shockwave Multiuser Server and Xtra"

Database Xtras

www.macromedia.com/software/xtras/Director/
www.integration.qc.ca/
www.datagrip.com/
www.paradigmasoft.com/

Chapter 15
Plan and Process

Being skilled in the intricacies of Director is one thing, but taking all these skills and putting them together to build a truly engaging piece is a skill in its own right. That's what this chapter is about.

Good planning and a good working process are not only important for successful collaborative work, but also for individual projects. As designers of interactive work, our field has become a hybrid of many other disciplines. Clearly a lot of what we do has its roots in the rich history of graphic design, but we also have to work in significant aspects of software engineering, product design, even urban planning and architecture. Creating a Director project usually involves design, copywriting, programming, animation, illustration, project management, information architecture and usability analysis. So it's easy to see that even if you're working on your own, things can get just as fragmented, because it's rather too easy to get immersed and comfortable in our work that we stop being able to see it from an outside perspective. By deriving each aspect of the work - the interactions, the imagery, the design, the text and the code - from the same initial concepts, your work can become much richer.

For the most part, the sort of things we'll talk about in this chapter are, well, stuff many of us would rather leave to someone else. I know you're here to learn how to create cutting-edge code, and push your Director skills to the edge, and that sweet-talking clients and creating a detailed process–plan may be one of the last things on your mind.

The fact is, though, that all the Director skills in the world won't amount to much without a clear concept, and a good plan. Even a collection of the most talented designers, coders and illustrators won't be able to create something that the client really wants and is pleased with if they all go off in their own direction on a project. That sort of work is important in its own right, but it is not often what your clients are looking for.

So in this chapter, we'll be discussing the importance of process, and of the right *sort* of process. As we've all discovered, interactive work changes as we build it. Ideas just turn up half way through; limitations rear their ugly heads long after they should have been accounted for. The ability to work a flexible process within a structure is arguably the single most important characteristic of truly groundbreaking work. As Bruce Mau puts it, *"When the outcome drives the process we will only ever go where we've already been."*

So, while it is important to plan your work, it is also important not to become a slave to that plan, and this is the sort of process we'll be looking at here. I believe that a Director project can be very much alive in its own right. Director's open architecture encourages this. It can accumulate its own inertia or develop its own drive. How many times has a bewildered Project Manager cornered you with the query, "But I thought you were going to do it this way?" The changes that occur during the process of a project – the life that project acquires can be very exciting and we should not fight these changes by always cutting back a project to its initial plan. We need to be able to incorporate them within a fluid process that enables the development of a fabulous piece of work, not one that restricts you into delivering half solutions and kludges.

In this chapter I will go over techniques for nurturing that life within a realistic professional environment. We're going to look at the steps in a typical project-plan, some guidelines for writing a brief, tips for meeting deadlines while still leaving the vital time for exploration, and talk about how we can nurture process within these steps to keep the project a living, growing entity. We'll be working through a five-step process:

- The brief: developing a brief that is going to deliver a project that at the very least meets the clients requirements

- The storyboard: using your storyboard as a framework for the creative developmental process

- Delegating workload: ensuring that every element works as a part of the whole

- Implementing and organizing the project

- Perpetuating the creative process through to completion

I'll also be dealing with some tips and tricks for organization – using naming conventions, and working with casts across a multi–author project. I'll share with you some of the best ways I've found for communicating effectively with clients. I hope that you'll find these suggestions enable you in your own working processes.

Step 1: The brief

If you are working on a professional project, you will probably be presented with a brief by the client. If you haven't been, then you must write one yourself. Even if you've been presented with one, don't be afraid to really work with it, and to push it quite hard until you're happy that the brief does exactly what it needs to do: enable a working solution. Working out a brief is very important, even for personal projects, because it gives you the opportunity to really think around the idea, to flesh out the concepts and the goals of the project before diving into the application.

A brief should pose the problem that the project is going to solve. It should establish the audience for the project, and it should detail any constraints for the project. Once you have a brief, you can start thinking about possible applications to solve the problem posed in it, and then through a series of scenario tests, see how different proposed solutions work.

Let's look at a classic example (although not specifically Director-related), of something that could have been alleviated with some proper work on a brief: mobile phone traffic update services. Several companies have created services designed to give you the traffic news for the region you are in. Simply punch in some details about where you are, and the phone gives you the best route. Although it sounds like a good idea, these services have been relatively unsuccessful. Consider a possible scenario, and an alternative to the proposed solution.

Imagine that the brief was: *build a traffic service that uses the mobile phone's browsing capabilities*. Now let's have a scenario:

> *Frank is driving to work and he wants to know which way to go to best avoid the traffic.*

A moving car may not be the best place to be fiddling with the tiny keypad on his mobile phone. Add to that the fact Frank will have to pay for every minute he uses his phone. If he flips his radio on to the traffic station, he can get frequent traffic updates for free, and keep his eyes on the road the entire time.

So that flags up an interesting question. If could get hold of a real brief, what would we find behind it? Well, it seems unlikely that what we would have found to be the driving force behind the idea was that people need traffic updates. If someone had researched that problem, they would have found that traffic updates are readily available, free, and don't impose upon the driver's control of the car. There wasn't a problem there. The problem the phone company needed to solve was probably something like: "How do we encourage people to use our phones?" There's a myriad of solutions to that brief; everything from stock quotes to flat pricing structures. Often it is the unspoken need that is at the base of the project.

When we write briefs as solutions without examining scenario and alternatives, we lock ourselves into a solution that may not be ideal. Phrased as a problem that needs to be solved and , considering the people who will be using our creation, we open up the path to innovative solutions, and can save the client a lot of wasted effort and money.

So, now we've established that a brief is vital, how do we go about developing one?

Researching your brief

Let's suppose that you are working with a client. You've been brought in to meet with the client, and to develop a brief from the ensuing discussions. Obviously, you need to really listen to them, because although they may not know how best to implement a solution to their needs, they do know *what* the problem they are trying to solve is, and they know their own company and their own customers. You should come away from these discussions with a really solid basis for creating your own brief.

Starting the dialogue with general concepts and goals will give you the freedom to come up with innovative solutions that really achieve what the client wants, rather than allowing discussions to be diverted into potential application solutions that don't necessarily meet the criteria of the problem too early on.

Really work at finding the *emotional center* of the project. The emotional center is the thing that the client really wants to say to their future customers (the people that will be using your product). You might ask the client to write a paragraph to explain the emotional center of the project: what are they trying to achieve? Who are their customers, and what sort of experience are they looking to give those customers? I also find that noting down the keywords that come up during these early discussions can be a very useful starting point.

Once you have a few keywords, and a clear idea of the emotional center, then you can start to build the brief. The brief should cover:

What the project is for	This is, after all, why you're talking with the client at all. What problem is this piece trying to solve? Your design ideas should come from the concept of the piece, not the embellishments you might add to help achieve those concepts. What's the underlying concept?
Who is it for?	Who makes up the audience it's aimed at?

What are the constraints?   You do need to find out at this very early stage about any constraints you might come up against.

What you *don't* need at this stage are details about the application of these concepts. If your client presents you with a brief that includes an application, *ignore it*, at least, ignore it at first,while you work from the brief to determine the best application with your team. If that application just happens to jive with the application the client has proposed, great, but if not, don't be afraid to come back to the client with suggestions for a different application.

Once you have all this information, you're ready to write your brief. The brief should not only help you analyze your project in abstract terms, but should also provide grounding for the various aspects of the project so that everything flows together.

Of course, you won't always be in the luxurious position of being brought into the project right at the beginning, so this approach is not always possible. Director developers are often brought into a project already well under way, to deal with a specific aspect of the project, and revamping the entire approach is just not an option. But you should still take that step back, and make sure that you're happy that the way the client has asked you to solve his or her problem is the best one. There's usually plenty of room for adapting the approach within a Director piece in most situations.

Writing the brief

There are many ways to approach a brief, but from my experience a brief is most useful when it answers the three questions we just looked at: Why? Who? Within what constraints? Here's a fictional brief, provided by a fictitious client. Lets apply the guidelines we've talked about to see how we could improve it.

> *A museum needs a kiosk that provides information about the exhibit, and lets people purchase related gift-shop items by credit card.*

This brief has already committed a couple of brief writing sins: it's straight in there with the solution (a kiosk that can take credit cards), hasn't identified whom the project is designed for, and hasn't really posed any problem. It's purportedly solved the problem without establishing what the problem is.

So, let's look at the people who'll be using this product. It's helpful to craft a few scenarios to help us identify who will be using it, and how they will be using it. This enables us to see the shortcoming of any brief, and encourages us to be open–minded to alternative solutions to the one proposed at the outset.

Testing the brief with scenarios

A little discussion with the client brings up a few scenarios for you.

Scenario 1
> *Children on a recent school trip weren't reading the text accompanying the exhibit, and so weren't learning what they could from the museum.*

We've got a 'who' and we've got a problem to solve. There are a lot of potential solutions to this, and undoubtedly one of them could very well be an engaging kiosk that provides the information to the children more dynamically and therefore engages them better than just text. But there are plenty of others:

- Vivid posters might provide the same information better, and to more than one person at a time

- Personal audio tours

- Booklets designed for children

- Some sort of portable interactive device: something the museum patrons could carry with them as they meander through the exhibit.

So then, what happens when we factor in the related gift shop items? Posters and booklets won't help people purchase related items on the spur of the moment and children can't use credit cards, so the proposed solution immediately alienates one potential source of the client's income. Well, maybe we could make a kiosk that accepts cash, or a personal interactive device that can be loaded with a preset store credit when the unit is rented. Then the children could buy related gift shop items while in the exhibit.

Let's look at another scenario with another set of possible users.

Scenario 2

An elderly couple wants to buy a poster of the painting that depicts an apple in front of the face of a man wearing a bowler hat, but can't remember the artist or the name of the painting when they arrive at the gift shop at the end of their trip. Besides, the gift shop is overrun with noisy children who, bored with the text descriptions of the paintings, have diverted their attentions to ransacking the gift shop.

Here, the problem isn't to do with reading the text, but with remembering it. We can also see from this scenario that the gift shop appears to be ill placed and overburdened.

A possible solution could be to build smaller gift shops near the exhibit spaces that only contained items directly related to the rooms they bordered. This would help ease the burden on the main gift shop, and inspire more spur-of-the-moment purchases when patrons saw paintings in the museums they particularly enjoyed. It wouldn't, however, solve the problem of dull text accompanying the paintings. Coupling vivid posters with these smaller gift shops could solve both problems. A personal interactive device that accepted credit cards or was loaded with pre-paid credit to the gift shop could also solve the same problem.

By ignoring the client's proposed application and examining the proposed brief through scenario and problem posing, we are really thinking around the problem, and have some alternative suggestions that may be better suited to the museum's problem. More importantly, though, we have a much clearer idea of what the problem that needs solving is.

So, now we're able to rephrase the brief along the guidelines we covered at the beginning of this exercise:

The museum's gift shop is always full, and many people complain of not being able to easily acquire the items they want. The museum needs a way to make it easier for patrons to purchase gift shop items related to the exhibits, as well as a more interesting way to explain the exhibition than the text currently accompanying the paintings.

The museum's patrons range from groups of children to elderly couples, and we need to create something that will interest the entire range of patrons, as well as enable them to make purchases quickly and easily while still in the exhibit space. The museum has up to $200,000 for the initial phase of the project, and three months to complete it.

By phrasing the brief as a problem to be solved rather than as a solution to be implemented, we have already started nurturing a more flexible process. We have a clear idea of the reasons behind the project, as well as the audience who will be using what we create. We know the constraints that we are faced with, and the goals the client wishes to achieve with this project.

Of course, the client will usually require something firmer than an open–ended brief before they will entrust their project to you. But it is my belief that the brief is not the place to firm up the details of the application. You can't get to the specifics of delivery until you have proposed a solution, and you can't propose a solution until you really understand the problem. Once you have a well crafted brief, you can open it up to the entire team, and then work out some solutions that you'll pitch to the client. After the general approach has been agreed upon, you can nail down the specifics in what is often referred to as the "statement of work" or "service-level agreement."

This brings up a sticky point in client and product management. Sometimes what is best for the client is not necessarily what he or she has asked for. Our job is often to give the client what he or she *needs*, not just what he or she *wants*. For this to work the client has to truly trust you and your team. We have all experienced the frustration of being forced to implement what we may consider a less than ideal solution to the client's problem, and the brief is the best point at which to propose alternative solutions.

This of course means meeting up with the client.

Approaching the client or manager

In this example the museum has very likely already hired a team of consultants who have decided this solution is the best option. They have undoubtedly uncovered some problems with alternative solutions, so you may not be in the place to significantly change the brief. Nevertheless, there are ways of managing these discussions that can make them very much more fruitful.

Tips for approaching the client
In general, when you have changes to suggest, it's better to come back to the client saying that you can and will implement their solution, and that you have some additional ideas. They'll feel that you're going to be giving them what they want, and you'll be demonstrating that you have gone above and beyond what was needed to make the project even better. It's even a good idea to use this approach when you're dealing with briefs from project managers or upper management. Think about it from their perspective. They have spent some time and money getting this idea together. They have a deadline to meet, and they are enlisting your services in

delivering their product by the proposed deadline. Your job is to make their lives easier by making the product better, not to complicate their lives by rethinking every one of their decisions. So, how do you handle this fact finding mission elegantly? It's a touchy situation, and one we have probably all experienced.

1. **Avoid the word "but"**
   Even when your ideas contradict the person you are dealing with, frame them so that they come across as perfectly aligned. It can be as simple as using the word "and" in place of "but". Ideally, it means presenting your ideas for what they really are: ideas for developing the project to its best possible framework, not fighting the client or manager's ideas with your own.

2. **Remember that you're a team**
   Be sure it doesn't come over as 'you against me'. You just need to remember that you are both working on the same project, and you both have the same goals. If the project is a success and is delivered on time, then you both win. Make sure this comes across in your language. So, for example, if you mean, "You asked for this, but I don't think that is the best way to do it," you could say, "Yes, I see what the goals of this project are, and here are some ways we can achieve our goals."

3. **Explore the context of the project together**
   A client or project manager will be a lot less leery of change if he or she feels it is what he is supposed to be delivering. Your suggestions, even if they involve a major rework, will receive less push-back if they seem in line with what he or she was asking for. And new ideas can be effortlessly integrated if they seem like they came from his or her initial idea. The way to do this is just to approach the conversation the same way we discussed approaching the brief. Start talking about the goals you deduced from the brief, and with your ideas in mind, start stepping the concept closer and closer until the other person gets the obvious "aha" insight him or herself. Treat the ensuing discussions that lead to a solution as a kind of shared exploration, which will help your ideas come across as more in tune with the project's goals. It will also open up the way for the client or manager him or herself to come up with ideas that really do solve the problem.

You may well be sitting there thinking: what does romancing my manager have to do with Director work? What do I care about mincing words? I am a Director author, not a client–relations manager.

Well, yes, it's true. In an ideal world you wouldn't need to spend valuable time romancing your managers. But it's still a good thing to do. Have you ever implemented a solution that you're not entirely happy with? How many times have you heard (or even said), "Well, I wanted to do it this way, but my boss made me do this, so..." An examination of project flow by the Communication Research Institute of Australia (www.communication.org.au) found that 50% of the time spent on projects were consumed by politics.

If you work on your own, freelancing your Director skills as a contractor, or if you work as part of a team, spending some time to think about how you approach the client or manager in a project will allow you and your work to go much further. As a freelancer, you'll be dealing directly with clients, so when you come upon a sticky situation, it's good to know how to make it work out. So, although manipulating relationships for the good of the project is not an ideal situation, it can often be the unfortunate reality.

So anyway, now you and the client are getting along splendidly, and you and your team have developed a pretty clear idea of the application that's going to meet the client's needs, let's get back to the project.

Step 2: The storyboard

Once you've written a good brief and your entire team has a very good idea of the problem that's being addressed, it's time to storyboard the specifics of the project.

So what are storyboards good for?

Storyboards really are a good idea. They enable you, your team and your client to:

- Visualize how the finished project will work

- Visualize how the process of creating the project will work

- Share ownership: garnering and focusing the creative juices of all involved parties

- Maintain a collective focus: ensuring that everything in the project ties in with the whole.

The first stages of the storyboard development will help the team come up with the specifics of the project to be presented to the client. I'm sure you've heard the horror stories about overzealous sales teams talking the client up on a solution that would be implausible to implement. By involving everyone early on, we come up with a specification that reflects the direction the team wants to take.

Focus and ownership

As we discussed earlier, producing interactive work involves a lot of different roles, many of which overlap, and it's important to organize your workflow so that you get the maximum input from each of these areas. It's incredibly important for the good of the whole project that everyone has a feeling of ownership for the project, and has their input early on in the process, so that you're all working towards the same goals. Only then can you safely leave room for the changes and growth that naturally occur during the process.

> *A storyboard is something everyone can participate in, before the investment of time, code and technology has made change harder to rationalize. The storyboard is a wonderful, low-tech way to get everyone involved in determining the flow of the piece.*

We've all experienced the problems that occur when all the roles of a Director piece are not involved in the initial concept building. Programmers brought in late in the game may make wonderful suggestions, or point out deficiencies in the plan, for example, but after so much time and effort has been put into the project, it is difficult to pull back and start again. And the last thing you need from the copywriter is something completely out of kilter with the rest of the project.

Visualizing the finished project
In the initial stages, don't worry about hammering the details of the storyboard down too tightly. As everyone starts to work on their own aspects of the project, a clearer picture will begin to emerge of the constraints that you will be working within. It's good to meet often to discuss these developments, and update the storyboard so that pretty soon it does contain specifics like stage-size and file names.

It's important that every piece in the finished project tells the same story; every individual aspect of the project, as well as every interaction must head toward the same story, so map interactivity as well as content onto the storyboard. Whether you're working in a group or on your own, you need everything to cohere. Even on a personal project, the distinct aspects of your piece can get just as disjointed working alone as in a group. Truly exceptional interactive work is interrelated at every level.

Visualizing the process
Once you've created a draft storyboard, with everyone's input, you can begin honing it into something more functionally useful.

Although the term is borrowed from filmmakers and animators, the storyboard for an interactive piece can be much richer. I use the storyboard as an enhanced sitemap, or in Director's case, movie map. Flesh out each section of the movie, detail the kinds of interactions that can take place, and where in the storyboard each interaction will take you. You can also start figuring out which media might be appropriate for different sections, and what each person will need to do in each section. At this point, gaps should become very clear, and you can take action to remedy them.

By the end, the storyboard will be a place to which everyone can refer to and remind themselves what they need to do, and how their own role fits into the greater picture of the project as a whole. While you don't want to become a slave to the storyboard, there's no way you could possibly imagine at the outset all the possibilities the project will need to cover, so you'll be updating the storyboard throughout the project. It's a kind of fluid, living document.

Once you've created your storyboard, make sure your team as well as your client has a copy. Just printing it out on large paper and putting it on poster board makes the whole process seem that much more in the works. It's also a good idea to design your storyboard in a program like Freehand or Illustrator – for one thing, you can import it into Director in one swift move should you need to. You could even put it on the Web for the client to see, so they feel confident that you are actively building their project (you won't get constant phone calls, "So how far are you now?").

Creating a storyboard

I'll walk you through a storyboard for a past Director project of mine, and hopefully you'll see how tightly integrated it became with the final product.

When I first started working in design, my work was largely based on educational projects. A few years down the line, I realized I had begun to drift away from educational projects, and I wanted to build another educational Director project to get me back in the groove of this sort of work. My goal with designhistoryinabox.net was to provide an educational site about design history for designers. So my initial brief was:

> Create a project that will help you get back into educational Director work. It will be aimed at people in the design community, fellow designers. It will also be self–promotional, and accessible to design-directors who need people to help create educational Director projects, people at museums for instance. And get it done before the summer's over.

> *A word about deadlines: even in personal projects where there are no deadlines, it is often a good idea to set deadlines for yourself. I've found that after the initial excitement of beginning one personal project, it doesn't take too long before some new idea becomes "the next great thing" and it can often be hard to stick with that first idea through to the end. I'm not the only one either; see the May 1st reboot (*www.threeoh.com*), set by a group of designers for putting up a new website.*

So, back to the project. I know that many designers have little patience with huge reams of text online, so I knew I wanted to keep the text descriptions down to a minimum. Besides, a picture tells a thousand words, so as long as the images I created painted an appropriate picture of each design era, I knew I could portray an immense amount of information without pages and pages of text.

I wanted to talk about the different eras and trends through design history, but I didn't just want to create a shell around other people's work; I wanted to create the work myself. I wanted this to be a simple, compact site that condensed all of design history into a tiny little box.

When I started researching design history in detail, I came up with over fifty different eras, trends and areas that I wanted to cover. I also knew I wanted this to grow as a collaborative project in the end, so I needed some way for people to submit their own designs to the piece. I started breaking these out into the different media and roles I'd need to fulfill for each aspect of the project; sort of a draft enhanced movie map. Pretty soon I had a huge list, and I knew I didn't want some ungainly side navigation bar with link upon link of info, so I had to come up with another way for people visiting the site to explore the information.

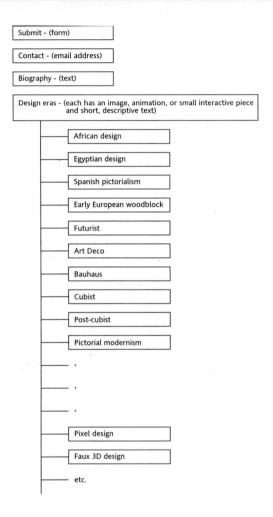

The goal began to emerge: I would create a project that condensed design history into a simple, compact interface, using my own art and sparse text as the vehicle to portray this information.

So I started working out the storyboard to put down my ideas for creating a compact and intuitive method for navigating the piece.

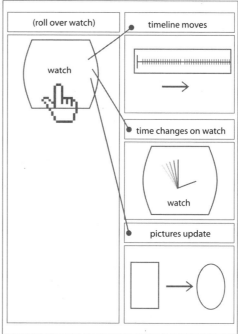

Storyboarding the layout

It's always tempting to leap right into the layout at this point, but I like to force myself to hold off on design until I've identified the way it will work.

The layout for this piece flowed pretty naturally from the concept behind the piece. I wanted to create a compact box in which to hold design history. I applied this rather literally and came up with the idea of an old letterbox, the kind that held lead and wooden type back when most printing was done by letterpress.

A box like this:

To hold type like this:

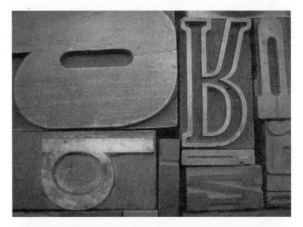

or this:

As this was meant to be an educational piece about design history, I decided to apply one of the oldest design guidelines to the letterbox: the golden rectangle, a rectangle divided in a certain ratio (around 1:1.6180) thought since Ancient Greek times to be particularly pleasing to the eye.

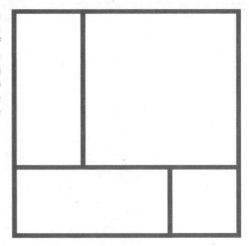

As you'll see when we get to the design, I fudged it a bit to make room for the timeline, but the basic construct is still the golden rectangle.

Once you've fleshed out the storyboard for the project, then you can it down into disparate elements, and from there, media elements and roles.

Storyboarding the elements
Now for the elements themselves. I wanted each piece, each 'thing' itself to stay the same, while the era of the piece changed to reflect the time in design history to which the person had traveled using this magical little box.

If I wanted to stay strictly literal, I could have simply used type in this box, and made the typeface and the material the type was made from update as we scrolled through design history. For example, we could have morphed from the language of cave painting to hieroglyphs to woodblock, to lead type, to digital type, from Roman letters to Garamond, to Futura, to Johnston to Benguiat, to Geneva, to Kottke's Silkscreen, to Eboy's PEECOL. The piece, however, wasn't to be about typography. I wanted it to be about graphic design in general, so I needed to select some graphical images to view through this history filter.

The inspiration eventually came from a Paul Simon song that was playing on my stereo as I got to this part of the process, some nonsense about "The penguin, the moon-glow, the Oreos...". At least that's what I thought he was singing about. In any case, I had my objects to put in this box: A penguin, a moon and a cookie. I would take these three objects and hurtle them through design history. The penguin could start as a Penguin a la Egyptian Ibis scribe, meander into some Cubist mutation, and settle down into a fat-pixel icon of a penguin. The moon and cookie would go through a similar adventure.

So there were the pieces. Now I had to work them into the media I was using (remember, the media is, in this case, part of the brief. In other projects, it won't necessarily be.) So then I had to start thinking about Director and it's interface. Director certainly used to be essentially timeline based, going back to its roots as an animation program. Traditional storyboards rely on the timeline as the action. A storyboard for an animation portrays how the images will change as time passes. Now, though, we can use Lingo and the cast to update elements on the stage interactively, irrespective of an overreaching timeline. In fact, most Director movies I've worked on are single frame affairs.

For interactive work, the interaction becomes the driving force rather than the time, so it is useful to approach the different panels in your storyboard based on the interaction that is causing the change. As you see below, "rollover watch" and "rollover image" are the driving actions in each of the panels. This is a simple piece. There are only four basic interactions that go on: rollover watch, rollover moon, rollover penguin and rollover cookie. We're not pushing the envelope of Director or really doing anything all that innovative; it's just a simple little piece that teaches a little about design history, so it was very easy to storyboard.

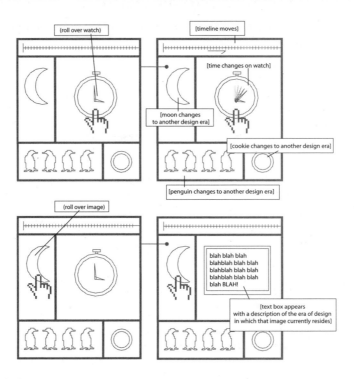

As you storyboard more complex projects, it may become less obvious how to organize your storyboard. Starting each panel with the interaction that drives it, and then organizing these panel sets into sections of the project can usually make a neat storyboard out of the most complex project. While I did this myself, in a shared project everyone could be involved in this process.

So you can see how the storyboard related to the final product in this case. Here are some snapshots of the finished director project. This is the splash page that shows the letterbox you've come across in this story:

And here is the interface you can actually play with:

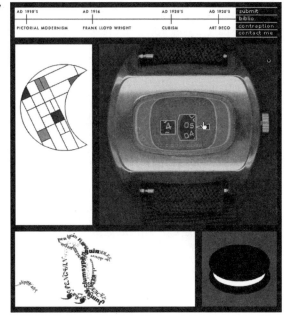

At this point it would be a good exercise to build your own storyboard. You could flip back to the project we built in the OOP chapter, and create a storyboard for that. There was very little interaction in that piece; we defined rules for the system and then hit the play button, setting the system into motion. If you break the process into steps, and think about the media used in each section of the piece, you could put it all together in a neat little package, and probably make something much more interesting to boot!

At this point in the process, you should go back into your storyboard and update it accordingly. While the storyboard is not the place to work out all of the details of design, it is a good place to put down the general layout once it has been designed, with graphical symbols to represent the different elements. This helps everyone on the team have a clearer image in their minds of what they're all working towards will look like.

Which brings us nicely to the next step in our process: The allocation of roles within the project. Once we've started to determine what exactly will be taking place in our project, we need to figure out who will be doing what.

Step 3: Delegating workload

Break down each section in your storyboard by role and by media. Let people suggest their own roles. Programmers don't just program, and writers don't just write. Everyone has ideas, and if everyone's ideas are integrated to fit, the project will be much stronger for it.

I firmly believe that everyone should have some input into, or at least some understanding of , every aspect of the project. This doesn't mean that everyone votes on how the design will look, or indeed how it will work, but it does mean that they will see the design at an early stage and that they will understand the reasons for designing it this way. It's a way of keeping everyone on the same page, so regardless of the specifics of their role in the project, they are building towards a unified whole. In the same way, everyone should have a basic understanding of how the back-end will be functioning, so that they can accommodate this process as best they can in their own work.

> *A big caveat: I am not advocating design by committee! Design is not a democratic process. Everyone should be aware of what is going on with the design, should feel free to offer suggestions and discuss what they can all do to make their pieces fit together. When it comes down to it, except for some unavoidable technical limitations, each person should feel that they are responsible for their own part of the project. Design by committee is a big no–no. By design here, I am not speaking only of the graphic design, but the design of the programming structure as well.*

With all this in mind, let's take another look at our storyboard for 'Design History in a Box', annotating it so that media and roles start to become apparent.

Breaking it down into media

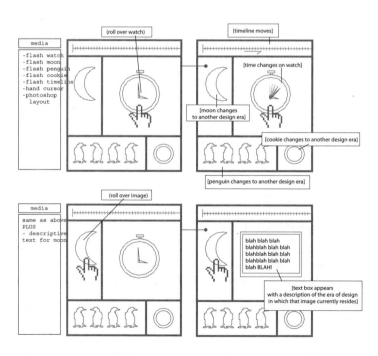

You'll notice that most of the media is Flash. Flash files are dynamic and small, so I tend to use Flash files for most of my vector cast members. When I built this project, a lot of what I wanted to do lent itself to Lingo rather than ActionScript, so Director was still the right choice for the authoring, and because I was initially designing a CD piece, size was not an issue. Flash 5 and the ActionScript that came with it wasn't around when I began this, and if I were to start this piece today, I may very well decide to build it entirely in Flash (actually, given my brief, I'd have probably built something entirely different). Either way, I often prefer to use Flash for the animation and Director for the authoring, and that is what I chose to do in this project.

Once we've figured out which media types are needed for the different areas of the project, we can then start to delegate workload based on the different media we'll need. In this case, we know that for each design era we will need a moon, a penguin and a cookie, as well as descriptive text for each object. The interface, the hand cursor, the watch and the timeline are all constants.

Now, many of us work on our own, so delegating roles to different people is not an issue. On a solo project, this is where you'd flesh out all the distinct roles you're going to have to play so that all aspects of the project will eventually slot together nicely. If you are working in a group, you'd allocate the roles using the same approach. We'd need a copywriter, maybe even a different one for each era. We'd need a designer to layout the overall interface and we'd need an illustrator to create the images themselves and a Flash animator to animate those illustrations that required it. Often, the same person handles the illustration and the animation, and, since this is the bulk of the work of the project, we may want to further divide the illustration/animation roles into subcategories. We could have one in charge of the penguin, one for the moon, and one for the cookie. Or perhaps we'd rather break it up historically, with different illustrators/animators taking different eras of design. The added benefit of this sort of delegation is that we'd be assured of more consistency between objects within an era. We'd also need a Lingo programmer, of course, and perhaps a project manager to keep it all moving together towards that almighty deadline.

Step 4: Implementing and organizing

By this point in the process we have a pretty clear idea of where this project is going (or so we think); it's bound to change as the project develops, but its good to start with a communal goal. In this scenario, the goal is:

> *Create a small box that contains design history within it. By fiddling with the watch in this box, the user can make the objects contained in the box morph through design history, changing from design style to design style as they zip through different eras. We want to keep everything short and simple. Action should be quick without being jumpy, and the text should be a short and easy read.*

Working out the organizational details

Now we can get down to the nitty-gritty of specifying the details of the project.. We won't be able to really work out the details until we're into the meat of it, but we can start by agreeing on some conventions. Building the storyboard has already pointed us towards a lot of the project flow.

For instance, looking at the storyboard, we can see two major functions in the movie. Rolling over the watch makes the timeline move, it makes the time change on the watch and it updates the images within the movie to the proper design era, as well as the text associated with each object for that era. Rolling over any of the objects brings up the text associated with that object in that time period.

We can also see on the size of the objects within the movie, their functions, and the maximum character count for any text description. At this point you can begin working in some naming conventions that you'll be using consistently throughout the project.

In this example, if each era is given a name we all agree on, then by adding the object's name and the type of media, the programmer can build a few modular scripts that will put everything in its proper place. The source for this script is included in the `dhiabox_basic.dir` file. There are a lot of other things going on in the movie; you'll find the following script in the MovieScript member.

In this movie I created three lists, one for each object:

```
—P=Penguin
—M= Moon
—O=Oreo

P_list = ["P_bushman", "P_egypt", "P_mali", "P_ghana", "P_block",
➡ "P_futurist", "P_artdeco", "P_bauhaus", "P_miro", "P_tanaka",
➡ "P_postm", "P_3d", "P_pixel"]

M_list = ["M_kenya", "M_spanpict", "M_earlyeur", "M_durer",
➡ "M_wright", "M_postcubist", "M_neth", "M_IntTypStyl",
➡ "M_igarashi", "M_kare"]

O_list = ["O_zulu", "O_celtic", "O_mack", "O_arch", "O_pictmod",
➡ "O_artdeco", "O_metro", "O_tube", "O_war", "O_lorenz", "O_wim",
➡ "O_woodward"]
```

The illustrator/Flash designer in charge of drawing and animating the individual objects, for example, names each Flash file with the *object name+design era*, and the copywriter names each text chunk as the *object name+design era*+*"text"*. I've simplified the object names down to the first letter of the object plus an underscore. So the Flash cast member for the bushman penguin would be named simply `P_bushman`. The text member associated with that flash member would be named `P_bushmantext`.

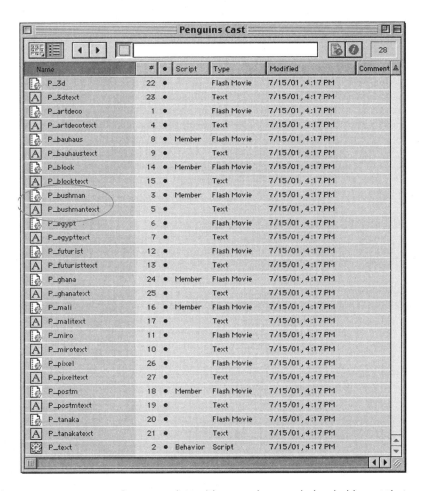

Now the programmer can craft some scripts with properly named placeholders at the same time as the illustrator/Flash designer and copywriter do their work.

Basically, the programmer needs to keep note of where in the lists the user is at any given moment in time. Another script (or aspect of that script) switches each Flash sprite in the Director score to the cast member with the name of that selection in the list. When we roll over that Flash piece, another script turns on the text which is named according to the name of the member of the sprite we rolled over + text. So, if the text field is in channel 8 of the movie, when we roll over any given object the following code runs:

```
On mouseEnter me
  sprite(48).member.text =
➡ member(sprite(thecurrentSpriteNum).member.name&"text").text
end
```

Rolling over P_bushman will make Director replace the sprite (a text member) in channel 48 with P_bushmantext. (You can find this script in text behavior.)

There are a couple of other things going on, such as moving the text box to the right place on the stage, along with the background and frame for the text box, but you'll be able to see this script working alongside all of that. That same script works for every possible incarnation of every object! By agreeing on naming conventions and by ensuring that everyone understands how the different aspects of the piece are going to work together, we can make everyone's lives much easier as we develop further.

Now, there is rarely just one person working in the Director environment. More often, we need to share our code with other people, so it is important to agree on some conventions amongst the programmers ourselves.

Conventions for sharing Director files

There are a number of ways you can organize your casts on a team project: using external casts, cast–less scripting, creating and updating lists on the fly. We'll look at those here.

Cast organization: external casts

I find it useful to allocate one cast for scripts, and then a few casts for the different categories of artwork. In the case of 'Design History in a Box', it might have been a good idea to create a script cast, a text cast and an art cast. Or to have organized them differently: you might have chosen to create a penguin cast, a moon cast, a cookie cast and a general interface cast.

If you're using casts, you'll need to save them as external files so you can share them. This is essential for maintaining consistency when a Director project involves multiple movies.

Working with external casts

1. To create an external cast, you create a new cast as you would any other, by clicking the cast selection button in the upper left corner of your cast and selecting New Cast...

2. Then select the External radio button, and depending on whether you want to use the cast in your current movie or not, check the tick box for Use in Current Movie.

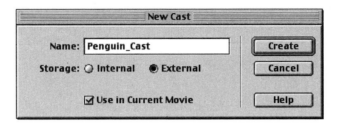

3. You can then save your external cast as you would any other file. Select the cast you want to save by opening it up and clicking somewhere in the cast, and when you go to save the file, Director will save the cast you are in rather than the Director movie.

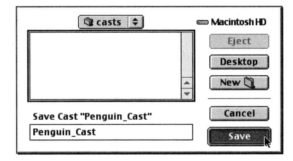

4. If you wanted access to that external cast from another Director file, you would just open up the cast the same way you would any Director movie.

There are a couple of things you need to watch out for when you're working with external casts. In the first place, keep an eye on your file structure. If you change the file structure of your Director piece (like creating new folders or moving the project to a different folder), Director will lose track of the cast and you'll need to link it back up again manually. Director will alert you that it can't find the cast.

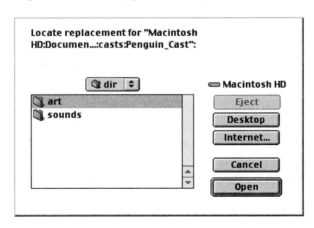

You can also run into versioning issues. If everyone on the project is working at the same location, you can all just share the cast from a central server. If you are all working in separate studios, however, you'll still be using individual copies of the same cast, so you'll need a way for determining which cast takes precedence. You'll need to sit down from time to time, discuss the changes you have made to the casts, and move all the new members into one super cast.

Having thought through the pitfalls of shared casts, you may well have decided that on your project you're going to minimize the number of casts you'll need to work with as a group. Director can directly reference files as they sit in their folders, rather than importing them into Director's casts. This will allow your illustrator/Flash designer and copywriter to simply save their work into a specified folder, and your programmer can code his or her work so that Director grabs these files from the folders to place them in the score without needing to hold every member in casts during authoring.

Cast organization: cast-less scripting
You can find in the source for this discussion in `dhiabox_cast-less.dir`.

You access file outside of director using the syntax: *member.filename*. So, if sprite 13 holds the penguins, then we could fill that sprite with the flash file `P_bushman.swf` with:

```
sprite(13).member.filename = P_bushman.swf
```

Of course, we wouldn't want to hard code like this. To make this script more modular so that it can work in a variety of circumstances, we would want to replace all the hard coded segments with references to general variables.

As you recall, `P_list` holds the names for all the different penguins that will be used in the movie. This list serves as the base from which we place the appropriate flash and text files in their appropriate channel in the score. It looks like this:

```
P_list = ["P_bushman", "P_egypt", "P_mali", "P_ghana", "P_block",
➥ "P_futurist", "P_artdeco", "P_bauhaus", "P_miro", "P_tanaka",
➥ "P_postm", "P_3d", "P_pixel"]
```

We access items in a list by referring to their place in the list. `P_list[1]` would be `P_bushman`. `P_list[6]` would be `P_futurist`. If we create a variable `P_listcounter` that holds the place in the list the penguins should be at, then we can access the external Flash file with the following:

```
sprite(13).member.filename = P_list[P_listcounter]&".swf"
```

> *Note that for this script to work on a PC you will have to set your Windows preferences so that the 3 letter suffixes (.doc, .txt, .swf) are visible.*

We then augment `P_listcounter` by 1 every time the numbers on the watch change, as the time flies by, Director figures out which Flash file to put in the appropriate slot. In this movie, there is a circular dial on the watch that contains all the numbers. As the dial rotates, a different number appears in the window. So I augment P_listcounter by 1 every time the dial rotates a certain amount. With the dial in sprite 4:

```
if sprite(4).rotation = -50.0000 then
    P_listcounter = P_listcounter + 1
    sprite(13).member.filename = P_list[P_listcounter]&".swf"
end if
```

It's actually better practice to use a local variable than keep repeating the entire segment of code P_list[P_listcounter]&".swf". So, I'd set a local variable P_temp = P_list[P_listcounter]&".swf", and update everything else to P_temp.

Lots of files in the same directory can get messy pretty fast, so we should create one folder for all the penguin files, one for all the moon files, and so on. Director holds the place that the movie is playing from in the @ symbol. So the path to the P_bushman.swf file, which resides within a folder named penguin, would be:

```
@/penguin/P_bushman.swf
```

In the context of our script, we would write that as:

```
P_temp = "@/penguin/"&P_list[P_listcounter]&".swf"
if sprite(4).rotation = -50.0000 then
    P_listcounter = P_listcounter + 1
    sprite(13).member.filename = P_temp
 end if
```

Changing this script to handle the text our copywriter has written would be as easy as changing every .swf to .txt, and ensuring that the copywriters and illustrators/Flash designers are naming everything according to agreed conventions.

I've left dhiabox_cast-less.dir with all the text members still inside the cast. If you wanted to apply what we've looked at here to the text members, you'd simply copy and paste each text description into its own text file, naming them as you go according to our conventions, and put them in a folder that you will then access from the Director movie. The text for P_bushman would be, then, P_bushmantext.

Cast-organization: creating lists on the fly
Using member.filename to bring external files into the movie in fact divorces a lot of the coding from the frequent updates that will be occurring to the Flash and text elements. Since the programmer, copywriter and illustrator/Flash designer have all agreed upon naming conventions, the programmer just needs to make sure his list accurately reflects the names the other two have given their files. But what if they decide to add a few new eras into the mix down the line? Then the programmer would need to update his lists to reflect those changes.

But there's really no need to do all this work when Director can do it for you. If you generate your lists on the fly, then you don't have to worry about incorporating every change into the code. By setting up your scripts to work within the file naming conventions and directory structure the team has agreed upon, the code can take on board any changes made by the copywriter or illustrator quickly and easily. (The source code for this example can be found in dhiabox_cast-less_makeList.dir. The script we are about to look at is in the MovieScript.)

The Lingo we will be using in this script is getNthFileNameInFolder, and the syntax for using it is:

```
getNthFileNameInFolder(folderPath, fileNumber).
```

So, to build a list for the penguins based on the flash files stored within the penguin folder, we could use the following script:

```
P_list = []
P_path = "@/penguin/"
P_list = makeTheList (P_list, P_path)

on makeTheList the_list, the_path
    repeat with i = 1 to 100
    n = getNthFileNameInFolder(the_path, i)
    if n = EMPTY then exit repeat
        the_list.append(n)
    end repeat
    return the_list
end makeTheList
```

We have set P_list equal to the result of the makeTheList handler, passing parameters for the list's name (P_list), and the path Director needs to follow to get to the folder it will build the list from (P_path). Here, the handler will repeat from 1 to 100. I used 100 because I doubt I'll ever create 100 different penguins. The script simply follows the path, grabs the file name of the first file in the penguin folder, and adds that name into the list. We defined P_list as an empty list by setting it equal to [], so the first entry will be the first item in the list.

It will then continue through each file in that folder until it can't find anymore, and then returns EMPTY. Then the handler exits the repeat loop and returns the list it has just created. P_list is now a list containing every name of every file in the penguin folder. And since the rest of the movie depends on this list, we don't have to change anything else in the movie. The list has always been the base for all the action; now we have just generated it on the fly rather than hard coding it into our code.

However, there is a problem. Chronological eras aren't, unfortunately, named alphabetically. The Art Deco period came a long time after the Egyptians were writing hieroglyphics, yet P_artdeco comes before P_egypt in our list, so our timeline is scrambled. So, let's amend their naming conventions. All we need to do is prefix each Flash file or text file with a number. And because everything is based on the list and Director builds that list according to the filenames in the folder, Director will accept these changes gracefully.

You'll notice that I have kept all the text members as members within the cast, and that they still use the member's name:

```
sprite(48).member.text =
member(sprite(13).member.name&"text").text
```

Since we never change the member's name, just the filename, the text will always be stuck on the first entry. In order to keep in line with this on the fly list making and cast-less scripting, you could rework the text update so that it works from the list directly, the same way Flash works from the list.

This method works great when you're running Director off of your computer or a projector on a CD, but if your project is destined to be a web site, you can start to get some lag as Director loads the new Flash or text file onto your computer and into the score every time it needs to bring up a new Flash or text member.

Cast-organization: updating casts on the fly (importFileInto)

One way to handle this is to let Director populate your cast with the external files on prepareMovie. That way, you get the benefit of having all your files kept external during authoring, which makes it easier for a team to share and update the files. Then, when it is time to create the shockwave movie, you run the following script once to let Director fill up the cast with the most recent versions of the file, comment out the cast update script, and make your Shockwave movie.

To save space, I'll just show the example for the penguins, but you would do the same thing for the Oreos and moons. The source for these scripts is in `dhiabox_importFile.dir`. First, the list needs to be defined, just as we did in the first example:

```
on prepareMovie
    P_listcounter = 1

    P_list = ["P_bushman", "P_egypt", "P_mali", "P_ghana",
➥ "P_block", "P_futurist", "P_artdeco", "P_bauhaus", "P_miro",
➥ "P_tanaka", "P_postm", "P_3d", "P_pixel", "P_bushman"]
```

Then you use `importFileInto` to update your cast with the most recent versions of the Flash files. The general syntax for `importFileInto` is:

```
importFileInto member whichCastMember, fileName
```

To apply that syntax to our scenario:

```
repeat with i = 1 to P_list.count
    importFileInto member member(P_list[i]),
("@/penguin/"&P_list[i]&".swf")
end repeat
```

As `count` counts the number of items in a list, `P_list.count` is the number of items in `P_list`. Here it will be 14. This script will run through each item in the list, importing the name of that item plus the `.swf` extension into the cast member with the name of the item.

This script exists to do the dirty work of updating our cast for us. It's a script designed to ease the flow during authoring, and not meant to go into the final product. So, when it is time to export the movie as Shockwave, we'd run the movie once to update the cast, comment out this helper script, and then export our movie as Shockwave. As long as our cast is updated before we make the Shockwave movie, we don't need this script to run every time a user calls up our movie.

In fact, if we left the script in the Shockwave movie, we'd get some unwanted results. Shockwave can only use `importFileInto` if it is preceded by a `preloadNetThing` command. Leaving this script as is would actually fill our cast members with blank spaces, as Shockwave would not be able to access any of the files we are asking it to import, since we didn't run a `preloadNetThing` first. We really don't gain anything in this movie by building the cast on the fly every time it plays on the Web, so it's smarter to just let Lingo build it once for you properly, and then export the movie with that static cast.

> *Just because you can do something (build a cast on the fly with Shockwave) doesn't mean you always should. If this project was made to be dynamic, changing according to what was within the folders on the web site, then we would want to build it dynamically. In this example, though, dynamic elements aren't needed and would in fact slow the end product down.*

When you start thinking of scripts as development helpers, as well as something that goes into the final product, you can start to streamline your workflow. If there is some laborious process you find yourself doing over and over, you may find that you can write a script that will do the work for you. You've probably done this in other programs as well. If you've ever used macros in Word, the Action palette in Photoshop, AppleScript with your Mac, or if you use a Unix or Linux command-line interface to interact with your computer, then you've probably already been building scripts to help your day-to-day workload. The same concept holds true in Director, and there is no reason why everything you script has to be designed to be included in the final product.

So, there were some examples that show how agreeing naming conventions across media types can really be important as you're developing a team project, to help organize your casts and scripts. Naming conventions can have greater scope than just the process for one project in development; if you're creating something that people you may never even meet will have to work with, it's a good idea to adhere to some more general principles.

Lingo naming conventions

It's an equally good idea to agree on naming conventions for sprites, casts, scripts, handlers, variables, and so on at the beginning of a project. For example, many Lingo programmers use:

> `g_variable` for a global variable
> `p_variable` for a property variable
> `the_variable` for a local variable
> `myHandler()` for a handler or function

This way another developer coming to the project can see at a glance what purpose a property, handler or a variable has at a glance.

It's also good to agree on conventions for commenting your work. I usually save multiple copies of the Director file, incrementing the number after the file name and commenting any major changes. We all know how hard it can be to come back to an uncommented script after a few weeks away from it. When code passes through many hands, proper commenting becomes even more important.

Using Lingo stylesheets for text handling

If you're going to be working with large blocks of text, contained within external `.txt` files and then imported into the piece, (the easiest way to automate substantial text changes), then you're going to need some way of regulating the formatting. (If you're not, then just set up a directory for the latest version of any text so that changes can be manually inserted without too much hassle.)

An easy way to keep text formatting consistent throughout the piece is by creating Lingo stylesheets.

For instance:

```
on beginSprite me
        sprite(me.spriteNum).member.color = rgb( 217, 217, 87 )
        sprite(me.spriteNum).member.fontsize = 13.5
        sprite(me.spriteNum).member.font = "Johnston ITC Medium *"
        sprite(me.spriteNum).member.alignment = #right
        sprite(me.spriteNum).member.antiAliasThreshold = #11
end
```

Create a different behavior script for each stylesheet, as above, and apply them as needed to the text. This ensures that all the text is formatted consistently, and if you need to change the formatting later down the line, you only need to update the appropriate stylesheet script, and all the text will magically update as needed. (Thanks to Buddy Miesler who showed me this little trick.)

Everyone has his or her own conventions. It's not important that you follow the conventions exactly as I've shown you here, just that you agree on conventions with the rest of the team that you're working with as early as possible in your project.

Step 5: Staying open to change throughout the cycle

With all this talk of conventions and delegating workload, a project can start to feel a bit constrained. While it's important that you plan and organize your projects carefully, it's just as important to leave room for the unplanned.   The most important aspect of a nurturing process is that you must always be able to regularly step back and look at your work from different angles. Just because a great deal of time has been spent on a specific aspect of a project doesn't mean it is a good solution. You should be willing to ditch what you've been doing and start anew at any point, and at the same time you have deadlines and objectives to meet. There are a few key approaches to keeping the process open enough to enable positive change, while meeting your goals and objectives:

Nurturing a fluid process

- Go back and edit that storyboard when changes occur. Don't just let certain segments of the project creep quietly away from the original goal. Keep everyone aware of these changes by updating the storyboard to reflect them.

- Process is fluid. It is growth, not restraint. The greatest ideas come about when we are creatively jamming with a particular concept. If we tie ourselves to a presupposed way of working, we will only go where we have already been.

- There are never bad mistakes. Save all your 'errors'; they may well become the basis for something else entirely. Often a lot of our best work doesn't make it into the final cut, so make sure you save these bits for later use. They may prove very handy down the road.

- Make time for experimentation. Our best work occurs when we're playing with what we've got, letting our working mind wander with the concepts at hand. If you really want to create groundbreaking work, make sure you plan for these dalliances. You don't want everyone to be so short of time that they have to kill every idea that can't be immediately applied to the goal at hand. A project allowed to evolve in its growth phase will be far superior to one that is forced to adhere to the ideas conceived before the project even began.

Meet deadlines

- Agree on a minimum deliverable. We do have deadlines, so it is a good idea to set up your project so that you have a minimum deliverable at an early date; a steppingstone to the bigger goals that might be able to take over. This way, the stress of meeting the deadline will be covered, and you'll have planned for the vital time-flow to make the work truly exceptional.

- Set a cut-off date. You should decide on a cut-off point at which no more new features or approaches can be integrated, a time at which scope–creep is no longer permitted. Be sure to document all of your ideas for use in other projects, or in case the client is interested in these improvements later on.

Keep an open perspective

- Step back. It's easy to get so immersed in a project that you miss the forest for the trees. By referring back to the storyboard throughout the project you can make sure you do always keep the general scope of the project in mind as you work on the nitty-gritty details.

- Get outside opinions. As early as possible you should get people who are not involved with the project to give feedback. A good method for getting user feedback early in the game is called **paper prototyping**, and simply involves laying out the project as a series of pages, removing all text hints from the storyboard and presenting it to a potential user. Ask them what they might do with the elements on the screen, and when they make a decision, show them the panel from the storyboard that deals with that piece of interaction. If users are constantly doing something you hadn't intended, or not doing what you had hoped they would do, it's a pretty good clue that your design is not as clear as you had hoped. By going through this process before any code has been written, you can make the necessary changes without incurring big loss of time and money.

- Test, test and test again. Once you have the project laid out in Director, even before all the code is worked out, you can use Director's print frames feature to print out different parts of the project for paper prototyping that gives the user a more intimate feel of the actual interface. Once you have the project working, you should implement a true test phase. This does not have to be an expensive procedure involving one-way mirrors and hidden video cameras. A simple camcorder pointed at the screen, or even a patient observer in the room can achieve many of the same results. It's best not to let one of the people actually building the project in the room. They can watch the video afterwards to make their own conclusions, but it is extremely hard not to tell someone what to do when they are floundering about your own design. If you are working in a company, grab people from a different department to test it out. At home you can enlist the help of friends and family. And students are often more than willing to spend an evening testing your work, if only for the real-world Interactive experience they'll be getting. If you do have a budget for testing, (which is the ideal), then it'll probably go a long way. We've been able to get people in to test for as little as £50 ($75) an evening. You'd be surprised how many people just love to give their opinions. Throw in a little pizza and beer, and you'll have some happy people who will be more likely to become users of your product when it is released because of their input into it.

- Throw out the storyboard! Ok, don't really throw it out, but have everyone retreat into his or her own personal space and play with the ideas they've taken from working out the project as a group. You may find some great discoveries during this time, and the research you'll all uncover could end up being vital to the project.

In the end, process is a very personal thing. I have talked about some techniques for planning and organizing your Director work, but there is no absolute right and wrong in process. As long as there is an open sense of shared ownership for the project, and as long people feel comfortable with exploring while they develop, whatever you specific techniques, you are on your way to nurturing the kind of process that makes interactive work excel.

And that's more or less all there is to beginning to work out a process that works for you and your team. I'll summarize the points we've covered in this chapter, taking a look at the process as a whole, by going through a case study of an unsuccessful process, and applying some of the ideas we've looked at here to figure out how we could have created a process that worked better.

Case study: process gone wrong

In this chapter, we've explored the various points through what I consider a positive process: designhistoryinabox.net. However, I've worked within just as many unsatisfying processes as successful ones. We often learn more from mistakes than from successes, so it is a good exercise to examine one of those less successful processes through the points we discussed in this chapter so that we can come up with some ways for improving process the next time around.

The brief

We came into the project with some givens; the goals of the project had already been determined. In fact, the technology behind the goals had already been agreed upon. All we needed to do was create a shell for this technology so it could be incorporated into their product plan. The brief we had was this:

> *Create a Director projector to be saved on a CD that references a database stored on the company's web servers. This CD is for the sales team, who will take it to meetings with potential clients and leave it with them. The clients will be able to rummage through the company's past work. CDs should contain up to date information, and much of the content will be taken from the database on the company's web servers.*

It started out well enough. We realized pretty early on that the initial organization of this project had been based on how the back-end was organized, not on how the users would approach the information on the CD. The information was broken down into categories, and some that appeared to us to belong in the same place were, in fact, split into separate sections because the back-end solution was divided up that way. This was because the case studies were based on work carried out by several departments, and the database was organized around these internal departments. The internal departments, as you might expect, had been structured in a way that made the company run as smoothly as possible. They were not divided up for transparency to an individual outside the organization.

This was fine for the company to run, but it caused problems when applied directly to the architecture of the project. An outside user isn't going to want to navigate a project by 'Sales' or 'Marketing'. They're probably more interested in seeing what type of work the company has done with companies like their own. But the brief we had been given detailed the sections of the project according to their internal departments as they were structured in the database. This brings up a good point about form and function.

So, we decided to take another look at the planned architecture, this time examining it from a user's perspective, not a programmer's. We re-examined the goals of the project, brainstormed category names, and wrote down each potential category and function on a separate flash card. We then brought in potential user after user and asked them to sort the cards into groups that made sense to them. Once we had achieved some sort of consensus on grouping and naming, we decided as a group how we would organize these sections. Rather than divide the navigation into sections like 'Sales' and 'Marketing', we divided it by industry: 'Aeronautics' and 'Mining', for example. That way the user could find something he or she knew about, and by seeing all the work this company had done in this field so closely related to his or hers, gain confidence in the abilities of this company.

Storyboarding

And then we had another problem: the back-end developers hadn't been involved at all in this process. Initially, some sections of the project had huge performance issues because we were querying so many different types of data, from so many different places. When we sent out queries for information, a script ran in the back to assemble all of the information, and once it had all come together, it would update the page. The database was dealing with the work the sales team had done in aeronautics, but was lagging far behind in the marketing efforts for that industry, and the user had an awful long wait before seeing anything.

This insight was just what we needed, but it came so late in the game that adjusting the project accordingly became quite a chore, and costly. In the end, we had to sacrifice some fluidity in the project because we had not fully understood the constraints imposed by the back–end solution. We broke up the components within the sections so that they could update individually This helped improve performance, but it was a late change, and the design and architecture implications this caused were never fully worked out before deadline.

So we had to go with a solution that wasn't perfect because the back-end programmers had not been involved from the beginning. If they had been involved in our initial architecture sessions, they could have pointed out this pitfall a lot earlier. Not only would we have saved money, but we would have been able to craft everything so that it all made sense to the user, while working with the back–end as efficiently as possible.

Delegating workload
The back-end programmers often came up with their own solutions to the same problems as we were working on. This became frustrating, as the work that came back from back-end was at odds with what the front-end were working towards. The back-end programmers had much to offer, but as the process was so disjointed, these alterations seemed more like sabotage than improvement. A sense of "us" and "them" quickly developed. Rather than accepting that our roles overlapped in many places, and that the project would benefit from our collaboration on those points, aspects of the project not officially in one group's domain were shuffled off to the other group. There were often front-end problems that the back-end could easily solve, but because they were the remit of the front-end, the files were bounced back to the front-end for minor edits. Obviously this was a waste of time as well as frustrating.

In the same way, when back-end made change requests to the front-end, the front-end often got defensive about these changes. Why were "they" messing with "our" work?

Implementation and organization
As a result of these two aspects of the project being so disjointed, it didn't end up being nearly as flexible as it could have been. What's more, the misunderstandings about templates and elements in the piece meant that each group thought they should have had more control over the final product than they ended up having. And no one was completely satisfied with the last-minute kludged fixes.

Continuing the cycle
The gulf between front–end and back–end on this project arose regularly and impeded a fluid and creative work process. The deadline was strict to the degree that each section had to be released for back-end programming as soon as it was finished. Since each solution was essentially frozen at birth, this pretty much killed the growth process that usually takes place during the course of a project. After one section was completed and programmed, we had to use the same solutions for every other section. As we continued to work on this project, we came upon better solutions later down the line, and either had to sacrifice that solution because it didn't fit in with what had already been released, or accept the inconsistencies these new solutions introduced.

The theme of the project soon became: "It doesn't need to be great; it needs to be on-time." This lowered morale, and gave the project an overbearing inertia. It had a life of its own, for sure, but that life was more of a dictator's than our own creation. A lot of very talented people worked on the project, but few of those talents had the atmosphere in which they could rise to the surface. I wasn't happy with my own work, and was even less happy with what the project became.

Conclusions

Of course, hindsight is 20-20, so looking back it's pretty obvious how things should have been different:

- First off, the entire team needed to be involved at the outset. Back-end development had a lot of positive input into the project, but it came at such a late stage as to seem a nuisance rather than an improvement.

- Secondly, the deadline was tight, and that couldn't have been changed. Rather than bite off a huge project and force it into fragmentation, we should have agreed on a minimum deliverable and fleshed out that mini project before embarking on the actual programming.

It's a lot easier to identify trends once they've done their damage than while they are developing. That said, we became aware of the fragmentation of process very early on, but the inertia of this project was so strong that none of us had the guts or the presence of mind to revamp the process mid flow.

Keep this in mind as you apply the ideas in this chapter to your own work. This chapter explores the ideal, the pie–in–the–sky process. Some sacrifices need to be made in real life, but it is important to understand the potential consequences of these sacrifices. By educating everyone in the importance of process, and not just focusing on an efficient project implementation plan, you can make your work experience much more enjoyable, and create the sort of environment that will develop truly innovative work.

Summary: Making your Director projects work in the real world

Director work involves many roles and many media. To be a Director author, you need to be a designer, a copywriter, an illustrator, a programmer, an information architect, an engineer and a usability specialist. When working alone on a project, it is important to consider all of these aspects of your work, and frame each role so that they all contribute to the same unified whole.

When working as part of a group, everyone should be involved in crafting concept from the outset. Everyone should have a sense of shared ownership for the project. They should feel that they are personally responsible for their own role in that project, and must understand the significance of their role in the overall project. Although not everyone will be involved in the design or programming on the project, each individual needs to have a basic understanding of the reasoning behind the decisions within each person's aspect, allowing reasons behind any compromise to be followed.

There are five key stages that you really do need to be aware of as you go, whether you're working alone or in a team. In the first place, you do need a brief, and you need to be happy with it.

The brief should:

- Pose the problem that your project is addressing

- Identify the audience your Director movie will have

- Identify any constraints that your project will have to work within

Once you have your brief, you need to work on the problem and deal with as many possible solutions as you can come up with to think around and through the problem. Run your brief through a few different scenarios of usage to be sure it is framing the problem ideally.

Then you need your storyboard. This is both a simple medium through which you (or the team) can identify and explore the concepts behind the work, but also should turn into a living document, an organizational aid that helps you make sure all the different aspects of the Director project are aiming towards the same goals. The storyboard can be integrated with a site–map or movie–map, and by tagging the storyboard with media and roles, it helps everyone find their place in the project as a whole.

Then you can allocate the workload. Allow the different people involved in the project to suggest their own roles. Interactive work involves a lot of overlapping roles, and programmers can contribute just as much to the concept of a piece as designers. By being careful not to simply assume roles.

Finally you're ready to implement and organize your Director movie. Make sure you:

- Keep developing your storyboard through this process.

- Make external, shared casts and divvy up your casts into logical categories. In fact, try to minimize the use of casts where possible by accessing your files directly from their folders with `member.filename` and `importFileInto`. You can even build lists on the fly from files in a folder using `getNthFileNameInFolder`.

- Really make Lingo work for you through the authoring process, and not simply to create final scripts. If you ever find yourself repeating rote tasks in your development process, see if a simple script can do that work for you. Be sure to comment your work well and agree on naming conventions at the outset. Use Lingo stylesheets to keep text formatting consistent, and agree on a process for handling text updates.

And finally, remember to keep open to change through the cycle. Process is fluid, not static, and you should always be willing and eager to re-examine your project. Make time for experimentation, and recognize that great achievements cannot always be planned. There is no such thing as bad "error." Often inadvertent tweaks of a project can send it in an entirely new direction, or become fodder for something else entirely.

By updating the storyboard as these changes occur, and by sharing your discoveries with the rest of the team, you help ensure that the project grows as a whole rather than fragmenting in increasingly divergent paths. Encourage the same kind of exploration in the rest of your team as well. In order to make sure deadlines are met, it is often a good idea to agree on a minimum deliverable so that the stress of the deadline can be put away at an early stage, leaving room for truly creative exploration. You'll still need to choose a "kill date," of course, the point after which no more new additions, the dreaded scope–creep, can be made.

I wish you the best of luck! Here are some resources that I'd really recommend to you if you'd like to investigate further:

Dust or Magic: Secrets of Successful Multimedia Design, by Bob Hughes, Addison-Wesley, 2000.

This idea of a communal, explorative process is nothing new. In fact, William Morris nurtured this sort of process in his work with the Art and Craft movement in the 19th century. He focused on the "soft" side of technology, the human side of human creations. He believed that a group of workers with overlapping skills could share workload in a particular way to make their creations more in tune with the people they were designed for. New Media firms now use the same process William Morris developed over a century ago to create outstanding interactive work. This is the basic premise for **Dust or Magic: Secrets of Successful Multimedia Design.** Although the technology discussed in the book, HyperCard for instance, is often dated, the process Bob Hughes describes in this book is in tune with the new media industry today. Everyone who works in interactive media should read this book; especially those involved with determining process at an organization.

An Incomplete Manifesto for Growth, by Bruce Mau

www.brucemaudesign.com/manifesto/print.html

These four pages are some of the most inspirational stuff on the web. In this manifesto, Bruce Mau offers 43 points for growth and process in work. His advice ranges from "Don't be cool" to "Make mistakes faster", from "Don't borrow money" to "Scat." Something to hang on your wall; I learn something every time I read it over.

Experience Design, AIGA

http://advance.aiga.org/expdesign/index.html

Experience Design considers the many roles of the designer in creating culture, and explores a more fluid definition of design than some more traditional definitions do.

> *"The experienced designer must combine the rigors of engineering with the inspiration of high art. He or she must become adept at the traditional skills of design, and engage in dialogue with the virtuosos in the world of social science, economics, architecture, theatre and the narrative arts."*

http://advance.aiga.org/who/london.html

The Communication Research Institute of Australia

Communication.org.au

The Institute has done numerous studies on process and project flow. They've mapped out the various stages of projects, including the amount of time usually spent on different areas of the project. Their research indicates that users of most interactive work are only able to do what they want to do in 60% of their interactions. That's not much better than chance, and this is stuff that has been consciously designed by professionals!

Chapter 16
Publishing
Shockwave

Creating the Director movie is only the beginning of the life of your multimedia work. If someone can only see your work when they're standing in front of your computer, your audience is extremely limited. You need to know how to get your work into a form that can be distributed. You need to publish it.

Many people associate Director with the CD-ROM era of computers, somewhere back in the early 1990s, and assumed that it would gradually disappear as the Internet kicked in. Not a bit of it, though: as recordable and rewritable CDs (CD-R and CD-RW, respectively) drives have dropped dramatically in price, and blank CD-R discs have dropped below US$1, the lowly CD-ROM, which can hold hundreds of megabytes and costs about the same as a 1.4MB old-style diskette is more popular than ever.

But Director isn't restricted from the Web. Shockwave is one of the most common and most versatile tools for delivering multimedia on networks. While Flash is more readily associated with the net, more and more people are beginning to realize the potential of Director movies with multimedia web work, because they really are more flexible and powerful.

In this chapter we'll look at creating Shockwave, the kind of things you should bear in mind when you're creating Shockwave files, how it works, the security issues and some of the network commands you can use. In the next chapter we'll look at two more publishing options, projectors and a slightly more unusual one: printing from your Director movie.

What's Shockwave?

Shockwave is an elusive term. Originally, every Macromedia product to do with the Web was some sort of Shockwave. In early 1996, there was Shockwave for Director, Shockwave for Authorware, Shockwave for Freehand, and Shockwave for xRes (Macromedia's first image-editing application). There was also the Shockrave.com web site, but as the rave music scene grew a little long in the tooth, it was renamed Shockwave.com and spun it off as a different company.

In early 1997, Macromedia bought a tool called FutureSplash Animator, renamed it Flash, and unleashed a storm on the Web. Shockwave for Freehand disappeared, as did xRes. Shockwave for Authorware gradually became the Authorware Web Player. Which left Shockwave for Director and the Director Shockwave Studio. Remnants of the original scope of Shockwave live on in the file extension for Flash Player files; SWF used to stand for Shockwave for Flash!

> *In this chapter we're going to use the term Shockwave only as it relates to Director movies. The way it should be used.*

Shockwave files (which use the extension `.dcr`) are essentially the same as Director (`.dir`) files with two exceptions:

- The scripts in a DCR files are stored only in their compiled form. The editable portions of the scripts are removed at the time the file is created.

- The files are compressed using a lossless technique on items like scripts and pre-compressed media like Flash cast members. Depending on user preferences, bitmaps and sounds may be compressed by Director during the process of creating the DCR.

Other than these two things, a DCR is essentially the same as the original DIR file it is made from. Shockwave files can be used at playback just like any other Director file, and even used as a movie in a window, or as a tool Xtra, although they cannot be opened or edited in the Director authoring application.

Depending on the types of data contained in the original Director file, the compressed Shockwave version is usually in the range of 30% to 70% of the original file size. Here are some examples of movie sizes before and after Shockwave compression (these values will vary slightly):

Movie contents	DIR size (bytes)	DCR size (bytes)	% of original size
Empty movie	11,614	1,528	13%
Text in a field cast member, single style, 19,000 characters	32,999	9,563	29%
Same text in a field cast member, multiple styles	42,360	11,223	26%
Text cast member, 19,000 characters, single style	34,400	10,477	30%
Script cast member with Random Movement and Rotation behaviors	37,821	5,665	15%
Bitmap image cast member, standard compression, 276.3K	210,613	169,123	80%
Bitmap image cast member, JPEG compression, 276.3K	211,909	25,087	12%
Embedded font cast member (Times, all characters)	33,306	21,221	64%
Shape (rectangle) cast member	13,150	2,350	18%
Same shape placed as a 10 frame sprite	13,290	2,417	18%

Movie contents	DIR size (bytes)	DCR size (bytes)	% of original size
Same shape as a 20 frame sprite with 2 keyframes	14,272	2,836	20%
Same shape placed as a 40 frame sprite with 4 keyframes	14,452	2,913	20%
10 (rectangle) cast members placed as 10 frame sprites	15,080	2,955	20%
Flash movie cast member (150K)	165,829	102,190	62%
Same Flash movie cast member placed as a 10 frame sprite	166,005	102,260	62%
Same Flash movie cast member as a 10 frame sprite, with a script cast member and two behaviors, Random Movement and Rotation	191,275	105,601	55%
Flash movie cast member (150K) placed as a 10 frame sprite, with a script cast member with Random Movement and Rotation assigned as a sprite behavior	191,435	105,662	55%

Shockwave movies can also make use of external compressed cast files. The uncompressed cast library file (CST) is given the .cct extension during the compression process. The primary difference between a Shockwave movie and a Shockwave cast file is that the movie file contains score data.

As you'll be well aware, a Shockwave file needs the Shockwave Player browser plug-in to play on a computer. The player performs many of the functions usually carried out by a projector (reading the score data, loading and unloading cast members from memory, and so on).

Because Shockwave movies are essentially compressed Director movies, the Shockwave Player can also play DIR and DXR (protected Director movies), and use standard cast library files. Generally, DIRs, DXRs, CSTs, and CXTs are not used on the Web because of their larger file size.

Shockwave files can actually be used in projectors and even in other applications. For the remainder of this chapter, though, unless I specifically state otherwise, 'Shockwave' will be used to refer to Shockwave playback in web browsers like Navigator and Internet Explorer.

How Shockwave works

When a web browser with the Shockwave Player installed downloads a Shockwave movie file, the Player automatically starts up. Once the Player is ready, the movie file can begin playback or continue downloading.

The Shockwave Player utilizes the Web browser's own cache for downloaded files, as well as its downloading mechanisms. When a Shockwave movie makes a request for data or links to an external file, that request is passed from the Player to the browser, where the request is queued along with any other files the browser is waiting to download. Most browsers have a limited number of simultaneous downloads that they can perform, and everything must wait its turn, even Shockwave movie requests.

A Shockwave movie has two possible playback modes: standard and streaming. Standard playback will wait for the entire movie file to download before it begins to play, although Lingo-executed data requests or links will not be acted upon until the movie plays. A streaming movie can begin playing before it has completely downloaded, but it is up to the author to ensure that there won't be any commands encountered that might cause an error, like referring to a property of a cast member that hasn't been downloaded yet.

So, when you're thinking about using Shockwave to reach your audience, there are a few questions you need to ask yourself:

- What percentage of the target audience is likely to need to install the Player? (Check Macromedia's site for the latest statistics?) And of that group:

    - What percentage will have a computer capable of playing the movie if they have the Player installed? Shockwave 7 was the last version to support playback on Windows 3.1 and non-PPC Macs. The heavy-duty demands of Shockwave3D playback can bring an older Power Mac or Pentium processor to its knees.

    - How compelling is the Shockwave content to the audience?

    - How can you best advertise the content so that they are prepared to go through the installation? (This isn't as much of an issue for a large number of viewers; the ActiveX control for Windows viewers with Internet Explorer will automatically install upgrades, but for new installations, the download is still over 2MB for the current version.)

- Can your audience install Shockwave? Children and less web–savvy members of your audience may find themselves lost in the install process despite Macromedia's attempts to create a seamless experience (not always entirely successfully) and the instructions that may seem clear to you.

- And if they are web savvy enough to install, can they? In many educational and business environments, students and employees are prevented from installing software on the machines they are using.

Installation issues

If it's been a little while since you did a new Shockwave install yourself, it's worth remembering that it's not, by any means, an instantaneous procedure.

When a Windows machine running Microsoft Internet Explorer loads a page with a Shockwave movie loaded into the browser, the user must navigate through a number of dialogs to get the player, more so if they don't already have the ActiveX control installed. They will be asked whether they are under or over 13, whether they would like to receive information from Shockwave.com by email, and whether they want automatic downloads to occur. When the Shockwave Player is fully installed, a page at Shockwave.com comes up, on top of the original window.

The Netscape plug-in process (used for all Macintosh installs) is slightly longer. Those on Netscape must first go to a download page at macromedia.com, and download an installer, or have something like the Netscape Smart Installer do it for them.

Then they must run the installer, closing all programs, including the browser containing the Shockwave movie. On completion of the installation, the browser is re–opened, the browser's memory allocation increased, and the process continues as outlined above for Internet Explorer on Windows.

As you might guess, this procedure can put off some potential Shockwave clients, because there are so many stages during the download process during which people might well just give up – if they even started downloading at all.

What Shockwave can do

Shockwave movies can do almost everything a regular Director movie can do. When it's used in conjunction with a projector, in fact, a Director movie saved in the Shockwave movie format can do everything a regular movie can do, because the file formats are virtually identical.

Shockwave movies can use every standard media type. 3D, bitmaps, Flash, sounds, and vector shape cast members are all supported in the standard installation. Some media types such as Animated GIF, QuickTime, and RealMedia are supported but require an Xtra to be downloaded from the Macromedia site (and it must be embedded in the movie, see **Chapter 12**).

Shockwave movies can use external cast library files and change the cast file associated with a particular cast, just like projectors can. Individual cast members can be linked to external media files on remote servers (some media types like QuickTime are always linked).

Shockwave can use Network Lingo to control the web browser, change the movie playing in the current page, pass messages and data to JavaScript, and preload media. It can store text data locally using the preferences commands.

A Shockwave movie can respond to mouse events, and to keyboard events when the movie is the computer's application focus.

Movies playing in browsers with HTTPS (Secure Hypertext Transfer Protocol) support can send encrypted data across the Internet, and can communicate with other Shockwave movies on the same computer or on other computers through the Shockwave Multiuser Server.

When a Shockwave movie is used in a browser, the way we normally think of Shockwave as being used, there are some special limitations and issues to consider.

What Shockwave can't do

A Shockwave movie can't copy files to or from the user's local hard drive. It doesn't have general access to the file system and can't determine specifics about the computer apart from the information found in the `environment` and other properties.

Each Shockwave Player instance is essentially a 1-window system. Movie in a Window (MIAW) commands are not supported in Shockwave, although other movies embedded on the same page or in other browser windows can communicate with each other through the Multiuser Xtra or the preferences commands. Some standard MIAW functions can be duplicated by using Linked Director Movies (LDMs).

> *For information on using LDMs, see Rob Romanek's article "Linked Director Movies" on Director Online:*
> www.director-online.com/accessArticle.cfm?id=439.

Shockwave security

There are two primary issues regarding security in Shockwave movies: **client security** and **content security**. Client security protects the person running the browser that the movie is playing in. In an ideal world, it prevents their computer from being trashed by a file they've run across on the Web, and protects any confidential data they transmit, like credit card numbers.

For sensitive data that is sent to a server by Shockwave movies (and vice versa), Shockwave movies can send data using the browser's own HTTPS protocol to achieve the same type of security the browser does.

In the interests of security, Shockwave's file-access capabilities are restricted. Shockwave uses the host browser's own cache for any files it downloads. You can't use the FileIO Xtra in Shockwave. In fact, anyone wanting to create a Shockwave-safe Xtra must go through an approval process, and only approved Xtras that have been approved as Shockwave-safe can be downloaded by the Shockwave Player.

Shockwave can access files on a local drive with its preference commands, but only text files in the system's Macromedia folder. No other files or folders can be accessed.

Shockwave movies run from the local hard drive (rather than a web server) can only access external files if the movie's path contains a folder named **dswmedia**. This prevents a movie from grabbing information from other files outside the dswmedia folder and sending it to a remote server.

Content security

Content security protects the media and scripts in your Shockwave movie from being used elsewhere. This is a tricky area – after all, anything you put on the Internet is, by definition, available to anyone who knows it's there and has access to it. If someone can download a file, there's a possibility that they can get at the data inside the file.

For example, media assets in a Shockwave movie are expanded into memory when they're played. In order to use a piece of media, a computer must decompress it, decrypt it, and, in essence, remove any protection from it during playback. Numerous tools exist to capture sections of a computer's memory, and a determined person with the right tools is going to be able to get at your media in this manner.

There are, however, a number of methods that have been devised over the past few years to prevent other Director users from casually ripping off media. Shockwave movies can't be opened in Director like a DIR file can, but they can be used as a movie in a window (MIAW) or Linked Director Movie (LDM). Both have been used to extract media and access movie data from otherwise protected Shockwave movies. None of them are totally secure, although they can slow down the process.

There is one area of your movie that can't be successfully extracted from a Shockwave movie (at least publicly): the original scripts. Script cast members are digested into a form called **p-code**, and only these instructions are saved with the movie. You should be aware that the compression process doesn't always fully compress all your text literals, though, so it's generally not good practice to save password data inside script, field, or text cast members.

Some developers spend a lot of time and effort attempting to secure their assets. My own advice is to decide what's most important to you: if it's getting your work seen on the net, then go ahead and do it. Just take all the precautions you can, and know that your content is unlikely to be 100% protected from someone absolutely determined to help themselves.

> *Earlier versions of the Windows Shockwave Player read a file called* shockwave.ini, *which could be used to open a Message Window during Shockwave movie playback. Intended as a debugging feature, it could be used to examine data structures and media within the Shockwave movie. Director 8.5 introduces a new Boolean movie property —* debugPlaybackEnabled *— which opens or closes a message window depending on its value. To prevent casual abuse of the Message window on Windows, set this value to* FALSE *before distributing your movie.*

Publishing a Shockwave movie

It's not hard to turn a Director movie into a Shockwave movie; it's a two-step process with a lot of options in the first step that you need to know about to really utilize the possibilities.

Before you actually create the movie, you need to decide which of these options you prefer, by selecting File>Publish Settings from the menu.

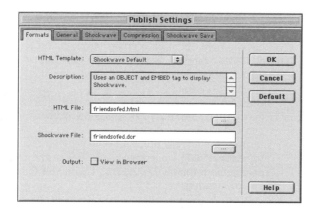

The Formats tab of the Publish Settings dialog defines what (if any) other files are created along with the Shockwave movie itself, where the files are placed, and whether a browser is opened to view the files when they're finished.

There are ten publishing templates installed with Director 8.5, but you can also create your own. The template definition files are in the Director application's Publish Templates folder, and instructions are available at macromedia.com's Director Support Center. The standard options are:

No HTML Template	The movie and its associated cast files are compressed into the folder you specify for the Shockwave file itself, without an HTML file.

You'll find this option useful when you're just updating the movie and already have the page created, or if you're using another application (Dreamweaver, for example) to place the movie into an HTML page.

3D Content loader   The movie and cast files are compressed along with an HTML page and another Shockwave movie; the **loader** movie. The loader movie displays the Shockwave and Intel logos together with a progress bar until the movie is loaded. The `sw1` parameter in the HTML document's OBJECT and EMBED tags indicates the name of your movie.

Shockwave Default   The movie and its cast files are saved along with an HTML page. The movie is loaded directly into the page using the OBJECT and EMBED tags.

Detect Shockwave   Generates a JavaScript routine that determines whether the browser has the right Shockwave Player installed. If it is detected, the OBJECT and EMBED tags are written into the page, and if not, a message comes up indicating that the player is needed.

Fill Browser Window   Uses the Stretch to Fill setting from the Shockwave tab to resize the movie to its maximum size within the browser window.

Loader Game   Displays small (12K) Breakout-style game in the loader, giving the user something to do while they wait.. As with the other loader settings, a parameter in the OBJECT/EMBED tag defines the name of the movie to be downloaded.

Progress Bar with Image   Uses the Image tab to allow you to choose a frame from the score to be displayed underneath a progress bar in a loader movie.

Shockwave with Image   The frame you select in the Image tab will be used to generate a JPG file image while the script determines if the browser is capable of displaying the movie (as in the Detect Shockwave setting).

Simple Progress Bar   A small (8K) progress bar movie is displayed until the main movie is downloaded.

Center Shockwave   Does pretty much the same as Shockwave Default setting, but centers the movie on the browser screen instead of appearing at the upper-left corner of the HTML page.

The two detection scripts, Detect Shockwave *and* Shockwave with Image*, have some problems. Neither works with Internet Explorer on the MacOS, because of IE/Mac's JavaScript implementation, which can't determine which plug-ins or versions are installed.* Shockwave with Image *doesn't work on at least some Netscape versions either. You should always test these setups on as many variations of browsers as you can.*

Some of these options will generate files in addition to the DCR, CCT, and HTML files you expect: the loader movie options create an extra DCR file, and options using the Image tab create a JPG bitmap file for display when a plug-in is not detected.

You can modify or study the loader movies to make your own. The DCRs and their source files are located in Loader Movies *in the* Publish Templates *folder.*

The General tab in the Publish Settings dialog controls the area in the HTML page allocated to the movie and the color used for the background. The Dimensions options let you choose the size of the DIR stage, set the size in pixels, or select percentages of the browser window size.

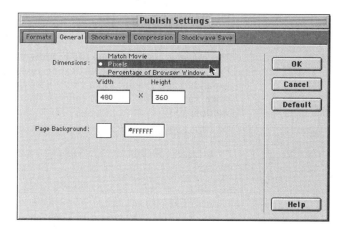

The Shockwave tab controls several different features:

Playback   Affects the Shockwave move as it plays. The Shockwave Player has a menu that can be displayed by right-clicking (or control-clicking) on the movie. The menu gives the user options to set the volume, stop, start, or pause the movie, and to save it to Shockmachine.)

Loading	Controls what is displayed when the movie is in the process of loading but hasn't yet begun playing.
Background Color	Controls the color displayed within the area of the Shockwave plug-in window.
Stretch Style	Determines how the movie is displayed within the HTML page. This style controls how the movie is scaled within the window that's set up as a result of your selection under the general tab.

The options are:

No Stretching	The movie appears in the window flush against the upper left corner. If the dimensions in General tab are smaller than the movie stage, the movie will be cropped. If the window is larger, the background color of the HTML page is used.
Preserve Proportions	The movie is aligned to the window based on the settings in the Stretch Position popup menus. The movie is resized proportionally so that it is at its maximum scale within the window, with the entire Stage visible.
Stretch to Fill	The movie is scaled non-proportionally (anamorphically) to fill the window. This may cause elements of the movie to become distorted.
Expand Stage Size	The movie is aligned within the window based on the Stretch Position menus. The movie is not resized, but the stage expanded and graphics that could have been clipped by the stage can now be seen, so long as they remain within the window.

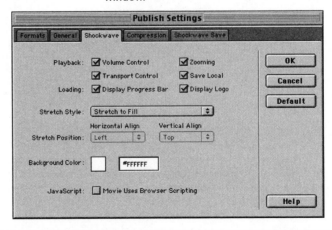

If a movie communicates with the browser's JavaScript engine, then the browser's Java engine will be started and this will delay playback beginning. If your movie doesn't use JavaScript browser scripting, you can leave the JavaScript checkbox off to speed up playback of your movie.

The Compression tab determines whether standard lossless compression is used for images in the movie, or whether lossy JPEG compression will be used. JPEGs are typically much smaller for most photographic-style images, but JPEG compression can cause problems with alpha channel transparencies in 32-bit images. Bitmap cast members can have their compression values set independently of the movie's defaults.

This tab also controls compression of audio in Shockwave movies. Unlinked audio cast members are compressed using the Shockwave Audio compressor (a variant of MP3). Smaller files can be achieved using other sound tools and importing audio tracks into Director; the lowest setting in this tab is 16 Kbits/second.

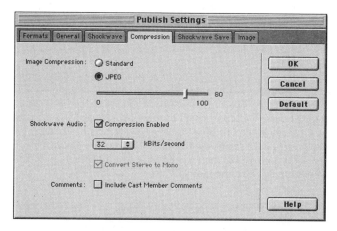

Some programmers use cast member comments to store data about the cast members used at runtime. If this isn't something you do, just leave this option off.

Finally, the Shockwave Save tab controls the settings used by the Shockmachine.

Publishing a Shockwave movie

Making a Shockwave movie isn't hard, but you can get better results if you're careful about what you choose. We'll run through a quick example here. Try using this selection of options, and see what you get:

1.   Open the movie you want to turn into a Shockwave movie with Director, (I'm using `wave99.dir`, which is on the CD if you want to use it) and select the Publish Settings dialog from the File menu.

2.   Select the Fill Browser Window from the HTML template drop-down list, and browse (...) to the folder that will hold your HTML Shockwave files.

3. Set the size and background color from the General tab. Choose Percentage of Browser Window from the Dimensions popup menu, and type 100 in both the Width and Height fields. Select a color for the Page Background, either by selecting one, or by entering the code (I'm using black here):

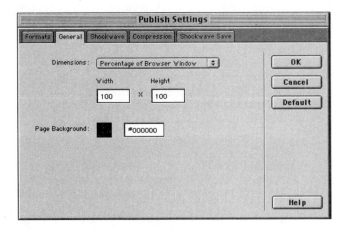

4. Select the Shockwave tab. Turn all of the Playback and Loading options off except for Zooming. Because the Fill Browser Window setting has been selected in the Formats tab, the Stretch Style and Stretch Position settings are unavailable. Set the Background color to something other than the one you used earlier – I used red (#FF0000). Then OK everything to close the dialog.

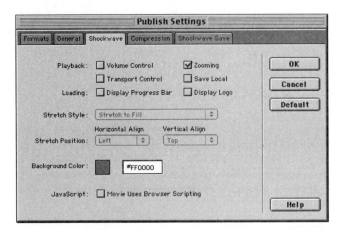

> *If you want the movie to scale within the Shockwave Player, you must enable the* Zooming *option in the Shockwave tab.*

Go ahead and publish it (File > Publish). The Director default browser will open once it's all done (unless you turned off the View in Browser option in Formats). The movie we've just made will scale to fit the size of the browser window when it's resized.

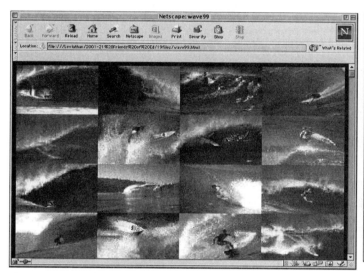 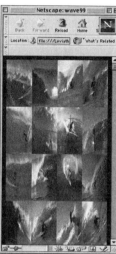

About the OBJECT and EMBED tags

Just like most other media types that appear on an HTML page, a special tag is used to embed a Shockwave movie.

Netscape plug-ins and ActiveX controls use different tags, so Shockwave movies actually need two tags, rather than the single tag you'd use for an image. The EMBED tag is used for Netscape plug-in compatibility. The OBJECT tag is used for ActiveX controls. Early attempts at using both attempted to use scripts to write one or the other tag, depending on the detected browser and the Player version. Several years of experience have produced a combination that's used by Director itself during the publishing process.

This is a sample of the combined OBJECT and EMBED tag generated by the default shockwave publish template (with the EMBED tag shown in bold face):

```
<object classid="clsid:166B1BCA-3F9C-11CF-8075-444553540000"
 codebase="http://download.macromedia.com/pub/shockwave/cabs/
```

```
➡ director/sw.cab#version=8,5,0,0"
  ID=screens width=480 height=360>
<param name=src value="screens.dcr">
<param name=swRemote value="swSaveEnabled='true' swVolume='true'
swRestart='true' swPausePlay='true' swFastForward='true'
swContextMenu='true' ">
<param name=swStretchStyle value=stage>
<PARAM NAME=bgColor VALUE=#FFFFFF> <PARAM NAME=swStretchHAlign
VALUE=Left> <PARAM NAME=swStretchVAlign VALUE=Top>
<embed src="screens.dcr" bgColor=#FFFFFF swStretchHAlign=Left
swStretchVAlign=Top  width=480 height=360
swRemote="swSaveEnabled='true' swVolume='true' swRestart='true'
swPausePlay='true' swFastForward='true' swContextMenu='true' "
swStretchStyle=stage
  type="application/x-director"
pluginspage="http://www.macromedia.com/shockwave/download/"></embe
d>
</object>
```

As you can see, the EMBED tag is inside the OBJECT tag. Browsers that use the OBJECT tag will ignore the EMBED, and vice versa.

The two tags duplicate data, but the format for each is different. The EMBED tag is more straightforward, with parameters of the tag such as the location of the Shockwave movie file (relative to the HTML page) looking like this:

```
src="screens.dcr"
```

The same information in the OBJECT tag is in a more structured format:

```
<param name=src value="screens.dcr">
```

There are some more significant differences between the two tags. ActiveX controls have a mechanism that performs major updates, not just minor ones, and the first parameters of the tag contain classid and codebase information identifying the type of control and where to find it on the Web, along with the version of Shockwave needed to play this particular movie. All the EMBED tag can do is point users without the plug-in to the Shockwave Player download page.

> *Notice that a number of the parameters in both tags aren't true parameters at all, but are actually part of a string assigned to the* swRemote *parameter.*

While it's certainly possible to create and modify the OBJECT and EMBED tags by hand, it's a whole lot easier to start with one generated by the Publish command.

Planning a Shockwave movie

Like any web-related project there are a number of issues involved in making the best Shockwave movies that you can. Shockwave makes creating interactive multimedia for the online delivery so simple that it's not unusual for people to simply take the files they might have created for a CD-ROM and save them as Shockwave movies. While that can be fine if what you want to do is create a playable Shockwave movie, but if you want to create a usable Shockwave movie, or one that can be easily transmitted across an average data connection, then there's more thinking to be done first.

Media

The biggest portion of a Shockwave movie is the media data. Bitmaps and audio are the two largest common components to be embedded in Shockwave movies (NB: digital video files are always linked rather than embedded).

It's important to spend some time figuring out how to make the elements of the movie as small as possible if you want to shrink your movies for the fastest downloads. The first aspect you will probably want to look is at the bitmap images you are using.

Compressing bitmaps

Uncompressed, a 100x100 pixel 32-bit image is nearly 40K. Depending on the image and the type and amount of compression, that same image can be compressed into as little as 1% of its original size.

Director's **standard bitmap compression** is a lossless scheme similar to that used by GIF images. It works best on images that use a large numbers of consecutive pixels of exactly the same color such as graphics. In an image where there are 100 identical pixels in a row, instead of storing the same color value 100 times, this type of compression will just store the color value once and the number 100. (So the uncompressed image and the original image are identical, and no data is lost, hence: **lossless**.)

JPEG compression is better for images where the colors blend into one another, or where the color changes from pixel to pixel (like photographs, for example). In JPEG compression, the image is analyzed for areas of similar color. Images that seem to compress hardly at all with run-length compression can be reduced to a fraction of their original size. Close examination of a JPEG image will reveal flaws in the image as a result of the compression, so this type of compression is called **lossy**.

It's up to you to decide and set the compression values for your images in Director. Here's a simple comparison of an image that began life at 32K as a 24-bit BMP file. The screen shot on the next page is from Fireworks 4's Export Preview dialog. The top frame shows the image with GIF compression, which is similar to the type used by Director. The bottom frame is the same image with JPEG compression. The amount of JPEG compression has been adjusted to make the estimated image size comparable to what the run-length compression would offer without any loss of image quality.

While the top image looks identical to the original, the JPEG-compressed image's edges are less defined, and neither the black lettering not the background are solid color. This type of image would work better if you use Director's standard compression.

You may need to override the JPEG setting (in the Image tab of the Publish Settings dialogue) for some images. Select the image in the cast window, open the property inspector panel and select the Bitmap tab. The compression setting allows you to use the default compression for the movie for this bitmap, to specify that the standard compression should be used, or to use a specific JPEG compression value.

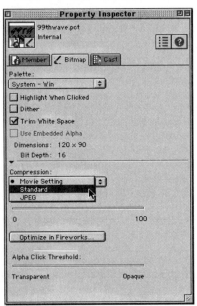

> *JPEG-compressed images that are imported into Director will retain their compression when they are exported. However, many people are confused by the fact that the* Member *tab of the* Property Inspector *panel shows the bitmap's uncompressed size. If you edit a JPEG in the Paint window, though, its compression data will be lost.*

Setting JPEG compression values through the publish settings dialog or the Property Inspector still doesn't give you any idea of what the image will look like when it's published as part of a Shockwave movie. To be sure what things will look like, you need to do one of two things: either compress the image with a tool like Macromedia Fireworks or Adobe Photoshop before importing it into Director, or use Director's ability to communicate with Fireworks.

Setting JPEG compression in Fireworks from Director

1. Open a new movie and import an uncompressed bitmap image into Director.

    > *Further compressing an already compressed image can lead to unpredictable results.*

2. Select the image in the cast window, open the Property Inspector and select the Bitmap tab.

3. Press the Optimize in Fireworks button. A dialog box will come up allowing you to modify the image. When editing is complete, Fireworks will open with the image of the selected cast member.

4. In Fireworks, you can interactively edit the compression value for the image and see what it will look like when it's published. Press the Update button when you're done and the Fireworks window will close. In the sample image on the next page, the Quality value has been set to 40%.

5. Switch back to Director and press the Done button in the Mix Editing in Progress dialog. The Bitmap tab of the Property Inspector will now reflect the JPEG compression value set in Fireworks.

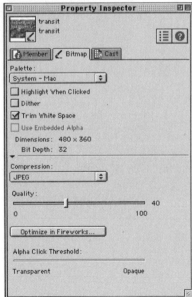

Compressing sound

The other big bandwidth hog in Shockwave movies is sound. In Director, you have several alternatives for bringing in compressed sound:

- Sound cast members can be imported as embedded (where the sound data is a part of the Director movie's cast files) or linked cast members. Embedded sounds can be compressed with the Shockwave Audio compression setting in the Publish Settings dialog. Sound cast members (both embedded and external) must be fully loaded into memory to begin playing.

- External Shockwave audio files can be linked to a placeholder cast member. Shockwave Audio files (SWAs) are **streamed;** they can begin playback before they are fully loaded into memory. MP3 files can also be streamed as linked Shockwave Audio cast members.

- RealMedia cast members can be linked into movies and provide an alternative for streaming playback. The user must have Real Media 8 (or later) player installed.

> *The RealMedia documentation is not included in the Director 8.5 release. You can find it at:* www.macromedia.com/support/director/soundvideo/realmedia_xtra/.

- QuickTime files containing audio only can be played through Shockwave movies when QuickTime is installed on the user's computer.

Only the Sound and Shockwave Audio formats are supported in the default install of the Shockwave Player. RealMedia and QuickTime both require the download of support Xtras before they can be played, as well as installs of their own respective players.

Embedded sounds are added to the Director cast just like any other cast member, and their compression is controlled through Publish Settings dialog's Compression, as we've seen earlier in this chapter. Embedded sounds are usually the ideal format for short sounds that are used repeatedly, like button clicks or other audio cues.

Shockwave Audio files need to be created and linked to a Director file in order for them to work. Shockwave Audio is preferable when the sounds are longer.

> *Any compressed audio format may fare poorly on older computers. The amount of processing power needed to uncompress sounds in real-time can cause stutters or gaps in audio playback if the processor is taxed beyond its capacity.*

Creating and inserting Shockwave audio files

The first step to using Shockwave Audio cast members is to get a sound into the SWA file format. This process is slightly different for each platform. On the Mac, you just open a sound file with the Peak sound editing software that comes with the Director Shockwave Studio. On Windows, you can use an Xtra.

1. Select Convert WAV to SWA from the Xtras menu.

2. In the Convert .WAV Files to .SWA Files dialog, press the Add Files button to bring up a file browser window, and select the file or files you want to convert. Use Select New Folder to determine where the converted files will go. Set the maximum Bit Rate and Accuracy for the conversions. The higher the bit rate, the better quality sound you'll get (and the bigger the file). Accuracy controls how fast the conversion process will go as well as the quality of the sound. Press the Convert button to turn the WAV files in your list into SWAs.

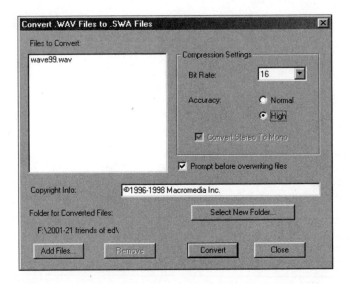

3. Now that you've got an SWA file, it's time to get it linked to the movie (you can find the SWA I'm using here on the CD). In Director, choose Insert > Media Element > Shockwave Audio from the menu. The SWA Cast Member Properties dialog appears.

4. You can use a relative file or absolute address to a SWA or MP3 file through the Link Address entry field; use the Browse button to find a file on your system or local drives (see the next section on URLs and File Placement).

You can also preview the sound using the Play button. The default volume for the cast member can be set here, and you can determine the Sound Channel to be used for playback, as well as how much of the sound (in seconds) must be streamed before playback begins (Preload Time). Press OK to complete the insertion of the SWA into the cast.

5. SWA cast members are totally different from standard sound cast members. They are treated as sprites and appear in the score when they're placed in the movie, rather than in the sound channels. They still need to be allocated a sound channel for playback (as seen in the previous step), much as a digital video does.

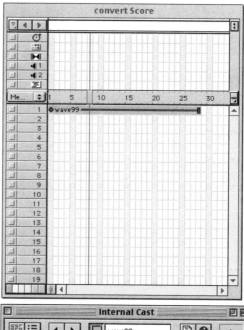

About URLs and file placement

A URL or Uniform Resource Locator, as you probably know, is simply an address to something on the Web. These are known as **absolute URLs**. All of the information needed to find a specific file on the Internet is contained in these types of addresses.

Most Web developers also use what is known as a **relative URL,** which is simply an address from one object to another. A simple relative URL might be something like: bunny.jpeg.

Because the URL is just a file name, the file this URL references is assumed to be in the same folder as the file it's referenced from. So if the file calling bunny.jpeg was at the absolute URL www.moshplant.com/trip/index.html, the browser would look for www.moshplant.com /trip/bunny.jpeg. You can also specify subfolders, so images/bunny.jpeg, would reference the JPG is a folder called image, which shares the same folder as the file. The browser would assume the image would be at: http://www.moshplant.com/trip/images/bunny.jpeg.

You can go up a file hierarchy as well as down. The relative URL ./bunny.jpeg goes into the parent folder of the original file, and would refer to www.moshplant.com/bunny.jpeg.

> *Another type of relative URL is the* **absolute-path reference,** *which begins with a slash character:* /trip/images /bunny.jpeg. *Absolute-path references always begin with the domain of the referencing file, then add the URL to the domain.*

If you're at all familiar with HTML development, you are probably aware of the difficulties of using relative and absolute URLs. Shockwave adds a little extra fun to the mix. In most web development, the HTML page is the basis for all URL references. With Shockwave movies, though, references made by the movie itself are relative to the location of the DCR file, not the HTML page it appears in. Just keeping the DCR and HTML page in the same folder makes it easier to keep track of everything. If the HTML page references a Shockwave movie from another folder, relative URLs in the movie can begin to get confusing.

Linked media

One way to keep Shockwave movies small is to only use what you need when you need it. Linking graphics, sounds, and other media into a movie means that you don't need to cram every possible thing you might need into a single Shockwave movie file. The downside to this approach is that you end up with more files to manage.

As we saw in the Shockwave Audio exercise, some media types are linked by definition. Others, like bitmaps, Flash movies, and Shockwave 3D can be linked to new files by changing their fileName property.

It's even possible to change an entire cast by manipulating the fileName. Switching from one external cast library to another is common practice to change the appearance of a movie by replacing all of the sprites with the matching cast members from the new movie. You can do this in Shockwave just as easily.

Linking external Shockwave casts

Our sample movie consists of three files which you can find in the folder Linking External Shockwave Casts. screens.dir is the main movie, with two sprites in the Score. One sprite provides a button with the test switch. The bitmap for that sprite is in the internal cast library. The other sprite provides the background image. Its cast member is cast member 1 of the cast library screens, which is linked to the external cast file night.cst.

There is one other file, transit.cst, but you don't need it yet.

> *For security purposes, Shockwave movies can only access external files on their local drives when the path to the movie includes a folder named* dswmedia. *This prevents images or other media outside the* dswmedia *folder from being accessed by the Shockwave movie, or having information about them sent to a server.*

1. The purpose of this Shockwave movie will be to switch the file for the cast library when the switch button is pressed. A script is placed in frame 5 of the Script channel to create a simple loop. To execute the cast change, a behavior is attached to the switch button. The script must detect the current cast library, figure out what the other cast library is, then change to the other cast library. This is the behavior that appears on the button:

   ```
   on mouseUp me
     otherCast
   end mouseUp

   on otherCast
     if castLib ("screen").fileName contains "night" then
       newcast = "transit"
     else
       newcast = "night"
     end if
     castLib ("screen").fileName = newcast
   end otherCast
   ```

   The mouseUp handler calls the otherCast handler. The first thing the otherCast handler does is to determine whether fileName property of the cast library used for the background image (castLib ("screen")) has the string "night" in it. If it does, we can assume that we want the transit cast next. Otherwise, we want to switch back to night.

   The final line of the handler does all of the hard work. Simply setting the fileName property of the cast library to the value of the newcast variable will change the background image once the cast library file is loaded.

2. We still haven't made this Shockwave yet, though. To do that, use the Shockwave Default setting in the formats tab of the Publish Settings dialog, and then publish your movie.

   This process creates three files: screens.html, screens.dcr, and night.cct. All three files will be placed in the same folder (assuming the Publish Settings were set up that way). If you had the View in Browser setting enabled, and the movie opened in the browser, though, you'll see that nothing happens when you click the switch button.

3. The reason nothing's happening yet is that the rest of the cast isn't with the files; fileName is switched, but there's nothing there. So copy the transit.cst file into the same folder as the DCR file.

4. Choose Xtras>Update Movies from the menu. In the Movies dialog, select the action Convert to Shockwave Movie(s) and Delete the original file (make sure you copied, not moved the cast file). Press OK.

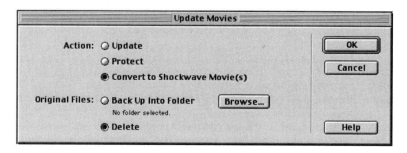

5. In the Choose Files dialog, Add the `transit.cst` file to the update list. Press Proceed, and a warning dialog will appear, letting you know that the copy of the cast file (you did copy it, didn't you?) will be deleted. When the compression is done, you can open the HTML file in a browser and switch back and forth between the two casts.

The files in the 10 ways to publish a shockwave movie folder on the CD-ROM accompanying this book show this exercise exported using each of the standard HTML templates in the Publish Settings dialog.

Network Lingo

Shockwave movies aren't just Director movies that play on the Web. They are actually capable of extracting data and files from servers, as well as controlling the web browser they are playing in. In some browsers, they can interact with the browser's scripting model. This is done through the set of commands known as **Network Lingo**. There are a number of commands and functions in Network Lingo, but here we'll look at some of the most important.

Working with the browser

A basic type of interaction with the browser is the ability to control what's being seen. Shockwave movies can do this in a couple of ways:

gotoNetPage   loads an entirely new URL into a browser window or frame
gotoNetMovie   replaces the movie it's issued from with a different movie

So, for example, if a movie named `goto1.dcr` contains the command:

```
gotoNetMovie "goto2.dcr"
```

it gets the movie `goto2.dcr` from the same folder `goto1.dcr` is in (per the URL rules) and plays it back in the same HTML page. The URL is always a string value.

If `goto2.dcr` executes this command:

```
gotoNetPage "goto1.html"
```

then the HTML page goto1.html replaces whatever is in the browser window or frame containing goto2.dcr. The gotoNetPage command can also use a second parameter, as in:

```
gotoNetPage "goto2.html", "_blank"
```

The second parameter allows you to specify a frame of an HTML frameset or another browser window. In this case, the goto2.html file would open in a new browser window.

These commands are used in the movies goto1 and goto2 that, along with their respective HTML files. You can find them in the network Lingo/working with the browser folder on the CD. The movies are virtually identical, consisting of three buttons and a script for each one. The buttons can open a new window, change the movie in the HTML page (the movies are colored differently so that you can see the change) or replace the HTML page (and the movie) in the main browser window.

 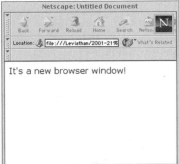 

User preferences

If people keep coming back to your movie, there may be information you need to maintain over a period of time. If your application is a game, for example, you might want to keep track of a user's keyboard preferences.

The simplest way to do this is to store the data on the user's drive. So long as it can be assumed that the only time the information will be needed is when the same user uses the same machine, a local file is an easy way to implement a persistent data feature.

Shockwave is limited in the types of files Lingo can use locally, for security purposes. Very limited. What Lingo can do is write text files to a preferences folder called in the Shockwave folder.

It's a very simple procedure to read or write a preference file. All you need to do is set a variable to the value of the getPref function.

```
preferences = getPref ("surftrio")
```

In this example, the variable `preferences` is given the value of the preference file `surftrio.txt`. For cross-platform purposes it's best to stick to preference files that have up to eight characters in their names; there's no need to specify the file extension.

The `setPref` command uses two parameters. The first parameter specifies the name of the preference file, the second is the data that's put into the file.

```
setPref "surftrio", field "pref"
```

This example takes the text data stored in a field cast member named `pref` and saves it into the `surftrio.txt` preferences file.

Take a look at the `prefs` movie in network lingo/User Preferences on the CD-ROM to see an example movie that lets you get and set preference file data.

Talking to the server

There are three commands that Shockwave movies can use to get in touch with servers;

getNetText   Performs essentially the same functions as an HTML form's GET method. A request is sent to a server, and the server returns data of some sort. The request might be a file name, or contain variables that are interpreted by the server before it returns data.

postNetText   Performs essentially the same functions as an HTML form's POST method.

These commands are equivalent to the `gotoNetPage` command, but instead of data returning to the browser, the data is returned to the Shockwave movie.

netTextResult Intercepts the data that comes back from the server.

The tricky part about using these commands is that network operations aren't instantaneous. The response from the server doesn't happen right away, you need to wait for the request to get there and come back.

Retrieving pages using the netText commands

1. To retrieve an HTML page in the message window, you need to use getNetText with a string representing a URL:

   ```
   getNetText "http://www.friendsofed.com/"
   ```

2. To test whether a network operation is complete, you use the netDone function. Without a parameter, the function just tests the most recent network operation (you can have several simultaneous operations going on).

   ```
   put netDone ()
   - - 1
   ```

   If the result is anything other than 1, then the operation isn't complete. Just wait a second and test again.

3. To see what is returned, use netTextResult.

   ```
   put line 1 to 4 of netTextResult ()
   - -"<html>
   <head>
   <TITLE>friends of ED | Welcome</TITLE>
   <meta name="keywords" content="friends of ED, flash, macromedia,
   motion graphics, actionscript, after effects, live motion,
   foundation, tutorials, expert, new masters, code, subnet, designer
   to designer">"
   ```

   The getNetText and postNetText commands can also send variables to CGI scripts and server-side processors, just like an HTML form. Variables and variable names can be appended to the URL for CGIs using the GET method. To get the HTML page with the stock quote for Macromedia from Yahoo!'s finance server, you'd use this command:

   ```
   getNetText "http://finance.yahoo.com/q?s=MACR&d=v1"
   ```

Both commands can also use Lingo property lists as a secondary parameter. The format for the same URL in this format is:

```
getNetText "http://finance.yahoo.com/q", [#s: "MACR", #d: "v1"]
```

or

```
postNetText "http://finance.yahoo.com/q", [#s: "MACR", #d: "v1"]
put line 49 of nettextresult ()
— "<td nowrap align=left><a href="/q?s=MACR&d=t">MACR</a></td><td
➡ nowrap align=center>1:00PM</td><td nowrap><b>18.07</b></td><td
➡ nowrap>+0.02</td><td nowrap>+0.11%</td><td
➡ nowrap>526,400</td><td nowrap align=center><small><a
➡ href="/q?s=macr&d=c">Chart</a>, <a
href=http://biz.yahoo.com/n/m/macr.html>News</a>,
➡ <a href="http://messages.yahoo.com/?action=q&board=MACR">
➡ Msgs</a>, <a href=http://biz.yahoo.com/p/m/macr.html>Profile
➡ </a><br><a href="http://biz.yahoo.com/z/a/m/macr.html">
➡ Research</a>, <a href="http://biz.yahoo.com/t/m/macr.html">
➡ Insider</a>, <a href="/q?s=macr&d=o">Options</a></small>
➡ </td><td align=center><a href="http://edit.finance.dcx.yahoo.
➡ com/ef?.intl=us&.done=http://finance.yahoo.com/q">
➡ <small>Choose Brokerage</small></a></td></tr>"
```

There amidst the links and other text is the important info you're looking for. You can write your own code to parse out information from any page you want, or even to create a new type of browser by using the link information in HTML pages.

If a Shockwave movie attempts to use getNetText or postNetText to access text data from a domain other than the one it's being served up from (or any server, if it's running locally) a security dialog box appears to inform the user that an access attempt is made.

You can find a sample movie (nettext.dir) that accesses text data on the CD, in network lingo /using NetText. Typing a URL in the upper field and pressing the get text button will load the data from the URL into the lower field.

> *These commands and the preferences commands work in projectors as well as in Shockwave. The primary difference is that projectors can only access HTTP and FTP servers, not secure HTTPS servers.*

Browser scripting with Shockwave

We've seen interaction with the browser, interaction with the server, and now it's time for the really ugly part: interaction with the browser's scripting model.

I say ugly, because this is the most error-prone and unpredictable part of Shockwave development. It relies on perfect communication between the Shockwave Player and the browser's scripting engine.

Browser scripting with Shockwave doesn't work with Mac Internet Explorer at all, because of the incomplete support for Netscape-style plug-ins in that program. ActiveX controls in Windows Internet Explorer support browser scripting in an entirely different way than plug-ins in Navigator. Browser scripting is something that, outside of controlled conditions, cannot be relied on. So, while these scripts will work on PCs and some older versions of Netscape (4.7 for example) you will have problems with newer versions of Netscape.

That said, how is it done? Messages are sent to the browser from the Shockwave movie using the `ExternalEvent` method. Unfortunately, this is implemented differently for plug-ins and ActiveX controls, so you'll need both JavaScript and VBScript to get it to work.

Going the other direction, from the browser to Shockwave, you can use just JavaScript and the `evalScript` method. Both methods have a browser script component and a Lingo component.

The sample movie in the Network Lingo folder is called `external.dir`. This movie allows you to send a string from the Shockwave movie to a field in a form of the HTML page, and sends a message from a form button in the HTML page telling the movie to change its background color. This is the HTML page code (the scripts and object names are in bold):

```
<html>
<head>
<title>Shockwave Talks to JavaScript</title>
<meta http-equiv="Content-Type" content="text/html; charset=iso-
8859-1">
<script language="JavaScript">
<!—
function changeField (fieldText) {
  document.Controller.Display.value = fieldText;
}

function changeBGColor() {
  theArgs = 0;
  document.myMovie.EvalScript(theArgs)
```

```
        }
//-->
</script>
<script language="vbscript">
sub myMovie_ExternalEvent(byVal aCommand)
  quote = InStr (aCommand, "'")
  aString = Right (aCommand, Len (aCommand) - quote)
  quote = InStr (aString, "'") - 1
  aString = Left (aString, quote)
  call changeField (aString)
end sub
</script>
</head>

<body bgcolor="#FFFFFF" text="#000000">

<div align="center">
<h3>
Shockwave Talks to JavaScript</h3>
<h3>h</h3>
<form name="Controller" method="post" action="">
<input type="button" value="Change Background Color" name="button"
onClick="changeBGColor ()">
<br>
    <textarea name="Display" cols="40" rows="3">Display field
</textarea>
</form>
</div>
</body>
</html>
```

The movie itself has the object name myMovie. The form is Controller, and the text field in the form is Display.

The send text to HTML button in the Shockwave movie has a simple behavior attached to it:

```
on mouseUp me
    ExternalEvent "changeField ('" & field "script text" & "')"
end mouseUp
```

When the button is pressed, a string is constructed consisting of the changeField function and the text of the Shockwave movie's text field. That string value is the parameter for the ExternalEvent command, which is passed to the browser for processing. Simple enough.

It's when the browser must intercept the message that the aforementioned ugliness sets in. For plug-in style browsers, it's not so bad. A JavaScript function in the head of the HTML document can catch the message easily:

```
function changeField (fieldText) {
    document.Controller.Display.value = fieldText;
}
```

The changeField function is the one called from the Lingo handler. The string value of the Director field becomes the variable fieldText, and the text in the text area Display is changed.

This doesn't work in Internet Explorer, though. To enable the ExternalEvent command (on Windows at least) you also need to intercept it with a VBScript. To do that, create a subroutine attached to the myMovie object:

```
sub myMovie_ExternalEvent(byVal aCommand)
    quote = InStr (aCommand, "'")
    aString = Right (aCommand, Len (aCommand) - quote)
    quote = InStr (aString, "'") - 1
    aString = Left (aString, quote)
    call changeField (aString)
end sub
```

This is a bit trickier, because rather than treating the string as a call to JavaScript and executing the changeField function, to VBScript it's just a string containing not only the parameters but also the function name, as in changefield ('text from Shockwave').

The VBScript subroutine looks for the single quote marks in the string and creates a variable called aString, which contains just the data inside the quotes. This variable is then passed along to the JavaScript changeField function with the call command. Both of these elements need to be present for the widest possible compatibility, but it still won't work everywhere.

Going the other direction is somewhat more straightforward. The HTML form button has an onClick property attached to it. When the button is pressed, the JavaScript changeBGColor function is executed.

This function is also simple:

```
function changeBGColor() {
  theArgs = 0;
  document.myMovie.EvalScript(theArgs)
}
```

The function creates a dummy value (theArgs) and addresses an evalScript message to the Shockwave movie object. In a movie script in the Shockwave movie, the evalScript handler receives the message:

```
on evalScript
  newColor = random (255)
  repeat while newColor = the stageColor
    newColor = random (255)
  end repeat
  the stageColor = newColor
end evalScript
```

When the movie gets the message, initiated by the HTML button and passed through JavaScript, received by the evalScript handler, it looks for a new color for the movie's background and sets it.

Creating web pages with Shockwave

As our dip into browser scripting indicates, Shockwave movies don't exist in a world by themselves. They are most frequently encountered though HTML pages, and as you've already seen, the OBJECT and EMBED are how you associate the Shockwave movie with the page. There are other ways, though, of getting your movie into a web page – using a page creation tool, for example.

Using Dreamweaver and UltraDev with Shockwave

Macromedia's HTML-editing tools, Dreamweaver and UltraDev support Shockwave. The Shockwave icon appears in the Common group of the Objects palette. Since version 4 of Dreamweaver and UltraDev shipped before Director 8.5, however, the OBJECT tag version information Dreamweaver uses is out of date if you're using it with Director 8.5 movies.

You can easily change the objects in the Dreamweaver and UltraDev palette by editing files in their configuration folder. The template data for Shockwave objects is contained in the Shockwave.js *file. If you make a duplicate of the file and give it a different name, you can use one object for Shockwave 8 and another for Shockwave 8.5.*

A common practice is to create the initial OBJECT/EMBED tags for a movie using the Publish command in Director. The HTML created by Director can be opened up in Dreamweaver or UltraDev, and the Shockwave movie can be copied and pasted graphically onto a page layout.

Dreamweaver and UltraDev expose the properties of the OBJECT/EMBED tags in a properties window when the Shockwave movie is selected in the editing window. Editing is somewhat faster because changing a value in the properties window changes it in both tags automatically. (A list-style view can also be viewed in the properties window by pressing the lower of the buttons on the left edge of the window). The properties window is a good place to add a name parameter, which is needed for browser scripting. In the image below, the name parameter has been highlighted in the properties window as well as the HTML pane of the main window).

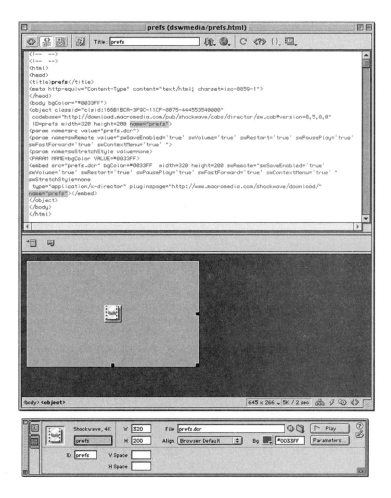

Simple Shockwave movies can actually be played within the HTML page (by pressing the Play button on the properties window), so long as the Shockwave Player is installed correctly. Network Lingo and browser scripting are among the unsupported features of UltraDev and Dreamweaver, however.

Parameters that don't show up in the default list for the object can be edited by pressing the Parameters button on the properties window. The parameters dialog can delete, add, or edit parameters for both tags.

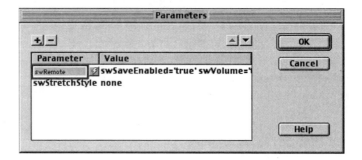

Summary

So, we've looked at a number of ways you can publish and manipulate your Director movies for the web, and use NetLingo commands to communicate to and from the server, and between browser windows. There will, of course, be times when you don't want your movie to be published on the web, so we'll cover projectors in the next chapter. We'll also look at printing from Director – it's one of those things that's often overlooked, but really can be useful.

Chapter 17
Projectors and Printing

On our course through this book we've already come across the Director projector, but we took it at face value without really considering what constituted a projector. So, that's what we'll do here. We'll define what a projector is, look at your projector options, take you through how we'd go about making one, and give you tips on how to ensure your Director projector projects go smoothly.

And, in order to be thorough with regard to publishing, we'll look at printing again. Again? Remember, we covered how to print using the Flash Asset Xtra in **Chapter 12**. We'll do a refresher on that meddlesome subject and take it a stage further to look at dynamic printing. We'll also cover some of your other printing options.

Projectors

Shockwave's not the only delivery mechanism for Director movies. Director predates the World Wide Web and the general populace's interest in the Internet. Its roots lie in the days before CD-ROMs, way back when floppy discs were king. It's still widely used for non-Web multimedia projects including kiosks, presentations, games, and even utility applications.

What is a Projector?

A Director projector is an application. It's a self-contained playback vehicle for the Director movie that can be distributed to just about anyone. You don't need to have Director to run a projector; all you need is a computer capable of playing a Windows or MacOS Director-created application - essentially, a Windows 95/98/NT/2000 computer or a MacOS PowerPC. Older versions of Director could create projectors that ran on Windows 3.1 and non-PowerPC Macs.

A projector at its minimum consists of a single file combining the Director movie and the playback engine for Director. Depending on the size, complexity, and purpose of the application, many other files may be involved in a Director project.

On Windows, Director projectors always have an EXE file extension, indicating that they are **executable** files. MacOS projectors have a file type APPL, which tells the operating system that they are **applications**.

> *Executable files like projectors are not cross-platform. In order to create a projector for Windows, you need to have the Windows version of Director. To make a MacOS projector, you need Director for the Mac. If you do cross-platform development, at the very least, you'll need a copy of VirtualPC running on a Mac, or (preferably) actual computers of both platforms available. You can do most of your development on one or the other, but projector creation and testing should be done on both. While you can make Shockwave movies that are cross-platform on a single system, you should still test them on both.*

Standard Projectors

Projectors always include at least one movie file in addition to the playback resources. They may also include other movie files and cast libraries. What really separates a standard projector from anything else, though, is its Xtras.

In **Chapter 11: Xtras**, we looked at how to embed Xtras in Director movies by using the **Movie Xtras** dialog's **Include in Projector** option. Xtras are generally included in the projector because it's easier to manage them and nobody's going to forget to include something.

As the projector application starts up, it has to load in references to the Xtras files, and to do that they must first be extracted from the application file. This takes time, and slows down the startup of the projector.

Fast-Start Projectors

A fast-start projector is one where you assume the responsibility for making sure the Xtras are in the right place, in an Xtras folder right next to the projector file. Instead of having to unpack all of the Xtras, the projector can get right to the task of beginning movie playback.

This means that you need to spend some time investigating the Xtras that are used in your movie and figuring out which ones are essential for supporting the media and functionality you require. This is a step you should be taking even for standard projectors, because Lingo-only Xtras won't be automatically included in the Movie Xtras dialog.

Capabilities

A projector is a true application. The possibilities of what you can do with one are not limitless, but they are exceedingly varied. While Director is essentially a multimedia development tool that is meant to work with graphics, video, and sound, Xtras give projectors the ability to do things that are beyond the scope of Director alone.

A primary limitation is speed. The Lingo programming language is an interpreted language, and while it's exceedingly fast at some tasks, it is not suited for extremely processor-intensive data manipulation. You won't, for instance, be writing the next version of Quake in Director; because it's built to be able to do so many things, it's not optimized for a specific, intensive task.

Director projectors have the ability to read, write, delete, and create files. They can communicate with HTTP and FTP servers to get text, graphics, and other types of files, and they can even control other applications through Xtras. You won't be writing the next big image manipulation application with Director, but you can write something that will allow you to assemble an image, save the image to the hard drive, and upload it to a server. You can write a tool that will download log files from a Web server and process them. It won't be as fast as a compiled C program that did the same thing, but it might be fast enough.

Making a Projector

The process of making a projector from a single Director movie is, in some ways, even easier than making a Shockwave movie – there aren't as many options.

Projector options

The options for creating a Director projector are not set using the Publish Setting dialog as they are for Shockwave. The options appear during the projector creation process, so we're going to take a look at them before we make our first one.

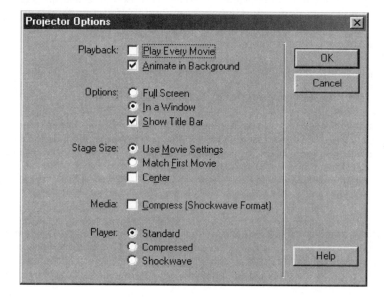

Playback

Playback options determine how movies interact with the user's system. As a projector file can contain more than a single Director movie, the Play Every Movie option will begin with the first movie added to the projector, and when it's done it will continue through other movies in order until all of them have completed (unless another movie is called by Lingo beforehand). If this option is not ticked the projector will play only the first movie in the play list. This is mostly used by those making presentations.

The Animate in Background feature tells the projector to continue attempting to grab processor cycles even when it's not the foremost application. So, the movie will continue running even when another program receives the focus. Otherwise, if unchecked, program execution halts until the projector window is brought back to the front. Sometimes, though, having this option ticked can result in a slower frame rate and stuttering and skipping when the projector is brought back to the fore (because, depending upon the system, there may not be sufficient computational power to keep the movie running).

Options

The radio buttons for Full Screen and In a Window control whether the other applications and windows visible on the desktop at startup are seen during movie playback. On the Mac, this is implemented through a single check box reading Full Screen. A Director projector, by itself, will not change a user's screen resolution to make any movie fill the screen, but will simply blank out the rest with the stage color. You can, however, get an Xtra to do this.

If the movie is run in a window, the Show Title Bar option is available. The title bar on the window makes it possible to close the window with a click or move it around on the screen. Without the title bar, the movie plays inside a window with no border.

Stage size

The radio buttons for Use Movie Settings and Match First Movie determine what happens in projectors with multiple movies. Typically, you'll only include movies of the same stage size. When that isn't the case, and a movie of a different size begins playback, the Use Movie Settings option tells the projector to change the size of the window to match the new movie. If Match First Movie is used instead, new movies of a different size will be either clipped or centered in the projector window.

The Center checkbox tells the movie to center itself on the monitor. If this option is off, the Stage Location value in the Movie properties tab of the Property Inspector is used for placement of the movie window. The manuals say that Windows projectors don't use this property, but they actually do. On multi-screen configurations, though, while MacOS projectors will pick a screen to center on, Windows projectors will center on the point that is the center of the total screen configuration, which may force the window to cross multiple monitors.

On the Mac (only), there is a Reset Monitor to Match Movie's Color Depth option. When the movie plays, the computer monitor will change to match the movie's color palette, and will reset when the application quits. This can also be done through Lingo on most modern computers (including Windows machines).

Media

Use the Media options to compress the projector's movie data. To make smaller projectors, you can use Shockwave-style compression on the media in the movie by selecting the Compress option. Images will be compressed using JPEG compression, sounds will be compressed in the SWA format (requiring you to include the SWA Compression/Decompression Xtras), and other media will be run-length compressed. This can significantly reduce the size of a projector, but it will adversely affect the playback of the movie, as media elements are uncompressed at run-time.

Player

The Media option controls compression of the movie and cast files; this setting affects what happens to the projector playback resources themselves. Like most options, it's a tradeoff between size and speed. The Standard option creates the largest projector, adding several megabytes to the movie data. A Standard projector is the fastest playback method.

The Compressed option uses run-length compression on most of the projector resources. Combined with media compression, it can make projectors much smaller than a standard, uncompressed version, but (as mentioned before) it will be slower to begin playback, as it first needs to uncompress.

Choosing **Shockwave** adds very little to the size of the media, and makes the smallest possible projector. It's not a truly self-contained application however, because it relies on the playback resources of the Shockwave Player installation on the same machine. If the Shockwave Player isn't installed, this type of projector cannot play.

Memory

On the Mac only, there is an option for Use System Temporary Memory. Mac projectors - like every other Mac application - have a memory partition setting that determines how much RAM they're allocated when they start to play. Multimedia can suck that memory up pretty quickly, and unless you modify the memory allocation (in the projector file's **Get Info** dialog), it can run out of memory, causing a crash. This option gives the projector a little bit of breathing room by allowing it to tap into the operating system's RAM allocation when memory availability is low.

Creating a Projector

1.   Open a file in Director (this example will use wave99.dir from the sample files for this chapter). Choose Create Projector from the File menu.

2.   Select the files you want in the projector and move them to the Playback Order pane with the Add button. The movie at the top of the list will be the first movie played. As movies are added to the list, an estimated projector size is displayed.

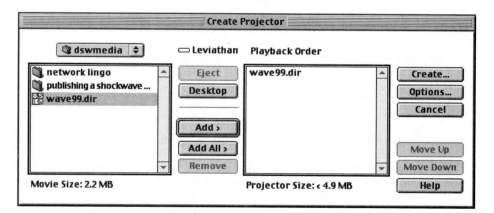

3.   Press the Options button to display the Projector Options dialog. Use the settings shown in the image below. Press OK to close the window.

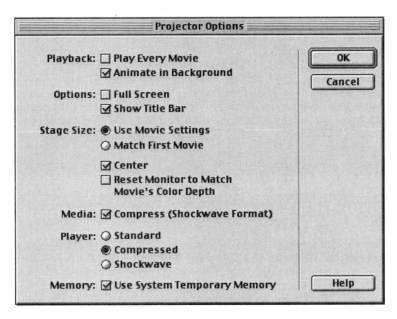

4. The Create Projector dialog should now contain a revised estimate of the final projector size (although it's not likely to be anywhere near what you eventually get). Press the Create button to complete the process. A standard file save dialog will appear letting you choose where you want the projector to be built. Once you've entered a name, hit the Save button, and the projector build process will begin.

Depending on the number of movie, cast, and Xtra files you've included in the projector, anywhere from two files on up can be added during the creation process. Some files may take significantly longer than others, particularly if you're using compression of any sort.

The original DIR file used in this example is 2.2MB. With the options chosen in this exercise, the projector is approximately 1.5MB. Without any compression, the standard projector and media are 4.8MB; with compressed media and the Shockwave Player option, the whole thing is just over 400K. (None of these numbers include the external SWA file, just the movie file.)

Stub Projectors

The larger a projector is, the longer it takes for the operating system to load and start playing the movie – we're talking about the projector's *uncompressed* size, here. If your movie file is several megabytes and you make a standard projector without compression, the projector can easily start ballooning over 10Mb and more. Take a look at the Director 8.5 application. It's less than 5Mb in size. The larger the projector is, the more RAM it takes up right out of the starting gate. You don't want to turn a large DIR file into an even larger projector, or you run the risk of running out of memory on a lot of computers.

The other downside to making a projector out of a large DIR file is that it takes a long time. Each time you make a new projector, you have to save the movie and cast files, then the projector build process. For large files, especially if you use compression of any kind, this can take several minutes.

Apart from splitting your movie up (see Dividing the Movie later in this chapter), the way to avoid making projectors whenever you have a minor change is to use a stub projector.

A stub projector consists of a projector with a very simple movie in it that has one essential command in either a frame script or movie script: go movie.

The go movie command is used to load a new movie into the projector. This is the sequence of what happens when a stub projector is launched:

- Projector unpacks playback engine, Xtras, and media (which consists of nothing in a stub projector).

- Projector begins playback of a very small movie.

- Small movie tells the projector to load in large movie.

Because the stub movie (the one containing the go movie command) is so simple, it's unlikely to change during development, so it can be built once, and barring any changes to the projector options, you might not need to make a new one. In fact, you can often use the same stub projector across multiple projects once you've built one that meets your needs.

Without Stub Projector

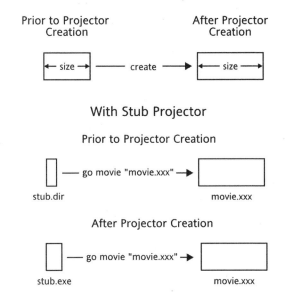

Note: in the above and following diagrams, the 'xxx' file extension means you must specify the correct extension to the movie files you use.

Splash screens

Director 8 introduced another feature intended to help cover up the time it takes for a projector to start up (and one that helps stop the user performing subsequent double-clicks on the projector before it loads). As soon as a projector file begins to run, it looks for a bitmap image with the same name as the projector file in its folder. If it finds one, it displays the image immediately and then continues to load the rest of the movie resources. If you use the default name Projector on the Mac, when it starts up, it looks for a PICT image file named Projector.pct. On Windows, Projector.exe will find and display Projector.bmp. Just substitute whatever name you want for the projector and make an image file. The bitmap image does not need to be the same size as the movie Stage.

> *The splash screen is always centered, no matter what the stage location of the movie is set to.*

Planning a Projector

Just because there aren't as many options to choose from when you're building a projector , don't think that means that it's any easier to do a projector-based project. It's just easier to make a projector file than a Shockwave movie. The actual process of creating a project involving projectors is actually much more complex, in part because of the number of files that are usually involved, and also because it requires more *planning*.

Dividing the movie

A typical Director rookie mistake is to make a single giant movie file, wrap it into a projector, and plunk the whole thing onto a CD-ROM. While it's entirely possible to make a 60Mb projector, it's not the most efficient way of working, particularly when you have the luxury of working with the (nowadays) nearly instantaneous access of a hard drive or CD-ROM rather than downloading files from the Internet.

The larger a file is, and the more pieces it has, the more memory it takes up and the longer it takes to load. The bigger the movie file and the more pieces it contains, the more slowly your presentation will run.

What can you do about it? Learn to use the go movie command mentioned earlier in the section on stub projectors. If you have a linear presentation, split the presentation into multiple movies and when each one reaches the end, just use go movie to move on to the next one.

movie1.xxx   movie2.xxx   movie3.xxx

go movie "movie2.xxx"   go movie "movie3.xxx"

Movies that are more compartmentalized, like a menu-style project, can also be easily broken into multiple movies, where any movie can go either back to a main menu or to any other movie.

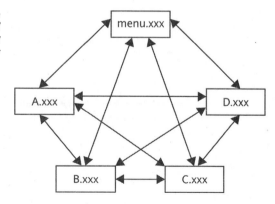

Data can be shared between movies because global variables are maintained in memory from one movie to the next. Another, more permanent option is to use preference files (introduced in **Chapter 15**), saved through FileIO or the `setPref/getPref` commands.

External casts

Moving media to external casts is another way to drastically reduce movie file size. Rather than having every single possible cast member loaded in your movie, group cast members by function or when they appear in the presentation.

External casts allow you to share the same media (including scripts) between multiple movies and are also useful for creating groups of commonly used cast members that you can switch while the movie plays. They also can aid in organizing your movie assets.

Linked media

Finally, divorcing the media from the movie and cast files entirely means that files are loaded only when they're needed. Using the `fileName` property for bitmap, Flash, and other media that is normally embedded in a cast prevents them from automatically being accessed just because a file is opened, whether the particular image is needed or not.

Take the example of an image browser with thousands of bitmaps, like a yearbook. You can import all of the images into a cast, but you can just as easily have them loose in a folder and use the `fileName` property to link a particular bitmap only when you need to look at it. It's a much more flexible and easy-to-update system, and it keeps your Director files lean and fast to load.

The price of perfection

All of this economy sounds good, but what is the catch? It means organization and planning. It means observing good multimedia planning techniques and putting together a chart ahead of the project. This will mean that you know where groups of files are going to go and maintaining those relationships to the main movie file, because linked media, external casts, and multiple movie files are all referenced by relative file paths, and those relationships need to be maintained on the distribution media, whether that's a CD-ROM or a hard drive.

Creating Projector projects

There are a variety of methods for creating projector-based projects. At some point, all of them include the process described in the exercise **Creating a Projector** earlier in this chapter. But, because a projector-based project often consists of more than just a single Director file, there are some other steps that you may need to take both during production and in the final stages prior to distribution.

- Finalize file placement. Ideally, this is done from the beginning of the project, by creating a single folder or volume that contains all of the resources needed for the project. If you don't do this as the project progresses, you may only find broken links after the project has been distributed. You need to make sure that each linked file (digital video, external media, external casts, and multiple movies) is where the file it's linked to expects it to be. This is a lot easier if you start with things in the right place rather than scattered across several drives.

- Assemble your Xtras. Make sure you've got them all added to the Movie Xtras dialog for inclusion in the file you will be using to make your projector, or add them to an Xtras folder in the directory that will contain your projector.

- Create a test projector. Make the main movie or stub movie into a projector and run the movie in place to ensure that the playback is fine outside the authoring system. Don't assume that because the movie runs fine inside Director that the projector will run the same way. This step also tests to make sure that all of the Xtras are included in either the projector or an Xtras folder. Don't put this off until the moment before you burn the CD-ROM - *testing is an important part of the development process and should be done throughout.*

- When you're ready to create a final distribution version (and at any point where you can during development), test the project on the media or machines it's going to be running on. Ideally this will involve not just platforms, but also the minimum (as well as 'standard') specification machines that you expect your users to have.

For a larger, projector-based project, this means deciding on how your distribution files are going to be packaged. Director has three ways to package its two file types:

- Standard Packaging. This means just putting the movie (DIR) and cast (CST) files onto the media. These files have all of the editing data in them, including scripts, uncompressed data for JPEG files, and more. Anyone with Director can open these files and access them (just as you can on the CD examples accompanying this book).

- Protected Packaging. Protected movie (DXR) and cast (CXT) files are stripped of their editable data and cannot be opened by Director.

- Shockwave Packaging. Shockwave movie (DCR) and cast (CCT) files are essentially compressed versions of the protected movies.

When you are ready to distribute a large, multiple-movie, multiple-cast project, one thing to keep in mind is that the Publish and Create Projector commands don't know anything about what you might be doing with Lingo. When you create a projector, only the movies and casts you add to the projector are affected by whatever projector options you choose. When you publish a Shockwave movie, only the movie you have open and the casts linked to it are compressed. If your project includes movies linked by go movie commands or casts linked at run-time through Lingo, those files aren't affected by your settings.

- Once you've made a decision on the packaging format, you're ready to complete the process of preparing your files for testing or distribution. If you're going to distribute your Director files as DIRs and CSTs you're done. Some developers do this when they're not particularly worried about people seeing their code.

- If you want to distribute your files in protected or Shockwave file formats, *duplicate the entire directory containing your project, which should include all movie and cast files, any linked media files, and any Xtras* - it can't be stressed strongly enough that you should keep an unprotected copy that is editable. Once the folder has been copied, choose Update Movies from the Xtras menu.

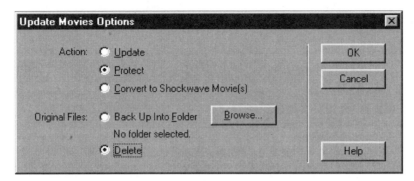

The Update Movies Options dialog is used to batch-process large numbers of movie and cast files. It has two sets of options. The first is used to determine what happens to the files: you can update them from an older version of Director, protect them (converting DIRs to DXRs and CSTs to CXTs), or turn them into Shockwave files (converting DIRs to DCRs and CSTs to CCTs). The second set of options determines what happens to the original files. They can be backed up into a new folder or deleted. Neither option affects any other files. This is the reason I prefer to copy the entire folder, the Back Up option doesn't back up anything except the movie and cast files. The directory structure is maintained for folders where movie and cast files exist, but no files or folders without movie or cast files are backed up. If you use this option, you lose the work you've done building that directory structure. I prefer to copy the project folder and delete the duplicates of the original files. Press OK to move on to the next step.

The Choose Files dialog is where you select which files to update, protect, or convert to Shockwave files. You can select individual files and add them to the File List with the Add button; when the Proceed button is pressed, the new files replace the original files and the originals are either backed up to the location chosen in the Update Movies Options dialog or deleted. If you're doing an entire project and you've duplicated the project folder (as suggested above), a simpler method is to open the duplicated project folder and use the Add All button with the "Add All" Includes Folders option checked. This will look in every folder and subfolder of the duplicated project folder and put any files found into the File List.

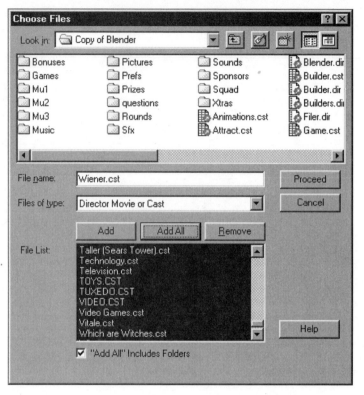

The process of updating files is fairly simple. Director opens each of the movie and cast files in the File List in turn, then resaves it in the new format, in the same location as the original (backing up the original, if necessary) and changing the file extension. The updated files are then ready to distribute.

> *Director automatically checks for movie files with the standard file extensions, trying all three of the possible combinations before admitting defeat. You can use this to your advantage in projector-style projects by using only the file name without a file extension in* go movie *commands.*

Distributing Projectors

Once a version of a projector project has been built, it's time to get it out to the world. For smaller projects, that can be as simple as putting an archive file on an FTP site so that someone can download the application. Many Director applications can run on CD-ROM drives, particularly now that CD-ROMs are many times faster than they used to be. Complex projects may require an actual installation of the software to be performed.

Creating installers

The simplest form of installation from the developer's point of view is a set of instructions to the user to simply drag a folder onto their hard drive. It's not usually the easiest for the end user, though. If you want the user to be able to install your project by double-clicking an icon, you have a few options.

Because of the differences in operating systems, most installation programs aren't cross-platform, and even where versions for both MacOS and Windows are available, they don't tend to do exactly the same things on both platforms.

Installers may need to do a number of things, like give the user options about versions of your program to install, launch supporting installers like Apple's QuickTime installer, install fonts, and give the user feedback about what's happening during the install. Windows' installers usually have to create registry entries and include the applications on the Start menu, as well as copying the files to the hard drive. Here are some of the many options for creating installers:

- **InstallShield**. This is probably the best-known installation tool for Windows. It comes in Express and Professional-level editions (about US$249 and US$999, respectively), which both include the ability to create installers by using step-by-step wizards and drag-and-drop techniques. You can create updaters and uninstallers, as well as full installers. www.installshield.com/

- **Installer VISE**. One of the only cross-platform tools for creating installers, VISE costs US$695 for the first year of a Windows subscription for unlimited distribution, with a yearly renewal of US$295 after that. The MacOS version is US$275 per year for up to 3,000 copies of a product. For 20,000 to 60,000 installs, it's US$1,500 per year. Installer VISE Lite, with fewer features, is US$295 for unlimited distribution or free for shareware/freeware. Both the Windows and MacOS versions are capable of integrating with the eSellerate software purchasing system. Find it at: www.installervise.com

- **Wise for Windows Installer**. Another popular commercial install system, which comes in Standard (US$449) and Professional (US$899) editions. It has many of the same capabilities as InstallShield and the Windows version of Installer VISE, and like them can be scripted, create dialogs that guide the user through the installation process, and has the capacity to create multiple language versions of the installer. www.wisesolutions.com/

- **Aladdin InstallerMaker**. One of the more popular MacOS installer development tools, InstallerMaker charges according to a licensing fee agreement that covers up to three products, with prices ranging from US$250 (for up to 10,000 installs) to US$1,000 (for 20,000 to 60,000 installs). Shareware and freeware developers can apply for a free license. Installers can have Internet registration built in, and there's also a feature to time out demonstration software. It's available from: www.aladdinsys.com/

- **Ghost Installer**. One of the many shareware and freeware installation tools for Windows, this is intended to give developers who don't need a lot of options the ability to create a simple installation but still has a wide variety of capabilities www.proggle.com/

It's entirely possible to create a Director projector that acts as an installer as well. You do need to know what you're doing, though. There are a number of tasks usually handled by installation programs that you can accomplish with a projector, but this can be a complicated process.

Checking out the system is a common enough task. Some information is available through the environment property, which contains values for the operating system and version. Other system properties can detect QuickTime. Other tools like the BuddyAPI Xtra **Chapter 11** can perform these tasks and more.

Creating custom icons on the Mac is a fairly easy matter. You can make a 32x32 bitmap and paste it into the Get Info window for a projector file. Using a tool like Apple's ResEdit, you can modify the masks that control its appearance in various highlight and selection states. The Iconizer Xtra from Penworks can be used to do the same thing for Windows: www.penworks.com

Copying files from a CD-ROM to a hard drive is something that can be done with BuddyAPI's baXCopy method or the fx_FolderCopy method of FileXtra3 (which is discussed in the **Xtras** chapter).

On Windows, Program Manager groups can be created and fonts can be installed using BuddyAPI's baInstallFont method. The Mac doesn't have an equivalent to the Program Manager, and just copying fonts into the System's Fonts folder makes them available to programs when they start up.

Both BuddyAPI and MasterApp (US$299) can be used to control other installer applications. www.updatestage.com

Professional-style installations can be done from Director, with some help from Xtras. It's not a trivial task, but it's a heck of a way to learn more about how operating systems work!

Printing

In a perfect multimedia world, you'd never have to worry about something so twentieth-century as printing. Or would you?

Actually, there are a lot of reasons you might want to have someone print something out from one of your Director movies. Kiosks can print out information for users to take away, like recipes or directions, and games can print out award certificates for high scores. If your movie allows salesmen to make custom catalogs with low-resolution images, then maybe you could enable a high-resolution printed version to be printed out. If a kid draws a picture with your application, why not let them keep a copy for posterity?

With the prices of color printers down below US$100, more people have the power to print than ever before. Here are some options to take advantage of that in Director.

Simple printing with `printFrom`

A Director movie's printing capabilities are surprisingly primitive. No effort has been made over the past several versions to improve or expand them. Or rather perhaps I should say *it*, because there's really only one printing command in Lingo: `printFrom`.

The `printFrom` command is very simple, and has few options. It can print one or more frames of the current movie and can print at three sizes. It doesn't bring up the standard print dialogs and it doesn't give the user an opportunity to cancel anything. The images (and text) it prints are 72-dpi bitmaps.

The sample movie (`printfrom.dir`) and the projectors made from it are simple movies, six sprites that you can drag around on the stage, and a print button. The script on the print button gives you the option of printing at 100% or 25% (if the OPTION key is held down while the print button is pressed) of the Stage size:

```
on mouseUp
  if the optionDown then
    printfrom 10, 10, 25
  else
    printfrom 10, 10, 100
  end if
end mouseUp
```

The printFrom command can have from one to three parameters. The first is the first frame to be printed, the second is the final frame to be printed (in the example above, only frame 10 is printed), and the last is a scaling value for the page.

You can print frames other than the one you're currently viewing (as in the example file). Be aware that the playback head does move to the frame(s) being printed. In the example movie, the print button only extends to frame 6, so it isn't printed when the printFrom command is used to print frame 10. A loop script holds the playback head in frame 6 until printing begins.

Because the playback head goes to frame 10 of the movie, though, it could move on to other frames or the end of the movie. A script in frame 10 returns the playback head to the loop once printing is complete. Without it, a projector made from this movie would quit.

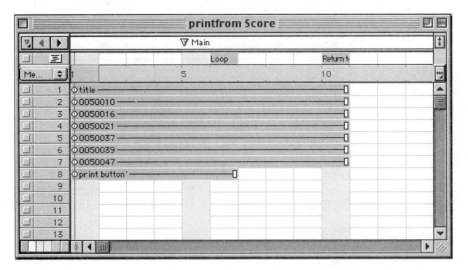

Using PrintOMatic

For more sophisticated printing projects. many developers have relied on Electronic Ink's PrintOMatic Xtra, a US$300 cross-platform tool is available from: www.printomatic.com.

PrintOMatic is an extremely full-featured - and sometimes frustrating - tool which goes far beyond the printFrom command's meager capabilities. With PrintOMatic, you can build multi-page documents, build in print previews and include external high-resolution files on pages.

PrintOMatic Lite

The Lite version of the Xtra includes several basic functions of the full version, including the ability to print specific sprites and cast members (of most types), strings, and even simple documents with previews and print setup dialogs.

Items can be appended to a document and printed, although you don't get placement and scaling control as you do with the full version of PrintOMatic. The unregistered version of PrintOMatic can be used royalty-free in projectors. A US$50 fee gets you some additional functionality.

PrintOMatic Xtra

The full version of PrintOMatic allows you to define frames on pages. When you define a frame, everything you add to the document at that point goes into the frame, so you can place graphics or text at specific locations on a particular page.

The drawPicture command is one of the most useful, because it allows you to define the rectangle that an image will appear in, or the point where the top left corner of the image will appear. It is not restricted to drawing images from the Director movie, it can also access external PICT, BMP, or EPS files.

The following script (presented only for reference) creates a new PrintOMatic instance, accesses an external EPS file and places it within a rectangle 3 inches (216 points at 72 points to the inch) square and 1 inch from the top left corner of the page, then displays a preview:

```
doc = new (xtra "PrintOMatic")
doc.reset ()
doc.setDocumentName ("Moshplant Logo")
doc.append ("")
doc.drawPicture("Leviathan:TRACTOR001:moshplant.eps", rect (72,
➥ 72, 288, 288))
doc.printPreview ()
```

Using just the drawPicture command won't allow you to generate a preview. The empty string in the append command tricks the Xtra into thinking that something is on the page.

On Windows, the PrintOMatic Xtra can be set to download automatically, like other Shockwave-safe Xtras. On the MacOS, at the time of because of writing, PrintOMatic can be manually installed for Shockwave, but it will not auto-download due to a problem with the Shockwave plugin.

Printing with the Flash Asset Xtra

Macromedia Flash added the ability to print from its player not long after Flash 4 was released, and it makes delivery of high-quality graphics over the Web possible in entirely new ways. For a more thorough examination of Flash Asset Xtra printing refer back to **Chapter 12**.

Creating printable Flash movies

Printing a Flash movie from Director is quite easy in version 8.5. Just pop a Flash movie into a Director sprite channel, and tell it to print:

```
sprite (1).print ()
```

> *The print command can only print shapes and bitmaps as opaque graphics, if you need to print Flash movies with transparency effects, use the* printAsBitmap *command.*

In the example movie numbers.dir, a 200x200 pixel Flash movie (created from numbers.fla) with 10 frames and a bounding box is imported into the Director movie and placed in sprite channel 1. A print button in the Director movie tells the Flash sprite to print.

When the Flash movie prints, each of its frames becomes a separate page. Unfortunately, the square Flash movie is scaled to fit the entire printable area of the page, which means the movie is stretched non-proportionally.

The scaling is determined by the aspect ratio of the bounding rectangle of the objects on the stage of the Flash movie and the printable area of the page. If they don't share the same proportions the movie will be distorted when printed.

The way around this is to edit the Flash movie. The Flash printing specifications allow you to define a printable bounding box in the Flash movie by defining a frame with the label #b. Graphics on that page will then determine the area of the page that is printed. In the example file bmovie.fla, a frame has been created at the end of the movie, given the appropriate label, and a rectangle is drawn to define the print area.

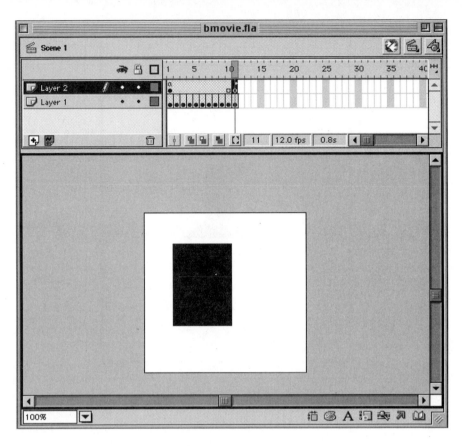

This rectangle, to the left of and slightly above the movie's center, causes a major change in what gets printed when the same print command is issued.

> *Printing commands can also be issued from the Flash movie's own scripts.*

You can even use the print command with Flash movies to print an individual movie clip. The numeral in the first frame of bmovie.fla has been turned into a movie clip, its instance is given the name one, and a bounding box has been defined that just covers the artwork for the numeral. The lower button in the Director movie bmovie.dir prints just the movie clip with this command:

```
sprite (1).print ("one")
```

The result is that the artwork for the number fills the page:

To print a movie clip, the clip must be the currently displayed frame of the Flash sprite, and it must have an instance name assigned.

Individual frames of a timeline for a Flash movie or a movie clip can be printed by giving them a label of #p.

Flash printing works on both operating systems in projectors and in Shockwave.

Although printing from Flash sprites yields high-quality vector shapes on printers, using Flash printing with the Adobe Acrobat PDFWriter only creates bitmap images.

Printing dynamic data from Flash movies

You're not limited to printing static frames of a Flash movie. You can use the abilities of movie clips and dynamic text to create styled text, charts, and more. In the `temp.dir` and `temp.fla` movies you can see how this is done.

The Flash movie `temp.fla` consists of just one frame containing two text entry fields and a movie clip with one dynamic text field. The movie clip has a bounding box frame in it (with a #b label), scaled to the same proportions as a standard sheet of paper. The dynamic text field has three characters in it, one in the regular font style, one bold, and the last in italic, to ensure that the font used for the field embeds all three versions.

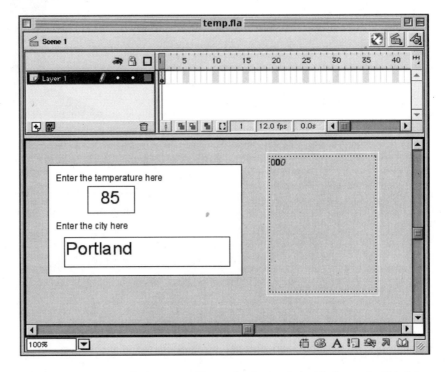

You'll notice that the movie clip isn't actually on the Stage of the Flash movie. This is important, because what we're going to use it for is a report that isn't seen in the Director movie, but *can* be printed.

The Flash SWF file is placed in sprite channel 1 of the Director movie, and a button is added in sprite channel 2. The script on the button gathers the temperature and city name from the text entry fields in the Flash sprite, then updates the dynamic text field in the movie clip instance named `report`.

```
on mouseUp me
  temp = integer (sprite (1).getVariable("temp"))
  city = sprite (1).getVariable("city")
  report = "<I>"
  report = report & the date & "</I><BR><BR>"
  report = report & "The high temperature today in <B>"
  report = report & city & "</B> is <B>" & temp & "</B>
➡Fahrenheit (<B>"
  report = report & ((temp - 32) * 5 / 9) & "</B> Celsius)."
  sprite (1).setVariable("report.reptext", report)
  sprite (1).print ("report")
end mouseUp
```

The two getVariable functions return the text data stored in the editable text fields of the Flash sprite (named temp and city). This data is then added to a Lingo variable named report, with HTML tags indicating italics and bold text (the dynamic variable in the Flash movie clip has its HTML Display option turned on).

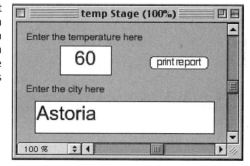

The report includes the date (derived from Lingo), the name of the city in bold, and the temperature in both Fahrenheit and Celsius (with the conversion made in the Lingo handler).

7/9/01

The high temperature today in **Astoria** is **60** Fahrenheit (**15** Celsius).

The dynamic text variable inside the `report` movie clip is named `reptext`. Its value is changed by the `setVariable` command, then the `print` command is issued. Only the off-screen movie clip named `report` is printed.

Much more complex types of dynamic data and graphics can be printed in both projectors and Shockwave now that Flash 5 is supported in Director 8.5!

> *All of the Lingo that affects Flash sprites is only functional when the Director movie is running. You can't affect variables when the Director movie is stopped.*

Summary

Projectors are a powerful way of distributing your movies and presentations - they are stand-alone applications that can be viewed by the majority of the world who possess computers. The stub projector is an advance on the Standard projector and can be the basis for a multi-movie, multi-cast project. Stub projectors, along with the `go movie` command, can also be used to create user-interactive experiences where multiple movies (or a single, large one) can be spliced together to follow a user's selection. Remember, though, that a wonderful user experience comes at a price - complexity for you, the designer-developer - which means careful planning is required.

As opposed to the complexity and interactivity that projectors provide, printing from Director remains a prehistoric experience, unless you're willing to invest in purchasing some additional functionality. Of the Xtras available PrintOMatic (which comes on the Director 8.5 CD-ROM in the Xtra Partners folder) is the most popular.

Chapter 18
Designing for
Interaction

Three members of the Antirom collective got together to write this piece about the way they create interactive user experiences, and the design processes behind some of their favorite work from the Antirom, tomato interactive and romandson studios.

We felt that a discussion of a number of Director pieces would be more helpful, and hopefully more inspirational, to you as a developer than simply bulldozing through the production of a single project, so the following discussions look at developing concepts that build on the ways that users interact with a piece, and the relationship between programming, interactivity, and creativity. It covers a number of sound-reactive interface projects, with the final three projects building upon on another, each informing the development process of the next.

In the beginning

In 1994 a group of Londoners were foolish enough to believe they could make an interactive CD–ROM all by themselves.

We were aided and abetted in this conceit by an American company called Macromind whose product, Director 4, was advertised as a state of the art interactive authoring environment. We came from a variety of backgrounds and possessed a range of media skills, film and video, photography, music, design, fashion, writing and so on. Some of us had even done a bit of amateur coding.

We wanted to get involved in what we had identified as a new and exciting form of expression: **interactive media**. We weren't impressed with many of the interactive CD-ROMs we had seen up until then. Many of them were run–of–the–mill educational or informational CD-ROMs, buttoned up, badly designed, and boring multi–mediocrity. We reckoned we could do better.

We were catalyzed by the release of BlindRom, a CD-ROM by the Dutch artist Gerald Van der Kaap first distributed with a magazine. For more information see www.xs4all.nl/~00kaap/blindrom.html. BlindRom gave us faith in what we believed: there was a different way to design for interactivity, that interactive media could be witty, intelligent, funny, perverse, and above all playful.

Director was the only tool that made it possible for us to even think about creating the kind of experiences we had in mind. Sure there were alternatives, HyperCard, SuperCard or C++, but none of these allowed a disparate group of wannabe interactive artists to so readily integrate video, stills, music, drawn animation, text and narrative, while still encouraging non–programmers to believe they could stick it all together with code.

This is the real achievement of Director, making coding look easy, beguiling everyone into thinking that they can code for themselves. By the time we realized the enormity and complexity of engineering interactive experiences we were already so far down the path that it just as easy to keep going as to stop. We ended up with a CD-ROM that contained a range of experiments in interactive media design and a reputation as experts in interactive media design.

Expertise is a relative thing. Actually, in our expert opinion, nobody knows anything about interactive media design. You can't know in advance what is or isn't going to work for the end user. You don't have the vast storehouse of established design solutions to refer to, like filmmakers or painters or novelists do. You're pretty much on your own, mapping out an unknown design space. You have little option but to explore the territory, to try stuff, to experiment. The best you can do is make your mistakes quickly and learn from them. At the same time, everyone's got a theory, so here is ours, based on the experiences we had at the Antirom collective and its subsequent incarnations in romandson, tomato interactive, studio 3 etc.

First, get used to the idea that what is radical and experimental one day can become a paid job the next day. We have found that personal creative experimentation and commercial work crossover all the time. That's what makes interactive media design so exciting. There's a premium for innovation. So use whatever downtime you have to try stuff out, especially weird stuff. Next time you sit down with a client you might find you've hit on something that fits.

Second, test, test and test again, test early and test often. You can't test too much. Testing is all about answering two key questions:

- Is the interactivity robust (will it crash)?

- Do people like to use it?

Never, ever, underestimate the capacity of programmed code to throw up errors when you're testing for robustness, especially when you're just starting to believe it's stable. The only way to ensure that code really is stable is constant and protracted testing. This means robustness testing for hours and hours.

The other kind of testing, user testing, will demonstrate pretty quickly which of your great ideas actually work for other people. This will always be hard for you, the designer, to predict. You simply don't have the necessary distance from an idea to evaluate it properly yourself. User testing is when you find out that nobody understands the navigation, the on–screen text is too small to read, the game is boring or too long, the audio is irritating and that most people want to turn it off. User testing can be a deflating experience for people who are designers of interactivity, but the earlier you start the easier it is to change direction based on your findings.

Third, think about the simple things. In spite of the diversity of interactive experiences, the user only has a few ways to interact with the computer. They can move the mouse around the screen, click a mouse button, or press keys on the keyboard. Maybe you've got microphone input. That's pretty much it. These are the basic user interactions, so this is where designing for interaction starts.

Interaction, the simple things

We started with these basic interaction opportunities and developed them into a range of different experiences. The focus of the examples that follow is on the key ideas: transforming simple interactions into a user experience though code.

Your user has to be interested enough in the situation you present to them to want to control it, and you have to spark that interest pretty quickly, before they quit out or wander away. The problem you have to solve is mapping the interaction to the interactive, ensuring rapid intuition and continuing interest from the second the user touches the mouse or the keyboard.

The mouse

One of the simplest things you can do with mouse movement is map the coordinates of the cursor to another variable, the volume of a sound channel for example. You can work with this simple idea to get some complex and involved results.

For example, in one of the Antirom pieces, we mapped the horizontal part of the mouse position (the mouseH) to two long sound loops set to play *on startMovie*. We mapped one sound so that it played at full volume when the mouse moved to the left-hand side of the screen and zero volume when the mouse moved to the right-hand side, with the intermediate volume levels in between. Then we mapped another sound working in the opposite direction, full volume on the right, zero volume on the left. This created the illusion that there was a sound on the left of the screen and another on the right of the screen and by moving the cursor left and right these sounds could be mixed dynamically.

The pseudo code looked something like this:

```
—sound1 with max volume on left, minimum on right

Set sound1volume= 255 - (the mouseh * (255/screen width))

If sound1volume> 255 then set sound1volume = 255
—stops sound1volume getting greater than 255, the maximum value
for sound volume

If sound1volume < 0 then set sound1 = 0
—stops sound1volume getting less than 0, the minimum value for
sound volume

—sound2 with max volume on right, min volume on left

Set sound2volume = the mouseh * (255/screen width)

If sound2volume > 255 then set sound2volume = 255
—stops sound2volume getting greater than 255, the maximum value
for sound volume

If sound2volume < 0 then set sound2volume = 0
— stops sound2 getting less than 0, the minimum value for sound
volume
```

The illusion of control is that of a simple sound mixer where the two sounds play at half volume when the cursor is halfway across the screen; sound 1 gets louder and sound 2 quieter as the cursor is moves to the left, sound 2 gets louder and sound 1 quieter as the cursor is moved to the right. Complexity from simplicity. There are a large (but not infinite) number of volume combinations produced by simple mouse movements. The user pretty much gets it straight away without instructions.

The hard bit is, of course, choosing the right sounds, but we can't help you there.

An obvious development of this side–to–side mixer is a mixer that locates sounds at discrete pixel coordinates. You can do this by mapping the sound level of a channel to the X,Y distance of the mouse cursor from a particular X,Y coordinate position. The code to calculate X,Y distance from point to point involves, that old chestnut, Pythagoras' theorem: in a right–angled equilateral triangle, the square of the sum of the right angle sides is equal to the square of the hypotenuse.

Any two positions on the screen, in this case the mouse cursor position and the 'source' of the sound, can be connected by a line which can then be understood as the hypotenuse of an equilateral triangle. The vertical and horizontal sides of this equilateral triangle are measurable as the difference between the vertical and horizontal coordinates of the mouse cursor and the vertical and horizontal coordinates of the 'source' of the sound.

```
Set horizontaldistance = the  mouseh - the loch of soundposition
- - - where soundposition is point data referring to the sound
source.

Set verticaldistance = the  mousev - the locv of soundposition
- - - where soundposition is point data referring to the sound
source.

Set horizontaldistance = horizontaldistance * horizontaldistance
- - - square of the horizontal part of the triangle.

Set verticaldistance = verticaldistance * verticaldistance
- - - square of the vertical part of the triangle.

Set totalsquare = verticaldistance + horizontaldistance
- - - add the two squares

Set distance = sqrt(totalsquare)
- - - find the squareroot, ie: the length of the long side or the
hypotenuse.

Set myvolume = 255 - distance
- - - map the distance of the cursor in two dimensional xy space
to a volume variable

if myvolume < 0 then set myvolume = 0
- - - make sure the value of the myvolume does not become less
than 0

sound(whichChannel).myvolume
- - - set the real sound channel volume to the mapped volume
value, myvolume.
```

We used this in the application that worked with the following image. The horse, sheriff's badge, and dollar icons are moveable sprites. Each has a sound channel mapped to its X, Y sprite coordinate property. Each sound is a long loop taken from a western movie sound track. The user can move the cursor around and mix the volume of three sound channels in a two–dimensional space. They can drag the sounds around to create different spaces for the cursor to move within. It's simple and engaging at the same time, as long as the sound files are well chosen.

The cowboys in the background are just there for illustration, which, with hindsight, might have been a mistake. If an object isn't interactive, then maybe it shouldn't be there.

Pushing buttons

Director knows which key is which on the keyboard, and when a key is being pressed.

We used this for the rom one CD-ROM www.romandson.com. Users press one of the numeric keys between 0 and 9 in the globe sound toy (all other keys are ignored). The value of the key is mapped both graphically, along the vertical axis, and sonically, as gong sounds of varying frequency. So when you hit a low number key, say 0, a sphere of light appears in the lower part of the screen area, and you hear a low gong sound. A high key, for example 9, produces a sphere in the higher part of the screen and a high frequency gong sound.

Time is represented as a loop and each key press event is positioned within this loop time. The information about when the key was pressed becomes a moment in loop time, and is mapped as a sphere of light on a 3D model that revolves slowly from right to left. The playback head, the point at which the light gives up its gong sound and the correct note for the vertical position is at the center front of the model.

The lights come around again as loop time loops and the 3D model revolves. When the light crosses the center of the globe the appropriate frequency sound plays again, but this time at half the volume. The sound volume is mapped to diminish over time.

The interactions are simple and immediate: press the keys and hear a scale of notes. Map this into loop time and the illusion is simple too: press the keyboard to put sounding lights on a revolving globe, with a playback head in the front middle of the globe.

What makes it intriguing is the way the sounds you have played already come back around to combine with new sounds to form complex and surprising harmonies and rhythms.

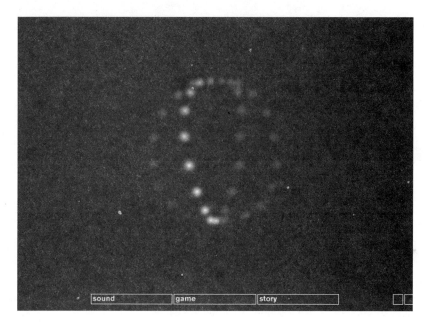

Sound reaction

Many machines have inbuilt microphone as well as the standard input devices, mouse and keyboard. You can read the input from the microphone using an Xtra such as GetSoundInLevel by Geoff Smith (www.physicalbits.com/PhysicalBits/Xtras/) or asFFT by Antoine Schmitt (www.asci.net/asFFTXtra/). The input gives you a range of values that describe the sound coming into the microphone. `GetSoundInLevel` measures the overall volume, whereas asFFT gives you the frequency ranges.

Of course, getting the user's input is only half the story. The most interesting thing is what you decide to do with it. One of the first projects we saw really develop the creative potential of sound input in Director was the Tota Hasegewa's Microphone Fiend CD–ROM.

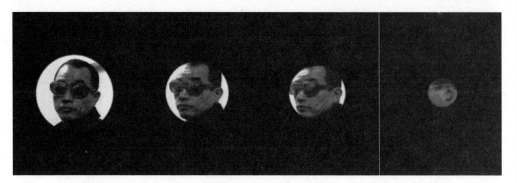

In one section the iris widens and a man turns towards the user according to the amplitude of sound at the selected input device. At the maximum volume the man moves his lips as if to say "Shut it!"

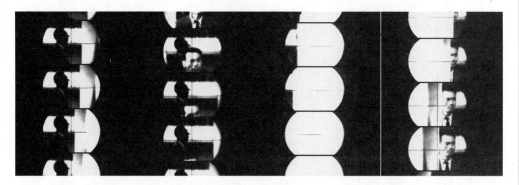

In another section a filmstrip rushes downwards at a speed that depends on the sound's amplitude. At a certain level of sound the strip is moving just fast enough to give the illusion of a moving image, something like a sound–activated zoetrope.

GetSoundInLevel allows you to query a specific sound input device, and the value returned corresponds to the amplitude of sound measured at that device. The beauty of amplitude is that it is immediate, crude and simple – you make a lot of noise and you get a lot of reaction, or, in our case, a big integer. If you are too quiet then nothing much reacts to you.

The team at tomato interactive have created a number of sound reactive pieces which have recently been published on the Foret L'ecoute CD–ROM.

Throwing some shapes

Vector cast members were first introduced into Director 6. Tomato interactive's Islamic project used them to develop an interactive toy from the aesthetic simplicity of patterns growing from rule–based geometry.

The user can specify the number of corners the central shape should have and the length of its sides. The sum of the corners and sides is the number of shapes that surround the central image.

The value of the sound level produced is mapped to the rotation of the shapes and their offset distance from the central point. The top row of digits on screen allows the user to chose the number of corners the central shape should have, the bottom row allows the user to chose the size and the sound level spreads the shapes around a central point. The user can vary the experience by setting different shapes of different sizes and animating them though noise.

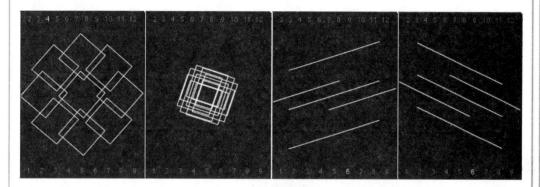

Time passed and commercial projects came along that enabled us to take sound reaction further. We showed the client Islamic as part of a pitch for a project involving an interactive menu system for a restaurant, because we wanted to use sound reaction if we were awarded the project. We were. The menu system, called Busaba after the restaurant, sits outside, and when it detects that it is not being used, activates animations that are reactive to sound. A large sensor button allows passers to activate the menu system, pulling it out of its sound reactive state.

We presented both Busaba and Islamic to clients whenever we thought sound reaction might suit their needs. The resulting work ranges from a nightclub opening for Home in London, in which images of buildings wobble in reaction to sound, to the launch of a new web site for Penguin Books. Tomato interactive has also produced the visuals for live concerts for a sextet called Instrumental, and sound reactive projections for Ron Arad during his exhibition at the Milan furniture fair.

We used the Xtra in the Home project to return the sound input level and map it directly to the frames of a very short piece of video. The equation goes something like this:

```
currentframe = maxframes * currentsoundlevel / maxsoundlevel
```

With a little more code this simple equation gives you a really compelling sound reactive interface. Tomato interactive used a piece of footage in which Dirk van Dooren, a fellow member of tomato, dances. The close relation of sound and dance bring the piece to life.

Tom applied the same method to short clips featuring 3D renditions of Ron Arad's furniture in action. The resulting piece has a beautiful, yet comical effect, that of chairs jumping around or springy vases uncoiling to the sound of the spectator.

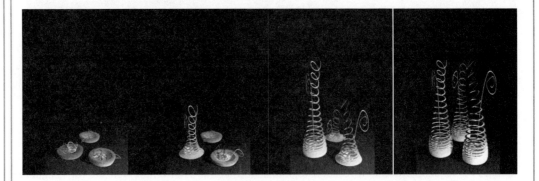

Another idea developed for the Home nightclub project uses a bit of code developed earlier for the navigation system of the tomato web site. We call it the 'wobbly code' because it creates the illusion of still images moving as if they have been projected onto the surface of water.

The basic principle behind the code is the division of an image into a grid of smaller, equal sized, segments. The rule applied onto the grid is that if one segment is enlarged then all other segments have to take up the resulting loss of size, be it in height or width. The 'wobble' is added by introducing a little equation that simulates inertia. The value returned by the sound level is used to affect a random segment of the grid. For more about the 'wobbly code' see Wobble by Joel Bauman in New Masters of Flash (it includes Director code examples).

We used a still image rather than video in this toy. All the photographs are of high buildings taken from ground level. The user can disturb these solid structures using the power of the voice – it creates an unsettling and intriguing effect.

After a fairly prolific period we found ourselves on the verge of repetition, somewhere we try very hard not to go, so we left sound reaction for a while and went back to the mouse and keyboard. A few weeks passed. There was a kind of intense calm in the office without the constant testing of our sound reactive interaction with silly noises, constant clapping and whistling. And then we found a new toy, the asFFT Xtra.

The asFFT Xtra allows you to get at more precise and complex sound information. You can specify the amount of a frequency, the 'bins' or slices, in a sound sample taken from a specified sound input device. Each bin represents the amplitude of the specified pitch of the sound sample at a given moment. The overall effect is that asFFT gives an image of the frequency of a sound, and not just its overall volume.

Although the asFFT Xtra gives a more detailed picture of an input sound than the GetSoundInLevel Xtra, we didn't find it better to design with. We remain unconvinced that experiments with the asFFT Xtra can go much further than the flashing graphic equalizer LEDs of 80's stereo systems. The GetSoundInLevel Xtra focuses on the simplest aspect of a sound, its overall volume. It is crude and very easy to understand, and this has been more useful in our work. The fact that a toy reacts to a user making noises is interesting. The fact that the user can make high noises and low noises to trigger different reactions from the interface is interesting, but not interesting enough. Still, the asFFT Xtra can still be put to good effect, adding subtle sophistication to a sound reactive interface. We used the asFFT Xtra for a project shown with the British Council in an exhibition in Stockholm. The exhibition was called New British Design. The project was called Wallpaper and set out to create sound reactive wallpaper that was projected directly onto a wall.

The designer's designers

romandson designed a sound reactive installation for Paul Smith's Covent Garden store in December 2000. It worked on an iMac robbed of keyboard or mouse. The only way users could interact with the piece was using the inbuilt microphone.

We wanted people to get the interaction method straight away, and we wanted them to want to engage with it for as long as possible. We came up with two types of experience, an attractor generated using the asFFT Xtra which modeled the microphone input as abstract patterns reminiscent of sound wave forms, and a game which used overall volumes from the GetSoundInLevel Xtra to drive a linear narrative towards a goal.

The pseudo sound wave forms help the user understand that sound is the interaction method. The response is immediate and subtle as the user modulates his or her voice.

In the second class of sound reaction in the Paul Smith project, overall volume data is provided by the GetSoundInLevel Xtra. This is used to interact with a linear Flash animation based upon a character created by the Paul Smith design team, R. Newbold. Mr Newbold is a stupid character who always puts himself in danger. Each one of the danger images is taken to its logical conclusion. Where Mr Newbold is foolishly holding a bomb with a lit fuse, for example, the animated version becomes a sequence in which the fuse burns down and the bomb explodes. The Flash movie is then imported into Director and volume information from the GetSoundInLevel Xtra is mapped to frame numbers within the Flash animation. The louder the user shouts, the further down the timeline the animation plays and the closer Mr Newbold gets to disaster. If the fuse gets all the way to the end the bomb exploding sequence plays through. The effect is of shouting a man to his death. It's horribly compelling, stupid and funny all at once.

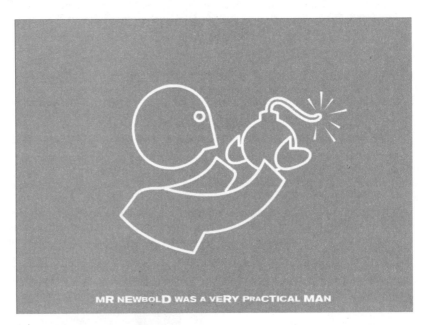

MR NEWBOLD WAS A VERY PRACTICAL MAN

One thing after another

The following three projects are connected. Each informed the next, which we think is representational of how works sometimes progress both creatively and commercially. It also demonstrates how personal work can inform commercial work, as well as creating openings, and that it is possible to work across many different platforms.

Cutting a disc

Tomato3 was created in 1999 during a quiet spell at tomato interactive. The concept was to produce a project that would represent the diversity of tomato output and would be used to attract clients. You can download it from www.tomato.co.uk.

Our creative starting point was to reject the drive of many multimedia producers for executables that try to recreate a cinematic experience. It's an obvious approach and we wanted to investigate other strategies. The idea we had was for a DA (desktop accessory, like the calculator on the Mac, for example.)

We wanted to emulate the unobtrusiveness of the desktop accessory, and the floating quality of structures that sit on the desktop allowing content to fold into and unfold out.

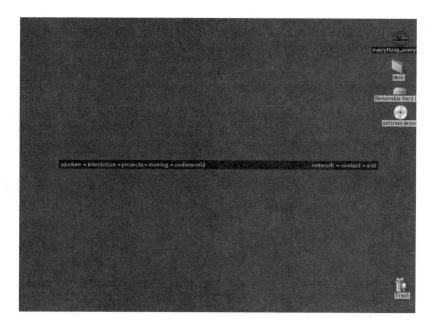

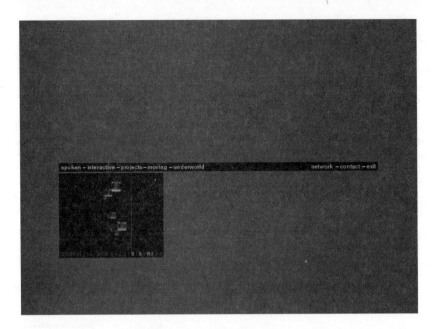

Clicking on one of the section's text buttons opens the relevant window, and clicking on it again closes it. While multiple windows are open only one is active at any one time. Clicking on a new window activated it and deactivated the previous window.

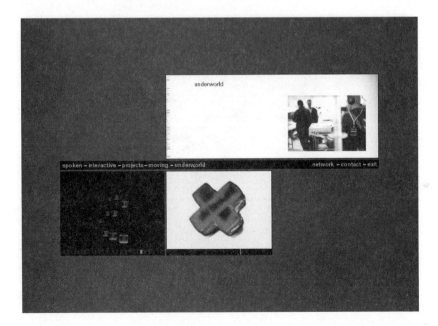

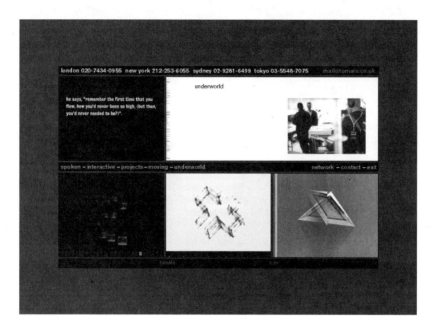

We used MIAW (movie in a window) code to do this. It allows you to create windows and control many aspects of them independently. We've used this technique frequently to separate navigation from content, not unlike using a frame set when you're producing a web site. It allows you to load a new stage without having to load the navigation, which is kept open in a MIAW.

We don't have the space here to go into MIAW code, but there is one thing we should mention, because it's undocumented (although it has appeared in the Macromedia Developers Newsletter): the `WindowType` property. This is very useful; it allows you to set the window style of a MIAW. You can create your own style by using a 1–bit image as a mask. We used this approach for a CD –based project created for a music promotion company called Mind Horizon.

The head shape is simply a 1–bit image that dictates the transparency of the window. This was coded like this:

```
(gMainWindow).windowType = member "mask"
```

gMainWindow being the window and member mask being the 1–bit mask.

Anyway, let's get back to the project in hand. Before we began developing tomato3, we had been working with Tom Hingston who had shown us one of the first CD business cards. This was very exciting, particularly the physicality of a non–conventionally shaped CD.

Talking to the replication company we were told that they could cut the CD to fit the size of our content. As we were launching the CD very close to the release of QuickTime 4 we had decided to include full installers of QuickTime for both Mac and PC. This put a lot of pressure on disc space, so we had to have a serious look at keeping the assets as small as possible. The most disc hungry aspect was the tomato video show reel. We did at least thirty test renders to achieve a good balance between compression and quality.

tomato three. london 020-7434-0955, new york 212-253-6055, sydney 02-9281 -6499, tokyo 03-5548-7075.

One other notable feature of the tomato3 CD–ROM is that can keep itself updated. When the user opens up the network section it checks to see if there is a network connection, then if there is, downloads a text field from the web site and rebuilds the navigation. This allows the content of this section to be changed remotely.

Consumer appreciation

After completing the tomato3 project the design team at tomato interactive began to see commercial possibilities for the mini CD format. However, marketing CD–ROMs for prestige clients like Levi Strauss always brings up the same problem: how to maximize distribution without devaluing the brand. To put it simply: if you give something away, people don't value it.

We worked around this with the mini CD by integrating it into the packaging of the garment. Then we felt it would be perceived as an overall strategy, and not just 'buy one get this free'. Tomato interactive suggested this to Levis, and were paired up with their new ICD brand. This new sub–brand was developing modern work wear that integrated technology into clothing. It seemed the perfect situation to build a manual for these hi–tech garments. As well as creating an interactive manual, the team also produced a section of links focused particularly on music as the jacket included a MP3 player.

deutsch
english
español
français
italiano
nederlands
svenska

information
>> WARNING <<
Introduction
Call Center
Components
Connecting
Eargear
Microphone
MP3 Player
Mobile Phone
Remote Control
TRC Gilet
Mooring Jacket
Beetle Jacket
Producer Jacket
links
change language

- Philips Mobile phone
- Philips MP3 player
- breathable
- temperature regulating
- detachable sleeves
- metallic coated
- basket weave nylon
- water-repellent

information
links
magazines
mp3 resources
ICD+
change language

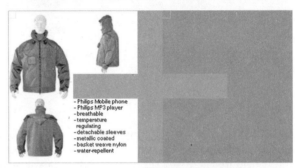

Philips Xenium GSM Phone:
- carousel menus
- voice dial
- 95 grams with battery

listen, download and play

Philips Rush

mp3

people sound

best buy

atomicpop

information
>> WARNING <<
Introduction
Call Center
Components
Connecting
Eargear
Microphone
MP3 Player
Mobile Phone
Remote Control
TRC Gilet
Mooring Jacket
Beetle Jacket
Producer Jacket
links
change language

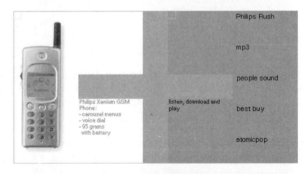

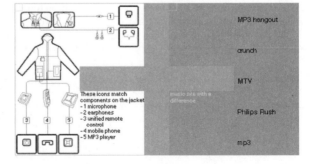

These icons match components on the jacket
- 1 microphone
- 2 earphones
- 3 unified remote control
- 4 mobile phone
- 5 MP3 player

music site with a difference

MP3 hangout

crunch

MTV

Philips Rush

mp3

It was built up of three movies in a window, like tomato3, but this time the structure was based on the logo. The navigation was placed in the left MIAW, the manual in the central MIAW and the links in the MIAW on the right.

As it was a European campaign, the CD had to be viewable in various languages. Language preference was set the first time the user played the CD and then stored in the system folder so that the disc would start up in the correct language (see **Chapter 2**, Lists). The language preference could be changed later on if required.

This language preference also determines the language of the links. The CD checked the language preference file on startup, if when there wasn't one, looked for an Internet connection and downloaded the correct data for the links according to the language selected.

A small bit of interactivity we introduced here was setting up the buttons so that the users didn't have to click directly them, by calculating the closest button to the mouse when it was clicked. We set this up by calculating the triangular distance from each button and putting them in a sorted list, so that the first button in this list would be the closest to the mouse. A bar was used to indicate the current closest button to the mouse.

Don't skip intro

Once we'd finished the CD, Levi Strauss asked us to produce a web site, www.Levis-icd.com. This was something we had hitherto avoided because we'd found that much of commercial web design was uninteresting. However, as we'd already created the CD-ROM, we decided to take it on and to use the opportunity to question some of the dominant creative approaches to building a web site.

The first thing we did was try to invert was the prevalent Flash intro approach; there seems very little point in presenting the user with a linear plug-in based introduction and then give them extremely bland content. The words 'Skip Intro' say it all. This has become a major issue since the introduction of Flash. It's not a question of Flash being a limited or limiting design tool, but rather of the limited imaginations of those with creative or financial control over commercial projects. It is really sad how the new media design industry has become progressively linear, rather then developing and experimenting with the potential of interactivity.

The design team decided to put all the dynamic content at the bottom of the structure, and keep the top as lo-tech as possible.

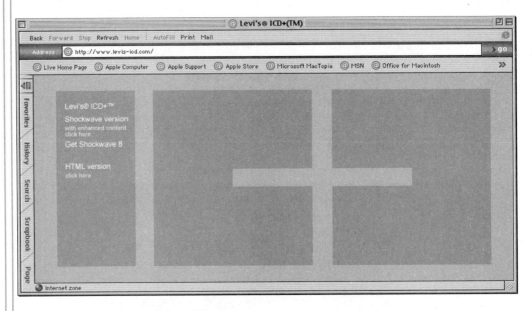

A key design issue was how to creatively represent the integration of the technological components into the garments. The solution was to use Che Tamahori's examples of keying through one image to reveal another (www.sfx.co.nz/tamahori/home/). Using this technique we were able to look through the jacket to a magnified X-ray image.

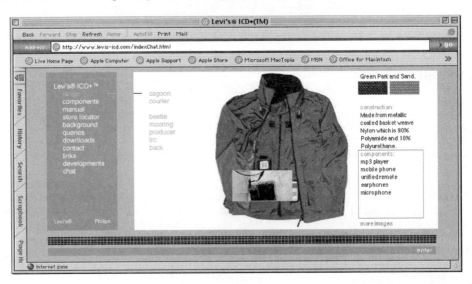

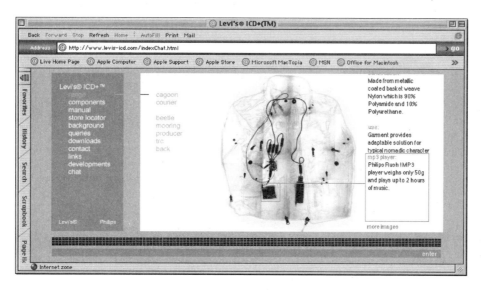

The keying was achieved using a mask ink effect. This ink masks a sprite dependent on a 1–bit member that is in the next cast member slot to the member that requires keying. The movement of mask was achieved by changing the registration point of the 1–bit mask.

The store locator uses a compiler that takes a small 1–bit images of European countries and creates a list of coordinates describing each country's shape. This allowed a slick morphing transition between selected countries – a very similar process to the 'ABC' example in the **Lists** chapter.

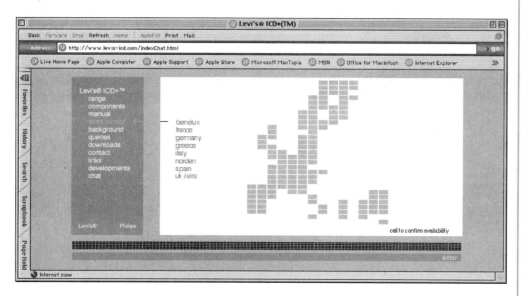

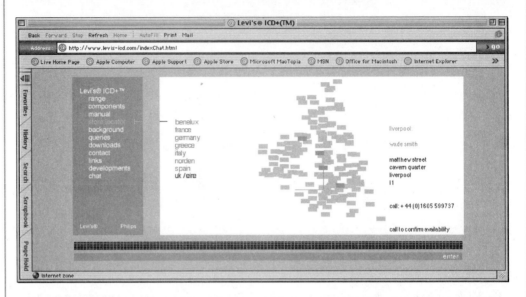

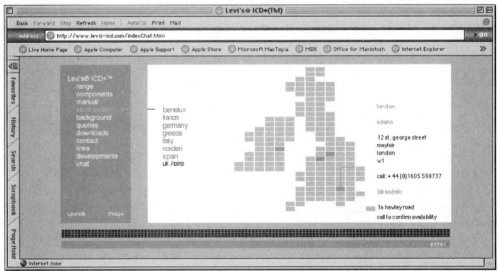

The logo was reinforced though a generic load movie, the movie used whenever a Shockwave movie was selected. As the preload movie began running it started downloading the requested movie, displaying the percentage loaded as well as the name of the movie requested.

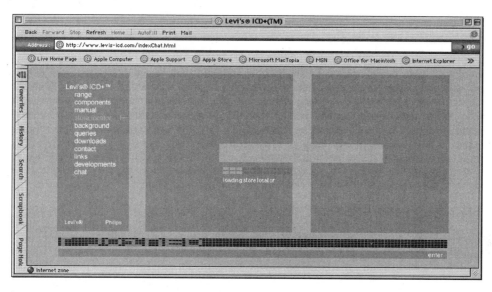

The movie knew the path of the requested movie as well as the name as it was embedded in the HTML page, and was loaded into the Shockwave movie using:

```
gmovie =  externalParamValue("sw1")
text =  externalParamValue("sw2")
```

Here sw1 and sw2 are parameters built into the HTML page. The nice thing about this approach is that the tiny preload movie (6k) is generic, so it loads very fast and is cached after the initial download.

We calculated the percentage of the download like this:

```
getStreamStatus( gnetid )

tatList = getStreamStatus( gnetid )

if (statList.state <> "Complete") then
if (statList.bytesSoFar > 0) then
percentDone = (statList.bytesSoFar * 100) / statList.bytesTotal
else
percentDone = 0
end if
else
percentDone = 100
end if
```

The last word

One of the ideas we hope we have managed to communicate in this chapter is that experimental work and commercial work are not opposed to each other in interaction design. Many projects in Director are marketable in one way or another – all you have to do is find opportunities for them in the real world. Sometimes opportunities have to be created, by showing clients experimental work that might be adaptable to a given commercial design problem, and exhibiting work in galleries or online, so that potential clients know what's available. The boundaries of interactive media are always being extended, as technologies develop and audiences become more sophisticated. Indeed, in such a fast changing environment, it could be argued that experimental work is a necessary prerequisite for commercial success.

Another point we hope that has come across is that, as far as interactive user experience is concerned, simple is usually best. This doesn't mean you don't have to work hard; simple experiences are often the hardest to design, and may include really complex code. But it does mean that for the most part, the user should know what they can do with an interactive as directly, quickly and as simply as possible. Having established this relationship between interactive and user you can then manipulate it how you like, including using it as the basis for building more complex experiences.

Finally, and most importantly, don't be shy about having a go at programming for yourself. Cobbling together bits of Lingo code while working on an idea can be very productive and actually quite a lot of fun. Think of it as the equivalent of scribbling in a sketchpad for a visual artist. You may not become the best programmer in the world, but you might turn out to be a great interaction designer and you might even come up with some ideas that no–one else has yet developed. The art of interaction design has only just got underway, and there are lots of solutions still to be discovered. So, get at it!

Appendix A: Director for Flash Users

Director 8.5 Studio

This appendix is intended for all those Flash users out there who are in the process of adding Director to their list of multimedia tools. It is written by one of only two purely Flash oriented designers who appeared in the Director 8.5 Beta. (The other one, as far as I could tell, was Manuel Clement of *Mano1* fame... anyone else was keeping quiet about it!)

As with most people moving from one software application to another in a related field, I went into Director not asking what it was, but needing to know the differences and similarities between Director and Flash. I needed to tease out which areas were similar enough for me to transfer my existing skill-set over (with a little modification), and which wereso different that I'd need to home in on specific areas of the Director documentation and learn them from scratch.

This quick-start to Director for Flashers is the result. It's intended to help people who started from the same point as I did on the Director journey. I guess the friends of ED Flash Foundation books helped a few people get into Flash, and now we, the authors, are in the same position with regard to Director as those readers were with Flash. This travelogue details how we found it – straight from the horse's mouth. I hope it helps you find your way in.

For those who just want the headlines, here they are:

The Interface   Perhaps the most daunting thing about opening up Director for the first time is the interface itself: all those windows! Once you've realized that many of them hold duplicate data, and that most of them can be safely closed during much of the development cycle, the interface starts to look a bit more approachable. One of my first impressions of Director is that its UI leaves plenty of room for the kind of streamlining that's come about in Flash.

Animation   Surprisingly (for me, if no-one else), Director has a much *better* animation system than Flash. You can set tween paths *with associated acceleration* and without ever having to touch a keyframe. As well as the surprisingly advanced low level animation facilities, the transitions and effects available (inks, etc.) in Director are much more varied than those in Flash because they work on the bit plane level rather than the vector level.

Behaviors   Director is a much easier environment to get into if you don't want to get your hands dirty with scripting. Director has drag–and–drop sewn up in a way that leaves Flash standing.

Lingo   For the Flash coder who wants to get into scripting, the bad news is that there is no 'standard' backbone to Lingo in the way that ActionScript is similar to core JavaScript and isbased on the ECMA 262 standard. Although this does mean that Lingo is something you'll need to learn from scratch, the good news is that it does support a dot notation format, so if you're comfortable with ActionScript, you won't be completely lost in Lingo.

Standalone apps   As well as web applications, Director is of course capable of creating standalone applications. The importance of this in building downloadable screensavers and desktop toys (these can include Flash components) is perhaps an important consideration for the expert Flash designer looking to gain a few additions to his or her skill set.

Multimedia

Finally, Director is a multimedia palette with a much larger number of colors. As the web world moves towards a broadband canvas that supports more and more content, Director is perhaps the only plug–in that contains video, hardware driven 3D, fast bitmap scaling and per pixel effects, and all within a recognized industry standard plug-in.

The Director Community

The software that people use to build their careers may very well look like 'just another application' to people on the outside, but those of us who use PhotoShop, 3D Max, Flash or Director for a living know better. There is always a community of professionals surrounding the programs.

In his introduction to *New Masters of Flash: 2002 Annual*, Jonathan Gay, the creator of Flash, talked about community, and pointed out how very much a part of Flash's success and perceived personality it is. Having been part of the Flash community for some time, I've got pretty familiar with the Flash community.

Flash is seen as the new kid on the block. Many (but by no means all) Flash designers are fairly young, and many are without a graphic art background. Motion graphics was too new to have a standard route, and this has been no bad thing. The golden period of Flash design has been about bringing motion graphics to the web – clever interfaces and crazy, unfettered designs. There is commercial Flash, of course, but many of the recognized talents within the industry, designers like James Paterson, Yugo Nakumura, Joshua Davis and Joe Cartoon, have been working with Flash simply for its own sake; creating something akin to a Flash underground of designers and developers challenging traditional HTML.

The Director community is different. Director has been around since the beginning of multimedia, and computers really did have 16 color palettes. Director has a long history of being the tool for creating CD–ROMs, kiosks and educational applications for the music and retail and promotional industries. This is reflected in the community, who to a Flash convert look a lot more polished and corporate. Even the Macromedia pricing of the two applications seems to reflect the difference.

Perhaps this has some bearing on the very distinct community feel. Perhaps it's also something to do with the fact that broadband development and design involves rather more than a 'couple of Flash designers a HTML guy and a server–side guy'. The amount of video, sound and other media pieces required to put together a broadband production tends to suggest a more planned route and process than the 'wow, here's a new interface concept, lets design a website around it' approach rife among the Flash community.

The relative maturity of Director also has its effect on distinct working practices within the two groups of designers. Although we are constantly told about web-safe palettes and bit depths, for example, no Flash designer I know takes a blind bit of notice of them. The assumption is that anyone out there with a graphics card that doesn't display at least a 16–bit desktop is unlikely to know about Flash or the web either. No one uses VGA and CGA displays anymore because even the old Matrox graphics cards of five years ago could display enough unique colors for us to safely ignore palette issues. The only remaining issue is possibly the relative brightness of PC and Mac displays, but apart from the few Photoshop graphic people who actually take the time to calibrate their monitors, no one actually cares (yeah, I know some other folks write whole chapters on web safe colors, but we're a little more pragmatic when it comes to the realities of web design!)

Director, however, goes back to when a Hercules 256 color card was the best money could buy, and the interface is littered with references to file formats that allow us to set bit depths and a myriad of low level bitmap stuff. Most Flash designers are by now used to just using JPEG/PNGs, or converting images to vectors if there's enough solid color. My advice is stick to it in Director unless there are compelling reasons not to (and I haven't found any practical ones so far).

Why is Director a good option for Flash designers?

Of course, anyone who already has the big Director 8.5 box on their desk has already answered this question, but it doesn't hurt to cover a few points here about the particular problems that Director solves. Flash 5 is designed for low bandwidth applications, and suffers in other areas because of this – in particular, **performance** and **lack of multimedia options**.

At the heart of Flash is a real time vector–rendering engine. Every frame in a Flash site is rendered from basic vector point and filled with data on the fly, and this takes lots of processing power even if nothing much appears to be happening. Although this factor is often sited as an advantage, and lots of designers have worked against this limitation to come up with killer Flash sites and applications, there are some things that just can't be attempted in Flash.

Another issue that quickly becomes apparent with Flash is that its potential for instability goes up with file size. Flash is designed with small applications in mind, and as soon as you start to load an application up with high bandwidth assets, the .swf file can become a little erratic and crash happy. Director, on the other hand, is tailor made for handling this sort of content gracefully.

Because Flash is aimed at low bandwidth applications it doesn't have anywhere near the same sort of multimedia support that Director has. Director is a generic multimedia engine. Its output can be either streamed across the web, or compiled into standalone, stable applications. Its native engine is bitmap based, which makes it much easier for computers to draw quickly because the images are effectively 'pre-drawn', and the image file is simply manipulated in memory. The Director plug-in can handle a greater number of different media elements, anf can handle them very efficiently; 3D support via hardware, video support and all sorts of other support that the 350k Flash plug-in just can't accommodate.

Of course, the emerging digital frontier has moved from simple internet connectivity to the Broadband Web, and Directors old CD–ROM heritage, coupled with its recent streaming abilities, make it better suited for this kind of work than Flash.

There are some broadband Flash sites around, and I had a look at some of them while I was researching this section. Broadband Flash takes every bit as long as similar broadband Director sites, and on occasion even longer, simply because most broadband elements (bitmap, video, 3D) are not part of the Flash plug-in's design focus, and don't stream as well as vector based content. The upshot is that Flash loses much of its streaming capability in migrating to broadband. There is a more subtle problem as well; performance. Broadband Flash requires a *very* fast computer to work well. Flash based streaming video and sound solutions are particularly slow, and a full screen update on a (pretty standard) 1024 x 768 screen is something Flash struggles with, even with sites that aren't broadband.

Director already equals Flash on the broadband streaming front, and is edging past it in the raw multimedia performance stakes. This is a contest well worth watching in the future as Macromedia develops the two programs.

Having said that, though, and despite the Flash versus Director debates you can find, Director in fact looks set to compliment Flash in many web and other applications, supporting it where Flash cannot handle the heavy multimedia streams such as video and hardware assisted 3D. If for this reason alone, knowing both applications is a valid strategy for future–proofing your skills base.

A Flash designer's first impression of Director

The good news is that Director and Flash have become much more similar since Director version 8 (so my Director contacts tell me). In fact, the basic Director interface is reminiscent of Flash 4. Director hasn't had the 'tabbed palette makeover' that came between Flash 4 and 5, and the main components (apart from the Director scripting windows) have a distinctly Flash 4 feel. Despite this, the Director interface is *much* easier to use for the non-programming Flash user because of its true drag and drop scripting. Additionally, the Director help system now looks much like the Flash one, and given that you will use it a lot early on (I know I did!) this is another bonus to fast learning.

More on all this later, but first, let's tackle the basic graphic interface stuff.

The Timeline/Score

The big joy of using Flash is its 'do it anyway you want to' philosophy when it comes to using timelines. You can attach scripts, sounds or graphic elements on pretty much any keyframe of any layer. This freeform nature of Flash has, perhaps more than anything, helped its ability to draw in converts from non–multimedia backgrounds; it's just so easy to chop and change timeline animations so that they reflect your own preferences. Have a look at this comparison between Flash's terminology and Director's:

Flash	Director
Layer	Channel
Timeline	Score
Graphic/button/movie clip	Cast member
Element on the stage	Sprite
ActionScript attached to a keyframe	Behavior attached to script channel
ActionScript attached to movie clip or button	Behavior attached to sprite

One of the biggest differences you'll come across in Director is that it *doesn't* volunteer the same freeform design. It has a much more structured timeline, there are specific channels dedicated to specific elements (called the **effects channels**). Although this in itself is not really a problem given that some of the channels in this group have no Flash equivalent, it does mean that you're more limited when it comes to sound, unless you're prepared to go digging into Lingo. (And in fact, if you do go digging into Lingo, you'll find that you can obtain much more control over your sound in Director.)

Most Flash users create a specific layer for the purpose of attaching scripts to the timeline (I call mine the actions layer), so the fact that Director asks you to do the same for your timeline behaviors (the behavior channel) is only prompting a good habit.

Being able to do things like changing the frame rate using the tempo channel is the sort of thing we poor Flash cousins wish we could do. Director's ink effects are *much* more useful than the equivalent Flash instance effects (because Director works at the bitmap level rather than Flash's vector shapes, which can only address vector tint, brightness and alpha transitions).

The real practical differences start when you begin adding things in the Director sprite channels (the channels that appear below the effects channels, and are also sometimes called **member channels**, or just **sprites).** You can hold several graphic elements at the same time per layer in Flash, but Director operates a strict 'one channel, one sprite' rule. Consequentially, you're likely to have a much larger number of channels in a Director score than you will in a Flash timeline.

This can be annoying if like me you like to place related graphics on the same layer in Flash; the Director alternative isn't just different, it requires a lot more forward planning if you want to manage your timeline in such a way that you don't start to lose sight of where stuff is.

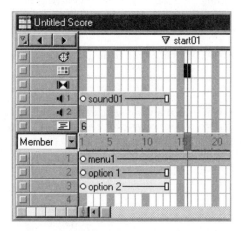

Director is miles ahead when it comes to fine tuning and editing the score, and controlling tween animation, as befits a true multimedia authoring tool.

For example, the spiral tween motion below took me 20 seconds to set up in Director. By moving points directly on the tween path, I can determine the sprite's direction and acceleration without having to touch a timeline. With Flash, I *have* to keep messing about with the timeline because there is no easy way to set up a path with acceleration in such an intuitive and graphic way.

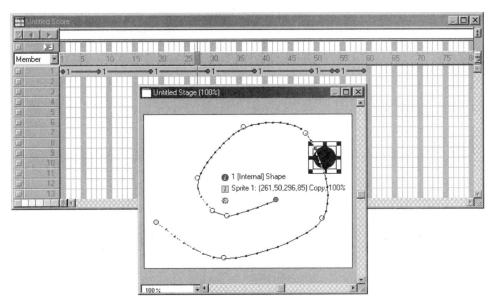

This is something that seems to be frequently overlooked. You'll probably hear a lot of: 'Flash is for the web and Director is for kiosks', but less often will you find someone digging around under the hood going: 'wow, I never knew Director was better for hand–drawn animation, particularly because it supports vectors as well; I just thought Director was something to do with bitmaps and video...'

The fact that Flash doesn't have this sort of low level animation usability is possibly one reason the Flash community go straight for scripting solutions. Animation in Director is all so intuitive that scripting isn't necessary as early on in the process – and even when it is, there's often a pre-built behavior that you can use instead of reaching for the Lingo manual. Really working with Lingo comes in when you're creating more sophisticated work, not the minute you need some animation.

I've already started looking back at some of my old animation heavy Flash movies and tried reworking them in Director, and some of this stuff is looking really neat, particularly when you start adding ink effects into the mix. (Another big bonus is of course the additional performance; Director is definitely faster.)

Movie Clips and Sprites

Director's implementation of the equivalent of a Flash movie clip is perhaps the thing that takes the longest to get used to for a Flash designer. When you're used to working in Flash, movie clips are your key graphical element. You're used to basing everything around them, and constructing your media out of loads of movie clips triggered with buttons or events. Even advanced scripted presentations rely heavily on movie clips, because they are the only true object–based graphical element with properties and methods. Movie clips are easy to create and modify in Flash because of the total reliance upon them; simply double click them from either the stage area or the library.

In Director the *sprite* or 'static graphic' seems to be the most basic element. To create the equivalent of a Flash movie clip in Director, you need a film loop, and creating one of these is a two-stage process:

- Create the film loop content in the main Director timeline.

- Select the parts of the timeline you want to make into the film loop and drag them into the library. Once the movie clip is created you can't edit it again (although you can copy its contents back onto the main timeline for re-editing).

> *There are a couple of ways to make your film loops easily accessible, but they're not the sort of things Flash experts will be expecting – you can keep the animation sequence in the score and create the rest of your movie around it, or you can place the animation sequence right at the end of your movie.*

This is a pretty major change to a Flash designer's free form workflow. Of all the things that I had to learn in crossing over to Director from Flash, this was the actually the hardest bit. Lingo and Havok (the Xtra that helps you create physic-realistic 3D environments) were easy in comparison.

The Cast window

The Cast window is broadly equivalent to the Flash Library window. The main difference is that the Director environment allows you to work with multiple casts and external casts. The similarities are far more apparent: Director's Cast window feels much like the Flash Library window (for those who can remember, it feels a lot like the Flash 3 Library window).

The Inspectors

About 60% of all your time with the Director interface will center on the Property Inspector. This is a context sensitive tabbed window, similar to the sort of thing seen in Flash 4.

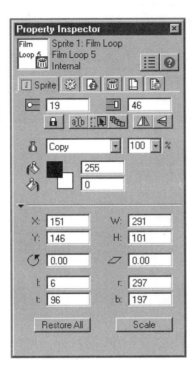

Only the tabs and requesters available for the currently selected element are shown (and if nothing is selected, the Inspector defaults to the tabs for the stage itself), making it completely intuitive as long as you understand the attributes of the thing you have just selected. It works in much the same way as Flash 5's tabbed panels, so it's not even something new to learn.

There are a few other inspectors for each of the more specialized functions; text, behaviors, memory, and even new 3D inspectors like the 3DPI Inspector that comes on the Director 8.5 CD–ROM (this has to be installed separately). Of particular note is the Behavior window – one of the greatest instances of parallel evolution I have come across; it's *just like* Flash's actions window, and even has something very similar to the normal/expert script editing modes.

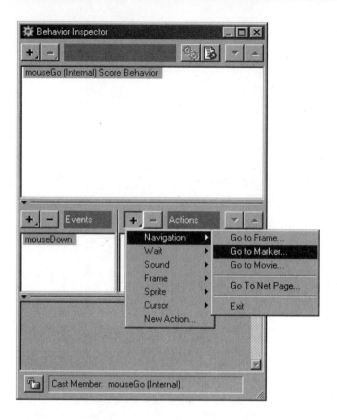

If you start a new script as a beginner, the Behavior Inspector window allows you to define your commands as event-action pairs selected from a set of drop down menus, like this:

```
on mouseDown, go to frame 20
```

The Behavior window

The great thing about scripting in this way is that you don't actually have to know an awful lot about Lingo; you just need an understanding of simple events and handlers (which is something the typical Flash user knows all about already). I found myself writing scripts for a few trial Director sites within a few hours of opening the Director box (and some hours before opening any of the manuals!) This is exactly the way you worked with actions way back in Flash 3 and 4, so it's not even new to a lot of us.

Using the basic functionality is a bit limiting in that it only allows you to build basic navigation and the most elementary media control commands (about the level of scripting of the Flash 3 dialect of ActionScript). I did find that the basic scripting methods discussed here were a good way to begin writing my own simple Lingo scripts, though. Once I'd got one together, I opened it up in the real script window (by pressing the 4th icon from the top in the Behavior Inspector), which looked to me for all the world like expert mode in Flash, and started dissecting the raw Lingo to modify the basic scripts I had created.

> *This is how I learned Flash in the first place, the best way to get into Lingo I have found so far. Create some 'drag–and–drop' Lingo and go in and start playing with it close up.*

The Paint and Vector Shape windows

The Paint and Vector Shape windows allow you to create bitmap and vector based graphics within Director – but I'd really recommend that you don't use them to create your finished media pieces. They're great for placeholder media, but as any web design person will already know, Photoshop and Freehand (or whatever your chosen bitmap and vector programs are), are miles beyond the sort of thing you can do in the Director content creation windows.

Most of the Director people I spoke to tend to work in external programs and then import all the finished assets into Director for building into the final presentation. What's more, Director's editing windows only support one level of undo; so if you're more familiar with something else, use it instead.

The only basic content creation window worth really working with (apart from the new Shockwave 3D window of course) is the text window, but this is just a basic text editor; I didn't have to consult the manual and I don't suppose anyone else will either.

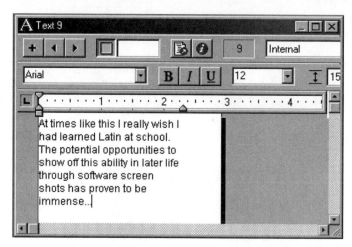

Although there are a few other windows lurking about, these were the only elements I had to address before I was well on my way in Director. As mentioned before, the only real problem I found is the lack of a movie clip object with the same ease of editing as we see in Flash. The next big challenge was learning Lingo.

Scripting in Director

One of the big advantages of Flash is the accessible scripting language. In a total masterstroke, Macromedia changed Flash's scripting language (ActionScript) into a syntax very similar to the only other computer scripting language that web designers might actually know; JavaScript. This immediately made the creation of scripting heavy Flash sites accessible to a large number of the existing web design community.

Lingo is very different to ActionScript in that it is not a new language, and so it can't really be changed in such a drastic manner. Lingo has a long user following and has matured over a long period. One of the few recent changes though is significant: as well as the rather strange (to new Lingo users) 'verbose' Lingo syntax, most commands can also now be expressed in *dot notation*. This will make Lingo particularly accessible to Flash designers crossing over. It's not quite a total implementation of dot notation however, and there are particular technical and historic inconsistencies.

Lingo syntax

Lingo commands are not grouped into objects as they are in Flash (the `Math` and `MovieClip` objects, for example). The fact that you can access ActionScript's functionality through dot notation makes for an extremely logically defined structure. If you think there ought to be a command to do something in particular, the chances are that there is one *and* you're halfway to the syntax.

For example, there are a lot of Lingo commands that handle vector shapes, such as `addVertex`, `antiAlias`, `backgroundColor`, `broadcastProps`, and so on. If you've been working with ActionScript, then you'll probably see these and expect to find a `vector` object through which you could call actions like `vector.addVertex`, `vector.antiAlias`, `vector.backgroundColor`, and so on.

The Flash object based action groupings are great for learning the language. They make it easy to find a command from a requester or a drop down menu, once you know how the groupings work. And, of course, once you have used a method of a particular object (like the `getSeconds` method of the `Date` object, for example) then you have a pretty good idea of the other commands that are going to be available to you, because you only have to understand the particular object to understand *all the methods of that object*. Learning Lingo is a little harder than learning ActionScript because it doesn't follow a full dot notation implementation through to the actual structure of the language syntax itself.

> *You can, of course, get an ordered list of commands by using the 'categorized lingo' button, which can be pretty useful if you're hunting around for a particular kind of functionality. It's not quite the same thing, but it's a step in the right direction.*

Lingo keywords

Lingo serves many more applications than ActionScript, and so there are particularly large subsets of Lingo (for 3D and video for example) that aren't comparable to anything you'll find in Actionscript. In short, the Lingo dictionary of keywords is HUGE! The boxed Director 8.5 release has two 500 page books (the *Lingo Dictionary* and the *What's New in Director Shockwave Studio*) that contain lists of Lingo commands... scary! Because there is no true dot notation hierarchy applied to command syntax, there's a lot of syntax to learn out there in Lingo world.

Verbose and dot syntax

The distinction between verbose and dot syntax is rather dialectical. Many Lingo aficionados use verbose syntax, while others prefer the shorter, sweeter dot notation. Some of the Lingo tutorials I have downloaded from the web even switch between the two styles throughout a `.dir` file. Confusing to the beginner to say the least!

Once I got into Lingo scripting, though, I found that it's much like any language; there are a few commands you use often and loads of more obscure ones you hardly ever use. If you're well versed in ActionScript then you'll find Lingo is essentially more of the same (albeit with a larger body of commands to get your head round). There are pieces of Lingo specific terminology that you'll need to get hold of, but they aren't complex. **Parent-child scripting,** for example, isn't that different from the Flash movie clip based animation hierarchies that ActionScript divas use all the time.

There are some things in Lingo that really make it worth the journey though – the greater number of events that your scripts can trigger on, Movies in Windows, 3D. Best of all though is the raw increase in performance that Lingo gives you over and above ActionScript; it's like test-driving a much faster car; exhilarating and fun!

Conclusion

At the time of writing, I have been working with Director for about a month. I can't say that the first couple of weeks were not hard going; they were. But looking back, that was just about unfamiliarity, not a lack of understanding of basic principles; if you know one multimedia timeline based tool you're a good way into them all.

I've already started to look at working with Director on some personal multimedia projects that just didn't get off the ground in Flash because of technical issues. One of my most ambitious is a multimedia version of a graphic novel I did years ago (it was cited as the first ever totally digitally created comic strip in *Computer Arts* way back when), and I'm using real time 3D (Character Studio et al) along with bitmapped images...

My first love in digital art was always 3D, and Director has finally brought this back home in a form that brings together all my favorite applications: 3D Max for the 3D object creation, Flash for the cool interface elements, and Director to bind the real time 3D together with pre–rendered 3D video, sound and any other media streams I might want to add.

So it's really not about choosing between Director and Flash. It's about saying 'Here's a project I want to do, what are the tools I can use to visualize this?' For me, things are really beginning to get interesting, because the stuff I had to pre–render three years ago can now be done in real time with some openGL hardware and a few alpha bitmaps to hide all the jaggies.

All the programs I worked with individually only a few years ago are fast becoming integrated in one big workflow, and that's the truly exiting thing, because as applications get more integrated, the possibilities for using them together exponentiate. And the program that looks set to come out from the shadows and integrate all this media into one big broadband delivery system is Director.

Index

The index is arranged hierarchically, in alphabetical order, with symbols preceding the letter A. Many second-level entries also occur as first-level entries. This is to ensure that users will find the information they require however they choose to search for it.

Index

Index

friendsof
DESIGNER TO DESIGNER™

Books
D2D
Code
News
Authors
Interviews
Web
Events
Contact
Home

You've read the book, now enter the community.

friendsofed.com is the online heart of the designer to designer neighbourhood.

As you'd expect the site offers the latest news and support for all our current and forthcoming titles – but it doesn't stop there.

For fresh exclusive interviews and videos every month with our authors – the new and future masters like Josh Davis, Yugo Nakamura, James Paterson and many other friends of ED – enter the world of D2D.

Stuck with a design problem? Need technical assistance? Our support doesn't end on the last page of the book. Just post your query on our message board and one of our moderators or authors will make sure you get the answers you need – fast.

New to the site is our EVENTS section where you can find out about schemes brewing in the ED laboratory. Forget everything you know about conferences and get ready for a new generation of designer happenings with a difference.

Welcome to friendsofed.com. This place is the place of friends of ED – designer to designer. Practical deep fast content delivered by working web designers.

Straight to your head.

www.friendsofed.com

freshfroot
motion web mindfood

stripes

seams & f

warhol

seven day itch

freshfroot is where friends of ED fertilise the designer mind. It's a visual search engine, a daily creative resource and a hard-to-kick addiction. Everyday the froot pickers, along with a select band of celebrity guest editors, search through the web's good, bad and ugly to bring you the diamonds – categorised, critiqued and instantly searchable. freshfroot rejects the usual search engine criteria in favour of daily themes that pull together stylistically similar works and images to provide the rock solid creative resource to complement the technical resource on offer in our books.

freshfroot is the place where Mike Cina, James Paterson, Golan Levin, Mumbleboy, Brendan Dawes and many other new and future masters go to share their inspirations and be inspired. It's the place everyone goes when they need fresh ideas fast. Submit your own found or created masterpieces, spout your opinions and share ideas in the discussion forum. Get involved, be inspired and escape the mediocre.

my froot

my froot

❓

shee

archive

a‑z a-z

📅 date

? keyword

search for: inspiration

james pate

forward

hybrid   revolution   brendan dawes

urban

playground

friendsof

D E S I G N E R   T O   D E S I G N E R ™

friends of ED write books for you. Any suggestions, or ideas about how you want information given in your ideal book will be studied by our team.

Your comments are valued by friends of ED.

Freephone in USA 800.873.9769
Fax 312.893.8001

UK contact: Tel. 0121.258.8858
Fax. 0121.258.8868

feedback@friendsofed.com

Director 8.5 Studio - Registration Card

Name _____

Address _____

_____

_____

City _____ State/Region _____

Country _____ Postcode/Zip _____

E-mail _____

Occupation _____

How did you hear about this book?
- ☐ Book review (publication) _____
- ☐ Advertisement (name) _____
- ☐ Recommendation _____
- ☐ Catalog _____
- ☐ Other _____

Where did you buy this book?
- ☐ Bookstore (name) _____
- ☐ Computer Store (name) _____
- ☐ Mail Order _____
- ☐ Other _____

What influenced you in the purchase of this book?
- ☐ Cover Design   ☐ Contents
- ☐ Other (please specify) _____

How did you rate the overall contents of this book?
- ☐ Excellent   ☐ Good
- ☐ Average   ☐ Poor

What did you find useful about this book?

What did you find least useful about this book?

Please add any additional comments

What other design areas will you buy a book on soon?

What is the best design related book you have used this year?

Note: This information will only be used to keep you updated about new friends of ED titles and will not be used for any other purposes or passed to any third party.

DESIGNER TO DESIGNER™

NB. If you post the bounce back card below in the UK, please send it to:

friends of ED Ltd.,
30 Lincoln Road,
Olton,
Birmingham.
B27 6PA

BUSINESS REPLY MAIL

FIRST CLASS   PERMIT #64   CHICAGO, IL

POSTAGE WILL BE PAID BY ADDRESSEE

friends of ED,
29 S. La Salle St.
Suite 520
Chicago Il 60603-USA